Rose Cottage Chronicles

UNIVERSITY PRESS OF FLORIDA

Florida A&M University, Tallahassee
Florida Atlantic University, Boca Raton
Florida Gulf Coast University, Ft. Myers
Florida International University, Miami
Florida State University, Tallahassee
New College of Florida, Sarasota
University of Central Florida, Orlando
University of Florida, Gainesville
University of North Florida, Jacksonville
University of South Florida, Tampa
University of West Florida, Pensacola

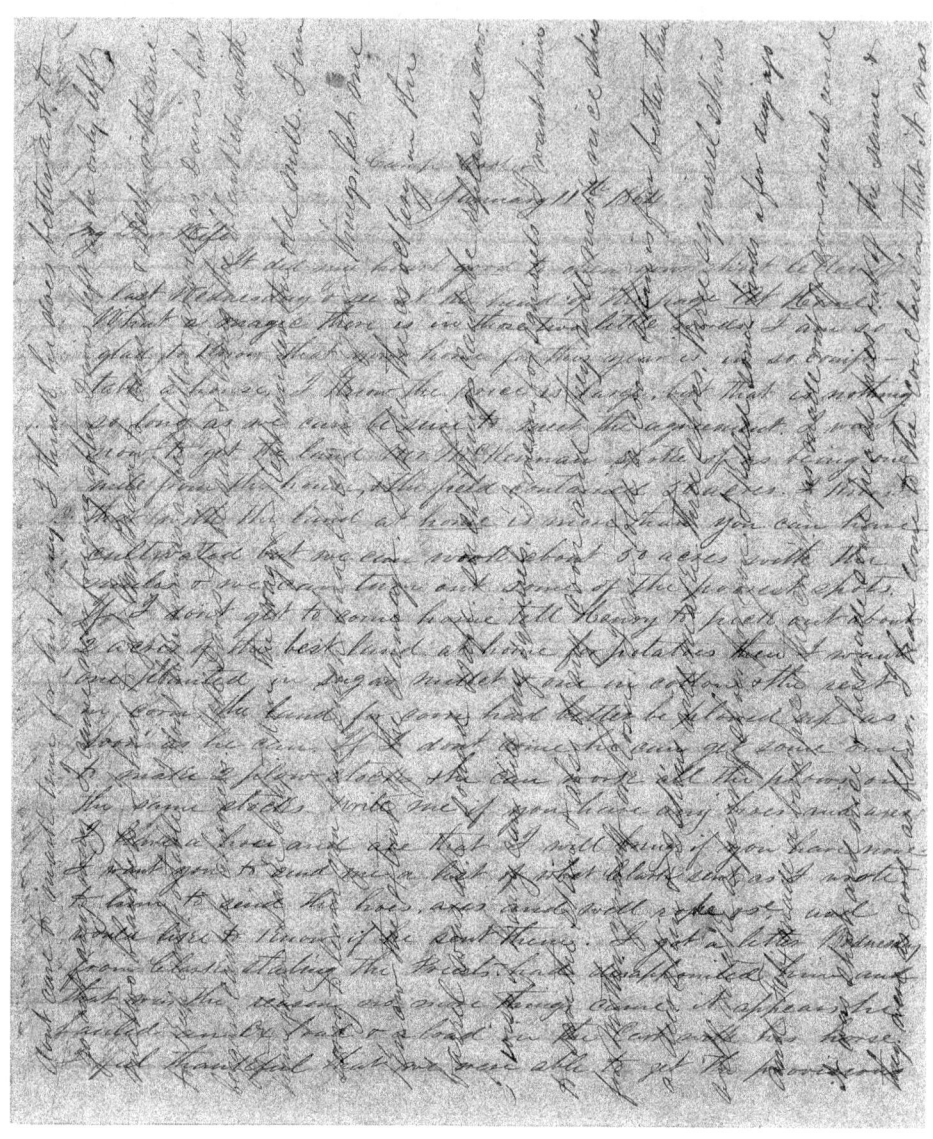

Letter from Winston Stephens to his wife, Tivie, 11 January 1864.

Edited by Arch Fredric Blakey,
Ann Smith Lainhart,
and Winston Bryant Stephens Jr.

Rose Cottage Chronicles

Civil War Letters of the Bryant-Stephens Families of North Florida

University Press of Florida
*Gainesville Tallahassee Tampa Boca Raton
Pensacola Orlando Miami Jacksonville
Ft. Myers Sarasota*

Copyright 1998 by Arch Fredric Blakey, Ann Smith Lainhart, and Winston Bryant Stephens Jr.
All rights reserved
Printed in the United States of America. This book is printed on Glatfelter Natures Book, a paper certified under the standards of the Forestry Stewardship Council (FSC). It is a recycled stock that contains 30 percent post-consumer waste and is acid-free.

First cloth printing, 1998
First paperback printing, 2012

Permissions appear on the last printed page of the book.

Library of Congress Cataloging-in-Publication Data
Rose Cottage chronicles: Civil War letters of the Bryant-Stephens families of North Florida / edited by Arch Fredric Blakey, Ann Smith Lainhart, and Winston Bryant Stephens Jr.
p. cm.
Includes bibliographical references (p.) and index.
ISBN 978-0-8130-1550-7 (cloth)
ISBN 978-0-8130-4438-5 (pbk.)
1. United States—History—Civil War, 1861–1865—Personal narratives, Confederate. 2. Florida—History—Civil War, 1861–1865—Personal narratives. 3. Stephens, Winston John Thomas, 1829–1864—Correspondence. 4. Bryant, Octavia Louisa, 1841–1908—Correspondence. 5. Married people—Florida—Correspondence. 6. Stephens family—Correspondence. 7. Bryant family—Correspondence. 8. Florida—History—Civil War, 1861–1865—Biography. 9. United States—History—Civil War, 1861–1865—Biography. 10. Welaka (Fla.)—Biography.
I. Blakey, Arch Fredric. II. Lainhart, Ann S. III. Stephens Jr., Winston Bryant.
E605.R77 1998
973.7'82—dc21   97-44236

The University Press of Florida is the scholarly publishing agency for the State University System of Florida, comprising Florida A&M University, Florida Atlantic University, Florida Gulf Coast University, Florida International University, Florida State University, New College of Florida, University of Central Florida, University of Florida, University of North Florida, University of South Florida, and University of West Florida.

University Press of Florida
15 Northwest 15th Street
Gainesville, FL 32611-2079
http://www.upf.com

Contents

Preface *vii*

Introduction *1*

1 My Own Little Home: Courtship and Marriage, 1858–1859 ⁃ 33

2 Life at Rose Cottage, 1859–1861 ⁃ 50

3 It Is the Duty of Every Man to Help Drive Back the Invader ⁃ 60

4 A New Captain, a Long Year, a Divided Family Reunited for a Day ⁃ 85

5 Farewell Little Bell; Farewell Rose Cottage ⁃ 186

6 Tragedy Strikes Again; and Again ⁃ 300

7 End of an Era; Farewell Dixieland ⁃ 354

8 The Sad Times Continue ⁃ 369

Bibliography ⁃ 375

Index ⁃ 379

Illustrations follow page ⁃ 84

Preface

Rose Cottage Chronicles differs from most published accounts of the Civil War, for there are no generals or political leaders on center stage here; no perceptive and well-placed Mary Chesnut, whose memoirs were published as *A Diary from Dixie* in 1905 and as *Mary Chesnut's Civil War* (edited by C. Vann Woodward) in 1981; no indefatigable John B. Jones, the writer of *A Rebel War Clerk's Diary at the Confederate States Capital* (1866); no pomp or pageantry. In fact, there is very little of what one normally expects to read when visiting this most tragic time in American history. What we do find is a complete picture of what most people in the Confederacy experienced, how they coped with the daily challenges unleashed by the war, and especially what it was like for women on the homefront. We hear from the men too, some in combat, some not, and the result is a balanced view of what life in the Confederacy was like. The diaries and letters of the correspondents capture the pathos and pain that millions experienced on a daily basis.

This is also a love story, an intimate account of the courtship and marriage of Winston Stephens and Octavia (Tivie) Bryant and the effect the war had on them. The courtship was prolonged, erratic, and stormy; the marriage was very nearly perfect and far too brief.

When Winston proposed to Tivie in the summer of 1856, he was a twenty-six-year-old planter, widely esteemed in Welaka, Florida, and the surrounding countryside. His intended was the daughter of the town's founders, James W. and Rebecca Bryant, who vehemently opposed the engagement. Their opposition was understandable, for Tivie was not yet fifteen years old. They immediately sent her to a school for young ladies in Massachusetts and made her promise to wait until she was eighteen before considering any proposal of marriage. Dutiful daughter that she was, Tivie agreed and departed for Boston that September for a fourteen-month stay. It was at this time that she began keeping a diary and also when she and Winston began the correspondence that is the focal point of this story.

When she returned to Welaka in 1858, Winston resumed his courtship. Winston and Tivie were married on 1 November 1859, even though her parents still had reservations, and moved into their Rose Cottage home, where they settled into a blissful marriage. A daughter, Rosalie (Rosa), was born on 17 October 1860, further enriching the lives of the happy couple. Three months later, on 10 January 1861, Florida seceded from the Union.

Winston's company was organized in September and mustered into service in November 1861. Although his unit was not to serve out of state and he was usually within a hundred miles of Welaka, his visits home were brief and infrequent, and the mail service was slow and irregular. Separated for long periods of time, both Winston and Tivie saved each other's letters, and almost the entire correspondence was thus preserved.

The couple revealed their deepest feelings to each other without any idea that their writings would one day become public. Tivie would have been mortified at this invasion of her privacy; Winston, on the other hand, would have probably chuckled and urged the invader to "have a good read." And it is a good read, even though their marriage lasted just four years and four months. Those few years brought events that most people never encounter in a long lifetime, and the story would be worth recounting even if it were confined solely to their remarks.

But there is more to this story, and the telling of the tale becomes more enriching and rewarding because several of their close relatives were also avid correspondents. On Tivie's side, we have the thoughts and experiences of her parents (James and Rebecca), her brothers (Willie, Davis, Henry, and George), and some of her aunts and uncles, including the indomitable Julia (Bryant) Fisher of Thomasville, Georgia.

Winston's relatives also have their contributions to make; this is especially true of his brother Clark and Clark's wife, the former Augustina Fleming, of the famous Hibernia plantation. We hear from another brother, Swepston, and from his mother, Mary Ann (Stephens) Gaines, as well. All of these correspondents were very well educated for the times, but, like most people of that era, they had their own unique ways of spelling.

The two families were divided over the war. Most gave their allegiance to the Confederacy; Tivie's father remained loyal to the Union; others attempted neutrality. There was nothing unique or even unusual in such variety of response, for thousands of families in the North and the South were torn apart by the war. What is unique is that each was apart from the others, except for Tivie and Rebecca, and each had different experiences and wrote from a different perspective, male and female, parent and child, Northern and Southern. This diversity, and the adversity each encountered, in large measure span the entire gamut of emotions that the war brought forth. Finally, this story offers a rare glimpse of northeastern Florida during those critical years, a panoramic survey of life in that region that is, in and of itself, a contribution to Civil War, Southern, state, local, and family history.

The introduction presents the cast of characters as they arrive and assume their positions in antebellum Florida. A detailed account of northeast Florida and the experiences of both families prior to 1858 is offered, but in 1858 the characters begin to speak for themselves through their diaries and letters. The account of the antebellum years 1858–1861 is continued in their own words with only a short introduction provided.

Chapter 1 covers the years of courtship culminating with the couple's marriage in 1859, and chapter 2 presents an overview of what the years 1859 to 1861, the last years of peace, were like at their Rose Cottage home. Chapters 3 through 7 deal with the wartime experiences of the whole family on a yearly basis from the autumn of 1861 to the end of the war, but two of the major members of the cast were silenced forever in 1864; Winston was killed on 1 March, and Rebecca Bryant died five days later. After that time the focus shifts to the experiences of Tivie's brothers, Willie and Davis, although other correspondents are also included. Chapter 8 concludes the study.

Some parts of the letters are not pleasant reading; language concerning the slaves and African-American soldiers will likely outrage the modern reader, but no attempt has been made to omit or modify words or modes of expression to make these offensive passages more palatable. The cast were unusual in many ways, but they fully subscribed to the prevailing ethos of their time and place when it came to racial matters.

This rich and varied collection owes its existence to Winston B. Stephens Jr. of Jupiter, Florida. As a teenager, Win became fascinated with the events covered in the 33 diaries and 863 letters of his great-grandparents. Later on he became convinced of their unique value, and in 1975 he donated them to the P. K. Yonge Library of Florida History at the University of Florida in Gainesville. Two other Bryant descendants also donated portions of the collection: William B. Parker Sr., husband of the deceased Rosalie (Geer) Parker (granddaughter of Davis Hall Bryant), who was planning to make the donation but died before she was able to do so; and Cordelia (Bryant) McIlwain (granddaughter of Henry Herbert Bryant).

The Bryant-Stephens Collection was used sparingly by various scholars from time to time, but the material consisted of a large mass of unorganized correspondence until professional genealogist and Bryant-Stephens descendant Ann S. Lainhart of Peabody, Massachusetts, became involved. Over a period of several years, she organized and transcribed that portion of the collection covered in this work. The transcript came to almost two thousand typed pages. To produce a manuscript of a publishable size, we have included only about one-fourth of the available material. (The collection contains material well into the twentieth century. Ann has written about earlier generations of the Bryant family in "The Descendants of Abraham Bryant of Reading.")

Ann, Win, and I have spent many hundreds of hours laboring over this collection, and "labor" is the operative word since much of the correspondence is exceedingly difficult to read. The shortage of paper in the Confederacy necessitated the use of cross-writing, a device that doubled the amount that could be written on a page but inflicts sheer torture on those who would attempt a transcription (see frontispiece). Numerous entries are virtually illegible, and while a few phrases have defied our combined and repeated deciphering attempts, nothing of importance has remained concealed.

The entries that have been selected appear in large measure as they were written. We have occasionally adjusted the punctuation, inserted a word, omitted word doubling, or corrected a misleading misspelling without informing the reader, but most grammatical mistakes and misspellings have been left intact in order to preserve the textual integrity. Proper names and places have been quietly corrected in some places and [sic] has been used only when an error of fact has occurred; the correction appears in the accompanying footnote. For easier reading, "&" has been replaced by "and" and "&c" has been replaced by "etc."

All journal entries are by Tivie, unless Rebecca is specified. Many journal entries have been omitted in toto, usually because they were repetitious or were concerned with mundane matters. This is particularly true of the journals covering 1862 and most of 1863 (Tivie and Rebecca kept journals simultaneously at this time), and the same is true for some entire letters. When entries from either source have been edited, three ellipsis points indicate the omissions.

I was selected to place this manuscript in the proper historical perspective. As the historian, I must take full responsibility for any errors of fact that remain, but as an editor I wish to stress that Ann and Win have been full participants in shaping this work in every way. They have shared in the research, and both have contributed heavily in this area. Although I wrote the introduction and the footnotes, we all edited and revised these portions just as we did all the other entries. This has been a team effort from start to finish and a rewarding learning experience for us all.

Arch Fredric Blakey
Yula Landing on the Suwannee River

Introduction

The United States acquired Florida from Spain in 1821, but almost a quarter of a century passed before the territory became a state. The most important reason for the long territorial status was that Florida's population was too small. In 1821 a territory could apply for statehood if it had 30,000 free inhabitants; it is doubtful whether there were 5,000 people (Seminoles not included) in Florida at that time. A special census taken in 1825 reported a total population (free and slave) of only 13,554. Yet more than 20,000 people moved to Florida during the next five years. The Federal census of 1830 recorded some 34,730 Floridians (free and slave), a substantial increase, but Congress also raised the requisite free population for admission to 47,700 that year.[1]

This rapid growth subsided during the next decade because Florida experienced trying times during the 1830s. Economic development and population growth were hampered by the great freeze of 1835, a long recession following the financial panic of 1837, and a seven-year conflict known as the Second Seminole War; from 1835 to 1842 almost all of the settled areas of Florida were adversely affected by this attempt to remove the Seminoles to reservations west of the Mississippi River. The population in 1840 came to some 32,600 whites and 21,800 slaves, a total of only 54,477.[2]

A second factor that delayed statehood was that Floridians were divided over the matter. The territory was extremely large geographically but was settled only in three widely separated areas. East Florida, the focus of this study, stretched from the Atlantic to the Suwannee River, and the residents favored statehood only if the rest of Florida were excluded. These divisionists, as they were called, were opposed by the settlers of Middle Florida (the region between the Suwannee and Apalachicola Rivers), who wanted the entire territory to come in as a single state. Many in West Florida, from the

---

1. Tebeau, *History of Florida*, 133–34; Fifth Census of the United States, 1830, Florida; Williams, "Florida in the Union," 1–2; Sidney Walter Martin, *Florida during Territorial Days*, 258.
2. Sixth Census of the United States, 1840, Florida.

Apalachicola River to the Perdido River, wished to be annexed by the state of Alabama.

Middle Florida was the most influential of the three regions. The five-county area centered around Tallahassee was the most populous and prosperous section of Florida. A land of large cotton plantations and large slave concentrations, these red hills constituted the true "black belt" of Florida.[3] Middle Florida was the political and economic center as well as the geographic and cultural center of the territory, and statehood proponents there were encouraged in 1837 when territorial governor Richard Keith Call proposed that a state constitutional convention be held.

The struggle for admission under the proposed constitution became a partisan fight. Democrats united in favor of a single state under the constitution, but Whigs everywhere opposed the provisions dealing with banks, and Whigs in East Florida remained committed to division.[4] Banks were in bad odor with most Floridians (all of the banks failed during the Seminole War), and the constitution placed severe restrictions on the chartering of any future banks and expressly forbade any bank officer to hold political office. Merchants and many large planters were dismayed by these provisions and supported the probank position of the Whigs.[5]

Another provision of the constitution aroused opposition in Congress. Senators and representatives from the Northern states were appalled that the document not only legitimized and protected the institution of slavery but expressly denied the right of any future state legislature to abolish the peculiar institution. Equally offensive, no free black could enter Florida, and all slaves who were freed by their owners had to leave within thirty days. These same passages were strongly defended by Southern congressmen, and the debate over Florida's admission added fuel to the ongoing national argument about the proper place of slavery in the United States.

In 1841 David Levy became territorial representative for Florida, and statehood advocates as well as avid Southerners found a new champion. This ardent Democrat worked unceasingly for the next four years, in Florida and

---

3. In 1830 more than 55 percent of the total population (19,133 out of 34,730) resided in this section.

4. The Whig Party appeared as an organization determined to defeat President Andrew Jackson in 1832. The Whigs were not a cohesive party and could not take a stand on any controversial issue without dividing sectionally; they tended to take a moderate position or avoid any position whenever possible until they self-destructed in 1854. They were generally people of property and more conservative in their views than the majority of Americans, but they conducted five presidential campaigns and won the office twice.

5. Under the constitution, banks could be chartered for a maximum of twenty years with no renewal and could engage only in the business of exchange, deposit, and discount. Williams, "Florida in the Union," 8–16.

in the national capital, for the admission of Florida as a single state. His appeal to Floridians included the powerful argument that it would be anti-Southern to oppose statehood, that it was their duty to enter the Union in order to protect the Southern way of life.

Ultimately, several Northern congressmen voted against admission, claiming that Florida lacked the requisite population. But Levy made a convincing argument that the population exceeded 90,000, and on 1 March 1845, both houses voted to admit Florida as the twenty-seventh state. The admission was part of a package; Florida and Texas came in to balance the proposed admittance of the free states of Iowa and Wisconsin. The addition of Texas would involve the nation in a war with Mexico the following year, and there was still considerable grumbling about Florida's actual population, but President John Tyler signed the bill into law on 3 March 1845.[6]

An examination of the 1845 state census reveals that those who doubted Levy's figures were correct; the free population of the state was only 36,707. Only if the 30,015 slaves were counted according to the Federal ratio (that is, as $3/5$ of a person each), for a combined total of 54,716, did the state meet congressional requirements for statehood. Be that as it may, Florida was now a state, the Seminole troubles were largely over, and the citizens experienced flush times for the next fifteen years.[7]

Appropriately, Levy was selected as Florida's first U.S. senator. He changed his name to David Levy Yulee at that time and took his place in the Senate as a firm ally of John C. Calhoun of South Carolina. Yulee joined that South Carolina school of politics that took the extreme Southern position that slavery was a positive good, a Christian duty, and could not be excluded from any public territory of the United States. In effect, the adherents of this view gave fair warning that any attempt to interfere with either the existence or the expansion of slavery would be thwarted, even if it meant the destruction of the Union. This radical viewpoint was endorsed by most white Floridians.

6. Williams, "Florida in the Union," 26–32; Dodd, *Florida Becomes a State*, 74–85. The statehood bill precluded any division of Florida in the future, but Texas was not so restricted, although it never acted on the opportunity to become several states.

7. Based on the incomplete census of 1845; tax rolls and accounts presented by census takers; and Dodd, "Florida in 1845," 29, the Florida population in 1845 was about 66,800. The results from two small counties are missing, but there were 36,178 whites, 529 free blacks, and 30,015 slaves accounted for in the year of admission, for a total of 66,722. Enumerating the slaves on a $3/5$ basis reduced their count to 18,009; that number, added to the 36,178 whites and 529 free blacks, yielded the 54,716 population figure cited. The Third Seminole War, 1855–58, is something of an overstatement regarding that conflict. It was limited to southern and southwestern Florida, which was very sparsely settled and did not involve any significant forces from either the United States Army or Navy. Nevertheless, a number of Floridians from the more populous areas of the state, including Winston, Richard, and Swepston Stephens, felt obligated to join the state militia forces to continue the attempt to remove the Seminoles from Florida. See Covington, *Billy Bowleg's War*.

The population doubled between 1845 and 1860, and although all sections of Florida shared this experience, East Florida became the leader during the 1850s. Duval County increased from 1,970 residents in 1830 to 4,056 ten years later, and Jacksonville grew from a small village to an important river port. Although smaller than St. Augustine in population, Jacksonville was the most important community in East Florida. Because of its location on the St. Johns River, it became the principal market for exporting cotton and other products cultivated in the area.[8]

The St. Johns River flows north, so upriver and downriver are the reverse of what one expects. When heading downriver on the St. Johns, one is heading toward Jacksonville, Mayport, and the Atlantic Ocean. The focus of this story is upriver from Jacksonville, south of Black Creek, Picolata, and Palatka, to Welaka, in Putnam County, about halfway between Jacksonville and Enterprise (see map 1).

Putnam was created from parts of St. Johns and Alachua Counties in 1849 and bordered Duval County on the north and Marion County on the south. Putnam was the smallest county in East Florida with a population in 1850 of 688. Palatka became the county seat in 1850 since it was the only town in the county, and it was a mere village at that time.[9] The population of the county more than doubled during the next decade.[10] Palatka had become a prosperous little community by 1860, much more diversified than it was in 1850. The urban population came to 294 free inhabitants and 319 slaves, but it was

---

8. T. Frederick Davis, *History of Jacksonville,* 82; Gold, *History of Duval County,* 123.

9. When Clay County was organized in 1858, it became the northern boundary of Putnam County. Residents of eastern Florida and even residents of Putnam County differed over the correct spelling of Palatka; some insisted on "Pilatka" even after the Civil War ended. Winston and Tivie also differed; he used the former spelling and she spelled it "Pilatka." We have opted for consistency here and use "Palatka" throughout. Similarly, we have corrected the spelling of all proper names in the correspondence where confusion might result, but otherwise we have recorded spellings as they were written by the correspondents. In 1850 only 35 people in the town were engaged in nonfarming activities.

10. In 1860 there were 1,664 whites, 32 free blacks, and a slave force that had increased fivefold to 1,047. Despite this large accretion of slaves, Putnam County was not a region of large slave owners, but cotton and sugar production was booming and plantations were on the increase. Eighth Census of the United States, 1860, Schedule I, Population Schedule, Putnam County. All of the free blacks in the county lived in the town of Palatka in both 1850 and 1860. This very small social class, numbering only 932 in Florida in 1860, encountered increasing difficulties from the 1830s on, but those in Palatka were the exception to the rule; they increased in numbers and in economic wealth during the 1850s. Equally striking is the significant increase in the number of transplanted South Carolinians compared to ten years previously. In 1850 they had accounted for about 9 percent of the county's population; ten years later the figure exceeded 19 percent. Native Floridians accounted for almost 48 percent of the 1860 population; and while those of Georgia birth were still second in overall numbers, their number had declined from 38 percent in 1850 to about 23 percent in 1860.

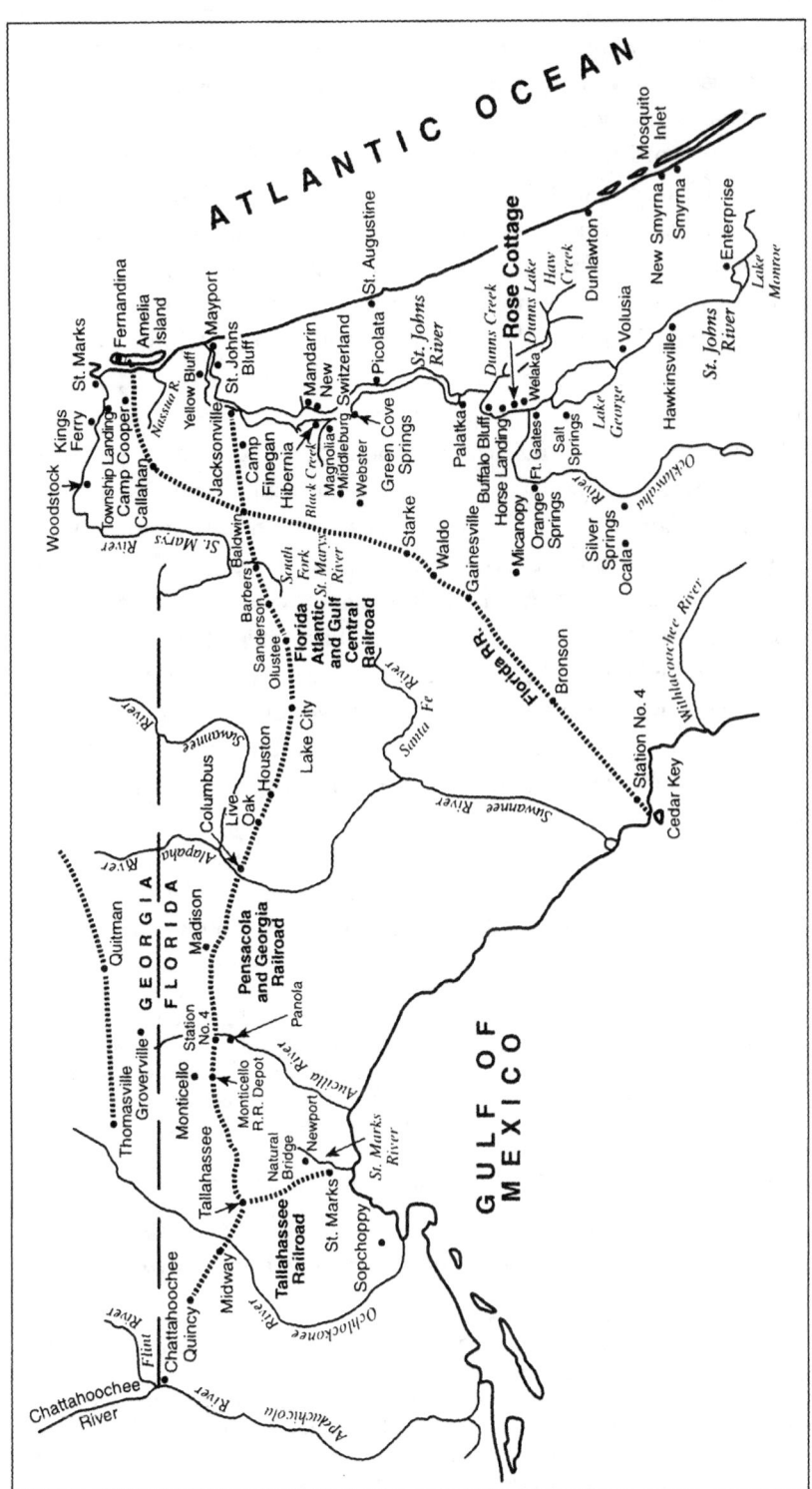

Map 1. East and Middle Florida during the Civil War. Source: An original map prepared by Arch Fredric Blakey and Winston Bryant Stephens Jr, from a variety of sources.

no longer the only town in the county.[11] Upriver, some eighteen miles south of Palatka and located at a sharp bend of the St. Johns, the new community of Welaka had come into being.

Welaka. The word meant "river of lakes" to the Native Americans of northeastern Florida and was their name for the river that whites later called the St. Johns. It was a name that appealed to the town's founder, James William Bryant, although some of the early residents would have preferred Bryantsville. The town was formed shortly after Bryant purchased a 500-acre tract known as Mt. Tucker on the east bank of the river on 6 July 1852. He also bought 2,000 acres on the opposite bank at the same time, paying $1,000 for the two properties. Both parcels were commonly referred to as the Crosby Grant, but only the Mt. Tucker portion became known as Welaka.[12]

Bryant was born on 7 January 1812, the second child (and first son) of Boston merchant James William Bryant and his wife, Ann (Andrews) Bryant (see the Bryant genealogical chart). During the next decade, the Bryants had six more children, and Ann was again pregnant when her husband died at age forty in 1826.[13] With the birth of this final child, Julia Maria, the thirty-six-year-old widow had the care and responsibility for seven children (two had died young), ranging in age from the newborn to her eldest daughter, who was sixteen. James was fourteen when his father died; as the eldest son, he had to seek full-time employment as soon as possible, and this he did in 1829.

Sometime that year, the seventeen-year-old Bryant departed Boston for South Carolina and became a clerk in the Taft mercantile firm in Charleston.[14] Bryant's father had been a cotton factor with Charleston connections,

11. The population mix for Palatka differed from that of the county; 41 percent there were Floridians, 14 percent were Georgians, and 13 percent were from the Palmetto State. Fully 32 percent came from other states and countries, and more than one-half of the latter were from areas that opposed slavery. This may be why the free black population of the county all lived in Palatka and fared well there while declining over the state as a whole. These figures were derived from a comparison of data for Putnam County from Schedule I of the Census of 1850 and Schedule I of the Census of 1860.

12. Deed Book A, 93–94, Putnam County Records, Palatka. Michael Crosby had received the land grant from the Spanish Crown in January 1818. The Indians called the river Weelaka; the French named it Rivière de Mai. The Spanish christened it Río de San Juan, and this was anglicized into the St. Johns River after Florida became a British possession in 1763. See Blakey, *Parade of Memories,* 1.

13. *Columbia Centinel,* 27 December 1826.

14. Stephens, "Reminiscences," written by Tivie early in the twentieth century, is part of the collection housed at the P. K. Yonge Library and described in the preface. There was no merchant by the name of Taft in Charleston in the 1830 census, and Bryant does not appear there either. This does not mean that Tivie was wrong in her recollection, but confirmation is lacking. Where it has been possible to check her "Reminiscences" for accuracy, Tivie was so correct that she must have referred back to the correspondence to bolster her memory.

BRYANT FAMILY 1786-1947

James William Bryant ——
(1786-1826)
md. Ann (Nancy) Andrews
(1790-1869)

—1. Caroline Ann Bryant ——
   (1808-1888)
   md. (1) Benjamin F. Perham
   (-1842)
   md. (2) Jared Everitt
   (-1875)

   —1. Frances Ann Perham
      (1835-)
      md. William H. Sharpe
      (-)
   —2. Alexander Paris Perham
      (1835-)

—2. James William Bryant ——
   (1812-1867)
   md. Rebecca Hathorne Hall
   (1813-1864)

   —1. William Augustus Bryant
      (1837-1881)
   —2. Davis Hall Bryant
      (1839-1914)
   —3. Octavia Louisa Bryant —— —1. Rosalie Bryant Stephens
      (1841-1908)   (1860-1883)
      md. Winston J. T. Stephens —2. Isabella Gertrude Stephens
      (1829-1864)   (1862-1863)
   —4. Henry Herbert Bryant —3. Winston Stephens
      (1847-1930)   (1864-1947)
   —5. George Perham Bryant
      (1849-1876)

—3. Lewis Henry Bryant ——
   (1814-1870)
   md. (1) Louisa H. Burritt
   (-1850)
   md. (2) Elizabeth
   (-)

   —1. Louisa Helen Bryant
      (1842-)
      md. Richard Tydings
      (-1890)
   —2. Julia A. Bryant
      (1844-)
   —3. William Henry Bryant
      (1846-)
   —4. Mary Bryant
      (1848-)

—4. Mary Frances Bryant ——
   (1823-1864)
   md. Samuel Seth Adams
   (1813/14-1889)

   —1. Wesley Adams
      (1843-1844)
   —2. Ann Elizabeth Adams
      (1845-1913)
   —3. George Henry Adams
      (1847-)
   —4. John William Adams
      (1849-1867)
   —5. Richard T. Adams
      (1851-)
   —6. Julia A. Adams
      (1853-1854)
   —7. Charles Darius Adams
      (1855-)
   —8. Mary Frances Adams
      (1857-)
   —9. Mitchel J. Adams
      (1860-)

—5. George Lawton Bryant ——
   (1824-1860)
   md. (1) Cecelia E. Overstreet
   (-1856)
   md. (2) Mary Ann Hankins
   (-)

   —1. Elizabeth B. Bryant
      (1851-)
   —2. George Ellis Bryant
      (1852/3-)
   —3. George Lawton Bryant
      (1860-)

—6. Julia Maria Bryant ——
   (1827-1876)
   md. (1) J. Ellis Fisher
   (-1854)
   md. (2) Samuel Seth Adams
   (1813/14-1889)

   —1. William Ellis Fisher
      (1854-1855)

and it is probable that the young man was also aided by close family friends, James Hall and his wife, Catherine (Davis) Hall.[15] Both the Hall and Davis families were prominent Boston merchants, and both had extensive contacts all along the Atlantic coast, including Charleston.

Within five years Bryant was in business for himself, and his relationship with the Hall family became even closer. In 1836 he returned to Boston and married Rebecca Hathorne Hall. The couple lived in Charleston for a short time but moved frequently during the next several years; their first son, William Augustus (Willie), was born in Massachusetts in 1837; their second child, Davis Hall, was born in Savannah two years later.[16]

In the interim, Bryant's younger brother Lewis Henry had moved to Jacksonville. In July 1839 he married Louisa H. Burritt, the daughter of lawyer-merchant Samuel L. Burritt and his wife, Louisa A. Burritt.[17] The newlyweds moved to the town of Madison in Middle Florida, about fifty miles from Tallahassee, and were joined by James and Rebecca sometime that year. James brought not only his wife and sons but also his mother, a younger brother, and two sisters who had been living with him.[18]

This was not an opportune time to come to Florida. The territory was in a financial depression, and the Seminole War further depressed prices and trade. Bryant rapidly discovered that he had made a poor choice and departed for Savannah and then New York in 1840. Late that year, or early in 1841, he decided to try Florida again and brought his family to the small community of Jacksonville. It was here that his third child and only daughter, Octavia (Tivie) Louisa Bryant, grew up.[19]

The town proper was quite small in 1840. The streets were sandy trails, some covered with sawdust. For much of the year, Jacksonville was a quiet place; the stores closed at dusk, and the townspeople usually went to sleep

15. The Boston City Directory lists J. W. Bryant as a cotton factor in 1816 and 1818.
16. Many of the birth, marriage, and death dates for the Bryant family are from a small book most likely kept by Julia Maria (Bryant) Fisher Adams and now in the possession of Cordelia (Bryant) McIlwain. Stephens, "Reminiscences."
17. Samuel and Louisa Burritt were from Connecticut and were among the most prominent residents in Jacksonville. In 1839 he became one of the original wardens and vestrymen of the St. Johns Episcopal Church. Unlike many Northern-born residents who had lived in the South for a long time, the Burritts remained loyal to the Union during the Civil War. After the war, he was elected to the October 1865 state constitutional convention as the representative of Duval County, but on 23 October 1865 he drowned with twenty-two others when the *D. H. Mount,* making her second run from New York to Jacksonville, went down off Cape Hatteras. Gold, *History of Duval County,* 115, 119, 155; T. Frederick Davis, *History of Jacksonville,* 361.
18. Sixth Census of the United States, 1840, Schedule I, Population Schedule, Madison County. These would be Bryant's mother, Ann (Andrews) Bryant, his younger brother, George Lawton, and sisters Mary Frances and Julia Maria; the Census of 1850 did not list them in Bryant's Jacksonville household, but they all moved to Welaka with him in 1852.
19. Stephens, "Reminiscences."

after the curfew hour of 9:00 P.M. But business was brisk during the harvest season.[20] By 1845 ocean steamboats from New York, Charleston, and Savannah made regular voyages south from Jacksonville to Palatka.[21] Although more than 400 residents lived in the immediate area, the Jacksonville business district was confined to one block on Bay Street, between Newnan and Ocean Streets (see map 2). Bryant initially moved into a house on the southeast corner of Duval and Market, across the street from where the Episcopal church would be built. Services began at the church in 1842. Bryant played first flute there; William Lancaster played second flute; and the choir was led by Dr. Abel S. Baldwin, who played bass viol. One of the singers in the choir was Harriett Reed; she and her husband, Arthur M. Reed, were the Bryants' closest friends in Jacksonville.[22] Reed owned a grocery and dry goods store on the northwest corner of Ocean and Bay Streets; and his twin daughters, Louisa (Lou) and Harriett (Hattie), born in 1841, became like sisters to Tivie.

The Bryants were visiting relatives in Massachusetts when Tivie was born on 21 October 1841. They returned to Jacksonville in mid-January 1842.[23] Shortly thereafter they moved across the street from the Reeds. Their home there, known as the Old Mills house, was located on the southeast corner of Forsythe and Ocean Streets. Much later Tivie recalled of this childhood home, "I rolled my hoop on a abutment along the river edge . . . when [there were] only two or three wharves there. Once after a storm the water rose nearly a block not far from the gate of Mr. Reeds house (and ours across the street), and Lou Reed and I rowed a boat across Bay street from Mr. Reed's store to a Mr. Kiel's. Also played ball with my brothers moonlight nights on sawdust down the middle of the street, two or three girls with us."[24]

20. T. Frederick Davis, *History of Jacksonville*, 82; Gold, *History of Duval County*, 123.

21. South of Palatka the river becomes narrower and shallower, and it was necessary to transfer to smaller steamers for the weekly upriver run to Enterprise on Lake Monroe. T. Frederick Davis, *History of Jacksonville*, 51–82; Rinhart, *Victorian Florida*, 55–56.

22. Gold, *History of Duval County*, 115; T. Frederick Davis, *History of Jacksonville*, 94, 396. The other two singers were Eliza Lancaster and Hannah Douglas, wife of William Douglas. Hannah's sister, Harriett Reed, also played the melodeon, a small organ that was carried to and from the church by one of the family slaves. Reed was one of the most influential men in Jacksonville. In addition to his mercantile business, he leased a plantation south of the city, and in 1857 he established the Bank of St. Johns, a private bank capitalized at $50,000.

23. Family papers indicate that Tivie was born in Newton, Massachusetts, on the date indicated. Although this may be considered a suburb of Boston, it was and is a separate town.

24. Stephens, "Reminiscences." Tivie was only five years old when the storm she describes hit Jacksonville in October 1846. The water rose more than two feet in stores on Bay Street, and this led to the bulkheading and straightening of the riverfront from Ocean to Pine Streets in 1848. Logs were squared, stacked, and held together by staples and chains to form a seawall, which was called the "buttment." Morris Kiel was a tailor, and his wife ran the family's small dry goods store. Actually, there were four wharves in Jacksonville in 1850, but Tivie no doubt remembered when there had been only two or three. See T. Frederick Davis, *History of Jacksonville*, 83.

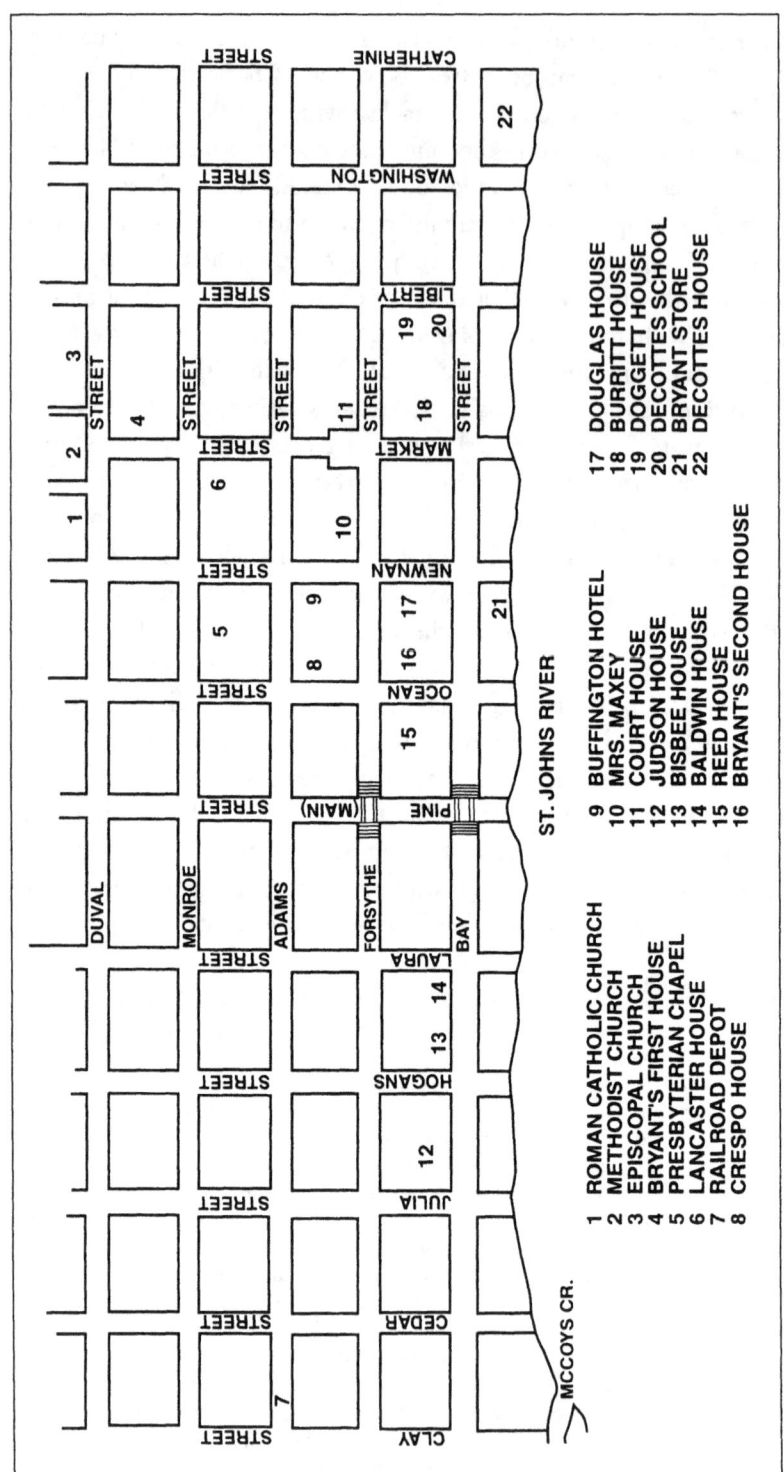

Map 2. Antebellum Jacksonville. Source: An original map prepared by Arch Fredric Blakey and Winston Bryant Stephens Jr., based primarily on the work of T. Frederick Davis, *A History of Jacksonville*.

Bryant worked hard all of his life and engaged in several different occupations. He was at various times a merchant and was editor and co-owner of at least two newspapers, but in 1850 he was known primarily as a lawyer. He was never spectacularly successful and apparently went bankrupt at least once; but the 1850s were prosperous years, and his assets in 1860 were valued at $9,000.[25] He also had business holdings in Havana and was frequently absent from his family for extended periods throughout the 1850s.

Jacksonville merchants began an extensive wholesale trade with Cuba during the 1830s. As early as 1835 Samuel Burritt embarked on this venture, and within five years Jacksonville became the wholesale distributing center for all of Florida. Timber was a very important export, and Jacksonville had a number of sawmills turning out rough and finished lumber when Florida became a state. Exports to Cuba included lumber, fish, and naval stores; the Florida firms imported sugar, coffee, fruits, salt, molasses, rum, and cigars. Bryant entered into this trade shortly after his arrival in Jacksonville, probably in conjunction with his brother Lewis, who was Burritt's son-in-law. When he was absent, Rebecca and young Willie managed the store.[26]

Like other businessmen in Jacksonville, Bryant supported the effort to secure the Florida Atlantic & Gulf Central Railroad for the city. When the road was finally completed, Jacksonville residents could "take the cars" (to use the expression of the times) to Baldwin (a key strategic point during the Civil War) and from there either go to Cedar Key or continue west to Lake City, about forty miles in the interior. At Lake City one could board the Pensacola & Georgia line and continue west to Tallahassee, about a hundred miles distant. Even though the Jacksonville road was not open to traffic until 15 March 1860 and the service was not always as advertised, most citizens agreed that it was a big improvement over the previous means of transportation, a stagecoach that bumped about for four torturous days on the Jacksonville-to-Tallahassee run.[27]

The railroad came too late to benefit antebellum Jacksonville, but river traffic flourished, and the community continued to prosper and grow. By

25. Eighth Census of the United States, 1860, Schedule I, Population Schedule, Putnam County. Bryant also served one term in the Florida House of Representatives, from 1856 to 1858. See Michaels, *River Flows North*, 421. Bryant's newspapers were the *Cuban Messenger*, located in Havana, and the *American Gas-Light Journal*, located in Bloomfield, New Jersey.

26. T. Frederick Davis, *History of Jacksonville*, 74. Lewis Bryant moved to Savannah in 1843 and to South Carolina three years later but was back in Florida by 1850. It became apparent to all residents in the northern part of the state just how important a port Jacksonville was after the naval blockade was imposed in 1861; soon a shortage of everything was the norm.

27. T. Frederick Davis, *History of Jacksonville*, 341–42; Gold, *History of Duval County*, 124–25. Jacksonville officially became a city in January 1859, when the charter of May 1840 designating it a town was superseded. Lake City was known as Alligator until the railroads were built.

1850 the business section housed twenty-five mercantile firms, and Bryant decided to sell out in 1852 and found a new town upriver. This was a lucky move, for two years later almost all of the Jacksonville business section, including Bryant's former house and store, was destroyed by fire.[28] By that time the new town of Welaka was firmly in place.

Not all of the family came to Welaka in 1852. Bryant brought his wife and three of his children: Willie, previously mentioned; Henry Herbert, born in 1847; and George Perham (Georgie), born in 1849.[29] Tivie and her brother Davis stayed in Jacksonville, where they lodged with a Charleston couple, Edward Augustus DeCottes and his wife, who were also their teachers. Davis received instruction in French in an old ferry warehouse located at Bay and Liberty Streets, and Mrs. DeCottes ran a school for girls out of her home on Bay Street (the number of students in addition to Tivie was not recorded).[30]

Jacksonville experienced a smallpox epidemic during the summer of 1853, and the Bryants were directly involved; in fact, James Bryant was the cause of the outbreak. Bryant had been in Georgia on legal business and contracted the disease there. He returned and became ill while staying at the Buffington House, the most fashionable hotel in Jacksonville. A number of his friends visited him before the disease had been diagnosed and soon became infected. Sporadic cases began to develop, and within weeks a severe epidemic was in progress. Many deaths among both blacks and whites occurred before it was over, and many survivors, including Bryant, were badly pitted by the disease. Although Tivie had been vaccinated, she too caught the disease, but she escaped without pockmarks.[31]

In November Bryant brought Tivie and Davis to Welaka. The family was now a sizable clan. Besides his wife and children, Bryant had with him his mother; a younger brother, George; and his youngest sister, Julia, who had just married Ellis Fisher of Satilla, Georgia. Several of Fisher's relatives were also on hand, and the two families built a sawmill, warehouse, wharf, and several small houses near the mill. While the town was being laid out, Tivie and the rest of her immediate family lived in one of the mill houses until White Cottage, the Bryant home, was completed (see map 3). White Cottage,

28. T. Frederick Davis, *History of Jacksonville*, 100–101. It may be that Bryant hoped to create a permanent home for his family in Welaka in addition to gaining wealth through this "boosterism" that was so common in promoting new settlements on the frontier.

29. According to Tivie's "Reminiscences," Rebecca lost another infant after the birth of Georgie.

30. Stephens, "Reminiscences"; Seventh Census of the United States, 1850, Schedule I, Population Schedule, Duval County; T. Frederick Davis, *History of Jacksonville*, 415–16.

31. T. Frederick Davis, *History of Jacksonville*, 97–98. Tivie did not refer to this event in her later writings; possibly she was ashamed that her father was responsible for the tragedy. But in a letter to Winston on 7 August 1862, she noted, "I have not much faith in vacination, as I know one whose arm took finely not long before he had it, and I was pronounced proof against it, as mine did not take and we both had it."

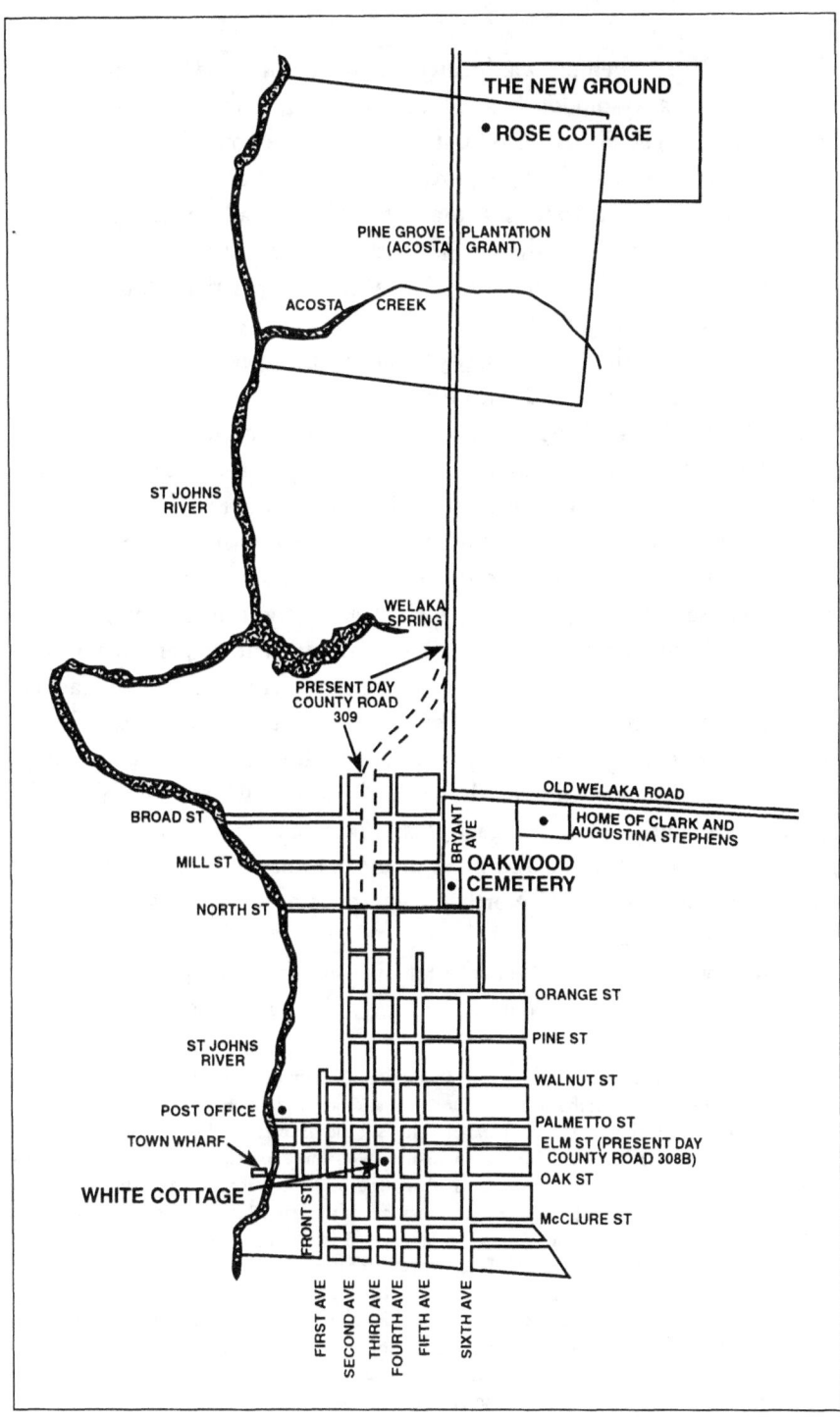

Map 3. Antebellum Welaka area. Source: An original map prepared by Winston Bryant Stephens Jr.

a large two-story dwelling, was located in what became the heart of the community. Bryant also sold lots to and built homes for his mother and his brothers and sisters. The Fishers also built more than one house.[32]

In July 1853 George Bryant purchased property north of his brother's holdings, paying $312.50 for a 256-acre tract known as the Acosta Grant. It would be on a portion of this property, the northern border of which was over two miles north of White Cottage in Welaka proper, that Winston would later build Rose Cottage.[33]

Julia Fisher's husband died in 1853, and the next year she moved to Thomasville, Georgia, and lived with her sister, Mary Frances, the wife of Dr. Samuel Seth Adams. George Bryant built a substantial house on his Acosta Grant (at an unknown location) but also decided to leave. He sold the property to Joseph Hastings for $1,319 on 1 May 1854 and returned to Jacksonville, but many more settlers arrived than departed during the 1850s.[34] The Bryants and Fishers who left Welaka, except for George, rented their houses rather than selling them, because Welaka was a good tourist area.

Many Northerners wintered at Welaka and other towns and plantations on the St. Johns, and some became permanent residents. They were drawn to this area for a number of reasons, the warm winters and its accessibility by water probably being the most important. In addition to the pleasant climate, northeast Florida was advertised as a health resort with "magical" sulfur springs, as a hunting and fishing paradise, and also as an exceptional place to gain wealth through trade and investments.[35] Many of these residents also spent their summers in the North, happy to be away from Welaka during Florida's "sickly season."

Growth was so rapid in Welaka that by 1860 the white population numbered 317 (55 more than Palatka), and sixty-six homes and stores had been

32. Deed Book A, 123–24, 149–50, 168–71, Putnam County Records, Palatka.

33. George Bryant bought the land from Domingo and Jany Acosta on 16 July 1853 (Deed Book A, 120–21, Putnam County Records, Palatka). He sold the property to Joseph Hastings in May 1854. See Deed Book A, 226–27. Mary Ann Gaines, Winston's mother, took out a 99-year lease with an option to buy the property on 27 December 1856. The rent was to be $100 annually for the first two years and then to rise to $180 for the remainder of the lease. After five years, Mary had the option to purchase the property for $1,500. In January 1857 Winston subleased the northernmost 100 acres from his mother to establish Pine Grove Plantation, renamed Rose Cottage two years later. See Deed Book B, 60–62, Putnam County Records, Palatka.

34. The sale is recorded in Deed Book A, 226–27, Putnam County Records, Palatka. Our speculation is that Bryant built the house on high ground south of Acosta Creek, but this is based solely on various entries in Tivie's journals. It was probably several hundred yards closer to Welaka than Rose Cottage, which stood 2.3 miles north of White Cottage; but all we can say for certain is that Bryant's house was somewhere on the road between Rose Cottage and Welaka.

35. Except for the claim that Florida was a healthy place, which it most definitely was not during the summer, the advertisements were accurate if exaggerated.

built. There were 137 slaves on the nearby plantations and farms and in Welaka proper, but only sixteen families were engaged in nonfarming activities. Like the rest of Florida, the Welaka area was inhabited by small farmers, although the small planter class was also in evidence.[36]

It was not just the river communities along the St. Johns that experienced a large influx of people during the antebellum years, for there was good cotton country in the interior of East Florida, particularly in Marion County. This county was created in 1844, shortly after the area was opened to settlement by the Armed Occupation Act, passed by Congress two years earlier. This law entitled any head of household to claim 160 acres as a homestead on lands formerly designated Indian territory. The land was free; one had only to work it for five years to acquire title, and hundreds seized the opportunity. In 1845 there were almost 1,500 people in Marion County, and Ocala (formerly Fort King) was the county seat. The following year the county also became the home of Winston Stephens and his family.

Winston John Thomas Stephens was born in 1829 on the family's 280-acre plantation along Goosepond and Millstone Creeks in northeastern Oglethorpe County, Georgia, some seventy miles east of Atlanta. He was the second of four sons born to Thomas Peter Goolsby and Mary Ann Jane (Taylor) Stephens (see the Stephens genealogical chart). Thomas was from a well-to-do family and attended the University of Pennsylvania, where he studied medicine before returning home to marry seventeen-year-old Mary Ann in 1826. Winston's elder brother, William Clark Taylor Stephens, was also born at home in 1827; his younger brother, Swepston Benjamin Whitehead Stephens, was born at home in 1833. The following year Thomas moved his family to Alabama. His fourth son, Minor Richard Goolsby Stephens, was born there in 1835.[37]

The Stephens clan (including Joshua, a younger brother of Thomas), arrived in Dallas County, Alabama, in August 1833 and purchased two tracts of land totaling about 240 acres (some fifteen miles west of present-day Selma). Two years later Stephens bought 320 additional acres near his plantation so that his total holdings came to about 560 acres. In February 1836 Thomas

---

36. Eighth Census of the United States, 1860, Schedule I, Population Schedule, Putnam County.

37. General Alumni Catalogue of the University of Pennsylvania (1917), 589; the marriage of Thomas and Mary Ann on 19 June 1826 is recorded in Smith, *Marriage Records of Greene County and Oglethorpe County, Ga.*, 201. It is rare to find the complete names for the Stephens children, but they are written out in full in the Orphans Court minutes of December 1845 concerning the death of Thomas Stephens. See Dallas County, Alabama, Probate Judge Records, Mscl. Probate Records, vol. F, 154, Orphans Court Minutes, LG 2627, microfilm reel 10, Alabama Department of Archives and History, cited hereafter as ADAH, Montgomery, Alabama. Goolsby was the maiden name of Thomas's mother, and Whitehead was Mary Ann's mother's maiden name.

STEPHENS FAMILY 1800-1947

Thomas Peter Goolsby Stephens ——
(ca. 1800-1836)
md. Mary Ann Jane Taylor
(ca. 1800-1875)

—1. William Clark Taylor Stephens ——
(1827-1904)
md. Augustina Alexandria Fleming
(1831-1900)

  —1. William Winston Stephens
  (1849-1910)
  —2. Lewis Isadore Stephens
  (1851-1914)
  —3. Mary Jane Stephens
  (1855-1930)
  —4. Charles Seton Stephens
  (1862-1915)
  —5. Edward L'Engle Stephens
  (1867-1944)

—2. Winston John Thomas Stephens ——
(1829-1864)
md. Octavia Louisa Bryant
(1841-1908)

  —1. Rosalie Bryant Stephens
  (1860-1883)
  —2. Isabella Gertrude Stephens
  (1862-1863)
  —3. Winston Stephens
  (1864-1947)

—3. Swepston Benjamin Whitehead Stephens
(1833-1907)
md. (1) Mary Ann Dunn
(1838-1860)
md. (2) Victoria Mills
(1843-1909)

—4. Minor Richard Goolsby Stephens
(1835-   )
md. (1) Caroline H. (Callie) Barnes
(1842-1861)
md. (2) Eugenia Richard
(1847-   )

Mary Ann Jane (Taylor) Stephens ——
(ca. 1800-1875)
md. (2) Lewis Clark Gaines
(1809-1861)

—1. Mary Gaines
(1841-   )
md. Jessup Branning
(-   )
—2. Lewis Gaines
(1844-1862)
—3. Benjamin Gaines
(1845-   )
—4. Rubannah Gaines
(1848-   )
—5. Ida Gaines
(1850-   )
—6. Alabama Gaines
(1854-   )

was killed when he fell from his horse during a fox hunt; his young widow now had to provide for her four sons, none of whom was yet ten years old. The estate, which included twenty-three slaves, was valued at $14,853.40. One of the slaves, a thirteen-year-old named Burrel, would in the future become the mainstay of Winston's labor force.[38]

For the next four years Mary Ann ran the plantation, but she did not have to do it alone. In addition to Joshua Stephens, she could also rely on Major Lewis Clark Gaines, the man who became her second husband. Lewis and his brother Phillip Pendleton Gaines were originally from Virginia, but they had been speculating in land in Washington, Sumter, Choctaw, and Dallas Counties, Alabama, during the early 1830s. Lewis first bought property in Dallas County in mid-1832 and continued to buy and sell property in the county for the next several years.[39] Gaines was a frequent visitor before and after Thomas Stephens died since he was the tutor for the Stephens boys after 1835. He sold his farm in June 1836 and soon moved into the Stephens home. In partial exchange for his room and board, he taught school and helped Mary Ann with the plantation books. Gaines also had six slaves; it appears that one of them was named Jane, and she was destined to become Burrel's wife and the property of Winston and Tivie Stephens in the future.[40]

On 2 April 1840 Mary Ann and Lewis Gaines married.[41] The census of that year reveals that Gaines had recently become a prosperous cotton

38. On 13 August 1833 Stephens bought two parcels of land: 159.75 acres for $199.69 and 79.71 acres for $99.04. On 15 December 1835 he bought another 79.70 acres for $99.63 and 239.51 acres for $299.39. His holdings came to 558.67 acres in all and were worked as two separate but nearby plantations. See Register of Certificates, Cahaba Land Office, Book 304, 318, 547. The estate was appraised on 24 February 1836; see Dallas County Probate Judge Records, Mscl. Probate Records—Accounts, Administrators, Guardians, etc., vol. D, 145–46, LG 2625, microfilm 3, ADAH, Montgomery, Alabama.

39. On 4 June 1832, Lewis Gaines bought 79.30 acres of land in Dallas County for $99.18. This was in Township 17, Range 8, Section 9. On 1 May 1835 Gaines purchased an additional 80 acres in Township 17, Range 8, Section 18, for $125.00. Register of Certificates, Cahaba Land Office, Book 304, 251; Deed Book D, 343; Deed Book E, 147, Dallas County Records, ADAH, Montgomery, Alabama.

40. Gaines sold his farm on 16 June 1836 for $475, but he and his brother continued to make land transactions for the next several years. They bought 120 acres for $150 on 2 January 1837 in Washington County and another 160 acres there for $800 on 7 January 1837. They sold both of these tracts for $1,327.40 on 1 June 1841. Many of the records for Choctaw (formerly Washington) County were lost in fires in 1857 and 1871, and it is not possible to trace all of the transactions of the Gaines brothers; but there were a number of other family members in that area at the time, and it is clear that they were moving a considerable amount of property. See Mscl. Probate Records for Dallas County, vol. E, 148, and Mscl. Probate Records, Washington County, Book H, 526–28, ADAH, Montgomery, Alabama. For the slaves of Lewis Gaines see Sixth Census of the United States, 1840, Schedule II, Slave Schedule, Dallas County, Alabama.

41. See Deed Book E, 293, Marion County Records, Ocala. No marriage records were located in Dallas or surrounding counties, and where they married remains unknown.

planter, and he proved to be a warm and generous father to his stepsons as well as to his own sons and daughters. He and Mary Ann had seven children, but their firstborn daughter, Mary (Minnie) Gaines, became the special favorite of both Clark and Winston Stephens and also of Tivie Bryant.

Although the plantation was a successful venture, yielding annual revenues of between $2,500 and $5,000, Mary Ann and Lewis were hampered by a substantial debt left by Thomas Stephens. The law required, for the sake of the minor children, that this debt be paid off within ten years or that the estate then be divided. In March 1844, unable to satisfy the debt, Lewis and Mary Ann appeared before the Orphans Court of Dallas County and asked that the estate be apportioned. Their request was approved, and the land was sold at public auction to the highest bidder on 21 December 1844 for a little more than $5,700; this money was distributed by the court during the January 1846 session, which also oversaw the distribution of the slaves (see table 1).[42]

After the legal affairs were concluded, the family decided to move to Marion County, Florida, not far from Ocala. Four years later both Clark and Winston had established their own separate domiciles nearby. Clark married seventeen-year-old Augustina (Tina) Alexandria Fleming in 1848, and the couple had a son, William Winston, the following year; but the godfather remained a bachelor.[43] In 1850 Winston's immediate "family" consisted of eight slaves.[44]

The fate of all of the slaves from the time of the death of Thomas Stephens to the arrival of the Gaines-Stephens family in Florida cannot be determined, but it is obvious that some had been sold and that the division mandated in 1846 had not been strictly adhered to. Clark received five slaves in 1846, including Banger, or Old Bangs, and Dicey, who were Burrel's parents, and Bill, Bob, and Mary. In 1850 Clark and Tina owned a fifty-year-old slave named Charley and a fourteen-year-old male named Brice, but the records are mute as to when they were acquired. Winston received five slaves as his

---

42. For an account of the sale of the plantation, which had increased to almost 1,000 acres, see Dallas County Probate Judge Records, Orphans Court Minutes, vol. F, 19–20, ADAH, Montgomery Alabama.

43. Tina Fleming was the daughter of Lewis Michael Fleming and his first wife, Augustina Cortez. Lewis's father, George Fleming, was born in Ireland and received 1,000 acres on what became known as Flemings Island in October 1800 for services he had rendered to the Spanish Crown. On the island he built a plantation that he named Hibernia, the Latin word for Ireland. He married Sophia Fatio, daughter of Francis Phillipe Fatio, who was one of the wealthiest planters in Florida. Lewis's first wife died when Tina was a child, and he married Margaret Seton. Both before and after the Civil War, Margaret took in boarders during the winter months at Hibernia. See Biddle, *Hibernia*. Clark and Tina married on 27 November 1848, and their son was born at Ocala on 26 September 1849. See Marriage Records Book B, 1, Marion County Records, Ocala.

44. Seventh Census of the United States, 1850, Schedule II, Slave Schedule, Marion County.

Table 1. Distribution, age, and value of Stephens slaves, January 3, 1846

Heir, age	Slave name	Value	Age
Mary Ann Jane Gaines, 46	Jess	$700	16
	Martha and	450	20
	child	150	1
	Jerry	450	12
	Total	$1,750	
William Clark T. Stephens, 18	Banger	$450	53
	Dicey	200	50
	Bill	550	14
	Bob	350	12
	Mary	350	11
	Total	$1,900	
Winston J. T. Stephens, 16	Burrel	$700	22
	Sarah and	400	26
	her child Jane	100	1
	Eveline	300	9
	Rachael	200	3
	Total	$1,700	
Swepston B. W. Stephens, 13	Joe	$700	14
	Sally	500	45
	Henry	250	7
	Fanny	200	5
	Jane	250	9
	Total	$1,900	
Minor Richard G. Stephens, 6	George	$450	50
	Sandy	400	55
	Melia and	500	23
	female child	100	1
	Julia	150	2
	Sammy	225	6
	Total	$1,825	
	Grand total	$9,075	

Source: Orphans Court Minutes, Dallas County, Alabama, January 1846 session, LG 2627, microfilm reel 10, vol. F, 154, ADAH, Montgomery, Alabama.

share of the estate in 1846, including a female named Eveline. Four years later she was not in his possession, but he did retain Burrel, Sarah and her child Jane, and Rachael. In addition he had acquired Big Jane (probably from Gaines), and she and Burrel had twin boys, Mose and Joe, born in 1849. Finally, he owned a slave named Tom, who was four years old in 1850, but how or when Winston acquired him is not known.

Of the eighteen slaves listed by Gaines in 1850, at least eleven belonged to Swepston and Richard, who were still minors. Of the remaining seven, some belonged to Clark, including Old Bangs and Dicey, previously mentioned. It is probable that Gaines leased out some of the slaves he and Mary Ann owned, so an accurate account is impossible to document.[45] At any rate, by 1850 Gaines and Mary Ann were established planters, and Winston and Clark were successful farmers.

Clark and Winston leased 80 acres of land from William Delk until 1854, when they jointly purchased the farm for $1,000. In August of the following year, Winston bought Clark's share (37.5 acres) for $400, as Clark had moved to Putnam County to the new town of Welaka. Winston and the rest of the family also decided to move there in 1856, but he continued to add to his acreage in Marion County.[46]

Marion County was settled by small farmers, but there were several large farms and one cotton plantation in existence in 1850. John H. Madison was the largest planter, but Gaines and his family were not far behind. Madison owned fifty-one slaves and 770 acres; Gaines and his family owned twenty-seven slaves and 586 acres. Neither Winston nor Clark listed their assets for the 1850 census, but Gaines reported that his plantation and slaves were valued at $7,000, second only to Madison in the county. Suffice it to say that Gaines and his sons were prominent people in Marion County from the day of their arrival.[47]

The correspondence does not reveal why they decided to leave this prosperous place, but the Gaines-Stephens family moved to Welaka in 1856, and

---

45. These numbers have been deduced from the Seventh Census of the United States, 1850, Schedule II, Marion County, and a number of references to various slaves in the correspondence.

46. The initial purchase occurred on 25 January 1854, and the 80-acre tract was located in Township 14 South, Range 21 East, Section 24. See Deed Book D, 564–65, Marion County Records, Ocala. Winston paid Clark $400 for his share on 27 August 1855. See Deed Book F, 473–74. Winston bought 80 acres from William Delk on 24 May 1859 in Township 14 South, Range 21 East, Section 23, for an unspecified amount of money. See Deed Book F, 707.

47. Seventh Census of the United States, 1850, Schedule I, Population Schedule, Marion County, and Schedule II, Slave Schedule, Marion County. Gaines also housed a carpenter and a stereotyper in 1850; most probably they were only temporary renters. For the land transactions of Lewis and Mary Ann, see Deed Book C, 454, and Deed Book D, 85–86, 132–33, Marion County Records, Ocala.

then the Gaines clan moved to Middleburg in Clay County two years later. It appears that Swepston, who attained his majority in 1853, followed the example of his two elder brothers. He apparently lived at home or leased a farm until September 1856, when he bought land of his own in Marion County. Like Clark, he married at an early age. His bride, Mary Ann Dunn, was just fifteen when they were wed in 1853; and they too had a son, Adolphus, within a year of their marriage.[48]

Even though he joined in the move to Welaka and also served with Winston in the Third Seminole War from 1857 to 1858, Swepston intended all along to return to Marion County and did so in 1859. Richard also returned to Marion County from Welaka at that time. Shortly thereafter, Richard married Caroline H. Barnes on 27 May 1860. Although the records are mute on this matter, Winston must have leased his farm from 1857 to 1859, and it appears that Richard leased it after that time. In the 1860 census he placed a value of $1,200 on the farm and $5,000 on his nine slaves.[49]

Clark and his family were the first to leave Marion County. They apparently rented a house in or near Welaka during the summer of 1855.[50] Clark was primarily a farrier, but by 1860 he was also a farmer. His farm was about a mile northeast of White Cottage. It appears that he leased the property from

48. Mary Ann and Swepston were married in Ocala on 1 June 1853; see Marriage Records Book B, 43, Marion County, Ocala. The only reference to her in the correspondence is when Tivie recorded in her journal on 26 February 1860 that Mary had burned to death. Only one entry in any official record regarding her death has been found; Schedule III of the 1860 census for Marion County, page 54, provides the following information: "Mary A. Stephens, age twenty-two, a native of South Carolina, burned to death, February 1860." Two sons—Adolphus, born in 1855, and William H., born in 1857—cannot be further accounted for, but Swepston was not a widower for long; he married Victoria Mills on 6 October 1860 (see Marriage Records Book B, 157, Marion County Records, Ocala). Vicky, as she was called, was the daughter of Archibald and Caroline T. Mills and was eighteen years old when she married. The family was from Georgia. The 1860 census listed their farm as worth $2,000, and the slave force of eight was valued at $6,000. Since one of the slaves was a hundred years old and two were under the age of ten, this seems to be a rather high evaluation.

49. Richard married Caroline, called Callie and Cad by Tivie and others. She was the daughter of David (deceased) and Henrietta Barnes of Marion County. Callie died in 1861, and Richard married Eugenia Richard of Duval County in January 1864. There is no record of a lease in the surviving records and no mention in the correspondence of what was done with the farm, but when Richard and Swepston bought each other out after their mother and her family moved in with Richard early in 1862, there was a disagreement between Winston and Richard over the transaction. Also, Winston still had part of his holdings; he told Tivie that she could always move back there after she left for Georgia in 1863. See Eighth Census of the United States, 1860, Schedule I, Population Schedule, Marion County; Schedule II, Slave Schedule, Marion County; and Marriage Records Book B, 154, Marion County, Ocala, for the data on Richard.

50. It cannot be determined exactly when they moved to Welaka. Tina gave birth to her daughter Mary Jane on 17 April 1855 at Ocala, and Winston did not buy Clark's share of the farm until August, so all that can be deduced is that they left Marion County for Welaka sometime during the summer of 1855.

Tina's brother, Lewis I. Fleming, and began clearing it in February 1860. He reported to the census taker that summer that he had farmed but 20 of his 60 acres and that his total crop consisted of only 150 bushels of corn, by far the lowest yield of any slaveowner in Welaka. Granted, his four slaves were not prime field hands. He owned one sixty-five-year-old man, a thirty-year-old woman, and two children, ages seven and one; but he also employed a white farm laborer named William Brown.[51] Still, he and Tina seemed quite content to rear their two sons and a daughter (see the Stephens genealogical chart) in these rather modest circumstances, although Tina did visit Hibernia plantation and Jacksonville occasionally.

Clark's younger brother was more ambitious. Mary Ann Gaines leased Pine Grove plantation (the old Acosta Grant) from Joseph Hastings in December 1856, and Winston leased the northern 100 acres from her the next month. Although he had a separate lease and his own slaves, the whole family lived together in the house built by George Bryant. Within a short time Gaines's health failed, and Mary Ann was also frequently sick and unable to run the plantation. In December 1858 they decided to move to Middleburg, where Gaines could teach school.

At that time, Winston took control of the whole estate, and the next year Rose Cottage became the official name of the plantation after he and Tivie married. Shortly after the marriage, Tivie bought 60 adjoining acres (referred to as the "new ground" in their correspondence), so the plantation consisted of almost 320 acres in 1860. In that year Winston reported that he and his slave force of ten (although two were too young to work) had produced 7 bales of sea island cotton, 200 bushels of sweet potatoes, 50 bushels of peas and beans, and 150 bushels of corn on the 60 acres then being cultivated.[52]

51. Although the lease was not recorded, we are convinced that the farm was the 60.59 acres owned by Tina's brother Lewis I. Fleming. This was in Township 12 South, Range 26 East, Section 3; see Deed Book B, 498, Putnam County Records, Palatka. For the slaves and crop yields, see Eighth Census of the United States, 1860, Schedules II and IV. Of the four slaves, only three can be identified. On 22 January 1858, Tina received two slaves from Soloman F. Halliday of Alachua County. The Hallidays had in large measure reared Tina after her mother died, and they obviously considered her part of the family. Halliday's wife, Mary J. (Fleming), Tina's aunt, had recently died, and it was her request that Sophie, twenty-eight, and her daughter, Domingo, four, be given to Tina. The elderly slave man was Charley, and a baby girl, Mary, was also listed in 1860. Brice, a male who would have been about twenty-four years old, was not recorded in the census data for Clark, but he was there in 1862, according to the correspondence. There was a male slave of that age living with Gaines in Middleburg in 1860, but whether or not he was Brice is unknown. Without a doubt, Clark raised other crops that were simply not reported on Schedule IV, which is well known for its inaccuracies. For the Halliday transaction, see Deed Book B, 172, Putnam County Records, Palatka.

52. As mentioned in note 33 above, Mary Ann Gaines leased the 256.75-acre Acosta Grant from Joseph Hastings on 27 December 1856. Winston subleased 100 acres from his mother in January 1857, the northernmost portion of the property; and Tivie purchased an adjoining 60.75 acres from the U.S. government in November 1859, just after she and Winston married. See Eighth Census of

Winston planned to clear and plant the whole 320 acres, and he made some progress in this direction before the war put an end to his efforts. Until the war came, Winston toiled in the fields with his slaves much of the time and closely oversaw the planting and cultivation of his crops, especially cotton. During the war he gave Tivie explicit instructions on what the slaves should do in managing his plantation.

The cash crop of Florida and the Lower South was, of course, cotton, but there were two different types or varieties grown and marketed. The most common by far was upland or short-staple cotton, which was grown all over the Southern states. Cloth from the short-staple variety was used for everything from common clothing to the sails for ships. It was this crop that made the South the Land of Cotton.

The sea island or long-staple variety, which yielded a much more luxurious cloth, could be grown only along the sea islands of South Carolina, Georgia, and northern Florida (hence the name) and along the banks of the St. Johns River as far south as Marion and Lake Counties. While the yield per acre was less than that for upland cotton, the price was usually more than twice as much for long-staple, so it was grown everywhere it could possibly be grown, and Florida outproduced both South Carolina and Georgia after the mid-1850s.[53]

The two varieties of cotton were so different, from planting to ginning, that they can be properly treated as two separate crops. For example, gangs of slaves tended the upland variety, while the task system was used for the cultivation of sea island cotton. The latter had to be picked from the boll, whose burrs could inflict severe cuts on the hands of the worker, while the short-staple had no burrs, and the entire boll could be snapped off of the stem. The whole short-staple crop matured at the same time and had to be picked quickly, or the crop would be lost. Sea island cotton could be picked

---

the United States, 1860, Schedule IV, Putnam County, for Winston's reported crop yields. While it appears that Winston assumed physical control of the entire acreage, he did not farm the southern part of the Acosta Grant, and it may be that the plantation called Rose Cottage consisted of only 160 acres. Winston owned Burrel, Big Jane, and their children, Mose, Joe, Jane, and Jess. He also owned Tom, Rachael, and Sarah but leased Sarah's daughter, Jane, from Nicholas Bradley of Clay County.

53. The price of upland cotton for the decade of the 1850s was $.11–.12 per pound, while Winston received $.28 per pound for his 1860 crop. Short-staple cotton was not profitable until after Eli Whitney invented a cotton engine, or gin, in 1793, which separated the small green seeds from the fiber. Long-staple was cultivated before the gin appeared since the large black seed could be separated from the silky fleece by hand relatively easily. Long-staple seed looks very much like a large apple seed except that it is more regular in shape and is covered with fine hairs. Long-staple was reportedly grown as far inland as Tallahassee (see Shofner and Rogers, "Sea Island Cotton," 376), but it could be grown commercially only in the areas mentioned above. The editors would like to thank Hugh A. Peacock for sharing his knowledge of Florida's sea island cotton experience with us.

up to eight times over a six-month period as the bolls matured. By and large, long-staple was much more expensive, difficult, and time-consuming to grow, and the entire rhythm of farming it was different from that of farming short-staple.

According to most accounts, the slaves were much better off when the task system was used. In the gang system, slaves usually worked from "can see to can't see" under the rigid control of a driver, overseer, or owner. Winston and his slaves also started early, 5:30 A.M. usually, but they were out of the fields by 5:00 P.M. or earlier. Also, their tasks varied from day to day for much of the year, and this helped to break the monotony that was so ubiquitous in the slaves' world. Burrel and the rest of the slaves usually worked five and one-half days per week for Winston and had half of Saturday to hunt or fish, rest, or work in their gardens. Except for Burrel, they never worked on Sunday, and on that day he worked for his God; he was the only permanent preacher in Welaka. Still, even though they had quite a lot of time off from work, they were slaves and subject to the will of their master. If it pleased Winston to do less work in the fields after he married than he had before, then the slaves had to work harder. Winston's slaves undoubtedly had a better life than most, since he rarely if ever used the whip, but the work was hard, and everyone experienced lean times when crops failed or the harvest was small.

Cotton may have been king, but corn was the indispensable crop; one could survive without the former, but there was no substitute for this daily staple. Two crops per year were grown, each taking about four months to mature. Grass was the main nemesis of both corn and cotton and had to be plowed and hoed on a frequent basis.

The basic Southern diet was pork and corn; everything else was secondary. Pretty much the whole hog was used (everything except the squeal, as the saying went), and this was also true for the corn plant. The ears, leaves, and stalk were all important to both people and animals. The ears went for food, of course, and made meal, mush, bread, pone, hominy, grits, or "roasenears" (roasted ears, or corn on the cob). Hogs were fattened on corn for a month or so before being butchered to increase their flavor, and they and other livestock also ate the leaves and eventually the stalk. Livestock also consumed the cob as fodder, and people used the cob in place of toilet paper. After the crop was laid by, peas were sown between the rows, and the stalks served to support the climbing pea vines after the ears were picked. Once the peas were harvested, the livestock was turned into the field to eat the stalks.[54]

54. Corn required less hoe work and thus was less labor-intensive than cotton. The phrase "laid by," used then and today, means that the crop has been cultivated by hoe or plow for the last time.

Winston's 1860 production of 150 bushels meant that he had to buy additional corn, for that amount would not feed fifteen people plus the livestock for a year.⁵⁵ Although there is no mention of any transaction in the journals, it seems likely that Winston bought some of the surplus that Clark produced. Since about fifteen bushels could be grown per acre, Winston apparently devoted about ten acres to corn, around half the acreage allotted to cotton. If that is so, he was following a pattern that became obvious shortly before and during the war; the cotton mania resulted in far too many farmers' literally taking food from their tables to produce the staple, and the result was that the whole region faced shortages and actual starvation at times. In this respect, perhaps Clark was considerably smarter than his younger brother.

Winston made up for the 1860 corn shortage with the production of sweet potatoes. Like corn, the sweet potato was essential; it too had to be produced twice annually, and each crop had to meet the needs of the farm for six months. Once the crop was made, potatoes were usually banked rather than stored in a building, although Winston used both methods of storage. In the former, banks of straw and earth were fenced off so that the hogs could be turned into the fields to dig for roots, and each bank normally contained from 10 to 15 bushels. A bushel of sweet potatoes weighed about 80 pounds, so Winston's 1860 crop produced about 16,000 pounds of solid food. An acre of land usually produced some 4,000 pounds of potatoes, so it is probable that three or four acres were allotted for the potato crop.⁵⁶

If Winston devoted but forty acres to cotton, corn, and sweet potatoes, what did he grow on the remaining twenty acres? The answer appears to be that peanuts, squash, string beans, black-eyed and crowder peas, cushaws, watermelons and muskmelons, turnip greens, cabbages, and Irish potatoes took up three or more; fruit and citrus trees including oranges, peaches, and plums covered several acres; and pasture for the animals accounted for the rest. In addition, there were blackberries, chinquapins, huckleberries, and sparkleberries growing wild, and everyone was always on the lookout for a bee tree. But even when this fare was supplemented by game and fish, there were food shortages after the war began.

---

55. The rations for the ten slaves were 2 bushels of shelled corn per week for a total of 104 bushels for the year. If Winston provided the same rations for himself and his family, an additional 40 to 50 bushels for the year, then he might just scrape by. But he frequently had visitors for extended stays, and after Rebecca and the boys moved in, this would not have been enough. Also, the journals and letters reveal that corn was used to fatten the hogs and was also fed to the horses and mules, so Winston undoubtedly had to buy additional corn from time to time.

56. Rosengarten, in *Tombee*, 75–79, presents an excellent discussion of farming practices on the sea islands, and conditions there were not very different from those at Rose Cottage.

Table 2. Slave owners in Putnam County, 1860

Name	No. of slaves

Large and medium planters

W. D. Moseley	114	Peter Monroe	8	M. Strickland	2
R. G. Mayes	88	Thomas Lane	8	S. Bronson	2
Mayes Simkins	69	Richard Tilles	8	**R. Bryant**	2
J. H. Verdier	47	Martin Manning	7	J. Higginbotham	1
A. H. Cole	42	Elijah Wall	7	James Bassford	1
Adna Johnson	39	N. W. McLeod	7	Geo. W. Priest	1
George Hawes	35	Norton Trowell	6	John Tiner	1

Small planters

		Morris Sanchez	6	W. Daniels	1
		Gran. Priest	6	W. Thigpin	1
Marquis Booth	26	E. Quartermain	6	Hannah Priest	1
Ch. Eatmon	24	A. J. Phillips	6	S. Saunders	1
James DeVal	24	R. R. Reid	5	C. Hemming	1
Nathan Norton	20	John Motts	4	W. A. Forward	1
E. Monroe	20	**Clark Stephens**	4	M. Christopher	1
G. W. A. McRae	19	Josh. McCardel	4	J. W. Woods	1
Ben. Hopkins	19	Calvin Gilles	4	M. D. Cleveland	1
T. S. Haughton	16	Thos Hicks	4	G. Lucas	1
M. Seigler	16	Charles Brush	4	B. G. James	1
Gabe. Priest	16	F. A. Giroux	4	H. Baronton	1
S. Tillman	15	John Register	4	E. Drummond	1
		J. Hawthorne	4	W. Jordan	1
		James Braddock	3	Henry Agnew	1

Slave-owning yeomen

		V. Sanchez	3	
F. M. McMeekin	14	J. McMillen	3	
N. H. Moragne	14	Ch. Lynch	3	
W. Johnson	12	P. Peterman	3	
H. A. Gray	12	H. R. Feasdale	3	
W. W. Dalton	12	L. Geiger	3	
James Eubanks	11	Miriam Roberts	3	
W. Priest	11	C. Ashley	3	
W. Rembert	11	W. Pinner	3	
J. R. Saunders	11	M. Morton	3	
L. H. Rosignol	11	G. Brice	3	
H. L. Hart	11	N. D. Currie	3	
L. Sanders	10	J. Livingston	2	
Win Stephens	10	N. Stephens	2	
R. S. Eubanks	9	G. E. Thomas	2	
E. B. Timmons	9	R. E. Syle	2	
E. Kernerly	9	L. Sparkman	2	
J. C. McEwe	8	H. Gaskins	2	
W. Norton	8			

Source: Eighth Census of the United States, 1860, Schedule II, Slave Schedule, Putnam County. The census data do not distinguish between ownership of slaves and slaves that were hired or leased, and this table does not either. The ranking here is determined solely by the numbers given to the census taker and can be misleading. For example, Rebecca Bryant is listed as the owner of two slaves when in fact she did not own any.

After 1861 Winston also planted short-staple cotton for the use of his family members, free and slave alike, as well as long-staple for sale. Had the war not come, he probably would have become a true planter within a few years; but in 1860 he informed the census taker that he was a farmer whose estate was valued at $8,400. In reality, he was referred to as a planter by his neighbors, and his farm was called, even by himself, a plantation.[57]

The label "planter" was used somewhat loosely all over the South. Benjamin Hopkins, Winston's friend and neighbor, owned nineteen slaves in 1860 but called himself a farmer, while Swepston and Richard listed themselves as planters in 1860 even though both had fewer slaves than Winston did.[58] Richard placed a value of $5,000 on his nine slaves and $1,200 on his farm; Swepston declared values of $3,000 and $500 respectively.[59] In truth, there were but eighteen planters in Putnam County (see table 2).

If the possession of at least fifteen slaves be taken as the minimum for planter status, the usual measure, then there were eleven small planters and eighty slave-owning yeomen in the county. A noticeable drop in cotton and overall production is apparent between small planters and slave-owning farmers and those labeled large or medium planters (see table 3).[60]

---

57. Eighth Census of the United States, 1860, Schedule I, Population Schedule, Putnam County. Winston listed the value of his farm at $1,000, even though the land was leased, and his slave force at $7,400.

58. Benjamin Hopkins, a native of South Carolina, was one of the most prominent men in north Florida. A highly respected lawyer and planter, he served in the militia against the Seminoles with the rank of general. Although born in 1800, he organized and commanded the St. Johns Rangers with the rank of captain. He died on 22 February 1862, and Winston took his place.

59. A comparison of the census data with that shown in table 1 indicates that Richard owned George and Sandy, both over sixty years old; Sammy, about nineteen; and three boys ranging in age from five to nine. The females included Melia, thirty-five; her daughter Jenny, fifteen; and an unidentified female of twelve. Swepston was not listed as a slaveholder on Schedule II, but he must have owned at least four of those he received in 1846. There is no record of when he acquired Archey and Solomon, whom he sold in 1855. But if in 1860 he still owned Joe (twenty-nine), Henry (twenty-three), Fanny (twenty), and Jane (nineteen), he could have conservatively estimated their value at $3,000. Hopkins placed a value of $9,600 on his nineteen slaves.

60. The key to production was not merely the number of slaves owned but the age of the slave force. As indicated in table 2, planter G. W. A. McRae owned nineteen slaves, but nine were twelve or younger, and two were fifty or older, so he had only eight productive slaves. Conversely, six out of farmer Elijah Wall's seven slaves were prime hands, and E. Kernerly had six out of nine in that category. Both yeomen outproduced planter McRae. Slave children under the age of six were given no chores, but within a year or two they would be required to carry water to the field slaves, feed the chickens, and perform other light tasks. By the age of ten or twelve, they would be counted as fractional hands with a regular routine of field work. When the males became eighteen to twenty years old, they would normally be referred to as full or prime field hands. Adult women were also counted as full hands except when they were pregnant. They were usually given lighter tasks for the duration of their pregnancy and returned to the fields shortly after they delivered.

Table 3. Overall production, Putnam County cotton growers (produce measured in bushels, gallons, and bales)

Name	Mules/hogs/cows	Sweet potatoes	Beans	Corn	Molasses	Cotton	Slaves
Wm. Moseley[a]	–/–/–	–	–	–	–	100?	114
R. G. Mays	15/250/6	1,500	2,000	2,500	–	75	88
A. Johnson	9/40/6	350	400	1,400	280	69	39
Mays/Simkins	12/200/–	250	300	2,000	–	80	69
A. H. Cole	5/150/25	150	800	1,000	–	64	42
J. H. Verdier[b]	13/700/100	100	50	800	400	60?	47
G. Hawes[a]	–/–/–	–	–	–	–	60?	35
M. Booth	3/25/25	–	100	500	–	15	26
E. Monroe	0/300/32	250	50	600	–	15	20
J. Saunders	0/120/20	250	–	300	–	13	11
M. Siegler	0/90/200	100	30	400	–	12	16
F. M. Meekin	0/14/20	100	150	120	–	12	14
N. Norton	0/200/80	600	500	250	–	11	20
E. Wall	0/135/40	300	50	600	–	11	7
E. Kernerly	0/22/50	250	–	250	–	10	9
Wm. Johnson	0/230/90	400	20	1,200	–	10	12
G. W. A. McRae	0/30/30	300	200	250	–	10	19
Wm. Priest	0/105/100	250	–	200	–	8	11
N. Trowell	2/2/50	300	–	200	–	7	6
Win Stephens	2/30/0	200	50	150	–	7	10
J. McEwe	0/0/30	200	30	150	–	7	8
E. Drummond	0/38/35	250	80	200	–	7	1
Gabriel Priest	0/84/15	100	150	350	–	5	15
T. S. Haughton	0/4/10	50	50	80	–	0	16
James Eubanks	0/120/5	120	20	50	–	1	11
L. Sanders	0/39/75	200	150	450	–	5	10
R. S. Eubanks	0/27/30	100	50	120	–	2	9

Source: Eighth Census of the United States, 1860, Schedule IV, Putnam County.
[a]William Moseley and George Hawes were not included on Schedule IV.
[b]The cotton production for J. H. Verdier was not listed either. Hence the number of bales of cotton attributed to them is only an estimate.

The number of slaves owned was most important in determining one's social status in the antebellum South, but this was not the only criterion. Winston was esteemed far beyond his years or for the number of chattels he owned. He was referred to as Colonel Stephens when he moved to Welaka, even before he saw service in the Third Seminole War. During that conflict he was a captain but was addressed as "Colonel" by all, including Tivie. Some of this deference was due to his stepfather's standing, for Gaines was in every

Table 4. Total slave owners in Florida, 1860

No. of slaves owned	No. of slave owners
More than 200	3
100–199	45
70–99	42
50–69	116
40–49	99
30–39	171
20–29	333
15–19	349
10–14	627
9	169
8	186
7	225
6	270
5	285
4	365
3	437
2	568
1	863
Totals 61,745	5,153

Source: Joseph C. G. Keanedy, *Agriculture of the United States in 1860; Compiled from the Original Returns of the Eighth Census* (Washington, D.C.: GPO, 1864), 225.

respect a gentleman planter; but Winston's personal qualities were even more important in determining his status. None of his brothers commanded the respect that he did, although all were educated and well regarded. Winston's education, wealth, deportment, and overall character placed him in the planter class, and he was clearly accepted into their ranks. He was also viewed as a planter by the founder of Welaka; James Bryant wrote his daughter Tivie that Winston was in every way their social equal.[61]

Winston and Bryant were highly regarded in Welaka and in northeastern Florida, but it must be emphasized that the area was only on the fringe of the cotton kingdom, and few of the truly large planters lived in that part of the state. In fact, there were very few large planters in all of Florida; only forty-eight owned more than a hundred slaves, and only three of them owned more than two hundred (see table 4). The 1860 census revealed that 1,954 of the

61. James W. Bryant to Tivie, 23 October 1859. One might be acknowledged as a gentleman even if one were not a slave owner. Bryant was also called Colonel even though he had never been in the military or owned a slave; like Winston, he had the overall talent, wealth, education, and character to command the necessary respect.

5,153 slave owners in Florida equaled or exceeded the number of slaves that Winston owned, which meant that 3,199 farmers owned fewer than he did. This placed him in the top third of the elite population of the state; viewed from a national perspective, over 70 percent of all slave owners in the country owned fewer slaves than Winston. Since an individual who owned but two slaves and nothing else was equal in wealth to the average free farmer of the North, Winston was significantly wealthier than the average American in the North or South and can properly be referred to as a planter. At any rate, whether he was called farmer or planter, Winston Stephens was an exceedingly happy man in 1860, for he had finally succeeded in making Tivie Bryant his wife.

The records do not reveal when the couple first met (probably in 1855 when Winston was visiting Clark), but the courtship was in full bloom by 1856. Sometime that summer, Winston proposed, and Tivie accepted his offer of marriage. However, when he asked her parents for their consent, both James and Rebecca adamantly refused and brought an end to the engagement. They did not object to Winston as a future son-in-law; in fact, both of them liked and respected him. His religious and political affiliations were the same as theirs, Episcopalian and Whig respectively, and he was obviously a successful and responsible gentleman. But he was twenty-six years old and Tivie was not quite fifteen, far too young in the eyes of her parents to engage in even a steady courtship, much less marriage. In addition, they hoped she would eventually marry someone with a background similar to hers, someone in the mercantile, legal, or banking business, and live in a city. The thought of her living in the country and being responsible for a husband and ten slaves during sickness and health was out of the question. Under no circumstances would they consent to any engagement or courtship in 1856. They sent Tivie to Boston to attend her uncle Richard Parker's school for girls and secured her promise that she would not marry anyone until she was eighteen years old.[62]

This was unwelcome news to the couple, especially to Winston; but both acquiesced, and Tivie left Welaka in August 1856, accompanied by Amanda Latham and her daughter Carrie. When she arrived in Boston the next month, she found a letter from Winston awaiting her. This letter and six others from him that year are missing. We have Tivie's response to his first letters, and then the correspondence was broken off. It is impossible to deter-

---

62. Richard Green Parker of Boston graduated from Harvard in 1817 and taught in a number of public schools until his retirement in 1853. After that time, he taught privately in his own home and published a number of textbooks on various subjects. In July 1849 he married Catherine G. Hall, Tivie's aunt; she was always referred to as Aunt Kate by family members in the surviving correspondence.

mine exactly what happened; all that can be stated with certainty is that on 18 December Tivie heard from her close friend Carrie Latham that "Mr S— was going to Tampa to fight the Indians."[63] Two days later she recorded that her mother had written and confirmed that Winston had decided to fight in what was called the Third Seminole War.

From 5 December 1856 to 27 January 1858 Winston disappeared from Tivie's writings. When they met again on 12 February 1858 at Welaka, she recorded that "I think I never saw a person so changed in looks." It had been eighteen months since they had seen each other, and if Winston had changed, so had she. In late 1856 Tivie clearly indicated that she considered herself engaged and had every intention of marrying Winston, as the following letter reveals.

[OCTAVIA BRYANT TO WINSTON STEPHENS]

Boston Oct 12, 1856

Dear Winston

I received your affectionate letter last week and I expect that you have received mine. I guess you thought it was a funny kind of letter and that I had been tipping the brandy bottle a little too much . . . but I hope you will excuse all deficiencies, dont you remember that I told you that I was a very poor letter writer. I do not think I will ever forget that ride and frolic out to the Plantation the day before I left although I was laughing and carring on so. I felt very sad. It was a great trial for me to leave my home and all that are so dear to me . . .

The question you asked me about where the house should stand is rather difficult to answer for it would be very pleasant living on the river and also pleasant living by Minnie.[64] If you will promise to keep her there I would prefer living near her, but I will leave it entirely with you. I will live wherever you wish . . . Give my love to darling Minnie and tell her I will write to her again soon and accept a great deal for your own dear self from

Your Tivy

---

63. The Lathams were very close friends of the Bryants. The family was headed by Mrs. Amanda W. Latham, originally from Woonsocket, Rhode Island. She had two daughters, Carrie and Emma, and a son, Horatio. Although Tivie and Carrie sometimes quarreled, both Emma and Carrie were among her closest friends in antebellum Welaka.

64. The house in question was the future Rose Cottage. Mary Gaines, Winston's half-sister, at this time was called Minnie by Tivie. The two were the same age and were very close, almost like family rather than friends. She and Tivie wrote each other often while Tivie was in Boston, and they renewed their friendship after Tivie returned to Welaka. At this time Mary was living in the George Bryant house on the Acosta Grant with her parents and the rest of the family, but she too moved to Middleburg in December 1858.

On 12 October 1856 Tivie decided to keep a journal or diary "dedicated to myself." Even in this most personal world, she remained a very private person. She rarely revealed her deepest emotions, but she was obviously shy and somewhat aloof, very religious, completely nonpolitical, and socially awkward; she had a negative self-image. Yet with intimate friends she was warm and loving, somewhat witty, and possessed of a good sense of humor. Tivie was, above all, a dutiful daughter; when she resumed her relationship with Winston over her parents' opposition in 1858 and 1859, it bothered her greatly. She hated having to write and see Winston in secret. She knew her duty and usually did it; torn between her love for her parents and her love for Winston, she had a rough time of it.

chapter 1

My Own Little Home
Courtship and Marriage, 1858–1859

On 27 January 1858 Tivie recorded, "Since I wrote in my last years journal, I have come home and had nice times . . . Today is the day the Stephens are to be mustered out and we expect them home next week." Winston was not in Welaka when she returned, but Tivie and all her group were frequent visitors to the home of Clark and Tina, and all references to "Mr Stephens" or "Mrs Stephens" are to them. She used "Col" or "Col S" as her reference for Winston.[1] Although Tina and Mary Gaines favored the match, Tivie made it quite clear early in 1858 that she did not consider them engaged and valued Winston only as a friend; but before the year was over she had again consented to become his secret fiancée. Still unsure of her emotions and bowing to her parents' opposition, she broke the engagement in February 1859 only to yield finally to his determined campaign in May.

Feb 12, 1858. In the morning before Julie and I were dressed Lou came running up stairs saying that the Stephens had come, they came last night. In the morning wrote to Minnie.[2] In the afternoon after practising Lou,

---

1. Winston, Richard, and Swepston were mustered out at Tampa with the rank of captain, second lieutenant, and sergeant, respectively. Each served for six months, from 28 July 1857 to 28 January 1858. See Florida Department of Military Affairs, "Special Archives Publication No. 76, Florida Military Muster Rolls," vol. 10, 5–6. Sometimes the correspondents used a period or a dash after title abbreviations and sometimes they did not.

2. Louisa and Julia Bryant were daughters of Lewis Henry and Louisa (Burritt) Bryant of Jacksonville; these two cousins of Tivie lived in Welaka with the Bryants from 1857 to 1860. Minnie is Mary Gaines.

Julie, and I went down for the mail and as it was not open we went to the Fawn *and while there a row boat came from Maj Gaines with Lt Stephens, Mary and some others but not the Col*³ . . . *after tea went down to Mrs Stephens had games and candy but could not pull the candy.*⁴ *Maj. Gaines and Col. Stephens were there, I think I never saw a person so changed in looks as the Col. I had a chance to speak but a few words to him.*

Feb 14, 1858. . . . *just before going to church received a letter from Col. Stephens.*⁵

[OCTAVIA BRYANT TO WINSTON STEPHENS]

White Cottage Feb 15, 1858.

Mr Stephens Dear Sir

I received your letter yesterday morning . . . I will now try and arrange all missunderstanding between us, by bringing up some parts of our conversations. You say that when I went away you understood that I was *engaged* to you. Do you not remember, I told you that I was entirely too young to think of such a thing, and also said that I knew Father would say the same, and when you consulted Father, did he not say that, I was entirely too young, and that if the *best* and *richest man* in the world should ask me to engage himself to me, he would not allow it at my age, but if in three years our views were the same towards each other, he would *then consent to our being engaged* and I understood that it was *not an engagement,* and thought that *you* did. I was also then a great deal younger in experience and thoughts and hardly knew my own mind, I did like you very much (as all girls have a sweetheart) but not as an accepted *Lover.* I was too young, and am *now* too young to judge for my happiness in future life, neither my character nor mind is yet formed, and should I engage *myself now to anyone,*

---

3. The *Fawn* was a small side-wheeler steamboat built by John Clark of Jacksonville for James Bryant in February 1855. The vessel at deck level was 56 feet long and 10 feet wide, was 15 feet wide at the wheels, and had a 10-horsepower steam engine. She was the first steamer built in Jacksonville and was to make regular runs on the St. Johns and Ocklawaha Rivers, but there is not much evidence to suggest that this took place. Apparently Bryant and John Bouse of Jacksonville used the ship for a while, but no reference is made to her after 1859, and Bryant may have sold her by that time; her fate after that remains unknown. See Mueller, *Ocklawaha River Steamboats,* 3; *Jacksonville Florida Republican,* 15 February 1855. Lieutenant Stephens is Richard.

4. Dinner was the noonday meal, and tea was the evening offering, currently called supper. It usually consisted of tea and cakes or bread and honey.

5. This letter is missing, but Winston obviously mentioned something about their engagement, and Tivie lost no time in clarifying their new relationship.

it might be not only a source of unhappiness to myself, but to others after marriage.

I shewed your letter to Mother, and she said she would leave it to me to answer, for she did not wish you to think that she had persuaded me differently from what I felt, I know that both she and Father would be pleased with this course.

We all esteem you as a friend, and wish you to visit the house as gentlemen do, but not in any other position as regards myself. We will always be happy to see you. I hope that we will still be friends. I hope I will see *you* and all here this evening. If this is not plainly understood by you, please let me know what parts, and I will endeavor to explain them.

I remain your Friend

Octavia L. Bryant.

Feb 17, 1858. . . . *Father and Col Stephens went down on the Darlington today*[6] . . . *after dinner received another letter from Col S— in which he says I had trifled with his affections.*

Mar 5, 1858. . . . *Julie and I went over to Mrs Stephens to see Mary, she had come in from the plantation* . . .[7] *Mary brought my letters to Col Stephens back.*

Mar 8, 1858. . . . *Tonight I carried Col Stephens letters to him, all that I have received from him, he seemed quite friendly, but we had no conversation. Mother wrote him quite a friendly note, to send with my letters. It is now I hope all settled between us.*

June 5, 1858. In the morning Lou and I had a lunch and started at half past six with Mrs Stephens and her family in a boat for the plantation. Soon after we arrived there, Col and Mr Clark Stephens went hunting, while they were away Mr Richard S— shewed us the Indian curiosities,

---

6. The *Darlington,* owned and operated by Jacob Brock, began regular service in 1852 between Jacksonville and Enterprise and became the best known of the early riverboats. Brock also owned the *Hattie Brock,* which began operation in 1857, and the *Silver Spring,* which began service in 1860. Other boats—the *Thorn,* for example—ran from Jacksonville to Palatka, but it was sometimes necessary for the Welaka residents to take a small boat to Palatka in order to connect with the steamboats. See T. Frederick Davis, *History of Jacksonville,* 358; Mueller, *St. Johns River Steamboats,* 193, 196.

7. The reference here is to the Gaines-Stephens plantation, then called Pine Grove.

and we sewed and had some music.[8] *Col was gone about two hours and came back with two deer. We all then talked awhile, then I played the piano again, and I think I never was more embarrassed. At first Col was cool and sad but at the dinner table began to be more attentive, after dinner Mrs Stephens, Mary, Lou and I took a short walk and Mary and I made each other confidential friends, after we went to the house we sat a little while with Mrs Gaines, then we females with Col and Mr Clark S— and children went to Magnolia Spring, going Col was very attentive to Lou, I was with Mary, the gentlemen went off and Mrs S—, Mary . . . and I waded in, Mary and I sat on a log with our feet in the water and talked about Col some, I made Mary a promise. While at the Spring Col gave me a flower and made a cup of a leaf for me to drink from, he walked most of the way home with Mary and me, and [we decided] that when we got to the house, we would give 45 minutes to rest, then have music, then watermelon, then music again. While I played he watched me all the time and when the melon came he began throwing seeds at me and I at him and we became quite friendly, Mr R and C Stephens went to the Landing to bathe and fish, and we had more music, Col then walked to the landing with Lou and me and was very pleasant and funny, and at dinner we all agreed to have a huckleberry party on Monday . . .*

July 5, 1858. . . . went to Mrs Stephens where we met . . . Mary, Col and Richard Stephens, several Gaines and others, danced had watermelon and cake. Col was very agreeable, he talked to me most of the evening and danced the first dance with me and the last. I enjoyed myself very much in deed, came home at half past 12, brought Mary home to sleep.

July 13, 1858. In the afternoon Mother received a very insolent letter from Col. I received quite a letter from Mary . . .[9]

July 18, 1858. Father surprised us this morning before we were up, he has been away just five weeks.

---

8. These Seminole Indian materials, collected by Winston in 1857 from a Seminole he killed, consisted of a buckskin shirt, hat, garter, pouch, baskets, beads, and other assorted accouterments. In 1975 Winston B. Stephens Jr. donated these items to the Florida State Museum in Gainesville, Florida. At the time of the gift, Dr. Jerald T. Milanich, the museum's assistant curator in archeology, and Dr. William C. Sturtevant, curator of North American ethnology at the Smithsonian Institution, examined the materials and commented, "They are unique and represent the most complete mid-19th Century Seminole Indian outfit known and they are among the oldest ethnological specimens from the Southeast United States." According to Dr. Milanich, "In terms of its historical and anthropological significance, the collection is priceless."

9. On 10 July Tivie recorded that she and her mother had received a letter from Winston and that Rebecca had sent a reply. These letters, as well as the letters mentioned here, are all missing. Most probably they were destroyed after Winston and Tivie resumed their engagement.

July 19, 1858.... After tea Father and I sat under the trees a long while and talked ... Father is going to Jacksonville on Wednesday and back to Cuba in two weeks.

July 20, 1858. In the morning I taught school as Father wanted Davis. In the afternoon had another long talk with Father about Col ...

July 22, 1858.... we met Col Stephens, he seemed very friendly, I guess he has not received Fathers letter, he was very lively and we all had quite a little frolic ...[10]

Aug 16, 1858.... We girls intended going to see Mary but Father said no. I wrote a note to Mary to come up, but she did not. We girls have been very low spirited and do not know what has happened. We fear something has happened between Father and Col. oh dear what is to happen.[11]

[OCTAVIA BRYANT TO WINSTON STEPHENS]

White Cottage Sept 2, 1858

Forgive my keeping you in such suspense but you know Yes or No are the hardest words in the world to say, and require a great deal of thought, and for one in my place it is very hard to tell which to say. You have heard my decision, I have made it, and I feel happier and yet I feel as though I had done wrong in acting so contrary to my parents wishes. I did not (as I have told you) wish to be engaged as young as I am, but when I found you were so unhappy I determined to give up my wishes, I hope that all will be right.

I will agree to be engaged to you secretly until I am 18, then I will ask my parents again and I hope gain their consent, if not, then I will tell them of our engagement; we will then be engaged a while and if *neither of us* see a *good cause* to prevent will be married, these are my present thoughts, and I hope they will suit you.

But are you not afraid you are running a great risk? are you not afraid that in marrying a girl of 18, you will be made unhappy when it is too late. to be sure you have known me a long time as a simple frolicking girl, but you have only seen me in company, you know nothing of my temper at home, I am quick, but I

---

10. This letter is missing, but Bryant wrote Winston on 21 July, and Tivie read it but did not record any of the contents. No doubt Bryant once again told Winston to desist.

11. It is obvious that James and Rebecca told Winston in July to stop his renewed courtship of Tivie and equally obvious that he refused. There must have been some tense moments, but other than Tivie's brief mention cited above, no one recorded them. Winston managed to see Tivie secretly in August and September 1858, largely because Tina Stephens approved and assisted in arranging their clandestine meetings at her house. Winston pressed his case ceaselessly, and his reward came early in September.

think easily cooled, and one thing that perhaps would trouble you, I am not of an affectionate disposition, my other traits of character I can not tell but I tell you of these to let you think of them and be prepared. I forgot to say in the first part of my letter that Father said that while I was as young as I now am he wished me to be governed by his wishes, but that when I was of age, he would make no objections to any engagement I will make, but try his best to make me happy, do you not think that is showing the right spirit, and do you wonder at my being backward after that but never mind we will let it rest as it is at present . . .

Yours truly

Tivie

[OCTAVIA BRYANT TO WINSTON STEPHENS]

White Cottage Oct 7, 1858

My dear—

You can not imagine how sorry and disappointed I am that I can not see you to day. I believe I could almost cry, I had set so much upon going with the girls. I had been anticipating it the whole week, but it can not be helped so I will bear it with patience. The girls are dressed and gone down stairs and I am trying to write before going to my work, but I expect every minute to hear Mother in her room. I write a few lines and then do a little work. I know this sounds silly to you but I want to let you know how I have to steal the minutes to write even these few lines. Please excuse this half sheet but smaller the note the easier carried. Dear Loulie will carry this for me. I feel really sad to have her leave us don't you?[12] Excuse this someone is coming.

Yours affectionately

Tivie

Nov 12, 1858. . . . After breakfast Willie, Henry and I went in a boat to the plantation, intending to stay an hour, but we spent the day. Col and Lieut Stephens were hunting but Col came home soon after dinner and walked to the Spring with us meaning Willie, Mary, Alabama,[13] and Henry and I . . . Col walked home with me, after tea Willie, Davis and I went to

---

12. Louisa (known as Loulie or Lou) and Julia Bryant made the trip to the plantation, but Carrie Latham was sick and a house guest of the Bryants so Tivie had to stay with her. Loulie returned to her Jacksonville home at this time but visited Welaka from time to time until she married in May 1860. Julia continued to live with the Bryants at Welaka.

13. This was Alabama Gaines, one of Winston's half-sisters.

Mrs Stephens and we danced until half past eleven when I was so tired. came home had a *delightful time* . . .

[OCTAVIA BRYANT TO WINSTON STEPHENS]

White Cottage Dec 11[?], 1858

My dear you know who

I have just rec you aff letter and right glad *delighted* was I to get it.[14] it sent "roses" to my cheeks which have not been there for six weeks. I am glad you have not seen me for this one reason that you wanted to see roses on my cheeks there have been none (except while blushing) until since I received your letter . . . I send by Rachael a little pin cushion for you to carry in your pocket for pins and to remember me . . . I also send you a ring which I have worn nearly nine years and value, it is thin now but will you not keep it . . . I do not know what plan can be made for us to meet, none I fear. I intended writing to you to day and ask if we could not trust Burrel (*a preacher*) to take our notes. I will always try and answer your notes, but if I do not dont think it was a want of inclination . . .

I am your affectiate Tivie

Dec 24, 1858. . . . *In the afternoon Julie and I went for the mail and met Col Stephens at the store. spoke a half a dozen words to him. he said he was very lonely* . . .[15]

Jan 1, 1859. In the morning saw Col on horseback and he waved. In the evening received a letter from him, we have been exchanging letters for some time but I have been afraid to put it in here . . .

[OCTAVIA BRYANT TO WINSTON STEPHENS]

White Cottage
New Years Day 1859

My dear dear "Old Man"

I was agreeably surprised this evening when Julie called me from the parlor and said "Rachael has something for you . . ." all but Julie and myself have gone to Mrs Lathams, I did not go as I have been more than half sick for the last few days, and Julie would not go without me . . . last night I went to bed directly after

---

14. This letter is missing.
15. The Gaines family moved to Middleburg, in newly created Clay County, at this time.

tea and had not been up long when you saw me this morning, and have been feeling like a "stewed monkey" all day, but feel stronger to night. This morning Ellen our cook came running in to my room and calling me,[16] saying she saw the "young man" as she calls you, so Julie and I followed her to the kitchen door...

You will wonder how Ellen should know anything about you, she heard a story, and asked me about it. I told her that Mother and Father would not consent to our union, she then spoke up in favor of me, and said why wont you have the poor Young man Miss Tivy, I would not mind what they say, if you love a man marry him, etc etc and offered to help me out and keep it secret, so I told her that I intended when I was 18 to show the folks who I loved, but did not of course tell her of our engagement, she said you should have the cake I made for you if she had to carry it, and said she would carry it Christmas night. I am glad you liked it...

Dear "Old Man" I do indeed pity you in your loneliness, but oh I cannot yet give up my single life, you know I did not wish to marry for years yet, but allowed myself to be persuaded by you and others to say one year, do not think that I love society and do not wish to leave it, no, I can not tell why, but I do not feel inclined to marry for sometime, although I love you and when I do marry I wish to marry you, I wish as you say that I had your feelings on the subject then would I gladly go to you now, but sorry to say my feelings are not strong enough. I speak candidly for I wish you to know the state of my feelings. do not think that I am loving you less and backing out, for no I love you more and more, and am more and more satisfied with the step I have taken. I wish I could see you often but I will be content...

Good night, Your Tivie

[OCTAVIA BRYANT TO WINSTON STEPHENS]

White Cottage Jan 29, 1859

... You asked me in your last letter about the windows, I am afraid I would not say to suit you, but any how if you leave it to me I would say four windows in the front rooms, and two in shedroom.[17] Well as it is eleven o'clock I will leave this until I receive yours. Good night "May pleasant dreams attend thee and holy angels guard thee."

---

16. Ellen was the Bryants' domestic servant. At this time she was twenty-nine years old and had an infant son. Tivie noted in her journal on 1 October 1858 that her father "had hired a cook for Mother." Ellen was leased annually for the next two years and was mistakenly listed as belonging to Rebecca Bryant in Schedule II of the 1860 census. The name of her owner is unknown.

17. Winston was planning the building of Rose Cottage.

Sunday, Dear Crabid old Bachelor for so you call yourself . . . I am going to service at Mrs Lathams at half past three. I suppose I will not see you there . . . I had been intending to go to Burrel's church for sometime but other services have prevented.[18]

[OCTAVIA BRYANT TO WINSTON STEPHENS]

Feb 13, 1859

My dear

The only way I can fix to meet you is this Wednesday afternoon Carrie, Julie and I will go to the graveyard and they will go together and you and I. there is no other safe way . . .

Your loving

Tivie

Feb 16, 1859. . . . went to the grave yard to meet Col, we had a long talk.[19]

Feb 17, 1859. . . . After coming home told Mother I wanted to have a long talk with her but it was too late to have it then. Oh I do not know what to do oh it seems as though I could not refuse Col again, but I feel as though I must.

Feb 18, 1859. In the morning I had the dreaded talk with Mother, she decided me about Col, oh it will be a great sacrifice, but I hope it will be all for the best.

Feb 20, 1859. I went to school in the morning, but not to service in the afternoon, I stayed home and wrote the fatal letter to Col.[20] *I cried myself into a severe headache, but went to tea. after tea went almost directly to bed. I never cried so much in my life.*

---

18. The location of Burrel's church is not known, but it was in or near Welaka. It was common for planters to permit their slaves to worship on the plantations, and the larger ones usually had a "praise" house for this purpose; but it was most unusual for a slave to have his own church and for both races to attend.

19. Winston attempted to convince Tivie that they should marry regardless of parental opposition, a move that backfired. Instead of defying them, she again broke the engagement, although this time it cost her a great deal of pain.

20. This letter is missing. Tivie did not mention Winston in her journal again until 10 April, but he sent her several letters during the ensuing months.

[WINSTON STEPHENS TO OCTAVIA BRYANT]

Feb 20[?], 1859

How easy to write the words, "we are free from any engagement" only a little slip of the pen, but oh how much it cost the one to whom those words are sent. You say that your father said he would never forgive you and he would keep such a promise, did he not tell you that if you would be controlled by him untill you are 18 then he would allow you to marry the man of your choice, and do all in his power to make you happy? does he keep one of his promises and not keep the other or does he regard promises as it seems you do, only made to have the pleasure of breaking them, you alas say you have told me you love me and do love me, "oh such love" such as my greatest enemy would offer, smiles and fair promises to my face and cut my throat if a chance offered with my back to him. such has been your love you said you loved me and I thought you too pure in heart and soul to deceive. It was the opinion I had of your character that drew my love towards you but oh how I have ben led astray by your smiles and sweet words of promises. Oh that God may when we both stand before him for judgement forgive you for the great and irreparable wrong you have done an innocent and unoffending heart. Go to your parents for forgiveness as it seems they are the only ones you care for or would make any sacrifice for, talk of bringing their grey hairs with sorrow to the grave and such as that. what do they care for bringing black locks to the grave much less grey ones. you think it best to part and not make the matter worse, pray tell me how it could be made any worse than it is now when it seems to me you try to write your letter with my hearts blood. Tivie I send you all your letters and other little gifts that were of little Value of them selves but they were treasured for the givers sake. take them and treat them as you have me caress and love them for awhile and then cast them from you as something useless and beneath you but one request I ask and that is read all your letters over carefully and see the extent of the wrong you have done me see upon what I built my hopes and then ask the question and answer it candidly which is the greatest wrong to forsake me or your parents. at least let it be a lesson to you in the future and never trifle with no mans affections. Oh Tivie you call your girlish affection how can you the second time tell me you were deceived in your love for me that was your first excuse now the same old tune. Tivie I must have a wife and if you cant be my wife I must find some one to heal the wound in some degree that you have inflicted. Bacheloring is more unbearable now than before as I could with pleasure do the house hold duties thinking that soon you would discharge said duties but now when I attend them it makes me feel how much I have lost, and oh bitter the pangs it brings to my already breaking heart, but enough you have ordered and I obey as I have done for nearly three years, you refused my last request, that of one more meeting. Tivie if you cant be my wife we must be as strangers. I sent your ring it is broken keep it and look upon it as all the vows you made and it is a fit representation of the heart you discard. Keep it and when you see it say I brought on this wreck the pin cushion you can keep for the old man, farewell, oh how painful the word. I forgive you and may God do likewise and may you never be treated as you have treated me, farewell, farewell.[21]

Apr 10, 1859. I went to Sunday school as usual . . . Col was there looking very pale and sick, Father talked to him after church. I was surprised . . .

[WINSTON STEPHENS TO OCTAVIA BRYANT]

Apr 10, 1859

Dear Tivie,

. . . Tivie you must know the strength and durability of my love when it holds up under so many disasters, and with so many to combat with and I would not care for all the opposition if I could meet them upon equal grounds, but you see that they can be with you while I am kept at a distance and forbidden the previlege even of writing. If I could only be with you as they are I feel confident that our mutual love would bear down all that opposes us.

Dear Tivie I feel sure you love me and to day you would willingly give me your hand in marriage if not prevented by so much influence against your wish, but Tivie you should look around you and see from the experience of the world who is most happy, is it those matches that are formed by parents and friends to suit their wish and purposes or is it those that are drawn together by mutual love, and that love created by the affinity of their dispositions? The relation between man and wife require love to create happiness and without love marriage is a curse and the parties pay the penalty of allowing themselves forced or persuaded into a union without loving each other as they should. Think of this matter seriously Tivie and rise above the oppression that would seperate us . . .

Answer me if you can, and believe me as ever Yours aff,

Winston

---

21. Over the next few weeks Winston sent Tivie several letters in this same vein, though not written in the heat of anger. By early April Tivie appeared to be softening again, so Winston continued to write to her and by the end of May had won her back.

[WINSTON STEPHENS TO OCTAVIA BRYANT]

Pine Grove Apr 17, 1859

Dear Tivie

... I am satisfied Dear Tivie from what I saw this evening that you love me as dearly as ever, and from that I build my hope oh how much I would give to meet you and talk this matter all over, we would both be so much better satisfied than we can be to write, as we cant say half we want to say, nor have what we say so well understood as we could to talk it, then if you can *do see me*. oh Tivie remember the last time we parted how happy we were in the promises made to each other and sealed by that angel of a kiss, now Tivie I propose to meet you once more at the same spot and let us after a mutual understanding part as happy and in as much confidence as we did then. I still have that same faith in you that I did then, it was shaken at one time but I find I blamed you for things that you did not do ...

your Winston

May 7, 1859. Bella, Josy, Henry,[22] *Julia and I started ... for Magnolia Spring on our picnic ... Col and I took a walk then came back ... to the Spring again, then got in the boats and had a race to Col's field, where we got some vegetables and Col shot me down two beautiful magnolias ... Col and I have had a happy time together ...*

May 17, 1859. In the afternoon Aunt Kate and I rode out to Col's, she and I had a long talk of the affairs between Col and myself. she is on my side ...[23]

[WINSTON STEPHENS TO OCTAVIA BRYANT]

Pine Grove June 27, 1859

My Dear Dear Rose Bud[24]

How delighted I was to see *Tivie* over at the Old Bachelors, oh how happy I feel in your society, your only answer to all my questions and caresses is done by

---

22. Josy is Joseph Hopkins; he and his brother Henry both served in the St. Johns Rangers (later Company B, Second Florida Cavalry), originally commanded by their father, Benjamin, and then by Winston. Bella is their sister, Isabella.

23. Richard and Catherine Parker were visiting from Boston.

24. Winston had a picture of Tivie, and he called it Tivie and her Rosebud in this letter. He is "talking" to the picture in this letter. He is the Old Bachelor.

those expressive black eyes and they speak volumes. I am requested to send her back. Now Rose bud be a darling good girl and let me keep Tivie while I am gone . . .[25] she will be so much company to me and I will keep her next to my heart while away. Oh how I hate to give her up, say that I may keep her for that short time, only the 8th of July . . . Much love . . . to Mother B. and a heart full of love to My Rose Bud. Good bye and may heaven protect you from more sickness, pleasant dreams.

Your affctionate Winston.

[WINSTON STEPHENS TO OCTAVIA BRYANT]

Pine Grove July 31, 1859.

My Angel of purity love and Goodness!

How are you? Forgive this offence and I'll be guilty of the like again the first time I feel like writing. You had as well bid the Sun cease to wander the earth with its heat, giving life to vegitation and thereby producing plenty for all Gods creation, as to bid the heart of Winston not to commune with the object of its adoration. No love it must speak where their is hope of spreading one ray of love and warmth around its idol . . . My heart feels that it has found a resting place where their is so much love, and where it will be protected from the storms of this cold and unfeeling world. "It is happy." it is content and its whole life shall be devoted to the one that has been so kind and by that means I hope to be able to repay in some degree the debt of love and sacrifice you make . . .

I am your loving and hoping

Winston.

"Two months and twenty one days."[26]

Aug 4, 1859. . . . In the afternoon Mother and I were sewing together in the dining room and she asked me if Wins had any idea of eloping with me, and said she judged from appearances that we had renewed the engagement, but she seemed very good humored . . . Wins walked home with us, Mother was quite talkative and polite.

---

25. Winston left for Middleburg on 29 June to spend the Fourth of July with his family and returned to Pine Grove on 8 July. Tivie obviously missed him and recorded on his return, "Bless him I was so glad to see him back."

26. This was the time remaining until Tivie's eighteenth birthday, and Winston obviously hoped for a favorable decision at that time. On 3 August Tivie confirmed in her diary that she intended to marry Winston.

Aug 7, 1859. The preacher did not come, so Burrel preached . . . had a very good sermon.[27] *After church . . . Wins came home with us and Mother lent him an over coat, and he started from here on his mule in a gallop . . . Mother seemed more friendly than ever . . .*

[OCTAVIA BRYANT TO WINSTON STEPHENS;
ON THE BACK OF A PROMISSORY NOTE OF WINSTON'S
DATED AUGUST 7, 1859][28]

My dear dear Wins

You do not know my love for you. I know I am reserved and timid now but one of these days I will endeavor to pay my debt with interest, you will teach me how to be affectionate by giving affection. "My love is sweet and secret"

Your own

Tivie

[WINSTON STEPHENS TO OCTAVIA BRYANT]

Pine Grove August 28, 1859.

My Dear Tivie

. . . My Dear I can see from your Mothers manners and bearing towards me and you that the opposition in that quarter has ceased and I candidly believe if she was spoken to and told what was to be she would not only give her consent to our union but make us so happy from now untill that time by allowing us the same happiness granted to all affianced lovers, in the free interchange of our affections. If your Mother still persevered in her opposition, she would stop our meeting and cut short that small amount of happiness that we are allowed to injoy at present, but you observe she makes no objections to our happy meetings, but presses me to enter her house whenever I go home with you. Now my Dear Dear love I dont say this hoping you will say something to your Mother to make an intire recconciliation . . . between us, but I wish to have you notice the change in our favor, and have you prepared to do what is your duty when the subject is named again by either of your parents. tell them plainly what you are determined

---

27. As mentioned, it was not unusual for whites to attend church with their slaves, but it was unusual for them to attend a black church and hear a slave minister.

28. Tivie meant this as her promise to marry Winston, although she did not confirm it until after her birthday.

to do and my word for it the road to our union will be smooth after that time ... Your Own

Winston

Sept 6, 1859. . . . *In the afternoon dear Wins sent a piece of venison dear fellow it will not now be long before I will eat the venison he kills at his and my own table. I wish for that time to come yet I dread it.*

[OCTAVIA BRYANT TO JAMES W. BRYANT]

Sept 6, 1859

Dear Father

You said some time ago you would not give your consent to my marrying anyone while I was so young, but when I was 18 I might marry whom I pleased, that at that time I did not know my own mind, that it was only a fancy and imagination. You afterwards told me that I must let you know when I wanted to get married. I am now I may as well say 18 and with as much "common sense" as girls of my age usually have and after three years thought have made up my mind that Col Stephens is the one to whom I would give myself. Yes Father *my* happiness depends upon my marrying him, and you can not say that one who has proved as faithful as he has is unworthy of me, and you acknowledged his worthiness three years ago when he asked for me in marriage, as you told him at that time that you had no objection to him, and that the only objection you had to our union was that I was too young, but if I was of the same mind and wanted to marry him when I was 18 you would have no objection and as that time has arrived and Col S— maintains the same position in society he did then, I can see no reason for an objection. Col S— has always wanted you informed upon the subject, but as he did not meet with the friendly advances your first consultation indicated, has not named the matter since the first of the year.

It may be useless to ask you, but once more dear Father, for my sake I ask you to consent, we would all be happier for it, I would feel much happier if I knew you had given your consent. I would dislike to marry without, but if you do not, I will be obliged to for my own happiness. It is no use, I have tried several times to give up entirely, but each time the same feelings have returned and with more force. I tried to do my duty to you as you wished, and Heaven alone knows how I have suffered. I know you would like to have me move in the most fashionable society and be admired and praised but I am not fit for that nor do I like it, I could not be happy. I want a quiet little home to myself . . .

I know Father that I have done many wrong things, but being separated from you so much and knowing our views were so different I allowed the power of love to draw me from the right path, but Father I think you would do the same were you in my place, so let "by gones be by gones" and come home. I will be one object less for you to work for and keep you away from dear Mother. Once more I beg of you to consent. With much love Yr aff Daught

Tivie

Sept 12, 1859. . . . Wins brought me a letter from Tina, he also gave me a ring, God bless him.
Sept 17, 1859. In the afternoon . . . met Wins then Mother and I sat on the piazza and talked of my marriage . . .
Oct 2, 1859. . . . Winston took tea with us, the first time for three years . . .
Oct 21, 1859. My 18th birthday. In the morning Mother made me a present of ½ doz silver spoons and a ladle . . . Winston took tea here after tea he and I played backgammon and I played the piano and we had some singing.

[JAMES W. BRYANT TO OCTAVIA BRYANT]

Havana Oct 23, 1859

My Dear Daughter

Your letter of the 14th Sept. was received by me on the 21st inst. and I regret excedingly that I was not advised earlier, that I could have spared your Mother, as well as yourself, much anxiety in reference to your marriage.

In taking the responsibility your Mother did without late advices from me, caused her much unhappiness, which could have been avoided. I approve the course she adopted, and should have advised it under the circumstances, had I known them.

I consider the greatest error committed by yourself in the whole matter from the commencement to the end to have been in not confiding your thoughts feelings and intentions to your Mother. The clandestine course from the inception of the attachment, until this communication to me, has operated unfavorably upon my mind and conclusions, and I most sincerely regret it.

I have never been prejudiced against Col. Stephens, but on the contrary have been more indulgent under all the circumstances than my natural disposition usually permits. I have invariably entertained a respect for him, believing he possessed integrity of character and wished to sustain it. But as you say, let "by-gones be by-gones" I suppose you are now married, or will be before this reaches you, and I can say that in receiveing Col. Stephens as your husband, I feel perfectly satisfied in his honor and position as a gentleman worthy his connections with you as any other lady and I never have had any objection to him personally . . .

Give my best assurances of friendship to Col S. and I most truly hope you may both be happy, and you may depend upon my Co-operation to that end.

Affectionately yours

J. W. Bryant

Oct 28, 1859. . . . [Winston] is to go to Palatka tomorrow to engage the minister. God bless and protect him. In five more days I will go home with him.

Nov 1, 1859. My wedding day. Winston and I were married at half past six in the eve, by Mr McMillan.[29] *Mary and Miss Smith were my bridesmaids, Willie and Dick were groomsmen.*[30] *had company after, etc, a little dancing music etc.*

Nov 2, 1859. Mother gave a dinner. all left on the boat who came last Monday. Winston and I went to the boat . . . Spent the eve quietly at Mother's. Winston had a very bad cold besides troubled with boils.

Nov 3, 1859. Came to "Rose Cottage" my own little home in the morning . . .

---

29. John C. McMilland, clerk of the circuit court and a resident of Palatka. At this time there was no minister in Welaka except for Winston's slave Burrel, who of course had no authority to marry anyone.

30. Unfortunately, Tivie never recorded the full name of Miss Smith or where she was from. In her 31 October journal entry, she noted that her brothers Willie and Davis had arrived with Miss Smith on the boat, so she was probably from Jacksonville. Since this is one of few references to her in the entire correspondence, it is odd that she was one of the bridesmaids. One wonders why Tivie's cousin Julia, for example, was not the logical choice. Willie was her brother; Dick was Winston's brother, Richard.

chapter 2

Life at Rose Cottage, 1859–1861

From the day Winston and Tivie moved into their honeymoon cottage on 3 November 1859 until they left it in 1863, the couple never lacked for company. In addition, they frequently visited friends and relatives, and when her mother was in Welaka before the war, Tivie visited her almost every day. Either Winston took her in the buggy or she rode Flora the mule and went by herself. Winston hunted and fished a large part of the time and usually had Henry or Georgie or one or two of the slaves with him. They killed deer, turkeys, ducks, squirrels, possums, raccoons, and occasionally bears and alligators. Several of the slaves, male and female, were permitted to hunt and fish without white supervision, and Burrel was allowed to keep a rifle in his cabin, which was against the law in antebellum Florida.

Tivie went fishing with Winston regularly, and they frequently went duck hunting. He was a fine woodsman and hunter; the number and variety of game he killed prove that he was an excellent shot. Tivie recorded that she was also considered to be more than adequate with both pistol and rifled musket.

The couple were in good health and physical condition when they married, although Tivie had occasional problems with one of her feet, and Winston sometimes suffered from boils and a recurring pain in his side. They were well matched physically, emotionally, and intellectually. Winston was 5 feet 8½ inches in height, weighed about 150 pounds, and had blue eyes, black hair, and a dark complexion. Tivie weighed about 100 pounds and was 5 feet ½ inch tall, with dark hair, a light complexion, and flashing black eyes, her most dominant facial feature.[1]

---

1. Before she married, Tivie and her friends frequently weighed themselves, and she recorded the results in her diaries. When Tivie applied for a pension for Winston's service in the Third Seminole War, she stated that he was 5' 8½" tall. According to her son Winnie, Tivie was 5' ½" tall. See "The Little Boston Rebel," by Winston Stephens, in the collection. Her weight varied from 98 to 113 pounds, according to the correspondence.

Winston had a zest for life and a good sense of humor, while Tivie was more serious and reserved, although she too loved to sing, play the piano, and dance. Neither used tobacco, and both drank only on special occasions. Both were deeply religious, but Winston sometimes felt that Tivie was too quick to censure actions that he believed were harmless flirtations. Still, he appreciated what a good person his wife was and made every attempt to meet her high moral standards, even abandoning profanity to please her.

Tivie encouraged Winston to improve his grammar and spelling, but she always praised his ability to write an interesting letter. He attempted to involve her in the business of running the plantation, but she was more than content to make Rose Cottage a happy home.

No photograph of Rose Cottage exists, but enough is known so that a full description can be made. It was considerably smaller than White Cottage, which was a large two-story structure (42 by 56 feet including the porch), but larger than the typical cabin of the time. The most common houses in antebellum Florida were either single- or double-penned cabins (one or two rooms), and this was true even on the eve of war. There were much more ornate structures in the larger towns and cities and on some plantations, but Florida was not a land of Southern mansions despite the prosperity of the 1850s.[2]

Rose Cottage was situated about 700 yards east of the St. Johns and could not be seen from the river. Located in the midst of a grove of live oaks, laurel oaks, water oaks, and tall southern pines, it stood some 25 to 30 yards east of the road to Welaka and about 100 yards north of Acosta Creek. The cabin was built of seasoned pine logs that had been cut to length and notched after the bark had been removed with a drawknife. It was then just a matter of stacking the logs to form walls and partitions, and Rose Cottage was a reality.

The gently rolling hills to the north and south along the road made for a beautiful view from the house. To the north and east was the "new ground" still being cleared, and to the west was the river field and then the low marshy area next to the river where the wharf was built. This field was prone to flooding and probably would have been phased out as the new ground came into production, but the war put an end to those plans. The land all along the river was left undisturbed. Scrub oak stood next to tall cypress, and palmettos and various types of shrubs covered the damp earth.

The house faced west, toward the road and the river. Tivie noted that she had a good view of the road from her dining room. When she was in her bedroom at the back of the house, Winston surprised her quite often when he

2. See Blakey, *Parade of Memories*, 23–29.

came home during the war.³ As was customary at the time, the kitchen was separated from the main house by a roofed hallway called a dogtrot. The main cabin was about 30 by 30 feet, and a roofed porch or piazza encircling three sides of the house was soon added. As was true of White Cottage, a main hall ran the length of the building, and the two front rooms served as the living and dining rooms. There were two bedrooms and a loft, which could be used as an additional bedroom. A storage shed was attached to the back of the house and could be pressed into service as a bedroom if needed. All told, the couple probably could sleep at least ten people in the cottage.

In addition to Rose Cottage, there were several other structures on the property. Somewhere to the south there was the original house built by George Bryant in 1854, apparently used for storage. In addition, there were a barn, smokehouse, large corncrib, cotton house, a mill house for grinding corn on Acosta Creek, and three slave cabins on the plantation. One cabin housed Burrel and Big Jane and their children: the twins, Mose and Joe, born in 1848; Jane, born in 1851; and Jess, born in the summer of 1855. Slaves had no legal rights of marriage; slave weddings occurred when the slaves asked for and the owner consented to the ceremony. Since Burrel was a minister and the only permanent one in Welaka, it must have been difficult for him to accept this arrangement, but he labored long and loyally for Winston and Tivie.

The other slaves included Tom and Rachael. Tom may have had a cabin to himself, for it appears that Rachael shared the cabin assigned to Sarah and her daughter, Jane. Jane had been sold to Nicholas Bradley of Clay County (the date of the sale is unknown), but Winston leased her on an annual basis so the family was not broken up. In 1860 Rachael and Jane were eighteen and fifteen respectively and worked in the fields. Sarah was the cook and supervised all of the youngest slave children with help from Burrel and Big Jane's daughter, who was nine years old in 1860.⁴ Sarah was married

---

3. We deduce this from the fact that there was very little traffic north of Rose Cottage. Buffalo Bluff, the Hopkins plantation, was there, but most of the visitors would have been coming from Welaka, some 2.3 miles south. It appears likely that the family would orient the house so they could see people coming, either from the porch or from the front rooms. The old road that passed their house is present-day County Road 309, and it became Bryant Avenue, the northern entrance to the town. Rose Cottage was on the high ground just east of the road, slightly north of the present entrance to the Acosta Creek Marina. There are numerous references in the correspondence that we believe locate the site, and we have also marked the boundary lines and walked the property, courtesy of current owner Don Tredinick. Although no trace of any building can be found, we are certain we are within 50 or so yards of where Rose Cottage stood.

4. Sarah gave birth to a second daughter, Mary Polly, on 4 July 1862. This information about the slaves was compiled from various entries in the journals and letters; Schedule II, Slave Schedules,

to Jacob, a slave belonging to the Hopkinses, but they did not live together.[5]

Winston had several plans for increasing the size and diversity of his holdings, but by the time he and Tivie married it was obvious that the people of Florida and other Southern states faced an uncertain future. The fanatical John Brown had tried to incite a slave rebellion in Virginia two weeks before their marriage, and sectional tensions were clearly at the breaking point.[6] It is also obvious from a few entries in Tivie's diary that she and Winston did discuss politics, or at least that he did so with friends and neighbors. Also, by March of 1860 at the latest, Tivie knew that she was pregnant, but she did not record anything in reference to her condition. This is not surprising, since intimate matters were rarely recorded by women at that time; but it is surprising that she did not at least mention the ominous political events that were happening on an almost daily basis in Florida.

As early as June 1860, when the Florida Democrats held their convention and declared for secession, it was clear what the future course of the state would be. The Whig Party had collapsed in 1854 following the passage of the Kansas-Nebraska Act.[7] There was no viable opposition party from then until 1860, when moderates in Florida affiliated with the Constitutional Union Party.[8] By that time Florida was largely a one-party state, and the Democratic

---

Oglethorpe County, Georgia, 1830, Marion County, Florida, 1850, and Putnam County, Florida, 1860; and the Dallas County, Alabama, Orphans Court Minutes of 1846.

5. When this happened, the couple were referred to as being the "board wife" or "board husband" of the other. Unless the distance separating the couple was substantial, this arrangement usually did not cause much trouble. However, Jacob did become a problem after Sarah and the rest of Winston's slaves were moved to Georgia. Jacob was the father of Mary Polly, but we do not know who Jane's father was. All that can be determined is that he lived in either Duval or Clay County in 1860, probably with the Gaineses or the Bradleys.

6. John Brown and his followers captured a federal armory at Harpers Ferry, Virginia, on 16 October 1859 in an attempt to foment a slave insurrection. Brown was captured, tried, and hanged early in December, and he became an instant martyr to many in the North. This was about the last straw for the South; radicals vowed that if a "Republican abolitionist" became president, they would secede from the Union, a promise that was tragically kept.

7. The Kansas-Nebraska Act of 1854 opened up the possibility that slave states might be created from public lands that had been closed to slavery since the Missouri Compromise in 1820. The Whig Party could not heal the breach between its Southern and Northern wings and disintegrated as a national party, although many, like Winston, continued to identify themselves as Whigs even after the war had begun. After the Whig demise, the sectional Republican Party appeared, and its anti-Southern stance was the major reason why the South seceded seven years later.

8. The Know-Nothing or American Party of 1856 was only a temporary refuge for former Whigs. They could identify only with the party's loyalty to the Union; the bitter denunciation of Catholics and immigrants, which was the main focus of the party, found little support in Florida. Many former Whigs did vote that ticket in 1856, but the party disappeared shortly after the election. The Constitutional Union Party in 1860 also served as a temporary refuge for moderates who hoped to avoid the issue of slavery expansion or contraction, which they were convinced would destroy the Union. This party also disappeared after the 1860 election.

Party was thoroughly controlled by secessionists. Yet moderates and Unionists in East Florida continued to hope that they could elect delegates to the next legislature. Winston was one of their aspiring but unsuccessful candidates, but that was in the future as he and Tivie set up housekeeping in 1859. Tivie's father was unable to attend the wedding, but the couple received his blessing in December.

[JAMES W. BRYANT TO OCTAVIA STEPHENS]

Havana Dec 18, 1859

My dear daughter

Your letter of the 15 November was not received until a long time after it was written, as you have been informed by your Mother I suppose.

I can hardly realize you are married, as all my associating, in thought, with you, are that you are yet "Tivie" in *my* house. But the *fact* stops all fancies and I must view you as a Wife—the duties which you are called upon to discharge are of the greatest responsibility. The duties of *a Wife* are arduous under any circumstances, but I trust in the position you have placed yourself you fully understand, and will discharge them—In selecting the retired position of a planters wife, in the country, where you find but few persons who observe the rules of polite society, there is danger of you becoming indifferent to the customs of those who live in more populated places. If I understand Col Stephens ideas upon these things he prefers a different style of life from that which many Florida planters appear satisfied to possess—therefore I trust you will aim *ever* to make his house in accordance with his taste, and with what should be yours. The name for your "log Cottage" is very pretty, and I hope when I do see it, that I may have some evidence that it is not "Rose Cottage" *in name only*.

Your Mother did write me very fully about the wedding, and I was glad that the event passed off so pleasantly.[9]

From the first acquaintance I had with Col Stephens, I liked him, and from that time I have but one cause for disapprobation and that perhaps, may be excused—However that may be, I have no inclination now to probe it. He is now your husband, and connected with me, and although I felt that he was wrong, his desire to possess you was an excuse which should perhaps be justification.

You write me that you are *very* happy—God grant that you may continue so—and I believe you can be provided you do not expect too much, nor too much be expected from you—There are few persons who are happy in this married life—*Too much is expected*. Human nature has many weaknesses, and unless allowances are made for them, disappointments must ensue—In your retired life you will have less trials than those who mingle in society, but guard against all

9. This letter is missing.

associations which are inconsistent with your tastes, and those of a refined character...

I am glad to know that Col. Stephens takes so much care for the comfort of your Mother in my absence—It is an attention which I appreciate above all things. I hope you will continue to make your visits to "White Cottage" as you have commenced, because while I am absent your Mother must be lonely—more especially since you have left her.

With kind regards to Winston and affectinate salutation to yourself I am

Your affectionate father

J. W. Bryant

July 25, 1860. Mother, Willie, Henry and Georgie left on the boat to go North...[10]

[WINSTON STEPHENS TO REBECCA BRYANT]

Rose Cottage Sept 12, 1860.

Dear Mother Bryant

Once more I will attempt to add a little to Tivie's letter, though I am now as before, lost for want of something to interest you. Tivie is in her usual *good* health and I am a little bilious but on the mend... I go from home to day on a political tour as my friends have forced me out as a candidate, after allowing myself to become a candidate for the Legislature, they now want me to run for the Senate. They have held a meeting in St Augustine and that body elected me and sent a delegation over to see if I would accept and we will not determine untill we get to Palatka, but I think I shall decline the last honor as I would be compelled to stay from home the most of the time from now untill the 1st Monday in Oct...

I remain yours aff'ly

Winston

[WINSTON STEPHENS TO OCTAVIA STEPHENS]

Palatka Sept 14, 1860

My Dear Darling Wife

I am well and trust you are as well as when I left you. There is no place like my home with my Dear wifes good and happy influence, and I most solemnly prom-

---

10. The Bryants remained in Massachusetts until October, except for J. W. Bryant, who was in Cuba.

ise never to allow any influence or circumstances to draw me away from my wife and home after this canvas and its results . . . They have forced me out for the Senate and in the morning I shall go over to . . . St Johns County where there is to be a dinner and muster and I shall meet Mr Chals. Hopkins and others from St Augustine—then I will return to this place and remain untill monday 5 PM when I will take the *Sumpter* for home . . .[11]

Your aff husband

Winston

Oct 1, 1860. I went to Tina's in time for breakfast. Winston returned from Palatka and St Augustine and spent awhile with us at Tina's in the morning, then returned to town to the barbecue and election, returned to Tina's quite late and we concluded to stay all night.

Oct 15, 1860. Mother, Henry, and George came from the North, where [they have] been since August.

Oct 31, 1860. Two weeks ago tonight our little baby girl was born.[12] Henry and George left on the boat for Jacksonville today, and Mother went to town to pack some things, and I alone with baby all day as Winston is away attending Court.

Nov 1, 1860. The anniversary of our wedding, married one year to day . . .

Nov 6, 1860. Winston went to town to the election, gone all day.[13]

Nov 7, 1860. In the morning Winston went to town with Mother to help her pack some things and Mother left on the boat for Jacksonville where she is to stay this Winter with the four boys.

Dec 6, 1860. Arrived at Magnolia at 12 o'clock waited sometime, when

---

11. Charles F. Hopkins of St. Augustine, a Whig leader in the area. The *General Sumter* was built in 1859 in Palatka and ran from that city to Enterprise until the war came. Mueller, *St. Johns River Steamboats.*

12. Rosalie (Rosa) Stephens was born on 17 October 1860.

13. Winston was not elected to either branch of the legislature, and neither was any other Constitutional Unionist in the county; Putnam voters sent Democrats E. C. Simkins to the Senate and G. E. Hawes to the House. Radical Democrats also elected secessionist John Milton governor. On the national scene, Floridians gave over 8,500 votes to the radical Southern Democrat John C. Breckinridge; but the moderate Constitutional Union candidate, John Bell, polled almost 5,500, an indication that many in the state were not yet ready for secession. Stephen A. Douglas, who favored compromise, received but 367 votes, and Abraham Lincoln was not on the ballot in Florida or any other southern state. The election of Lincoln resulted in the secession of South Carolina in December, and the rest of the Deep South soon followed.

Dick and Lewis came with the conveyances, arrived at Webster, Mary was married between 8 and 9 o'clock, there were about 300 persons there.[14]

Dec 13, 1860. Took the Darlington for Jacksonville arrived between one and two o'clock a.m. Willie and Davis met us at the wharf. In the evening Willie and Winston went down town . . .

Dec 16, 1860. Winston left as soon as he ate breakfast, for home . . .

[WINSTON STEPHENS TO OCTAVIA STEPHENS]

Rose Cottage Dec 18, 1860.

My Dear Wife

I arrived safely on monday and met Joe or Joe met me with the mule and no saddle and I sent to Genl. Hopkins to borrow one and Joe returned with a request for me to go up to the house which I did, as I was feeling rather wolfish in the craw about that time, so I rode up and had a chat with the *good* folks and discused the all important subject over their breakfast,[15] and I broke my fast with venison stake and beef stake and other good things on the table, after which I marched home where I found all in good health. I got sarah and jane in the house and they cleaned up in a jiffy, and then I took possession of my lonely abode, and I am getting on about as well as could be expected, but every thing comes aucward as it has been so long since I was an old Bachelor . . . I met several letters on my arrival . . . one from Erwin and Hardee reporting sales of five bags of my cotton, three at 28 cts and two at 26 cts, which is good sales under the existing circumstances.[16] the net proceeds of the cotton was four hundred and ninety two dollars, nearly one hundred to the bag . . .

Yours with much love, Winston

Dec 23, 1860. Henry and I left Jacksonville for Welaka about four o'clock in the afternoon . . .

---

14. Dick and Lewis are Winston's brother Richard Stephens and his half-brother Lewis Gaines. Mary Gaines married Thomas Jessup Branning of Middleburg, the son of John and Mary Branning. The Brannings had been in this area while Florida was still under Spanish rule. They were a numerous and very influential family in East Florida. Webster was the new name for Whitesville, Florida; it was named for Daniel Webster in November or December of 1859 and reflected the strong Union feelings in the area. For a history of the region, see Blakey, *Parade of Memories*.

15. A reference to the secession conventions that had been called forth by the election of Abraham Lincoln. The Florida legislature voted unanimously on 28 November 1860 to hold a special convention in Tallahassee on 3 January 1861. South Carolina left the Union on 20 December, Mississippi went on 9 January, and Florida was the third state to leave, on 10 January 1861.

16. Robert Erwin and Charles H. Hardee were cotton factors in Savannah, Georgia.

Dec 26, 1860. *Burrel and Jane left on the boat for a Christmas visit . . .*[17]

Dec 31, 1860. *Burrel and Jane returned and brought the news of Maj Gaines illness with pneumonia . . .*

Jan 7, 1861. *Heard of Maj Gaines death.*[18]

Jan 14, 1861. *Winston and Lewis and Ben Gaines came. Ben came home with us, Lewis stayed at Tina's.*[19]

Apr 19, 1861. *Early in the morning Brother Willie surprised us from Jacksonville, he had arrived at Welaka the night before . . . he came up on business. After I had give him some breakfast . . . he and Winston went to town and did not get back until nearly two o'clock . . .*[20]

May 3, 1861. *In the morning Winston went to town and brought me a box and letters from Mother and Father. Father in Jacksonville but going back to Cuba to day, he and Mother sent me two handsome presents.*

June 9, 1861. *Quite a nice rain. Winston went patrolling in the morning.*[21]

June 24, 1861. *. . . rec'd a letter from Mother speaking of a narrow escape from drowning of Willie and Georgie and being ordered off by the blockading vessel . . .*

This letter is missing, but in it Tivie learned from her mother that the war had at last had a direct impact on the family. Willie was an avid Confederate, and his father was equally strong for the Union, but the rest of the family had not yet decided where their loyalty resided even after the firing on Fort Sumter in April 1861. In this respect the Bryants were typical of many in Jacksonville.

---

17. Burrel and Big Jane went to Middleburg to visit family as well as their former owners, Lewis and Mary Ann Gaines.

18. After Gaines moved to Middleburg in 1858, he quit farming, hired out all but eight slaves (a cook, housekeeper, manservant, and five young people), and taught school. Following his death at the age of fifty-one, most of the family moved back to Marion County. Mary (Gaines) Branning and her husband remained at Middleburg, Ben moved in with Winston and Tivie, Lewis stayed with Clark and Tina, and the rest of the family returned to Ocala in 1862.

19. Although Florida had seceded by this time, Tivie made no mention of that event, and life went on as usual. This was true after Florida joined the Confederacy in February 1861 and even after the war began with the firing on Fort Sumter in April. Ben Gaines was Winston's half-brother.

20. Willie had made up his mind to join the Confederate army and most probably wanted Winston apprised of his rental property in Welaka. It is likely that they talked about who would look after the Bryants' private property in Jacksonville. It does not appear that Davis had made up his mind about his future by this date. Instead of following his initial impulse to join the fight, he apparently took Willie's clerical position until Jacksonville fell to the Union forces in March 1862. At that time he joined up, and after that date the protection of their property in Jacksonville and the collection of the various rents owed the Bryants proved to be impossible.

21. Slave patrols were supposed to be conducted regularly in Florida, but unless there was some anxiety in the white community about a possible slave revolt, this was not done. There was little fear of a slave uprising in Welaka before the war, but this changed as the Federal threat intensified.

Most Floridians were strongly for secession, but this was not true of Jacksonville, and the question was debated openly and thoroughly in the homes and the streets of the city for most of 1861. The Bryant debate ended in May when James left for Cuba, but he was soon to learn that Willie had joined the Confederate army. James remained loyal to the Union and found himself cut off from his family for the duration of the war. In due time he would learn that all of his sons save one had donned the rebel gray. He was unusually lucky in that they all survived the war, but his wife and son-in-law did not; he was to see them just one more time, in December 1862.

Willie was the first of the family to join up, but it was just a matter of time before Winston, Davis, and finally Henry entered the ranks. Willie joined the Jacksonville Light Infantry, which was reorganized as Company A of the Third Florida Infantry. Although his company was not officially mustered in until 10 August 1861, Willie was in the field by June. Davis, George, and Henry visited him at Fort Steele in Mayport several times that summer and obviously had a harrowing experience in June.

chapter 3

It Is the Duty of Every Man To Help Drive Back the Invader

[WILLIE BRYANT TO REBECCA BRYANT]

Rebel Tent June 21, 1861

My dear Mother,

I am happy to inform you that after a very tedious trip we arrived here yesterday just before 1 o'clock;[1] We were travelling the whole time from 12 o'clock of the night before, with the exception of about 4 hours, when we laid by for some rest, and breakfast, and because *we could get no further,* I must say the delay was not enjoyed in any particular; The breakfast consisted of parched-corn, coffee without "sweetening," some rice boiled without salt, and some mullet ditto, and for once I found a meal that others could eat, and I could not *any* more than courtesy required; no, "I'd have fought first . . ."

With much love to all—

Willie

July 3, 1861. In the morning Winston went for his bees, and saw a negro at the field and had to shoot him to make him stop, he had him brought here and sent for the Doctor, he and young Allen came and carried him home . . .[2]

---

1. The headquarters of the Third Florida Infantry were in Fernandina, but Willie's company was sent to Mayport, at the mouth of the St. Johns River. Under the command of Captain Holmes Steele, several companies dug trenches, erected palmetto log works, and set up four 4-inch cannon for the defense of the place that was soon known as Fort Steele. See Gold, *History of Duval County,* 128. Holmes Steele was a medical doctor. In the Eighth Census of the United States, 1860, Schedule I, Population Schedule, Duval County, he was listed as age thirty-four, born in South Carolina, and having a wife, Rebecca (twenty-three, born in Florida), and a personal estate valued at $10,000.

2. In 1861 Bryan Gardner, of the Fernandina firm of Gardner and Branch, commenced a large turpentine operation in Welaka. He rented White Cottage for $9 a month, and his slaves soon

[WINSTON STEPHENS TO OCTAVIA STEPHENS]

Rose Cottage Sept 1, 1861[3]

My Very Dear Tivie

You may think very strange of my commencing this letter to day, but the truth is I have been thinking of you until I could not refrain from writing any longer. I feel quite well and I am happy to say my very *extensive* family are too.

I arrived late on wednesday P.M. and did not have the pleasure of meeting a pair of *pouting* lips, such as you *sometimes* present when in the best of humors, but instead, loneliness greeted me on every turn and at last I turned from the house and have since devoted myself to the mill. It goes quite hard with me as it has been so long since I did such hard work, but I suppose I will get use to it by the time I finish the job, Jane and the two small boys have dug about one third of the ditch. They will have to pick cotton next week but will perhaps get over in time to work one or more days on the ditch, but that will depend upon the weather as the cotton has opened in last few days more than formerly and if the sun continues to shine it will take them all the time to keep up with it.[4]

Good morning Old Lady

caused concern among the residents of Welaka. He and his overseer, a young man named Dan Allen, were not able to stop some of the slaves from wandering about and stealing things; but according to the correspondence, this is the only time one was shot. Gardner was a native of North Carolina who listed himself as a forty-year-old turpentine farmer in the 1860 census. Gardner and his partner, Thomas H. Branch, a twenty-three-year-old native of the Tar Heel state as well, owned an all-male work force of 25 slaves, ages seventeen to forty-eight. In addition, Branch owned 11 males from nineteen to sixty; all 36 were valued at $18,000 in 1860. It appears that Gardner began operations with the firm's labor force but added Branch's 11 when Fernandina fell to the Federals early in 1862. Whatever the numbers, his labor force had a sizable impact on the residents in and around Welaka, especially when food supplies ran short. Gardner's surname appears frequently in the correspondence and in the newspapers of the times. In the index and text of *War of the Rebellion: A Compilation of the Official Records* (cited hereafter as *OR*, with appropriate series, volume, and page identification) he is cited as an "unidentified civilian." Winston B. Stephens Jr. finally found his full name in the Putnam County land records, Palatka. For the rest of the data, see Eighth Census of the United States, 1860, Schedules I and II, Nassau County, Florida.

3. On 28 August Tivie left Rose Cottage for an extended visit to friends in Jacksonville. Winston accompanied her but returned home two days later.

4. Winston had purchased a cotton gin that summer, and although he tried for over a year to get someone to set it up for him, he never got it going. In addition to the gin, he was building a new grinding mill. To drive the gears operating the mill, he intended to use water power; hence the ditch. He referred to the whole operation as "the mill." It is obvious that he had every intention of expanding his productivity in both cotton and corn, although he knew that future cotton crops would be determined by the vicissitudes of war. Even though the Confederacy never officially announced an embargo on cotton, state governments and planters and farmers alike decided to hoard the crop in the mistaken belief that this would force England and France to intervene and officially recognize the independence of the Confederacy. This policy, coupled with the Union naval blockade, soon caused widespread shortages in the Confederacy. In 1862 Winston grew short-staple cotton for home use as well as long-staple for sale, as factory thread that was scarce in 1861 was virtually nonexistent a year later.

I have just put down the axe and now take up the pen to finish this. the pen is much the lightest but I think I can trace a line with one about as well as the other ... Jane is the proudest negroe on the River as she has picked over 30 lbs of cotton pr day this week ... you can buy what you are in need of and if any money left get ½ Gal Fluid, you will not have money for Factory thread ...[5] I want you to kiss your Mother and Rosa for me and then let them kiss you for me. Give much love to all. I have two pigs in a pen in the yard and I want you to make Mother and the boys promise to come up Christmas and help eat them ... your aff husband

Winston

[OCTAVIA STEPHENS TO WINSTON STEPHENS]

Jacksonville Sept 7, 1861

My dear Winston

I was *very* glad to receive your nice long letter on Thursday, and glad to hear that you were well for I had felt anxious about you ever since I left ... I am very sorry for your sake that you are lonely, but I must say I am glad, that I am missed by you, but then the worse people are sometimes the more they are missed. I hope you will not look for me next Monday ... Rosa has made more visits than I, she is much admired, she is the prettiest baby I have seen, nearly everyone asks whose baby she is, dont you feel proud...?

There was a report here the other day that there was a fleet in sight of Fernandina, and every body, or a great many are beginning to think of leaving, if times get "skcary."[6] Mother may go home with me, but I believe most of the reports are false, storekeepers are even packing up goods. The men have been drilling right here at the Court House this afternoon, I declare it made me feel dreadfully to think what they were drilling for, you do not know how glad I feel when I think you are not in any company, and I hope and pray you may never be in any.

I suppose you know all communication is broken off between the North and South, but Mother was fortunate enough to get a letter from Aunts Kate

---

5. The fluid was whale oil. Because of the blockade, substitutes had to be found, and one replacement was alligator oil. Before the war was over, both the Stephens and Bryant clans were involved in this activity. In 1864, when the Federal occupation of Jacksonville commenced, kerosene replaced the various substitutes for those residents who swore loyalty to the Union. In the interior, kerosene was not available until after the war.

6. The rumor was false. The only place in Florida that would see actual fighting in 1861 was Pensacola, where the Federals remained in control of Fort Pickens; but Jacksonville's turn came in March 1862.

and Mary last week, and they had heard from Father since Mother had, he was better . . .[7]

Your ever affectionate

Wife

[WINSTON STEPHENS TO OCTAVIA STEPHENS]

Rose Cottage Sept 10, 1861

My Dear Wife

. . . You have surely forgotten My Dear when you say you feel so glad that I do not belong to a Company. dont you remember I signed Genl Hopkins list some time ago? Well, that same Company was organized on Saturday and 45 men were present and elected their Officers. Genl. Hopkins Capt., Myself 1st Lieutenant, Capt Gray of Palatka 2nd Lt, and Mr Peter Peterman of Palatka 3rd Lt.[8] I could have ben elected Capt if I had allowed my name in opposition to Genl Hopkins but I thought the Genl entitled to it and would not suffer the men to use my name. I had an opponet for 1st Lt a Mr Braddock he got 12 votes and I got 33 which is a nice majority.[9] You remember this Company is for home service and is not to be sent to any part of the State but on the coast near our homes, say from Indian River to St Augustine, unless some point near by is invaded when we offer to go and help drive back the invader and then return to our usual range. Now My Dear I dont intend to Join any other kind of a company but I do think it is the duty of every man to help drive back the invader when they come so near as is contemplated in the organization of the Company . . .

You ask me if I dont feel proud of Rosa. I say not more so than before you left as I am not disappointed, I tell you she is the greatest baby in the Southern Confederacy and she has got the greatest Mother in the same scope. Give much love to all and bring Mother if you can. Good evening My Dear Kiss Rosa for me and as many more females as you please but no males if you please . . .

Your aff husband always, Winston

---

7. Aunt Mary was Abigail Mary Hall of Boston.

8. The unit, originally called the St. Johns Rangers, was organized on 7 September 1861, mustered into Confederate service on 15 November 1861, and reorganized on 4 December 1862 as Company B, Second Florida Cavalry. Henry A. Gray, owner of twelve slaves, also operated a boat out of Palatka. After Winston was killed in March 1864, Gray was promoted to captain and finished the war in command of the company. Peter Peterman was a Palatka merchant and did not serve long; he was replaced by William W. Shedd, also of Palatka.

9. John Braddock is the most probable guess here. The only other Braddocks in the company were Joseph and William, the sons of James A. and Winny Braddock, who lived near Welaka. Had it been either of them, Winston would probably have used their full names since he knew them well. It appears here that he did not know this Braddock at all.

Sept 16, 1861. Arrived at Welaka about 7 o'clock. Winston and Clark were at the wharf to meet us. Winston had breakfast at home ready for me . . .

Sept 21, 1861. Winston went to the Priest's settlement to drill, gone nearly all day.

Oct 22, 1861. Tina's 30th birthday. Winston started early out in the country with Gen Hopkins to buy horses for their company.

Oct 28, 1861. Winston went to town in the morning to get the mail and about 9 o'clock who should come on the mule but Mother, Henry and George also came, a very pleasant surprise, as I did not expect them until next Mon . . .[10]

[REBECCA BRYANT TO DAVIS BRYANT]

Rose Cottage Oct 29, 1861

My dear Davis,

I am here safe and sound . . . I found Tivie well and cheerful, notwithstanding she has five sick negroes to attend to, and those five include the best in the place—Burrel, Rachel, Sarah the cook, the little girl that waits about the house and the youngest boy, Jess.[11] She does not *appear* to feel as sadly about Winston's going as I thought she would—I know however she always conceals her feelings—but she does not dread the future as I do—She is young and hopeful yet, I can no longer build castles . . .

Mr Burritt told me on Sunday that he had spoken to you about writing to your Father by the vessel that is going to Nassau—I hope you or Willie will write—I shall write a few lines in the morning and enclose with this, hoping the vessel will not leave before it reaches you—If there is no opportunity to send it before you leave please destroy it . . .

I wish I knew if Willie went to Fort Steele to-day—Oh me! it is a long time to Christmas—Every one has been in bed nearly two hours and I must follow their lead—Good night may Heaven bless you and my dear Willie whereever you go.

Mother

Oct 30, 1861. Winston left on the boat for Palatka with Gen Hopkins and others to have their company mustered into service.

---

10. After this date, Rebecca, Henry, and George lived with Tivie at Rose Cottage until they were forced to evacuate late in 1863.

11. The "little girl" was Jane, daughter of Burrel and Big Jane. She helped Sarah set the table and clean up after meals.

[WINSTON STEPHENS TO OCTAVIA STEPHENS]

Porterville five miles from Palatka Nov 3, 1861.

My Dear Wife

... as some of the Boys have no blankets I shared with them and slept quite cold last night, and then some two or three had no blanket and had a colder bed than I did ... We are in Capt Porters yard five miles from Town,[12] where we have a good pasture for horses and a pleasant place for the men, I say pleasant I mean about as pleasant as we could expect. Friday night we had rain just after going to sleep and we got up and crowded in the house and roosted on the floor ... some horses have just left camp for Capt Hopkins and a friend of his from Georgia, who are expected by 10 oclock. I am to meet him with the men I have in camp. The Gentleman desires to become an honorary member of the Company and will present us with a nice bugle. I think it could have been done some other day but the Capt made the arrangements ... and I had to comply. We have not hird from the mustering Officer and cant tell when we will muster. We are recruiting some men every day and think we will have a good Company ... I want you to have the potatoes dug by the cotton and the hogs turned in at once and make Burrel get the four or five hogs from Welaka ... and hunt the Hammock for the rest of my hogs and if they find any *they* must go in a pen and be fed. I dont want the potatoes by the lot dug. Make Burrel bank them. I have a fine Mare which Cost $200 and she is only four years old and gentle ... Give love to Mother and the rest kiss Rosa for Pa Pa and accept many kisses [and] much love from your aff Husband

Winston

[OCTAVIA STEPHENS TO WINSTON STEPHENS]

Nov 5, 1861

My dear Husband

... Would you not like to look in upon us to night and see how we do without you? and what we are doing? Well I can tell you what we are doing now. we have a nice cheerful fire with the horse in front of it drying Rosa's socks etc,[13] and a table out in the middle of the room and Mother sitting opposite me writing. Henry and George sitting a little to one side studying, poor Ben in bed where he has had fever this afternoon.[14] Rosa asleep, now if you were only here our picture would be complete, though we would rather have Ben with us too. As for getting

---

12. J. W. Porter, a farmer born in New York, lived some five miles northwest of Palatka.
13. A clotheshorse was a simple frame upon which clothes were dried.
14. Ben Gaines, Winston's half-brother, lived with Winston and Tivie for several months.

along, we do that pretty well but I assure you I miss you sadly, but I can not help thinking that you will be home soon *to stay*. I can not realize that this is only the beginning of *worse*. Rosa has not yet forgotten how to say Pa Pa, though she is too often reminded to forget how to say it, if she does not forget to whom it applies. The first night you were away when I took her into bed Mother had not yet got in and she looked all around and kept calling for Pa Pa and made me feel right sad, she has been very cross for two or three days and nights, I am quite certain that there is another tooth coming, she has been better today, and slept quite well last night. just as I finished that sentence she awoke, I took her up and she went right to sleep again . . .

Burrel began digging potatoes after dinner yesterday. I do not know how near done they are, he said he wanted to get the hogs in and get those from town before he went on the Coast, which will be Friday morning, but I think he will not, for Clark wants him to come over Wednesday night to help him kill his beef early Thursday morning. Tina spent to day with us. I had beef enough for half ration, and we are intirely out of meat, have had chicken for dinner twice, no fish to be caught by *any body*. The boys started before breakfast the other morning for the Ocklawaha and did not return until afternoon, and got a mud fish and cat. I one little squirrel and a brim . . . the tide is so high that no one catches any fish.[15]

Last Saturday night Gardners negroes took the rounds, one came here (early in the eve) one at Clarks and two at one of the Priests, for potatoes. Burrel had been to Clark's and saw the fresh track in the road and got over in the patch (*by the lot*) and sure enough they had grabbed the best hills of three rows. I sent the measure to Mr Allen, and I hear he has found out who it was, but I do not know yet of the punishment, the one that went into Tina's chicken house has been laid up a week, one of them came here Sunday morning but Burrel made him leave and Sarah says he took a good look around before he left.

Well here I am again after a very good nights rest, I hope you slept as comfortable, we wished when we got into bed that you had one as comfortable, Rosa slept very well and woke up *very good* natured, but I tell you what we had a time of it after breakfast, thank gracious she is asleep now, you have no idea how she has changed in behaviour, I guess you will think, oh yes its her not the baby, but I try all kinds of ways with her, but of no avail, you had better come home and take care of her . . .

Rosa is still asleep so I will not wake her to send you a kiss, Mother sends her love, I wont send mine, for you have it already, provided you are a *"good boy."*

Very affectionately

Your Wife

---

15. When the tide caused the river to overflow its banks, the fish went into the newly opened feeding ground, and it was rare to catch one out in the river proper. That is still true today.

[REBECCA BRYANT TO DAVIS BRYANT]

Nov 5, 1861

My dear Davis,

... I am *rejoiced* that you are not going to join any company.[16] It really made me feel miserably to think of your being so far from *all* of us, in case of sickness or accident—It is bad enough to have Willie where he is, and while you remain in Jacksonville he has frequent communication with you—if you left, we would seem to be more widely scattered with no connecting link. I think Winston will feel disappointed, as he seemed desirous to have you accept the office of Sergeant, but no doubt he will think you judged right, under the circumstances. I hope he will be as well satisfied as he anticipates, and that their head quarters will be at St. Augustine. Welaka looked forlorn enough, I assure you, the morning I arrived and every thing *here* appeared different from what it ever did before, but now the negroes are all up again, we begin to get straight and I feel more reconciled, more at home than at first ... Today I have commenced attending to [the boys'] studies, which they dislike now as they have run wild so long, but think they will soon get into the way of studying and will enjoy their play the more. It was necessary to do something to keep them from such constant and familiar intercourse with the negroes ...

With much love
Mother

[WINSTON STEPHENS TO OCTAVIA STEPHENS]

Camp Porter Nov 10, 1861.

My Dear Wife

Your very long and affectionate letter was duly received on last Wednesday night and you may rest assured it was perused with no little interest and considerable satisfaction ... I hope this may find you as well as when your letter was written, but let me caution you about Rosa, dont let her have fever in cutting her gums for any length of time before you cut her gums with a sharp knife. It looks cruel but my dear sometime life itself depends upon it.[17] I would come home some day and be with you but I must put up with my camp for the reason, if I should come home it would give the men an excuse to do likewise, and in that

---

16. Davis had been offered the position of sergeant in Winston's company, but he apparently took the position that Willie formerly had with the Jacksonville merchant firm of Bloodgood and Bouse.

17. This myth was believable because the infant death rate was high when the children were first weaned and in some cases were given bad milk (without effective sterilization); since teething occurred at the same time, it was thought to be the cause of death.

case we would not have our company together when the Officer came to muster us in. We are not mustered yet, but Capt Hopkins started this morning down on the Darlington to Jacksonville after the Officer to Muster us. I have 38 Men in camp with me and there is about 20 in the neighborhood ready when the Officer comes and we are receiving recruits every day. Capt Norton failed to organize his company yesterday and we have some of his men and expect to get more. Mr McLeod of Palatka will take the place offered to Davis.[18]

The Darlington brought some exciting news yesterday, it reports the Yankee fleet of 32 sail had commenced an attack on Port Royal and that the Fort had sunk their best ship and the others had been obliged to retire for repairs, but there is no doubt but it will be a long seige. But I trust the Fort can hold out. It was also reported that a fleet had fired on Brunswick but I could not ascertain what was the force or what the result. We have a force (so reported) of 20 thousand at the first and 30 thousand at the last named place and the forts were considered impregnable.[19] The St Johns and St Marys did not come as they [were] conveying troops etc to the relief of those two places.[20] I presume the next place to be tried will be Fernandina, but I sincerely hope they will get enough in the fights above mentioned to require them to return to some Northern Port for repairs, so as to give more time for preperation on our coast.[21] I had a regular

---

18. Nathan Norton, a forty-year-old Palatka planter, and R. H. McLeod. McLeod served for the remainder of the war and finished as first lieutenant of the company. See Florida Board of State Institutions, *Soldiers of Florida*, 203; although inaccurate in many cases, this is still an indispensable source in locating Floridians who served in the war.

19. The Federal naval attack against Fort Walker and Fort Beauregard, which protected Port Royal, commenced on 7 November 1861. Under the command of Flag Officer Samuel Du Pont, some 75 warships bombarded the forts into submission that day and landed about 12,000 troops. Port Royal, South Carolina, was about halfway between Charleston and Savannah and served as a coaling station for the rest of the war. Possession of this port allowed the Union navy to continue the blockade with increasing effectiveness. Brunswick was not captured, but the offshore islands of Wassaw and Tybee were, and this allowed the Union to seize Fort Pulaski in April 1862. Possession of this fort threatened Savannah, but no serious attempt was made to take the city until early 1864, and that attempt failed. Sherman, however, made his famous march later that year. Unless otherwise specified, all information concerning battles, leaders, and campaigns is taken from Faust, *Historical Times*.

20. The *St. Johns* and *St. Marys* were in regular commercial service between Palatka and Savannah prior to the war, along with the *Welaka*, the *Seminole*, and the *Magnolia*. The *St. Johns* burned at her dock in Jacksonville, but the hull was raised and rebuilt, and she became a blockade runner with the outbreak of the war. She was captured by Federal forces on 18 April 1863 but returned to her regular run after the war under the name *Helen Getty*. The *Magnolia* ran for only a short time before her boiler exploded, killing Captain William McNelty and several passengers off St. Simons Island, Georgia. The *Welaka* was wrecked on the St. Johns bar; and the *Seminole*, like the *St. Johns*, burned at her berth in Jacksonville, but she was not raised. The *St. Marys* had several close escapes and was scuttled twice by her crew, in March 1862 and February 1864, to avoid capture. She was raised after the war and resumed service on the St. Johns River under the name *Nick King*. T. Frederick Davis, *History of Jacksonville*, 359; Hayes, *Samuel Francis Du Pont*, vol. 1, 375.

21. Winston was correct in his assumptions about Fernandina, which fell to the Union early in 1862 and remained under Federal control for the rest of the war.

soldiers dream on Friday night. I thought I had returned and after saluting you Rosa called Pa Pa and smacked her lips for a kiss, but alas I awoke and had a soldiers bed and bedfellow. You may think I love this life better than my quiet home with those dearer than life itself, but you are sadly mistaken it is only two things that induces me to make the sacrifices I am making. One is a duty I owe to you and the other is a duty I owe my Country, but if God permits me to return safe to my home after this term I will remain there only when I am compelled to assist to drive back the enemy from my State and then it shall be done as an independent Volunteer. I wrote a short and hurried letter by Capt Hopkins to Davis in answer to his which I rec'd the same time I got yours. I am glad Davis is not going to join us because I think some one of us should be free and as he can make it pay him better than any of us, I am glad he does so.

I send by Darlington in the morning some bagging and in the roll there is a bottle of Castor oil, be careful when it is unrolled that the bottle is not broken. I want Burrel as soon as he returns to cut off 5 yards and make a bag and weigh 440 lbs of seed cotton and pack it in the bag and put it on the wharf and write to Mr Smith to mark it to Parson and Levingston, Orange Springs, and send it by the first barge that goes up the river . . .[22]

I should indeed like to look in upon you and make one of the circle so as to fill up the picture. As soon as we are mustered I shall come home for a few days but dont expect to come before for the reason already given. Tell Ben to shoot Gardners negroes if they come about the place and I will be responsable for damages . . .[23]

Winston Stephens

[JULIA FISHER TO DAVIS BRYANT][24]

Thomasville Nov 11, 1861

My dear Davis

I take the few moments of recess at school, to acknowledge the receipt of your pleasant and most welcome letter some time ago. I have had not a moment of real leisure, and as you know this, you will ask no apology from me *my dear boy*, this is no time for mere words—I fear that before this reaches you, you and Willie may be ordered off to the coast, as all our men are, *now*—this is a terrible time—

---

22. John Parson and J. L. Livingston were cotton factors who also manufactured cotton gins. Seed cotton had not been ginned; it was sold at reduced rates to factors or others who could gin it. It was a lot more profitable to sell lint cotton, but if a gin could not be had, then it was best to sell cotton as seed cotton. In the future, Winston had his cotton ginned at the Priest plantation, near Welaka.

23. Of all the family, only Winston used the term "negro" consistently. As the war progressed, all of the Bryants, including Tivie, used "nigger" in reference to black Union troops; but Winston, the lone slave owner, never used that word in print.

24. Julia (Bryant) Fisher, previously mentioned, was the sister of James W. Bryant.

God pity us, *and protect our brave boys*—Paris and you and Willy,[25] may possibly be thrown together—there will be no better or braver soldiers in the army *than our three boys,* and none in any army *dearer,* I could not wish you away from the place of danger, for *duty* and *honor* demand that every true man should "take his life in his hand" and stand ready to defend his family and his country, but I pray God may be with you all, and shield your dear heads from harm. If I were only a man, how gladly I would take my place with you ...

At such a time as this, I would not weaken your heart or hands by useless expressions of love and fear; you know that our fondest love, and earnest prayers go with you, and when you think of any of us, let your heart grow strong for our sakes—have no fear or anxiety about *home*—the women will manage at home, while the men are doing their part in war—God bless you my dear *dear* Davis, and keep you in safety—Your Grandmother and aunts *all* of us are full of anxious love and care for you boys, but I trust all may be well—Yours with fondest love Aunt Julia

[OCTAVIA STEPHENS TO WINSTON STEPHENS]

"Rose Cottage" Nov 14, 1861

My dear Husband

You dont know what a state of suspense and anxiety I have been in ... I have watched for you every day since [last Friday morning] from daylight until I went to sleep at night until last night. I wrote a note to Mr Smith (whom I suppose you know has been to Palatka) and his reply made me feel worse than ever,[26] for he not only did not send me a letter from you, but said that you were to go to Jacksonville yesterday to muster in, and told Ben of the fleets attacking two or three places, and I of course supposed and do suppose that you will hurry to Fernandina or St Augustine, and oh you dont know how I feel when I think of it, would to heaven you had never left me. It seems so long since I heard from you, it seems as though you miss every chance of sending to me ... oh I dont know what I would have given to have seen you last night, the boys carried my note to Mr Smith after supper and we sat up until eleven waiting for them, and I began to feel really sick from suspense, and felt as though I was going to hear something unpleasant. Joe waited in town all Monday morning waiting for the boat, and Tuesday morning Ben and Georgie went over to see if any news of the boat had come (for we supposed her aground as it was very foggy). *they* found Mr Smith

---

25. Paris Perham was the son of Benjamin Perham and Caroline Ann (Bryant) Perham. Benjamin died in 1842, and Caroline then married Jared Everitt. Paris was twenty-three years old in 1861.

26. M. Smith was a Welaka merchant who served in Company B, Second Florida Cavalry and ended up as first lieutenant. Before joining Winston's company in 1863, he carried the mail between Welaka and Palatka.

getting ready to go to Palatka, so it was too late for me to think of sending anything, so I concluded to wait patiently until his return . . .

Burrel and *Henry* left last Friday morning with Clark and the three boys for Smyrna.[27] Ben missed his fever on Thursday, but looked badly and I thought he ought not get up in the middle of that night for the first time and start on such a journey, but said nothing to him, but Burrel did not want him to go in such a condition and spoke to Clark about it, and he gave up that night, Burrel said if Ben went he should take Tom, but when he found Henry could go in Ben's place said he would not take Tom, I felt very sorry for Ben, but was glad he did not go, for he looked so badly, Mother broke his fever with quinine. I believe I wrote you that Joe had one the same day that Ben had his second, he did not have any more, all I gave him was ginger tea while he had the chill and fever, I made some of "Old Maria's stew" that afternoon but no one has needed it yet, Sarah gave up again last Monday night, she had never been free from her fever since the time you were here, I dont know what to do with her. Rosa has got to be pretty much herself again, but I have to be very particular about her diet, her tooth does not seem to come forward very fast, if at all, she tries very hard to talk, she jabbers a great deal, calls a bonnet hat or anything to put on the head bahtah and loves to eat her "ta ta" with a fork very much, I wish you could see her dont your heart have a yearning for her sometimes, dont you ever feel a "honcing" to see her. If I only knew when to expect you I *perhaps never,* oh I do hope this hateful fleet will pass us by . . .

I believe I wrote you that I was to send Burrel to help Clark kill the steer, well they hunted for it most of Thursday morning, and at last gave up and Clark divided his beef with me which was not enough quite for the rest of the weeks allowance.[28] I gave them syrup this week as Burrel said potatoes hurt them, Jane said gave them heart burn, they have been possum hunting often, one night Jane and Rachael went with them and killed a fine possum, Ben has killed a few squirrels for us, they started fishing but found that some one had stolen their poles. I have killed quite a number of chickens yet have had no meat some days . . . Mother sends love and says we are doing our best to keep up our spirits, and that Rosa has not learned to love her as well as you yet. Do make haste and come

---

27. Smyrna and New Smyrna, some four miles to the north, are part of present-day New Smyrna Beach and were about twenty miles south of Dunlawton. The inlet known today as Ponce de Leon was then named Mosquito Inlet. Mosquito Inlet was used by Confederate blockade runners early in 1862 to import arms, but Smyrna was viewed by Welaka residents as a source of salt and saltwater fish.

28. The weekly ration for the slaves was as follows. Burrel got 3 pounds of pork; the other adults received 2½ pounds, except for Sarah, who got 8 pounds for herself and the children. If meat was not available, the adults received 1½ quarts of molasses and ½ bushel of corn. They were also to receive peas occasionally. This ration list was folded in one of Tivie's diaries and is about what most planters furnished their slaves. However, Winston's slaves were permitted to hunt and fish and had their own vegetable garden, so they undoubtedly fared better than the average slave in Florida.

home, dont let the Capt *boss* you too much and keep you there, when you can come. Good bye my dear husband, God bless, protect and bring you back safely to us is the prayer of your

loving Wife

Nov 16, 1861. *Burrel and Henry returned from the Coast just after dinner . . . they brought 30 fish. After tea Mother and I were sitting sewing in my room when who should walk in but Winston he came on horseback.*

[REBECCA BRYANT TO DAVIS BRYANT]

Welaka, Rose Cottage Nov 19, 1861

My dear Davis,

I cannot express my disappointment at not hearing from you or Willie by yesterday's mail . . .

Winston expects to remain at home until a week from tomorrow (Wednesday) as they now await the Governor's orders. They mustered in with 58 men and were complimented by the mustering officer as being as orderly and good looking a set of men, for their numbers, as he had mustered in since he had been performing that duty. Winston seems to be very well satisfied with them as a company.

Henry has had a trip of nine days to Smyrna since I wrote last . . . instead of three barrels of fish for each family as . . . expected, only about thirty fish and a bushel of racoon oysters for our share.[29] The sand flies were so troublesome from sunset to day light that it was impossible to sleep—they worked their way through the blankets. Henry looked rough and tough notwithstanding, and his tongue seemed to be hung in the middle all the next day.

Tuesday P.M. Hurrah, Hurrah!! Just as I laid down my pen to go to dinner table the boys came running in with a large bundle and a letter; "from *whom*," I asked eagerly before I could see the handwriting, and was answered by both at once, "from Davis." I assure you my heart leaped for joy as I pulled the treble communication from its envelope, and devoured its contents, before my dinner . . . I am delighted to hear of your visit to the Bar, it must have been such a pleasure to Willie as well as yourself.[30] I was thankful too that you have obtained

---

29. Raccoon oysters were from oyster beds that were exposed to the sun at low tides. Raccoons invaded the beds in large numbers and had a feast. These oysters were not thought to be edible by most Floridians during peacetime, but the war changed this attitude.

30. The shifting sandbar at the mouth of the St. Johns River near Mayport had long been a barrier for oceangoing ships. At times there would be one channel, and at other times there were two; but much of the time neither would permit the passage of a vessel that drew more than 10 feet of water. See Buker, *Sun, Sand, and Water,* 69–74.

so good a situation *in Jacksonville*—and I am also pleased to learn that letters have gone to your Father, with a prospect of hearing from him.[31] O, that he might be able to leave his business and come back in the vessel for a visit, if only a short one. I feel very sure that our letters will reach him and will be a great source of gratification to him . . .

With much love to Willie and yourself, I remain
Most affectionately
Mother

[REBECCA BRYANT TO WILLIE BRYANT]

Rose Cottage Nov 27, 1861

My dear Willie,

 . . . We have just said goodbye to Winston who returns to his camp for a month, if not longer. O, these partings in these times of danger are trying indeed! Tivie bears up bravely however, she makes a first rate soldiers wife—I never was intended for one, or if I was, my resolution has all been spent, year's ago. However I do not grumble much, when I can help it. Tivie says I must tell you to begin with, that you and Davis must be *sure* to come at Christmas, that she will have pig's feet, pig's jowl, pig's brains and all sorts of pig. Winston killed 8 hogs last week, none very large but all in good order, altogether weighed 599 lbs. He managed to cure it all before he left, except what we ate, which was *considerable*. Some more are to be slaughtered for Christmas I believe. You know it will be five weeks from today. . . !

Mother

[WINSTON STEPHENS TO OCTAVIA STEPHENS]

Palatka Dec 1, 1861.

My Dear Wife

 . . . When we got to the river we found that all the boys had crossed but those with me, and we had to wait some time for the flat, but eventually got over and arrived in this place about 5 p.m. all OK. I did not stay in camp that night but slept at Lt Grays, but on next morning we call'd the Roll and found we had recruits enough to make 74 rank and file. we have the men divided into Messes of eight men in each mess fixed off with camp equipage etc and they are all very well

---

31. As mentioned, Davis apparently took Willie's job with Bloodgood and Bouse in June, but he evidently secured a better position at this time. It is not certain where James Bryant was in late 1861 and early 1862; he may have been in Cuba or New York, but he was not in Florida until the Federals invaded later in 1862.

satisfied. We *hosifers* have formed a Mess and Felix does the cooking and pays attention to our horses and we pay two dollars pr month for said services . . .[32]

It is now about 4 pm and I will tell you how I have spent the day thus far. At my usual time I got up and washed and dressed for breakfast which we had about 8 oclock, then Mr Connel came in and shaved me, after that I put on my sunday clothes and at ½ past 10 oclock we formed the Company in lines and marched them to the Episcopal Church where half of the seats had been left for us, and there I listened to one of the best sermons preached by Mr Crane that I have hird for a long time . . .[33] We have not received any orders yet, and now Genl. or Capt Hopkins speaks of coming up home for a few days as he has had fever since his return to this place. "Now see" he curses Welaka and says this is a healthy place but he runs from this to Welaka because he has fever here, how convinent.[34]

We had glorious news from Pensacola! On the 22nd of Nov Lincolns fleet of seven vessels commenced their fire on a steamer of the C.S. and Fort Pickens assisted them and the fire became general on our fortifications and Genl Bragg returned the fire slowly but with good effect and they fought through the 22nd and 23rd and the Federal fleet became so much disabled that they had to put out to sea and one of the vessels the Magara had to be towed out by a steamer and a breach was made in one of the bastions of Fort Pickens. The report of Genl Bragg says they seem to have enough of it as two days have elapsed and no more appearance of an assault. And Bragg says he can stand all they can send against him. Our killed and wounded in the engagement is put down at 16 men mostly Georgians.[35] Now this is a glorious victory but I look for another tryal with a larger force before long.

Genl Lee commands in Fla and he has been to Fernandina and after a careful inspection of the premises he has instructed the Commander to hold it at all hazards and ordered considerable more work in the shape of fortifications

---

32. "Hosifers" was a play on words and meant "officers." Felix was Benjamin Hopkins's slave.

33. Private James R. Connell was a South Carolina–born farm laborer from Welaka who served throughout the war, and E. P. Crane was a Palatka Presbyterian minister.

34. Winston soon regretted these words, for Hopkins died of fever on 22 February 1862.

35. Brigadier General Braxton Bragg was in command of Confederate forces at Pensacola. The first bloodshed in Florida came at Pensacola in mid-September when the Federals attempted to burn the Confederate blockade runner *Judah*. They had previously raided and burned the dry dock without suffering any casualties, but this raid resulted in the death of 3 Federals, and 8 were wounded. On 9 October the Confederates attacked Fort Pickens by landing on Santa Rosa Island but were unsuccessful. They had 18 killed, 39 wounded, and 30 taken prisoner; they killed 14 Union troops, wounded 29, and captured 20. On 22 November only 8 men died despite the firing of some 5,000 artillery rounds; casualties for the Union were 1 dead and 6 wounded; the Confederates lost 1 man to gunfire and 6 more who smothered when a magazine caved in; 21 were wounded. The bombardment the next day resulted in the destruction of a large number of Confederate naval installations, but there was no loss of life. William Watson Davis, *Civil War and Reconstruction*, 126–36.

erected.[36] I would not be surprised if this company is ordered some where near that we can assist if necessary, but this is only my supposition. I will however keep you posted if possible and I dont want you to make yourself unnecessaryly uneasy about me if you fail to hear when you should. I will write by every opportunity I see but it may be as before and then you know it is not my fault.

I am in good health and the prospect is that we will remain so as the season is so far advanced. The Company improves finely in drilling, we drill twice a day at 10 am and 3 pm and it occupies with other duties nearly all the time. Be careful with your meat this warm weather . . .[37] Give Mother and the boys love Ben and Clarks family Kiss Rosa and accept many from your aff husband

Winston Stephens

[OCTAVIA STEPHENS TO WINSTON STEPHENS]

Dec 3, 1861.

My dear Husband

. . . I have at last had my turn of chill and fever. I had a decided one on Sunday, while you were writing to me I was wishing for you to bathe my poor old head and as Mother said to pet me, I had two chills or fevers before but so slight that I was not certain, thought it was a cold and Rheumatism, as it came on just before dark and my old bones and head acheed so until I went to bed, but Sunday dinner time told tales on me, Mother insisted upon my taking quinine on Rosa's account, and yesterday I missed, but to day I do not feel right and fear I will have it again, I have a cup of pepper tea by me, and I have a "stew" ready to take when I feel decided symptoms, Mother has only enough quinine for two pills, I was very obstinate about taking it at first but gave in upon Rosa's account, I think her other tooth nearly through, she looks very well now. Joe has had two chills, I gave him a "stew" last night. Sarah has been down a week or more. Tom and Jane are well again. Burrel has had a very bad cold but I believe is about well, they are now fussing over the potatoes again, we are loosing the whole very fast.

Ben wrote a letter to Ma on Saturday and I began one to her yesterday, so she

---

36. On 5 November 1861 General Robert E. Lee was placed in command of a military department that embraced the coasts of South Carolina, Georgia, and Florida. His immediate concern was to protect Savannah after the fall of Port Royal, but he also sent navy lieutenant William A. Webb from Savannah to Fernandina on 12 November to complete the batteries there and to help train the men who were to service the guns. Lee inspected the works on Amelia Island and Fernandina in mid-November and ordered additional works constructed, assigning the task to navy commander Charles McBlair. See Nulty, *Confederate Florida*, 31–32.

37. Warm winters could mean the loss of vitally needed meat through spoilage, and it was especially difficult to dress out beef without loss because of the sheer size of the animal.

has decided to go to Marion, I am sorry, but thats all I can say.[38] I think Ben is anxious to go to see Ma Christmas although he has not told me so. I fear you are going to get orders just before Christmas and cant come home, I have *four* eggs towards the egg nog but what will we flavor it with. if we have some cold weather I want to kill some hogs (if you say so) the week before Christmas so that I can have the chitlains, souce, etc already when you all come . . .

I blazed out at Burrel last Saturday about wishing the old beef gone. I guess he thought I was "spunky" all of a sudden, but I did not care, I told him I was tired of hearing grumbling etc.

Well I must stop. All send love but none so much as your

U*naffectionate*

W*ife*

[WINSTON STEPHENS TO OCTAVIA STEPHENS]

Camp Hopkins Dec 4, 1861

My dear Wife

. . . We learned this morning that Genl Trappier had arrived at Fernandina and had gone on to Tallahassee and as Capt Hopkins had written to Gov Milton I think it probable we will have some orders of some kind by Saturday . . .[39]

We are well and gitting good living so far. Lt Gray is acting QuarterMaster and makes a good one. I have no news of importance to communicate to you. I hope you all are well and doing well. We had a heavy rain night before last and last night it was cold to pay, but I sleep with Joseph Hopkins and by putting our blankets together we do finely.[40]

The steamer goes soon and I have to drill the Company so good by my Love. I cant say when I will be with you love to all and kiss my Dear babe. Your

Aff husband Winston Stephens

---

38. Part of Winston's farm in Marion County, the home of Swepston Stephens for the past several years, was bought by Richard Stephens early in 1862 and became home for Mary Ann and her family for the rest of the year.

39. Brigadier General James Heyward Trapier had been given the Florida command on 22 October 1861, but the attack on Port Royal delayed his arrival until late in November. He and Governor John Milton, who took office in October 1861, differed as to what section should take priority. Trapier originally favored the defense of East Florida, particularly Fernandina, but became convinced by Milton that a Federal threat up the Apalachicola River would end with the loss of Middle Florida and even the lower part of Georgia. Trapier decided to make his headquarters in Tallahassee, but the truth is that Florida really did not have a Confederate commander during the whole of 1861 except for Bragg in West Florida.

40. Private Joseph Hopkins, previously mentioned, was the youngest son of Benjamin and Susan Hopkins. He and his brother, Henry T., served throughout the war.

[WINSTON STEPHENS TO OCTAVIA STEPHENS]

Palatka Dec 5, 1861.

My Dear Wife

I received yours by Capt Hopkins yesterday about 1 ½ pm. I was glad to hear from you, but sorry you have the fever and hope you are clear of it before this. I send you 33 grains of Quinine which cost one dollar now and hard to get even at that price. I want you to take enough to break the fever if you have it after you receive this. I would come up to day to see you but last night just as I was about to open my mouth to ask my "Boss" if I could come he assigned me to some duty for to day and I then held my tongue, but perhaps if I were to come up to day I could not come Christmas and if you are not sick any more I had rather come then than now. I send you some calico for four shirts but I dont want you to work on them until you are well as I have got more calico shirts already made since I came down here . . . let me know how you are and dont hide your real feelings and if you are no better I will come up. I am in fine health and we have comfortable quarters in houses, the only thing I miss is a fire place. We have no tents yet from Government but Cpt Hopkins has five that he has promised the Company. Bless my Dear Rosa . . . I am glad to see she is improving so fast and to hear she has so much good luck with her teeth. I think if you continue to have fever you had better wean Rosa, but your Mother knows best. If you can take it the Quinine will be more effective in solution . . .

I am glad you spoke so short to Burrel and if they trouble me I will hire the whole of them out and you may tell him so . . .[41] Love to all. Kiss Rosa and accept as many as you wish from your old Man Winston.

Dec 6, 1861. Winston surprised us just as we were going to bed and just as I had received a bundle from him sent by Jacob.

[REBECCA BRYANT TO DAVIS BRYANT]

Rose Cottage Dec 9, 1861

My dear Davis,

. . . I regret the discontinuance of the Savannah steamers, more especially on account of the uncertainty of hearing directly from Willie. I hope however he will be able occasionally to send me a sheet through you, by Darlington. We hear that

---

41. One of the ways that slave owners gained obedience from their chattels was to threaten to hire them out; this was particularly effective when the owner mentioned an individual who was known to be a hard taskmaster. Other means of control included scoldings, isolated confinement, whippings, or the ultimate threat: the owner could tell the slave that he was going to "put you in my pocket"—that is, to sell the slave.

the Darlington however, is to run between Jacksonville and Brunswick, and that Capt B—s *new* stmr is to run up the river. We learn from Winston that the Sumter is to run to Jacksonville and to come up the river every second week, running to Silver Spring alternately with Capt Gray's barge—therefore you need not fear being detained here for want of an opportunity to go down.[42] I do not know on what days the new steamer is to arrive and depart from either place.

Winston took us by surprise again, last Thursday night, arriving about nine o'clk, just as Tivie and I were preparing to retire. Tivie had written him of her having chill and fever, and as there were some men to be sent across the river with two horses, Winston asked permission to accompany them and remain a couple of days at home—Yesterday he recd. a note from his Capt. saying that as he had recd. no orders from the Gov and the Commissary's stores were getting low, he had given furloughs to about 30 men and Winston could remain here until he heard from him again if he wished. His negroes go back and forth frequently which gives us an opportunity of hearing from the camp. Winston looks well and is in good spirits—The company have the use of three houses in Palatka and the Officers have Felix to cook for them, so that they are very comfortably fixed there. What a pity to disturb them!

10½ o'clk, a.m. Henry has returned bringing me your note enclosed with Willie's of 4th and 5th—I am *powerful* glad to hear from you both—am particularly glad to learn Willie's health is so good . . . The disunion of the mails is as disagreeable in its results as the disunion of the States—Well, we must take it all as it comes . . . All send much love and none more than

Mother

[WILLIE BRYANT TO DAVIS BRYANT]

Rebel Hall Dec 11, 1861

Dear Bro.

The very devil is to pay in Camp this a.m. in anticipation of an order for furloughs to be stopped; the squad with a fur "detailed" go to-day however, it is my turn also, but not wishing to go for any special purpose, and having no money, I have allowed some one to go in my place, trusting to luck to be able to go when I wish to; There is no doubt that the furloughs will be stopped, and it is hard and unfortunate, and I trust may not last long. I will not be able to write Mother this week so please state my fears of being unable to be with her Christmas. I have written Father, but The Pilot Boat has not yet gone out . . .

42. Captain Jacob Brock, owner of the *Darlington*, put the *Silver Spring* in operation in 1860. She ran upriver from Jacksonville to Silver Springs and Enterprise during the first two years of the war, but her career is largely unknown. The *General Sumter* was used by the Confederates as a coastal steamer until she was captured in 1864. Mueller, *St. Johns River Steamboats*, 193, 207.

We have not seen a sail since I wrote you, or anything else interesting. This sojering is profitable eh! 4 mo's ago yesterday, I entered the service and have rec'd $32—and a little something to eat, for it; our rations are now reduced to flour and meat alone; the Coffee will be missed, sure . . .

Yours,

Willie

[REBECCA BRYANT TO DAVIS BRYANT]

Dec 17, 1861

My dear Davis,

. . . We shall *expect* you between 11 and 12 o'clk on Sunday night—I shall sit up in order to send Henry with a mule to make a fire at Winston's landing, as we find on refering to the Almanac that the moon will be just rising. Winston says you had better ask the Capt. to blow his whistle about a mile below. Winston goes early tomorrow morng. much to our regret . . . Tivie wishes a little whisky, not over a pint, for an Egg nogg, and says dont forget to bring your flute . . . As to presents—I think the most acceptable to Tivie just now would be 9 or 10 yds calico for a dress—she has a handsome cashmere and others too good for every day wear . . . Neither Henry or George own a knife now and I suppose that is almost indispensable or considered so by boys of their age—Don't get expensive ones, they will soon lose them . . . I hope you may get a glimpse of Winston on his way to Fernandina . . . God bless you

Mother

Dec 18, 1861. Winston *left at daylight for Palatka and Fernandina.*

Dec 22, 1861. Mother and I sat up until one o'clock waiting for the boat expecting Davis and not only he came but Willie too.

[WINSTON STEPHENS TO OCTAVIA STEPHENS]

Camp near Fernandina Dec 22, 1861

My Dear Wife

I take pleasure this morning to inform you that I am well and no one sick in camps. We arrived at this place all safely on Thursday night about 11 oclock and found Capt Hickman to receive us and deliver us 16 Tents and poles, which is enough for our Company.[43] The day I left I got down to the flat before any one

---

43. Captain Enos Hickman of Enterprise was a staff officer in the Quartermasters Department of the Third Florida Infantry for a short time. The records do not reveal anything about his service except that he was mustered in on 23 July 1861. The company was ordered from Palatka to Fernandina on 17 December for training in expectation of the Federal attack that came three months later.

else and had it bailed out before any one arrived, and then had to wait until about ten oclock before we started over and it was twelve before I landed. I then got on Pet and rode in Town as soon as possible, when I arrived I found Capt H[opkins] quite sick and the Company was to be gotton ready by ten that night, so I had to fly around at a rapid rate ... To resume my travels, we left Palatka at 10 oclock that night and arrived in Jacksonville at 4 am and at about 7 I walked up ... and found Davis in the land of nod ... I had him up in a short time and [he was] surprised to see me but appeared glad ... I took a cup of Coffee butter and bread with pleasure and considerable comfort, after which Davis walked down Town with me and we left on the Cars at 9 am ... I arrived at Baldwin at 11 am and had to wait until eight pm before the Cars left for this place and we arrived here 11 oclock. We had our Tents all up and baggage and supplies stowed by 12 or one oclock and then I went to the land of *Nod*. We are on the main land half mile from the draw bridge and I think six miles from Fernandina. I like the place better than on the Island and in fact I like it better than in Palatka, only I would like to be that near you. We have the sand flies here when it is warm and no wind blowing, but that is seldom now. The object of our being placed here is to protect the Rail Road and the bridge as it is supposed the Yankees may attempt to land on the main and take possession of the Road which would cut off all communication with the Island and by so doing they could starve the forces into a submission, as they could at the same time blockade the water communication with their War vessels—two rifle eight pounders are being mounted at the draw bridge to prevent the approach of Gun boats up from Nassau bar. If we have any fighting to do the rail road will afford us considerable protection as it will make a good breast work. If any of the Yankees attempt to take the bridge by land I think they will have something to do ...

We have 68 men here and left 15 in Camps at Palatka to take care of our horses till our return. I wish I had known it and left Pet at home. I hope you may all have a fine time christmas, and that Davis may not be allowed to have the blues while there. I ordered my shot gun home and I want you to ask Henry to keep them all clean and loaded so they will shoot and tell Clark and you can tell your Mother but I want it carefully kept, but carefully watched. I heard just before I left Palatka that six of Gov Moseleys negroes had been heard to say if Lincoln did not free them by 20th of January they would free themselves.[44] Now My Dear dont let this give you unnecessary uneasiness but I want you to be safe, and to be so, the guns must be loaded and Henry and George can do all the shooting—Tell Clark that the men may establish a patrole and be on their guard, dont let the negroes hear of it dont say any thing before Jane. I am not afraid of my negroes, but Mr Gardners negroes may take a notion if they are consulted, to

---

44. Former governor of Florida William Moseley of Palatka was the largest slave owner in the county.

join in the fray. If I forgot to tell you how long to give the negroes give them from Wednesday to Monday morning . . .[45] Kiss My Dear Rosa and accept much love from your aff husband—Good bye and God bless my Dear Wife

Winston Stephens

[OCTAVIA STEPHENS TO WINSTON STEPHENS]

Christmas Eve 1861

My dear Husband

Here I am seated here to *write* to you instead of sitting by you *here* and having a nice time, you dont know how much I do miss you and more since Willie and Davis have been here . . . Last Sunday night Mother and I sat up for the boat, and at eleven o'clock woke the little boys and Tom and sent them with the mules to the landing and about one o'clock they came. Mother and I went out and met Davis and went in the house and I began pulling out of the fire some potatoes, when I looked up and saw a big soldier standing in the door, and "to be sure" it was Willie, and when *he* came I could not help looking for you, thinking that if good fortune had sent him she might have sent you, but no I suppose she thought we would then be too happy. Davis is to go down to morrow and Willie will stay a week with us they have wished so often for you, the morning after they came Willie looked around and said he wanted to see something that looked like you and I showed him . . . your old straw hat. Clark and his family spent to day with us and we are to go there tomorrow. Henry and George went home with them this eve we drank your health this morning in egg nogg. Mother has just said give her love and say we wished for you to day. we *darkies* had a Christmas frolic getting the pig out of the big pot it was cooked to pieces, but it was very nice to the taste. Burrel killed six hogs on Thursday the *whole* weighed 294 lbs . . . Burrel killed his two pigs on Saturday one weighed 68 lbs the other less . . .

Well my darling I dislike sending you such a mean letter but I must close for it is getting late, and I think Rosa is going to wake, she has looked so cunning to day in her new dress and sack I made and a pair of new shoes Davis brought. he also brought her a new dress, and me some rice and a broom. Willie and Davis send their remembrances, and said I must give their oft repeated regrets about your not being here. No letter came this week from any one.

Good night, pleasant dreams and a warm bed to night and a merry Christmas tomorrow.

Lovingly

Your Wife

45. This was time off for Christmas vacation.

[WINSTON STEPHENS TO OCTAVIA STEPHENS]

Fernandina Dec 26, 1861

My Dear Wife

I have not seen a line from you since I left and I begin to feel quite anxious to see your *fist* on paper ... We were ordered to this post on the morning of the 25th and the Cars were sent out for us and it took us all day to fix up camps, so you see my Christmas was not an idle one if not a pleasant one. If I live I will see the next is differently spent. We are now quartered with the fourth Regiment, Col Hopkins commanding. We are only temporarily attached to this Regiment. Capt Hopkins thinks we will not be here more than one month and if longer I can get a furlough of one week each month.[46] This is a dry and apparently a healthy place and I feel contented at present but the insects will be desperate here in warm weather. Some of the Companys have Mumps and measels, but we have given orders for our men to keep themselves seperated and I hope by precaution to avoid these diseases.

Capt Hopkins will start to Tallahassee in the morning to get our State pay which is for 26 days. The pay in this service is not so much as it was in the old by about 25 or 30 dollars and I will not make so much by a good deal as I expected, my pay is $100 pr month but out of that I have to pay for my rations, servant hire, washing etc which will reduce it to about $85 pr month. I shall be as equinomical as possible and try to clear all I can and if Burrel makes a good crop we will come out all right. I hope you are not alarmed about what I wrote in my last but you know it is best to be on the lookout, keep those boys at home or about home on Sundays.

We have about three thousand men on the Island including the Mississippi Regiment who are incamped near the Draw Bridge about six miles from Town.[47] Maj Hopkins took *tea* with us to night and told me there was eighteen Cannon mounted ready for action and they are erecting more on their batteries, he thinks he can keep the Yankees back or sink their vessels.[48] If they land they will have a hard road to travel as the ground is favorable to our ambuscade we are to have the fun of whipping the Yankees at this place for these reasons — 1st when Connant left here and went on to Washington we had no defences and he made a report to that effect and then was the time for them to strike but they have waited until we are ready to receive them and they know it and is hardly worth the lives they

---

46. Colonel Edward Hopkins was in command of the Fourth Florida Infantry Regiment, and Captain Benjamin Hopkins was in command of Winston's company.

47. General Lee ordered the Twenty-fourth Mississippi Regiment to Fernandina on 18 December. See OR, ser. 1, vol. 53, 201.

48. Lieutenant Colonel Charles F. Hopkins, former captain of the St. Augustine Marion Artillery, had recently raised and was in command of the First Florida Infantry Battalion. He was later placed in command of the Tenth Florida Infantry Regiment. Winston had served with this St. Augustine citizen during the Seminole War when Hopkins's rank was major; and just as he referred to Benjamin Hopkins as both captain and general, he did so with Charles Hopkins as well.

would spend in taking it.[49] The Blockader came up near the fort a few days ago and they sent some small shot at them and drew them on until in range of the heavy guns, they then turned one of the big guns on them and they were off in Bull Run time.[50]

I went out to the light house late yesterday and took a look at the Blockader and she looked as large as life but did not come in reach of our gunns . . .

Sergt McLeod who is one of our mess received a box to day *full* of fixings for Christmas, such as pies pound cakes sweet cakes sausages and all the good things too tedious to name and had like to have foundered myself to night . . .

Give my love to Clark and family, Mother and family and say to them we are fat and saucy.

Good night my Dear Wife and Daughter and God bless and protect you all. Your aff husband

Winston Stephens

[OCTAVIA STEPHENS TO WINSTON STEPHENS]

Dec 31, 1861

My own dear Husband

. . . I am sorry you had such a dull Christmas, seems to me I have missed you more than ever since the boys have been here. I am afraid you will be kept at Fernandina a long time and can not afford to come home often. I suppose it will cost 12 or 15 dollars. Willie says you might take two weeks in two months and then you would be able to stay a decent time with us, but that seems a long time between visits, but I suppose I would then be much better off than some folks, and may thank my stars if I see you that often. oh well I will hope again that something will turn up or change the order of things. I am sorry you are disappointed in the sum of your pay; I feared it would be so, and Willie told me of it after he came, every one must go for patriotism. with so little I dont see how we can come out straight as you say . . .

Oh I hear that Mr Tydings and Lou are to be in Jacksonville this year.[51] Mother sends love and wishes you a "Happy New Year" and hopes the next New Years night you will be seated at your fireside, and your store houses and barns full.

Good night my darling may the Lord grant Mother's wish.

Ever affectionately
Your Wife.

49. "Connant" is a reference to Larkins Conant, a Fernandina Unionist who had been a small farmer before the war.
50. A reference to the Union rout at the first battle of Bull Run or Manassas in July 1861.
51. Tivie's cousin Louisa Bryant married Richard Tydings, a Methodist minister from Thomasville, Georgia. During the war they lived near Monticello, and Tivie visited them in 1863.

[REBECCA BRYANT TO DAVIS BRYANT]

Rose Cottage Dec 31, 1861

My dear Davis,

I send you herewith a daguerreotype of your Father, which was taken in the Autumn of '45 and was *then* considered a good likeness—Both Tivie and I have good ones, taken at a later period and I thought you would rather have this than none . . .

This is the last day of 1861—where shall we all be at the close of the next? Echo answers where . . . ! Your visit here affords us pleasant reminiscences and was I suppose a source of more gratification to us, than to you, as your stay was so very short in comparison with the trouble and expense you had in coming.

I hope Willie has enjoyed his and think he has in a quiet way . . .

Write me next year, and accept much love from

Mother

[WILLIE BRYANT TO WINSTON STEPHENS]

Rose Cottage Dec 31, 1861.

Dear Winston,

I have been here now 9 days enjoying the hospitalities of yr home, and have had a good time of it, but regret very much that you have not been here, as I counted so much on it; I was greatly disappointed on my arrival at J'vlle to learn how I had missed you, and that you had been ordered to Fernandina; and I expect if you could get off one of my old fashioned "swears" it would do you good, at the arrangement; but as you have left the "old lady" so well provided for yr mind should be as easy as any husband away from a young wife. I am glad to see you so independent of Old abe; these times especially are farmers to be envied.

I have knocked around but little, powder and shot being so scarce, and have spent most of the time with the women and children, but havn't entirely succeeded in captivating yr lovely daughter; she is hard to win, and very coquettish, I must say, and I think I am as usual the most struck of the two; she's a great girl, certain! I have been over to Welaka several times and it makes me sad to see the place . . .

Well, good bye! If the Yankees come attend to them; I feel whatever may happen to us that "Divine Providence and Davis" will take care of the folks.

Yrs alway

Willie

1. Octavia (Tivie) Louisa (Bryant) Stephens, 1857.

2. Winston John Thomas Stephens, 1857.

3. Mary Ann Jane (Taylor) (Stephens) Gaines and her son, Winston John Thomas Stephens, ca. 1852.

4. Octavia (Tivie) Louisa (Bryant) Stephens with her children, Rosalie and Winston, ca. 1868.

5. Rebecca Hathorne (Hall) Bryant, ca. 1860.

6. William Clark Thomas Stephens, ca. 1870.

7. James William Bryant, ca. 1865.

8. Henry Herbert Bryant, ca. 1867.

9. William (Willie) Augustus Bryant, ca. 1866.

10. Davis Hall Bryant, ca. 1867.

11. George Perham Bryant, ca. 1867.

12. Winston Stephens's dress uniform and company flag.

13. White Cottage, Welaka, Florida.

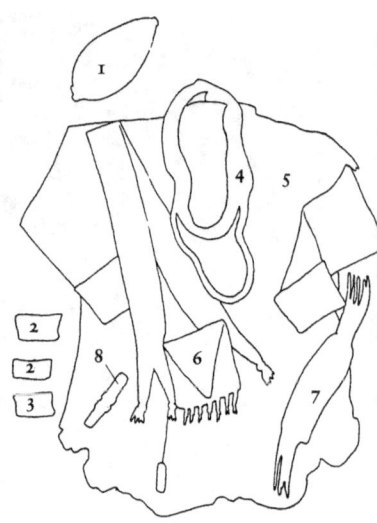

14. SEMINOLE ARTIFACTS, CA. 1857.

1. Beaded Scotch-style hat of European origin; similar European trade items are known from the Iroquois and from the South Pacific; none are documented.
2. Two split palmetto, double weave baskets with lids; about six others from the southeast are still in existence; all are twentieth century.
3. Buckskin medicine pouch; unique.
4. Strand of 420 blue faceted beads strung on the original buckskin thong; such beads are common from nineteenth-century Seminole archaelogical sites.
5. Buckskin shirt; may be rarest in existence. No others are known from the southeast. There are two calico Seminole shirts in the Berlin Museum (pre-1846) and one cloth shirt in the University Museum, Cambridge (1870s). Construction details of the shirt are ancestral to similar techniques present on well-known, colorful twentieth-century Seminole shirts.
6. Beaded, triangular flat pouch with beaded shoulder strap; red and blue cloth is stroud; each bead is individually attached to cloth. There are about forty similar pouches from the southeast, but only one or two are of this vintage (as indicated by the pointed pouch flap which is typical of the early specimens). None of the other early specimens are documented as to tribe.
7. Finger-braided garter with seed beads worked into design; perhaps thirty are known from the southeast, none are this old.
8. Buckskin-wrapped medicine stick; unique.

chapter 4

A New Captain, a Long Year, a Divided Family Reunited for a Day

There had been very little fighting in 1861, but that changed dramatically the next year. Lincoln proclaimed in 1861 that the war was being fought to restore the Union with slavery intact; before 1862 ended he declared that the Emancipation Proclamation, which abolished slavery in the Confederacy, would go into effect on the first day of 1863.[1] The war had now become a revolution, and both sides vowed to fight to the finish.

There was little sign that a Union victory was possible in the East in 1862 or even two years later, but in the West things were looking up. The Confederate forces in Kentucky and Tennessee under General Albert Sidney Johnston were far too few to hold their positions, and the whole line collapsed in February 1862. Johnston retreated rapidly all the way to Mississippi, and troops were rushed there from all over the Confederacy to shore up the line. Almost all of the fighting men in Florida were sent, and the state was virtually defenseless by the spring of 1862. When the state was invaded in March, many Floridians complained bitterly that they had been abandoned by the Confederacy and left to their own fate.

Once the Federal naval blockade was in place, Floridians felt cut off from the rest of the Confederacy, and in truth they were; no rail connections existed between Florida and Georgia, and the line from Pensacola to Montgomery, Alabama, was of no use when Pensacola was occupied by Federal forces in May 1862. Further, the lack of interstate connections militated against the long Florida coastline's being used effectively to end the economic boycott by

---

1. Although Lincoln personally condemned slavery as a moral evil, he realized that the institution could not be eliminated in the United States without a constitutional amendment. But he knew that if he could cripple or abolish it in the Confederacy, it would end everywhere in the Union. He did live to see the Confederacy defeated, but the Thirteenth Amendment was not passed until he had been dead for more than eight months.

running the blockade. Even if armaments and other vitally needed supplies could be landed, it still was a major problem to distribute them where they would be most effective.

In east Florida, for example, it was fairly easy to avoid the Federal ships and land at Mosquito Inlet. A contraband cargo was unloaded there in March 1862, but with the Federals in control of the St. Johns at Jacksonville, the only way to move the cargo from Smyrna to any destination out of state began by hauling the goods some twenty-five miles overland in wagons to the St. Johns River. The next stage was to transport the cargo up the Ocklawaha by small steamers to Orange Springs and there transfer it to wagons for another twenty-five-mile journey to Waldo, where it was at last possible to reach the Florida Railroad. Once the goods were moved by rail to Baldwin and there transferred to the Florida Atlantic & Gulf Central, they were shipped to Madison, offloaded into wagons again, and hauled another twenty miles to Quitman, Georgia. From there they could be sent anywhere in the Confederacy by rail, but it could easily take a month to get the goods out of Florida.[2] And if the Federals sent gunboats upriver to Welaka or captured Baldwin, they could prevent even this route's being used.

With the Union invasion of 1862, war at last came to the St. Johns region. The halcyon days at Welaka were over and would never return to Rose Cottage. Before the year ended, Winston would skirmish with Federal gunboats, Willie would fight in the Tennessee campaign, Davis would see action around Fernandina, and James W. Bryant would find that it was well-nigh impossible for him to see his loved ones. The only way he could come was by Federal gunboat, and his own son-in-law was pledged to shoot him unless he came under a flag of truce.

Bryant tried to reach Rose Cottage in May but did not succeed in his mission. It was rumored at that time, and printed in several newspapers, that he was the Federal military governor of Florida. This charge was false, but his sister Julia Fisher publicly denounced him. Bryant was finally able to meet with his wife, sons, and son-in-law, Winston, at Palatka in December 1862. For the Bryants, the year 1862 ended in better fashion than it began, but even this proved to be poor comfort in the long run.

At Rose Cottage, once the Christmas festivities of 1861 were over, most of the male members of the family dispersed again. Tivie continued to record the events in her diary, and Rebecca decided to keep one too.[3] Entries from her

---

2. William Watson Davis, *Civil War and Reconstruction,* 198; Nulty, *Confederate Florida,* 24.

3. Rebecca Bryant wrote four journals in the collection. The first contains entries from 11 June 1852 through 27 October 1852. The second begins with a few entries from 26 May 1858 and 25 June 1858. Rebecca began again in the second diary on 1 January 1862 and continued almost daily through the last entry in the fourth diary on 1 October 1863.

journals are preceded by [Rebecca] to distinguish them from Tivie's, and 1862 begins with her thoughts about the new year.

[Rebecca] Jan 1, 1862. at Rose Cottage, Willie left us this morning. at 8 o'clk having been with us 9 dys. Our family now consists only of Tivie, Henry, Georgie, myself and Rosa—The year has opened with bright sunshine, quite a contrast to our national affairs and domestic prospects. Memory has been busy with the past all day and sad thoughts have intruded themselves in spite of all my efforts.

[WINSTON STEPHENS TO OCTAVIA STEPHENS]

Fernandina Jan 2, 1862

My Dear Wife

. . . I was glad to hear that you all had been so agreeably surprised by Davis and Willies visit and glad to hear you had such a good time generally. I am in fine health with the exception of a cold which is very common in camps, my cold is much better than it was yesterday. Some few of the men have fever with their colds and some of the Regiment have pneumonia, Mumps, Measels and a variety of other Contagious diseases too tedious to mention . . .[4] We try to keep our men seperated as much as possible from other Companies to avoid the various diseases—We have itch in camps but I shal hold myself aloof from the men as much as possible to avoid catching it if possible. The general health has improved in the last few days . . . This has the appearance of a healthy place. We have to drill about four hours every day which gives us exercise enough to keep us from getting lazy and the Company has very much improved since our arrival here . . .

I think I told you not to transplant the peach trees unless you had good seasons, but I want you to have it done at once and have them *well watered* about sunset every evening until you are sure they will live, also the Plum. the three large trees by the old place you can let stay, but transplant all the rest, and if this dry weather continues until you receive this tell Burrel to examine the new ground and if the bushes are dead he had better set fire to it and burn it off and let Tom haul the rails before the woods are burnt, tell him to try and get a windy day as it will burn better and be careful and not let the fire burn him out when the woods gets afire . . .

It seems a long time to wait for a letter, from one Saturday to the next, but I suppose I should feel thankful to have one that often. Does my Darling Rosa stil lisp her Pa name or can she talk plainer. I would give any thing to see you both

---

4. By this time, men in both armies had lost their boyish enthusiasm about the war as they saw their comrades die by the thousands from numerous diseases without ever seeing battle. Just being in the army killed twice as many men as were killed in battle, and that was true of Winston's company, which saw two die in battle and four of disease.

and have the pleasure of your society if only for a short time, but I cant tell you when that will be as Lt Peterman has the promise of the next furlough. I think we will be removed before very long and perhaps to Smyrna, if so I will come home, I will perhaps be able to tell you more about the change in my next . . .

Yours ever

Winston

[WINSTON STEPHENS TO OCTAVIA STEPHENS]

Fernandina Jan 4, 1862

My Dear Wife

. . . We had news by Telegraph that a fight commenced near Charleston on Yesterday and the Yankees were driven back, but had gotten reinforcements and had commenced the fight over. We are looking constantly for news but as yet nothing has arrived—Also we have news of the fight at Pensacola and hear we losed one man by the bursting of one of our own shell—but dont know the damage done on their side . . .[5]

I cant tell how long we will be here but Capt H— thinks we will return to our horses in the first of February—if so I will see you then if not before—If it was not for the boys that came in on my account and the horses I am responsable for I would resign My Commission and come home—but my Dear I was the cause of several men coming in the service and it would not be treating them right to leave them, by remaining I am not afraid of losing any thing in the horse business. I have purchased a barrel of syrup and it will be landed at the wharf by the first barge down the river. My wife I have and do appreciate your worth and have ever done so and you may rest assured this will leave me the same as ever and hope we may ever be to each other as we have been. You say you cant see how I am to come out of debt this year. This I can say, If I am spared my life and my family I shal feel thankful and be satisfied. If I am left any poorer than now I hope my Wife will not love me the less and with health and your love I can support you and my dear Rosa any where—This difficulty if it lasts will be the means of the sacrifice of much property and I may be one of the sufferers, if so we must learn to bear it. I can bear any thing, but it will be hard to see you any worse off than you are—We must hope and trust for the better times. You cant say more of Rosa

---

5. There were sporadic attacks against Charleston from time to time, but no serious naval attack was mounted until April 1863. The attack failed, and the Federals tried a combined land and naval attack three months later. This too failed, although the city was effectively blockaded after July 1863. Charleston was not occupied by Federal forces until after the rebels evacuated it in February 1865. There was a short artillery duel at Pensacola on 1 January 1862 with no deaths reported, but even though the *Official Records* do not mention a death, it could be that one man was lost, as Winston reported here.

than I like to hear and you must give me in each of your letters the particulars of our home and those so dear to me . . .

Love to all and many kisses to you and Rosa. I wish so much I could give them.

Your ever affectionate husband

[Rebecca] *Jan 7, 1862*. *My dear husband's birth-day—Oh that I could spend it with him! He has lived half a century, and I cannot expect he will be spared many years longer. May we both live so that we may be permitted to meet in Heaven . . .*

[OCTAVIA STEPHENS TO WINSTON STEPHENS]

Jan 7, 1862

My dear Husband

I was doubly glad to receive *two* such nice long letters from you this week . . . I hope your cold is well by this time, and that you may not have any of the various unpleasant diseases you speak of especially the itch, you had better wear a *big piece of asafoetida* around your neck as you used to in old times, or something, you will surely fall a victim to some of them. I have never heard you say that you had had the mumps so think you have not. I think you have exercise enough to keep you well if that will. I suppose Sunday is the same as any other day, or do you have more time?

Henry and George transplanted two rows and a half of peach trees last week, and we had a nice rain on them Saturday night and Sunday. I will not put out the plum trees until next week as we have so many peach trees to attend to some of those in the back yard were dying but perhaps we can save them. Burrel burned off the new ground a week ago after rolling my logs,[6] he is now hauling rails himself and put Tom to cutting logs with the others until he gets some rails hauled then they are to "follow behind him with the fence . . ." he says he thinks he will be ready to start ploughs in three weeks . . .

I have just put Rosa to sleep, she tries to say a great many things now, she says "de papa don" for dear Pa Pa gone and often says it by herself while playing, she said it a little while ago. then we heard her say "peas ma'am" she says "tart" for Clark and "Teet" for Tina. I cant write how she says Uncle and Aunt . . .

6. Logrolling could become a community affair and a recreational event, but most of the time it was killing work for slave and free alike. Some of the logs could be "snaked" out by mules, but when the trunks were so close as to prevent this, the only option was to pick them up and carry them out, or burn them in place if they were thick enough. As in a fireplace, at least three logs stacked together are necessary to get a good burn.

I hope the negroes will not try what you wrote about, perhaps they know that their intention is known and they will not try it at least for some time. Last Sunday Mother had them . . . all up here and read a chapter in the Bible etc and intends continuing it. they have not given the least trouble so far, and Burrel seems bent upon his duty . . .

Mother sends lots of love and says we are looking anxiously for your next furlough. oh Taylor's howling reminds me a tree fell on him on a hunt the other night and nearly finished him but he is recovering. two weeks ago Clara ran into a light wood stick or something and made a *terrific* gash under her fore leg but she is getting well as I told Burrel of it and he put tar and grease on it immediately . . .[7]

Your loving Wife.

[REBECCA BRYANT TO WILLIE AND DAVIS BRYANT]

Jan 7, 1862[8]

My dear, dear boys,

. . . this is your father's birthday—I know he will think of us and feel sad at the prospect before him—It seems hard that the few years he has now to spend on earth should be past so far from all those he loves, after a life of such untiring effort and perseverance. But I know we both must need this discipline or it would not be alloted us, and we must endeavor to profit by it. I hope the present year may terminate more happily than it has begun with our dear children . . .

Tivie and boys send love and I send much more to both my dear boys—

Mother

[WINSTON STEPHENS TO OCTAVIA STEPHENS]

Fernandina Jan 10, 1862

My Dear Wife

. . . I am very well weigh 158 lbs which is more than when I left home by several pounds—The men are not so well as we have about 6 or 8 sick with cold . . .

We are to be paid for one and half months next week by Maj Teasdale for our Confederate service, which will help some.[9] Let me know when you get the Syrup

---

7. Taylor, Clara, and Watch were the Stephenses' three dogs.

8. Rebecca quite often wrote to Willie and Davis collectively because of a shortage of both envelopes and writing paper. The letters went to Davis in Jacksonville, who forwarded them to Willie at Fort Steele.

9. Major H. R. Teasdale was quartermaster for the District of Florida. He was a thirty-two-year-old merchant from Orange County.

and be careful when you have it opened. Tell Burrel not to get behind in his cleaning up but to make those boys moove about with life...

Give love to Mother and boys also Clark and family and kiss My Dear Rosa and accept many and much love from

Your Old Man

[OCTAVIA STEPHENS TO WINSTON STEPHENS]

Jan 13, 1862

My own dear Husband

... Mother received a letter from Father to day, he was in New York then 25 days ago, and was going to Washington to see how matters stood, and see if he could come if we all thought best.[10] Mother asked me if she had better tell him to come here, I told her yes for the present anyhow, that I thought he might find some business soon. I think the boys have written urging him to come and as we or *I* have Mother here. she will want him with her for a time at least. do not think my dear that I intend having them all on your hands always, for I hope that all will be different before the year is out, that we will all be settled down cosily. Father's business in Cuba has failed or broken up, he says his health is good, but his cough still hangs on. Mother has seemed so much happier today. I dont know when I have seen her laugh so heartily and often and *easily* as she has to day, she says she has been feeling very gloomy and sad about him for the last week or so. when we saw this new moon we were to gether, and I said now let us wish, and to night she said that she wished that before the moon fulled she might hear from him soon, but did not think of it until she mentioned her wish to night, and sure enough the moon will full tomorrow or next night.

You will probably think it queer that I am writing to night but I wanted to write most of my letter to night as Rosa may be sick tomorrow. Our baby has had three fevers and has a bad cough, real [bad], every other day *chill* and fever, on Friday she was not out of my lap an hour from breakfast until night, most of the day on a pillow with a scorching fever, and seemed to feel so sick. I ate my dinner in the room with her in my lap. we gave her oil, and quinine Saturday night and morning early, but she talked and noticed a great deal all the time, when the one before she would not open her eyes wide or notice any thing or any body, just laid there and let me bathe her head and hands. she looks badly and is quite weak, but the days between is as lively as ever. she has been so funny to day, oh I so hope she will not be sick to morrow. I will give her quinine again to night, there is no appearance of any more teeth. I think she took her cold at night, for I am awake a great part of the night trying to keep her legs covered but I can not

10. This letter is missing.

do it. I tuck in the bedclothes to her crib and that wont do, I take her in bed and put my arm across her and that wont do. she coughs a great deal just before day. I am giving her honey for it after first boiling it a little to get some of the fermentation out.

Tuesday morn. Well my dear it is now eleven o'clock, I have put off writing until this late to see whether Rosa had her fever or not, she has just gone to sleep apparently quite bright and well and as it is now three hours or more past her chill time I think she is going clear . . .

I have the potatoes bedded, there are five large beds, three of yams, they were beginning to sprout in the bank, the negroes have begun on one bank of Hayties and we will soon.[11] The work gets on nicely, Burrel is now rolling logs, half the field or more is bulging with heaps. Taylor is able to walk about some but very stiffly . . .

All are well now. I am looking forward to 1st February with hopes of seeing you. Good bye. With lots of love from

Your own

Wife

[WINSTON STEPHENS TO OCTAVIA STEPHENS]

Fernandina Jan 14, 1862.

My Dear Good Wife

How glad I was to receive your nice, long letter and see you all were well and every thing progressing so finely. I do sincerely think I have the best little Wife in the whole world. (Tell Mother to except present company for her sake) You cannot concive how happy I am to know I have such a treasure as yourself and our dear Rosa. If every one loved home and their family as I do, there would not be so much room for complaint among the sex you belong to, but some are destitute of all honor to their Wives, or love of home as I have evidence of here in many cases. Men come here and forget the embraces of their dear Wives and throw themselves away upon the common *strumpet,* but My Dear "though I say it that should not say" You may trust your old man as God knows my marriage vow has been kept and I have never felt the least inclination to break it so help me God. I am constantly thinking of you and ours and wishing to be with you and I

---

11. There were several different varieties of sweet potato, including the common yam or Spanish potato that Tivie called Hayties. As she mentioned, both slave and free ate them, but the more preferred variety was called Leathercoat. The record does not reveal how many different varieties were grown at Rose Cottage. Winston also grew Irish potatoes, but the mainstay was always sweet potatoes. Rosengarten, *Tombee,* 78–79, has an excellent summation of the potato varieties available.

often take *you* out of my trunk and imagine you are before me and reality.[12] Genl Hopkins has not returned and I am in Command as usual and find it rather tedious, but the men are generally a good set and less troublesome than any Company in the Regiment—We went out on Batallion drill this morning for the 2nd time and we were highly complimented for our solderly appearance and prompt action—Yesterday Genl Lee reviewed the Troops on the Island—and this Regiment (the 4th) received the best praise as they were the best drilled and our Company received praise from Genl Lee for our proficiency in drill considering the short time we have drilled and I would be better satisfied here but some of the men are clamerous about leaving their horses and they take the pains to come to me with all their grivances as they think I can redress them. This makes my position unpleasant and when the Capt comes I am going to explain to him and he must become responsable for his own acts, as it was him and not me that offered their services here. Our Company has not improved in health but they are complaining generally of colds, some fever etc, no measles etc yet but they are in the adjoining camps and I dont see how we are to miss—"Now to your questions"—

I have not had mumps. and sunday is the same as any other day here, last sunday however I attended church in the a.m. and pm and heard the Rev Mr Baker who is a good preacher . . .[13] I am glad Mother does call the negroes every Sunday and feel greatful to her for it. Tell Burrel to continue his duty as a good servant and make a good crop and I will make him a nice present at the end of the year . . .

Poor Taylor! I hope he has recovered, also Clara. They must be careful for if Taylor is killed the coons will eat the corn up . . . Give my love to Mother and the boys tell the negroes howdy and accept all you desire from your aff husband for yourself and Rosa—Give love to Clark and family—Yours as ever

Winston Stephens

[REBECCA BRYANT TO WILLIE AND DAVIS BRYANT]

Rose Cottage Jan 14, 1862

My dear boys,

. . . I will commence by saying, what you doubtless already *suspect*, that I am nearly beside myself with delight in hearing from your Father.

---

12. The ambrotype Winston refers to has not been identified.
13. Reverend Archibald Baker was an Episcopal minister in Fernandina. The South Carolina native was fifty years old at this time, a widower with four young children and nine slaves.

I have had more gloomy forebodings about him the past month, than ever before I think at times it has been only with much effort that I could be cheerful. I suppose you did not receive any letter from him as you do not mention it. I am very glad Davis, that you wrote him so promptly—and I hope he will be induced to come to Florida—Yet he will not be contented to *remain* here doing nothing, and what can he do? But he *must come* any how, unless he has something positively lucrative and certain in view, which is not probable—I shall enclose my reply to him with this, that you may send it . . .

Yr Mother

[OCTAVIA STEPHENS TO WINSTON STEPHENS]

Jan 22, 1862

My very dear Husband

Again this week I have no direct news from you but was glad to get one last night which ought to have come last week, and know that you were well then . . . I have but little time and writing with Rosa in my lap, pulling my paper, and hands, so you must excuse writing. Rosa is fretful this morning she missed her fever the day I wrote to you last and has not had a return, but her bowels have been quite troublesome. I can not find any teeth, but think some must be coming. I am beginning to wean her, she has not nursed through the day for two days. The boys drove up a cow last week so I give her boiled milk and bread or rice she will not eat much, but gets two *"jugs" full* when she goes to bed and a good deal through the night, she has a restless spell about every night . . . Tina . . . is *enormous.*[14] I tell her to expect *double,* but her health is still good only she is very helpless she thinks she can not go until March . . .

Burrel and Jane are ploughing, began Monday. they have not rolled all the logs in the new ground as they are very large, I told him to wait until you came and perhaps you would have a "rolling," for they were all straining. I am glad I made them stop when I did for after that on Sunday last he was laid up with his back . . .

All send love, Rosa is asleep. I send all the love that is due a *good husband*

Ever affectionately

Tivie

---

14. Tina was pregnant with a boy who would be named Charles Seton Stephens. He was born on 14 March 1862 in Welaka.

[OCTAVIA STEPHENS TO WINSTON STEPHENS]

Welaka Jan 24, 1862

My own dear husband

... I heard yesterday ... that the horses were in a starving condition, nothing but crab grass hay, no corn, so Clark advised me to send two bushels of corn to Isham Stanley and request him to feed Pet with it until I heard from you ...[15] I am scribbling this off while the darkies are shelling the corn, and Rosa is plaguing me. She is better than she was, but I have to diet her on milk in different ways and bread or rice on account of her bowels. I have pretty well weaned her in the day, this is the fifth day she has gone without, she gets a good quantity at night. Sarah is sick to day, every one else well ...

Well my dear I must close now. with my best love and prayers for your safe return to us. Ever your loving Wife

Tivie

Jan 25, 1862. *Winston surprised us just as we were sitting down to dinner. He came on the* Darlington.

[REBECCA BRYANT TO DAVIS BRYANT]

Rose Cottage Feb 10, 1862

My dear Davis,

... My disappointment in getting no letters from any one to-day has given me the dumps. It seems an age to wait until next Monday ...

We are all pleased with the change in the weather, especially for two reasons, it enabled Winston to kill another pig thereby giving us some fresh meat and has frozen up the sandflies for a time. I declare! I *have* had an adventure since I wrote. We all went to pass Thursday at Mrs Stephens' having Winston's horse to pull the buggy—coming home Winston stood on the back of the buggy and drove. The horse is not accustomed to going in harness and it is difficult to make him turn his *body* enough to clear the trees—when about a quarter of a mile from Mrs C Stephens,' trotting briskly, we came to a sudden turn and between two trees and Winston could not bring the horse round quick enough to avoid the right hand one, consequently we smashed in to it and broke both shafts and split the swingle-tree! We expected every moment the horse would kick, but he stood

---

15. Isham Stanley was a thirty-seven-year-old Welaka farm laborer who worked for Granville Priest. Born in South Carolina, Stanley joined Winston's company during the Third Seminole War and again in April 1862; he died of disease the next year.

perfectly quiet when Winston spoke to him . . . Winston thinks he can make two shafts and repair the damage so that it will carry us to town . . .[16]

Much love . . .

Mother

Feb 13, 1862. Winston started before day and went turkey hunting and returned before 8 o'clock with a turkey weighing 23 lbs. After breakfast he went back to town to load the waggons for camp, his waggon went also. I sent some of the turkey etc for his dinner over to him, he did not return until after tea as he had been hunting with Clark and C— killed a deer.

Feb 16, 1862. Before we were dressed in the morning a Mr Donaldson came from camp Dunlawton saying that Capt Hopkins *was so sick that he and Josey had come for Mrs Hopkins.*[17] After breakfast Winston went to Mrs Hopkins to help her arrange to start.

Feb 17, 1862. Winston started as soon as he finished breakfast for Dunlawton.

[WINSTON STEPHENS TO OCTAVIA STEPHENS]

Dunlawton Feb 20, 1862

My dear wife

I arrived here about 4 oclock on Tuesday and found Capt Hopkins very sick and not expected to live . . . poor man! He is so very much reduced in flesh—he gets up to stool from four to five times a day and it is very dark and offencive. We are using injections of gumerabic and the blisters have drawn well and we give him brandy in boiled milk and arrow root and the Dr says that is all that keeps him alive.[18]

I send the waggon home and I want burrel to haul the manure out and plant the old field [in] corn as soon as possible—fix up my trunk blankets and if you can fix me up a small matras and musquito bar I will thank you as we are ordered to Smyrna and they are bad there, also send the box with *fixings* if convinient, send every thing over to Welaka as soon as you can get them ready and Sergt Mizell will bring them down.[19] I cant return now and dont know when I can. We

---

16. The visit took place on 6 February, and Winston began repairing the swingletree the next day. It took him a week to fix it. Swingletree, singletree, and whiffle-tree are all names for the crossbar to which the traces are fastened.

17. This is either Private George W. or John F. Donaldson; both brothers were Marion County farmers and served for the remainder of the war.

18. Gum arabic is the gum of the acacia tree, and arrowroot is a nutritious starch obtained from the plant of the same name.

19. Sergeant John Mizell was a farrier from Marion County who served until 1864, when he took the oath and went home.

have been ordered to Smyrna . . . and we will go up as soon as the Capt's condition will permit . . . I rode out yesterday to kill a deer and killed a very large Panther but no deer—the men have no meat and I went on their account and to day I have sent out for some pork. I am suffering so much for want of thinner clothing . . . send my light linnin coat and vests . . .

Much love to all—Yours Very truly
Winston Stephens

[WINSTON STEPHENS TO OCTAVIA STEPHENS]

Dunlawton Feb 22, 1862[20]

My Dear Wife

Our Capt died last night at 11 oclock. Poor Man he suffered very much for about three hours before his death, but the last few moments he was easy and died without a struggle. he was in his mind up to the last and made his will just before he died but I think Mrs H— is dissatisfied as she says he gave some of her property to the children—he gave her Felix and Wife and the two youngest—and Miss Bella, Harriet, and Henry, small Frank, and Joseph, John Bull, then he wanted his debts paid and what was left divided between Bella, Henry, and Joseph, except the lots—those he wanted for the use of Mrs H. I will go to Smyrna next week. you may keep the shot gun and shot *but* send other things. The waggon will not start back here before Thursday—I send Lt Peterman with a detachment of men to bury Capt H— and they will take him to Palatka.[21]

I am quite well—I send you some shells, send the bag back—Your aff husband

Winston

[OCTAVIA STEPHENS TO WINSTON STEPHENS]

Rose Cottage Feb 24, 1862

Well my dear husband I have just finished my part of the cooked things (or things to be cooked), and taken my seat on the steps to begin my letter to you but it is so dark that I can hardly see the lines . . . the cake and Pone look very rough, but hope they will taste better than they look. I had forgotten that I said I would

---

20. As Rebecca noted in her diary, Jefferson Davis was inaugurated president of the Confederate States of America on this date. The provisional government was replaced by the "permanent" one at this time.

21. Hopkins is buried in the Westview Cemetery in Palatka. The tombstone is engraved, with his former rank, "Gen. B. Hopkins, C.S.A." Winston's grave is also there; he was originally buried in Lake City but was removed after the war. Why Tivie did not have him interred in the Welaka graveyard is unknown.

not send anything and wish now that you had not asked me, I am willing to do anything for you, but I never like to have anything I do go where there is a chance for it to be commented upon, well all I hope is that my husband will not think any the less of me because I can not quite come up to other wives, I may improve, I am young yet. Burrel brought me your letter on Sunday while we were at dinner and I assure you I was glad to get it, the week was a long one to me. I was very sorry to hear of Captain H—'s situation, but was surprised too that he was alive. I have heard since that he was dying Friday afternoon, and suppose that all is over now . . .

Just as I finished the above sentence one of the men of the company came in to get the mules (as they were passing with the Capt's body) to go on to the bluff as their horses had broken down . . . I declare that I can not imagine that Capt Hopkins has been carried past here a corpse. Mrs Hopkins must feel thankful that she was with him at the time of his death . . .

I am sorry to hear that you are ordered to Smyrna, for I fear the Yankees will be ordered there before long. We heard bad news this week from Tennessee. Fort Donelson was surrendered, but Gen Johnston had retreated about 15 miles from Nashville, and had rec large reinforcements of soldiers and inhabitants and it was thought there would be another desperate battle, there are several reports but that was the latest and I believe the most true . . .[22]

Much love to all. Your loving Wife
Tivie

[WINSTON STEPHENS TO OCTAVIA STEPHENS]

Enterprise Feb 28, 1862

My Dear Wife

You see we are on the St Johns once more, I received orders at Smyrna last night and to night I am here—My Orders are to divide the company into detachments and station them at various places that I may think best and watch the river, and not allow the enemy to come up the river and surprise the party at Smyrna. I shall station some at Volusia and some at Welaka and as I am *boss* I think I shall stay near Welaka—I suppose I will be home in less than two weeks

---

22. Fort Donelson was surrendered to Brigadier General Ulysses S. Grant on 16 February 1862. General Albert Sidney Johnston of the Confederacy had sent half of his forces to the fort, and the loss opened up Nashville to attack. It was evacuated on 23 February. Both Kentucky and western Tennessee were lost for the Confederacy, and Johnston swiftly retreated all the way to Corinth, Mississippi. This dire turn of events was what caused the withdrawal of almost all of the Confederate troops in Florida. In early April, Johnston's reinforced army turned north and struck Grant at Shiloh, Tennessee. Johnston was killed in this battle, and Braxton Bragg, promoted to major general, took command of the army in June. Reinforcements were once again rushed to Corinth, including Willie Bryant's unit, the Third Florida Infantry.

... I am feeling tired as I rode from Dunlawton yesterday to Smyrna and from there to this place today. Give much love to Mother and boys and accept lots for yourself and Dear Rosa.

Your Aff husband
Winston Stephens

[OCTAVIA STEPHENS TO WINSTON STEPHENS]

Mar 2, 1862

My dear Husband

I have just laid our baby down to sleep, and now sit down to have a little chat with you. I rather think though that I will do all the Chatting, if it can be called so, and it ought not for how much pleasanter it would be to have you here so that we could talk in earnest, this way of sending questions and answers by letter is slow business, but being able to write and read letters is a great blessing, yes letter writing was a great *invention*. I dont know what I would do if I could not hear from you. You dont know how much I want to see you, the weeks are very long ... I suppose when you come home you will be Capt as I hear that you will most probably be elected to that office. The night that the men passed here with Capt Hopkins body, four men stopped in the yard and got Jane to cook them some supper ...

I sent your trunk over to the store yesterday to go with the provisions ... I send your bedding too as you have not countermanded your order. In the left hand corner of your trunk (which you cant help seeing, you will find a box of cake, in the right hand corner back part, you'll find a kettle of lard, which I intended to fry your *fish and oysters*) inside of that kettle is a cup of butter, in the back part of the trunk is a box of eggs. I found that the pies would not keep this weather. I hope you will get all this safely, and that they will taste good. I am sorry the Pone is burned ... was in rather a hurry to get it done and cool to put in the trunk, the one I baked for you last week was too dry to be good, but I hope this is better. I made some quite nice pies last week for you, but of course we ate them as there was no way to send them. Speaking of the pies etc my flour is getting very low, as you said you were going to get more. The syrup is some of Barnes' and perhaps you know as well as Tina and Burrel that his syrup is watered, generally, this is thin, but has a good deal of sugar in it.[23]

I will now finish what I was saying about the storm. Well it was terriffic, the roar of the thunder and falling of the trees was awful ... The fields are sights to behold, Burrel said tell you that if you could see you would almost be willing to declare the field has not been cleaned up. I think it worse than before they rolled at all, it did not do much damage to the corn, he is getting them rolled up pretty

23. E. Sylvester Barnes was a Welaka shoemaker.

fast, but there is a great deal of grumbling about the hard work, and I had some words with Jane and Rachel about things they said day before yesterday, before the boys, they have said little things before, and Henry would not say anything until now he thought it had gone or was going too far. I thought Jane had said a good many things that Rach had said, and threatened to either send her home or have her punished if I heard any more, she said for one thing that she had rather be whipped to death than worked to death, and they or Rach said you used to have to work before you were married but you had not since, and couldn't see why you couldn't ask help to roll logs unless you were afraid you would have to feed them. They were neither of them impudent but yesterday Jane the same as called Henry a liar. I have not said anything more to her, the work is hard and I fear will injure Burrel for his back troubles him so much. I will tell you more of it when you come . . .

Rosa sends a kiss. I send love and kisses in lots to my dear Husband, lovingly your

Wife

[WINSTON STEPHENS TO OCTAVIA STEPHENS]

Enterprise Mar 4, 1862

My Dear Wife

. . . sorry you have had so much trouble in the first place with my *fixings* and in the second with the darkies—never mind I will fix up their account and settle it for them. I will come home some time next week and hav'nt time to write you a long letter as I will start to day for Volusia and am in a hury preparing to leave . . . The trunk and goodies were rec'd and very acceptable and no remark made only in the praise of them—Dont fear that I shall ever despair of My Wife for she is the best I have ever seen. I want to get home and see you and be with you as much as possible and I think I shall be about Welaka for some months, this is only supposition as we have traveled around considerable lately—Good news for the Confederate States—We have the Carolina, Cecil, and three Sailing crafts now inside of the Smyrna bar.[24] The Steamers are loaded with arms, powder and other things to equip about 15 thousand men, one of the sail vessels has 1,000 sacks of salt—the others I have not learned what they have—I am to keep watch

---

24. These two small, fast steamers carried some 10,000 guns from Nassau to Smyrna destined for the chief of ordnance at Savannah, Georgia; but Florida units seized the weapons for themselves. The state of Florida received but 1,289 of these guns for the official arming of state troops. See Nulty, *Confederate Florida*, 16–17; Anderson, *By Sea and by River*, 218.

at Welaka and Volusia for the enemy and if they approach I am to send an express to Smyrna etc. I think we are yet to have trouble on this River, caused by the shipment of these goods. If we do I will have a chance to fire my gun in defence of my Country and My Dear family and you may rest assured that one will fall when she fires . . .

Kiss my Dear Rosa and accept much love from your aff
Old Man.

[CAROLINE EVERITT TO REBECCA BRYANT]

Groverville Mar 5, 1862

My dear Ruby,[25]

Yours was duly recd. and was very welcome. Since that time Paris came home from Camps for one day, he came home to arrange his business, the great preparations made to attack Savannah caused many troops from Darien and other places to be ordered there, Paris, as well as others, knew that the conflict would be terrible, and he prepared for the worst. I staid with him till he left, and tho' we all were calm apparently, yet you may imagine what our feelings were, day after day we have expected to hear that the attack had commenced, but so far hear nothing of any such movement . . . I can only cry, oh! that we may have peace blessed peace, that we never appreciated. Yet I do not know that this War could have been avoided. Mr E. and myself were not strong Secessionists. I was anxious for a Compromise, so was Mr Everitt, but he gave up at last that we must not hope for justice, and like the rest, we go in for doing all in our Power for the War . . . I can only think of our dear boys safety, and of our country . . . Mother and I have read your letter over and *talked* of *you* today. I am glad indeed you have heard from William.[26] What a state of suspense you have been in, and your boys gone! You have had a sad time . . . I want to see you so much, when this war is over, perhaps, we will meet. When the War is over!! When will that be? God bless and keep you, and all your dear ones, my dear sister. Write when you have time and inclination to yours ever truly.

Caroline

25. Rebecca was called Ruby by both sides of the family. Caroline, the oldest of the Bryant clan, was Rebecca's sister-in-law.
26. James William Bryant, Rebecca's husband, was called William by his wife and sisters but always signed his name as James W. or J. W. Bryant.

[Rebecca] **Mar 6, 1862.** .... *Receive a letter from Davis saying that the Federals have possession of Fernandina—and that they are preparing for an attack in Jacksonville—Many families leaving the place.*[27]

[WINSTON STEPHENS TO OCTAVIA STEPHENS]

Volusia Mar 6, 1862

My Dear Wife

I start this morning for Ocala for the purpose of procuring teams to transport the contraband property at Smyrna to some point of more security.[28] I will try to return here by Monday night or Tuesday and then I will come down to Welaka unless something transpires while I am absent to prevent. You have no doubt heard the news—Fernandina has been taken, the Darlington taken, St Maryes taken,[29] and the enemy landing on the RR and making for Baldwin, but our troops had met them and the fight was raging when the Courier left.[30] I know their object is to cut off the transportation of this property and now if we cannot get off we are going to run it up the interior if we can and if not destroy it if we cannot keep them back. I want you to be governed by your Mother—dont despair but bare up like a good Wife and I shall be true to you so long as life lasts— If the enemy comes when I am absent, do the best you can to save yourself, Mother, and our families, then all the provisions you can and negroes—you had better I think tell Burrel what is going on and tell him if they come for them to

---

27. The letter referred to here is missing. With the withdrawal of almost all of the troops from Florida to wage war in Tennessee, the decision was made to evacuate a number of vulnerable areas, including Fernandina. The order to evacuate the town and all of Amelia Island was issued on 25 February, and the Federals entered the town just four days later. Pensacola, on the west coast, and St. Augustine and Jacksonville on the east were taken by the Federals in a matter of days. Of all Florida cities occupied by Union forces, Jacksonville received by far the worst treatment. Invaded and occupied four times, the city was in ruins when the Federals commenced their final occupation in February 1864.

28. As previously mentioned, the primitive transportation facilities made it very difficult to move this cargo. It had to go overland to the St. Johns River; then up the Ocklawaha to Orange Springs; then overland to Waldo, where it could be picked up by the Florida Railroad and carried to Baldwin; and from there transferred to the Florida Atlantic & Gulf Central to be sent to Madison, off-loaded, and hauled overland to Quitman, Georgia. Once in Quitman, it could be sent anywhere in the Confederacy by rail. There was no railroad connecting Florida to Georgia until too late in the war to make any difference. Nulty, *Confederate Florida,* 24; Shofner and Rogers, "Confederate Railroad Construction," 217–28.

29. Fernandina was taken, but the *St. Marys* escaped for a short time. She was trapped in the St. Johns River when Jacksonville was occupied a few days later and was scuttled by her crew before the end of the month. For an account of the chase and capture of Jacob Brock and the *Darlington* on 4 March as well as the shelling of the last train out of Fernandina (it made good its escape), see Hayes, *Samuel Francis Du Pont,* vol. 1, 351–52.

30. There was very little fighting at this time. A few skirmishes in and around Jacksonville resulted in several deaths, but there was no big battle anywhere during this invasion and occupation.

take to the woods and not come in until they go and tell him if they get him they will treat him worse than he was ever treated and I think you may trust him—tell him I want him to keep the others out of the way—let the work proceed until you hear of their approach and manage the best you can . . . I would like to come to you but duty takes me off—but knowing you as I do I go with a light heart so I know you will do the best you can and be content that I am doing all I can, love to Mother and boys and many kisses to my Dear Rosa and my own dear Wife, secure the powder if they come by burying or some way—good bye and God bless and protect you all. Your aff husband

Winston Stephens

March 8, 1862. *In the morning* buried some provisions *to keep from the enemy if they come. In the afternoon,* Henry and George went to Clark's *to see if there was news from Jacksonville as we had heard two boats had passed, they were going to Ocklawaha with cotton. After supper,* buried the silver and powder.[31]

[OCTAVIA STEPHENS TO WINSTON STEPHENS]

March 9, 1862

My dear Husband

. . . I was glad to hear that you had gone to Ocala, and wish you could stay there until the enemy leaves these parts . . . My dear do be careful, dont think you must fight them anyhow, for you have so few men, what could you do against four or five thousand. I hear there are five thousand but suppose all those will not come up the river, too many though for you to manage.[32] I think the fight near Baldwin was only a rumor, for I think the boat that carried you that news brought a letter from Davis which said they had possession of Fernandina, but we must not listen to any reports about their being at the mouth of the river etc and there was no chance of their having to leave Jacksonville for some days at least, he had only ten minutes to write but wrote considerable.

We are prepared for the "Yankees" or rather prepared to see them, which I hope we will not do, I shall try to be brave but guess I'll be tolerably "skeered," for I tremble just talking of their coming, night before last I woke up shaking dreadfully I suppose from dreaming of them. The negroes seem troubled about their coming, declare they'll take to the hammock . . .

31. Family legend has it that Tivie's silver baby cup was dented when it was run over by a carriage in the spot where it had been hidden from Union troops.
32. There were almost four thousand Federal troops in Florida when the order was given to evacuate Jacksonville in April 1862.

I shall expect you certainly on Wednesday, if you do not come before, but if you hear the enemy are coming dont come unless obliged to. I have many more fears for you than myself. Rosa is well and asleep. Goodbye, God protect my dear husband is the constant prayer of your

Wife

[Rebecca] **March 10, 1862**. *Henry and George go over to town in the morng. for Davis' articles—In the afternoon Davis arrives . . . Jacksonville surrendered! The Confederate Gov have decided to abandon the defense of E. Florida.*[33]

[WINSTON STEPHENS TO OCTAVIA STEPHENS]

Volusia Mar 10, 1862

My Dear Wife

I arrived in camp last night from Ocala and found all well but considerable excitement—The Hattie arrived from below soon after I landed and brought the inteligence that the enemy were expected every hour in Jacksonville and thought it unsafe to go so far down. Now my Dear I cant come in several days more, but will as soon as I get every thing organized and ready for the reception of the enemy if they come up this far. If they come up the river and stop any where about you I want you to take the mules and get back from the river. I dont think they will stop but if they do I dont want you where they can insult you and I will write to Clark to assist you in carrying out any plan to keep out of reach. I am nearly crazy to think of what might happen to you—take to the woods, any thing but disgrace by the poluting touch of those scoundrels. We are going to plant some guns on the river and scatter the Company on the bank and I think if they will give us a few days to mature our plans that we will stop them. I think if you and your white family could get back out of their way that Burrel can carry on the farm and make his escape when they approach . . .

---

33. On 7 March 1862 the mayor of Jacksonville, H. H. Hoeg, published a proclamation to that effect. When the news reached the city that Fernandina had been occupied and that a large invasion force was on the way, panic gripped those who supported the Confederacy and many fled the city, but those who were Unionist or who had become apathetic or disillusioned with the Confederacy welcomed the news. On 9 March, Willie and his company passed through the city on their retreat from Fort Steele at Mayport to camp seven miles west of Jacksonville. Martin and Schafer, *Jacksonville's Ordeal by Fire*, 71. On 11 March four Federal gunboats crossed the St. Johns bar and anchored in the river. On the same day, the Confederate commander, Brigadier General James H. Trapier, ordered the destruction of the sawmills, lumberyards, an iron foundry, and a ship under construction. That night a mob of irregulars and refugees from Fernandina set fire to the Judson House, the fashionable hotel on Bay Street, and several homes of known Union sympathizers. Federal forces occupied the city on 12 March.

Tell Davis I leave every thing to him and for your sakes not to leave you to come here—I think you all had better get as far back from the water as you can as I feel sure they will not go out in the Country. I'll trust Davis and tell him to save you, Rosa, Mother and the boys and if he cant save the rest to let it rip—save all the provisions you can as they will be scarce, plant no cotton but all corn and tell Burrel to keep out of their way. Oh how much I want to see you—good by and God bless you all—I will be careful and try to live to see you all. Your affectionate husband

Winston Stephens

[OCTAVIA STEPHENS TO WINSTON STEPHENS]

March 12, 1862

My own dear husband

I hardly know what to write and how to write to you my poor heart is so full of anxiety for you, seems as though I can not concentrate my thoughts on paper, do not think though that I have given up to the blues and dumps, but no one knows the anxiety I feel when I think of your situation, but as I can not better it I try to trust in Providence, and if any poor mortals ever prayed earnestly I have for your safety. I know they are heard, and hope and pray that they may be accepted and granted. Oh I can not bear to think that it may be otherwise. Well I ought not to write this way to you, for your burden is hard enough to bear . . .

I think you may as well give up and come home as to try and keep the enemy back for they have a very large force, Mr Lewis Roux stayed on in Fernandina a day or two as a sort of spy, and passed himself off as a union man, and the enemy told him they had 25,000 men, and 21 gunboats, that they expected a hard fight and came prepared to conquer all Florida and establish a territorial government.[34] I suppose you heard that the Government has abandoned this State and the Governor has ordered all the regiments that are mustered into the Confederate service away from East Fla. What is to become of us. I think we will have to leave or be made Lincolns subjects . . .

I think we are safe enough here if the Gun boats come up for they can not see us from the river, and they probably will not come from Welaka here. I think there is no fear of my being insulted if any attempt should be made I think whoever did should rue it, if they come we intend to be civil as long as they are so, Mother thinks she will not be insulted, that she is *too old* and she will be "spokesman." We have taken care of a small portion of the corn and a barrel of meat,

---

34. Louis Roux and his brother George were prosperous commercial merchants in Fernandina. This number was five times the size of the largest force that ever invaded Florida; the 1864 invasion force numbered a few more than 5,500 men.

and *the bale* of cotton. Burrel thinks that some of the corn we thought killed will yet come out, he is getting along finely. I would not like to leave the negroes if I should leave, for it would give them more of a chance to be unfaithful, and if faithful I would not like to leave them . . .
God bless my husband.

Your Tivie

[WINSTON STEPHENS TO OCTAVIA STEPHENS]

Volusia Mar 13, 1862

My Dear Wife

. . . Oh! what a dark hour in this our Country and I fear we have not seen the worst by a good deale—but I have hope even now when every thing is so unpromising. I think our cause a just one and I believe that the God of battles will yet crown our arms with more and greater Victories and that the cause will yet prosper. Nothing of a common nature can be achieved without an effort and some sacrifice—and in this great struggle we must suffer in proportion to the benefit we are to derive from the struggle. One thing gives me more trouble about this matter than all others, and that is that this State is to be abandoned to the enemy and if true I fear we will have a rebellion in this State, as the people are determined not to go out of State and leave their families to the mercies of the enemy and fight for others and your good for nothing *old Man* is one of that number. I will not abandon my family for any cause. What I most fear is this, that you my beloved wife should fall into the hands of the enemy and that they might treat you as they did a poor girl in Fernandina. A poor man that was left had a Daughter ten years old and the second day after they got possession three of the men took her in the scrub and ravished her and when it was reported to the Oficer he merely made them mark time one hour—Now if that is to be the rule I want my family out of their way—Keep a close watch and if they come up the river take the mules and waggon and dont trust negroes but ask Davis to secrete you in some place and he can furnish you with provisions as long as the enemy are in the neighborhood and let the negroes make a corn crop and next fall I will take you so far from the water that you will be safe . . . Write by every opportunity if only one line to say you are safe and well—Kiss our Dear babe and tell her Pa Pa wants to see her very much and ask her to Kiss Ma Ma for me. I wish I could see Davis and talk this matter over with him but I want him to stay by you all until I come when I hope he will have some plan matured with Mothers help by which all of you may be placed beyond the reach of the enemy—We feel like we can make quite a stand here . . . Give much love to Mother and boys and accept your husbands whole devotion for you and Rosa.

Winston Stephens

[JULIA FISHER TO REBECCA BRYANT]

Thomasville Mar 15, 1862

Dearest Sis,

If the news is true that reached us yesterday from Madison, I fear this may not easily reach you, as I understand the mail communication is stopped—we understand too that a portion of Jacksonville is burnt, and three men killed—(unionists) and last night we heard the town was in the possession of the Federalists.[35] We are very anxious of course, about you and Tivy, Lou and Richard, but more particularly about our dear boys Willy and Davis . . .[36] I see no chance but to stand our ground, and trust to Providence—but though I could not oppose them, and would not unnecessarily exasperate them, my tongue should be palsied before I would ever say one word of concession—God help us to forgive them, but I am sure He will protect our cause, for we only fight in pure self defence—I trust our boys may get out of the reach of danger—I do not think they will trouble women and children, but the negroes may give you trouble . . . If the boys think it best for you to leave, come here dear Sis, *at once*—You and Tivy and boys, and any negroes you want to bring—we can all find room here . . . Darling we can only commit you and your dear children, dear Winston included, to the God we put all our trust in—may he protect us, and *especially* our dear boys on the field . . . Yours dearest ever—

Julia (do write)

[WINSTON STEPHENS TO OCTAVIA STEPHENS]

Volusia March 17, 1862

My Darling Wife

. . . I was glad to hear you were safe and that the Enemy had not reached our home, but I fear we are not to be allowed much longer to call it so—I would give so much could I come to you now, but I cannot come yet, as the Officers all appear to consider my presence of great importance. I wish I was considered of less importance, then perhaps I could go to you, and not be missed at this point— My Dear, Lt Gray tells me the enemy have been out two miles from the St Johns and that they had killed chickens and stolen some coffee and one negroe man,

---

35. This account is partially accurate in that the city was in Union hands, but no one had been killed, and very little of the city had been burned at this stage. Although dated and biased in dealing with Reconstruction, William Watson Davis, *Civil War and Reconstruction*, 157–62, gives a good account of this and subsequent invasions.

36. Tivie's cousin, Louisa (Bryant) Tydings, and her husband, Richard, previously mentioned, were in Jacksonville; Willie's unit was about seven miles west of the city at Seven Mile Camp, soon to be named Camp Finegan; and Julia probably thought Davis was in Jacksonville, but he was at Welaka.

and they say they intend to take all the property of those that are in arms against them and I feel sure they will keep their promise and I fear they will not respect the wives of soldiers. Several men joined them in Palatka who know me and know the position I am in and where I live which makes me uneasy on your account—Do my Dear go from home if they stop any where near Welaka . . . one thing I do hope and ask of you dont let them get near enough to insult you—for my sake go from home back in the Country when they come. I had rather lose every thing in this world than to have you in their power—I will not trust them and I dont want you to trust them . . . I had thought if you were surprised that you could tell them some fine story and keep them from finding out that your husband belonged to the army—I have just heard that they were burning the property in Augustine of all those in arms against them.[37] If Davis will save my family I am his slave if he wishes the rest of my life—I think I shall go crazy if I hear of any thing of that kind has happened to my Wife . . . Dont be uneasy about my safety as we will fight them Indian fashion and can have a better chance to save our selves . . . If Mother can sell the cotton she can claim it and dispose of it as they will steal it if they find out I own it and you had better destroy my letters and then they cant learn any thing from that source—I am coming home soon any how—If we never meet on earth I hope we may meet in heaven where there is no wars—Give my love to Mother, Davis and boys—and write every chance—Kiss Rosa for me and do try to be cool in any emergency—Your loving husband

Winston Stephens

[OCTAVIA STEPHENS TO WINSTON STEPHENS]

March 19, 1862

My own dear husband

. . . You can not think of the different plans etc we have had and thought of to day, at one time I thought they would send Rosa and I to Ocala *any how,* as you have such fears for me, but all think it entirely unneccessary and in fact "jumping out of the frying pan into the fire" for the enemy will go there next for they know that Marion is the richest place . . . so as Clark is going to stay and be parolled if necessary, and he says he will protect me, so I am going there right off and stay and if the enemy come I will hide and they are not going to *hunt me up*. Mother and the boys will stay at home as long as permitted, everyone thinks without being molested, if they come to burn why then they'll burn, but much quicker if no one is there, we will have to meet them at some place why not now have it over, do not think that I trust them, for I do not, and will keep out of their way. I will be safe enough, for Clark will give up so easily that they'll not trouble any thing of his, we can not go to Ocala, and if your life is spared we will get together

37. This was just a rumor.

somehow and somewhere . . . oh if I could only talk with you . . . do give up, come home, parole and let us try and be happy here for the present at least, the State will be conquered any how, so give up now as many others have had to do, territorial government will be better than none and we have none now . . . My dear if you lay down arms now they will parole you all, think, do my dear. Think of our baby and me, if you and my property should be taken away what would become of us, when if you should come home you might save all. You need not talk of the defence of your home and country for you *can not defend* them, they are too far gone now, so give up before it is too late . . . I have tried to write in good spirits to you, for I had *some* hopes of our State's being saved, but now *all* that hope is gone, I tell you I am miserable, and I say come to me, and let us bear what comes *together* . . .

You speak of our going in the woods and not letting the negroes know where we are, it is impossible and we are afraid to go far for fear they may cross from Dunns creek and find us.[38] No my darling I think it best as it is arranged. I dislike to leave home but will as you have such fears for me . . .

Once more I say give up. I will take care of myself. I shall hope to see you soon. My prayers shall be constant for your safety. Ever yr loving

Wife

P.S. . . . My dear I cannot destroy your letters. I have them packed away as my choicest jewels . . .

Tivie

[DAVIS BRYANT TO WINSTON STEPHENS]

March 19, 1862

Dear Winston

. . . Your fears for Tivie, particularly, caused me to feel my responsibility greater than before . . . You may be sure that in *any event* I shall not forget that I have a *Mother* and *sister* under my protection (the boys I have no fear for) and I shall make *any sacrafice* for their benefit . . .

---

38. Tivie was apparently aware of the Federal attempt to salvage the *America* in Dunns (Cresent) Lake. Dunns Creek connects the St. Johns River to Dunns Lake, into which Haws Creek flows. The *America,* namesake of yachting's oldest and most illustrious trophy, was one of the most famous ships in the world. Built in 1851, she was purchased by the Confederacy a decade later and renamed the *Memphis.* She was towed upriver by the *St. Marys* to prevent capture and scuttled. Unlike the *St. Marys,* she was immediately raised by the Federals, given back her original name, and placed in blockading service until she was sent north for repairs in October 1862. She returned to duty the following January and served until she was sent to Newport, Rhode Island, in May 1863 as a training ship for the U.S. Naval Academy. Hayes, *Samuel Francis Du Pont,* vol. 1, 375–76, vol. 2, 57, 347, 503–4, vol. 3, 90; *Official Records of the Union and Confederate Navies* (cited hereafter as ORN, with appropriate series, volume, and page numbers), ser. 1, vol. 12, 638–40, 643.

I am terribly disappointed that you have not been here as I depended on seeing you before deciding what I should do in all respects and would give *anything* if you were here now, but will do *what I can,* and pray it may be for the best . . . *Take care of yourself* and I'll try to take care of all here. Yrs ever

Davis

[Rebecca] **March 21, 1862.** . . . *Winston arrives a little before nine, having ridden 60 miles! He retraces his steps to his brother's place to pass the night.*

March 22, 1862. *Winston came last night after all had gone to bed . . . In the afternoon Winston and Davis ran bullets.*[39]

March 23, 1862. *Winston quite unwell.*

[Rebecca] **March 28, 1862.** *Winston improving . . . Davis and Henry arrive about 4 o'clk, having gained some important information—The 3rd Regiment to which Willie belongs is stationed 7 miles from Jacksonville. Mr Tydings has been arrested and is confined at Tallahassee . . .*

[Rebecca] **March 31, 1862.** *Very warm. Write letters to Willie and to Julia to send by Winston who leaves in the morng. for Tallahassee. Sandflies bad!*[40]

Apr 1, 1862. *Winston left soon after breakfast for Tallahassee and Davis, Henry, and Tom went to Buffalo Bluff to put him across the river, they did not return until late in afternoon, brought some ducks . . .*[41]

Apr 14, 1862. *Winston arrived from Tallahassee about 8 o'clk in the evening, had seen Willie and brought letters from him.*

[Rebecca] **Apr 16, 1862.** *Winston left after breakfast for a probable absense of two weeks. Davis preparing to leave tomorrow on the Gov. Milton.*[42]

Apr 22, 1862. . . . *Davis came back about 11 o'clk at night, could not get to Jacksonville on account of the enemy.*

39. It was standard practice at that time to make up new ammunition by melting lead and running or placing it in molds of various calibers or bore size. There was no standard rifle in either army, but the most common were the .58 caliber Model 1861 Springfield and the British Enfield .577 caliber, which could accommodate the .58 bullet. Winston had several rifles including a .577 caliber Enfield, a short Enfield, and a Maynard.

40. Presumably Winston was going to make a case for Richard Tydings, but there is no reference to this in the correspondence. Tivie also became pregnant again at this time.

41. Buffalo Bluff was about six miles north of Rose Cottage and was the location of the Hopkins plantation. Once across the river, it was only five miles to Palatka, but the land was low, and the trip could be made only during the dry season. From Rose Cottage to Palatka was only ten or eleven miles as the crow flies, but the meandering river almost doubled the distance by water. Even so, there was no way to travel all the way overland without difficulty, for much of the land was swampy.

42. The *Governor Milton* was built in 1858 and captured on 9 October 1862 by Federal forces near Lake George. Captained by Paul Canova of Jacksonville during 1861 and 1862, she made the Jacksonville-to-Enterprise run with the rest of the riverboats. Mueller, *St. Johns River Steamboats,* 204.

[*Rebecca*] *Apr 23, 1862.* . . . *the* Hattie *has gone up the Ocklawaha and the* Milton *about to follow, and Davis decides to go on the latter and proceed to Orange Springs and thence in some way to reach Jacksonville . . .*

[*Rebecca*] *Apr 29, 1862.* . . . *A year ago this day my dear husband arrived in Jacksonville from Cuba and left on the 3d. May, expecting to return in a month, but I have not seen him since and have no prospect of a reunion!*[43]

[*Rebecca*] *May 2, 1862. Quite cool in the morng. Winston arrives about half an hour before dinner. He states that the 3d. Reg. Florida Volunteers are ordered to Tennessee—that all males from 18 to 35 years of age are ordered into the service for the war!*[44]

[JAMES W. BRYANT TO DAVIS BRYANT]

May 5, 1862 On board USS *Seneca*

My Dear Son Davis

I supposed you was at Welaka until I was told you was at Jacksonville. I was surprised to meet you but glad to see you in good health. You and Willie have taken positions in this civil struggle in opposition to the views I Entertain, but I believe you are both conscientious in your course. Pursue always in life the Path which you think is consistent with duty, honor, and justice, and I shall always respect you as *men,* and my love for you as *children* will be increased, if possible,

---

43. Her husband was much closer than she knew. On 3 April 1862, aboard the gunboat *Ottawa,* the ship's commander reported that "a Colonel Bryant and a Mr. [Samuel] Fairbanks, both gentlemen of character and influence in this section of the country, go to Fernandina in the *Hope,* to look after some slave property which has deposited itself there, they understand." Within a month, Bryant would try to reach Welaka. *ORN,* ser. 1, vol. 13, 705.

44. The Confederacy passed the first of three conscription acts on 16 April 1862, for all males eighteen to thirty-five. Eleven days later the age was increased to forty-five. The Union later enacted a military draft as well, but the results were not good for either government. In February 1864 the Richmond government extended the age range, making it seventeen to fifty. For the last year of the war, about one-third of the soldiers in the rebel armies in the east were conscripts. One could avoid service by hiring a substitute (though this provision was repealed in December 1863), by paying a $500 commutation fee, or by obtaining an exemption. Although Clark could have been exempted as a farrier, he was enlisted in that position by Winston in May 1862. However, his active service was brief; he was sent home on sick furlough on 20 June 1862 and was given a medical discharge on 25 November 1862. According to acting surgeon James S. Meredith, Clark had a foot injury and also suffered from "disease of the acetabulum" (the cup-shaped socket in the hip bone, which rendered him "unfit to perform the duties of a soldier." Meredith, a contract physician from Tampa, had served in Captain William J. Turner's company of Independent Florida Volunteers from April 1861 to March 1862 before entering Winston's company. Winston and Meredith may have known each other as boys in Alabama; they were certainly good friends at this time, and Winston was much distressed when Meredith was killed in 1863. See the Seventh Census of the United States, 1850, Schedule I, Population Schedule, Shelby County, Alabama; the household of David Meredith lists a twenty-year-old medical student named James. Since Winston's father was a physician, we believe that the boys were friends although nothing in the collection confirms this.

in the Knowledge that you possess *genuine* integrity . . . You will hear from me again soon. Any letters sealed or unsealed for me, sent on board the Seneca or other Gun boat addressed to me *at Fernandina* will be forwarded . . . by the officer of the Gun boats.

I would be very glad to have a good private talk with you, but will wait for a short time. This is Enough for the present—seeing you in good health, and knowing that all the family are well is a great cause of happiness to me to day.

I shall Expect frequently to hear from you if only a few lines—Give much love to Willie

Yours Ever Affectiontely

J. W. Bryant

May 6, 1862. Winston left soon after breakfast for Camp five miles below . . .[45]

May 11, 1862. In the morning Tom took Mr. Glisson in the boat to carry orders to Lt Grey, returned in the afternoon with the news of two gunboats at Palatka. Winston went right over to town to arrange to burn the turpentine if the boat came, returned while we were at supper and started for camp soon after.[46] *12 o'clk Winston returned for spades and with the news that Father was on the Gunboat at Palatka and intended coming for Mother. Winston staid only long enough to write a note to Clark.*

[Rebecca] *May 11, 1862. . . . Late in the day Winston receives a message from his Lieut—that two gunboats are at Palatka. W. goes to town to place a guard over the turpentine there, returns to tea and leaves soon after for camp—About midnight he returns again for a time—Had heard a report that my husband was at Palatka coming here for his family! I doubt the truth of it.*

[WINSTON STEPHENS TO OCTAVIA STEPHENS]

May 11[?], 1862

My Dear Wife

Your Father is in Palatka and I dont know how he intends presenting himself but he told several in Palatka . . . that he was going to come up to my house for

45. Winston moved his company to Horse Landing, some four miles north of Welaka, where the river is shallow. There is also another Horse Landing near Mandarin, which was used as a camp during the war, but Winston stayed within two miles of Rose Cottage during the month of May.
46. This was the turpentine that Bryan Gardner had stored at Welaka Springs at the northern outskirts of Welaka. Private D. W. Glisson was mustered in during the December 1862 reorganization and served for the remainder of the war.

his family. If he comes under a flag [of truce] (which I think he will) then I will allow him to come but none of the rest shall if I can prevent them. I want you in the morning to tell the negroes that the boat will perhaps come and tell them to keep out of the way until she goes down the river and manage everything as coolly as you can and break the inteligence to your Mother as you think best, be cool and fear not for me as we have a good place and can keep out of danger. The boys can let the guns be taken out of the way.

May 12, 1862. Between 2 and 3 o'clk p.m. Mr Wm Priest came for a gun of Winston's and said the Gunboats were coming up and Winston wanted us to leave home so we prepared for camping out and took to the woods but returned soon after sundown as we heard no guns firing.[47] *When we got home, found one of Mrs Hopkins negroes here with letters from Father to Mother and me. The boats got aground and turned back, one was too large to come up.*

[Rebecca] *May 12, 1862. . . . On our return we find a negro here from Buffalo Bluff with letters for me and Tivie. They were written on the gunboat while they were aground—and my dear husband has been expecting to see us all but was obliged to return ungratified—And so near us!*

[JAMES W. BRYANT TO OCTAVIA STEPHENS]

May 12, 1862[48]

My Dear Tivie

Having scrawled off a Note to your Mother, and the Boat yet being aground, I will write a little to you, and say how sorry I am not to see you and little Rosa. It will not be long however before I shall return and then I can be more Certain as I will come up in a smaller Gun boat. Whenever a Gun boat comes up, by going to the landing with a white flag, or sending off a boat with a white flag, or

---

47. William Priest of Welaka was forty-one years old in 1860. At that time he and his wife, Martha, had eight children and owned eleven slaves; he listed his total wealth at $6,500. He did not serve in the army, but his son James and his nephew William served in Winston's company from April 1862 until the end of the war.

48. On 6 May 1862 the captured *Darlington* arrived off Jacksonville from Fernandina under a flag of truce for the purpose of exchanging army prisoners and landing any civilians who desired to remain in Jacksonville. Lieutenant Commander Daniel Ammen of the Union navy reported that "the presence of Mr. Bryant prevented any action on the part of the local [Confederate] authorities. They evidently fear his influence, and, pending the arrival of instructions from Tallahassee, neither he nor the citizens desirous of returning were permitted to hold intercourse with their acquaintances. I shall therefore direct the return of the *Darlington* to-morrow to Fernandina and the *Isaac Smith*, accompanied by the *Patroon*, will proceed up the river, taking Mr. Bryant as passenger. I have directed Lieutenant Commanding [J. W. A.] Nicholson to facilitate the wishes and movements of Mr. Bryant as far as in his judgment they were in accordance with the interests of the Government of the United States." ORN, ser. 1, vol. 13, 804–5.

putting up a white flag anywhere, there can be communication had with the Vessel, or You Will be safe from any injury, *unless* the Boat is fired upon, in which case *no house* where a secessionist lives will be spared. The horrible system which some persons propose of shooting *individuals* either as sentinels, or upon Boats as steaming, must be put down, or it will induce a retaliation of the most bitter vengeance, and the retaliation will be tenfold. The house of Every person in arms against the Government will be destroyed, and his property of Every kind taken. Open Warfare is Expected, but the Government do not intend or wish to Prosecute a war upon individuals, nor destroy property of any private Persons who conduct themselves properly in their Positions.

The Captain has just Come in and says he shall not attempt to go up any further! It makes me very sad. My Expectation was to have been with you all within a Couple of hours, and now I must go off for Probably a month.

Your Mother can send open letter, address the outer envelope to the Commanding officer at Jacksonville, for me, and he will forward it to Fernandina.

I believe we are getting off, so I must send this ashore at once. God bless you my dear daughter, Kisses for Rosa and *all* of you. Yours Ever affectionably

J. W. Bryant

... A longer delay permits a P.S. In regard to myself I can only say that I am Engaged in East Florida, and I have no doubt but this District will soon be Engaged in its industrial Pursuits, with the ports of Fernandina, Jacksonville and St. Augustine *open to commerce;* the blockade will be withdrawn so soon as a Civil Goverment is Established, and that will be soon.

It gives me great pain to find Winston, Willie and Davis, all engaged in opposition to me, but I hope there will be a speedy End to this terrible war, when we can be again united.

[REBECCA BRYANT TO DAVIS BRYANT]

May 13, 1862

My dear Davis

... Yesterday eveg. I was surprised beyond expression to receive a letter from yr father, written at Buffalo Bluff. Only think of his being so near us and not able to come to see us for a half hour! The steamer got aground or they wd. have come up. But if they had the St. John's Rangers would probably have fired on them so perhaps it is "all for the best ..." your father writes that he saw you at Jacksonville ... I want to know what you have determined upon, whether Willie has gone out of the State with his company, and where and how we are to write to him. Tell me the substance of your interview with yr father ... He says the gunboats that may come up the river will do no injury unless they are fired upon.

My great fear is that they will be—but I must *hope* that I shall be able to see him under flag of truce, if he returns. My time is up—God bless you—

Mother

[Rebecca] *May 14, 1862*. . . . A letter from Davis confirms my fears that Willie had left with 3rd. Reg . . .

[WILLIE BRYANT TO REBECCA BRYANT]

Montgomery, Ala. May 14, 1862

My dear Mother,

Contrary to my expectations we are thus far on our way to Corinth, sure enough, and in about a week I suppose will reach there: I fully expected the fight would be over there before this and that we would not get beyond Georgia. Our officers and every one else feel sure that our Regiment will not be sent into the field under it's present discipline, and that it will be some time before it is prepared, and we will be used to guard prisoners: I suppose you will be better satisfied with the last arrangement, and as I am still in good health and spirits I hope you will feel easy concerning me until you have greater cause for the contrary. We commenced our march from Midway (between Tallahassee and Quincy) on last Friday a.m. 9th and marched to Chattahoochee 33 miles; arriving there at 2 o'clk Satd'y p.m. after a toilsome trip; Sunday a.m. we got on 3 Steamers and reached Columbus on Monday at dark; Tuesday a.m. (yesterday) we took the cars for this place and reached here at 10 o'clk last night, where I *suppose* we will remain till to morrow a.m. tho' the transportation is not sufficient for us anywhere and we arrive and leave at any hour; We were to have remained at Columbus at least 2 nights and a day, but the first morn'g 5 companies had an hours notice to leave at 10; I was much disappointed for I expected to write you and several others long letters from there . . .

Columbus is in many respects a very handsome city, containing about 15,000 inhabitants, and the surrounding country is hilly and very northern in appearance, and quite a treat from our low flat woods. Montgomery is quite a place and very city like and businesslike; I am much pleased with it. We remain here till early to-morrow a.m. As soon as I reach the end of my journey I shall write Davis or you where to direct to me . . . Again let me enjoin upon you to have as little fear as possible for me—I am sorry I can do nothing for you, but must leave it all to Davis and Winston. I shall take the best care of myself. Goodbye again dear mother. Much *very* much love to you all. Tell the boys to continue to try and be men, and *gentlemen*. With true affection

Willie

May 20, 1862. The first thing in the morning saw the smoke of the turpentine burning and thought something unusual was to pay down the river, so Henry went over to see Clark and heard that Winston's company had an engagement *with a gunboat yesterday,* none killed on our side, *the boat turned right back. Winston returned home about the middle of the afternoon, brought a* bomb and a piece of one which burst near him.[49]

[Rebecca] *May 21, 1862. After early breakfast the boys to camp with Winston to bring the boat back. They return about 6 o'clk bringing news that the 3d. Reg. had left and Davis joined a new company commanded by Capt. R. Harrison!*[50] *This deprives me of all hope of seeing him ...*

[WINSTON STEPHENS TO OCTAVIA STEPHENS]

Horse Landing May 23, 1862

My Dear Tivie

Clark comes up and brings you a fine piece of bear that we have just killed. I shot him 8 times and Wm Stevens five, 7 of mine took effect and 3 of his.[51] I suppose the bear will weigh four hundred clean — save the oil for cooking — let the negroes have what you cant consume by the time it will spoil. I dont think I can come up until after Monday as that is about the time the Yankees comes up ... love to all and kiss to Rosa — Your aff husband

Winston Stephens

---

49. The gunboat *Isaac Smith*, with Lieutenant J. W. A. Nicholson in command, was fired on by Winston's company north of Welaka on 19 May. After running aground on 12 May, Nicholson was ordered four days later to proceed upriver above the mouth of Black Creek, where the *Patroon* was anchored, and as much farther south as he thought advisable. On 19 May he had reached a point very near Rose Cottage when about fifty rounds of small-arms fire hit the ship. Although twelve rounds penetrated the bulwarks of the ship and Nicholson raked the woods with grapeshot and explosive shells, no one on either side was injured. The *Isaac Smith* then departed. Winston and his company had survived their first fight. See ORN, ser. 1, vol. 12, 477, 705, 804–6.

50. Captain Robert Harrison was in command of an independent cavalry company that became Company K, Second Florida Cavalry upon the organization of that unit in December 1862. Before the war he had practiced medicine and farmed near Fernandina. Harrison was promoted to major upon the formation of the Second Florida Cavalry Regiment and served for the rest of the war.

51. William B. Stevens was the twenty-three-year-old son of Naaman (Naman) and Susan Stevens, and he served in Winston's company from 1861 to 1862, when he transferred to Company H. Naaman also served in Winston's company as a farrier.

[OCTAVIA STEPHENS TO WINSTON STEPHENS]

May 23, 1862

My dear Winston

I was so glad to get your note this afternoon . . . The bear must have been a noble fellow, for the piece you sent was nearly all fat, could get but little lean . . .

Rosa and I spent yesterday with Tina, I went to help her make Clark some shirts, and we had a very pleasant and cosy time. Little Jane had fever and I left her there over night, and I thought this morning that she had mumps, but as it seems to move to her eye and head now, I think it only cold. Mose has had fever two nights, Sarah is out to day. I tried to get salts from Mr Smith but he had none. I got a bottle Peppermint and one of Carminative, if he should come to you for the money, can you not get salts or oil from your Dr or Palatka? I mixed my last dose of salts for Mose and it was thrown away by accident . . . I shall think of you when I eat the bear meat and hope you are able to enjoy some. Well good night, may angels give you sweeter dreams than I had last night, for I dreamed you were going off somewhere, which I hope will not come true. Rosa kissed me to night for you as usual, so just consider that kiss sent, and one from

Your affectionate Wife

You know who

[Rebecca] *May 24, 1862. . . . Between four and five o'clk p.m. Winston comes home sick. He brings letters from Willie and Davis of old date but most welcome. Davis is stationed between Fernandina and Baldwin. Willie is now I suppose in So. Carolina!*

[JULIA FISHER TO REBECCA BRYANT]

Thomasville May 25, 1862

Dearest Sis:

Do forgive me my long silence: every day I wanted to write and every day pressing duties and immediate cares prevented . . . but dearest you are the only one I have so wholly neglected, . . . but *dear Willie was not,* and my last letter reached him just before he left E. Fla. to come to Mid Fla: a letter from him a few days ago written partly at Columbus, and partly at Montgomery says my letter "inspired and nerved him, as my letters always did," and I was thankful it reached him in time: *God bless our dear boy:* he was on his way to Corinth to join Beauregard as you will have heard ere this . . . I do not know the name of his company or Capt, only that it is the Fla regiment. I will find out, and I mean to write him *at once,* I tried to get others to take hold and form a society for the relief of the sick soldiers:⁵² all held back, so I got the girls together, sent them out as *agents,* and weekly they meet at my house, and bring supplies . . . we have sent lots of supplies to different Hospitals, and I have made appointments to meet ladies at important points through the country on the rail road at stated times, and send supplies . . . people all seem willing and glad to assist me . . . we have two rooms fitted up lately opposite my house for passing sick soldiers, and friends send me in supplies, and I see that they are attended to, and if I need help, call upon my neighbors . . .

Willie wrote me . . . [that] he might I suppose, have been 2nd. Lieutenant: he also told me that he could have accepted offers and remained at home, *I glory in his determination,* though I pity you, and suffer for him: poor old Mother too feel it keenly: but dearest, though I know "the applause of the world" could not repay you or him, as you say, for one pang, yet there is a principle allied to our very religion: a spirit that lifts us above all common ties and affections: life is a little sacrifice, but we offer *more than this* the dearest hopes and affections of life upon and for this principle: *honor and liberty:* I would rather my boys should *die* in such a cause than *live to witness its defeat:* God grant they may never suffer *that,* the keenest and severest pang their proud heart could suffer. It may seem almost presumptuous what I have been and still am attempting, but the work fell into my hands; I am a thankful willing instrument, and I should feel that my life and labors were *well* paid for, if I only lived long enough to know that our liberty was won: I will not neglect other duties, Mother and my little ones here, but I am willing to suffer and *die* if it can only aid what is a cause of far more importance: a cause the success of which would counterbalance the suffering of this generation for the sake of the next: you could give your children up to *God:* and your country *is next to your God:* in my heart they seem connected: no other love would cause me to yield that: yet I pity *a Mothers's heart:* it *is* hard: but are you not willing to suffer if need be, rather than lose *all? dear Tivie too:* but tell the darling child since she cannot *change* the facts; to meet them boldly as she can since they *must be met,* let us thank God *our men do not shrink* and we will not *for their dear sakes.* I trust Davis will accept if he can get any honorable position at home, I would have been glad if Willie had, yet I glory in his spirit: Winston too, I earnestly echo your prayer, *may he be spared many years to you.*

You said in one letter something about your not being able to do much good now etc, and my being useful: dear Sis, I realize *all the time* that though God uses me as an active instrument often in his hands, I effect less *real* good than *you*

---

52. Julia created a Ladies Aid Society whose members worked to relieve the conditions in Confederate hospitals. She was unflagging in her efforts, and her work eventually came to the attention of high Confederate officials, including Jefferson Davis. In addition, she taught school and took care of her mother, who was ill and in her seventies at the time. An ardent rebel, she was soon to denounce her brother James Bryant for his Unionist stance.

have *always accomplished:* your quiet, steady influence, your patient fortitude, and cheerful submission always heretofore, now you are sorely tried, yet you will come out of the furnace like gold, while I hurry away, life and labor on in the midst of a thousand thoughts that only *busy,* do not *sanctify my heart,* you turn in solitude *to God,* and are daily growing nearer to him; while I benefit some, I offend some and for every word of praise given, I know I have one of criticism if not condemnation: *I do not admire or like myself,* yet I must fulfil my destiny, and carry out (like William) my strong angelic impulses: You darling are like *a perpetual sweet incense* though burning, yet always fragrant still, our darling blessed little Ruby. Mother sends much love . . .

[Julia]

May 26, 1862. *Winston the same . . . Dr. Meredith and Clark came in the afternoon . . .*

[Rebecca] **May 27, 1862.** *While at breakfast Joe returns with my letters, did not reach town till Mr. Smith had* left. *Dr. M. goes to camp and they are sent by him to be forwarded by first opportunity. Winston better.*

[Rebecca] **June 1, 1862.** *Morning extremely warm, at 4 ½ o'clk Winston and Henry with two negroes leave for the camp . . .*

[OCTAVIA STEPHENS TO WINSTON STEPHENS]

Rose Cottage June 8, 1862

My dear Husband

. . . Georgie has had two fevers. And Sarah is sick or has been, perhaps she'll be up tomorrow, the rest all well. Have we not had some nice rains? I think the corn looks much better, oh I tell you we will make lots of eatables. What do you think I did, I staid with Tina two days and a night. Mother spent the first day with us. we had a cosy time of it, we sat up that night only until nearly one talking of old times . . .

Mother is very low spirited this morning, she just sits down and thinks worse than I have ever seen her. I dont see any prospect of peace being made in June . . . Rosa has just given me a hug and a kiss for you. Mr Bright has not brought the beef yet and we are about out.[53] I hope you will bring the deer you promised to kill for me. All join in love to you, wish to see you.

Affectionately

Tivie

53. George W. Bright, a Welaka blacksmith, was also a small rancher and farmer. In 1860 he owned 40 milk cows, 90 beef cattle, and more than 100 hogs. See Eighth Census of the United States, 1860, Schedule IV, Putnam County.

[Rebecca] *June 9, 1862.* . . . *A letter comes from Winston reporting a fight at Richmond which lasted 3 days, the Confederates drove the Federals back 3 miles with a loss of 75,000! Our loss about 15,000. The contest to be renewed when they had buried the dead.*[54]

[Rebecca] *June 12, 1862. A fine day. Mrs Stephens and family pass the day here. While at dinner Davis gives us a delightful surprise! He brings a letter from Willie written on 14th May at Montgomery Ala. on his way to Corinth which he expects to reach in a week.*

[WINSTON STEPHENS TO OCTAVIA STEPHENS]

Horse Landing June 12, 1862

My dear Wife

. . . I send you an article cut from Savannah paper, written by your Aunt Julia. You can see what a true Woman can do when necessary. I glory in such material but I can feel for your Mother and all the family—but a Traitor should be spurned no matter what the ties. You shall hear from me as soon as I come back. Your Loving husband

Winston Stephens

Savannah Republican Friday May 30, 1862[55]

Mr. Editor

In your last issue, I see a communication under the head of "Florida News" in which it remarks that, "J. W. Bryant, formerly a lawyer of Jacksonville, and subsequently editor of the *Cuban Messenger,* now Federal Military Governor of Florida was on one of the gunboats." If this be true, I desire to state that an old white haired mother, now over three score years and ten, of whom he was the pride and idol in former times, and sisters, who once loved him with the fondest devotion, now utterly denounce him forever! At such a crisis the offending "right eye" shall be *utterly plucked*

---

54. This was the Battle of Seven Pines or Fair Oaks, 31 May–1 June 1862. Major General George B. McClellan's peninsula campaign began in March 1862, and by May, his 105,000-man Army of the Potomac was in sight of Richmond. When he reached the Chickahominy River, McClellan divided his army, and the Confederates under the command of General Joseph E. Johnston struck the smaller portion during the afternoon of 31 May. The Union forces retreated, and the battle resumed the next day. Johnston was wounded, and General Robert E. Lee took command of the Army of Northern Virginia. About 42,000 men from each side were engaged in this battle; the Federals took 5,031 casualties, and the Confederates suffered 6,134. Lee launched the "seven days campaign" (25 June–1 July), drove McClellan away from Richmond, and ended the Federal peninsula campaign for good.

55. Julia Fisher's letter appeared on the front page, column two.

out, the right hand cut off *though it should cost our life*. The family that would have but clung the more closely to him in our hour of adversity, repudiate him now, and with him, the dark shadow of infamy he would cast! There is a higher principle than human love of life honor and liberty. On that principle, we will sacrifice not only life but all the hopes that make life dear.

For the sake of his relations, I desire to state that he has two sons, and an only son-in-law, fighting in the Confederate service. They will, if such a thing be possible, atone for his deriliction.

Justice

Thomasville, May 27, 1862.[56]

[WILLIE BRYANT TO DAVIS BRYANT]

Mobile, Ala. June 15, 1862

Dear Davis,

... The Mobile papers copied a paragraph from the Savannah Rep. a short time since mentioning the expedition of the Yankees up the St. Johns and their being fired into by Stephen's co. and that J. W. Bryant, Federal governor of Fla. was with them; letters too from Fla. have stated that Father was with the Yankees; I of course feel sure that Father has taken advantage of an opportunity offered by their gunboats to get home and the fact of his being on board being known has given rise to this story; but ... since I have been without any letters all this time, and until now have heard nothing to relieve or cheer me, but young Scott recd. a letter from his mother at Jacksonville saying that Father had come to Jvlle and been refused permission to land and that he had afterward gone up the river and the boat fired into and he had then rtd. to J'ville;[57] I truly hope I may *sometime or other* get a letter giving a true and full statement of the matter and that I may be able to vindicate his character; I have spoken to almost all whose opinion I cared a straw for and none of them believed the statement to be correct, but Father is so widely known and the report has had such an extensive circulation that it will at least injure his reputation; I wrote the folks at Thomasville

---

56. The charge that J. W. Bryant was the Federal military governor of Florida was of course false since no such position existed, but the accusation was carried in a number of out-of-state newspapers during late May and early June 1862. See, for example, the *Milledgeville (Georgia) Southern Federal Union*, 3 June 1862. That paper reported not only that Bryant was the military governor but also that Winston's company had fired upon the gunboat he was on. While not true, this report was surprisingly close to the truth. Had the *Isaac Smith* not run aground on 12 May, the engagement reported by Tivie in her diary on 20 May would probably have occurred a week earlier, and her father would have been on board.

57. Either Private Edmund G. Scott or his brother, James E. Scott; both served in Company H for the rest of the war. Mrs. Scott was correct in saying that J. W. Bryant had been to Jacksonville.

soon after I saw the account. It does seem as if Father is doomed to be tortured to death by misfortunes of every kind. I have written Mother several letters since leaving Fla . . . I am low spirited and gloomy beyond measure, and have been so for some time, and unless I can find some way to rouse myself and be interested, I don't know what in thunder I will turn into, but I feel that if I could only get some good letters I should be able to cheer up some.

Thro' the means of the Gov. of Alabama we have been stopped and retained in this state, and attached to the "Army of Mobile," and will be, I suppose 'till Mobile is attacked or the danger over; we are very well situated 2 ½ miles from the center of the city, and the ration list is pretty good, but the duties are pretty tough for this warm weather; I ought to be very well satisfied to remain here, but I am tired of the monotony of this d——d camp life, have no social associations which I really enjoy, and I want to be where there is something to encourage and stimulate a man; I'll swear I pine for it, and it is playing the devil with my disposition; I must have active employment and the excitement to live, and I wonder that I have not sought after it in an artificial way, but my morals have been better since leaving Fla. than ever before; temptations have of course been more numerable, but I have not felt the inclination to yield . . .

The ladies are pretty, but have very genteel manners and appearance: they are as numerous as blackbirds, and late in the afternoon walk out in crowds; but I am surprised to hear so little music; there is quite a pretty little park in the best of order, which is a great resort and very pleasant. The ladies here are very kind to soldiers. I have attended church twice, but the walk is too long and hot to go often. I must undoubtedly hear from you soon and will write again, for the present good bye . . .

Yrs Always affectionately
Willie

June 16, 1862. Rain most of the day. Winston came home in the afternoon from a scout to Blk Creek, in a hard rain. Rosa had fever.

June 18, 1862. Davis left us directly after breakfast to return to his company. The boys went fishing in the morning. Winston left us for his camp late in the afternoon . . .

June 30, 1862. Winston left us for camp in the morning and from there is to go near Jacksonville in a few days with his company.

[Rebecca] June 30, 1862. . . . Henry goes to town for mail in the afternoon — brings me a letter from Julia which causes me much unhappiness

from the allusion to a piece she has published renouncing her brother for his political course!!

[Rebecca] *July 1, 1862*. . . . . Tivie and I pass a lonely day—she in the knowledge that her husband is leaving for a long time and I not knowing what will become of mine in this new and bitterest trial!

[Rebecca] *July 4, 1862*. The anniversary of American Independence—Oh that it might be celebrated by the acknowledgement of the Independence of the S. Confederacy—Sarah gave birth to a fine girl this morng. about 6 o'clk. Mother and Child doing well.[58]

[OCTAVIA STEPHENS TO WINSTON STEPHENS]

Rose Cottage July 6, 1862

My dear Husband

. . . I have been (not quite "head over heels") in beef, but most all hands have been busy all day with the beef trying to save it. there was so much of it and so many different parts to cook at once that we have had our hands and pots full. I have just a little while since taken off one big pot full of bones and put on another . . . I did not weigh it as Burrel began on it before I was up, suppose it made no difference as the price was set, it was a tremendous one, the hind quarter that Clark took weighed 96 lbs, I sent Tina a basket full of bones this morning as I had more than I could possibly save as they were spoiling. I hope I will be able to save the beef. I had it out doors most of the morning but rain, or a good sprinkle made us take it in in a hurry and it has not rained to day . . . but how long I am coming to the good news, now dont shout when I tell you that you are a negro and colt better off than when you left. yes Sarah gave birth to a little girl on the morning of the 4th of July after a *whole night* of *hard* labour . . .

Pet's colt was born last night. Burrel says tell you that you have a fine colt here and he thinks you'll be so proud when you come home you wont know what to do. I dont know whether it is a *boy or girl* . . .

You must not stay off too long. You did not make me any *promises* before you left. I'll promise to be a *good girl* . . . I hope it will not be long before we will see you, please dont get to kicking too hard against orders and get carried to Tallahassee or be Court Martialed or anything of that sort. Rosa sends a kiss. Ever aff-ly

Your Wife

---

58. Sarah named her daughter Mary Polly.

[WINSTON STEPHENS TO OCTAVIA STEPHENS]

Camp Hateley July 6, 1862.[59]

My Dear Wife

You will see that I have arrived in Camps all O.K. My Camp is nearest Jacksonville and I am in two miles. I have a beautiful camp ground, but the water is not so good... The Regiment or a part of it is in half mile with a branch between us and Capt Row has part of his command near the Regiment but on the other side of the road. We number but 420 men and Capt Chambers is about four miles farther out but he is going up to Magnolia.[60] We have the most glorious news of the whole war on the arrival of the Cars yesterday, I saw the Confederate flag flying and thought something good was coming and sure enough. We have whiped the Yankees at Richmond capturing 30 thousand and no telling how many killed and McLelland had asked Lee for an armistice of two days to bury the dead and Lee had replied, let the dead bury the dead, the only proposition I will listen to is an unconditional surrender.[61] I say well done Genl Lee, as the object was to gain time and get away and our good brave Genl has defeated his army and has now defeated his cuning and will likely capture the whole army...

Give much love to Mother and the boys also to Clark and family. Kiss Dear Rosa and accept as many as you wish from your Old Man

Winston Stephens

[REBECCA BRYANT TO DAVIS BRYANT]

Rose Cottage July 13, 1862

My dear Davis,

...I recd. a letter from Willie... I am very impatient to hear from him again as he had not then recd. a word from us, but had seen the notice copied from the Sav. Republican of your father's being Mil. Gov. of Fla. and was in a dreadful state of suspense, though he did not credit the report... I did not *then* know of Aunt Julia's published renunciation, but the eveg. of the day my letter went off, I

---

59. This camp was initially named for Colonel John C. Hateley of the Fifth Florida Infantry, but it was renamed Camp Stephens for Winston around the middle of July 1862. Apparently it was about two miles west of Jacksonville on the north side of the railroad.

60. Captains Samuel F. Rowe (also spelled Rou) and William E. Chambers commanded independent cavalry companies that became Companies F and C, respectively, of the Second Florida Cavalry when that unit was organized in December 1862.

61. The "seven days campaign" was one of the worst weeks of the war. Confederate losses totaled 20,141 with 3,286 killed, 15,909 wounded, and 946 missing. The Federal total was 15,849 (1,734 killed, 8,062 wounded, and 6,053 missing). Contrary to the news Winston received, Lee had sustained a bloody defeat at Malvern Hill on 1 July, the last battle of the campaign.

recd. one from her in extenuation of her course, which she thought I would deem too severe. It seems from that that Willie wrote to her about the same time he wrote to me, but had not seen *her* publication. She wrote to him immediately and, I suppose, in the same strain that she wrote me. If he receives hers before he hears any thing from us contradictory of that statement, it will add greatly to his distress. In *any event* he will be deeply mortified by it, and I feel more on his account than my own, because he is so far from us all and has not the consolation of our sympathy, or the means of knowing what we know. I hope you have written encouragingly, or rather that you have written so particularly about your father's visit to the river that he will be comforted.

I suppose you must have done so when here or at Jacksonville, because Tivie tells me you saw Aunt J—'s paragraph while you were here. I wish I could send you her letter. It cost her a great deal of suffering to publish her renunciation, but her zeal for the cause she has so warmly espoused led her to believe it necessary. I shall never cease to regret the step even if she retracts it—It was entirely too hasty and was *in any circumstances,* uncalled for. I replied to her letter last week. She wrote me that almost every one about her knew the strong affection she entertained for her brother and therefore "watched and doubted." In reply I asked her if she could not for his sake bear to be watched and doubted until she could learn *the truth* from us—that she knew that she could *live down* the suspicion, but that the infamy of his mother's renunciation would cling to him long after this cruel war was ended and he was in his grave. I told her that I presumed she was excited to it by the fanatacism of those around her—that I believed *I* understood her feelings perfectly, but I feared others would not. She mentioned that she feared she shd. lose a portion of the love that I and all my children had for her—But I told her that she wd. not, certainly so long as she evinced the loving spirit she did for us, I thanked her again warmly for her kindness to Willie, (she sent him a small sum of money and intended sending more . . .) and I told her that Tivie said *you* expressed yourself about the matter precisely as I did. She had been most terribly provoked by an Editor in Thomasville who published the most shameful falsehoods about your father and she went to him accompanied by an influential gentleman friend of hers and told him that if he published any more she would *certainly kill him*—that although she had renounced her brother *politically,* no one should censure him falsely and live. This she says she "regretted, *as a christian,* but could not recall it, for she *meant* it." And she says many christians sustained her in it. The world generally will not make the distinction she does between renouncing him *politically* and entirely—because she says it is "forever," in her paragraph. And if it should come to your father's eye, as it doubtless will or has I do not know what the consequence will be—I sometimes fear he will leave the country altogether and not allow us to know where he goes—I have, at times, the most dreadful apprehensions of its effect upon him and long to be able to say one word of comfort and love—But weeks must pass before I know the result. My only trust is in Him who can give us all strength to bear our trials if we will ask it in the right spirit. And we know my dear Davis, that all these events are ordered by Him, and are designed for our future welfare—*He* cannot err, let us try to profit by the chastisements He sends. I feel certain that your father would give us satisfactory reasons for the course he has pursued, if he could freely communicate with us, and I wrote this to your Aunt Julia—I also wrote the substance of his letter to you—It is *possible* she may retract what she has published, since she prefaced her renunciation with the words, "if this be true"—I think she ought to do so, but I fear there are many who saw it who will never know that it was unmerited.

Winston is now near Jacksonville at Camp Finnegan, he left us a fortnight since[62]—I gave him your address and hope he has written you . . .

Much love from Henry, George and Mother—Do you not think the War will be ended and our army disbanded by the middle of October? Even that time seems to be an age to wait for. But we will try to be patient as the signs of the times are brightening . . .

That God will protect and bless you is my constant prayer
Mother

[WILLIE BRYANT TO REBECCA BRYANT]

Mobile Ala. July 13, 1862

My dear Mother,

Again have I allowed too long a time to elapse without writing you, and again conscience smitten take up my pen; I have had every reason to suppose that each succeeding day would bring me full intelligence of Father, and waiting in the vain hope, with my mind so full of it, time has slipped imperceptably by, and . . . now I must write with my mind in a state of much doubt and anxiety . . .

I have rec'd but two letter from Davis . . . These two letters contained accounts of Father's arrival, and tho' they contain nothing to cheer me, would have afforded me much relief from doubt. A strange fatalety attends all my letters from Fla, and only mine, some rascal is undoubtly at the bottom of some of it

---

62. Camp Finegan, named for General Joseph Finegan, was the principal Confederate camp in East Florida. Located about seven miles west of Jacksonville, south of the line of the railroad, on the high ground just south of present-day Marietta between the north fork of Wills Branch on the west and Cedar Creek on the east, it was home to infantry, artillery, and cavalry units simultaneously at various times. Winston, however, was at Camp Hateley rather than Camp Finegan. When he left Rose Cottage on 30 June, he told Tivie he was going to Camp Finegan and probably reported there only to be ordered to Hateley. As is obvious here, by 13 July Tivie and Rebecca did not know where he was, and two days later, on 15 July, Tivie had not received Winston's letter of 6 July informing her of his change of camp. This is a good example of the difficulty people had in communicating with each other even when they were not far apart.

and I truly wish that he may suffer double the amount of crushing thoughts and anxieties that I have endured for the past two months.

I do not know how to write you about Father, my spirit is so weighed down by the sad circumstances attending him, and would not do so did I not feel that I should. I learn enough from . . . Davis' letter to assure me that tho' he is not actively engaged against the South, and the Cause I love dearer than life, still, he is with the enemy in feeling, and hopelessly committed to them, and of course I cannot retain my former feelings of unalloyed affection towards him, but still I revert with satisfaction and pleasure to thoughts of the kind, instructive father he was to me, and the generous, high-minded, energetic, public-spirited, and sympathising man to the world, and regret with keen anguish that he has blindly pursued a course against all that he should hold most dear, and which will undoubtedly be a finishing blow to prevent entirely the social enjoyments among his family and friends, which he has so hoped for, for his latter days, and for which he has so untiringly striven to attain for so many years, against innumerable and almost overpowering disappointments and misfortunes; I can see nothing cheering for him in the prospect of the future;—I will add no more! few have suffered more than our family by this unnatural and horrible war, this is a tirrible blow, and I would have parted with life, O, so willingly, to have averted it . . .

I hope Winston is getting along well and near you, tell him to be vigilant, we won't be obliged to stick this out very much longer. Much love to Tivie—the dear old lady! and that blessed little one of hers with those bright eyes, and funny little mouth; she must be very interesting now; much love, and a hearty how-dye to the boys, no longer the "little boys," and tell them to be manly and industrious; and to you, dearest of mothers, an ocean of love, and a thousand of kisses, from your "soldier boy" who desires to live to prove that he loves you more and more as he becomes able to appreciate you; God bless you all, and grant us peace at last is my prayer—Ever affectionately,

Willie—

Monday morn'g—

. . . I have rec'd letters from Several tho' all quite old. I have yours written by Davis and a P.S. added by him at J'vlle and am delighted to know he had been able to visit you—I think with you, that Father is conscientious and hopes to effect some good by his course but he has certainly pursued one injurious to himself and will never be able to make his peace with the South and be able to live among them as he would wish . . . My letters this morning have raised me from a dull gloomy and desponding state and I now have a comparatively light heart, I am happy in knowing you are so well and comfortable—

Good bye again—With much love
Yrs always affectionately
Willie—

[OCTAVIA STEPHENS TO WINSTON STEPHENS]

Rose Cottage July 15, 1862

My dear Husband

... Oh I do want you home so much I dont get used to your being away at all, I feel lonely with out you and cross and good for nothing, seems to me I did not see hardly anything of you when you were home last, as you were sick and I was thinking so much all the time of your going away that I could not talk much to you.

I have just given Jane and Jesse a *dressing* for their impudence and behaviour yesterday while I was away,[63] every time I leave home Mother has trouble with them, but I never thought much of it, but this time I had told Jess to keep away from the house, but he came up and troubled so that Mother threatened that if he did so again she would whip him if no one else would, and he sat on the front fence and said he wasn't afraid of Miss Bryant. whenever Mother tells Jane to do anything Jane looks as though she could bite her head off, I think the negroes do not like at all having my folks here ...

Mother received letters from Willie and Davis yesterday. Willie was still in Mobile. Davis wants your address, I suppose his is the same, but he heads his letter "Camp Cooper."[64] Mother wants to know the name of the commanding officer at Jacksonville and if there is any communication now with the Gunboats by flag of truce. Do you ever go to Jacksonville? if you do *beware* and dont go to see pretty girls too often ...

Did you remember your birthday when it came ... ? 33 years old, what an old man you are getting to be. Dont you feel old? You appear much older than you did a year ago ...

Well I guess I will stop now. With a great deal of love I am

As ever

Yr loving Wife,

---

63. This is the only time that Tivie recorded that she had whipped any of the slaves, and it is doubtful that she would have tried to whip any of the adults. Winston probably used the lash, as almost all slave owners did, but there is no reference to this in any of the correspondence.

64. Camp Cooper was named for James G. Cooper, a major general in the Florida militia. He and Joseph Finegan represented Nassau County as delegates to the secession convention. The letters from Davis, and later from Winston after he was located there, together with a military report by Union Major Galusha Pennypacker (OR, sec. 1, vol. 14, 358), place Camp Cooper on the west side of Harts Road (approximately the line of present-day US 17), one mile north of the Harts Road railroad junction, present-day Yulee.

[WINSTON STEPHENS TO OCTAVIA STEPHENS]

Camp Hately July 15, 1862

My Dear Tivie

I have not rec'd a line yet, but I feel sure you have written and I am waiting patiently for it to turn up in Camps . . .

I would give a great deall to be with you and pass a few days if no more, but I must not indulge in having the hope of a Furlough for some time yet, and when I come I will be able to stay longer, be careful of your health during the warm months and walk every day . . . It is rumored that two more Regiments are ordered out of the State, the 8th and 5th, which will leave in the State only the Independent companies.[65] It appears the intention of Genl. Finegan [is] to abandon the State, but as long as they allow the Companies the independence to act We will keep them out of the State, or at least try[66] . . . I have had some trouble with one or two men about getting whiskey, one came in yesterday while I was in Town and cussed Lt Gray and he struck at him and crippled another man who tried to ward off the blow. I have had the man grubbing all the morning and think they will do better in the future. I have made Swep 2nd Corpl . . . We get a plenty of corn and our horses are improving. I hope we will have fodder on the train to day.

What kind of people live at the Crespo House?[67] I had to go in there to receive the money for the men and I rather think from appearances that *things* are conducted rather *loosely* as they were *very familier* with some of the *male gender,* some of them are good looking and rather facinating to some but I am all right and you may rest easy, but I think some wives are cheated of some affection and attention they should have. Man and Woman are both frail beings and weak in that particular point, but I know our union will never be disturbed or jared in that way and oh how thankful I am that I have a wife I can trust any where. I have seen so much of that kind of weakness that I am disposed to suspect, but with you I have perfect confidence and it would require a great deall to shake it, but I suppose if once shaken would never be restored, and I hope we will avoid

---

65. The Fifth and Eighth Florida Infantry Regiments departed for Virginia and, along with the Second Florida Infantry Regiment, fought in every major battle from Second Bull Run (29–30 August 1862) to the surrender at Appomattox (12 April 1865).

66. Brigadier General Joseph Finegan assumed the command of Middle and East Florida in April 1862, replacing Brigadier General James H. Trapier. Finegan was born in Ireland in 1814, came to Jacksonville during the 1830s, and built a sawmill there. He later moved to Fernandina, practiced law, and became a business partner of David Levy Yulee in building the Florida Railroad before the war. In October 1862 his command was reduced to the District of East Florida; he had very few troops to deal with Federal naval raids along the coast and was unable to offer any resistance to any serious invasion.

67. The Crespo House in Jacksonville was a hotel at the corner of Adams and Ocean Streets and was apparently a house of prostitution at this time.

any thing to cause suspicion. I want Joe to watch the mules when burrel is done working them, all the spare time I want the negroes to do some kind of work such as the mill, the new ground and fencing, scraping the lots for manure etc so as to keep them busy. I expect to live at that place next year and want arrangements made to suit. I will stop as you will be tired of this scribble. love to Clark and family and mother and boys. I remain your loving and aff husband

Winston Stephens

[WINSTON STEPHENS TO OCTAVIA STEPHENS]

Camp Stephens July 24, 1862

My Darling Wife

... I am well and my Company are in reasonable health. I returned from Tallahassee yesterday and find that we are certainly to be formed into a regiment but the Genl assures us we are not to go out of the State. I cant tell what is the programe, but it has appeared to me lately that the object was to abandon the State to its fate and make a strong and determined stand near the border and especially near Richmond. We gained a Glorious Victory at Richmond but not such a success as we were led to believe at first ... We are getting all the advantages in the late battles. Maj Genl Polk [sic] is chief in Command of the Northern forces and McLelland is in Command only of one division.[68] This is going to act in our favor as it will get them to quarrelling among themselves—but I fear we are to have a few more hard fought battles ... I will be up soon and will not send you any money as I will bring it. I am a good boy and will be. Love to all and Kiss Rosa and accept all you wish from your Very aff husband. how dee to Burrel and the rest, Good bye and God bless and protect you all.

Winston Stephens

[OCTAVIA STEPHENS TO WINSTON STEPHENS]

Rose Cottage July 27, 1862

My own dear husband

... I am not surprised to hear that you are to be joined to a regiment, for I have expected it for a long time, but I am vexed at it, the next thing you will be in Tennesee or Virginia. I am sorry you think we are yet to have more fighting for I

---

68. Major General John Pope was given command of the newly created Army of Virginia. McClellan was reduced in rank from general in chief of all Union forces to commander of the Army of the Potomac in July 1862, and Major General Henry W. Halleck became general in chief. Pope was defeated by Lee at Second Bull Run, 29–30 August, and the armies were once again under the command of McClellan as Lee undertook the first invasion of the Union in September 1862.

was in hopes that this last great battle was the last, and that it would not be very long before matters would be settled, and I have you at home. I think the Yankees, English, and all ought now to be satisfied . . .

I hope our letters will now go and come as quick as our last came. I am astonished at your going to Crespo's. I think you must have been bad off to go to those Minorcans for pity sake dont go there again. I think it very queer that you [and] the pay master went there, for your sake as well as mine dont get your name out for going to such places. I am glad to hear that you are a good boy so far, but dont stay until the temptation gets too strong to be a bad boy, what *I* call a *bad boy*, if you are ever tempted remember what you have told your little wife, remember your oath as you have called it. I pray almost daily that you may not be tempted, but may ever be true to me as I to you, that is all I ask when you know from my own actions and words that I am untrue to you, then you can act as you please, as you say I hope there may never be anything to cause suspicion of either of us. I guess this war has been the cause of many being tempted who would not have otherwise been, but if my dear husband comes out clear I shall not care for others, whatever you do dont deceive me, but let me know all, men are more "frail" in that particular than women . . .

Rosa has kissed me for Pa Pa. Good bye I hope to see you very soon. Ever your loving

Wife Tivie

[REBECCA BRYANT TO DAVIS BRYANT]

Rose Cottage July 27, 1862

My Dear Davis

. . . a short letter from Aunt Julia . . . enclosing one from Col Dilworth in reply to hers requesting him in case anything shd. happen to Willie, saying he was one of the best young men he ever knew[69]—After enumerating his many good qualities, he winds up by saying that "he is respected by all as a gentleman and a soldier . . ." A sister-in-law of your Captain Harrison called to see Aunt J— a short time since and spoke of you as being a great favorite of Capt H—. She said that he had said he had never felt so much interest in any young man before. You may be assured that such expressions about my sons from those who have an opportunity of knowing them and whose position gives weight to their opinion is very gratifying to me and I fully appreciate the treasure I possess in my children . . .

---

69. Colonel W. S. Dilworth commanded the Third Florida Infantry Regiment until the end of the war. Dilworth was a planter from Jefferson County; in 1860 he owned forty-six slaves, which he valued at $48,150, and real estate worth $25,000. Originally from Georgia, he and his wife, listed as C. Dilworth, had three young children at that time.

I have spent nearly all my Sabbath in writing—"these things ought not so to be . . ." I intend in future to write on Saturday and add P.S. on Sunday . . .

Much, much love from all—Yrs. most fondly
Mother

[WINSTON STEPHENS TO OCTAVIA STEPHENS]

Camp Stephens July 27, 1862

My Darling Wife

. . . My position as Commander of this Post is an unenviable one as . . . some days Ladies that appear to have seen better days come out and beg for something to eat, and the Government feeds so scanty since we have been down here that I have to refuse them, as my men barely get enough, we spare them a little corn and that is about all. I go in Town very frequently on business connected with my Command, but not on pleasure . . . I think some of my mess mates like to go to Town to see the pretty faces of some of the Girls, but your old man has other fish to fry, in fact he is getting too *old* for *such things,* 33 think of it! I do feel old but hope I'll not be discarded on account of my age as it was known some time ago. I was really so busy that the 13th passed by without my thinking of it so that expecting of it did not make me feel older . . .

Tell Mother that no communication is allowed with the Gun boat unless they should come up under flag of truce, then I would receive them and could send off a letter. No boat is allowed to go to them unless Genl Finegan should send to them on special business, if she sends a letter I will get it off if a chance presents itself. I may go over to Augustine under flag of truce and could send it then. I am glad you mustered courage enough to whip Jess and Jane and hope you will not allow them to suffer so long any more without correction, whip them to hurt and you will not be troubled to repeat the dose often. My Dear ride as often as you wish and when the colt gets a little older I had rather you would ride Pet but I do hope you will take exercise on foot, as it is better for you in your situation, please walk some every evening and ride when you please . . .[70]

My Wife you dont want me home more than I want to come home sometimes I am tempted to quit any how but that will not do as long as I can help it. They talk of putting us in a regiment, if they do the men have determined to run me for one of the field Officers, but I am trying to prevent it as I dont want the position. I will come up I expect before we are formed into a regiment. Capt Dunham will be here soon with his Artilery Company—Give much love to Mother and the

70. Tivie was pregnant with her second child, Isabella Gertrude.

boys and Clark and family[71] . . . Give My Darling Rosa a thousand kisses and then she can help you to as many as you wish—I remain as ever your devoted

Husband

Winston Stephens

[JULIA FISHER TO REBECCA BRYANT]

July [?], 1862

I found your letter awaiting me last night. I would not open it, till today when I was rested and calm enough to read it. I dread the keen pangs that at times pass like a flash through my very heart: You are a *dear, kind, forgiving angel*: while I acknowledge I have been, even as you say, harsh and hasty, yet looking back I see no other way I could have done, but I did not expect your love would or could survive it: my darling sister, I love and honor you for your devotion to Wm. God bless you for it: if I were his wife I should do so too, though I might think him wrong: but I feel now, as at first *keenly*, that he has inflected a grievous wrong on all his family, and that the "harsh and hasty" measures I took, *he forced me to take in self defense*: It was unnatural *in a sister,* as many of my friends say, but I had to choose between him and what I conscientiously believe to be right: my prompt acknowledgement of my position and feelings, saved me and the family *here* at least, from being compromised: It was *himself,* not me, that gave his enemies the power over him: he must have known the consequences: still if he is not Gov of Fla, my remarks had not force: *"if this be true"* I put in italics; a saving clause I do not want forgotten: but oh how much he caused all to suffer; and why is he on the other side *at all?* Still, dear sister, do not let me hurt you, in seeking to justify myself: I suffer continually in remembrance of what I have done, yet though seemingly harsh [and] hasty and I allow unnatural, I believe I did what was for the best, and right: only I regret that I even took any position that compelled me publicly to avow my opinions: I wish both had died before we were this opposed for the first time in life . . .

[Julia]

71. Captain Joseph L. Dunham commanded Company A of the Milton Light Artillery. Before the war Dunham had been a prominent merchant-banker in Apalachicola, Franklin County.

[WINSTON STEPHENS TO OCTAVIA STEPHENS]

Camp Stephens July 31, 1862.

My Darling Wife

... this morning the Two Gun boats made there appearance again and ran up in some half or ¾ of a mile of Town with Decks clear, guns run out and every thing ready for action and your old man on the wharf with 17 men armed and some few without guns. *bless Genl Finegan* he has not arrived until in the past few hours some guns arrived. Its a shame and if I am treated so again I will throw up my Commission and come home. The Gun boats left after spending a few hours looking at us. I hope they may come after we get ready for them. The Artilery Company will arrive tomorrow and they have good guns ... Love to all I am yours always. God bless you ...

Winston

[OCTAVIA STEPHENS TO WINSTON STEPHENS]

Welaka Aug 3, 1862

My very dear Husband

... What will you *think* when I tell you that I am again at Clark's I was sent for again last night to come over to day and help eat another turkey, and as Mother thought it would do me good to come I came. I wished for you heartily when I was enjoying a piece of the fine gobler. oh if you could only come home and stay. I was so glad to get your loving letter the other night, I was just sitting down to supper table when I saw Mose coming grinning with a letter in his hand, I hardly dared think it was from you until I saw the hand writing ...

I believe all is going on as well as usual at home, Rosa is very well, but just as full of mischief as she can be, so you may expect to hear me scold at her pretty well when you come, she is forever into mischief her tongue is going the whole time. Sarah came up yesterday and cooked, her baby seems to be very good. Mother was sick two days last week but seems well again, seems to me I am good for nothing, just a ride to town and back nearly laid me up, I could not sleep and was almost sick the next day ... Burrel has 18 shoats in the river field, he and Henry had a hunt for the others yesterday but could not find them. I must close. Do come as soon as you can, you dont know how much I want to see you. Goodbye my dear ...

Ever your loving
Wife Tivie

[WINSTON STEPHENS TO OCTAVIA STEPHENS]

Camp Stephens Aug 4, 1862

My Darling Wife

As Felix starts up to Welaka in the morning I will write you by him instead of the mail. Felix comes up to see his wife.[72] I did not tell him how bad she was but have assisted him in getting off as he could be mail carrier as well as visit his family. I am well and the health of the company as good as usual... Genl Finegan is to pay us a visit this week and arrange things generally, the Artilery Company (Capt Dunham) arrived a few days ago and stoped out 7 miles from Town. Captain Richard arrived today and camped in half mile of me.[73] I hope the intention is to block the game on the Gun boats and not allow them to come up this high... I cant tell when I will get off. I can allow others to go but cant allow myself to go, as the regulations specify that the Commander of a Post must not be absent but 7 days at a time and I could not come home in that time, but I expect to be relieved of the Command in a short time and I will be glad to get rid of the responsability...

... Love to Mother boys and Clark and family. Howdy to negroes. Kiss Rosa and accept much love from your old Man.

Winston

[OCTAVIA STEPHENS TO WINSTON STEPHENS]

Rose Cottage Aug 7, 1862

"My own love"

I have just finished my breakfast and sit down to begin my letter as I expect Tina over this morning and I want to write as much as possible this morning... We are all about the same as usual. Henry complains a good deal, Mother thinks it on account, or connected with his voice changing as that has been the case for some little time, he has taken medicine two or three times, but seems the same, complains of his head. I have felt better the past two days than I have for sometime.

Rosa is sitting by me rocking and making believe that a piece of paper she has is a letter from you, and keeps saying, "ead pa pa" for read pa pa, she is very

---

72. The Hopkins slaves were in a rather poor condition. Susan Hopkins had most of them in Marion County, but Sophie, Felix's wife, and several other slaves were still at Welaka or at the Buffalo Bluff plantation north of Rose Cottage. Tivie noted in a letter to Winston on 15 July 1862 that Sophie was very ill but that her mistress did not believe it.

73. Captain John C. Richard, Company A, First Florida Infantry Battalion, reorganized as the Tenth Florida Infantry Regiment in 1864.

cunning sometimes, but oh she is so mischievous gives me more trouble than a little. I dont know what I shall do with her, she is so hardheaded, I fear she will give us a good deal of trouble. I must say I can not look forward to the addition of another one with much pleasure, for what shall I do with two, when one seems to keep me in a perfect boil most of the time, and seems to me I loose instead of gaining patience. Day before yesterday Rosa fell out of the dining room door just missing the platform and yesterday fell off the steps just missing if she did not strike the duck trough. she seemed to feel badly yesterday and Henry who picked her up thought she struck, but her head did not look at all red, I would not let her go to sleep until her usual bedtime, but she cried out a good many times last night, and took up most of our bed, as she came in there quite early. Mother and I do not sleep together now, when she was sick she slept in her room and we have only slept together one night since, as it was warm we gave it up until cooler weather. I like being alone as I cant have you. In speaking of Rosa I forgot to tell you some of her sayings the other day I was spreading the corn out to dry, and she was sitting in your chair rocking in the house when she said very soberly, Ma Ma "payin torn" thinking I suppose that I ought not to put my hands in it as I would not allow her to play in it. I was in the Kitchen the other evening when the first thing I heard her calling Tivie, Tivie, and she says it so cunningly. Yesterday she had the cat rather tight around the neck so that her teeth showed and she said cat "laugh" and in the morning she walked up to me and said Ma Ma "pitty morning," the morning before Mother and I were saying what pretty mornings we had now, she has now got down and is hunting for some mischief.

You must be greatly taken at the Crespo House as you ask me again about them. I dont know about girls, but I know the family are low Minorcans, I used to know some girls of the family years ago, they are all married, were long before I was. I hope there is no particular attraction there . . .

Do you get any melons or any kind of fruit? we have not had a melon for a week or more, we are not going to make any pumpkins or Kushaws this year.[74] Burrel and Tom are now working on the dam, the others in the New ground. I guess things are going on as well as could be expected. Sarah's baby seems to be quite a smart little thing and very good so far. the other young *stock* are doing well . . .

Well good bye Rosa is asleep but I send a kiss for her, and you may be assured you have the best affection of

Your own

Tivie

[Rebecca] **Aug 9, 1862.** *A warm morng—I am depressed with the constant fears for Willie which crowd upon me in spite of all my efforts . . .*

74. Cushaws, or cushaw pumpkins, are a striped, semisweet variety of long-necked squash.

[GEORGE BRYANT TO DAVIS BRYANT]

Rose Cottage Aug 10, 1862

My dear brother.

As Henry wrote Willie a short time ago, and told him about every thing, I think it is time for me to try and tell you something about what we do here in this part of the world. This morning Henry, Willie Stephens, and I went to see if we could'nt get a few gallons of Alligator oil; but we did not succeed in getting any; Henry shot at a fine fellow with Winston's riffle, we do'nt know whether he hit him or not, but we think he did, we did not see any more of him.

Henry and Willie have gone fishing . . . They took Taylor and the gun expecting to kill some squirrels, Henry has killed four out that way lately; Rosa is very fond of them, when she sees Henry bringing them she says, Henry got querrel . . .

Sunday morning. Henry and Willie got back yesterday a little while after sunset and brought fifty three fish, they were small but sweet. They killed a very large fox as they were coming back; he had quite a fight with Taylor after he fell. Mr. Stephens went up to the Ocklawaha river and killed a fine bear; he has just sent us a piece . . .

All send a great deal of love. I still remain

Your affectionate brother
George.

[OCTAVIA STEPHENS TO WINSTON STEPHENS]

Rose Cottage Aug 12, 1862

My dear Husband

. . . I am in the beef business this morning and my mind is pretty well stirred up, and I hardly know what I had to say, we got a beef weighing 315 lbs from Bright and will have to pay $18 for it. Burrel and Tom drove this one here before killing it and I hope we will have good luck in saving it, the weather bids fair for it, as regards sunshine. Burrel is going to put the hides in tan . . .

Mother, Rosa and I spent the day with Tina yesterday, Clark was to start off to day on another alligator hunt of a week or more, he killed a large though not fat bear last Saturday on the Ocklawaha. I had a fine baked piece and it was as tender and nice as any beef I ever tasted, and came just in the nick of time as we were out of meat.

This is Henry's fifteenth birthday, Georgie had one last week, I think when you come we will have to celebrate all together . . .

It is six weeks to day since you left your camp down here, it is as long a time as you have ever been away from me and I tell you I want to see you as much as

I ever did in my life. I can not help looking for you all the time. I pine for you, but I seem to grow *larger* instead of smaller . . .

Rosa and I both send love and kisses to you.

Your loving

Wife

[Rebecca] **Aug 13, 1862.** . . . *about 8 p.m. Winston arrives to our great joy . . . He has heard too that my dear husband is in Massachusetts.*

[Willie Bryant to Davis Bryant]

Camp near Chattanooga Aug 16, 1862

Dear Davis

I have written you but one letter since arriving here 4 weeks ago, waiting in the vain hope of something interesting turning up; but even now find myself in want of it. We are still at our old camp ground, tho' thousands of others have been moved, and in readiness to move on short notice, with as little definite knowledge and prospect as before; The waggon trains from Tupelo for which we are told we are waiting before advancing, have not yet arrived; our brigade at present only comprising the 3d. and 4th. Fla. have been assigned to Maj. Genl. Saml. Jones division, who is *somewhere,* but at present we are under the orders of Genl. Hardee at Chatanooga . . .[75]

I spent nearly a day at Look Out Mountain this week and tho a very fatiguing trip on foot, enjoyed it and got a good dinner too . . . It is pretty hard getting along on Flour 2 meals of rice sometimes, and reduced rations of bad meat, but we still make out; when we move again we give up our tents and all but a very few cooking utensils . . . I write you once in awhile, and all of interest when I can and occasionally shall expect a letter from you—Good bye for now! Take good care of yourself, as I do—Yrs always affectionately

Willie

[Rebecca] **Aug 18, 1862.** *Quite cool—This the 26th anniversary of my marriage! As I reflect on the changes that I have passed through, I recall much to be grateful for, many short comings of my own to regret, and many dear, departed and absent friends to lament. No mail today . . .*

---

75. Major General Samuel Jones was at this time in command of the Department of East Tennessee. Major General William Joseph Hardee was in command of I Corps of the Army of Tennessee, which included the Florida regiments. The Third Florida Infantry was reorganized on 8 May 1862, and Willie transferred from Company A (the Jacksonville Light Infantry) to Company H at that time.

[WILLIE BRYANT TO REBECCA BRYANT]

In Camp Aug 24, 1862

My dear Mother,

I wrote you not long since that we wd. soon cross the Tennessee river and join the army to advance toward Nashville so you will not be surprised to learn that we are now encamped 4 miles beyond Chattanooga; we crossed on Wednesday p.m. and after marching a distance of about 8 miles that afternoon (from our old camp) over this hilly country and dusty roads, we were pretty well tired out when we camped that night; the first days journey was of course hard on us, unused to a hilly country too, and then we were all overloaded in our anxiety to carry luxuries; the first night we camped on the side of a hill so steep that we lay with our feet down against trees or large stones to keep from sliding; the next morn'g we went about 1 ½ miles and soon after were obliged to change camp and retrace our steps some distance to get into our right position, and have now been stationary two days, which has made us fresh and better than new and ready for another move; we are all over now but must wait several days longer for all the waggon trains to cross, and a road to be cleared out, before we can take up our line of march; our first start is to climb up a very steep mountain, and then for a number of miles the road is comparatively level and good, I am told; we are camped at the foot of what is termed "Walden's Ridge," under a perpendicular cliff of more than 200 ft in height, and in a thick hammock where if it were not for the countless stones we might possibly imagine ourselves in Fla, the growth being principally pine, oak, and hickory; we are now without tents and with scarcely any cooking utencils for such a number of men, carrying only what the demands of nature actually require; when we move each man carried his bread and meat for 2 days (or longer) already cooked in his haversack, his canteen of water by his side, and his bed and wardrobe on his back; I have reduced my wardrobe to 2 flannel shirts, 2 prs wool socks, 1 pr drawers, 2 prs pants, 1 thick Jacket, 2 silk hadkfs, and have an oil cloth besides; With other little things, I carry in my knapsack a box pills, a small quantity of E. Salts, some cayenne pepper, a btl linement and plenty of soap; when we wish tents, two make a tent of one blanket and a bed of the others and sleep together, and I am now writing under such a tent— hurrah! letters have arrived and I hear my name called out; sure enough I have one, and from you dearest Mother, it bears dates of Aug 8th. 9th. and 10th. but was not mailed by the p.m. at Welaka till the 17th. and consequently was only 6 days or less in reaching Chattanooga.

Your letter as you say is written in a sad and desponding state, but it gives me joy to hear from you and I am glad that you write me as you feel, and should complain if you did not, for I know your situation and feelings and almost yr thoughts, and did you try to make me think differently about them you could not; I expect you to write *just as everything is* with you; I only wish you had a more hopeful disposition, and some of the "trust-to-luck" and a little of the "don't-care" which I possess, and O! if you only felt the enthusiasm in this cause which I do, and could feel as willing to give me up as a sacrifice for it as I am to suffer it, I wd. feel so differently, and it seems to me wd. be perfectly happy; and I do often and earnestly pray that as your lot is so hard that you may have some change of feeling, and the comfort, and support of the Holy Spirit. I have been better satisfied ever since leaving Mobile than I have ever been before in the service; I am fond of excitement and change, and to see all that I can and to realise varied sensations, am willing to endure trials and hardships; I glory in experience, and with my determination am unsatisfied until my wishes are gratified; I know now that I can endure as much as most men, and with more fortitude and cheerfulness, and take a pride in it; I still retain my good health and my strength increases and feel no fear to take my position among men under any circumstances; I am not yet satisfied and willing to stop. The service has been of incalculable benefit to me in health and experience; I have seen and learned much that I would never have done in a quiet and easy life which will be of benefit to me in after life, if I am spared, and am willing to take the chances and have the conviction that all will be well; it is only the thoughts for those I love that gives me any uneasiness or trouble; try to feel satisfied that my wishes are only being fulfilled that I know the worst and am willing to endure it to have them gratified, and resign me to it as cheerfully as possible; for your sake I shall be prudent and careful under all circumstances. Without me you still have much to comfort you, and hope for in yr other children, and may God help you to feel so, and soothe your thoughts and troubled spirit.

You speak of the sorrow you will feel in leaving yr children as if something that will occur, and it pains me to know that such a thought has entered your mind; none of them would be willing to live away from you, and their happiness, if nothing else, will demand that they be with you always; if I am spared my life shall be devoted to you, and tho' I do not now feel toward my father as you wish, I do not entertain such an extent of feeling as I infer you suppose, I cannot but respect his memory and retain affection for him and still expect to share many joys with him, tho' my love and feelings of pride and honor have recd. a severe blow from his course . . .

With much love and many kisses to you all I am

Yours always in love
Willie

August 26, 1862. *Winston left us soon after breakfast to return to his camp at Jacksonville. Rain.*

[Rebecca] **Aug 31, 1862.** My dear Willie's birthday—God bless him! O! that I could know where and how he is to-day...

[WINSTON STEPHENS TO OCTAVIA STEPHENS]

Camp Stephens Aug 31, 1862.

My Dear Wife

I have but a minute to write and must necessarily make this short... I arrived in Camps all O.K. and found all in Moderate health. But I have to write you bad news when I got to Jessups I heard of the death of Louis.[76] he started down to take Sweps place and got to Jessups and stoped for a few days and went out hunting and the horse frighted, the gun started to fall and struck a tree and went off and killed him dead, he only spoke once saying Oh Lord. poor Boy how sudden and unexpected and what a blow to poor Ma. Sister and Jessup was going up in a few days from the time I passed... Much love to all...

Your aff husband
Winston Stephens

[WINSTON STEPHENS TO OCTAVIA STEPHENS]

Camp Stephens Sept 4, 1862

My Dear Wife

I seat myself this p.m. that I may write you a more deliberate letter than the hasty sheet sent you before. I find it impossible to write without interuption as I have ben interupted already.

Your long, interesting and affectionate letter found me in good health free almost from any symtom of cold and you may rest assured that if I die of cold it will be one that is to come. My Command is not so well, Swep is sick the Dr is sick and about 9 or ten others, some have been threatened rather seriously though to day they are all on the mend. The Dr has no medicine for the sick and that is one reason why we suffer as we do...

I have just ben called as a Courier stands with orders near my tent. The orders are that I hold myself with 25 men in readiness to march on saturday morning, with three days cooked provisions for myself and men, I dont know where we are going and therefore cant inform you but suppose it is to scout the coast so as to allow Capt Dunham [to] see the Country—I will write you if any thing turns up worth hearing...

76. Lewis Gaines was Winston's half-brother and was only seventeen years old when he was killed. He was nicknamed Toady. Jessup Branning was the husband of Winston's half-sister, Mary.

I got a letter from Mr Greely stating he had purchased the uniform and had got me a cheap one what do you think of that?[77] We had a report in circulation that we were to be sent out of the State in a short time but its all false I think . . .

Sept 5th 4 pm. My Dear I have just sat down to finish this. We had more glorious news to day by the Cars. Kirby Smith has defeated Genl Nelson of the Federals at Cumberland Gap capturing his whole force 10,000 men, our loss was not as heavy as could have been expected, but in the last days fight between McC— and Pope with Genl Lee our loss was heavy and a dispatch was received to prepare for 8,000 wounded.[78] You will see by the despatch that they had three days fight. It is thought that by this time that Buell has surrendered or [been] defeated.[79] The 7th Fla was in the fight at the gap—God is surely with us as we are all the time victorious and our cause is prospering . . . When you hear from this part of the world again you will hear that the St Johns River has been blocked on the Yankees as my scout is in connection with that object. I cant give you the particulars as I am sworn to secrecy, but dont be uneasy as I will take care of myself and you shall hear as soon as I return . . . Good bye lots of Love to all and many kisses to Rosa and love to you

Yours aff
Winston Stephens

[REBECCA BRYANT TO DAVIS BRYANT]

Rose Cottage Sept 5, 1862

My dear Davis

This is your *birthday,* and I will commence a letter to you and finish it on Sunday morning. We are now having most delightful weather, after much that has been disagreeable and I hope you are enjoying the change. I think you have had a regular north-easter, from the course of the weather here . . .

Tivie sends much love and hopes this is the last birth-day you will ever pass in camp—and I heartily respond to that sentiment. We are to pass tomorrow with

---

77. Jonathan Clark Greely, a Palatka merchant, opposed secession but served in Winston's company for most of the war. He served one term in the Florida legislature before returning to the ranks, but in February 1864 he joined his family at Fernandina and took the oath of allegiance to the Union. Greely, "Musings of Mellen Clark Greely," 1–5. The uniform was donated by Winston B. Stephens Jr. to the Florida State Museum at the University of Florida, Gainesville.

78. Major General William Nelson was badly beaten by Major General Edmund Kirby Smith at Richmond, Kentucky, on 30 August 1862; but his entire army was not captured, and he withdrew to Louisville to reorganize. The Second Battle of Bull Run, 29–30 August 1862, resulted in Federal casualties of some 16,000 killed, wounded, or captured against Confederate losses of some 9,200; this victory enabled Lee to invade the North and brought on the Battle of Antietam in September.

79. Major General Don Carlos Buell, in command of the Army of the Cumberland, was in timid pursuit of Bragg's forces throughout the month of September, and he was removed from command after the Battle of Perryville in October 1862.

Mrs Stephens. I have begun teaching her two boys, three days in the week—they come in the morng. and study with Henry and George two hrs. in the am and one p.m. I proposed it partly for their sake and partly for my own, as I require something to divert my thoughts from the gloomy channel into which they constantly flow, despite of all my efforts, when my mind is not occupied entirely and it is all I can do to be useful here now to any one—Henry looks very thin and sometimes pale, but I think it is caused by his rapid growth principally. He has a good appetite and is sufficiently active for the season—I think the cool weather will increase his flesh.

Sun morng ... Tivie recd. a letter from Loulie Tydings last Monday—they are living in a place belonging to one of his uncles (Dr Adams' brother) where they are making salt. Mr Tydings superintending the negroes for him. The place is called Sopchoppy and is some distance from Tallahassee.[80] Lou expresses great anxiety to hear about you and Willie and indeed all of us, and we were rejoiced to hear from her. She says they are cut off [from] the world and fears she will not be able to hear from us—Tivie wrote to her immediately.

We look with renewed impatience for tomorrows mail, hoping for favorable news from Tenn. and from Virginia. It seems to be the general belief that if we do not gain our Independence in the next two months, the War will be indefinitely prolonged; perhaps for the whole of Lincoln's term of office ...

The boys send much love—Henry says he will write soon—Ten thousand kisses and blessings for you, my dear boy, from

Mother

[OCTAVIA STEPHENS TO WINSTON STEPHENS]

Rose Cottage Sept 7, 1862

My dear Husband

I was agreeably surprised to hear from you ... but it was sad news indeed that you wrote me, so we will never see our poor "Toady" again in this world, and what a sudden death. I can scarcely realize that it is so, he was a good boy. I hope he has gone to a better world. Poor Ma, I fear it will be very hard for her to bear, her health has been so feeble, and her constant anxiety about her sons that are in the service. I am glad Mary was going to her so soon, and hope her being there with the little baby will serve to direct Ma's thoughts some that her grief may not take too great a hold on her ...

---

80. Sopchoppy is about thirty miles southwest of Tallahassee and some five miles from the Gulf of Mexico. Salt making was very important after the outbreak of war, and Florida had the best natural resources for furnishing the product. Salt was produced from seawater all along the west coast throughout the war, although the facilities were constantly raided by Union forces. Sopchoppy was far enough inland to escape destruction, and the probability is that Tydings made good money while he was in the business.

The corn is all gathered in and we have not near as much as we had last year, Burrel says he got 17 loads from the field here at the house, that you can judge how much the wagon holds, and not quite two from the "little field" and a small quantity of *very small* pumpkins and kushaws, some as large as *your fist* very few ripe. we have three pumpkins cooking for our dinner to day, and fear that will not be enough, they are about the size of cocoanuts. I think if we dont do better another year we had better give up ... In mentioning our misfortunes in the crop I forgot the cotton, the catepillars are ruining it.[81] Burrel says they have stripped leaves and blooms, that it looks as though it had three frosts on it ...

I guess I will stop now and write to our poor Ma ...

Ever affectionately

Yr Wife

[WILLIE BRYANT TO REBECCA BRYANT]

Camp near Sparta, Tenn, Sept 7, 1862

My dear Mother,

I wrote you a few days ago from Dunlap, since then we have come thro' the Sequatchie valley and crossed the Cumberland ridge ...

Our march thus far has been a forced one, sometimes traveling 17 miles pr day, and of the most trying nature, owing to the nature of the country and the scarcity of water; we are invariably aroused at 3 o'clk in the morng. to start, and keep going till after dark, and every 2d or 3d night are obliged to be up late cooking rations ahead; the regmt. rested 2 days at Dunlap, I wrote you, here we rest and to cook 3 days rations from 10 o'clk this a.m. till tomorrow a.m.; It was the intention for our army to attack Buell at McMinnville, where he had fortified himself, and then to follow him in retreat to Nashville, but he evacuated McM— before we could get there and retreated to Nashville and we are now informed that Nashville will soon be evacuated also, Therefore our army is now destined for Kentucky, and I think it is supposed that by a certain arrangement of the confederate forces that the Federals will be unable to concentrate theirs into a large army again; I am sorry for this change of plan for I dislike the longer march into Kentucky and wished very much to see Nashville; our point of destination is undoubtedly *Louisville* now ...

I am otherwise in good trim, accustomed to walking and my feet are now hardened; yesterday I was obliged to knock under for awhile, however, as I had become weakened from diarrhoea caused by drinking some cider and eating fruit,

---

81. The corn ear worm was also called the cotton boll worm or simply the boll worm when it attacked the cotton plant; it did retard the yield but did not completely destroy the crop as the boll weevil did later on.

and from bad water and the scarcity of it, I had some fever also, but stopped at a house till the cool of the evening, when the kind lady offered me some food and I eat some corn bread, milk and honey and came on to camp, then took some medicine and went to bed and this morng. woke up all right and marched 8 miles by ½ p 6 when I stopped at a house till 9 and got some breakfast. The worst of our trip is over, we are now over the mountains, in a good country and where water is more plenty, and will not be so hurried.

East Tenn is booked in my memory as the most abominable section of country I have known; The hardships we have endured passing thro' have increased my dislike, but the people are a lazy, ignorant, overreaching and cold hearted set; when they would sell us any thing it was at the most exorbitant prices, and old and young would combine to cheat us and take advantage of our situation, they wd. not only charge 10 and 15¢ pr doz for peaches and apples rotting on the ground, and 50¢ pr qt or 10¢ for a little cupfull of cider, but actually wd. sit on the fence with little loaves of corn bread no bigger than "*your*" two fists to sell for 50¢ and $1 each; my feet were horribly scalded by my wool socks, a very smiling and benign looking dame "to oblige me," let me have a pr of their cotton ones, of the cheapest sort and which I have sold many of at 10¢ and a bit, for the moderate sum of *one dollar,* this is the 3d. day I have worn them and they are all holes already; I got a better to-day from a fellow soldier for 50¢ which I shall carry for a similar necessity.

But thank Heaven we are now in a fine country and where the people are glad to welcome us, and kind, and if I would happen to become at all sick I would not hesitate to stop—

This whole section of country is beautiful and grand, and very fertile, and tho' at a heavy cost I am glad that I have been able to see it . . .

I hope and pray that you are all well and may continue so—I am sure I feel a sense of gratitude for my being so blessed in health—Oceans of love to you all, *you know,* from

Willie

[OCTAVIA STEPHENS TO WINSTON STEPHENS]

Sept 9, 1862

My own husband

. . . Rosa has not had fever since the day I wrote you, she had another tumble off of the steps this afternoon, she tried to throw the chicken off and she went rolling off too, right on top of a puppy, and cut her lip inside and skinned it outside. The night that Rosa had fever I dreamed of your having a chill, I hope it was not true. I wonder if you ever dream of your poor little wifey? I dream of you every night and I think Rosa dreamed up and said in the same whining tone she used to when you went out "Ma Ma Pa Pas done . . ."

Mother has just *poked* her head in the door, and says I must give lots of love to you and hopes you are enjoying these beautiful moonlight evenings. I said yes in bed sound asleep, when I am walking up and down the path every evening enjoying the moonlight, I think of you asleep. I believe you never had romance enough to enjoy the moon anyhow, perhaps your romance had worn out when I knew you. Speaking of romance, the cotton has been picked over once and got 189 lbs . . .

I have one stocking nearly finished and have not knitted steadily on it. I think I will have one if not two pair knit before you come home again, besides other work. All are well here now . . .

Good night and God bless and protect you. With much love I am

as ever your own
Tivie

[WINSTON STEPHENS TO OCTAVIA STEPHENS]

Jacksonville Sept 11, 1862

My Dear Wife

I returned last night and can say to you that so far I am unharmed. I went down to May Port and carried out my orders and I was shelled for more than an hour with my men not over ¼ mile but no one was hurt, the sand was nocked in their faces but no danger done, they fired 62 shots at me and while I was keeping the Gun boats down there Genl Finegan crossed some cannon and had them mounted at St Johns Bluff and this morning they opened the ball and have been fighting some four or five hours but no news as to results, they continue to fight and God grant we may succeed . . .[82] Love to all and as many kisses for you and Rosa as you wish from

your Aff husband
Winston

82. On 6 September General Finegan arrived at St. Johns Bluff with Captain Robert H. Gamble's Light Artillery, a section of which was commanded by Lieutenant F. L. Villipique. He attached to this artillery force Battery A, Milton Light Artillery, commanded by Joseph L. Dunham; three infantry companies and a few irregulars under Major Theodore W. Brevard; Captain John C. Richard's company; and Winston's and William Chambers's companies. The commander of the *Uncas*, L. G. Crane, reported that he encountered a company of rebels at Yellow Bluff, and after "killing and wounding several thereof and scattering the rest, I returned to my station." He reported that two days later the rebels attempted to burn Mayport, but he was able to contain it with little damage. Crane's intelligence was excellent; he knew the commanders and the size and location of the units facing him; he warned that something should be done before the enemy build-up became too strong. *ORN*, ser. 1, vol. 13, 301–2.

[REBECCA BRYANT TO WILLIE BRYANT]

Rose Cottage Sept 14, 1862

My dearest Willie,

... You always write cheerfully to me and make light of your privations and toils, but a hard march of 150 miles, without tents or many cooking utensils must be a severe test of any man's philosophy and powers of endurance. I have been hoping most earnestly for a telegraphic dispatch, a newspaper paragraph, or *something* on which to base a conjecture where you are. A month has passed since the last recd. from you was written—how much must have occurred in that time to bring you either joy or sorrow! I have endeavoured to comply with your wish that I shd. believe that all was well with you until I *knew* to the contrary— But my hopes and fears are constantly alternating and I must confess the latter often predominate, in spite of my efforts to the contrary...

I can conceive what you must have suffered by being 6 wks. without letters, when I find it difficult to be cheerful under a trial of half that magnitude—2 wks without a letter from you, is as much as I can bear patiently. The newspapers of Aug 30th. inform us that Buell had fallen back in the direction of Tupelo, but it seems probable if troops had been engaged with him since that movement or if there had been any decisive action at Nashville since you left that we shd. have heard of it by telegraph the past week as there have been persons from Palatka passing up the river. Telegraphic despatches recd. at Gainesville are brought to Orange Springs, thence to Palatka, and we got the news of the Richmond victory in that way in 3 days. I receive letters from Davis quite regularly now every alternate Monday... You were mistaken in supposing you had expressed to me your opinion of Aunt Julia's cause toward yr Father, I have looked eagerly for it and from the dates of yr letters, I think I have all you have written me since that time—I suppose you wrote Davis and thought you had said the same to me— Aunt J— speaks of recg. one from you, and that you were just to both herself and yr father. She seems much gratified by mine to her—it was more forbearing and affectionate than she dared to expect... Henry was much pleased with your commendation of his letter. George intends writing to you—He has just returned from a visit to Mr Stephens' boys, he went on Friday P.M. to return yesterday but the storm prevented—I teach those boys with mine three days in the week— Reading, spelling, writing and arithmetic is all I profess to teach. Henry however has commenced Nat. Philosophy and Astronomy. He has also been building a crib for his corn crop which is now gathered—It is the only way in which I can be useful now and I need something to draw my thoughts from my wearing anxieties and mental burdens. Tivie and Rosa are both in good health—Tivie sends much love and a kiss—and from me dear Willie accept ten thousand kisses and blessings.

Mother

[WILLIE BRYANT TO DAVIS BRYANT]

20 miles in Kentucky, Sept 14, 1862

My dear Bro.

I have wished to write you often . . . Tho' I wd. probably have found more time and been able to write more but for a badly sprained shoulder (my right) which kept me behind with the waggons . . .

This is the 17th day since the regt started, and we have marched a distance of a little more than 200 miles, crossing 2 ridges of mountains on the way, and when we start again tomorrow will have rested but 3 whole days and part of a 4th.

What we have suffered on this march those only can know who have experienced it, it is impossible to describe it, or for the mind to realise it by description; many a poor fellow has been killed by it and is buried by the road side, and I am only surprised there are not more, thousands have been left sick at houses and hospitals established along the road, and by the side of the road to make their way *somewhere* the best they could, and many of the hardiest and strongest are of the number; it has been terrible, terrible, and no man of us will ever forget it, or think of it but with pain . . . the scarcity of water, dusty roads, heat, and hunger have *all* been just till a few days past; the average of the march is about 16 or 17 miles pr day, some days they have driven us 22; O! it has been inhuman! but thank Heaven it is now better with us, the country has been good for the past few days, and it is but 28 miles to Bowling Green where we are destined for the present, 2 days will take us there—Our rest to-day, and having time to wash our bodies and clothes, and nurse our lame feet is delicious, but last night we were cooking till very late, and will be obliged to to-night, as without any apparent excuse they are not to issue rations till dark—I would not have Mother know what I have endured for worlds; I must confess that *once* I was throughly discouraged, and wished myself out of the service and home. I was following with the regt. and was sick, and as long as a man can walk he is forced to keep up with the regt. Our march has depended intirely upon Buells movements, and I suppose still will, he managed to elude us by 2 days at McMinnville Tenn and we have been forced to get around him; at Bowling Green we cut off the R. Road commtn. between Nashville and Louisville, and Price is on his other side,[83] his only escape is thro' Kentucky into Missouri; the report of his being hemmed in [in] Tenn proved false; Our army consisted of about 60,000 men, 3 divisions, Cheatham's,

---

83. Major General Sterling Price and his Army of the West were not factors in the coming battle.

Buckner's, and Anderson's (ours) but Cheatham's has gone to reinforce Kirby Smith . . .[84]

Good bye again—Yrs always affectionately

Willie

[HENRY BRYANT TO DAVIS BRYANT]

Rose Cottage Sept 20, 1862

Dear brother

I intended to write to you the last time Mother wrote but Georgie and I had to make a little house to put our corn and fodder in, so I thought I would put off writing until this week . . . When Col was up here I went deer hunting with him once, the dogs started one a little above the Mill dam but we did'nt get a shot at it, as we went up around the head of the branch towards Browards lake,[85] the dogs would run through and come out on the other side, but just as we got to the end of the scrub we saw two deer jump and run towards the place the dogs ran in, Col jumped off his horse and ran back and just as he got around to see where the other one was, he saw something shake its ears but thought it was Clara and would not shoot it, it was a yearling deer and began to run along in the edge of the bushes, he shot where it would have come in one more jump, but it stopped just as he shot so he shot in front of it, after he shot, it came out within twenty steps of him and stopped and looked at him, he called to me to come there as quick as I could, and I thought the deer had gone on so I galloped around to him as quick as I could, and when the deer heard me coming it ran back in the scrub, I gave him my gun and rode around to the other side of the scrub and then came through but could not start it again, while we were after the yearling the dogs ran on after the doe, when we were ready to follow them we could not hear them barking at all, they ran her into a little bay on the branch, we went there and blew the horn but they would not come; Col says he is sure they caught it because he wounded her badly, the dogs did not come home until some time after we did . . .

84. Bragg had about 46,000 soldiers when all of his divisions were united, but only 16,000 were in action at the Battle of Perryville. Major General Benjamin Franklin Cheatham had been in the Battle of Shiloh, and his division was engaged in every major action from Stones River to the fall of Atlanta and the Battle of Nashville. Major General Simon Bolivar Buckner surrendered himself and Fort Donelson to his former West Point classmate Ulysses S. Grant on 16 February 1862. He was exchanged during the summer and given the Third Division in Hardee's Corps during this Kentucky campaign. Brigadier General James Patton Anderson assumed divisional command after the Battle of Shiloh and performed creditably at Perryville and heroically at Stones River.

85. Lake Broward is four miles due east of Rose Cottage.

Last Tuesday afternoon, while Georgie and I were saying our lessons, Sarah called me and said she saw some turkeys in the field up towards the old house, I took my gun and went out by the cotton house and then through the field towards the river, as I was going I saw the turkeys run towards the fence so I hurried on and got over the fence and walked along on the outside, I had not gone far before I saw them just inside within twenty yards of me, but they saw me and ran back down the fence a little ways and began to fly up on the fence, I crept along the fence until I thought I was within gun shot then I raised up, there were four up on the fence, I shot at the nearest one but when I went there I found *two*. So the first time I ever killed a turkey I killed two at one shot. I think it was pretty good luck . . . Your aff brother

Henry

[OCTAVIA STEPHENS TO WINSTON STEPHENS]

Rose Cottage Sept 21, 1862

My dear husband

Mr Smith arrived at last with two letters from you, I received them last Friday, you cant imagine what a relief it was to my mind to get those letters, for I was in a great state of anxiety about you for I had heard of your trip down the river and your fight with the boats, and that six men were killed on our side, and I thought if you were not among that number you might suffer in a few days after . . . What a narrow escape you and your men had from the shells of the Gunboat. Oh how thankful I am and you ought to be that you escaped. I shall be in constant fear the whole time now . . . for I fear that blocking the Gunboat will not be such an easy thing as you think—for the fiftieth time I say will we ever have peace? When I feel that you are not in danger I do not realize the troubles half so much, I suppose I have my share of the anxiety to bear. You say we must certainly have peace soon. God grant that we may but I have but little hope, for that has been said so many many times. If it is true about Pope and McClellan there are plenty more men in Yankeedom that may make better Generals than them.[86] We have certainly gained a great many victories (if we can believe all) for which I am very thankful, but, oh

---

86. After his success at Bull Run in August against Pope, Lee invaded Maryland. McClellan was once again given command of the Union forces and struck Lee at Antietam on 17 September 1862. Had Lee won at Antietam, it is possible that England and France would have officially recognized the Confederacy. If that had happened, the Confederate States of America would probably have endured. Lincoln shipped Pope out west after his defeat and relieved McClellan for good when he failed to pursue and destroy Lee's army after Antietam. Still, Antietam was a Union victory, and Lincoln used it to present the preliminary Emancipation Proclamation, which declared that slavery would be abolished in the Confederacy after 1 January 1863. Tivie's observation was correct: there were great generals in the North, but Lincoln had not yet found them.

such loss of life and seems to me to no purpose, if we do ever have peace how few there will be to realize it and how many of *them* will be desolate and unhappy. God grant that I may never be one of that number . . .

You ask me what I think of your uniform. I think it a great pity that the wives of *confederate officers* have to wear unbleached *homespun* chemises, when their husbands can afford to buy *uniforms*. You told me to manage things to my liking, I have sent with others to buy some factory thread, Clark and I counted it all up etc, and it would be cheaper to buy the thread and have it woven at 10 cts a yard than buy the cloth at 50 cts, and we are obliged to have the cloth, and the Winter will be over before we can get our cotton ginned, and spun at home, and having it spun elsewhere is not very cheap. I hope it will be to your satisfaction, I could not wait to hear from you again as I am behind the others in sending already . . .

I wish to heaven you could come home. My dear you say you will be cautious, it is easy enough to say it when you are quietly writing, but I am so afraid that when you are excited you will forget in your enthusiasm for your *country* how dear your life is to more than yourself. Mother sends love and says she was rejoiced to hear from you after a week of anxiety that you were safe and well. All are well yet except Sarah who has had fever and has five *"risings."*[87] Rosa sends a kiss. I hope I shall be able to hear from you a little oftener hereafter. once in three weeks is rather trying. Good bye "Do take care yourself My dear" as ever

yr loving
Wife

[WINSTON STEPHENS TO OCTAVIA STEPHENS]

Sept 21, 1862
In Camp near "St Johns" Bluff[88]

My Darling Wife

. . . I am in good health and fine spirits as every thing seems to work under the direction of Divine Providence—We have the game plaid out with the Gun boats on this river, the first fight you have doubtless had the particulars. the second took place on the morning of the 17th at 5 a m and lasted till 10 a m. In which time the Gun boats therein [fired] as estimated between one thousand and 12 hundred shots and our guns replied very slowly only throwing some 50 shots. the boats then retired. Our loss was 2 killed and 2 wounded. Capt Dunham lost one man and Maj Brevard one, the bateries received no injury during the firing, but

---

87. A rising is another name for a boil.
88. St. Johns Bluff rises about seventy-five feet above the St. Johns River some six miles inland from the mouth of the river.

the shell and shot fell like hail.[89] It was certainly Providential that we did not have more injury on our side. The Enemy was hit several times and forced to retire, but returned the Friday next day after the 18th and fired 18 shot and retired before we fired a gun. And on Friday one boat came up in long range and our big guns was about to open on her when I asked the Capt to hold on and not let them get the range of his best gun which he did and after looking at us for a short time she turned around and went back and then all the boats went out over the bar but two large side wheel steamers. Some think they have gone for reinforcement and others that they have given up, but I am of the first opinion, as they feel it a burning shame to have allowed us to mount guns in sight of them and drive them back when they try to pass—The only fear I have is they will get guns of longer range than we have, which will allow them every advantage and we may lose men and not be able to retaliate—Capt Chambers and myself are about three miles and a half from the boats, acting on the rear to prevent a land attack which I do not fear as they have not got the land force to spare for this place, Genl Finegan is down here looking at the positions etc, he has asked for a regiment from Georgia. I am not a favorite as I am a Whig and I came near offering my resignation as he refused to give my men good arms, but he has consented to give me 60 Enfield rifles and Maj Teasdale has promised to get me some sabres. The old granny thinks I have done a little more than I should have done and he is afraid I will get more credit than some of his Democrat friends, and I think he would like to see me whiped. I shall try to prevent such a disaster as I will not expose my men until I am armed. We have 3 8-inch guns or Columbiads, two 32 [-pound] rifle, two 8-inch short siege guns mounted ready for action, and the last fight we had none of the 8-inch ready. We have over 300 infantry in the Batallion and one Independent Co of 117—Chambers and My Cavalry 227 men, besides about 150 that work the guns making our force now 794 and we will have one company more next week on this side and two companies on Yellow bluff on the opposite.[90] you see by this that we are pritty strong and if we get the Georgia Regiment we will be ready for any thing, but I dont like sending our men out of the State and then having to call for help from some other State . . .

I rode out this morning with Capt Chambers to fix some pickets and got down to look at the two Gun boats in the river and my mare ran off and lost my overcoat (not the blue one) but I hope to find it . . . I hope Rosa has not had return of fever I know she will be well cared for and shall ask you to be careful,

89. Major Theodore W. Brevard, commander of the three infantry companies engaged at St. Johns Bluff, began his Civil War career as captain of Brevard's Partisan Rangers, which he raised in summer 1862. He was promoted to major of cavalry in 1862, colonel of the Eleventh Florida Infantry Regiment in 1864, and brigadier general in 1865.

90. Yellow Bluff, or New Berlin, is on the west bank of the St. Johns, about four miles upriver from St. Johns Bluff.

but do take care of your own health and you had better not ride on horseback anymore and walk every evening. I wish you would tell burrel not to allow an ear of corn fed only when obliged and tell me how the peas promise. I want them all saved nicely and the cotton too. I want to know about the hogs and how things generally look once a week . . . Give love to Mother and boys and the Darkies tell howdie . . . Good bye and God bless you kiss rosa for Pa Pa. Your loving old man

Winston Stephens

[OCTAVIA STEPHENS TO WINSTON STEPHENS]

Sept 27, 1862

My dear husband

. . . Last Monday morning I heard of the fight with five Gunboats and their defeat at the Battery with three men only killed on our side. My hopes and spirits raised greatly, thinking the boats would not try it again very soon and if they did the Battery could stand it well, as I thought they would never send more than five boats, but Monday afternoon I heard that the boats were at the Bar waiting for larger ones to try it again, so that they might stand off a long ways and give your side shots which I fear will damage you greatly, and I know the high tides which we have now will help them much, I wish the Battery had never been erected. I am glad though that you have to scout instead of remaining at the Battery for I suppose there is less danger . . . All of us are well now, Sarah is up again and her five risings dwindled down to two. Burrel is at last well again after going with Henry to Palatka and having two teeth out, I am doing pretty well, but can not stand half as much as when I was *with Rosa*. I have a sore throat but no cold . . . I fear if this weather continues all will be sick, October was the month last year . . .

Who do you want to have shoes, if you can not get any shoes for Rosa I shall have to try and make some of buck skinn . . . She will soon have to wear shoes most of the time, I have one pair of my stockings done, I began them the first day of this month, and have done a great deal besides . . .

The boys have just returned with a nice string of fine large fish. I wish you could dine with us, but I guess you get mullet down there, which I wish for often . . . we are at last enjoying green crowders they are very fine.[91] Are you not going to let us enjoy some potatoes before very long—when the green peas are done? How often may I give the negroes peas? Every thing *seems* to go on very smoothly. Pet looks miserably, but the colt and mules [are] rolling fat, the mules tried to run

---

91. Crowder peas, also known as hay peas, were used for both food and fodder. The small brown peas are packed tightly in the shell—crowded together, so to speak; hence the name.

away with the wagon the other day. I can not keep the puppies fat, they and Pet seem determined to look like hard times . . .

I suppose there is no use to ask you when you expect to come home, for I guess you can not tell yet. Mother sends a great deal of love, but not more than does

Your own

Tivie

[OCTAVIA STEPHENS TO WINSTON STEPHENS]

Rose Cottage Oct 1, 1862

My own dear Winston

What has become of you? I can not imagine why I do not hear from you, all I can hear is that there is no fighting going on down where you ought to be, for which I am very thankful, for if I knew there was fighting going on and not hear from you I would be more miserable than I am, as it is I fear that you are off some where on a scout, for I think if you were sick you would let me know in some way . . . I guess you will think this great scribbling, for my hand is very unsteady, as I took a notion this morning to try and have one of my "duck fits" as Henry calls them . . .

Capt Smith has gone up for the Hattie and said that if Clark and I would have some wood on the wharf by Friday he would pay any price so I sent Tom this morning with Clark to haul as Burrel said Tom could be spared.[92] I hope it will suit your notion. oh how glad I will be when you come back, to have things your way and take the responsibility from me, for everything I have done I fear may not suit you, though you wrote to have things to my liking and you would not complain . . .

Good bye my dear, God bless and protect you wherever you are, is constantly the prayer of

Your Wife.

92. Joseph F. Smith was from Palatka.

[WINSTON STEPHENS TO OCTAVIA STEPHENS]

Camp St Johns Bluff Oct 1, 1862

My Dear Wife

... We are being drawn more and more under a rule of Despotism every day and sometimes I fear we are to have hard rule until this war is over. Civil law is thrown by the board for Military dictation and some men seem to forget their obligations to their fellow man after getting in position. I hate to write with my feelings that I have at times but I must let it out and I suppose you will make allowances for me. We have been treated badly in some respects since we were moved on this side of the river. I had on my yesterdays report 15 men on sick report and one Lt which is McLeod. I have but six tents for 90 men and the rain falling nearly constantly. I sent some men after lumber and Genl Finegan had them turned back and they have to sleep in the woods with a blanket over them and their clothing all wet, sometimes a plenty to eat and then again nothing, this morning we got a beef but for the last two days we had nothing but dry bread. The men look to me and you may imagine my feelings with a hungry crew and as hungry myself with them calling for something to eat. I dont complain of my men for they stand it as well as men can and all of them know I do all I can, but it makes my position unenviable ... Our whole Comissary and Quartermaster's business is managed badly and all have more or less favoritism to show and that spoils every thing. And to cap the climax, my Dear Wife has given me a cut that I dont think I deserve—When I was at home you laughed at my coat and made all sorts of fun of it and I supposed you would take a pride to know that I had changed to a better one when thrown in Company—but instead of that you censure me for getting a new suit when my Wife has to wear *yellow* homespun—I ask you the question did you ever ask me to get you any thing that I did not get if I could ... ? I have cautioned you about my debts and only asked your cooporation with me to get clear of debt but I have never intended you should not have what you wanted, but on the contrary I have taken pleasure in getting you what you have asked me and you have been one of the most equinomical women I ever saw and you have asked for as little as any one could get along on. I have often thought you wanted things and would have anticipated your wants but I dont know enough about womans wants to know what you require. And I hope you will always make your wants known frankly and they shall be gratified if possible. I have sent after some flannel and will send it if it is in Jacksonville ...

We have some days six boats and some days five and some of them very large. They are about four miles from the bluff but we sometimes go in one mile while on picket duty. I think one of these days or nights they will try us again but if they dont come with an overpowering land force they had just as well stay away as we have good guns and a plenty of them and then we have a batery on Yellow bluff to keep them back if one or more should pass this bluff. We are not as strong as we wish to be but we can kill four to one in these woods. I'll finish in a P.S. when Silvester Barnes starts.[93]

Oct 4, 1862. Just as I was folding a letter to Winston, Tina came with my letter sent by Capt Canova and said that the Yankees had taken St John's Bluff and that Winston's and Capt Chambers companies were swimming themselves and horses across the river . . .

[OCTAVIA STEPHENS TO WINSTON STEPHENS]

Rose Cottage Oct 4, 1862

Well my dear . . . The nearer my time gets the more I dread it and fear you will not be here, if I should be taken sick before the time I dont know what I would do the doctor is so far off I might die before he got here, and no "Granny" here. I hate the idea of having to depend upon Dr Currel at the time anyhow.[94] I hate the idea of the whole affair, and how soon the time will come, the nearer the time comes the more I remember of the other time, at night when I go to bed and nothing to take my attention it all comes to me vividly. I have become pretty clumsy. Burrel and Georgie had fever yesterday. Colds seem to be going the rounds now, I got off with only a slight one. Rosa has kept well so far and has been merry enough all the morning, has now gone to sleep . . .

I must close now. Come soon to your loving Wife

Tivie

[Rebecca] *Oct 6, 1862. . . . About 11 o'clock p.m. Winston arrives having had a very hard time getting here—swimming creeks, no ford etc—He*

---

93. Winston was not able to add a postscript, for just as he finished this letter, the Federal attack began. Brigadier General John Milton Brannan arrived at Mayport on 1 October with more than 1,500 troops and six gunboats. Three gunboats proceeded upriver but were driven off by the artillery at St. Johns Bluff. Colonel Charles Hopkins, who had been placed in command by Finegan, ordered the ordnance destroyed and the place evacuated the next day. Rain prevented the gunpowder from exploding, and the Federals were able to capture the guns intact on 3 October. Brannan advanced past Yellow Bluff, which had also been evacuated; occupied Jacksonville for the second time; proceeded upriver and captured the steamer *Governor Milton;* and then returned to Jacksonville on 9 October. Brannan left two days later with several Jacksonville refugees and 276 "contrabands," a designation applied to slaves who ended up in the Union. Prior to the issuance of the Emancipation Proclamation, this scheme was used so that the runaway slaves did not have to be returned to their owners. The second battle of Jacksonville was over, and no further activities of importance happened in the area until March 1863, when the city was occupied for the third time. See *OR*, ser. 1, vol. 14, 131, 142.

94. Dr. Currel was mentioned frequently in the correspondence, but no first name was given, and no one by that name appeared in any of the county records or in the Federal census. He was a drunkard and not very talented even when sober.

confirms the news of the surrender of the Bluff—but it was no fault of the men, the enemy's force was overwhelming.

Oct 7, 1862. Clark and Tina came to spend the day with us, just before dinner Old Jacob came and said the Gunboats were coming up.[95] In the afternoon Clark and Winston went to watch the movement of the boats, did not come back until after supper, then slept under the cotton house for fear of a surprise in the night. Tina and her children staid here. Rain.

[Rebecca] Oct 8, 1862. Mrs Stephens and whole family here all last night and to-day. Winston with Capt Canova and others having formed a plan of attack on the Darlington start after dinner to go up the river but the D—n coming down with the Milton prevents their going—Henry goes out in the country to inform Capt Canova of the return of D—n with the Milton—The men from the Gunboat open Mr Smiths store and carry off great quantities of articles belonging to Mr Smith, Mr Brown and others . . .[96]

[REBECCA BRYANT TO DAVIS BRYANT]

Rose Cottage Oct 11, 1862

My dear Davis,

I wrote you a brief letter last Saturday and promised to write to day if I had any thing to say. When I closed, we had no details of the engagement in the river with the gunboats, and were very anxious about Winston, although we learned from the Capt. who bro't up the Milton that he saw his men crossing to Jacksonville before he left. About 11 o'clk on Monday night Winston reached home. It seems that he was detained in crossing till the last, being obliged to protect the retreating forces with his cavalry, and when he reached the river, the Milton having left, there were only two flats to cross in and he supposed the gunboats wd. be upon them before they could all get across. Therefore he sent Lieut. Gray with 30 men across and he brought the remainder up on this side. He and six others were compelled to swim the Haw Creeks—there are three, and they were so swollen that the haw-bushes were not discernible until they were among them and entangled so that it made it very difficult for the horses to swim and some of

---

95. Jacob, a Hopkins slave, has been previously mentioned; he was at the Hopkins plantation, Buffalo Bluff.

96. This was the first Federal landing at Welaka. The sacking of Smith's store and warehouse was the first hostile act taken against a Welaka resident. Most of the Federal force returned to Hilton Head, South Carolina, on 11 October, but the gunboats continued to ply the river. William Brown and several other residents had goods stored at Smith's warehouse and lost them at this time. The *Darlington*, in Federal hands, was in pursuit of the *Governor Milton* and captured her on 9 October at Hawkinsville (now Crows Bluff), some forty miles south of Welaka. The Federal gunboat was the USS *E. B. Hale*. When the *Hale* departed Welaka, it took on board Dan Allen with his personal effects, he having given the Federals useful information concerning the rebel steamers.

them with their riders came near drowning![97] W's mare which was small (not the one you saw here) became so much exhausted that he had to throw away his gun and finally took off everything and turned her loose. He has not yet heard whether she got through safely as he came in to Mr Braddock's and got a horse to bring him home.[98] One of the men who lives near there was to look out for his gun and mare when the water subsided. On Tuesday the day after W. arrived, Mr and Mrs Stephens came by invitation to eat a fine turkey which Henry had killed the afternoon before—About an hour before dinner old Jacob came from the Bluff to inform us that the Darlington and one gunboat had gone up towards Welaka— W— and Mr S— left immediately after dinner, sent Mr S—'s two boys over here that all might be together and we women and the children were expecting a visit from the Feds, all the afternoon and eveg. Before we retired our two gents paid us a visit of a few minutes, told us that the gunboat was anchored out opposite the wharf at Welaka—that the Darlington had gone up the river, it was supposed in pursuit of the Milton and that they shd. not sleep at home that night. I assure you we all slept with one ear open that night . . . On Wednesday afternoon the Darlington came down with the Milton—Eight or ten men came on shore, broke open Mr Smith's store—took a quantity of oranges he had, part of a bbl of syrup, all his clothing they cd. find, in fact every thing they could lay hands on and scattered his papers every where . . . The enemy also destroyed all the boats around the wharf—cutting them to pieces, as they did we are told all along the river . . . God bless you my dear boy!

Yrs always affectionately

Mother

[WILLIE BRYANT TO REBECCA BRYANT]

Bryantsville, Kentucky, near Lexington, Oct 11, 1862

My dear mother,

After a very long time, which seems an age, an opp'ty offers to send letters . . . We have had a tough time, certain, and for a few days I was unwell, but fortunately we were on picket and I could lie in camp, and by taking medicine was soon better than before, and am now in better health and flesh than you ever have known me, I think; I have endured exposure to nearly all weather now,

---

97. Haw Creek is at the southeasternmost corner of Crescent Lake on the present-day boundary between Putnam and Flagler Counties. Winston had to ride some thirty-five miles from Jacksonville toward St. Augustine and then another thirty-five to forty miles southwest to reach the creek. From there to Fort Gates, where Winston crossed his troops, is about fifteen more miles. From Fort Gates he turned north for the trip to Rose Cottage, a distance of about five miles. Haw Creek had three branches where Winston crossed, and for this reason some called it Haw Creeks or Haws Creek.

98. James A. Braddock had a farm near Welaka.

heat, cold, rain, hunger, thirst, fatigue to prostation, without being really sick, rheumatism or colds, and am to-day, a cold misty fall day, and after marching thro' rain and mud all yesterday, and sleeping on the wet ground last night with a single wet blanket over me, the better for the service, but I have even more than all this to be thankful for, and I trust I am fully sensible of it, and grateful to almighty God. I have been in a most terrible fight and *came out without a scratch;* yes! my wish has been gratified, we have met the enemy, have been victorious, and I know what I am under such circumstances; preceding events I must skip; on Weds'dy the 8th at 2 oclk P.M. our brigade consisting of the 1st and 3d Fla. and 41st Miss. was led into action, and in as hot a fight as any at Shiloh till after 6 when darkness closed the conflict for the day, and us; The fight took place near a little town called Perryville, at midnight we were relieved by fresh troops who have taken up the fight and since then have been marched 15 miles, and as there is a large quantity of captured stores of all kinds here, I think we will be kept here several days and get well rested and fed before marching again.[99]

Our regmt. gained great credit and a name, we fought bravely and suffered severely, our list of casualities being 102 out of 247 taken on the field, but four were killed or dangerously wounded, comparatively; Charlie Hemming, my little and only chum, was wounded below the right shoulder, I have just written his father; Wesley Wethington, whom I found out a few days previously to be a nephew of Dr Adams, was seriously wounded in the face and head and I fear may not recover; I shall try and write Dr. Adams. I went to the poor fellow as he lay on the field that night and was able to be of great comfort and assistance to him and saw him safely to the hospital.[100]

I am thankful that I was able to minister to the comfort of many poor fellows, both friends and foes, that night, and was all over the field and among them from just after the fighting ceased till our regmt. moved at midnight; the night was a splendid moonlight night and I had an opportunity of seeing a battle field as I

---

99. Major General Don Carlos Buell left Louisville, Kentucky, on 1 October 1862 with about 50,000 men and headed toward Harrodsburg and Bardstown, communities southwest of Frankfort, the provisional Confederate capital of the state. Bragg's intelligence was faulty, and he hurried to Frankfort in the belief that Buell's army was there. Elements of the two armies collided at Perryville on 8 October, and a desperate close-quarters battle raged for the rest of the day. Confederate casualties totaled 3,396 to the Federals' 4,211; but since Bragg left the field to the Federals, they could claim a victory even though their losses had been higher. Buell did not pursue Bragg, and this resulted in his dismissal on 24 October 1862. Major General William S. Rosecrans took command soon after and fought Bragg at the bloody Battle of Stones River on the last day of 1862 and the first two days of 1863.

100. Private Charles Hemming, son of Charles C. Hemming of Jacksonville, and Private John Wesley Wethington, also of that place. Hemming and Willie transferred back to Company A, Third Florida Infantry, but Wethington, who was discharged earlier in 1862 for being underage, reenlisted in time for the fight at Perryville and served there in Company H, Third Florida Infantry. Wounded twice at Perryville, he finished the war in the Fifth Florida Infantry Battalion. He was the nephew of Samuel S. Adams of Thomasville, who was married to Mary Frances Bryant, Willie's aunt.

have read of it; I have seen one in all its points, I left nothing unseen, and never will I forget it: I of course had many narrow escapes, men shot down on *every* side of me, balls striking near me and once as I lay on the ground taking aim a ball so filled my eyes with dirt as to blind me for some time, but that was the nearest I came to being hurt, not once a shot thro' my clothing.

Perhaps you wd. like to know my feelings and how I acted; for an hour before we fired we lay on the ground under a hill exposed to shot and shell which killed and wounded several, and were whizzing and striking uncomfortably close, I was almost *perfectly* cool and free from any nervousness and I think from *all* fear; when in action, which the other was play to, I felt considerably excited and a *little* dread, at first, but no fear, and to test myself, exposed my whole body needlessly, but soon saw the worse than folly of it and became cautious, and hereafter, should I ever be again engaged shall be as much so as possible; I think that you feared, and I thought too, that I would be much excited and rash; *impartially*, I am satisfied with myself. I was very generally reported and believed to be killed, and had the "satisfaction" of *hearing* it told; a *Henry Bryan* son of Col. Stephen Bryan was killed; I fear that the news and exaggerated reports will reach you before you get this or see the list of casualties . . .[101] Much love to all and a thousand kisses for you and Tivie and give little Rosa a share too—

Very affectionately
Willie—

[WINSTON STEPHENS TO OCTAVIA STEPHENS]

Middleburg Oct 15, 1862[102]

My Dear Wife

I send back these few lines to inform you of what the Enemy have threatened to do and I have no doubt they will do it if they have an opportunity—they say they intend to force the negroes to go with them, that they intend to pay the expense of the war with the negroes and that they will make us suffer in the distruction of our property as much as they can. They took some negroes by force in Jacksonville and they even took women that refused to go—I hardly know what to advise you to do but I want you at least to call the negroes together and tell them what they may depend upon and tell them when the Gun boat is about my place or Welaka they had better keep on the watch and run into the

---

101. Stephen Bryan was the largest planter in Clay County; in 1860 he owned ninety slaves and lived near Orange Park. He moved his large family to Alachua County in 1863 because of the Federal threat and sold out and left the state before the year was over. See Blakey, *Parade of Memories*, 60–68. His son, Henry, was in Company B, Third Florida Infantry, when he was killed on 8 October 1862.

102. Winston left Rose Cottage on 13 October to rejoin his company.

woods if they come to the house—If Sarah will cling to you they may not take her as they have allowed some to stay that did so, several negroes have been shot in this neighborhood—one was killed last night. I wish Clark would kill the Officers if they land and I think they will be afraid to come out—the neighbors should band together for mutual protection and I think they can keep them from coming out—I wish you were out from the river and I should not be alarmed. I think the mill had better stand awhile and let us see what they will do—let Burrel and Tom split rails and the rest can be imployed on the new ground and fences—unless you can find a place back in the country and you think it best to move the negroes to it. I do not fear much for any thing but them and the provisions and cotton—I dont think they will disturb you or Mother but they will take all the property of mine they can get—as I am a Rebel Capt . . .

Much love to all and a kiss for you and Rosa, Good by and May heaven protect you all. your loving husband

Winston Stephens

[Rebecca] Oct 17, 1862. Rosa's birthday! We all pass the day at Mrs Stephen's—I go to the office with the boys and go into the house also—sad and desolate all around! Yet there was a melancholy satisfaction in standing once more beneath that roof where I have enjoyed so many happy days.

[WINSTON STEPHENS TO DAVIS BRYANT]

Camp Finegan Oct 19, 1862

Dear Davis

. . . I hope you may never have the misfortune to be placed in the same position I was on the Memorable 2nd. You have no doubt had many and various accounts of our retreat from the St Johns Bluff and I fear that my power of writing events will fail in this instant when I attempt to give you some of the details of that masterly retreat, no one that has any knowledge of the Bluff will dare say the retreat was not masterly, when they understand our force and situation and that of the enemy. You know the Geography of the country and I will only give you the retreat, etc. On the 1st the Gun boats moved up and commenced bombarding our bateries on the bluff and under cover of that fire landed a large force variously estimated at from three to four thousand men—I think about 32 hundred in all.[103] My Pickets were stationed near the landing place and reported the landing etc. Col Hopkins had several days before reported to Genl Finegan that the enemy were being reinforced in Gun boats and transports and

---

103. The Federal force consisted of 1,573 infantry plus the crews of the gunboats, about triple the number of Confederates.

called for reinforcements and on the 1st ordered Capt Dunham to bring over his command from Yellow bluff. Capt Dunham sent over detachments numbering some 120 men from three companies . . . but refused to come with his artilery and ordered Lt Villepigue to remain at Yellow Bluff. On the morning of the 2nd. my pickets . . . ascertained the enemy were flanking us and our force was so small we . . . remounted and marched back to our incampment some four miles and I thought we would make a stand at that place but after resting a very short time we were ordered to remount and continue the march in the direction of the Bluff, the Enemy following rapidly for their force. Capt C and myself went in and saw Col Hopkins and proposed to have two of the field Howitzers and mount them on a high and commanding hill which he agreed to and we went to work[104] . . . but about 9 o'clock that night I was sent for by Maj Brevard and told that a counsil had been held and that myself and Capt Chambers were the only officers not at the Council and that the unanimous decision was to give up the Bluff and that in trying to move the two guns they had got them boged in the mud and could not get them out—I was ordered to bring my command out which I did and mounted my company, then I was ordered by Col Hopkins to bring up the rear and protect the command from an attack which I did, arriving at the ferry about 9 or 10 o clock Friday morning. You can better imagine my troubles than I can write them, think of men giving out, sick and lame all had to be helped and I had it all to do—poor fellows I pitied them and did all I could to help them, but in spite of all my efforts some few were left on the way, but near Jacksonville and have since got in safely—I got up so late that I was afraid to attempt to cross my company at Jacksonville and had to go up as high as Fort Gates to cross and swim several creeks and I came near being drowned in Haws creek and lost my mare, though I may get her yet.[105] I found all at home anxious but well. I remained a few days at home and then returned to my duties in camp—The whole trip was trying and hard and my men and horses are worn down but thank God we keep well. I was opposed to leaving without a fight but I am sure now it was for the best to come off—but if we had been reinforced by the Artilery we could

---

104. Captain William E. Chambers was in command of an independent company that was soon designated Company C, Second Florida Cavalry. The Confederate position was strong and could have inflicted much damage on any ship, but the position could easily be flanked by army units that could be landed in the rear of the bluff. Winston was correct when he reported that the only way to hold the place was to stop the Federals with reinforcements, which should have been sent by Finegan when Hopkins asked for them.

105. After Winston lost his horse he proceeded to James Braddock's farm, borrowed a horse, and led his command to Fort Gates. The Fort Gates ferry was and is about three miles south of Welaka. The ferry, at that time operated by Theodore Dukes, has been in continuous operation since 1856. Winston sent his command across and then rode to Rose Cottage. From St. Johns Bluff to Rose Cottage is about 110 miles. He left Jacksonville at noon on Friday and arrived home about 10 P.M. Monday night, covering about 30 miles a day, excellent time considering the terrain.

have given them a good fight—The trouble is that if we fought we had to succeed or be taken prisinors owing to the situation of the country . . . yours ever.

Winston

[OCTAVIA STEPHENS TO WINSTON STEPHENS]

Rose Cottage Oct 23, 1862

My dear husband

. . . I hardly believe the Gunboats are going to pay us a visit for they have staid away so long. I have concluded to stay here and run the risk of their coming for I know of no place to go to and I thought by the time we could get moved the Yankees if they were coming would be here and do all the damage they wanted . . . The negroes seem much afraid of the Yankees and keep a watch for them, and say if they catch them they will have to do it with a bullet . . .

You may be sure Mother is anxious now as we have heard of the great battle fought in Kentucky. The Savannah paper has begun again about the prospect of Foreign intervention but I have no faith in it, but I wish to heaven that something would stop the war. I begin to fear again that we will have to give up as I hear our soldiers in Virginia are so poorly off for clothing that if they do not have ready assistance they will have to disband, there are some stirring letters in the Savannah paper about it, one from Aunt Julia. Mother and Tina are high for doing something, but I think we can do no good worth counting, as I believe there is no such thing as stirring up the country people, and without their help we could do nothing but knit a few pairs of socks . . .

I was sorry to see you did not enjoy your visit more when you were here, you did not seem yourself. I hope it was not my "crossness" altogether. I knew I was more cross than I used to be but did not know I had got so bad, I hope your next visit will be more pleasant, perhaps by then some of my troubles will be over and I may be better natured and you may have another little one to make you happier. I have heard that women in my situation are always more cross and I hope it may prove so in my case and that my husband will again love me as he used to. I hope you do not see so many prettier and more agreeable persons in your travels around as to wean you from me . . . Rosa is full of fun and often asks for you, and says "ait soon PaPa tum . . ." I rec a letter from Loulie this week, the Yankees had threatened to break up the salt works and ordered them all to leave before the next Saturday. Mr Tydings wanted to leave as soon as possible and were going to visit in Thomasville in November, Lou sent her love to you . . .

Well I guess you have had enough of me for this time so I'll close. Mother and the boys send their love, and Rosa and I love and kisses

Affly
Your Wife

[WINSTON STEPHENS TO OCTAVIA STEPHENS]

Camp Finegan Oct 23, 1862

My Dear Wife

I seat myself to write you a letter and hope you will be repaid for the trouble of reading—I am well, thats right so far! We are generally well but on short allowance which makes soldiers in bad humor, but I am in good humor as I have just had dinner—Baked beef, potatoes (at one dollar pr bushel) and rice with a little sugar for desert. we have no syrup since the *run*. We have to purchase feed for our mess servants which makes bill of fare pretty high . . . We are in camp eight miles from Jacksonville and with the whole command under one rule— That rule is Col C. Hopkins. We are satisfied with him as our ruler but Finegan has made his rules quite *military and formal*. Old Barny finds public sentiment changing in favor of Hopkins and against himself and he is in quite a pet and is trying to get up something sustaining for his case and he is like a drowning man, he will clutch at a straw and Finegan is drumming up every thing to throw blame on others and rid himself of part of the load. Madam rumor says he intends to have me Courtmartialed for going up the river, but I dont believe it. Enough of *Finegan and his*.[106] The Yankees behaved more like rogues and black hearted scamps in Jacksonville than they ever have on the river before. They sent out a man who represented himself as quartermaster and he took any and every thing he wanted for his department, then came out the soldiers and rob'd what they wanted, then came armed negroe men and demanded what they wanted and swore and shined around in uniform quite extensively and last came the sailors and got their share of the spoils. They not only took things but they broke and destroyed furniture and smashed in doors and windows etc to a great extent . . .

Watch every thing closely and I want Henry to shoot any run aways about my place. Give my love to Mother, boys and Clark and family. Kiss Dear Rosa and wifie can take a kiss from Rosa for your Aff husband

Winston Stephens

[Rebecca] Oct 28, 1862. Cloudy—It is a year to-day since I came to stay with Tivie! The war seems now no nearer its end than it appeared then—

---

106. Finegan had a mixed career during the war. He was strapped for troops while in command in Florida, but at this time he probably erred in not supporting Hopkins with the available reinforcements. He did little at Olustee in February 1864 but shuttle his troops into battle as Brigadier General Alfred H. Colquitt requested them. The victory was not followed up with vigor, and Finegan was replaced by Major General James Patton Anderson, even though he had won the battle. Finegan was sent to Virginia and placed in command of a Florida brigade. There he and his men performed excellently for the remainder of the war. All in all, he was an able commander, but Winston obviously had little use for him.

and my boys farther from me and in constant danger. We know not what a day may bring forth much less a year . . .

[WINSTON STEPHENS TO OCTAVIA STEPHENS]

Camp Finegan Oct 29, 1862

My Dear Wife

. . . I had the pleasure of meeting Genl Finegan Yesterday and we had quite a tongue lashing and every one standing by said I got the best of him. At any rate he stoped talking and said there was no use of talking more about the matter and today he met me in a good humor and seemed better pleased with me than I have ever seen him, so I suppose my independent talk did me some good that time. I had my mind made up to make him respect me or I would not respect him.[107] The Genl blames the Commanding Officer and some spicy articles have appeared and the Genls side has so far got decidedly the worst of it . . .

I am sorry you have to stop your riding but My Dear I am glad you think it best as I have thought so some time but I would not say so as you would perhaps think I did it to stop your going to Tinas so much and to be candid with you, I think you get a part of your bad humor by seeing Tina show her temper so much and I know your situation is some cause of ill humor, but My Dear as to not loving you as much as ever I say if it is possible I love you more than I ever did, not because you are sometimes cross but because I know that no one is perfect and you can compare creditably with any wife and I have hoped you will get rid of your little bad humor and then we can be so happy—It is our duty to try and cheer each other and get the other in a good humor when the other is out of humor. We are all frail creatures and subject to ere and the best of us will do wrong at times. Never let it cross your mind that I will ever be drawn off by any other woman or women. You know the promise I made you before the alter and rest assured that vow is sacred with me and if I am cool at any time it will not be that I love you less, but that something has troubled me. When I was home last I was not aware that I was not myself, but I do admit I was troubled about many things and my mind was constantly trying to plan for the future for you and those that are dear to me, remember my situation when I was last home and I must think you cannot blame me for being troubled and perhaps I appeared changed . . . I want you to let me know again when you look for an increase and I will ask for a furlough at that time and if I am refused I will resign and come any way as I must be with you if possible on that occasion. I want you to have some Dr with you and I must say I had rather have some one besides Dr Currel . . .

107. Arguments flared between officers in both armies and were usually resolved, as this one was. But so many official charges were brought in the Confederate forces, it appeared at times that almost all of the officers were prima donnas. Winston and Finegan had no more trouble after this encounter, but Winston never liked or respected his superior.

Give love to Mother and boys and accept much love and many kisses for you and Dear Rosa from your ever Affectionate husband

Winston

[OCTAVIA STEPHENS TO WINSTON STEPHENS]

Rose Cottage Oct 31, 1862

My own dear husband

... Burrel has had to give the sows up ... I think these in the field look very well now. I wrote you that we had another shoat up, we killed the one we had up when you were here last Monday, he was plenty fat enough for fresh pork, you see I am better off than some folks, I have *bacon* in my smoke house. I hear that Burrel has some very fine, he has killed all his, he was afraid the Yankees would do it for him, Sarah's breast is getting better, big Jane is sick with a dreadful cough, though I think is better to day, we think Mother had a slight chill night before last, and this afternoon she took cotton seed tea and is well so far to night, though feels as though she had been sick. Rosa is very well, looks quite fat and rosy, and talks a great deal, says a great many funny things, yesterday morning I went to her bed to take her out and she said "dont take 'Osa' out" so I went on dressing and a minute after said "Ma Ma Osa too sick" and a few days ago we heard quite a fuss behind the bed and found out she was trying to carry the cat to her *chair* and afterwards heard her telling the cat about telling Ma Ma chair, she says a great many things through the day to make us laugh, she nearly lives out doors now making sand cakes. She goes to sleep now in her crib every night, by my lying down awhile with her, I had trouble at first, but by repeating some little story to her have got her more resigned, and the last two nights have not even done that though she says every night that she wants to go to sleep in Ma Ma's lap ...

This is the last day of October and no telling what may happen two months from now, oh how I dread to have the end of each month come, oh that I were only as I was nine or ten months ago. I dread the event enough, but when I think it probable that you will not be here it makes me feel worse, my health continues pretty good but I suffer a good deal with my back and tire easily and sometimes I feel as though it would take very little to *tip me over*, but pshaw there is no use talking about it. It has yet to come and I have it to bear. I lived through it once and may again, but it is horrible, horrible, horrible ...

Well I guess I will close as my back and side ache, and I am pretty tired generally having trotted around considerably to day. Good night God bless and protect my dear husband

Ever affectionately
Tivie

[Rebecca] *Nov 1, 1862.* Sat. Quite warm. The anniversary of Tivie's marriage. What changes in 3 years! Write to Sister Julia to-day inclosing $5. for soldiers clothing.

[WILLIE BRYANT TO REBECCA BRYANT]

Knoxville Tenn. Nov 1, 1862

My own dear Mother,

... First let me repeat that we are camped 2 miles from Knoxville, where we arrived on Friday pm Oct 21, and are expecting orders daily to leave; where for we are not permitted to know; most conjecture Mobile, or near, many, Murfreesboro Tenn, *some* Augusta Geo. to be convenient to Charleston and Savn'h; *I*, Mobile: at all events we leave here in a day or two for Chattanooga and as soon as I can, will inform you more fully. Secondly, I am in the best of health, and fat for me, tho' to my disappointment I find I am not one of the fat kind and can't get up to 150, tho' I don't know how much I do weigh now; Yes, on striking a balance I find myself a gainer by my trip into Kentucky, and that is more than most can say; now it is over I am glad I went, but I don't want to go again ...

I was too busy attending to the wounded on the battlefield that night to get many trophies, but I have a carnelian ring,[108] which I took off a young chap's finger "who I knew had no further use for it," which I wish to send to Rosa by first better chance, a good pocket knife, and a canteen and tin cup which I cut from a dead Yankee while chasing them at "double quick," I also took a haversack with some parchd. coffee and hard bread, which was a rarity and I enjoyed it and the more so as I lost mine that night with two days rations in it. Tuesday 4th. I left this open for something more definite to turn up and Yesterday we moved 7 miles, and am camped now on the line of R.R. preparatory to moving to Chattanooga, which may be 2 days or more ... We will be kept in Tenn I think. I have walked to town—5 miles—this a.m. to get an overcoat ... which makes me comfortable, except in shoes, which I will get soon—I, with hundreds of others, lost my knapsack and blankets etc at the time of the fight by the bad management of the Officers in command, but I had on a good suit and got along pretty well and since then have bought and drawn till I am not in need longer; but many thousands have been obliged to sit up by the fires night after night to keep warm until their eyes, faces, feet, and hands have terribly swollen by excessive heat and cold.

We had a storm of snow and sleet soon after our arrival here which lasted 2 days and nights, and being without tents gave us fits; after writing you that Sunday P.M. I rode in a heavy snow and then sleet storm from before dark till after 9 o'clk; cold as it was I rather enjoyed it, and the sight next day was beautiful; and

---

108. Carnelian is a reddish, translucent variety of quartz. The ring has been lost.

that night I was out on foot thro' the freezing mud and water till past 10, having been sent off with waggons after forage early that a.m.—Rheumatism gives me no trouble, but we all have had colds now; mine is going off now however, and as we have some tents now and I this overcoat, I think I will be free in the future as I have been; I have slept many nights on the wet ground with a wet blanket *over* me thro' a cold rain, and been wet for days and nights often; my flannel shirt and heavy wool socks helps me all right—I think I may now say I have gone thro' everything which I will ever have to endure in the service, and as I am better in health and strength than when I entered I feel no uneasiness for the future . . .

Good bye—Kind remembrance to Mrs Stephens, and other friends, and tell her I have a big pack of big stories to tell when I get back; she knows my "capability"—Love and kisses to all

Yr loving son always Willie

[WINSTON STEPHENS TO OCTAVIA STEPHENS]

Camp Finegan Nov 4, 1862

My Dear Wife

. . . I want you to send out to Mr Granville Priest and see if he will gin my cotton at once and if he will I want it carried out as I can sell it for 40 cents at the river and I fear the Yankees may destroy it or take it and I had better sell. do make them push it up if Mr Priest will gin it. Some think the Yankees will occupy this State this winter but I dont think they will unless they can take Savannah or Charleston, but we had better prepare for them and for that reason I want to get my cotton off . . . Let Burrel hunt the hogs about the Bluff. I hope you will make pork enough to do. Give love to Clark and family. Also Mother and boys, and accept love and kisses for yourself and Rosa. As ever your loving husband

Winston Stephens

[OCTAVIA STEPHENS TO WINSTON STEPHENS]

Rose Cottage Nov 8, 1862

My own dear husband

. . . We had the pleasure of riding in our buggy yesterday, we got it home the first of the week. I intend to ride often now as I find it much easier to me than even walking, though shall keep up my little walking, as regards the expected time, it ought to come between the 21st of December and the first of January if nothing unusual brings it before. I can not well count from before the 21st of March up after the 1st of April. oh I do hope you will be here I can not bear the idea of being sick and you away. I think if you give your reasons, *the particular* reason when you ask for your furlough that it will be granted without resigning . . .

oh how anxious I feel when I hear of your going on those scouts, do they ever send any one else on scouts? seems to me they always pick you out, but I had ten times rather have you do that than be in Virginia or Kentucky. I hope Finegan and others will respect you more instead of disrespecting you, and I hope they will favor you more . . .

Rosa talks much more now and much plainer, yesterday morning she asked if you were coming to day, and this morning said "by by pa pa tum tiss Osa" then she had the cat in her lap and wanted to know if you would kiss kitty. I told her I thought you would have a decided objection to that, you will find her much improved in every way when you come again . . .

Mother sends love, Rosa and I send lots of love and kisses.

Yr loving

Wife

[REBECCA BRYANT TO DAVIS BRYANT]

Rose Cottage Nov 8, 1862

My dear Davis,

. . . Although Winston has no idea of moving this Winter, I cannot give up the idea of seeing you the last of this month or first of next. I say the *first* of Decr. because Tivie will probably be confined about Christmas holidays and it wd. not be pleasant for you to be here then. We *all* want to see you so much we cannot think of yr giving it up. Tivie says she has been looking forward to it so long, you *must* come. My anxiety and dreadful suspense about Willie seems to increase my desire to see you. I have not a line from him later than Sept. 7th. and it appears you have none later than 14th . . .

With an ocean of love I am ever

Yrs fondly

Mother

[Rebecca] **Nov 9, 1862.** *The coldest morng. of the season, a light frost last night — Read a sermon . . . in the morgn. After dinner I review my dear Willie's letters, written since he entered the service of the Co States. How vividly they bring his image before me! How shall I prize them if I never receive another from his hands!*

[WILLIE BRYANT TO REBECCA BRYANT]

Alisonia Tenn on the Chga and Nvlle R.R. Nov 14, 1862

My dear Mother,

... I am very desirous of recv'g further news from you tho' happily I can feel no anxiety; I want to know where Davis and Winston are—At last my good health has been affected, for the past ten days I have been much troubled with diarrhoea, which with slight fever and want of proper nourishment has made me very weak, and just sick enough to be right "blue," and long to be able to lounge around home; but for the past three days I have avoided duty, and dosed plentifully, and this p.m. am pretty straight again; I shall continue to dose and be careful until my liver and whole system are in perfect order again, and in three days I think I will be all right. Very mild weather we have had has cured the cold I mentioned.

I weighed in Knvlle the day I wrote you and weighed 139 lbs; I think I look as if I wghd. more—If we remain in Tenn this winter I know we will all feel the cold very sensibly, and . . . the government is unable to furnish clothing for all of us, and even if it could be bought our pay would be insufficient; accordingly quantities of clothing etc are being prepared for the soldiers in the different states; a good supply will soon be sent from Monticello for the two companies in this regmt. and I being in one come in for a share if I need any thing; other regmts. are sending two men from each company home, or elsewhere, to bring or purchase clothing etc, and I think such an arrangement will soon be made in ours; but better, application has been made for a furlough for the regmt; I do not suppose it will be granted but if we should be permanently stationed anywhere we would probably be allowed it by squads, at any rate if the thing be possible *I* must have a furlough this winter, and if I see no probability of getting it in a "natural" way soon, I shall try all the hooks and crooks I can devise;—When ever I have a "regular attack of reflections"—as I frequently do—about home affairs, and think how long a time has elapsed, and how much transpired, since I saw you last, it seems as if I could not endure the seperation much longer; since I have found out how little it is appreciated, my desire for self sacrifices for patriotism has considerably subsided; I find but few in the service who have as little selfishness and the right kind of patriotism as I, and who can appreciate it, and I have been greatly disappointed and decieved, and hereafter I shall "look out more for No 1"; to my sorrow I have found out that in the service as in all matters of the world, true moral worth and uprightness profit but little for promotion, the most impudent, cunning and obsequious boot lickers, are the most favored; at any rate I have the self satisfaction of knowing that thro' all the low meanness, selfishness and vice that I have been surrounded by, that I have maintained the dignity and demanded the respect of a gentleman; but I am not fortunate in possessing the right kind of disposition to work my way up in the world, nor can I, or *will* I learn it; proud, sensitive, quick to resent a wrong or slight, reserved toward those in whom I detech anything low and mean, and a good judge of human nature and not *very* "democratic," I can't accede, or rather concede to the demands of the world and be what is termed *popular,* in all spheres; in fact I am particularly unfortunate in this respect, and wish I was differently constituted to an extent; I fear now that I am adding to my natural stock of misanthropy, and gracious knows that is large enough; O! how I do long for a *social* change, to be among those from whom I can receive a kind act or favor without feeling that it is done thro' some selfish motive, or myself obligated . . .

I missed sending this yesterday a.m. but will send it now to be mailed in Fla. by a discharged soldier, I will also enclose the cornelian ring for Rosa, as I do not know when I will have a better chance; it is a trophy from the first battlefield I ever was on; perhaps before the war ends I may be able to give her one of more value . . . I hope all is well with you and to hear fully soon; do let me know just how you are all situated—Good bye—With much love to all Ever affectionately

Willie

[WINSTON STEPHENS TO OCTAVIA STEPHENS]

Camp Finegan Nov 20, 1862

My Dear Wife

. . . The camp is in an uproar with fun and the noise would indicate contentment and I believe that most of the boys are satisfied but some are not contented. You would be amused at some of the tricks they fix up on one another and some of them get the hardest falls and bumps you ever saw, but as it is in fun they have to laugh it all off and try to pay off in the same coin.

I am tired and not feeling so fresh . . . I have ridden about 30 or 35 miles to day looking at the positions on the river . . . I made no discoveries to day worth notice. The Gun boats have not been up since Saturday. I intended in my last to tell you how I wanted the potatoes put up. I want you to put them up in banks as usual only I dont want straw put over them, put bark and a little dirt merely enough to cover them. I hear that my way of bedding them heats them and makes them rot . . .

Good by, I hope to be with you before long, love to Mother and boys and many kisses and much love to Rosa and My Dear Wife

Your ever aff husband
Winston Stephens

[OCTAVIA STEPHENS TO WINSTON STEPHENS]

Rose Cottage Nov 21, 1862

My dear husband

Clark arrived yesterday afternoon and brought your nice long letter and I assure you I was rejoiced to get it, for I had not heard from you for two weeks, and it seemed as though there was no probability of my hearing soon by mail as they were so uncertain, my hope was in Clark's returning, I felt quite certain I would hear by him. I was glad to hear such a good report of your health, I was afraid that I might hear of the continuation of your cough, fearing you might have neglected it as before. nearly every one around here have or have had colds, we are still blessed with good health, Georgie has had quite a sick time this week besides fever has had some kind of eruption, dont know whether it is erysipelas or nettle rash or what it is, he has escaped all to day, and is quite bright tonight and is playing on the floor with Rosa, if we have fevers now I dont know what we shall do for medicine for Clark has informed us that cotton seed tea is injurious and I had placed great confidence in it, though luckily have not used much of it, and had determined not to take it myself. I hear that Clark was quite troubled for fear I might have had chill and fever and taken some while he was gone, for he thought I would certainly take it, if I had, and he heard of a case of abortion being brought on in five minutes, and almost death, from a lady's taking the tea, from what he heard it is a dangerous thing, for both sexes. I think you or I had better drink some when my trouble is over this time, *dont you?*

Clark is going to see Mr Priest about the cotton, Burrel has been waiting for frost to pick the last of the cotton . . . The pea field is eaten out and I am anxious for frost that we may turn the stock into the potatoe patch, the hogs jumped the fence like a dog and Burrel had to shut them in the lot last Sunday until Monday when he hauled rails and made the fence higher, I have killed only one hog as I thought you might not want them killed so soon . . . I have already patched up your old pants and given them to Burrel and Tom, I do not want to give him those pants of yours, he wants a coat, I think they can do very well, if they leave on that account after the pains I have always taken about their clothes let them go, some times I almost declare I wont puzzle my brain so much about them for they dont appreciate it one bit, though I know they are better than most negroes . . .

What do you think? Rosa has just gone to bed she had a nap coming home in the buggy and has just acknowledged that she was ready to go to bed and it is nine o'clock, she does not seem to take after you in that respect, she seems to like to sit up. I must write you some thing she said the other day. I was dressing and had but few garments on and she said "aint big Ma Ma?" so you cant say now you have a little wife, when she thinks I am big, a day or two ago she came to me holding on to one finger and said "I beeve I tut my finger" and sure enough she had sliced quite a piece off of her finger.

Never fear that I will get tired of reading your letters, no matter how long they are, it would be well if you loved to write them as well as I love to read them, I read them over and over until I get them almost by heart. I must close now, I hope you are now having a pleasant dream of me, I still continue to dream of you, it is so pleasant to see you in my dreams if I can not in reality. I want to see you *very* much. I get dreadfully homesick lovesick or something for you sometimes. oh if this war would only end. Good night my dear, how much happier I would feel if I could have a good night kiss from you before going to bed.

Ever your loving

Wife

[REBECCA BRYANT TO WILLIE BRYANT]

Rose Cottage Nov 21, 1862

My own dear Willie,

I am, and have been in such an agony of suspense for the last five weeks, regarding your whereabouts and condition, that I have determined to wait no longer for advices *where* to address you, but send this as I did my last written five weeks ago, to Chattanooga—I think it must reach you sometime, by that route, if you are *any where in Tennessee*—We learn by the papers, that Gen Bragg's army has left Kentucky—I cannot account for me having no letters from you—Yesterday I recd. a Tallahassee paper sent by Winston which had a list of the casualties in the 3d. Regt. at the battle of Perryville. You can judge how eagerly and yet trembling I perused it—Thank Heaven your name *was not* there, and I fell upon my knees to thank our Heavenly Father for his mercy . . .

We are promised a mail next Sunday—the first for two weeks and I hope, still hope, though so many times disappointed. This much I do know with certainty, that you have been in a terrible battle, and I believe you to be uninjured—but O! how much you must have suffered from fatigue, exhaustion, perhaps from hunger and thirst and other causes that I know nothing about—Yes, you have been in the horrid carnage of the battle field, and have seen your comrades fall around you, not knowing but your turn would be the next! It is what you have wished for you hoped that it might not be your fate to pass thro' the War without it, you wished to share all the dangers, privations and trials of this conflict and you certainly have been gratified—Now if there is an armistice which is talked of confidently, may we not hope you will visit us? The hope may prove as delusive as a hundred others have before—but it seems as if we must have a respite from our misery soon—If these fiery trials make us all sincere Christians evermore, then indeed we shall have reason to bless God for them . . .

Tivie sends an ocean of love—Rosa is asleep.

Mother

[Rebecca] *Nov 25, 1862. Clear and not so cold—Quite warm in the middle of the day—Henry goes to town and returns with 3 letters from Willie, 1 from Davis 1 from Aunt Julia, 1 from Winston, and 7 newspapers! God be praised that our dear Willie is in perfect health notwithstanding the dangers he has passed through—and he is deeply grateful for it. Davis is well too and expects to be with us soon! George has a return of his eruption to-day.*

[Rebecca] *Nov 28, 1862. . . . About 7 ½ o'clk p.m. Davis arrives! We all talk fast enough from that time until 10 o'clk, when we retire happy.*

[OCTAVIA STEPHENS TO WINSTON STEPHENS]

Rose Cottage Nov 30, 1862

My dear husband

. . . I am very anxious to hear from you now as you wrote in the latest that you were sick with cold and fever. I hope by this time you are all right again, and able to join in some of the frolics which were going on when you wrote, or dont you ever join in them? I can not imagine you frolicking, it is such a long time since I saw you frolicsome. Since the day after receiving your letter . . . I have been half sick with a dreadful cold and about as sore a throat as I ever had, but managed to keep about scarcely able to speak at all, when I did just about a whisper, to night I feel much better, and hope I will soon be all right. I began dosing from the first as I found it jarred me so much and made me feel so badly, that I was afraid it might bring on something else, and I try to be very careful for I am as afraid that something *might* happen before you come. oh how near my time is now, I can not bear to think of it, I wish it was over for I am so good for nothing, I shall look for you in little over two weeks, I am so anxious to see you. Rosa had fever yesterday but has been tolerably bright to day. I have just put her to bed, I gave her some oil to day and hope there will be no need of any more medicine. Georgie is still on the sick list, or rather is a convalescent as he has missed his fever and eruptions yesterday and to day he looks pretty well bleached after two weeks sickness, he would have fever one day and that singular eruption with fever the next, the day that he had the eruption he would be taken with a pain in the stomach and in a short time this stuff as he calls it would come out on him and worry him terribly with itching.

I have written all this and have not told you that Davis is with us, he arrived here last Friday night and will stay this week with us, then will make you a visit on his way back to camp, he will probably be at your camp on Monday the 8th Dec...

We have had some pretty cool weather here this last week. I had four hogs killed, they made pretty good meat, good sized pieces but none too fat for rations, I made some sausages, a few, and hope you will like them when you come, but do not expect you to enjoy them as much as I before thought as Clark says you have plenty down at camp. I shall not feel that you enjoy any eatables at home, as I hear you live like Lords down there...

Yr loving
Wife

[REBECCA BRYANT TO WILLIE BRYANT]

Rose Cottage Nov 30, 1862

My dear, dear Willie,

My heart was relieved of an immense weight on Tuesday last by the receipt of *three* letters from you... I devoutly trust and earnestly pray that the same Merciful Power that has protected you thus far, will preserve you through coming dangers and restore you in safety to us, before many months.

You have endured *every thing but* wounds from the enemy—You say you are the gainer in health by it and I am thankful indeed for that, and hope you are. I trust you will not be subjected to a continuation of such trials and privations, though I know you will not enjoy much *comfort* while in the service. We are now hoping to hear again soon, informing us of your destination—I wish the change might bring you a little nearer home, so that we could hear more regularly and frequently from you. This week has been the happiest I have passed in a long time. The same mail that brought your letters, also brot. one from Davis, saying he wd. be with us soon and accordingly he arrived on Friday eveg. about 7 ½ o'clk. He looks well and says he is stronger and weighs more than ever before. He will remain with us 5 or 6 days longer... I thank you dear Willie for writing me so promptly and so much of your own feelings after the battle; if I could have recd. your first letter in the normal time it would have saved me many sad hours. I hope our mail will not always be so tardy. But when letters *do* come how welcome they are...

To-day has been delightful with us, after several days of cold. I should be very glad to hear of the 3d. Regt. being ordered farther South for I anticipate a severe winter. Tivie sends much love and says she wishes you "a Merry Christmas"—I had not thought of such a thing—but I have often recurred to *last* Christmas and the pleasant visit we had from you and thought of you as you rode off from us the morng. of the 1st. Jany.—Oh that we might see you before another New Year! But a truce to vain wishes—I will try to be patient, as you are under all you have to encounter. We expect to have a visit from Winston about the 20th. of December, that will come soon after Davis leaves us . . . God bless you my dear boy—

Mother

[WINSTON STEPHENS TO OCTAVIA STEPHENS]

Camp Finegan Dec 1, 1862

My Dear Wife

. . . I have obtained a Furlough of one month to be with you during your illness, I will start on the 13th or 14 and it will take me about three days to get home I will be with you if life lasts at or about that time . . .

I start tomorrow to Tallahassee to attend the Court Martial of My Deserter and perhaps I will get back by Saturday I will not write any more unless some one comes direct home. Mr Greely is attending the Legislature as he is a member of that Hon body. I am glad to go during the session as I will see the *Eliphant*.[109] I think My Deserter will see him before he gets out of the scrape he is into. I will try and make the case as easy as possible for him under the circumstances . . .

I dont intend to drink cotton seed and dont want you to. If *God* sees fit to give us children we will with his help take care of them. Saturday I went with Maj Scott to the *Crespo*, but I find him like myself as he told me he would not be seduced from his wife for any price.[110] I told him of the report about them before we went, but as he had promised to call there for Capts Chambers and Bird we did so, but my Dear we stoped only a few moments and no harm shall come of it and nothing but business can ever induce me to go.[111] I hold my little or *big* wife too sacred for such creatures as they and I want you to know I think more of myself. If I thought you really suspected me of such a thing I should be unhappy

---

109. To have "seen the elephant" meant to have seen the world or to have become more cosmopolitan. See Partridge, *Dictionary of Slang*, 256. In mid-nineteenth-century America, the phrase was associated with the Oregon, Santa Fe, and other trails west and meant that the individual had undergone a rough ordeal and lived to tell about it. A rough equivalent today might be "Now I've seen everything." It is interesting that, by the mid-1870s, it meant exclusively "to have been seduced." During the Civil War, it normally meant to have seen combat.

110. Major William Washington Scott, on detached duty from the First Florida Infantry Battalion, was in command of Camp Finegan at this time. He was promoted to lieutenant colonel in 1864 and served in the Tenth Florida Infantry Regiment under the command of Colonel Charles Hopkins during the last year of the war. Scott lost an arm at Hatcher's Run, Virginia, in February 1865.

111. William Chambers has been previously mentioned, as has Captain Pickens B. Bird of the Second Florida Infantry Battalion.

and could not live with you under such circumstances. I want our lives spent with the same confidence and I will avoid all collision of a suspicious kind. I would not do such a thing if I had no other restraint but my dear Daughter, but having one such as you are makes it impossible to tempt me.

I do hope you will not feel that Mother is in my way, for I do assure you I feel that I could not rest satisfied if she was away, I hope she may never feel that she is in the way and if she ever mentions any thing tell her that I feel more than paid by her company and kindness to you and my interest. *Dont you allow Miss Stephens to sit up so late . . .*

Give love to Mother and boys Clark and family and kiss Rosa and tell her papa [is] coming to kiss her. Good night and God bless you, I dont often dream of you but I constantly think of you.

Your loving Husband
Winston Stephens

[WILLIE BRYANT TO REBECCA BRYANT]

Head Qd. Army of Tenn. Murfreesboro Tenn. Dec 4, 1862

My dear mother,

I last wrote from Alisonia on the Nashville and Chattanooga R. Rd., promising to write George soon, a promise I have not fulfilled, owing to numerous duties, and the difficulty in getting writing material, however, I will "owe him a letter all my life rather than cheat him out of it"—as I heard a fellow say concerning some money, once . . . I have good news for you, Mother! I say *you* because I consider it good mostly for the relief I know it will give you; Through the influence of Jason Fairbanks I have been detailed as clerk in the Office of General Bragg's Adjutant Genl., Col. Brent, and am installed in my new situation![112] So, you need have no more anxious fears about my health, or life; I have now no guard duty to perform in the rain and cold, little exposure to endure, and no tedious marches or ½ rations to make, nor Yankees to fight, "against superior odds and numbers," *also* no orders from pompous and half witted officers to obey; just think what a list of evils I might sum up that I am now clear of!

I have been in the office three days, and find my situation very honorable, and agreable, tho' the duties are at present very confining; as matters are at present arranged there are two offices, Col. B—'s, and the clerks', and I am in the office of Col. B—, with him, and Jason . . .

---

112. Jason Fairbanks, a civil engineer before the war, was the son of Samuel and Juliet Fairbanks of Jacksonville; Colonel George W. Brent served on Bragg's troubled staff until Bragg was replaced. Willie's position was a good one, but some staff members were more or less constantly bickering and sniping at each other for the entire Kentucky campaign.

Murfreesboro is quite a place, and the general appearance of the houses is neat and tasty, some very handsome; the place shows many of the ravages of war, but pretty and well dressed ladies drive around in handsome carriages and exchange calls etc; a large and handsome house just across the street has a great many callers, and my attention is frequently distracted by the refreshing sight of pretty and merry girls; the people tho' are very disaffected, and incline to *Unionism* in sentiment—There are different opinions concerning it, but I think it is intended, and that there must be, a terrible battle at some time between here and Nashville; the Yankees are mighty saucy already, and some skirmishing is going on . . .

Friday a.m. 5th. There is quite a snow storm this morng. and already everything outdoors is wrapped in a sheet of snow. O! how nice! to be sitting in a warm room watching the white flakes as they fall, instead of being obliged to tramp through them in the cold, as many soldiers are doing to-day—I have been unwell again, as at Alisonia, but have been taking medicine, and got rid of the fevers, and I think, will soon be all right again, as I am not at all exposed now. Write me immediately at this place care Genl. Bragg and I think I will soon get it—From what you wrote some time [ago] I am becoming anxious to hear from Tivie—

I dont yet know Davis' whereabouts—I hope now to be able to keep up quite a regular correspondence with every body—Much love to you all, and "the promise of more soon"—from, Yrs always affectionately

Willie

[Rebecca] **Dec 5, 1862.** *. . . Just before dark Winston arrives—He brings the welcome news that he has seen my dear husband and has promised to take me to Palatka to meet him on Sunday next—We pass the eveg. in happy communication with Winston and Davis—*

Dec 7, 1862. Mother, Winston, Davis, Henry and Georgie went to Palatka to see Father *who was to be there on a Gunboat. Rosa and I went to Tina's to stay until the folks returned. Very cold.*

[Rebecca] **Dec 7, 1862.** *A very cold morng. and high wind. Nevertheless Winston, Davis, Henry, George and myself start in a canoe for Palatka at 7 ½ o'clk. The wind being against us we do not arrive until after 1 o'clk—Find the gunboat opposite Palatka—Go to Mrs Lynch's where we find rooms engaged for us and we soon made happy by the arrival of my dear husband.*[113]*—We are most happy in being again together all but Willie and Tivie. Pass the afternoon and eveg. in the natural interchange of family en-*

---

113. Charles G. Lynch, his wife, Mary, and their daughters Adeline and Harriett ran the St. Johns Hotel in Palatka. Charles died in 1862, and his widow operated the business with the help of her daughters and three slaves after that time.

quiries. I am pleased to find William in better health than I expected but with a troublesome cough—He remained with us until 9 o'clk next morning when we go with him and others to gunboat and pass half an hour, then leave for home. Davis bids us goodbye on the wharf and starts for his camp while we are on the gunboat—Arrive safely at home just at sunset, find Tivie well as usual but anxious for our return. We bring several presents for her and the eveg. is passed in talking of our pleasant reunion—

[JAMES W. BRYANT TO REBECCA BRYANT]

On board Gun Boat Uncas Dec 9, 1862[114]

My dear Ruby

My heart is full of happiness from the Events of the last few days. The circumstances which conspired to afford me the meeting we had were indeed remarkable, and had I endeavored to prepare for the interview I could not have arranged matters better. Although my stay with you was short yet so much was realized that I should have almost feared to have remained longer under the present condition of things for fear of something occurring to mar the Entirely pleasant intercourse we all Enjoyed. It would have been more complete could I have seen Tivie and Rosa, and Willie, but having the Knowledge that the two first were well, and so far as we could Know, the confidence that the latter was also, together with the Satisfactory news from Thomasville, I had nothing really to detract from a full Enjoyment of the fondest and happiest Emotions of my heart. May it not be long before we meet again and under Equally if not more agreeable circumstances . . .

In Consequence of our late arrival off Jacksonville, we passed on to the bar, but the *Cimarron* had left for Fernandina, and I cannot go until day after tomorrow.[115] Our boat is now on the way to Jacksonville but we shall anchor this side of there for the night, and in the morning I may have an opportunity to land for a short time, but I fear not because the Captain wishes to be soon at the bar

---

114. Commander M. Woodall, United States Navy, recorded on 11 December 1862, "I send the *Uncas* to Fernandina to convey Mr. Bryant, an agent of the Government, who has visited this region. He was up the river when the *Water Witch* left, and being very desirous to get North at the earliest possible moment to communicate the result of his mission personally to the President, I felt it a public necessity to advance him on his route without delay." ORN, ser. 1, vol. 12, 478. As far as is known, Bryant was not an agent of the government and was not on an official mission. He knew the upper reaches of the St. Johns thoroughly, however, and could have been of significant help to naval authorities.

115. There were several gunboats that operated more or less regularly in Florida, including the *Cimarron, Paul Jones, Water Witch, Patroon, Hale,* and the *Uncas* and *Isaac Smith,* previously mentioned. When and on what ship Bryant left is unknown, as is his destination. If he was an agent, then he would have headed for Washington; but if he was simply acquiring transportation for personal reasons, as we suspect, then he returned to New York.

tomorrow. I shall have an opportunity however to send this letter on shore to be forwarded to you.

It was a great satisfaction and pleasure to find you looking so well, and also Davis and Henry. What a fine stout fellow he is becoming; George I hope will rally soon and become rugged also. Winston looks unchanged, time has not marked him at all—how I wish I could have seen Tivie and Rosa! But I will not repine, although I cannot but regret, after so much gratification.

I hope you arrived safely without suffering from cold. Tivie I know welcomed you back most cordially. Of course you told her how I expressed my wish to see her and her pet . . .

There will not be much delay, I think, in having letters forwarded to me through some of the Officers of the Gunboats who will probably land occasionally under flag of truce at Jacksonville, or the letters can be sent off with a white flag to a Gunboat at any time when at anchor. I shall be anxious to hear from Tivie.

The visit to Palatka was an agreeable one to the officers of the Boat, it softens the asperities of the war to visit occasionally in such a manner, and in no way lessens the prosecution of the Warlike Operations. When honor and Chivalry Exists there is ever generous and friendly feelings Expressed at proper times and places . . .

And now I will close my dear wife indulging the hope, *Expectation* I will say, of seeing you all soon, and under happy circumstances—Give Kind messages of love to all and believe me as ever

Your Affectionate husband

J. W. Bryant

[Rebecca] **Dec 13, 1862.** . . . *Retire to my room at 8 p.m. Looking back upon the past 3 weeks, my heart swells with gratitude for the happiness I have experienced and I indulge the hope that the severest trials of the War are over.*

[Rebecca] **Dec 14, 1862.** *I was awakened this morning at 3 o'clk to attend to Tivie who was quite ill. At 3 ½ o'clk she presented us with a fine little girl* . . .

[REBECCA BRYANT TO WILLIE BRYANT]

Rose Cottage Dec 14, 1862

My own dear Willie,

I wrote you a fortnight since, when Davis was here, and inclosed a few lines from him—Since then we have been made very happy by a visit from Winston who came two nights before Davis was to leave—He brought us the joyful news that he had seen your father under "flag of truce," had a very satisfactory chat with him of 1 ½ hours duration—He then obtained permission from the commanding officer at Jackvlle. Maj. Scott, to come up the river and arrange for me to go to Palatka with him and meet your father there . . . Burrel was the only negro who went with us and W— and D— took the oars alternately, Henry occasionally giving aid to Burrel—A bitter cold morng. it was, wind and tide against us—but we arrived at P— about 1 ½ o'clk. P.M. found the Uncas there with white flag flying—Yr father had been ashore and engaged rooms at Mrs Lynch's (who by the way is now a widow) and all met there, escorted by Lieut. Mc'Eaddy of Capt. Dickison's Co now stationed near Palatka.[116] He was very courteous to us, as were other gentlemen who dropped in to see yr father during the afternoon and eveg.—Your father looked quite as well, perhaps better than when you saw him last—but he has a very bad cough—it appears to give him no anxiety however, as he says it has become chronic and does'nt affect his lungs. He remained with us until the next morng. about 9 o'clk when the Lieut. from the Uncas came in a fine boat and took us all on board to visit the Capt—Davis excepted, he had to start off for his camp at that hour, having a long two day's and half ride before him and expecting to pass one night in Jackvlle.—Father's conversation was perfectly candid and unrestrained with those he met and nothing unpleasant occurred in the whole time—He says when he returned to the North last Spring he told every one at Washington that he wd. take no official position, either civil or military so long as the War was engaged against Southern institutions—He says he knew he could not do any thing in Florida without plenty of money, unless he went into the field, and he did not then feel equal to it, he was too old, his constitution too much broken—For the last six months he has been engaged in some business in N. York—has obtained a patent for a cap, very desirable for soldiers or civilians . . . He has also an interest in a Gas Co—but he says he shall enter into nothing that will confine him to the U. States—He wishes us to decide where we want to live and he will conform himself to my wishes—He hopes to be here again in 2 or 3 mths. in times of peace.[117]

He brought all of us some small but useful presents, such as shoes for the boys, hkfs. etc Winston is much pleased with a fine water proof haversack he gave him—When he left N.Y—he did not expect to come up the St. John's but tho't he could perhaps send a small box he had with him—I carried your ambrotype down with me which gratified him much—I thought of carrying yr late letters but did'nt suppose we shd. have more than two or three hrs. together—

---

116. W. J. McEaddy was third lieutenant in Captain John J. Dickison's independent cavalry company, which was to become Company H of the Second Florida Cavalry in a reorganization in December 1862. McEaddy served for the rest of the war and was second lieutenant at its end.

117. This was the last time James Bryant saw his wife and son-in-law. It appears that he barely made a living during the war, for he was not financially able even to visit his surviving family until several months after the war was over.

and perferred to *engross him myself*—knowing I could repeat almost verbatim what was of most interest to him.

My heart has been full of gratitude to the Giver of all good the past week— Winston has been at home and seemed much relieved by the posture of affairs— This morng. we have *another* great cause for thankfulness—Our Tivie has another little dark-haired daughter, and is in all respects very comfortable—If the mail which comes this afternoon brings me favorable news from you, my cup of joy will be overflowing!

Dear Willie, you know my thoughts are ever with you, by day and by night— We wished for you often, very often at Palatka—We have no dates from you later than Novr. 4th. We look anxiously for news of your coming nearer to us, or perhaps getting a furlough—I do'nt like the idea of yr remaining in Tenn. all winter—

I suppose Davis will write you this week—I must close and write a few lines to him—God bless you ever! All send abundance of love and kisses—So does

Mother

[DAVIS BRYANT TO WILLIE BRYANT]

Camp Cooper Dec 21, 1862

Dear Bro. Willie

... I hope you have the situation with Jason (or Bragg as you please) you mention in your letter ... as I fear the exposure as private to *weather* as severe as it is in your region now, and will be for some time to come, to say nothing of exposure to *bullets* will prove too much for you, and I think there is no *reason* now why you should decline a position of that kind, since you have endured much more than many soldiers and more than could be expected of you. All of your letters to me have been hurried, lately, in fact since you left Mobile and it was a great pleasure to me to read yours to mother when I was at home ... I have lately had two appointments, on a small scale, but they are in "ascending progression," I was first made 4th. Corp'l (I declined the position of 1st corpl in the summer) and on the appointment of Soutton (a mess-mate) Adjutant of our regiment, I was offered—and accepted—his place as clerk and commis'y of the company, and am now quite comfortably situated in that capacity.[118] I could have had the appointment of 2d. Sergt, and would have much prefered it but for being thrown in contact with the *itch* and other such diseases of a loathesome nature

---

118. Corporal M. Soutton was named adjutant for the Second Florida Cavalry Regiment and served for the remainder of the war. Ten independent cavalry companies, including Winston's, were being organized into the Second Florida Cavalry Regiment. Winston's St. Johns Rangers became Company B, and Harrison's old company, in which Davis served, became Company K.

while on picket and other duty. The field officers of our regmt. are *appointed* at last; Caraway Smith for Col.; Lieut. McCormick of Chambers Co. Lieut. Col.; Capt. Harrison Maj. and Soutton Adgt. and I understand we are to be "reinforced" here by two companies soon, which will be quite a relief . . .[119]

My visit home was a complete success. Everything combined, for once, to make it satisfactory—I spent eight days very pleasantly at home, and the evening before I was to start on my way back—no, *two* evenings before I was to leave, Winston gave us a very pleasant surprise by stepping in upon us suddenly and, of course, entirely unexpected, and after having been with us some time and finished supper informed us that he was detailed to come *from Jacksonville,* to take mother and the boys (provided of course they were willing) down to Palatka to meet father who had been granted permission to go there in a gunboat, and pass a part of two days and one whole night on shore, and he was to be there at 12 o'clock Sunday, that was Friday . . . We were under no restraint whatever and in the time we had, from 2 o'clock that day until next morning at 10—we talked a good deal you may know, and more than once wished you was with us . . . He talks as nearly right as can be expected, and in fact *nearer,* I do wish you could have talked with him. He is exactly with us excepting he wants "*us*" to return to the Union under guarantees etc . . .

Take care of yourself and I'll do the same.

Yr aff bro
Davis

[WILLIE BRYANT TO DAVIS BRYANT]

Murfreesboro Tenn. Dec 21, 1862

Dear Davis,

. . . How dreadfully must Mother have felt after hearing of the battle of Perryville and not knowing whether I was hurt or not, and in looking over the list of casualties not knowing but my name would appear; it is a d——d outrage that postmasters will be so careless in forwdg. letters! On Mother's account principally did I take this situation, and am I glad of it; she need feel no anxiety now whatever about my life, health, or comfort and our communication will probably be more regular.

For fear you may not know yet, I will inform you of the pleasant fact that I am detailed as a clerk in the office of Genl. Bragg's Adjt. Genl.; . . . my situation is

---

119. Colonel Caraway Smith assumed command of the Second Florida Cavalry Regiment; his staff consisted of Lieutenant Colonel A. H. McCormick of Company C and Major Robert Harrison of Company K, Second Florida Cavalry.

much better and more pleasant than the rest of the clerks of my age, 5 of them are in the clerks room by themselves, while I am in the office with Col Brent, Fairbanks, and another very clever gentleman just arrived, Where I can know and see all that is going on, and am continually coming into contact with all the "Biggest Bugs"; the duties are very confining, and generally from 9 a.m to nearly 10 p.m everyday I hardly have time to think, but they are such as I like, and it will not always be so . . .

O, what a luxury it is to be once more where I can keep clean, shave, associate with gentlemen only and "feel like a white man," to say nothing of being free from exposure to this d——d climate, and relieved from the dog's life of a private! Murfreesboro is much more of a little city than I had supposed, and in times of peace must have been a right nice place, tho' now, as is everywhere else where soldiers have been any time, it is a miserable, uncharitable, and nothing-to-be-got-itable place; nor can I say much for its secesh proclivities, and the elegant dresses and kid gloves which the ladies wear, prove they must have improved their late chance of patronising a yankee market by supplying themselves from Nashville. There are lots of very pretty ladies here . . .

Yrs always affctly—

Willie—

[Rebecca] **Dec 25, 1862.** *Winston goes hunting with his brother before breakfast Mrs Stephens and family come early—wait dinner for Winston until nearly 2 o'clk . . . The day brings reflections of a varied character both pleasing and sad—Yet I feel that I have much to be grateful for—I long for an opportunity of attending divine service—*

[REBECCA BRYANT TO WILLIE BRYANT]

Dec 26, 1862

My dear Willie,

I wrote you a hasty letter on the 14th. the day Tivie's second daughter was born—by the way, she is to be called, Isabella Gertrude . . .

My heart does yearn so often for one long free, face to face interchange of loving words with you—I do not believe you can realize how long this separation has appeared to me. When Davis was here and when we were at Palatka with your father I continually thought, O if Willie were only here for a couple of hours even . . .

I have not heard from Davis since his return to camp. Yesterday Christmas was a very busy day with me, which prevented gloomy reflections to some extent—Winston being at home and Tivie well enough to be about her room, he wished to have a big dinner for his brother Clark and family . . . As I have been housekeeper for the past two weeks, was anxious to have all go on well—but could not help reverting to the last when we dined together at Mrs Stephens'— She spoke of it too, and wondered if you would think of it—I well know that your thoughts were with us, and wished I could know what you were doing, whether you were *well* and able to enjoy *any* recreation—We drank the health of absent friends in a glass of lemonade, and in the eveg. as all sat round the pie after our guests were gone we talked of you . . .

Tivie sends much love and says the cornelian ring sent to Rosa will be highly appreciated—that when she becomes a young lady she shall wear it on her watch chain as it will *probably* not fit her finger—Winston says if you shd. come he believs that luck would change and he wd. kill a deer with you . . .

Good night dear Willie—May angels guard you by night and day—A thousand kisses from

Mother

[Rebecca] **Dec 28, 1862.** *A fine clear cool morng! Have prayers in Tivie's room for the first time since her sickness . . . The baby quite sick towards night.*

[Rebecca] **Dec 29, 1862.** *Morng. cool but pleasant. Baby still sick—Tivie goes about the house a little to-day. Mr Smith brings letters from Palatka— one from Willie informs me that he has a situation as clerk to the Adjutant in Gen Bragg's army, for which I am truly thankful . . .*

[Rebecca] **Dec 31, 1862.** *. . . Winston arrives just at dinner time brings a fine lot of oranges—Succeeded in getting salt at $8 per bush. Baby not so well again . . . The year closes with much brighter prospects for me than it opened—Heaven be praised for the many mercies of the past month!*

chapter 5

Farewell Little Bell; Farewell Rose Cottage

Rebecca's hope for brighter prospects was not to be; the Emancipation Proclamation went into effect on 1 January 1863, and the war to restore the Union became a revolutionary struggle to abolish slavery in the rebellious states before restoring them to the Union. This pretty well eliminated any chance that England would recognize the Confederacy and intervene in the conflict; if the South was to win independence, it would have to do so on the battlefield.

Southern leaders were fully aware of this, and the year 1863 witnessed the most determined effort to attain victory that the Confederacy waged, but by the middle of the year it was obvious to some that the effort had failed. The Federals continued to have success in the West from the first of January to the last of December. The bloody battle of Stones River opened the campaign; Grant's capture of Vicksburg on 4 July cut the Confederacy in half; and his assault on the Confederates at Lookout Mountain in November made for a very happy Thanksgiving celebration for the Union. At year's end, Federal forces were poised to strike the heartland of Dixie.

In the East the Confederates fared much better, but Lee's defeat at Gettysburg, occurring simultaneously with the Vicksburg surrender, certainly lowered Southern hopes. The blockade also became more effective, and shortages of everything became widespread.

The year also brought much sadness to Rose Cottage. The Stephens' loss of their newborn infant began a series of hardships that culminated in the abandonment of Rose Cottage before the year was over. For the family, as well as for most in the Confederacy, the setbacks simply meant that they were undergoing another severe trial. They would continue to fight, and there was much confidence in Confederate households as the new year began.

[REBECCA BRYANT TO WILLIE BRYANT]

Rose Cottage Jan 2, 1863

My dearest Willie,

Words cannot express to you my joy at receiving your letter of Decr. 4th. and 5th. written at your new *place* of *business* in Murfreesboro'—Yes, indeed it was "glad tidings of great joy," to me and most devoutly do I thank the "Great Giver of all good" for the many mercies he has granted us the *past month*—it has been the happiest of the whole year! You left us here on the 1st. Jany. one year ago, and since that time how much we have both endured, though our sufferings have been of a widely different character ...

Winston is still with us, having had a furlough for a month, he leaves us in a week. Tivie is rapidly recovering her strength. She rode over to pass the day with Mrs Stephens yesterday, where our whole family assembled to a fine "New Year's dinner." The baby is very small but has dark eyes and hair and will I think be pretty ...

Farewell dear Willie—Do not forget the Great Being to whom you owe so much and in your prayers remember her who always loves and prays for you

Mother

[WILLIE BRYANT TO REBECCA BRYANT]

Winchester Tenn. Jan 6, 1863

My dear Mother,

Ere you receive this, you will have learned of the dreadful battle of Murfreesboro' and that our troops were obliged to fall back, which accounts for my dating from this place, Gen Bragg's Hd. Qrs. being now here; he with his staff arrived yesterday p.m. but I did not reach here until a little while ago and I now hasten to write you, as I know you will be desirous to hear from me as soon as possible, after such an important event ...

Now for the battle... !¹ our Cavalry ... cut the Enemys line of commtn. with

---

1. The Battle of Murfreesboro or Stones River started on 31 December 1862 and lasted until 2 January 1863. Bragg attacked Rosecrans's right flank and got very much the better of the battle that day, Rosecrans's forces retreating in some confusion. Bragg expected the Federals to retreat and did not resume the attack the next day. On 2 January, finding the Federals still in position, Bragg attacked that afternoon and was bloodily repulsed. Bragg retreated that night and left Rosecrans in possession of the field, permitting him to claim a victory. It was tactically a stalemated bloodbath, but it was a major defeat for the South. It marked the last time the Confederate Army of Tennessee would take the offensive except for John Bell Hood's suicidal attacks in 1865. After this it was a case of gradual Union advancement and slow rebel retreat in the West. Casualties rivaled those of Shiloh and Antietam; Federal losses were 1,730 dead, 7,802 wounded, and 3,717 missing; while Confederate losses came to 1,294 dead, 7,945 wounded, and 1,027 missing.

Louisville and they were obliged to come out to get forage and provisions, and having that a large force had been sent from this army to Miss. concluded to attack our army with their full force and obtain possession of the rich country from which we were obtaining a large amount of supplies; on Friday Dec 26th. they attacked our cavalry, which slowly fell back before them to the line on which Genl. Bragg intended to give them battle; the right flank extending a few miles East of Murfreesboro, and within 2 ½ miles; up to Tuesday skirmishing was kept up pretty briskly; on Tuesday, there were several sharp fights, and on Wednesday a general fight ensued, which was terrible; Thursday there was more fighting but at intervals, it was very severe tho'; on Friday and Saturday, the weather, which had been rainy and bad for several days, became so much worse, that but little was done on either side, and on Saturday night the order for a retreat was suddenly given, and We now occupy a line many miles in the rear, to the South.

We whipped the Enemy, for they were the attacking party, and except at one point—on our right—where they had a strong entrenched position, we drove them back several miles, and there we kept them in check, and after the first hard fight they showed little disposition to renew the attack; The fighting was most desperate and severe, and the loss on both sides heavy, theirs much greater, particularly in killed, which was so much so as to make it remarkable, and again, that so many were shot in the head and breast, showing a precision of aim, having driven them from the field we were able to see all this, and prisoners confirmed it. We are also able to judge very accurately of their force engaged, which was between 60,000 and 70,000, probably as much as 65,000 men, with a large amount of artillery; our force I *know* did not exceed 35,000, and as we heard they were to be reinforced from Kentucky, I suppose Genl. Bragg thought it best to fall back.[2] We had punished them so severely that they were "skittish," and thought the retreat some ruse, and up to yesterday morng. had not occupied Murfreesboro. Could General Bragg have held Murfreesboro it would have done wonders for him, as it is it is unfortunate, occurring so soon after the Kentucky campaign the moral effect on the troops and people is bad. Col. Brent being chief of staff was obliged to be on the field all day, Fairbanks was away, and a Lt. who is in the office, proper, with us has a horse and was anxious to be out most of the time, and consequently I was obliged to remain in the office very closely during the time the fight lasted and did not manage to get out on the field at all; I found time however to go to the Hospital occasionally; The sight there was dreadful, and with as little excitement to sustain me I found that I could not bear to remain long at a time; the ladies of Murfreesboro were very kind to the wounded. Many men who were not wounded caught colds during that severe weather which will kill them; of course they could have no fires at night while so close to the Enemys lines, and in the cold rain for two nights it must have been very severe; and once

---

2. Rosecrans had about 47,000 men to Bragg's 38,000.

for nearly the whole day our Regt. with others was obliged to lie flat on the wet ground, and you know in this country it is not like wet *sand,* only "damp" but muddy.

At first I was almost crazy to return to the Regt. and go into the fight, but the sight of the thousands of wounded, with their tales of suffering made me glad afterwards that I had not been there and thankful for the pleasant duty which thus prevented it—I think now that I can be satisfied to retire from the service with only "the Laurels of Perryville to encircle my brow . . ."

Good bye—Much love to all, and *two* kisses for little Rosa in return for the one sent me . . .

Yrs Ever affectionately
Willie

Jan 11, 1863. Winston and Clark left for Camp Finegan. Bell very sick all day.

[Rebecca] Jan 12, 1863. Clear and cold—Baby no better—Tivie sends for Mrs Stephens who remains all night to assist in nursing her—The baby appears a little relieved towards night—Mrs S— sits up with her until 12 o'clk Tivie and I afterwards divide the night.

[DAVIS BRYANT TO WILLIE BRYANT]

Harts Road, Fla R.R. E. Sta.[3] Jan 12, 1863

Dear Willie

. . . During the past week we have had quite an interesting affair, and it has "done me good." Our picket discovered one gunboat and two large transports with two schooners in tow going up [the] Nassau river, last Wednesday afternoon, and we knew at once, of course, that they were after the lumber at Holmes' Mill—of which there was about *700 feet*—and immediately set about devising ways to disappoint and surprise them.[4] It is about 10 miles from here to the Mill *the last five* miles being by water, and through marsh the whole way, so that we can see the Mill distinctly across the marsh by daylight, it being only three miles in a direct line. When the boats were seen they were only 10 miles below, but the Capt. determined to try to beat them there and destroy the lumber before they

---

3. Harts Road was the name of the road that went from Jacksonville to St. Marys, Georgia; but it was also the name for the present town of Yulee. Davis is at the Harts Road station, or Yulee, at this time.

4. Holmes Mill, the property of merchant Henry E. Holmes, was a large sawmill operation located on the Nassau River in Duval County; the machinery was estimated to be worth at least $50,000 in 1860. Eighth Census of the United States, 1860, Schedule I, Population Schedule, Duval County; Gold, *History of Duval County,* 150.

could get up . . . and accordingly chose ten men to go with him, me among the number . . . We had not gone two miles, however, when such a dense fog settled on the marsh that we could not see one hundred yards ahead . . . but as this was our only chance to effect the object we determined to venture as we were . . . We managed to effect a landing about a hundred yds below the mill and on walking up discovered they were not there. Louis Roux and I were then deputised to go to the house and make known the object of our mission[5] . . . we set to work with cotton and Rosin that we found convenient [and] in less than no time the whole mass was in flames . . . As soon as it was well underway we put back and were lighted the whole way by the flames, and landed "in triumph" on this side, thinking it was a pretty nice trick . . .

Before we left for the mill the Capt had ordered the balance of the Co. under command of the 1st Lieut. to start that morning before daylight for a bluff on the river and there await the return of the boats[6] . . . On arriving at the bluff, we ascertained that the boats with the vessels had grounded nearly opposite that place—but out of reach . . . in seeing the fire, they had stopped in plain view and sent the gunboat "a Kitin" up to see what it meant. Towards the close of the afternoon she came "tearing" back and imagine our satisfaction on seeing the other boats turn about and follow in her wake, disappointed as they must have been, returning empty . . . *ten men* at the last moment asked permission to go to a deep gulley some of them had discovered, about two hundred yards below us "and went." The gunboat anchored about ⅓ of a mile above in a place from which she could rake the whole bluff and there waited for the other boats to pass. One of the Strs. came a long away ahead of the other and passed within good range of our long enfields but only three men were to be seen on deck and the Lieut. concluded to let her pass knowing we would have a better chance at the other. It would have been rather an impudent move any how, for as I lay on my belly the deck seemed to be considerably above me, But after she passed the bluff I saw a good many coming out to look, and behind the cabin etc showing that they had seen us, when the fellows in the gulley opened fire on them, and of all the falling down and scrambling below you never saw the like, but before our boys had time to reload they commenced firing small arms from the boat . . . Before this however, We on the bluff had fallen back and in *mighty* quick time to get out of range of the gunboat supposing she would commence operations immediately but she didn't say a word . . . Please, excuse my "prosiness" and remember that such an affair is a rarity in these parts . . . The thing might have been bettered had we known the ground well, but I think all considered it was a "glorious victory . . ."

5. Louis F. Roux of Fernandina was later promoted to sergeant of Company K, Second Florida Cavalry, and served for the duration of the war. The mission was to destroy the lumber at the mill.

6. First Lieutenant John D. Jones was killed two months later in a skirmish not far from Camp Cooper.

"Our mess" is now *nicely* settled in our log house, We have it lined with the old tent. Have a nice open stove and more other conveniences than I can enumerate. So that while in camp we live like lords.[7] Our picket duty is now so heavy, though, we have only 3 *days* at a time in camp, spend half our time on picket.[8] However, we have good accomadations at almost every station, and get fish and oysters in abundance. Besides picket guard we have to keep camp guard which brings a private one, occasionally, several nights in succession and "non com." officers every other night, So you can see if we did not have some comforts our duty would be *killing*. We drill nearly every day too. I am more and more satisfied every day that cavalry is the best service, for a *gentleman* by all odds. I now weigh 131 *lbs* and am stronger *generally* and more active than I ever was before, and am considered generally "much of a man for my inches." I'll stop at that I reckon, particularly, as I can think of no more to bore you with . . .

Yrs ever affectly
Davis

Jan 13, 1863. Bell no better, sat up with her again all night. Sent for Dr Currel he arrived a little after 10 o'clk a.m. Tina went home in the afternoon . . .

[Rebecca] *Jan 14, 1863. Still warm—Baby about the same—Dr C— gives her calomel. He goes home late in the afternoon. Tivie and I up with her by turns all night . . .*

[Winston Stephens to Octavia Stephens]

Camp Finegan Jan 15, 1863

My Dear Wife

. . . We arrived in camps the evening of the 13th sound in limb and health good as when I left. My soar hands have improved some though I am suffering with the left front finger and have not ben able to go out on drill since my arrival . . . I found the men generally well and anxiously expecting me and when I got in sight there was a general rush and a hoop, and I really felt proud of the reception as the demonstration appeared sincere and the boys faces wore a pleased expres-

---

7. It appears that Captain Robert Harrison or his successor, Captain F. J. Clark, of Company K, Second Florida Cavalry, oversaw the construction of the log cabins that served the troops stationed at Camp Cooper after 1862.

8. An advance outpost was called a picket and usually consisted of a lieutenant, two sergeants, four corporals, and forty privates, who formed a scattered line far in advance of the main army camp. This duty was the most dangerous work for infantry. Since they were the first to encounter any enemy movement, they were also more likely to be captured, wounded, or killed. Picket duty was rotated regularly within a regiment, but when only limited forces were available, as was true in Florida, one company usually was on picket most of the time.

sion. I find things materially changed since I left, every thing is done on a strict military rule, and Col McCormick has been very strict . . .

The Pay Master has just arrived and now we will have a little cash. I paid out $500. this morn and expect to continue the same practice until I am clear of debt. A telegram informs us that a desperate battle was fought at Vicksburg and the Yankees repulsed and 5000 lost by them on the field, though they are collecting a heavy Morter fleet to try once more the Gibralter of Rebeldom.[9] God Grant they may loose their thousands at each attempt. Our men are determined to hold it and they are being reinforced daily . . .

The Pay Master is here and we will be paid in a few hours. Love to all and many kisses to our Daughters. I remain your loving husband

Winston Stephens

[Rebecca] *Jan 16, 1863. Tivie's dear little baby still very sick—We send again for Dr Currell—he sits up with her until 2 o'clk when there appears to be a change for the better and we hope the crisis has past.*

[OCTAVIA STEPHENS TO WINSTON STEPHENS]

Rose Cottage Jan 17, 1863

My dear Husband

My letter to you this week must be short as our little Bell has been *very very* sick and I have put off writing for the crisis to pass, until now it is almost past the time to write, all think now the crisis is past and she is a little better this morning, oh how I dreaded having midnight come but thank Heaven it passed well for our dear little one, and I hope now strongly for her recovery. The morning you left you had hardly got to Clark's when we took Bell up and found her appearing *quite sick,* and I noticed a red spot behind her ear, that place spread through the day towards her nose, we were up that night with her and Mon morning I sent for Tina, for some time she thought it the bold hives but gave up the idea when we found her face and neck swelling greatly Tuesday morning. I sent for Dr Currell, he can not exactly tell the matter, he staid Tues and Wed. Tina went home Tues afternoon . . . and came back Thursday and has been here ever since, we sent again for the Dr Friday morn (yesterday) and is here now, the disease very much resembles the scarletina, but we can not tell what it is, we have been

---

9. The Vicksburg campaign was a tough one for the Union commander, U. S. Grant, who made his first attempt in October 1862. Three months later Grant was forced to abandon his campaign to take the city from the north. Several other unsuccessful attempts later, he decided in April 1863 to cross south of Vicksburg and take it from the south and east. After fighting two major battles, he had the Confederates bottled up in Vicksburg by the middle of May. He laid siege to the city until the commander, Lieutenant General John C. Pemberton, surrendered on 4 July 1863.

up all night every night since you left, you would not know her, she is very much prostrated and of course pale, her bowels have been a great part of her disease, she has been in continued pain somewhere, we cant tell exactly where the whole week, sleeps only a few moments without jumping and crying, her voice is now very weak, I forgot to say that red eruption has moved all over her body and is now going off at her feet, her little privates were *dreadfully* swollen and looked blistered, we have not until this morning been able to move her the *least* bit without her screaming and it seemed almost death to change her napkins, we have kept her mostly on a pillow, she still seems to have pain somewhere, but Dr says she is much better and he has now gone home, we are now giving quinine to keep her strength and I do hope and pray that she will continue to improve. I am about as you left me, not quite so strong but no worse in any other way, but my nerves are so unstrung that I can scarcely guide my pen as you can judge from this writing. Rosa has a bad cold, I hope it may not prove to be the scarletina the baby has and Rosa and Charles get it. Big Jane is quite sick with the same she had last Summer, the Dr has prescribed for her. I must close and take Bell that Mother may rest as she did not sleep a wink last night. I hope the baby will be well when I write next. I feared having dreadful news to write you this morning. Tina had promised to write to you this morning but when I found the baby better I felt that I could write. I hope to hear from you very soon.

Ever aff-ly
Your Wife

Jan 18, 1863. Bell not so well again sent for Dr Moragne of Palatka.[10]
Tina went home in the morning.
Jan 22, 1863. Bell doing very well.

[OCTAVIA STEPHENS TO WINSTON STEPHENS]

Rose Cottage Jan 23, 1863

My dear Husband

I am happy to say that our little Bell is much better than when I wrote last, though I consider her very far from well. I am almost afraid to think her recovering for fear she may be taken suddenly away, at times she seems much worse than others. I would give so much for a good Physician. she does not seem to have much if any fever now, the red eruption has been all over her body and left with the exception of her feet and hands, which you would hardly believe were the

---

10. Dr. N. H. Moragne was a planter and medical doctor who came from South Carolina to Florida in the mid-1850s. Unlike Currel, he was well trained, but he lived too far away to be of help to Tivie at this time.

same poor little things they are so swollen, and the tops of her feet are yellow blisters, she looks now precisely as though she had the jaundice *very* yellow, but suppose little babies never have it, at first I thought her skin was yellow after the disappearance of the red, but now her water stains her clothes a bright yellow and I think it some disease, the day after I wrote you she seemed worse and I sent for Dr Moragne . . . and the Dr said he would be here Monday morning if Capt Dickison would let him, and no Dr yet, luckily she got better again. She has a very bad cough, she has been sat up with every night since you left, until last night, she slept part of the night in bed with us, Tina has been over several times and relieved us or I believe I would have given out entirely . . .

I can not write much as I find it troublsome to my eyes which are troublesome from sitting up by the firelight, they had just begun getting well from their former weakness, every morning Rosa's eyes are shut tight from her cold. Although she has been very fretful, at times she is funny. to day I was washing her and she pointed her finger right in my face and said "see that old lady" with such a comical face. The baby is quite fretful and uneasy tonight so I will close and relieve Mother. With lots of love I am as ever your

loving Wife

Tivie

Sat. morning. My dear I am sorry to say that our little one is not so well this morning and I have sent again for Dr Currel, God grant that he may help her, oh that you were here, but I pray that she may be spared to see you when you can come. I can not write more.

lovingly yr

Tivie

[Rebecca] *Jan 24, 1863. The baby appears very sick, had a restless night—Send for Dr C— and Mrs Stephens—Dr C— could not come—Mrs Stephens comes and proposes different remedies but still the child grows worse rapidly—Before sunset we give up all hope and about 6 o'clk send for Mr Stephens who has just returned from Lake City—About 7 o'clk the dear little sufferer breathes her last very quietly—After sometime we persuade Tivie to go into another room with Rosa—Mr and Mrs Stephens sit up by turns all night—Being much exhausted I retire at 10 o'clk and sleep until daylight without waking.*[11]

[Rebecca] *Jan 25, 1863. Henry goes off at daylight to . . . make all arrangements for the burial of our little darling. These arrangements are not*

---

11. It was an ancient custom to sit up all night with the dead, most likely to make certain that the person was truly dead.

completed until nearly sunset—Mr Smith reads a portion of the burial service and Mr and Mrs Stephens take the little one in the buggy just before dark. Tivie nearly distracted for a time.

[WINSTON STEPHENS TO OCTAVIA STEPHENS]

Camp Finegan Jan 27, 1863

My Dear Wife

Yours of 17th has just ben received and the contents noticed and I cannot express to you the anxiety I feel and shall continue to feel until I hear again from you. I shall trust in God who giveth and in whose hands our dear child must rest. If I should lose her I shall think it a punishment because I have ben so much taken up with my Dear family that I have not paid the devotion to him that I should. I know how much you and Mother must have suffered during the time you write about in your letter, and oh how much that dear babe must have suffered. I would that I could be the sufferer and not my babe that cannot express its wants and explain where are its pains, but Gods will be done and not mine. I hope the crisis had passed as you thought and that dear Belle is now recovered and that I may see her lovely face again . . . I wish I could be with you so that I could divide the watch necessary in such cases. I do hope you may not have any more cases. I am quite well and doing as well as circumstances will admit. This wicked war is the means of so much unhappiness and distress, and yet our Enemys appear disposed to try every means of subduing us to their will but so far they have failed and in all the recent moves they have ben foiled and defeated . . .

I feel that we are obliged to have peace during the Spring and God grant it may soon come. The disposition appears to be to place us on an equality of Regulars and they take it regular giving new orders each day and they grow more and more strict and I pay but little attention to some of them and would not be disappointed to be called to account and I dont care as I will not make Regulars out of my men and they will not accept a Resignation and I dont care much what happens. I am doing my best to get rid of Genl Finegan and We hope to succeed and then I will be satisfied. Catholic religion has controlled the organization of this Regiment and other denominations have ben tolerated only where it could be used to elevate the other Church. Now I am for rebelling against such things. I do not believe in bringing Church matters in this trouble and I will fight it to the death . . .

Love to Mother and boys and to you and our dear children accept a husbands and Fathers whole devotion as ever yours your loving husband.

Winston Stephens

[REBECCA BRYANT TO WILLIE BRYANT]

Jan 30, 1863

My own dear Willie,

Our hearts were gladdened . . . by the receipt of your letter of the 6th. from Winchester. I looked anxiously for it the Monday previous, having heard or rather seen, by the papers, that the Federals occupied Murfreesboro . . .

Aunt Julia wrote in her last that she wd. be obliged soon to relinquish some of her labors for the soldiers and attend more to home matters—She had done an immense deal of good. I have never told you that yr father had not heard of her publication in regard to him—but said he understood she got into a newspaper controversy about him. I explained it all to him, defending Aunt J—'s course, as she had done to me. Davis was present too. He expressed regret and said she was foolish, but showed no resentment. It appeared very differently to him hearing it from me in the way he did, from what it would if he had seen it in print or been told of it in N. Yk. or Chastn . . .

God bless you
Mother

[WILLIE BRYANT TO REBECCA BRYANT]

Tullahoma Tenn. Jan 30, 1863

My dear mother,

. . . Father's fortunate and satisfactory visit is the source of great happiness and satisfaction to me, and I am truly thank[ful] for it, on your account, most particularly, and that such a succession of satisfactory events have caused you such relief and joy . . .

You ask concerning my plans for the future; I am yet unable to form any, whatever, can scarcely "build a small air castle" these times; *but,* when the war ends,—if it ever does—and if I am alive, I shall commence immediately, if not sooner, to make preparations for *a home; where,* is almost immaterial to me; Florida has no particular bonds on me, and no longer possesses any particular charm, and I now think I shall never live there again, or at least in E. Fla.; I like the state of Georgia better than any I have seen; but I should in any case go to a city, the field is better suited to my tastes and qualifications, and temperament, and it has been a great mistake in Father's life that he did not continue his early business in a large place; I am already so changed in disposition, however, that before much longer I may also be changed in tastes, and be content to seek a quiet life, with slow, but sure gain, and I hope most truly I may; but much of my life will be wasted by this infernal war, and when it ends, I must commence again just where I did at 16 yrs of age, and will be obliged to "hurry up my cakes," ("so to speak.") to get a start before late in life; but my rule now is to "take things as they come," and make the best of them, and for the present I am very well satisfied to have a whole body, sound constitution, and plenty to eat and wear, and if the war *should* end, and *I* should come out all right, I think I will be able to manage others affairs well enough to turn them to some good account . . .

Every thing promises a cessation of hostilities, if not a termination of the war, at no far distant day, and I hope no darkening cloud may arise to destroy it. "Genl. Joe Johnston" is here now; he commands the Department, which places him over Genl. Bragg; as I write, a very good band is serenading him, not far off, and playing "Home sweet home," sweetly.[12] This Tullahoma is a miserable little muddy Rail road station, and I wish we were almost anywhere else . . . Well, my paper is nearly out, and my eyes, and interesting matter gave out long ago, and I will wind up for this time . . .

Willie

[OCTAVIA STEPHENS TO WINSTON STEPHENS]

Welaka Jan 31, 1863

My dear dear husband

Ere this you are sharing the grief which now bows my heart down in sorrow, how unfortunate that we should have to bear this grief apart, the very time when we should be together to try and comfort and sustain each other. It is a hard duty which the Lord has called upon us to perform that of giving up our little one which he had so lately given us, I often wonder if it is as hard for you as it is for me to say "Thy will oh Lord not mine be done." his will *must* be done and we have to submit. I know that he knows best, he saw proper to take our darling notwithstanding my prayers for oh if any poor mortal prayed I did, that she might be spared to us, from the bottom of my heart and incessantly, and feeling that he had the power, if he thought proper, but no he thought best to take her to himself and oh how hard the grief is to bear, but it is a blessing to know that she was perfectly pure and unspotted from sin and will go to Heaven where she will feel no more pain . . . I was looking forward with so much pleasure to a few weeks when she would begin to take notice and laugh, and to the time when you came again to see her improved but all that pleasure was taken from me. I suppose we must be thankful that Rosa is left to us, but oh my heart pines for my little one . . . you dont know how I long to have you here, yet I know you would

---

12. Braxton Bragg remained in command of the Army of Tennessee until he was decisively defeated by Grant at the Battle of Missionary Ridge on 25 November 1863. Shortly thereafter, General Joseph Johnston took command of that army as well as the Confederate Department of the West, and Bragg went to Richmond as a special advisor to Jefferson Davis.

miss our little one more if here, for our room seems so desolate, every thing I look at has a sad appearance. My dear I dont know that I ought to have written so much in this strain but it seemed to unburden my heart and it seems so full. I know you feel sad enough.

Big Jane is not well yet, she helps Sarah spin, she is greatly troubled about herself, thinks it is going to "carry her off," she is I think getting better by degrees. I think she ought not to plough very soon. Burrel has been quite sick with fever this last week, but is going about to day, Tom and Rachel have kept the ploughs going . . .

Ever yr loving
Wife

[WINSTON STEPHENS TO OCTAVIA STEPHENS]

Camp Finegan Feb 2, 1863

My Dear Wife

Yours and Tinas were received the same day though yours was written first. Tina communicated to me the sad news of the death of our Dear Isabell. God has given us two dear children and has seen fit to take one of them to his bosom, let us my Dear Wife bear up under this severe trial. It is indeed hard to think our loved one is no more, that I shall never see her loved face again, but it is so. I had tried to school myself from what you wrote for the sad event. I know she is in heaven and what is a loss to us is her gain be comforted my Dear that he has left us one other to love . . . Give love to them all and mother and boys, and accept much love for yourself and Rosa, and may God in his mercy protect you. Your affectionate husband

Winston Stephens

[OCTAVIA STEPHENS TO WINSTON STEPHENS]

Rose Cottage Feb 8, 1863

My dear husband

. . . I have not heard from you in two weeks, and such long and sad two weeks they have been to me. I can not help looking for you all the time, I look out of the window very often hoping that I might see you, and my heart jumps at every little noise hoping that it might be you coming, you dont know how I long to see you, some times I get so lowspirited I dont know what to do. I thought when you went away this last time that I would not feel your absence so much as I would have our little darling and Rosa to take up my attention, but that little one was taken from me and I miss her *so much* besides you, and Rosa has been so fretful that she has worried me a great deal, she frets, and is illhumored the whole time, and it would take a perfect Job to get along patiently with her, sometimes I think this affliction sent upon me as a punishment and I try to be resigned and try to do better, then again it seems too hard and I get cross and wicked and seems to me almost desperate. I was looking forward to so much pleasure with our little "Bell" . . .

I must not write any more this time for this ought to be off. Rosa has just given me a hug and kiss for you, so you may imagine yourself hugged and kissed by her. I wish you were near enough to have them in reality. With a great deal of love I am

Your loving

Wife

[WINSTON STEPHENS TO OCTAVIA STEPHENS]

Camp Finegan, Feb 8, 1863

My Dear Wife

I am again in this Camp after a week of hard labour, on last Sunday I started on a scout and that night I was overtaken and sent on one of much more length and importance but which failed of accomplishing the object for which it set out. It seems that a steamer went up the St Marys and had on board 150 negroes and some white men, they landed at Albertis Mills near Kings Ferry and carried off some negroes, some sheep, some provisions and carried on a general thieving expedition and went out before we even got the word.[13] It cost me a weeks hard riding when I had two large boils which made it any thing but pleasant . . . I went to Lake City on Thursday but found that the Court had ben adjourned until next Tuesday. I start up tomorrow and will perhaps be there for one month but continue to direct your letters as usual and they will be sent direct from this place, the trip will cost me a great deale as board is from three to four dollars pr day . . .

The *beast* Hunter has resumed the Command on the Coast and he has sent the St. Augustine people as exiles from their homes.[14] Eighty three came out by way

---

13. Kings Ferry is about thirty miles up the St. Marys River from Fernandina, and E. R. Alberti had a large lumber mill there. Alberti estimated the value of his mill in 1860 at $48,000 and his slave force at $28,980. Eighth Census of the United States, 1860, Schedule I, Population Schedule, Duval County.

14. Major General David Hunter was placed in command of the Department of the South early in 1862, and on 9 May he declared that slavery was abolished in his department. Lincoln repudiated the policy, but Hunter then raised two black regiments, the First South Carolina Volunteers and the Second South Carolina Volunteers, under the command of white officers, Colonel Thomas Wentworth Higginson and Colonel James Montgomery. Hunter stayed at Hilton Head, South Carolina, but included these two regiments in the force that he sent to invade Florida early in 1863. This was the first time African-American troops were used in combat in the state. All abolitionists, especially Union officers, were referred to as "beasts" by most Confederates.

of Fernandina on last Thursday and have gone up to Lake City, but I suppose they will scatter through the Country where they can get shelter, Poor people theirs is a hard fate and none but a beast could send them from their homes. He gave them three days rations and Genl Finegan will provide for them until their friends are able to take care of them. We look for another boat load of them this week. They will send all out that will not take the oath of allegiance to the United States . . .

I want Burrel to plant corn soon and I want him to prepare the land well and manure all the pine land so that we can make a plenty I want him to finish planting corn by the 10th March and the cotton also if possible. He must plant the branch corn last as that is a wet place and the cold will be more likely to kill it. You had better have the lots in Welaka raked around to keep off fire and the mill place on the branch to save the timbers, after the potatoes are used out of the little room I want the irons and stones belonging to the mill put in the room to keep them out of the weather. Pet is looking badly and does not eat as we have no fodder, the other horses look well. I hope you will make a good crop this year . . .

I know you have felt the loss of our Dear babe more than I have as you were with her and I have ben constantly engaged since and I have forced a calmness that was hard to sustain when my thoughts have wandered to you and ours, I feel that God thought best to strike this blow for our good and let us profit by the lesson. Oh how I wish I could be with you I want to see you so much, bear up My Dear and pray God to spare our Dear Rosa . . . love to all, and accept much love and many kisses for yourself and Rosa

Your aff Husband
Winston

[WINSTON STEPHENS TO OCTAVIA STEPHENS]

Lake City Feb 11, 1863

My Dear Wife

. . . You may allow Burrel to manage the planting and allow no one to disturb him and I think he will do better than if interfered with . . . do the best you can and one of these days God being my helper I will protect and care for you as a husband should a Dear and affectionate wife. Dont allow Tina's influence over you to become too great as I do really fear it for both of our sakes. I like Tina in some respects but she is dangerous to our happiness in some respect. I hope dear Wife you will understand what I mean and not misconstrue my words. no one that has not that depth of love that I feel for you can tell how much I am interested in a continuation of our love and affection for each other. I feel that my life would be a blank without your love and confidence, and I want nothing to mar that feeling . . .

Love to all as I must close. accept kisses for you and Rosa and a heart ful of love from your loving Husband

Winston

[OCTAVIA STEPHENS TO WINSTON STEPHENS]

Rose Cottage Feb 14, 1863

My dear husband

. . . Your latest letter spoke of going on the scout to Kings Ferry, when will all these scouts end? seems to me the war is no nearer the end now than it was months ago, seems to me we had as well live together under Lincoln's Government than to live seperate most of the time under this Government, and are you now much more free than negroes, and the discipline becoming more and more strict. I suppose before long none of the soldiers will be allowed to go home at all, that will be great doings . . .

Please do not be so dont care about your military matters, for if you should be called to an account for disregarding orders I would care, and what would you make by it, you say you can not resign your commission, so you had better be resigned where you are and not make things worse by disobeying orders, for I fear you will get yourself deeper into trouble than you think, you might be put out of office and made a private and then I am sure you would be worse off. I fear you are not going to have such great times down there as you have been having, as you say the Gun boats shelled so much, I guess from that too that there is no communication and that Mother's and my letters will not go to the North . . .

I guess Burrel is getting on well with the farming as he always seems busy and going ahead. I have planted the Garden out in the front yard. Rosa dropped some of the beans, and is always crazy about planting, so now I have given her a few beans and a hoe and sent her out to planting them, so hope now to write in peace.

I want to write to Loulie this week. I received a letter from her the other day. Mr Tydings has an appointment near Monticello and their prospects no better than last year, the prospect is a larger family and no prospect of any thing to live with.[15] poor Loulie, but she ought to be glad, and suppose she is that she has her husband with her these troublesome times even if they do have to live on other folks . . .

Ever your true and loving

Wife

15. Richard Tydings had resumed his vocation as minister and teacher, having been forced out of the salt manufacturing business by Federal raids. For the rest of the war, the Tydingses lived in Panola, slightly southeast of Monticello in Jefferson County.

[REBECCA BRYANT TO WILLIE BRYANT]

Rose Cottage Feb 14, 1863

My dear, dear Willie,

... My last was perhaps written in a sadder tone than usual—the sickness and death of Tivie's baby cast a gloom over us all. Since then nothing of much interest has occurred here, excepting a trip Henry made up the Ocklawaha with Mr Stephens. Mr S— was going to purchase corn for himself and Winston— Burrel and Tom were to have gone in the canoe, but it was very inconvient for B— to be spared at that time as he had lost some time by sickness, and Henry proposed to go in his place. They were absent from Monday at daylight until Saturday eveg. last week. They camped out all the time—had one day and night of the coldest rain we have had this winter and were drenched to the skin, before they could get to a shelter. Henry took no cold, though he thinks he never *felt* so cold in his life ...

Have you an opportunity of attending church where you now are? I always think on Sunday that your thoughts are turning homeward more than on other days. Not much I would like to hear you and Davis sing some of the good old psalm tunes, accompanied by Tivie on the piano! She has not opened the instrument for months. She is becoming more and more weary of Winston's absence from home and thinks she would be glad to have peace on almost any terms. We have lost too many valuable lives to give up *now* without our independence and I *hope* the end is not far off—but it does not appear to be so near as it did two months ago. I trust we have all learned some lessons by this War which will never be forgotten.

I must wind this up and retire for the night—Sweet sleep and pleasant dreams to my dear Willie—and a world of love from us all

Mother

[DAVIS BRYANT TO WILLIE BRYANT]

Camp Cooper Feb 14, 1863

Dear Bro. Willie

... If you can't *communicate* regularly I do wish you would quite frequently drop me a line or two, if no more, just to let me know where you are and what doing etc, for it takes a long time for me to hear *of* you through others, and knowing that you are in a "squally latitude" I cannot but feel anxious, I do hope that on mother's account particularly you will not be *unnecessarily* "fighty," as she seems so much relieved to think that you are less exposed, generally, than before, and besides ... I will have a chance, even here, to do fighting enough for both of us, before the winter closes ...

One night, at about 11 o'clock, about two weeks ago, one of a picket stationed on the St. Marys river, 5 miles from Camp, reported a gunboat passing up.[16] We had expected the Yanks would come that way if they ever came after us, so the Capt. with all the men that could be spared from camp (29 and three officers—25 were on picket 8 on detached service and some had to be left at camp on account, particularly, of 9 negroes we had caught a few days previous on their way to Fernandina) . . . We had gone about 1 ½ miles when we met another of the picket who said the Yanks were landing just above, but that the remaining two of the picket were at a gate of the field in which they were landing and through which they must pass coming this way. The Capt. feeling secure carried us on at a gallop intending to dismount us at a certain branch and there ambuscade them, but just as we were approaching our intended ambush—about 1 ½ miles from the landing—imagine our surprise on being "opened on" by a line of Yankees about 60 yards long, then whooping and yelling as soon as they fired the first volley. The head of our column was not over 30 yards from them . . . The shock was terrible, and frightened our horses so that they took us "skitin'" through the woods in all directions. Two or three were thrown, but it is only a wonder that all were not. The Capt. was riding ahead with the 1st Lieut. and almost instantly commanded "Right about retreat!" and when we were gone about 150 yards called a halt. The buggers were firing all the while as fast as they could load, and as the bullets were whizzing by and *patting* the back all around us—the place being open level pine woods—it was decided advisable to fall a little farther back, particularly as we knew we could not check their advance at that place. We fell back about 50 yds farther and collected in the road, when one man was found to be wounded and our 1st Lieut. and another man missing. We then moved about a mile back behind a swamp on the road leaving a guard on the road. I was acting as clerk at the time . . . so the Capt. sent me with one man to camp to have the ammunition commissary store etc removed several miles back, thinking it probable another force might intend coming on camp from another direction, which might have been done easily, as we are stationed on a narrow neck which it is impossible for us to picket at every point. I went off with the waggon and negroes that night, 8 or 10 miles and did not know any thing further until the next day when I returned with the waggon etc. On going to the ground the next morning the company found the 1st Lieut. dead as he had fallen the night before, and the other missing man had gone to a house near by, severely

---

16. Colonel Thomas W. Higginson, with about a hundred men of the First South Carolina Volunteers (Colored), put ashore at Township Landing (present-day Crandall) and marched south toward Camp Cooper hoping to surprise the Confederates. After a march of about two miles, however, his force collided with Captain F. J. Clark's men, and a skirmish, called the Battle of the Hundred Pines, took place. Clark replaced Robert Harrison when the December 1862 reorganization took place. He resigned the following December, and Company K, Second Florida Cavalry, was commanded by Jesse N. Jones for the rest of the war.

wounded in the arm and hand. The other was shot through the wrist.[17] I neglected to mention that while we were halted the night before, three of our men fired a round each, and on examination that morning evident marks of one of their men having been either killed or badly wounded were found, also, a hat canteen broken ramrods and various other articles were strewed along the road in their retreat to their boat.[18] They had evidently commenced their retreat, firing as they went, from the time of their first volley, as they did not advance a step over the line they first formed and the trees were cut by shot in all directions from there to the gate. How they could hear us coming ½ a mile and were drawn up at right angles with the road, and the woods were very open. There was at least 250 of them. They burned the dwelling house of the place where they landed and took off several negroes. It seems the two pickets reached the gate just after the yankees had passed, and before they could get around them to give us notice the firing commenced. Two or three days after that, or *nights* rather, the same Gunboat passed up again. This time, however, continuing up. Twenty of us with the Capt. "laid wait" for them on a pine Bluff about 30 ft. high, where the river is only about 200 yds wide, maybe not over 150. She came down with a rush, at about dark, but the moon was full and shining brightly, shelling and *graping* as she came, and I can tell you it felt kind of funny when they were passing around, for she had a long sweep at us, and directed her fire at the Bluff as soon as she came in range. When she came within good shot the Capt. fired the signal gun at her and we all opened on her, and continued until she passed out of range, when she checked down and cut away at us with a vengeance, when we "changed base," and waited till she was satisfied and went on down. From some St. Augustine people who have been expelled from the place by the yanks we learn that we, at least, killed a Captain of them, as they heard in Fernandina, and gave the particulars, so I don't doubt it . . .[19]

We had rather a novel though tough time last week . . . receiving and transporting to the depot here, or about a mile from here, about 20 families from St Augustine and their luggage. They were landed under a flag of truce at one of our picket stations opposite Fernandina. Some on account of disloyalty to the U. States as the communication expressed it and others on account of having relations in the Confederate States and C.S. Army. It was a miserable day cold and rainy, and they were brought in open launches. We had to scour the country, which is not thickly settled, for conveyances of any and all kind, and as they

17. First Lieutenant John D. Jones was killed, and at least two privates were wounded, but their names were not recorded.

18. Higginson, *Army Life in a Black Regiment,* 75–76, reported that Private William Parsons of Company G was killed, and seven were wounded, one of whom died.

19. Higginson, *Army Life in a Black Regiment,* 90, reported that Jack Clifton, master of the army gunboat *John Adams,* an old East Boston double-ended ferry boat, was killed in this engagement.

had to be *hauled* about 12 miles it was 11 o'clock of one of the darkest nights I ever saw before they reached here and we had to give them our houses and take the rain and cold until next morning when they were sent up on a train sent for them. It was enough to have killed ordinary people but they stood it well. All but about three are Minorcans, and there were some mighty pretty girls amoungst them. There were about 30 children. Only four or five men, old or crippled. The yankees gave us one days notice of their intention, and *them* three days cooked rations . . .

    I am advised to finish my letters by to night so "adios"

Your ever affe bro
Davis

[WINSTON STEPHENS TO OCTAVIA STEPHENS]

Lake City, Feb 17, 1863

My loved Wife

    . . . I will perhaps get through here this week and return to camps. I do want to see you as bad as I ever did in my life and dont see how I am to be patient until I can have a furlough but I suppose I must learn to bear many things that is hard . . .

    I send you some garden seed you had better select a good place and plant about half now and the rest I would keep for fall, sow the cabbage in a rich spot and they should be planted in rich land so should the other things if you can. Burrel can get a good spot in the branch field I guess. It appears your letters find me very slowly, only three since I left and the last one nearly two weeks since I got it. I fear we are to have no mail facilities at all. I wish I had something good to send you, but nothing presents itself. I see many pritty ladies here, more than I have seen since the War commenced. They will have a fishing frolic on Wednesday and that night they speak of a ball, but I shall not attend either, seeing them on the Streets with young men carries me back to our happy days of Courtship. What a blissful time we have had, so little to mar our happiness, we have ben peculiarly blessed for surely none have been more happy than you and I. God grant that a lasting reunion may soon take place.

    Love to Mother boys Clark and family. Many kisses to you and darling Rosa and all the Love my heart contains.

Yours always
Winston Stephens

[OCTAVIA STEPHENS TO WINSTON STEPHENS]

Rose Cottage Feb 21, 1863

My own dear husband

Seems to me Fate is against me, I am denied even the pleasure of *hearing* from you, it is not quite two weeks since I received your last letter but it seems three or more, my not hearing from you regularly seems harder to bear now than ever, seems to me some times I want to start right off and hunt you up. I do wish you could be at home, I feel our separation now more than ever before, my situation, and the pleasure I would have after all was over used to fill my thoughts a great deal, but now all is indeed over, and what pleasure have I? no thoughts but sad ones, I keep myself employed at something the whole time when awake, I have been fixing the garden and doing things to try and make our home look pleasant, but no matter what I do there still seems to be a great void in my heart, night is the worse time, when Rosa has done all her fretting and frolicking for the day and gone to bed, all is quiet and I sit down to my knitting my thoughts have full play, and I assure you I am not happy, I know I have a great deal to be thankful for but I can not say I am happy now . . .

Henry and Georgie are spending the day at Tina's, this is Lewis' birthday. I have not been there since New Years day, when we were all there together, and have no inclination to go. I went over that way once in going to the graveyard, we little thought New Years day when going over that road so happyly and merrily that the next time I went over it would be to visit the grave of our dear little "Bell" who was then out for the first time. I often thought that she might be taken sick and die, but I was not prepared for it to come so soon. it seemed to me I would be thankful to have kept her even as she was, a corpse for the idea of putting that sweet little form *under the ground* to decay seems too too hard, it is all so mysterious. I know not what to say, hardly what to think . . .

I can not help looking for you every time I hear the dogs bark, and at night when I hear the yard gate open I listen for you to come up the steps, how many times my poor heart beats with hope for nothing. I dont know what I would want to do if I have to go another week without hearing from you for sometime now I think my nerves are stretched to the highest pitch . . .

How does Pet get on now? I suppose when she got rid of her milk she began to pick up, the colt looks well, will not stay out in the woods, but jumps the fences and often gets to where they are ploughing and goes ahead of the mules and troubles them much in ploughing. he is shedding and we spun some of his hair the other day, it would make nice heavy winter cloth. I must bid you good night, With much love from your

Good for nothing
Wife

[Rebecca] Feb 24, 1863. Very cool. Henry returns bringing a letter from Winston inclosing one from my dear husband of Jan 28th . . .

[Winston Stephens to Octavia Stephens]

Camp Finegan Feb 24, 1863

My Dear Wife

. . . I wish so much I could be with you in your trials to share them with you, but at present it is otherwise decreed and I hope you will bear the seperation with as much patience as circumstances will pirmit. I cannot be allowed to come home for some time yet as two of my officers will have to go before I can come, one of them will start in about three weeks and will be absent 15 days then the other will be allowed to go and he will not have less than 15 days so you will see unless something turns up I will not be home in 6 or 8 weeks. I would to heaven that I could change things otherwise for your happiness will insure mine but knowing of so many tryals placed upon you and your continual uneasiness makes me feel more restless than otherwise. I hope soon that we will have a permanent change for the better for I cant see how this War is to continue much longer. The Federals are placing the black troops among the white ones and that is creating so much dissatisfaction that they are afraid to risk an engagement with our forces at any point . . .[20]

I want you to write me all the particulars about the place now and how the stock looks etc, every thing of that nature will interest me . . . We are getting on a little better here and the Col fishes for my good will quite strong and I manage to get on as quietly as possible. We are getting some fine hay and my horses look pretty well. Pet is improving and is quite lively. Dont think my Darling that I love you less for writing you in the manner I did on the first page, but it is because I love you so dearly that I write for your benefit. God knows man is not more devoted to Woman than I am to you and I have changed my course very much for your sake and I think I have the right to ask you to be as you were when we were married. You can surely govern your temper some when so much is at stake, think of our Dear child, it is to be raised by you and I and it will take more after your training than mine as you are to be with her more and the example of a Mother is very material in raising children. I will try the Genl for a furlough as soon as I think I have any chance. You cannot want me home more than I want to

---

20. Black troops had been authorized by Congress in July 1862, but few had been recruited until the Emancipation Proclamation was enacted. After 1 January 1863, African Americans served in ever increasing numbers and in combat capacity, usually governed by white officers. They served in segregated units called U.S. Colored Troops, were misused by whites in hundreds of ways, and were not even given equal pay until 1865; but they refused to quit, and ultimately almost 200,000 served in the military forces of the Union.

come... Love to all and many kisses to you and Rosa and accept oceans of love from your aff husband

Winston Stephens

[REBECCA BRYANT TO WILLIE BRYANT]

Mar 1, 1863

My dearest Willie,

Your most welcome letter of Jany. 30th. and the newspaper *for Rosa,* reached us a week ago to-day—I need not say that yrs. was read over and over with great interest, for you know I hope, that the sight of yr handwriting sends a thrill of joy to our hearts *at all times.* I often wonder if it is possible that mine *can* produce such a sensation of delight in yours...

Aunt Julia wrote very affectionately and thankfully on having recd. a letter from yr father, written on the river, the day after we parted at Palatka—she says it was as kind and affectionate as he ever wrote her, merely alluding to the past, and she gives me credit for "bridging over the great Gulf" that lay between them. She says he speaks of wishing to go to see Mother, but that it *cannot be* while the War lasts—it would compromise both. She says that neither he or I have any idea of the intensity of the feeling in the interior. The day after hers and yrs were recd. Tivie got a letter from Winston, enclosing one from yr father to me dated Jany. 28th. He had heard nothing from us since we parted—was especially anxious to hear about you and Tivie and desired me when I wrote to give his love to you but flattered himself all was well with us, as "bad news travels fast..."

Tivie has learned to card and spin—I can knit though very slow at it—All our soap and candles are made at home too. Dont you think we will do to live in the Confederacy? I want to move away from these sandflies most certainly... much love to you from all of us.

Mother

[WILLIE BRYANT TO DAVIS BRYANT]

Tullahoma Tenn Mar 1 1863

Dear Davis—

... I rather wish you would take the situation in the Quarter Master Dept ... for the reason that you can be gaining knowledge all the while instead of "losing it," and it will enable you perhaps to get into something better, which should be a matter of great consideration with us; everybody is trying to better their condition, and in this war, as in every other worldly business, gain is sought for by all; if you don't take the situation some one less worthy will; I find that "patriotism" is like every thing else in this d——d selfish world, a devilish nice thing to talk about, beautiful theory, a clever humbug that deceived the "soft ones," but the *practice* is soon "played out," and people "can't afford it," and I don't see how we can afford it any better than every body else around us; my *personal inclinations* still lead me to be the same fool I have been all along, to risk everything, and suffer everything for the cause, but when I take a "business view" of affairs, as others do, I see the folly of it; I must say it would be more *satisfactory* to me for you to stick it out where you are, unless very unpleasantly situated, but my *judgement* advises you to do otherwise if you can. I can retain my situation here, and make a good thing out of it in many ways, tho' I see no early prospect of a *pecuniary* gain; but the general knowledge which I glean, and the standing I can gain among those in authority and power, I can, if I choose to exert myself turn to good account; then too you know I am proud as the devil, in spirit, and sensitive, and not of a disposition to take well with the "world generally," tho' I can get along first rate where all are *gentlemen* . . .

I must close . . . Good bye!

Yrs always affectionately,
Willie.

[JULIA FISHER TO JAMES W. BRYANT][21]

Thomasville Mar 1, 1863

My Dear Brother,

Your letter reached me safely and caused me great pleasure as well as surprise: I hardly know how to define my own feelings: you *know* how dearly I loved you *always* and I never dreamed of any circumstances separating us; but you know how strongly from the first my feelings were enlisted in the cause of "Secession," the glorious cause of *right*! I know you did not approve of it, or view it as I did, but never doubted but that ultimately like many of our Conservative men, you would unite with us: would to God you had! Your family, your friends, all here, and as one of your old political friends lately said any position you might choose in your adopted state, Florida: but at any rate, I would choose poverty and suffering with *the South* rather than honor and wealth with *the North:* It has become a part of my religion: the shameful and cruel abuse of power at the North, then degradation and weakness, makes me feel for them only hatred and contempt: but I could not forget my almost idolatious love for *you:* when all believed that you had accepted that military position which would have divided us *forever*

---

21. This letter was sent by Julia Fisher to Rebecca Bryant to send with her next letter to James Bryant. In her 24 April letter to Davis, Rebecca says that she found this letter "objectionable" and that she and Willie decided "that it would not be proper to send it." Letters sent under a flag of truce to the north had to be unsealed, and the information might have become public and proved an embarrassment for the family.

here, I felt bound, publicly situated as I was, and to avoid compromising others connected with me in my efforts to avow my sentiments and defend myself and family from our enemies, (for there are always enough glad to find a point of attack on any prominent person). On *this* platform I could meet them and it was well known that though politically we were opposed, I would permit no one *personally* to attack you . . . however let "bygones be bygones"—I trust this war will soon close, and we may be like ourselves again: You are *magnanimous:* I appreciate the generosity that could enable you to overlook my wrong done you: I still think you did *us* great wrong, and exposed us all to needless and severe suffering, yet there was a terrible load on my heart, a continual incubus that was never removed night or day, sleeping or waking, *till your letter came:* I would dream of you, and it seemed as if in case of your death, I should lose my mind: I think I should: *now* whatever may befall either of us, *we are fully reconciled as brother and sister,* though politically we are separated until the country I would cheerfully die for, gives me the right to meet you as of old: You speak of coming to see us: why my dear William, you do not dream of the intensity of feeling in the interior: Your life would not be safe: the people only recognize you as one among a people they have a right to hate: even after a peace is declared, you could not find it pleasant here: Years must pass before this intense bitterness can partially die out: what have we not suffered? how can it be forgotten? our family here, have so far been fortunate . . . but our poor soldiery! there naked feet and almost naked limbs! yet how like heros they have fought and conquered! oh William, if you could only share with us the glory of our suffering, in this true cause of simple justice and right! Yet forgive me dearest brother, I know I am too much blinded by my impulses: I know how you were situated, and that in your love for the old union, you were naturally sincere: I may wonder at, and regret the cause you have pursued, but I have no right to condemn you, unless you had accepted the post rumor assigned you, and it was only on *that* ground I ever publicly condemned you: I said *"if":* I shall not attempt to write again at present: Ruby (our dear little Ruby) will keep you appraised of everything: I want to tell you once more how much your letter relieved my heart: I was (and am) prepared to make any necessary sacrifice for my country, but it was unnatural for me to feel anything but love for *you:* I love you and *always must* love you with my whole heart, but if you were arranged against us, as we feared and thought, every feeling yields to that of honor and patriotism now: after this unhappy war ends, I trust we may meet again: I shall make an effort: Mother and I can come to Fla on a visit: she feels just as I do: loves you *dearly,* but feels that not till peace is declared can she hope to see you . . . I am thankful to know that you are doing well, and that you dont have any thing to do with politics: *here* it is a matter of life and liberty, death or disgrace: *there* shameful oppression: God bless you my dear *dear* brother: let us forget everything only that *we have,* and *still do* love each other truly, and that whatever may have been, *and may yet be,* only remember *the dear old days and our old love:* our love, our blessings, and our prayers follow you *everywhere forever:*

Yours lovingly still
Julia

[OCTAVIA STEPHENS TO WINSTON STEPHENS]

Rose Cottage Mar 2, 1863

My dear husband

... It seems that you thought I had written some thing in one of my letters especially to make you feel badley, I dont know what I have written and I dont know what motive you could think I had for wishing to make you feel badly, for that would not make my grief any the less. I am sorry you thought so. I know I have felt very badly and suppose in writing have expressed some of my feelings for my heart felt over burdened yet I could not express to any one my real feelings. My grief for a time seemed to darken my very soul and sent from me all my good reasoning. The evil spirit got into me, for I could not submit, at times my heart rebelled and I almost doubted the good intentions of Providence, and that there was any hereafter and had souls, it seemed to me that if it were not for you I would wish to be laid by the side of that little one, and forget everything. I love Rosa but sometimes think perhaps she would be better off if raised by some one else. I suppose in some such mood I wrote to you, I am becoming more reconciled, and hope all the bad thoughts will leave me, you ask me to be as I was when we were first married, I am just the same being, but then had never been tried. You always think and say that I imitate "some one else," because I have a temper and not much patience with children but you are much mistaken, she has more patience than I have. I have never imitated her in anything excepting when I knew her judgement or experience was better than mine, I hope Rosa may not take after me, she is this minute talking of you, wants to know if I am writing to you and talking something about kissing you ...

Burrel sends "heap of howdies" to you and says he will get through planting cotton by Thursday, and has a days planting of corn to do up here, have sent for more corn ... He says the cane has not come up so very well and when he goes down to plant corn he is going to (plough it I believe) and says he will get done planting every thing by a week from Saturday, he covered the corn with the plough, he says the mules look very well, have not fallen off much ...

All send love so does your aff
Wife

*[Rebecca] **Mar 9, 1863**. Still warm. Henry is out before day and returns at 9 o'clk with a turkey weighing 18 lbs. H— and G— go over to ask Mrs S— and family to come over and help eat it. Tivie preparing to go to visit Winston in his camp.*

[GEORGE BRYANT TO WILLIE BRYANT]

Rose Cottage Mar 14, 1863

My dear brother Willie

... Tivie is preparing to go down to Jacksonville to pay Winston a visit, and she is going to mail this letter at Baldwin, she is going to start tomorrow, she will go in the buggy to Waldo, and then take the cars and go to Camp Finegan. Henry is going as far as Waldo to bring the mule back. They expect to reach Waldo in time to meet the cars. Felix, Mrs. Hopkins' negro man, is going with Tivie to Camp Finegan, he cooks for the mess that Winston is in and he had leave to come home and see [his] wife. Tivie does not know how long she will stay there ...

We have heard that Davis passed several days at Jacksonville the week before last. He went with the intention of putting our most valuable things in the hands of Mr. Burritt, but we have not heard from him since to know how he found things. Winston's colt is getting to be quite a horse, he is turning a light grey and is very tame. His hair is so soft that we save it to put in thread to make socks, it looks very much like woollen. Tivie can spin very well now, she has been spinning thread of which she is going to have cloth made.

Henry and I went Turkey hunting last Monday morning and killed a large gobbler, and Henry went again the day before Yesterday with Joe and killed one as large. Rosa is quite interesting, she talks a great deal, and she is very funny sometimes.

It is pretty late so I will leave this for to night. Good night! I hope you will have pleasant dreams. All send much love. This is from

Yours affectionately

George

*[Rebecca] **Mar 15, 1863**. ... Tivie, Henry and Rosa start in the buggy at 3 o'clk p.m.—Felix walking ...*

[DAVIS BRYANT TO WILLIE BRYANT]

Camp Cooper Mar 15, 1863

Dear Willie

... During the past few weeks we have had the company of a detachment of Chamber's Company (30 men) and an artillery Co. of four pieces—12 lb. houitzer and 2 6 lb. rifled pieces—and 65 men, to guard the St. Marys river, as we had reason to believe the yankee boat intended going up after a quantity of lumber and other stuff, but a few days ago the detachment was sent for, and yesterday the artillery co. was taken off to Jacksonville, or as near there as prudent just now. I believe the next news from there will be that the poor ill starred old place is leveled to the ground, as it is again taken possession of and occupied by the yankees and garrisoned with nigger troops.[22] The last account was that two regiments of the devils had been placed there and were engaged in fortifying the place, and it was Finegans intention to shell them out as soon as he could concentrate his forces at the Seven miles Camp, so we are in hourly expectation of hearing big guns in that direction.[23] Of course in shelling them out he supposes the town will be burnt, and in my opinion that is the only way he can oust them, as their Gunboats are placed in position to protect them in town, and Therefore it is impossible to drive them out. Two gunboats—I think was the number—first went up very rapidly and stopped at B— and C—'s wharf before any, or many, were aware of their arrival,[24] (and they were not expected as not one had come as high as town—and only once in sight for three weeks before) and immediately landed a regmt. of niggers, rushing them out to all the entrances to town to "pen" all who happened to be there, and they did catch several ... Jno. Drysdale who, has been quite sick and living there—and several less important personages, Jack Butler escaped by the skin of his teeth.[25] As he was crossing "Bisbee's bridge" he heard the niggers "tearing" up the road behind him, whooping and yelling, to stop up that outlet. The next day, I think it was—Genl. "Barney"—as he is entitled by some of his disaffected subjects—mustered his little force at "Camp Finegan" ... (Winston's and Chamber's cavalry cos. and about 300 infantry) and tried to bag the outposts but owing to some mistake the infantry did not move fast enough and, in consequence, the cavalry was left to do the whole and succeeded in merely driving them in under cover of their Gunboats ...

22. The third occupation of Jacksonville began when Colonels Thomas W. Higginson and James Montgomery, commanders respectively of the First and Second South Carolina Volunteers (Colored), landed at the city on 10 March 1863. Confederate General Finegan asked for reinforcements and proceeded to the camp that bore his name. Before the Federals evacuated the place on 29 March, there were several skirmishes, and each side suffered casualties.

23. As mentioned, Seven Miles Camp was an early name for Camp Finegan.

24. "B— and C—'s" is a reference to the mercantile firm of Cyrus Bisbee and Anthony Canova.

25. Jonathan Drysdale was a former army officer from St. Augustine, and John G. Butler was a Duval County timber merchant before the war.

In regard to the folks at home I suppose you are as well posted as I, as every letter I get mentions their having written you, and mine are often two weeks coming. They were all well at last accounts. How I wish they were all at Thomasville. Winston and I tried to fix upon some plan when I was at his camp, but it is next to impossible for them to move over from that side to carry any thing with them, therefore he is determined to put it off until it will warrant the sacrifice he would have to make . . . All is quiet just around here now, though there is no knowing how long it will remain so. If those niggers are brought out into the State as they say they intend, you'll hear of some of the "damdest fights" you ever heard tell of, as every man of us is determined to do his best towards *wiping them out completely.* As long as my letters can reach you certainly I will keep you posted on matters here. I reckon this will do for the present. I hope to hear from you soon, and am anxious to do so as your last was so short, and matters so changeable.

Yr. Aff. brother
Davis

[Rebecca] *Mar 16, 1863. Cloudy until noon. George kills some birds in the field from which we dine. After dinner he goes to town on an errand and hears that a man brought a report of 3,000 of the enemy landing at Jacksonville and fighting there on Friday and Saturday—There is some doubt of the truth of the report—but O how anxiously must I await Henry's return—Perhaps Tivie will come too. What is in store for us, God alone knows.*

[Winston Stephens to Octavia Stephens]

In Camp at Mooney's place 5 miles out from Jacksonville.[26]

Mar 16, 1863

My Dear Wife

I can feel this morning how very anxious you must be for my welfare, as you have no doubt heard ere this of the fight at Jacksonville with all its exaggerations that follow such events. I wish I could send this direct to you and I did ask to be allowed such a thing but was refused and now I have to trust to the slow process of mail. On Tuesday the yankees and negroes in transports accompanied by three Gun boats came up to Jacksonville and Lieut Gray and the pickets barely had time to get out before they had landed and were going in every direction trying to capture all they could, Lt Gray lost his sword, uniform and papers etc. He then

---

26. George Mooney was a machinist born in Ireland in 1822. In 1860 he and his wife, Ella, had two children and eight slaves.

sent an express out to camps and I was sent with my Company and the rest followed, nothing was done that day of any consequence but that night Genl Finegan with some reinforcements arrived and Wednesday morning we were thrown in line of battle and the Cavalry went on the north side and the Infantry on the three miles branch and so as to cut off the retreat of the enemy and we were to charge them, every thing went on quietly until we got to . . . the plank road when the yankee pickets fired upon Lt Gray who was thrown out in advance. I then formed my Company under the hail of bullets and . . . moved up near the road pouring a fire into their lines and they began soon to give way and Capt Chambers about this time formed his Company on my right and across the road and they broke like wild animals, not waiting for a charge. The Infantry had not moved up fast enough and consequently all of them got away except those that were killed . . . We lost Dr Meredith who was shot through the head and two horses killed and one wounded. Mr McLeod a brother of Lt McLeod was struck with a spent ball on the thigh but was not hurt much. Jessup had the stripe of his pants on the thigh cut into by a ball. Poor Dr Meredith did not know what hit him, he lived about five hours after he was shot but was not sensible nor apparently in pain. We have lost a good friend and a Valuable Phisician.[27]

3 P.M. I was cut short by an expressman riding in to Camps stating the Yankees were advancing but after getting ready and going down we learned that after exchanging a few shots they returned to Town. I am to go down this evening to ambush them and I hope to get some of the scamps. Capt Dickison is coming up and has offered to send this up to you. I want you to arrange so that the negroes can go at once into the woods if they come up as high as you are and get Clark if the Yankees stay up there to try and get the negroes across the river and send them up on the road to me, but I hope it will not be necessary to break up, tell Burrel all about it and tell him I shall depend upon him to take care of the rest of the negroes. The negroes in arms will promise him fair prospects, but they will require him to take up arms against us and he will suffer the same fate those did in Town that we killed, and the Yankees say they will hang them if they dont fight. I think it a good plan for Clark and Henry to secrete some provisions where no one knows of it but the whites, that is the older ones and not any of the negroes, or perhaps if they were to do such a thing it might create the suspicion of the negroes. I want Burrel to see that I have the utmost confidence in him. Tell him to keep something hid away so that if they are forced to take to the woods they will have something to live on, and you had better consult Clark about the

---

27. Private D. C. McLeod served for the remainder of the war, and this was apparently the only time he was hurt. In his official report of 14 March 1863, General Finegan used almost the identical words that Winston did in describing the loss of Dr. James Meredith. Finegan noted that they "had lost a valuable life in Acting Surgeon Meredith." In the same report, Finegan officially commended Winston and Chambers for their valor and leadership during the fight, and he repeated his praise in his report of 31 March 1863. OR, ser. 1, vol. 14, 226–29, 850.

cotton. I want you to take care that none of the negroes or the mules fall into their hands. I hope Capt Dickison will be able to keep them from going up above Palatka as his Company will return to that point. The Yankees or negroes ... threaten to do big things but they will not fight and if they come up a few resolute men can drive them back, they will steal every thing they put their hands on so you had better get Henry to bury every thing some place and what money you keep put it around your body. I would not wear any jewelry or show any thing that will tempt them ... We are getting strong as we have some 16 Companies and some Cavalry is now arriving from Ga. I think God being our helper that the Yanks and negroes will be cleared out of Jacksonville in a few days. We look to God and trust in him to sustain us in this our just cause. I want you to put your trust in him and he will not forsake you. If I fall it will be in defence of a just cause. I hope very soon to see you when we will be fearing no enemy. This I regard as our greatest tryal ... If I should have any thing happen to me Davis will close up my papers for you ...

May God in his goodness protect you all. love to all and many kisses to Rosa and yourself. Good bye, tell the negroes howdie.

Your loving husband
Winston Stephens

Mar 17, 1863. *Arrived at Waldo just in time to meet the cars. Henry started right back by way of Orange Springs ... Arrived at Camps three miles from Jacksonville in the afternoon. Winston and Swep met me at the cars and came here to Mrs Mooney's with me, had been here about half an hour when Winston had to go to Jacksonville, after having one skirmish, as a report came that Maj Brevard was surrounded, the negroes were again driven back.*

Mar 18, 1863. *Saw a good deal of Winston ...*

Mar 19, 1863. *Saw but little of Winston as he was officer of the day. I wrote to Mother. The people were ordered out of Jacksonville.*

Mar 20, 1863. *Winston went with others to Jacksonville, had no fight ...*

Mar 21, 1863. *As the camps were moved back to Camp Finegan Swep took me to a Mrs Flynn's to stay,*[28] *Winston came there after supper to spend the night with me.*

Mar 23, 1863. *The Genl with 1000 men, Winston among them, went to Jacksonville with the 54 lb gun, no one hurt, they ret— just before night.*[29]

---

28. This was most probably Catelina Flynn, wife of George Flynn, a Duval County farmer.

29. Where Tivie got this information is unknown, but the next day the Confederates did mount a 32-pound gun on a railroad flat car and commenced shelling Jacksonville with deadly effect. On 25 March Colonel Higginson, with about 1,500 men, moved out against the Confederates, but the

Winston stopped awhile, the Genl came in for water. Winston came after supper to stay over night . . .

Mar 25, 1863. The troops went to Jack— again, killed some Yankees. none on our side hurt, 15 guns and other things were found . . .

Mar 26, 1863. The troops went to Jacksonville again had no fight. Willie surprised us in the afternoon from Tennessee. Winston stopped a long while on his way back to camps. Willie went with him to supper and then returned and spent the eve and Willie went to camp to sleep.

Mar 27, 1863. Winston and Willie came about 11 o'clk, Winston went to Jacksonville on Picket until Sun. Willie stayed until after dinner, then started for Welaka . . .

[OCTAVIA STEPHENS TO DAVIS BRYANT]

Mar 27, 1863

Dear Davis

Before you receive this you will have heard of Willie's being in Florida . . . Willie left here this afternoon for Welaka on one of Winston's horses, he arrived here yesterday afternoon. I was much surprised and delighted to see him, he requested me to write to you and say that he was left by the cars the other day, therefore could not come to see you, he will pass through Baldwin on the 10th . . .

I am very anxious about home as one of Transports with niggers have gone up the river, but I hope they will not go above Palatka, I am so glad Willie has gone up there.

I heard the day before I left home that some troops had landed at Jacksonville but it came from two or three men who were not at all reliable and it was not believed, but after I started and heard the report confirmed I came on, for I could not bear the idea of going back and being weeks without hearing from Winston, for it was more than I could stand when he was not in so much danger. I do not know what to say or think, my lot now seems very hard, yet I have a great deal to be thankful for.

Winston left me this morning to be away until Sunday afternoon on Picket duty near Jacksonville, he has been with me every night since I have been here and I have seen him for a few minutes sometimes through the day. Now that the danger has come so near I long more than ever for peace, but when shall we ever see that happy time . . . ?

---

fire from the 32-pounder plus Gamble's Light Artillery proved to be too much, and he retired after taking seven casualties. The continuous artillery bombardment, coupled with constant probing assaults by Confederate cavalry and infantry, induced the Federals to evacuate the city on 29 March 1863.

I believe I have told you what Willie wished me to, my mind has been so troubled for sometime now that I am more forgetful than ever. I wish I could hear from you before I start home. I must say good night. With much love

I remain

Yr aff Sister Tivie

[Rebecca] *Mar 28, 1863. . . . A gentle rain sets in just after supper and in the midst of it Willie arrives! He is thin, having been lately sick, but Heaven be praised he is here at last . . . !*
Mar 29, 1863. Winston returned from Picket duty in the afternoon and told us of the evacuation of Jacksonville by the Yankees, he staid to supper.
[Rebecca] *Mar 29, 1863. A rainy, dark day—but in the interchange of mutual feelings and thoughts we forget the weather. We are so completely absorbed in Willie that the boys' Sunday lessons are omitted—All retire early.*
[Rebecca] *Mar 30, 1863. . . . The boys all at home during the morng. cleaning guns etc—After dinner . . . they go on the river to fish and return at dark with a fine lot of brim and perch. We pass the eveg. in listening to Willie's relation of many incidents connected with his march into and from Kentucky—*
[Rebecca] *Mar 31, 1863. . . . Willie and boys go to town immediately after breakfast, return before dinner with two squirrels—Mrs Hopkins and Bella have arrived in Welaka . . .*
[Rebecca] *Apr 2, 1863. Very cold—The boys and Willie start before daylight to hunt turkeys—return without any—After breakfast go out and kill a squirrel. Soon after dinner all go in the boat to Welaka to see Mrs Hopkins and Miss Bella—return at sunset having enjoyed the afternoon.*

[WINSTON STEPHENS TO WILLIE BRYANT]

Camp Finegan Apr 3, 1863

Dear Willie

I was all ready to start up to day on 10 days furlough, but Col McCormick says he cannot allow me to go until he returns so I will have to wait here about 10 days before I start, as his furlough is for that time. Tivie will be so badly disappointed and in fact I am myself as I wished very much to be with you part of the time during your stay . . . You cannot imagine the relief from my mind experienced when the Yanks left Jacksonville. I feel more easy than I have for many days and feel that Tivie is not in so much danger here. You can see by this that it is not necessary to move any thing for the present. You must come down so as to spend a day with us if you can. Tell Mother I am so sorry to throw the duties of my household on her for so long a time, but it is impossible for me to get her up home until I come. You must excuse the haste of this as I have to go down to escort Barney and Staff to Jacksonville and the bearer is waiting. Love to all, and Howdie to darkies.

Yours as ever
Winston Stephens

[REBECCA BRYANT TO DAVIS BRYANT]

Rose Cottage Apr 7, 1863

My dear Davis,

Willie has been with us nine days and leaves tomorrow—He has gained strength and recovered his appetite here—and altho it is very hard to part with him, I am truly grateful for this visit... He lost all the flesh he had boasted of in a sickness of 10 or 12 days before he left Tullahoma, but is looking much better than when he came. It was fortunate for *me* that he came when I was almost alone, as the boys are absent nearly all the time during the day and Henry frequently stays over night at Mr Stephens' with whom he has formed a partnership in the Alligator business. Willie however would doubtless have enjoyed his visit much more if Tivie and Winston could have been here. One of the men from Winston's camp passed here on Sunday and left a letter from Winston to Willie, inclosing your last to him, and giving us the joyful intelligence that the enemy had left the river. I regret that you were so worried by the report that they had been up here—I know you must have suffered great anxiety—They came no higher than Palatka but we were in constant dread of them paying us a visit, after we heard what they had done below... I am as ever yours most fondly.

Mother

[Rebecca] *Apr 8, 1863. A pleasant morng.—Mrs Stephens and children come to pass the day—Willie busy with sundry little matters, preparing to leave us—He goes about 1 o'clk p.m. leaving an aching void in his mother's heart...*

[WILLIE BRYANT TO DAVIS BRYANT]

Welaka Apr 8, 1863.

Dear Davis—

I suppose you think that as I could not expect to see you while in Fla. I might at least have written you a long letter while up here, and I think so too, but somehow I havn't...

I of course am sorry that we cannot see each other this time, but I could not make the time hit right, and I reckon we can "bore it"; had I not got left at Lake City the Wedsy a.m. I intended coming down, I should most probably have run down to your camp that day. I spent 4 days at Thomasville on my way out; I could not get across to the R. Road in Fla. owing to the crowds of passengers, and Sunday intervening—when there is no traveling—I was necessarily compelled to make my visit then, tho' I intended to on my return; I had quite a pleasant time tho' I was unwell, and not in the mood for enjoyment . . .

Lake City, Friday night 12 o'c—

Arrived here at ½ p. 10—too late to see any "honest folks"—d—n it! . . . Spent 4 hours to-day with Winston and Tivie—They will go home on next Tuesday or Wedsy . . . I got yr letter—It's too devilish bad we couldn't collide; but we must hope for the best—Keep a stiff upper lip, Bub—I may write you, look out for a letter soon . . . Good bye—Yrs always afftly

Willie

[Winston Stephens to Davis Bryant]

Camp Finegan Apr 8, 1863

Dear Davis

As we were disappointed in getting off the day we anticipated I have concluded to write you these few lines in addition to Tivies. Lt Col McCormick would not consent to my going home before he had his furlough as I had my Wife so near me and said I could better afford to wait than he could. I was more anxious to get home at that particular time on Willies account than any other, and now I will see him only a short time on his return. I could have been with him some three or four days if I could have gone at the time I proposed, but I suppose Mother saw more of him by my not going as in all probability we would [have] spent part of the time in the woods. I have concluded not to move yet but to try and work my crop and if the Yankees return I will send my negroes and other property they would likely take off from the river to some place where they are not likely to visit. When I go home I will arrange for such an emergency—but hope they will not return. They destroyed many buildings in Jacksonville but I am not familiar enough to repeat the names so that you can know whose houses they did burn . . . My men were first in the Town and I sent them in every direction and they did all they could to arrest the fire . . . We are diging pits in the Town to shoot the Yankees if they land any more, some think it will bring them back but it appears to me they have gone to stay, at least I hope so and if you could see the work they did to prepare them for holding it and then the destruction of the Town and the haste in which they abandoned it you I think would have the same opinion. hoping to hear from you soon

I remain Yours truly
Winston Stephens

[Rebecca] **Apr 17, 1863.** *A fine morng.*—*About 10 o'clk Winston and Tivie and Rosa arrive to our great joy. All have bad colds and are glad to get home. The boys return from fishing with 2 fine trout and all enjoy our dinner highly—*

[REBECCA BRYANT TO DAVIS BRYANT]

Rose Cottage Apr 24, 1863

My dear Davis,

... I regretted your not seeing Willie as much I believe as you could have done. I would willingly have spared some days of his visit to me, if by that means he could have gone to you—but the Wednesdays could not be made to come in right, and he could not get an extension of furlough except by telegraph, and if refused, could not *then* reach his post in time. Tivie, Winston and Rosa arrived safely a week ago—much to my satisfaction you may be sure, for George and I had been by ourselves nearly all the time after Willie left. Henry had slept at home only two nights in eight, having been up the river with Mr Stephens to buy corn, and to O. Springs to sell their Oil. Mr S— found the waggon too weak to haul it to Waldo and reckoning the ferry wage and other expenses incident to the trip found it would be nearly as well to sell it for 4 dolls. per gall. at the Springs as for $6 at Waldo—They carried 21 galls. and Henry's share of the profits was $28. They expect to commence selling Oil again in about 10 days and to carry a much larger quantity to the R. Road ...

All send much love
Mother

[WILLIE BRYANT TO DAVIS BRYANT]

Tullahoma, Tenn Apr 25, 1863

Dear Bro. Davis—

Here I am back again and so fully reinstated, and deep in work that I can hardly realise that I have been absent at all—To-day is Saturday; I arrived here a week ago yesterday p.m. ...

Of course I did not enjoy much pleasure on my furlough as I found affairs in such a condition in Fla., but it was a great satisfaction to me to be there at such a time and I was thereby saved much anxiety; my being unwell too during the first of my visit prevented my feeling like enjoying many things that I would otherwise have enjoyed and then too I had but 10 days at Welaka and 5 at Thomasville out of 30; I was not half satisfied with my trip and must try it over before very long if I have to go on a sick furlough . . .

Paris was at the Cars at Sav'h . . . I immediately went around with him to his quarters; after tea we went to the Theatre where I met several I knew; knocked around next day . . . took a stroll up town to commence to pass the time pleasantly away with more oysters and whiskey . . . getting supper at a restaurant, and as it was raining, for the want of something better to do we went to a wedding, a regular democratic one, and among the guests were seven fast girls, we looked on for awhile and "sparked" the girls when I concluded to "pitch in for devilment" and led the bride out for a "quadrille" where I did her Justice, sure,—I mean in *dancing*—having nothing else to do, and it being too far to go up for drinks we staid there till after 1 o'c; . . . Paris is a d——d smart fellow, a good deal older than I am in every way, quiet or rather reserved in his manner, seldom laughs, and has a sort of careless, dissatisfied look, and possesses the great tact of using "the world" and making it respect him, takes it as a matter of course; with his tact I would soon possess wealth and power; I like Paris, tho' we would not agree in many things, and we would each improve by being together . . .

Hardee's Corps, which has been camped here, has moved up 16 miles within the past two days, to establish our line in front of the enemy at Murfreesboro, the troops are in fine condition now and the weather good. We have a splendid army now of at least 50,000 men and are anxious to bring on a fight; every preparation is being made for a battle, which must come off soon and be terrible terrible; I shall wait until the thing is fairly started when I intend to take a hand; if we can whip the Yankees here it will serve much to end the war, and will be the last great battle of the war; there will be over 60,000 troops on a side engaged in the next fight; Genl. Johnston is here and he commands the Depmt. which includes this and several other armies—and being an old and fortunate commander—having been wounded 12 times—the troops are greatly inspired by his pressence.

If I get off to go in the fight I shall write you a few lines just before starting—I am glad that you have been promoted; anything is better than a d——d private; the time when it was an honor to be a private has "played out"; I wd. rather be 2d. than 1st. Sergt if the 1st is any account. Our loss in Jv'lle has completely "busted" us; my watch and our dressing case are, I believe, all that we have left of the stock there . . .

Good bye for now—Perhaps I can get a "furlough wound" and see you soon.

Yrs always affectionately
Willie—

[JULIA FISHER TO REBECCA BRYANT]

Thomasville Apr 28, 1863

Dearest sister:

... When I went to Sav last I was carried to the "City Orphan Asylum," and also a private one: and to the "Widow's Home," a fine building occupied by poor old widows: also another widow's Home for those who had children and were destitute: fortunately I had donations enough with me, of food, to share with all, though my first care was the "Wayside Home" for soldiers: this is a fine Hotel converted into a Home for passing soldiers, and they have every comfort there, *gratis:* I had promised them to assist them if they established it, and have supplied them with a great deal: partly donations, partly bought ...

The folks of Sav, asked me to buy a cow for the orphan asylum, and I begged one of a rich friend, and the president of the R.R. is to send me a special car to ship her this week: he is very kind: are not these things better than money to me? a poor soldier had two little motherless children sent to him in camp (the mother having died,) and I gave a free pass for a poor Aunt to go and get them: I was so thankful I had the power, and in other similar cases: they will pass anything or anybody free for me: and even Gen Mercer made an exception to a general order of having all boxes examined, in favor of my shipments: therefore I must hold on ...[30]

I had a letter from Willie today! such a nice cheerful letter ... how much we love your boy! and it is really touching to see Mother's affection: she shows so little for others, is generally so apt to see faults in all, even in *me* (who she really thinks a great deal of!) but *Willie* she speaks of with so much tenderness: speaking of Willie's words the other day, that "Paris was his superior in some things," she said with tears and great warmth, "show me *one point* in which that boy has a superior in Paris or *any one* ... !" Willie's devotion to you is remarkable, and that has doubly endeared him to all of us ...

I am glad Willie heard from his father, and very thankful that Wm. is so situated as to give no cause for anxiety: how his heart must long for home and *his wife and children:* much love to dear Tivy and boys: Kiss our little Rosa and for yourself darling from all of us *fondest love:*

Yours ever Julia:

[WINSTON STEPHENS TO OCTAVIA STEPHENS]

Camp Finegan Apr 29, 1863

My dear Wife

... I arrived safely on Monday just at dark and found all as usual, I had no accident or delay on the road. I staid at Mrs Thomas' Sunday night and slept in

30. Brigadier General Hugh Weedon Mercer was in command at Savannah for most of the war.

the same room with two girls and the old Lady and the old Lady talked pritty plainly.[31] I had gone over to night to call on Mrs Greely who is at Mr Prices and spent a short time pleasantly . . . She made me a nice present in the shape of a palmetto hat, one of the best I've seen. She made the present in consideration of the kindness I have shown her husband, I think! Mr Greely had his little boy at camp and I took him up before me and on our way to Prices he asked me if I would give him my little Girl. It appears she made quite an impression on the young fellows mind or heart as he has constantly talked of her since he met her on the road . . .

I found that our troops were filling up the Bateries the Yanks made, but we are not fortifying the river as is reported up there. I find my Co has not been relieved from duty at all as they Picket, Drill and Every thing else. I will have a chance of telling some one of this before long as Genl Finegan gave two orders to have the Co rest but it has not been done . . . Love to all and accept oceans of love to yourself and Rosa. Your aff husband

Winston Stephens

[OCTAVIA STEPHENS TO WINSTON STEPHENS]

Rose Cottage May 1, 1863

My dear husband

. . . Mother and I spent yesterday and last night with Tina, we went to see what Mr Smith had to sell and it was so late when we got back that I was easily prevailed upon to stay. I am afraid you will think me extravagant although I only bought me one thing a clock, and paid ten dollars for it, I asked Tina (of course) about it and she thought it a moderate price so I took it, as you were not there to ask, for I wanted a time piece so much, but I am afraid it has got injured in coming over in the buggy for the Pendulum came off and I thought I fixed it on right but it will not run. I might have known that if I had anything to do with it something would happen. I guess Clark can tell me [what is] the matter with it, it is an eight day clock, with brass works, if it will run well I will not think the money thrown away . . .

You will perhaps be pleased to know that Rosa has become a little better behaved than when you were here, her cough is well and an eye tooth has made its appearance, and the other stomach tooth trying to come through but oh how I dread her having the whooping cough and feel quite certain that she will, for Polly no doubt has it quite badly and I think Jess just taking it, poor little Polly it is hard for her . . .

With love I close

Your aff

Wife Tivie

31. Undoubtedly this was Mary E. Thomas and her daughters, Jane and Judana.

[WINSTON STEPHENS TO OCTAVIA STEPHENS]

Camp Finegan May 4, 1863

My Dear Wife

... Old Lady, I want to see you mighty bad. how do you feel on the subject? golly I would give lots just to have one pouting smack, and I would give any thing I've got to have you serve me as you did you know when and you sayed you would kiss me din't you, that was a kind act and duly appreciated by your old Man. I hope you have had plenty of rain and that the crop looks well. We had a fine rain here last night and we feel thankful as we had orders to Drill and it would have been bad on account of the dust had we not had the rain, and then those planting around here wanted it badly ...

Love to Mother and boys and Clark and family and howdies to negroes. and lots of love to you and Rosa. Your aff husband

Winston Stephens

[OCTAVIA STEPHENS TO WINSTON STEPHENS]

Rose Cottage May 5, 1863

My dear husband

... I guess from the looks of things in my garden that these rains have helped your crop, I heard it had the cotton, we have had a splendid season for potatoes ... All the sows have pigs except your little white one, we have not yet found out how many, one brought six up, Georgie saw the bunch but could not count them they were so wild.

Clark and Henry begin alligatoring again to day ... I wrote in my letter that my ten dollar clock would not run, after finishing your letter and one to Ma I fixed it again and it does finely now, and is such a comfort to know the time, I hope you will not "begrudge" me the ten dollars, although I was sorry I paid so much after I had done it. Oh I forgot, Clark got fifteen bushels of corn for you, they got quite a number of trout that would have helped greatly if they had kept.

Big Jane has fever, Jess and Polly the whooping cough, the rest are well ... We are going to have (or try) some huckleberry cornbread for dinner, if it is good I shall wish you had some, we enjoy your orangeade very much and wish you had it every time ... Good bye.

Affectionately
Your Wife

[WINSTON STEPHENS TO OCTAVIA STEPHENS]

Camp Finegan May 7, 1863

My Dear Wife

... On Tuesday we had a Telegram stating a fight was going on at or near Fredricksburg and that we had made a capture of 1500 Cavalry in Tenesee. Yesterday Genl Lees Official dispatch informs us that he had ingaged the Enemy near Fredricksburg and after one of the hottest fights of the War he had driven the Enemy across the river, gaining a complete victory and capturing 25,000 men and they were stil coming in. and also Yesterday a confirmation of the capture of Wheeler's Cavalry 1500 of the Enemys Cavalry. and a *rumor* that as many more had been captured in 8 or 10 miles of Richmond. Madam rumor has it that the yanks sent 3,000 cavalry to see if our forces had been withdrawn about Richmond and our forces allowed them to go in a few miles without meeting any force when Stuart surrounded them and bagged the party, some stating it to be 3,000 and others 1,500. We have without any doubt gained another victory on the Rappahannock and captured the Cavalry in Tennessee but the other I question very much, as it appears to me impossible to get so near Richmond and not discover some of our fortifications. A fight is now considered imminent in Tullahoma with Rosencrans and if we are successful there I think the hardest of our fighting over[32] ... I think you had better get Clark to buy you some two or three beevs and kill one and mix the bacon and beef so as to make the bacon hold out, tell him to engage three and you can have one killed when you want it. I had rather do that than wait until all the bacon is gone and then have only beef. I hope you are having plenty of rain, as we have had good rains down here. Tell Burrel to be sure and keep the sows gentle and mark the pigs young. Love to all and howdie to negroes. many kisses to you and Rosa from your loving husband

Winston Stephens

32. The Battle of Chancellorsville, 1–4 May 1863, is Lee's masterpiece; indeed, it was one of the most daring plans in military history. Lee and General Thomas J. "Stonewall" Jackson defied every principle of military tactics yet gained a tremendous victory over the Army of the Potomac, commanded by Major General Joseph Hooker. Still, this tactical victory did not change the strategic goals of each army and really accomplished little except in morale. In addition, Jackson was wounded by his own men and died a week after the battle, on 10 May 1863. The death of Jackson proved to be a loss that could not be surmounted; the Army of Northern Virginia was never again the force that it had been. Federal casualties came to 1,606 killed, 9,762 wounded, and 5,919 missing, for a total of 17,287. Lee's forces had 1,665 killed, 9,081 wounded, and 2,018 missing, for a total of 12,764.

Major General Joseph Wheeler's cavalry were busy in the West; after the Battle of Stones River, Rosecrans's Army of the Cumberland regrouped around Murfreesboro while Bragg's Army of Tennessee occupied a line around Shelbyville on the Nashville & Chattanooga Railroad. Cavalry units from both armies engaged in various raids for several months, until Rosecrans took the offensive against Bragg in late June and forced him to withdraw some eighty-five miles during the Tullahoma campaign. By July, Bragg had retreated across the Cumberland plateau and taken a position behind the Tennessee River.

[OCTAVIA STEPHENS TO WINSTON STEPHENS]

Rose Cottage May 14, 1863

My dear husband

... I hope that you did not allow Mrs Thomas' plain talk to disturb your rest, or that you did not have to take a dose of *"Morphine"* to make you sleep the Sunday night that you speak of ...[33]

You want to know how I feel about seeing you, I want to see you as much if not more than you want to see me, I think more, you are too much taken up to think much of me now, but I long for you all the time, you think you love me best because I am not as affectionate as some folks, but the affection is abundant but stays shut up in my heart, will not flow out freely but I often wish that I could show more affection, but I love others, you especially to be affectionate to me. But see here you know what you said you'd give any thing for, you must be careful, you'll be away a long time, use cold water, you said that was a good remedy. I am going to send you orange juice enough for three or four drinks as a *cooling drink,* your bottle you left has not all gone yet, but is getting a little old, I will send you fresh, I wish I could send more ... I hope you will not think I dont want to see you when I give my excuses for not promising to come to you, in the first place I think as times are so quiet and Gray and McLeod have their furloughs now you will get a chance to come home soon, then the greatest reason is that Rosa has the whooping cough and I could not carry her any where, and I can not bear to go off again and leave Mother here, when I know she would like to go herself and take the boys off on a visit, and we can not all go together, unless we go in the Old wagon, then we will want a great deal of cloth and I am spinning hard, expect soon to be weaving, and with all my efforts fear we will still need, and I am afraid to travel over that road again with that old buggy, and to go the other way costs money, so I think you will have to ask Barny for a furlough next month, if none of these things were in the way I would like *very much* to go, but I feel that I ought to stay and Rosa's cough will put an end any how I guess ...

The sows have twenty five pigs. Henry's has seven, your little white just has some I guess as she has not been up for two or three days, they are said to be fine pigs ...

Did you sign your letter my lover with as much depth of feeling as you did four years ago? I can mine with a deeper. Well good bye my dear.

As ever your
loving Wife

33. "Morphine" was their secret word for sexual intercourse; most probably, this was Winston's creation.

[REBECCA BRYANT TO DAVIS BRYANT]

Rose Cottage May 14, 1863

Dear Davis,

... Mrs Hopkins and Bella are still in Welaka and do not think of leaving for a long time, I believe Bella keeps up her ideas of dress and fashion pretty much as she did before her father's death, it occupies a large space in her thoughts and conversation. What a pity it is that so many amiable young ladies neglect to furnish the upper story! I do hope if you and Willie ever marry you will select something more than a doll or a belle, something useful as well as ornamental—Speaking of the useful—Tivie has a mania for weaving since her visit down the river and I have given her $12 to purchase a loom—She expects to have it next week and if it does not require more common sense and physical force than she represents as necessary, I intend to learn to weave—She is quite an adept at spinning. Would you like to see me in a dress of my own weaving...?

Rosa we think has the whooping cough—but at times she is full of fun—The other children are having it mildly, and I hope she may...

Love from the boys and Mother.

[WINSTON STEPHENS TO OCTAVIA STEPHENS]

Camp Finegan May 17, 1863

My Dear Wife

Your long and affectionate letter was received last night and it was the first line or news I have had of you since I left ... I have not been obliged to borrow a dose of *Morphine* [but it] would be a better application than you propose, I will try to get along without but I think if you will study my comfort and interest you will not allow any one to keep us seperated so long as before ...

I am glad you will get some cows from Braddock and hope you have not been disappointed. you can use your own judgment about the loom but you must not sell any cotton unless you get 20 cents in the seed for it and that cash. I am glad to see so good an account of the sows and hope they will raise them ... I am not willing that your Mother should pay for the loom. I think you had better get a good one and you will find it cheaper in the end. I will gratify this notion of yours ... and you shall have all the money you want for the enterprise and hope you will *love me a little* for not scolding you. In two of the letters I received from you there seems to be something hid and you seem to have something that you want to complain of and stil you leave it unexpressed, do for my sake if you pity or love me have full confidence and tell me candidly of all your troubles and let me share them with you. I love you deeply and tenderly, and would rather die than willfully wrong you . . . I am glad to see by your first letter that Clark and Henry had got the corn. I am glad you have a clock to give you the time . . . I am glad to hear Rosa has cut her eye tooth but poor child how much she will suffer with that horrid cough I hope she will soon get over it . . .

I'l close I remain your affectionate husband always. love to Mother and the boys and Clarks family, and accept a kiss and love for yourself and Rosa . . .

Winston Stephens

[WILLIE BRYANT TO DAVIS BRYANT]

Tullahoma Tenn. Sunday May 17, 1863

Dear Davis

. . . My visit to Florida was far from complete, especially as I was unable to meet you, and although there was much to detract from the pleasure of it, the satisfaction of being there at such a time, and that I now enjoy in reverting to it, is great. Had I been here at that time I would have been wretched. You can form no idea of the strange feeling I experienced and the great relief, in being freed from military restraint and "dispotism," and having an opportunity once more to mingle "socially with the civilized world," after my long and barbarous existance as a private in a large army; *for 10 months I had not held half an hours conversation with a woman,* not two conversations with the same woman; that alone shows that I must have been unfortunately and unhappily situated; just think of that for me, and weep O, my brother! My senses seemed to have become dulled and my feelings blunted and numb and at first when I roamed thro' the old familiar woods with my dog, and rifle on my shoulder, with the freedom of early and happy days, I could not fully realise it, and I felt as if I could not fully arouse myself, my mind and thoughts seemed painfully contracted and unable to comprehend every thing and you have undoubtedly experienced that same indescribable sensation . . . I felt as if I dared not let my feelings "thaw out," and allow myself to enjoy too much the pleasant scene around me, for fear that it would be too hard to leave them when necessity compelled, and it was hard; I had tasted deeply of the pleasure of home and friends, and it had revived and increased my old appetite . . .

My duties have heretofore been very arduous, the most so in the office, but lately I have been "promoted" and am now "brevet act adgt. Genl"; you have never heard of that "statue?" before, have you! nor I either! so to explain myself; Col. Brent has left us and been assigned to duty in Richmond Va . . . I am at present *the* man of the office . . . and I am wanted to attend to duties of a higher order, which require more head work, knowledge and good sense, so I turn over my old duties to some one of my own choice, and in future shall be the gentleman clerk of the establishment, with no more to do than I choose; and shall wear good clothes and have considerable leisure, shall cultivate my already good standing and acquaintance with the first officers of the army, and thereby keep the best company and ensure my chance for something better in the future . . .

Yrs always
Willie

[Rebecca] *May 22, 1863. A heavy rain last night is followed by a cloudy morng. Rosa's cough very troublesome—This is my birthday—a half century old! I have past more than two thirds the usual period of human life . . .*

[WINSTON STEPHENS TO OCTAVIA STEPHENS]

Camp Finegan May 22, 1863

My Dear Wife

. . . I was very agreeably surprised yesterday to have a call by Davis. He has received the appointment of Clerk in the Q. Masters department at Lake City under Capt Routh a Gentleman from Va.[34] The position I think will be an agreeable one if the man is as pleasant and gentlemanly as I have heard and I hope Davis may like it. Davis was very much dissatisfied in Capt Clarks Co and his position had become any thing but pleasant, as the Capt would not speak to him and had said some very hard things about him. I think from what Davis told me Capt Clark suspected him of getting the good will of the men for his promotion to the detriment of the service, which every one that knows Davis will know to be a false supposition. Davis says the Capt is ignorant, jealous and selfish, failings not very enviable . . .

I am not feeling as I wish to as I have head ache, back ache, and I am very nervous, making me feel badly generally. I do wish so much you were here that I might have your company. It does appear to me that I cant be happy away from you, I feel that I want you by me more than I ever did in my life before. I fear from all that I can learn and see that there is to be a struggle in this State during the summer months and fall months unless some thing should turn up to give us peace before that time. I have some little hope that the banishment of Vallandingham will cause a revolution in the North.[35] He has ben banished for two years to the Tortugas Island, but since the sentence I think they have changed it by banishing him South until after the War and now his friends are having large

---

34. Captain (soon to be Major) H. S. Routh was acting chief, Quartermasters Office, Lake City, Florida.

35. Clement Laird Vallandingham was the outstanding Peace Democrat of the times; he blamed the war on Lincoln and the Republican Party and urged that peace be proclaimed because the war could not be won. In May 1863 Lincoln banished him to the Confederacy, and he became much less influential as the war news began to favor the Union.

meetings declaring the course pursuid by the Military illegal and Despotic and they have also taken out a writ of "habeas corpus" which will take it out of the hands of the Military and place him before civil court. One of the parties have got to yield or they will have war among themselves. The news from Jackson Mississippi yesterday was cheering. We had Grant between Genl Pemberton and Genl Johnston and the fighting was severe but not decided. Grant was trying to retreat to the River near Vicksburg, his loss in days fight was 6,000 our los heavy, we were being heavyly reinforced, Johnston commenced the fight with only 9,000 men and Grant had 40,000 to 50,000 men.[36] We are defeating them at every point and it does appear from the threatening attitude of England that matters will become bright for us in a few months. The federals destroyed a great deal of property in Jackson and captured some 2,000 negroes, but I suppose with our force on both sides of them they will lose the negroes and perhaps themselves, they will certainly have to abandon the property they have stolen to be able to get out of the trap they have got into . . .

Give love to Clarks folks and Mother and boys and accept all I have for yourself and Rosa. I remain your affectionate husband

Winston Stephens

[OCTAVIA STEPHENS TO WINSTON STEPHENS]

Rose Cottage May 26, 1863

My dear husband

. . . I have received two nice long letters from you since I wrote . . . I will answer your first letter first. I am very sorry you were feeling as badly as you spoke of in both letters, and wish that I could go immediately to you, but I can not, I hope you are better now but my dear dont say you "dont know what might happen," please do not think of it nor allow anything of the kind to happen, there *must* be plenty of ways to cure, how is it that it has not been the case before, you had not been from [home] long, did you not have *attention* enough when at home! You ask me in your last at what time I had rather go down to Jacksonville, I had rather you would come first and then we will see about the other, although I say I am going, by that time Rosa will probably be a little better . . . some say it will not spread after the first stage, or few weeks, the last of June Rosa will have had it a month and a half, poor child, she is having a hard time of it, she coughs badly, whoops a great deal and You can hear her a long ways, how she dreads it

---

36. Grant's final Vicksburg campaign, a military masterpiece, lasted from 1 April to 4 July 1863. He was soon to strike Jackson, Mississippi, defeat Joseph Johnston there, turn back west and defeat Lieutenant General John C. Pemberton at Champion's Hill on 16 May, and drive him into the earthworks around Vicksburg within the next day or so. Grant laid siege to the city from 22 May until Pemberton surrendered on 4 July 1863.

when she feels that she is going to cough, after a spell of coughing she is completely prostrated for a short time, I have to keep a lamp burning all night . . .

Rosa came in just now . . . poor child she has just been awakened by a fit of coughing, but gone to sleep again, when she thinks she is going to lose her breath she dances up and down, the worst will be over now I guess in three weeks, two weeks more before the height. Polly is getting better fast, Jess and Jane progressing slowly. Sarah is sick again, and having a great deal of *toothache* this time . . .

We are having a plenty of rain, and Burrel is pushing along, and says the crop is looking finely, he told me Sunday that the cotton was doing as well as it could do, and the "corn was so green and dark in some places that it fair looked" I have forgotten the rest of the expression, and the cane looks finely too, he thinks you would be pleased with it now . . .

Clara gave birth to *one* puppy, yesterday, your little white sow has 7 pigs six all white and one black, one of the others died, we think the sows mashed it one night, there is one that has only three, they are fine ones certain. We have robbed the bees the Gum was full and it was very nice, the thickest I ever saw. I tried all sorts of ways to manage to send you some but could not without too much trouble to whoever carried it . . . I have just been to dinner, we had huckleberry bread and Rosa said PaPa has'nt had any of this, she is very fond of them raw but not much cooked, she is full of mischief she filled my journal for me the other day, and yesterday she was washing her apron she is now trying to sew my work . . . Mother sends a great deal of love. Rosa sends a kiss she kisses me every night for you. Your aff Good for nothing

Wife

[WILLIE BRYANT TO REBECCA BRYANT]

Tullahoma, Tenn. May 30, 1863

My dear Mother—

. . . my labors are lightened at last, you may hear from me oftener than heretofore. Yes, I am about to realise my expected deliverance from the *drudgery* of my duties, and enjoy a little more time as my own. The Clerk who was to assume the principle part of my old duties has arrived, and I have him pretty well installed; he writes an excellent hand, and will do first rate, but spells badly, and as I am to supervise his work and control the work of his desk, if he isn't pleasant and don't suit me *personally*, I can "oust" him . . .

I am the right hand man now of the concern, and general reference; I am at last reaping some reward after my long toil, and able to turn my knowledge and experience so gained to a good account . . . Until since my return I have never intended that my situation here should be permanent, but . . . thought I should return to the Regt., and intended at least to go into every fight with it, if I could get off; knowing your aversion to such a course, I avoided saying any thing about it while in Fla., but now I can allay any uneasy feelings you may have on the subject, for the Regt. left for Mississippi last Sunday . . .

Much "ever so great deal" of love to you all, and a kiss in return to that little witch Rosa—

Yrs. ever affectionately
Willie

[OCTAVIA STEPHENS TO WINSTON STEPHENS]

Rose Cottage May 31, 1863

My dear husband

. . . I want to begin spinning again tomorrow, Sarah's wheel has been lying idle a week or more, and I have been spooling and twisting on mine for two weeks so that I have not spun any, . . . and will send for the loom tomorrow, and at the same time the thread to be warped, when that returns then comes the trial of my ability, and I hope I will be able to succeed. I can beat Sarah at spinning, not in quantity but in quality . . .

Our poor child is now sitting in my lap dreading and trying to keep back a coughing spell, but it will come in a few minutes, I asked her some thing just now and she could have answered it in one or two words, but after waiting some time said, "I cant talk when I coughing." It is over with and I have put her down, whenever she wants to cough she says she wants to go to sleep and when she coughs if I am not by her she runs for me, it serves her badly, sometimes when coughing she dont seem to know what she is doing, she dances and slips and all sorts of things, the other night she slapped me in the face, she keeps her eyes shut all the time and some time after, and the tears drop on the ground, her eyes look badly, at times much swollen. I feel like a "wet rag" in the day from loss of sleep, and sometimes in the night I can hardly rouse myself to take her up, sometimes I have to lie down and hold her up, I can neither sit up nor open my eyes, I did not know I could be so much over come by it. I heard Rosa say out in the piazza just now, "I pect Papa come drecky" Mother said I wish he would . . .

I am very anxious to hear from you and hear what is going on down there, I fear Gen. Finegan's arrangements will prevent your coming at the time appointed. I wish he had let the Gun boats alone. I hope we may see some *splendid* news soon, something that will end the war. I think as I said sometime ago that the whole world are going to fight and put an end to this miserable world, at times I am almost sick of it. Georgie cut his bee tree yesterday and got hardly enough for a taste around, our bees have become insulted and left . . .

I hope you have been able to cool off and without Morphine, I am anxious to hear from you, I wish you needed it when away no more than I do. Do try and come home very soon, I will get ready to go back with you.

You have lost another little pig and Henry one, they *"came up missing,"* I am sorry to inform you that we have only corn enough to last us three or four weeks, Clark is going to get him some more, and I am going to ask him to get me some. I have been very economical with portions of it, though lately have used some for huckleberry puddings but not extensively then, Burrel says he has been careful with it, never the less it is gone. Well my dear husband I must close, I hope to get a letter from you by Clark when he goes for the mail, With much love I remain

as ever your loving
Wife

[REBECCA BRYANT TO WILLIE BRYANT]

Rose Cottage June 1, 1863

My dear, dear Willie,

... Henry had his first *regular deer hunt,* about 10 days ago ... Mr Stephens killed a fine buck and a turkey—and Henry caught a very large bass as they returned—We had a good share of the venison, which was a great treat. Mr Stephens and Co sold 31 galls of Oil ... a fortnight since, of which Henry's share of profits amounted to $31 and some cts. Mr S— will finish his ploughing tomorrow. He and Henry will go for the mail on Thursday, hunting Alligators on their way down and back—and Mr S— intends to get the mail regularly now ...

Rosa is having the whooping-cough pretty badly—the poor child's eyes are so swollen as if she had been on a spree and the cough has not yet reached its height ...

Tivie says your wish in regard to her being clothed throughout in homespun is likely to be realised very soon—The first cool autumn days will find her thus bedecked, and by that time, I hope to be able to *weave* something that will answer for a negro, if not for myself. Henry has gone out in the country to-day to bring in a loom, and if it answers the purpose and I am not more stupid about learning than most people are, shall be able to assist Tivie. Perhaps I may weave you a pair of pants ... ! I hope dear Willie that the changes in your Office will not make the situation less agreeable to you and induce you to return to field duties—May *something* happen to terminate this War before that event takes place ... !

Tivie sends much love ... I am always your most affectionate

Mother

[WINSTON STEPHENS TO OCTAVIA STEPHENS]

Camp Finegan June 1, 1863

My Dear Wifey

Your long and affectionate letter was received by me yesterday . . . It was such a long, nice letter and one of continued affection thoughout, no complaining, no murmuring or discontent or apparent unhappiness, that letter made me feel better and more happy. I do wish so much it was in my power to relieve my Dear Rosa of that awful cough, but with care I hope she will soon be through the worst . . . I went up to Lake City as I wrote you I should and the Dr Filled two teeth and sayed in five or six months he would fill two more, Dr Bostwick did the work.[37] I am very much pleased with him as a Dentist and when you pay that visit to Lou you must make up your mind to stop over one day in Lake City to have your teeth fixed for I am sure to have it done unless you are decidedly opposed to it, which I hope will not be the case. On the 30th May we had a grand turn out of all the Military of the Post and Genl Finegan came down and reviewed us, he brought down about 40 Ladies and some Gentlemen to witness the show and Davis was one of the favoured ones and one of the Ladies escort. We had quite a shower just as the Ladies made their appearance on the field, they were in waggons and I never saw so many hoop skirts in two waggons in all my life, they had a canvas with them and I furnished an oil cloth to some of them so that they managed not to get very wet. We, I mean the Military then formed line of Battle and our brass band struck up a lively tune and the Genl then passed down our line and after he had returned the Command was given by Plattoon right wheel and the whole line moved pass the Genl in review, the Cavalry first, the Artilery next and the Infantry in the rear, the Drums beating and band playing. I was in the lead and I must admit I felt all eyes were on me at that time, but I sustained myself manfully and passed my Command by in fine stile, first in a walk and then in a trot. The Ladies sayed they would be willing any day to take the rain to see the turn out, which was complimentary. Everything passed off well and the Genl and ladies took the Cars down to Jacksonville and spent some hours down there, I was invited but did not go . . .

You ought to know I did not mean really to ask any one for *Morphine* but was only jesting, though I really wanted some *very* much, but I dont intend taking any from any one but you, I was well attended to when at home! Since I was sick I dont feel so bad off as that destroyed that feeling, I am glad to see you consent to come, for it is an evidence of your affection for me and a desire to gratify my wishes. I will not be able to come this month as the Genl is looking for Genl Beaureguard and will not furlough any more Officers until he comes . . . As soon

---

37. W. M. Bostwick, formerly of Jacksonville.

as Burrel can spare big Jane from the field I want you put her to spinning and weaving and I dont want you to make yourself sick. Keep her and Sarah at it all the time and they can keep plenty of clothing and I think Burrel can soon manage without Jane . . . I want you to tell Burrel to plant peas in the corn, commence on or about the 8th . . . You may tell Rosa Pa Pa has had any quantity of berries but not bread made of them, but we have had some genuine pies and good ones at that . . . Give love to Mother, boys and Clarks family and accept all you wish for yourself and Rosa from your Aff husband

Winston Stephens

[OCTAVIA STEPHENS TO WINSTON STEPHENS]

Rose Cottage June 7, 1863

My dear husband

. . . Rosa has just said of her own free will that she was going to send you a kiss. She had quite a high fever yesterday I gave her a dose of oil this morning and hope that will put an end to it, I had stopped giving her any thing for her cough thinking it did no good and thought her cough was getting better, that may be the cause of the fever for yesterday morning I thought she seemed more stuffed up with plegm and that I would give her something, and in the afternoon she had fever, she does not cough so often as she did a week ago and excepting during her fever has been very much brighter. I think the worst part is now passing, she still coughs and whoops badly but not quite so often, I hope she will now get well fast, she has had a time of it. I think she will not have it again, certain.

I am glad you were so well satisfied with your trip to Lake City, you did not tell me who you saw or much about it. I am glad Dr Bostwick's work suited you, he has had his hands in my mouth, and hope it will be a long time (if ever) before he or any other Dentist will have any thing to do with my teeth. I would like very much to please you and have my teeth fixed but you dont know what a *horror* I have of any thing of the kind, the front tooth of mine that is now so broken and decayed was the only one I had ever had filled and that one by Dr Bostwick . . .

I have got my Loom started and have woven a *whole yard* and little more, the thread is very rotten and troubles me a great deal . . . The whole cost me $12.75 . . . I wish I had begun a long time ago. I would like weaving very much if the thread did not break so much.

Burrel is going . . . after corn tomorrow having it already engaged and will begin planting peas as soon as he returns, we have hardly corn enough to last this week, the corn in the field is still looking well . . .

I remain as ever your loving
Wifey

[WINSTON STEPHENS TO OCTAVIA STEPHENS]

Camp Finegan June 7, 1863

My Dear Wife

... We had one of the grandest times yesterday I have seen since the War commenced. Genl Beaureguard came down to Review the troops at this place and with him came his own Staff Genl Finegan and his Staff and about five waggon loads of ladies with their *Staff*. I think without any exageration there must have been 75 to 100 Ladies. We gave a salute to the Genl of 9 guns fired from Dunhams Artilery, and My Co., Capt Chambers, and Capt Row formed an escort for them. The day was suffocating and we had to be in the broiling sun and Dust that almost suffocated for about two hours "that part of it was dreadful." The Genl complimented the Command and said if the War continued he would be glad to lead us into battle as he knew we would win Laurels, after they all got back to the cars they went on down to Jacksonville. I did not go again as I was so tired and dusty I felt I could not injoy myself. Davis was along and was devoted to some pritty miss, and appeared to injoy himself very much, but said they were unlucky in getting a waggon that broke down. Genl B— is a man about 45 to 48 years of age, hair quite Grey, keen eyes a little crossed just enough to notice, but not enough to make it unpleasant, rather good looking, small but erect and soldierly in his appearance but looks very Fancyfied, taking him altogether he does not look like the *lion* that he is ...

I know you will succeed in your weaving as you *love it*. I hope you will find corn handy but I think it is a scarce article. Tell me when you write how many Watermelons you are going to have and how this rain makes the crop look, pinders and all and do hurry up the pea planting while the time is right as I want them planted in the dark night of this month ...[38]

Good bye My Dear Wife and be a good Girl Dont work too much as I want you well and strong when I come home Howdie to Darkies,

Yours Aff husband
Winston

[DAVIS BRYANT TO WILLIE BRYANT]

Lake City June 8, 1863

My dear Bro.

... I have expected daily to write you since I came up and particularly since receiving your last but have been either very busy or very much engaged with

---

38. Pinders are peanuts. Winston, like most farmers of his time, planted different crops by different phases of the moon.

pleasure. For I happened to strike the commencement of a round of Gaiety, and have been lured back into my old habits . . . I am *very* pleasantly situated. Find Capt. Routh a mighty clever *considerate gentleman,* would rather be with him than any one I have ever had business dealings with. He is a young married man—about 28 or 30 yrs of age—a native of Louisiana and originally from New Orleans, in fact was there up to the breaking out of the war . . . I am constantly busy during the day but have thus far had nothing to do in the office at night, though I may occasionally have to write evenings hereafter . . . We have had gay doings since I came up. I have made several calls—through necessity of course—have been invited out several times and *gone,* have been in one *big dancing affair* and have been on two picnics to Jacksonville. The first picnic was got up to go down to Camp Finegan to witness a review of the troops by Genl. Finegan—The Genl. furnishing the cars and of course extending the invitations. After the review, which took place more than a mile from the R. Road, and to where we went in waggons we went down to town, took dinner in the market and walked all over town. Had a *splendid* time notwithstanding it rained all day nearly and wet us all. The other was last Saturday. In this instance we were invited to go by Genl. Finegan down to Camp Finegan and witness a review by *Genl. Beauregard,* and afterwards go to town as before. We had a delightful and—to me—very satisfactory time there also. There were two Car loads of people and mighty big loads at that, many having to stand up all the time. Both passed off very quietly however I would not have missed the last affair for *considerable*—Genl Beauregard is a very pleasant unassuming man. Though I did not have the honor of an introduction to him still I was near him a good deal, and a part of the time was conversing with a young lady at one end of a seat which he was engaged "similarly" at the other. So I became about as well acquainted with him as if I had been introduced. I did not ask an introduction for the reason that a great many worthless *shoats* did annoy him . . . The Genl. expressed himself much pleased with the troops and affairs here generally, and is determined to give us better means to act with here. He was *charmed* with the St Johns . . . Eight Ladies are here from Madison now, . . . and a wild time I *could* have if I wished to give up to such, but I must "desist," I wish you could have been with me the other day—though I don't know that you could enjoy yourself with these *girls* (as most of them are) as I do, as I have made up my mind to take the "half loaf" rather than "no bread," and usually do pretty well . . .

I am very often asked about you. Take Care of *yourself*

Yrs ever affctly

Davis

[OCTAVIA STEPHENS TO WINSTON STEPHENS]

Rose Cottage June 10, 1863

My own dear husband

... So you have seen the great yet little Beaureguard, I think it was a hot sight, did you speak with him? or were you not that much *honored,* but had to be satisfied with *waiting on him.* I should like very much to have been there, to have seen my husband better in my estimation than all the Generals, though I would have liked to see *the* Gen too. I hope he may *not* spur Gen Finegan up but let matters be quiet, and I hope he or any other Gen may never have the pleasure of leading you to battle, I hope those laurels may stay unwon, that the war may stop before there is a chance or need for that, though there is but little to hope on ...

I dont want you to make fun of my efforts, but if you are really afraid that I will do too much, I can tell you to be perfectly easy about that, I wish I could feel that I was doing enough to be in that danger, although I am always striving I never seem to accomplish anything, for Rosa and *other little interruptions* (here *she* is now) prevent my doing much ... when I think how little I do to help anybody I feel ashamed of myself, it seems as though I am of but little use to anybody. Rosa is sitting in my lap with the cough rattling in her throat and she trying to keep it back and dreading it, she sends a kiss to you, she is I think getting better slowly, she coughs about as hard as ever but not so often ...

Burrel says our corn is doing well, that the melons do not look so well since the continued rains the melons seem to have dropped, that the pinders look well, only a little gray now but he will soon have them clean, the cane looks only tolerable now, he began planting peas to day, would have begun Monday but went for corn, he needs no hurrying up that I can see about anything, for he always seems to be pushing ahead as fast as possible and always calculating something else ahead, he is very anxious to have the crop clean when you come but says he can not get ahead of the grass, for the rains keep it growing. I know how it is by my garden ...

Good bye my dear husband be a good *boy,* I *try* to be a good girl in all respects. With lots of love I remain yr loving

Wife

[WINSTON STEPHENS TO OCTAVIA STEPHENS]

Camp Finegan June 15, 1863

My Dear Wifey

... I am feeling well, though I am constantly sick at my stomach and last night lost my supper, I feel I suppose like a woman in family way. I had a dream a few nights ago of getting a *representative* and you were the mother, that is the first time I have ever had such a dream with or about you and I hope you will *appreciate* it. I wish I could hear from you oftener . . .

My Company now for duty is smaller than it has been in a long time, I have some 25 men home, What do you think of that? We are getting plenty of fodder now and pet looks well and is getting fatter every day. My horse does not look quite so well as before he was stolen. one of the Infantry stole him and rode home three days before he was caught, poor fellow I think he will suffer for his trip as he is in Lake City being Court Martialed. horses are now worth from 800 to 1500 hundred dollars. My horse and pet are worth 2,000 dollars. Tell Burrel I want him to try and get through with his ploughing by the time I come if he can so as to gin the cotton while I am at home as I want to dispose of it. If the Yanks should go up the river I would loose it and I dont feel like losing it now as it is worth so much and it has ben on hand so long . . .

List of things sent you in bag made one bottle castor oil roled in two pair drawers, two pounds black pepper in over shirt, one Bottle paregoric in 2 pair gloves and pr pants, 2 handkerchiefs, pacage of soap roled in Jacket, one Jacket with large white buttons, one pair pants. Some of the things are old clothes Davis gave me for the negroes, but if you think Henry would like them to hunt in give them to him. I shall be impatient for this month to come to a close as I do want so much to clasp you in my arms and press those sweet lips, and hear the prattle of My Dear Rosa and press her to my heart. I dont think most of men love their families as I do mine. This service has placed many tryals and temptations in my way but I have passed through all unscathed and I feel that is more than most married men can say to their Wives and tell them the truth. I hope my wife will forget the past when I have shown myself so true and devoted to her since our union. I was a wild recless fellow when single but after I engaged your affictions and before I was married I changed my habbits and since my marriage I have never done you an injustice in that respect. I admit I am sometimes more wicked than I wish to be, but I do try to keep my temper and do right and to all mankind as I would have them do to me . . .

Give love to all Clarks folks and also to Mother and the boys and accept all you wish for yourself and Rosa from your Aff husband

Winston Stephens

[WILLIE BRYANT TO DAVIS BRYANT]

Shelbyville June 16, 1863

Dear Davis,

. . . Your letter beside being very interesting in details gave me great satisfaction in the knowledge of your being so very pleasantly situated; By Jove, how much good it did me! and coming at this particular time, when I am in low spirits and in rather an undecided state, it does me more good to know that you are so well situated . . .

My duties have been much lighter and more agreable, and I have enjoyed my liberty much, but the bad state of affairs between me and some of the other clerks has increased; vacancies had to be filled in the office, I had no friends to reccommend, and my enemies succeeded in getting some of their low bred set detailed, the accession to their numbers emboldened them and we have had a regular rupture, their "force" is superior and they have at last succeeded in annoying me, as my present pay does not admit of my cutting loose entirely from them and taking my meals elsewhere; there are now nine of us clerks 3 of them are avowed enemies to me, 3, "aliens," 2 "friendly," and but 1 an "ally" upon whom I can depend. General Bragg has a chief of Staff now, who stands between him and the acting adjutant general here; the Chief of Staff, Brig. Genl. Mackall,[39] is a strict, arbitrary old cuss, and has his head full of theories on the business of the A.A.G. office, he has just been making some alterations in our duties which are unpleasant to all, and a parcel of d——d absurdities, and plays the devil with the freedom and liberties of my situation I have gained, in many respects, for I have [been] something more than a clerk . . .

Genl. Mackall is a stern, manouvering, tyrannical old cuss, and has caused much dissatisfaction among Genl. Bragg's staff, and Col. Brent and some others have left in consequence, and if he continues in his course almost all the others will do the same . . .

"So no more at this present"—Kind remembrances to all friends, and keep me cherished fondly in their memories—Adios—

Yrs always affectionately
Willie—

[OCTAVIA STEPHENS TO WINSTON STEPHENS]

Rose Cottage June 18, 1863

My dear husband

. . . We are all doing nicely. Rosa still continues to improve in regard to her cough she coughs more seldom and I think does not whoop quite so much, she does not cough more than twice through the night now, I think if she does not take cold now she will get well fast, Polly took cold last week and now coughs nearly as bad as ever. Rosa talks of you a great deal. The other day I said something about your having clabber at camp and to day we had some and she said, PaPa gets clabber at Camp but I get some here, yesterday the drawer was open

---

39. Brigadier General William W. Mackall was a West Point classmate and close friend of Braxton Bragg.

and she turned to me and said "are these Winston pants?" and to day she wanted your sow, she is full of mischief nearly always up to something, she is now asleep, she calls Tina's home and said to day at dinner that she liked to go to Tina's when no one was talking about it. I think she will be glad to see you and I hope she will not be so backward as she has, I often talk to her of frolicking with you to try and get her in the notion and prepare her to be easy and frolicksome with you when you come, I have played with her more lately for I sometimes have thought perhaps she would be better if I would frolic with her, but never can get started. I tell her she will soon be equal to you in eating clabber, she made her supper last night and dinner to day off of clabber, passed her saucer three times, she lives on that and bread and milk, and that is what keeps her from being pulled down more by the cough. Tina sends me a quart of sweet milk and over two of sour every morning or I send for it, the cows are a great help to Tina . . .

Burrel has gone this afternoon to Brights to get a beef, oh how I dread it and have been for several weeks, I intend trying to pickle some of it, especially as we are having such bad weather for drying it. I guess you will have to pay thirty or thirty five dollars for it. I hope we may have good luck and not loose the least bit of it . . .

I suppose you want to know how I get on with my weaving, and if I dont tell you you will think me smarter than I am. I get on slowly, but hope to get the piece out before two months, instead of making me sick it has done me good so far, for it gives me exercise, and better appetite, and trying to hurry on occupies my *mind so much that I have* not time to be so gloomy. I have not much time now for gloomy thoughts, for my hands and mind are full of what I have to do before you come, to get ready to return with you, as I suppose you have not changed your mind on that subject . . .

Well I have nothing more worth saying so will close with lots of love from your little daughter and

Wife

[OCTAVIA STEPHENS TO WINSTON STEPHENS]

June 19, 1863

My own dear husband

You dont know how happy and thankful I feel at this moment as I received your letter and bundles . . . a short time ago, everything came right that you mentioned in the list . . . Your letter is such a dear one it makes my heart feel so much lighter, your expressions seemed to come from your heart, you have never before spoken quite so plainly of your fidelity to me, that makes me happier than all else, you dont know how I feel sometimes when I am a little blue and think perhaps you might be tempted and be untrue to me, for I feel that there are so few who are true to their wives in that one respect, I think of that every day in my prayers and pray that if you should be tempted you may have the strength to forbear, that prayer has been granted so far and may it always be, I have always thought I had one of the best husbands in the world and I wish I was more worthy of that husband, if my worth consisted in my fidelity to you I would certainly always be worthy, but there are many things in which I am but hardly perceptable yet, I have got over most of the wicked feelings I had after our little babe was taken away and feel better and hope to continue in the same, I do *appreciate your* dream, but still am selfish and wish they might all be of me, you did not know you had such a jealous wife as not to wish you to dream of such with another did you? I can not forget your actions before we were married, but I do not feel about it as I used to, especially since you have been tried so well and proved faithful. I am always glad to have you injoy yourself and go any where if you will be a *good boy* . . . Good bye my darling I long for you to come home.

Your loving
Wife

[WINSTON STEPHENS TO OCTAVIA STEPHENS]

Camp Finegan June 23, 1863

My Dear Wifey

. . . I am sorry to see you have such bad time in getting your beef and curing it, it does appear that you always have such weather for such work. I am truly glad to hear such fine news from the crop and hope the Yanks will allow us to use what we make. Some think they will come out and destroy all that is in the country . . . We had a Telegram Sunday and one today they say Genl Lee is 6 miles beyond Chambersburg in Pennsylvania and had captured lots of property . . . Hooker has gone after Lee.[40] We are expecting glorious news from that direction and the Yankees are wonderfully frightened, in New York they are ringing the bells and getting up the regiments to send out. I think that is the way to stop the war make them feel what we have felt . . .

I am sorry to have to give you this in exchange for your nice and long letter but so it is this time. I find that I may expect if the War lasts to have to remain from home a long time as the Genl does not love me. Give love to all the folks and dont be uneasy about the Gun boat Capts Chambers and Dickison are in the way and they will swallow the boat rather than have her go up. Kiss Rosa and tell her papa likes to hear of her thinking of him so much. Good by my love and God Bless thee — Yours always

Winston

40. Hooker was replaced by Major General George Gordon Meade, who fought at Gettysburg on 1–3 July.

[WILLIE BRYANT TO DAVIS BRYANT]

Tullahoma June 27, 1863

Dear Davis,

I wrote you on the 17th. from Shelbyville, and now, 10 days later, I am writing again from Tullahoma; —d—n Tullahoma! —the fact is just as it appears, I have very suddenly changed my base. Affairs up here have assumed a very stirring and interesting aspect, and ere this reaches you you will have heard of the devil to pay. Day before yesterday the Yanks suddenly threw forward a sufficient force, and after a short fight gained possession of two mountain gaps; they pressed on, and yesterday there was a pretty sharp fight; to-day, particularly this p.m., there has been considerable skirmishing at different points; the Enemy is making a general advance, and the battle is most probably imminent; it is expected that a big fight will come off tomorrow.

The Enemy's getting possession of those gaps so easily is quite discretable to our troops, especially the Cavalry outposts, and the fight yesterday resulted to their gain. Late yesterday p.m., Genl. Bragg finding the Enemy had gained the flank of his fortifications around Shelbyville, determined to move his Hd. Qrs. etc back to his stronghold at Tullahoma, accordingly this a.m. at 6 o'clk, we all left, Genl. B— and staff coming down on horseback, (23 miles) and we clerks on the R. Road . . .

I was sorry to give up our comfortable quarters and pleasant situation at Shelbyville, particularly just as Sunday was coming, and I hope we may soon be back again. Shelbyville is a strong union town, and the Unionists there were tickled to death at our leaving this morning; some of them would say "skedaddling, eh!" "Shelbyville will again be in possession of the Federal soldiers by to-night," etc . . .

The Yankees have about 50,000, our force is not so large, but General Bragg would rather fight them than not, and we feel no apprehensions for the result; I hope they will continue to follow us, if they do they will catch thunder "sure as you're a foot thick."[41] Good bye for now, more soon. I wrote mother yesterday p.m. that we would move, and of the signs. Direct here unless you know better.

Yrs always affectionately

Willie

41. Rosecrans's Tullahoma campaign was an unqualified success; at a cost of some 560 killed, wounded, and missing, he forced Bragg to evacuate several formidable positions, forfeit large quantities of supplies, and retreat some eighty-five miles beyond the Tennessee River. This attack also prevented Bragg from sending much-needed reinforcements to relieve the troops at the siege of Vicksburg.

[OCTAVIA STEPHENS TO WINSTON STEPHENS]

Rose Cottage June 28, 1863

My dear husband

Your letter and saddlebag were received in good order yesterday . . . I expected to hear decidedly about the time of your coming, I shall begin looking for you *in earnest* on Thursday the 2nd. you dont know how anxious I am for you to come. Burrel says it seems as though you had been gone five months. I am much obliged to you for the salts. I would like very much to know if you wish me to make that suit for you before you come, but think you certainly do not intend wearing it this summer, it is very handsome cloth, and will make my Old man look finely. I am almost afraid Barny will not let you come as there is a probability of the Yankees coming, but I hope he will and will give you as long a one as you asked for . . .

Well my dear I will not write any more this time as you may not get this. I hope to see you before this week is out, and I hope you may not have much rain, just as I wrote that a tremendous clap of thunder came, and frightened Rosa pretty badly, the other day she turned perfectly white, and came pretty near it this time. come soon as old Barny will let you to your

loving "Old Lady"

[Rebecca] July 1, 1863. . . . Soon after dinner Winston arrives in a hard rain. He brings me a letter from Davis who writes cheerfully and sends many articles of use to me and boys. He writes that his Aunt Julia is to be in Lake City this week—would that I could meet her!

[Rebecca] July 2, 1863. . . . Henry comes before sunset with two letters for me, one from my dear husband, forwarded by Davis, and one from Willie written at Shelbyville, where the Hd. Qrs. are now. My husband's letter rejoices my heart.

[REBECCA BRYANT TO WILLIE BRYANT]

[Rose Cottage] July 8, 1863

My dear Willie,

. . . I heartily approve of the course you propose to adopt, by way of relief—I think with you, that a few lady acquaintances wd. be a "powerful" remedy. "It is not good for Man to be alone," nor for *men* to be always together in herds, without a mollifying influence—(I did'nt intend a pun in the sweet name of Mary.)

I suppose that Davis is in this regard, far more pleasantly situated than you are—and from his last letter, he has enjoyed quite a season of gaiety . . .

Tivie had made her calculations to go down with Winston when his furlough expires, which will be on the 20th, and we were talking of some plan by which George and I could get to the R.Rd. en route for Thomasville about a fortnight after they left, when the mules would not be so constantly required at home . . . and it is *possible,* tho' by no means certain, that we may all manage to go together. I find that Winston intends that Tivie shall be absent, visiting himself and Loulie as much as 6 weeks—So much has been said about George visiting Loulie and perhaps Thomasville, that I do not like to disappoint him entirely, neither do I like to be alone for *so long a time*—George has had two trips to Salt Springs and one to O. Springs lately, camping out each time—and he is in all respects so much better than last Autumn that I am not so desirous of his having a change, *immediately*—Therefore, one of my plans is to keep him here until Henry's engagement with Mr Stephens is fulfilled and then let them both go together to Thomasville, stopping a day or two with Loulie. But Tivie is very anxious that I should go visit Thomasville too, while she is absent—Winston says that if Henry will come over once in a while and take a look at things about the place, he is not afraid to leave it without any white persons and if I find there is any reasonable expectation of my being able to get back, when Tivie returns, I may conclude to go. If Florida is invaded this Autumn, Winston would send Tivie into Georgia, and if I happen to be there already, it would be so much the better. The long and short of it is, that we can't decide yet what is best, but will have to come to some conclusion next week . . .

God bless you my dear Willie!

Mother—

[GEORGE BRYANT TO DAVIS BRYANT]

Rose Cottage July 8, 1863

My dear brother Davis

It has been a long time since I wrote you last so I thought I would write you today to let you know that I had not forgotten you, I know that you have not forgotten me because you sent Henry and me the line and hooks for which we are very much obliged to you; The hooks are just the size we wanted . . .

Last Friday I went to Orange Springs with Burrel and Tom to get the buggy wheels that were sent there to be fixed, and some other things . . . It began raining before we reached the mill so we were wet; and when we reached the mill it rained harder. When it stopped raining the sun was down and it was late in the night when we got to the boat. We worked a long time before we could make a fire; we staid by it until the moon was two or three hours high then we got in the boat and Burrel paddled down while Tom and I slept until day light then we took the oars . . . we drifted a long while we ate our breakfast; as we were drifting a tin cup fell in the water and Tom in catching it tipped the boat, and Henry's gun fell over and it is there yet; so we lost a great deal more than we gained by our trip . . .

This from your affectionate brother

George

[WILLIE BRYANT TO DAVIS BRYANT]

Chattanooga Tenn. July 8, 1863

Dear Davis—

Before this you know of the change in our locality, and therefore will not be surprised at my writing from this place. Yes, "Rosy" was too much for us, and our unfortunate army is again in disgrace, "Rosecrans stock up" and Bragg stock at a "discount," but, it must be admitted General Bragg is a "master hand" on a retreat, which is considered a valuable qualification in a general; "Bully for Bragg!" but it's a devilish pity his army can't appreciate it, the boys say "that thing has played out." I think I wrote you last after our return from Shelbyville to Tullahoma, and yet I am not sure; however, I will Commence back from there; the Sunday, Monday and Tuesday we were there there was but little skirmishing going on, principally occasioned by the Enemy attempting to destroy the R. Road and Bridges in our rear, the weather and roads were in too bad state for large movements; Tullahoma wore a busy appearance, and the troops and everybody were in a high state of excitement in eager anticipation of the promised battle, but Rosecrans refused to accept the several offers of battle made by Genl. Bragg, and continued the safer course by moving to destroy our line of communication; Genl. Bragg having a long line to protect, and an inferior force, could not do so without too much weakening his main body, and was therefore continually obliged to fall back to protect his line; Tuesday evening a sudden and general movement began to take place, the greatest activity prevailed, but except to those in command and the staff officers, the whole thing was enveloped in a mystery, most persons supposed that Genl. Bragg intended to swap bases with Rosecrans and would push on to Nashville, but in that they were wrong; at about 9 o'clk I found out a retrograde movement was on foot, and at ½ p. 10. I got on a special train with Genl. B. and staff in a couple of hours we were at Decherd; all day Wednesday we lay at Decherd, Genl. B. failing to draw Rosecrans into a battle; Thursday forenoon the retreat commenced; thinking we would only go 5 miles to the foot of the Cumberland mountains, I concluded to walk for the exercise instead of taking the cars, tho' I had a transportation ticket to Chattanooga; the wagon train stopped but a short time there . . . when it commenced the ascent of the mountain, I determined to take the trip, and kept on with them, we travelled all that night and the next day, that night camped for several hours and then moved on again, reached Bridgeport early next morning (on the Tennessee river) where I found Genl. B. and staff . . . and then went on 2 miles to our wagon camp; the following forenoon (Sunday) we again took up our line of march for Chattanooga, arriving here the next noon,—Monday—after an arduous and trying trip over 3 mountains, and the worst roads you can imagine; all along with me grumbled and swore terribly at the hard trip, and starvation, and had it not been one of my own choice I too would have joined them, but as it was, such is human nature, that I enjoyed it, rather; so here is Bragg's army, back again at the same point where nearly a year ago he organised it for that ever memorable Kentucky campaign; Bully for Bragg!

Much may be said in extenuation of this retreat of Genl. Bragg, and it's necessity easily explained, but that Rosecrans should so easily render untenable a position deemed a strong one naturally, and strengthened during our occupation of it for 8 months, seems strange, and indicates a want of capacity or knowledge *somewhere;* however it may be, the people and the army are greatly dissatisfied with General Bragg, and their confidence in him still lessened, and I am compelled to say I feel with them to a great extent, and on account of his bad management, or bad luck,—which ever it may be—I never want to fight under him again.[42] The retreat, as a retreat, has been well executed and almost completely successful, but the loss of valuable territory, with its valuable crop which would have sustained our army a long time, and just as the extensive wheat crop was being harvested is considerable, nevertheless, so it is, and we can only make the best of it. The Enemy has not pursued us to the opposite bank of the river, our army is now entirely across on this side and it may be some time before the Yanks will come farther. The intention for our future movements are of course unknown, if not unformed, as yet.

Affairs in the office are now somewhat more pleasant and I am still doing first rate, tho' not satisfied, tho' I suppose for that matter I never would be; had I some rank,—which I certainly deserve—or some prospect of it, I would feel very differently, this war has now got to be an old thing, and a business, and the reflection that I stand just where I did when I entered the service is now somewhat mortifying to me; had I been willing to make a sacrifice of some honor, principle, and feeling it would now have been differently with me; I have the satisfaction of knowing I "have not," but that does not satisfy me entirely, by a good deal . . .

42. Unfortunately for Bragg, many of his senior general officers viewed him with contempt and did not cooperate for almost the entire duration of his command. Had not Bragg been a special favorite of Jefferson Davis, he would have been relieved after the Tullahoma campaign.

We are just as busy as we can be just now and I cannot add much more to my letter of last night. We have to-day recd. the particulars of the fall of Vicksburg, which is truly a heavy blow to us, how heavy it will prove no one can tell; could we but have followed ere long, as it is, there is no knowing how much longer the war may be protracted, that the Federals will receive new encouragement from this success, none can deny . . .

Well, so long! Yrs always affectly,
Willie

[REBECCA BRYANT TO WILLIE BRYANT]

Rose Cottage July 19, 1863

My dear Willie,

. . . Since Winston has been here his Company have been removed to Camp Cooper and Capt Clark's to Camp Finegan. This is far from being an agreeable change to *us*. Letters will be doubly as long in reaching us from Winston, and the time necessarily consumed in travelling back and forth, the number of creeks to swim etc will prevent the men who live in this part of the country from coming home as often as before, thus depriving us of one of our chief sources of information. Then again, it is a death blow to all Tivie's plans of a visit down the river—here she will have to stay and make the best of it. We could endure it all very patiently if we could see any encouragement to hope for peace . . .

Much love and good wishes from all to my dear Willie—
Mother

[JULIA FISHER TO REBECCA BRYANT]

Thomasville July 20, 1863

Dearest Sis:

I have suspended my labors, settled business matters, and for the first time in two years am taking rest: I feel such a sense of relief, but it is only temporary; I know as soon as I am mentally and physically able again, some new work will be appointed—and who could wish to remain inactive at such a time if their services were needed, and they could give them? I hope Davis has written you before this, and if so he has told you of my meeting him: he could not tell you however the great pleasure it gave me: *you* can imagine that, but much as I enjoyed it, I wanted to transfer my privileges to *you* . . .

Since the fall of Vicksburg, and the attack on Charleston etc, our people generally are much depressed: in yesterday's Sav paper, an article of mine came out which I wrote Friday, hastily: I enclose it: Dr. Adams came to tell me today that it took well up town: one old gentleman declares himself a "Julia Fisher" man! The fact is too many are ready to *give up: it won't do* . . .

Dear Sis though I write so poorly and so seldom, my heart of hearts cling fondly to you: you are *dearest and best* to me: Kiss Tivy and Rosa for me: love to boys: tell Henry he must come next time and bring *you*

Yours fondly: Julia:

[WINSTON STEPHENS TO OCTAVIA STEPHENS]

Camp Cooper July 23, 1863

My Dear Wifey

I arrived in camp this p.m. about 3 o'clock. I found all that are here in tolerable good health but 3 of them who are quite sick . . . I am not prepared to give an opinion of the camp as I have not seen enough to form an opinion. The camp itself appears to have good houses for men and good stables for horses and the water is about the same as Camp Finegan. The duty is very heavy, requiring some of the men to remain on duty 6 days at a time. They have an opportunity of getting more to eat than at Camp Finegan, but the men are all dissatisfied. I think I shall like the place only being so far from home—the men having so little chance to get home . . . I find that you could have come with me as there is a good place I am told in one mile of camp . . . I want you and Mother to make your arrangements to go on contemplated visit and you can let me know when you can come best and I will see if I can get a room for you. I am anxious to have Mother go as she stands in need of recreation . . . I saw from New York papers that a riot had been going on for two days, from 20 to 50 thousand engaged the Police were ordered out and the mob drove them off then the Military was called out . . . Several were killed on both sides and the Mob burned a great many houses pillaged the stores and private houses. The Gov came from Albany and addressed the Mob and told them he would Telegram to Lincoln and have the conscript act suspended (as that was the cause of the riot) but it did not satisfy them and he then issued a Proclamation declaring the City and County in a state of insurection . . .[43] I hope the feeling will continue until the whole north will rebell and stop this War. I find that the Northern papers state that Napoleon B. has signified his intention to recognise this Government and he has given the People of Mexico

---

43. The New York draft riot was in response to the Federal conscription act passed on 3 March 1863, whereby all able-bodied men from twenty to forty-five were liable for service. Riots occurred in most large cities everywhere in the Union, but New York was the worst and received the most publicity. The riot was put down quickly; some troops went directly from the fight at Gettysburg to New York. The drawing of the draftees' names was resumed in about a week.

notice to that effect, and it is thought the other nations will follow suit.⁴⁴ Yours truly and aff

Winston Stephens

[OCTAVIA STEPHENS TO WINSTON STEPHENS]

Rose Cottage July 26, 1863

My dear husband

Again I am seated to write to you, when I wrote my last letter, I thought there would be no occasion for me to write to you as soon as this, for I expected to be with you, but it has been ordered otherwise, and we are again separated, oh when will there be an end of this, I wonder if we will ever live together at home any time again. Events look more gloomy than ever I wonder what you think of the present state of affairs. I think the Confederacy nearly a goner. I had just begun to have a good deal of hope that we would gain our independence, but things are now worse than ever. I suppose we have at least got to have the war a year and a half longer . . .

We did not get a beef . . . Burrel fears we will not be able to get any after a little, he says there are none to be had. Burrel has packed another bag of cotton weighing 410 lbs, the gin troubled him a great deal besides the weather, it seems very hard work for mule and all the mules fall down a great deal. Burrel says you have him now in the worst place he has been in in his life . . . Big Jane is now spinning hard, not now, but week days, she spins six broaches a day and Sarah her four, so the thread comes in faster but I am cut nearly entirely out of my spinning as they keep the one pair cards in use. I card a little when Sarah stops to get dinner, then a little while after the horn blows before my dinner and at night, but that is very little for such slow work, Saturday afternoons I have the cards to my self, even that helps but little . . .

I asked Rosa what I must tell you for her, she said "send a kiss to him." Well I will close for this time, Mother and the boys send love, Accept a husbands full share of love from

Your Wife.

---

44. Napoleon III took advantage of the American Civil War to send troops and establish a puppet government in Mexico. But he was forced to remove his troops in 1865, and the government fell. He was sympathetic to the Confederacy, as was the British government, but the probability of foreign recognition ended with the Union victory at Antietam, and there was no possibility of foreign help after the Confederates lost at Vicksburg and Gettysburg.

[WILLIE BRYANT TO DAVIS BRYANT]

Chattanooga Tenn. July 26, 1863

Dear bro. Davis—

... There is nothing new with me: I still continue plodding along in this office, my duties are not heavy but I stick close to the office; were there more attractions in this "delectable" place I could easily find time to enjoy them, but as it is, an occasional ride is about all I participate in, except going to church; I did not go this a.m. as my wardrobe is far from elaborate just now, and the Q.M. Dept., or Chattanooga cannot replenish it to my taste. Col. Brent has just retd., and will resume his old duties as a.a.g. tomorrow a.m. much to the delight of all concerned ...

This war presents an illustration of life and the ways in this world, in a reduced size, and the longer I live the more impressed I become in my belief in good and bad luck, and the more I see how unequal it is distributed; wealth first, then influence, and lastly tact, can command honors to some extent, as I *am not blessed* with either of the requisetes to any extent I cannot hope to succeed; I claim to have some small share of "merit" but that is always at a discount, and seldom current with dame Fortune, and as I am not a proficient financier, I find it d——d bad stock ...

Affairs look gloomy for the Confederacy just now; the fall of Vicksburg was heavy for us, our fall back from Middle Tenn. was heavy, Lee's loss was heavy in Penn., affairs at Charleston look heavy, and all together make a weight sufficient to depress our spirits; that is natural, but not cause enough for despondency; the farther we draw the Enemy from where he can use his combined forces of gunboats and the army against us, the more sure is our success ...

Yr's always affectionately
Willie—

[WINSTON STEPHENS TO OCTAVIA STEPHENS]

Camp Cooper July 27, 1863

My Dear Wife

I have just had role call for the night and every one has left my room and now I am quiet and alone I will spend a few minutes in converse with you. As I finished supper and came into my room I lit a candle to write but just then the Dr came to the door and through courtesy I invited him and he came in with his pipe in mouth and then Gabe Priest came along and in he walked with his pipe in his mouth and I had to bear it all until the bugle had to be sounded and Gabe had it to blow, then I had to attend roll call leaving the Dr in the room but when I returned I found the room vacated and the air somewhat pure. I feel thankful I have no one living in my house that uses the filthy weed, while smoking they spat over the floor as *Soldiers* are not particular. My room is a log house about 12 by 15 feet with door in one end and chimney in the other, no window but I punched off a few boards to day to let in the air. The houses are generally small but lots of them not requiring the Co to use any tents. I have two men quite sick . . . Maj Harrison goes up the Road on Wednesday and wants me to see some of the Country before he goes as I will be left in Command of the Post when he goes. The Maj tells me I can increase my Co to 150 men, I am receiveing some recruits and will have several transfered to my Co if the Genl will allow it. I want to get the largest and best Co in the State. My men are becoming better satisfied every day and they do not mind the duty but say they had rather do it [here] than at Jacksonville, but a few are not satisfied and want to go back. I am well pleased so far with what I have seen and with Maj H—, but I dislike being without the news so long. We get no milk or butter but can do well in the meat line and we have plenty of peaches. I often wish for you and can bring Rosa before me in my imagination waiting for the peach to be pealed and then hear her say tarta PaPa. I wish it could be real and not imaginary. I can see you sitting down now writing to me . . . hope it will be a better and longer one than this . . . Good night my love! pleasant dreams. I finish in the morning—Good morning Mother Stephens . . . I had a dream last night and thought I was taking some *morphine* but some how I failed and woke up disappointed . . . I will be able to come once in two months and will be home that last of Sept or the first of Oct but if you want to go up the road and run down here to see me I can get a good place in one mile of camps. Give love to all the family also Clarks folks and accept lots of love for you and Rosa—Good bye my dear Wife and may heaven protect you and yours Yours as ever

Winston Stephens

[OCTAVIA STEPHENS TO WINSTON STEPHENS]

Aug 2, 1863

My dear husband

. . . I want very much to hear from you as soon as possible upon one subject, I have got quite in the notion of making my visit to Lou and I want you to write me plainly whether or not you wish me to stay here, you said in your last that I might if I wished, but have you thought of all the inconveniences my leaving would make, the negroes will have full control of the corn, do you think they would burn any quicker if I was not here? I want you to write me plainly your *wishes* about it . . . we can not go for four weeks at least as I think Burrel will not get through with the mules before then, but I write about it now, for it takes nearly a month to get an answer from you by mail. Burrel thinks you have bagging enough for all your cotton, we think there is not more than three more bags, if that is the case he ought to get done in three weeks . . . Good bye my darling . . .

Your loving
Wife

[WINSTON STEPHENS TO OCTAVIA STEPHENS]

Camp Cooper Aug 4, 1863

My Dear Wife

. . . I think I could read a letter from you every day with unabated feelings of interest and Love—Your last was of good length considering I had left home only one week before, giving you but few changes to account for. One of your sentences gives me no little uneasiness and that is about *beef* now my Dear Wife I am generally of a sanguine temperment and look on the bright side of things more than otherwise—but I must confess the beef question or meat question gives me great uneasiness and the only fear I have for this Country is that the Speculator will get such a stronghold on the edibles that the Soldiers family will be made to feel the anguish produced from starvation. Who will stay and battle on when he knows his family are starving? not I! last year a large beef could be purchased for 18 or 20 dollars now they can hardly be obtained at any price—what has caused this change? I answer runing the blockade and others speculating at home! you see the man who runs the blockade cannot pass Confederate money out of the Confederate States and the consequence is he offers first 3 dollars for one of gold and so on until now gold will bring 13 to 15 dollars for one and continuing to go on up—the Speculator at home takes advantage of this state of things and refuses to sell things only at the same depreciated rate, the consequence is that our money is going gradually down and if the Government dont do something soon we are lost.[45] The fighting population has been sold by the Speculator, I am aware that he sells himself also, but he cant stop, his love for gain is so great that he becomes reckless and risks all to make a fortune . . .

Another great battle is expected in Virginia as Grant will be obliged to do something. Lincoln thinks now Grant will crush out Rebeldom—We will see when the two armies meet. It will be a hard fight that whips Lees forces on Virginia soil. Mediation is stil spoken of and the Paris papers say Napoleon will or has proposed to other Foreign powers to join him in asking for an armistice

---

45. The blockade did not deprive the Confederacy of the means of survival, but it certainly caused major shortages of every description in Florida. The breakdown of the transportation system in the state and in the Confederacy was the real reason for the widespread suffering, although Winston did have a point about ruthless speculators.

and he will upon the refusal of the North to an armistice at once acknowledge the Confederates. I have noticed in late Northern papers that they fear foreign inteferance now more than ever. We will never settle this question by arms—but we must stop fighting and talk it over and come to terms in that way—and the sooner the better for both North and South. We can maintain our position and so can the North for an indefinate time and nothing gained on either side—but every thing lost . . .

My Company are improving a little though I have considerable sickness yet. The Dr thinks they are all out of danger. I am now in fine health. I have ben out fishing once and got a mess. Oysters are not good now but will be soon. I shall petition the Genl to be moved in the Winter and hope I may be changed with Capt Dickison . . . If you see the mules are failing stop awhile and let them rest. I want to see you bad enough now and I dont know how it will be in two more months, tell Rosa her kiss is accepted and appreciated and she may let you give her as many as she wants for me. I do all my writing now and it gives me more imployment. love to Mother and boys, Clark and family and accept your Husbands devotion and heart overflowing with love for his aff Wife

Winston Stephens

[OCTAVIA STEPHENS TO WINSTON STEPHENS]

Rose Cottage Aug 5, 1863

My dear husband,

Just now I do not feel in a letter writing mood, for I have just got pretty tired from putting the beef out, and the chickens worry me no little in trying to get the corn which is drying. I did at last get a beef yesterday, it was not a large one, 35 dollars for this one and the same for the one before, we have had fine weather for beef, but this morning was cloudy, but just now it is shining nicely and I hope it will continue so . . .

I am glad you are so well pleased where you are and that you have such a comfortable house, it would be nice for Winter if you have to be in the service then as I suppose of course you will. I hope you will continue to like the Maj, and that he will be lenient, and let you come home often. I hope you may have your wishes in regard to your company having it the largest and best, but then if you do I fear you will be called upon too readily . . .

You will judge from my last that we folks have got quite a fever for visiting, I think the fever on Mother as high as mine, but I fear we will not go. I have a great deal to do, and it will be such a long trip to go to Waldo in the wagon, and now the wagon is broken, but Burrel says he will have to have it fixed before he gathers corn, but as I wrote you in my last I want you to say candidly if there is any reason why I should stay . . .

I have been doing something that I am afraid may not suit you, three men at different times have stopped here and wanted food for their horses and as they could not get it anywhere near I let them have a feed, shall I refuse them hereafter? if not what must I charge, I dislike to refuse them. I charged the gentlemen that were here to day fifty cents a piece for their horses feed, but nothing for their dinner. the gentleman insisted upon my taking a dollar, I did not find out his name, but he belonged in an artillery company under Bragg . . .

Henry will be sixteen the twelfth of this month; the Militia was to have been organized the first, will he have to join as soon as he is sixteen? Tina thinks none will be called from home excepting in case of an emergency and when that is over return home again. Clark has the blues again as his paper said no white man discharged or not, excepting Clergymen and ferrymen were exempt. Can you not write us all about it, what your knowledge of the matter is . . . I think if we fight much longer we will come down as low as slaves, and I think we had better give up, and have our husbands with us, slavery if such it will be, will be much harder when we are subdued after our husbands are killed. oh how I wish the war never had started . . . That little potatoe mouth of ours has just given me a kiss for you, she seldom ever forgets you at night, last night she said "you dont get any kiss" I hope only the ones we send you. I know Mother sends love and Georgie says I must not forget to always send his. I have none to send, you have it already. Good bye my dear,

Lovingly your Wife

[REBECCA BRYANT TO WILLIE BRYANT]

Rose Cottage Aug 5, 1863

My dearest Willie

. . . I have a strong inclination to go to Thomasville and Tivie says she will not leave me here alone, but it is impossible to get a conveyance for all of us to the R. Road, and the mules cannot be spared to make two trips over there. I should not be surprised if we all had to pull up stakes and move into Georgia this Autumn, unless the affairs of the Confederacy brighten very much in the next two months.[46] Winston had to buy fifty bushels of corn this year, at $2. and will not make more than half enough for next year—It seems a pity for him to stay here, and yet it is difficult for him to move, or even decide on a place, situated as he is . . .

Tivie and George send much love—Henry is still with Mr Stephens, at home only from Saturday night till day light Monday. I must close with an ocean of love to you from

Mother

46. Rebecca's prophecy came true earlier than she expected; Winston decided in September to move his family to Thomasville.

[WINSTON STEPHENS TO DAVIS BRYANT]

Camp Cooper Aug 11, 1863

Dear Davis,

... I send you enclosed in this one hundred dollars to keep for Tivie and you will please hand it to her when she arrives—I send this not knowing how much *Confederate* she will have with her—she has State money that I dont want her to spend, please get this in smaller bills if you can as it will save her trouble.[47]

I had a letter from home and Tivie wrote that Mother would go to Thomasville on a visit provided she "Tivie" would go also and she wrote to me for my opinion and I will write in the morning for her to go. I suppose they will come along about three or four weeks from this, and as they have to stop over one night in Lake City you will have a nice time of it and I must say I will envy you the visit. I am going to try to prevail on Tivie to have her teeth worked on and I wish you would unite with me in trying to prevail on her to have them fixed, if I could be there I could carry my point, I will try to get off to see them but fear I will fail. Tivie will return and stop two or three weeks at Mr Wingates on her way back home.[48] I have not been over to his house, but I am told they are nice folks . . .

Several of my men . . . are sick, as the Doctor has no medicine and we cannot give them such diet as they require. I lost one of my men yesterday—a Mr James Futch, a nice young man and a good soldier.[49] He died of Typhoid fever after an illness of 30 days. I am having more sickness now then I have ever had, in fact I have had more sickness the past month than all my service together. I have 20 men unfit for duty. I would make application to be sent to some other place had we not come here so recently . . . Mother will let you know when to look for them and have rooms for them.

Yours truly
Winston Stephens

[Rebecca] **Aug 12, 1863.** *Still warm—About 9 clk a.m. Mr Stephens sends to Tivie that cannon have been heard in the direction of Palatka and*

---

47. There were several currencies in circulation in Florida: Confederate bonds; Confederate treasury notes; state treasury notes; and corporation and fractional paper notes issued by cities and businesses, although these had about disappeared by 1864. The state notes, guaranteed by the public lands of Florida, were worth four or five times those of Confederate issue, and Winston did not want Tivie to spend Florida notes out of state.

48. William and Margaret Wingate lived about one mile east-northeast of Camp Cooper on property known as the John Wingate Grant.

49. James Futch was the son of Joshua and Lavina Futch of Putnam County; all the members of this extensive family were farmers who had moved to Florida from Georgia in the early 1840s.

she sends Tom to move the cotton. We put our silver and other valuables out of sight . . .[50]

[OCTAVIA STEPHENS TO WINSTON STEPHENS]

Rose Cottage Aug 12, 1863

My dear husband

. . . What do you think, I am sitting in the dining room watching the field and road for the yankees for Clark sent word this morning to know if I had heard all the firing of cannons, we had heard something but thought it must be thunder, and as Clark offered me the oxen and I thought intended it as advice I sent Tom and Mose over to move the cotton . . . we have nevertheless buried our silver and are partly prepared if they should come though not expecting them much . . .

"Aracious alive" as Rosa says the musquitoes "nigh about eat a feller up," and it is monstrous warm, I tell you this sort of weather makes a body feel very worthless, I am not worth much, I feel often as though I would like to do as you do I guess part of your time lie down and read some pretty stories, I guess you are pretty nearly out of stories now, and wont you miss them when they are all read . . .

I have forgotten to ask before if Mrs Capps moved to Camp Cooper too, I suppose so though, she will not leave the service as long as the war continues, she is of *so much service* . . .[51]

Thursday morn . . . Sarah is down at last, reported on the sick list this morning, Big Jane spinning but hardly able, I gave her a dose of oil a short while ago, as she has been taking blue mass, I would give a great deal to know what to do for her. I am starching my thread this morning, something I expected Sarah to have the pleasure of doing, I am disappointed in my dye again, it is too light . . .

Well my dear I must close this I am sorry to have to send you such a mean letter, but it cannot be helped this time. Mother and Georgie send love. Rosa sends a kiss, and accept as much love as you wish from

Your devoted

Old Lady

---

50. This was a false alarm; the Federals did not return to the region until early in 1864. In February they occupied Jacksonville for the fourth and final time and raided up and down the river for the duration of the war.

51. Elizabeth Capps, wife of Private Michael Capps of Winston's company. Evidently she went with her husband wherever he was sent; she may have washed and sewed for the company originally, but Tivie and Winston both remarked later that her reputation was poor, and the probability is that she had become a prostitute.

[WINSTON STEPHENS TO OCTAVIA STEPHENS]

Camp Cooper Aug 12, 1863

My Dear Wifey

... I was surprised in reading yours to see what a change had come over you! You at one time appeared to dread or rather wished to avoid going from home and now I can see by the earnestness of your letter that your heart is set on the visit. Now I would ask how is it possible for a doating Husband to refuse such a good wife? You have my willing consent to go and the purse strings are in your hands, all I have to ask is that you will not spend a dollar of the State or Bank money, but use confederate. I have to day sent one hundred dollars up to Davis that you might not be short of funds . . . If he does I think it would be safest to take what money you want and deposit the rest with Davis telling him about the State and Bank moneys not to be used. You might be robed on the road and Davis can place in the chest or in some safe place until you return, let me caution you about carrying money. Keep it on your person as the trunks will be stowed in the baggage train and other Keys might fit, these times you will have to watch . . . I want before you go to have it distinctly understood with Henry how much the negroes get and as the mules will have a pasture to run on Henry can carry the corn house and the Smoke house key and arrange for Henry to go over once or twice a week and see how things go on and if the Yanks should come while you are off have the negroes etc got out of the way and let Henry represent the place as belonging to Mother and State. She is on a visit and we living with them, I think there will be no harm in fixing up a story in such a case, all your Valuables pack up and you had better leave them with Tina, or get Henry to burry them if the yanks come, arrange every thing just as though they were sure to come while you are absent. Your Mother must write to Davis when you will arrive at Lake City so that he can meet you and secure room for you, and I want you to write me when you will take the Cars and I want it to be on some Wednesday that I may see you if possible at Baldwin and perhaps get to go on to Lake City with you. I have given this subject my intire thought and know that if we were to wait until we could go from home without some detriment, We would never go, for things never go on so well when absent as when we are at home, but it is a while when we can afford the means and now you have the means you had better go and besides it gets Mother off and I know she wants so much to go and it will be a benefit as well as a pleasure to the whole party. I have seen Mr Wingate and he thinks you can get to stay two or three weeks on your way home. You can arrange to come on a head of Mother and stay with me and then meet her on Wednesday and go home together. If you can count up the time of your return so that Henry can meet you it will be best as to risk by mail he might not get it. I want you if you can stay at least two weeks and had rather have you three, and I hope to be able to return home with you, but set your heart on seeing or having me with you until you come down. You can write me from Lake City when to look for you and I will have to meet you . . . Tell Burrel to keep up close with the cotton and in your absence I shall trust to his care every thing, knowing he feels an interest in what I have "this will incourage him." I have 20 men sick and they continue to get sick every day, I think caused by continous duty and exposure. I have to keep up 7 picket posts and to day the Infantry goes off and I will have 3 more which requires in all 42 men and I have only 58 fit for duty, so that the men will have to stand guard every night for nine nights and then rest only three and go on again. I send to day six men to the Hospital . . . Return many kisses to Rosa and thank her for hers and love to Mother and Boys and Clark and family and accept your share of kisses and love from your ever Aff Husband

Winston Stephens

[OCTAVIA STEPHENS TO WINSTON STEPHENS]

Aug 15, 1863

My own dear husband

. . . Yes my heart is now set upon going, the folks all write so urgingly for me to come and if I do not go now I dont know when I can again at least not for a year, I want to get off just as soon as possible on account of my interesting situation but this morning came to that conclusion that we would have to put it off a week longer than we expected[52] . . . I wish I could keep *myself down* a month, for I will have to alter all my dresses, I dislike very much putting it off but Mother seems to think better. If we take the cars on Wednesday we will have to leave here on Sunday, which probably will be three weeks from tomorrow the 6th. of Sept, it will add much to our pleasure if you can meet us as you wish at Baldwin and go to Lake City. I wish you could make the entire visit with me, you were very kind and thoughtful in sending that money to Davis for me, I appreciate *all* your actions in this matter, but feel I can not express my feelings as I wish I would not have used any of the money put up for *anything*. I have a plenty as I have not paid out any since you left, I will do as you said about leaving it with Davis, it will be a great relief to me too. I do hope you can come home with me, I think four weeks will be as long as I can stand it from home unless I *grow* slower than I think, seems to me now I am almost large enough for three months. I guess you need not expect us before three weeks from next Wednesday, you will hear from me again . . .

As ever your aff
Wife

52. Tivie was again pregnant.

[WILLIE BRYANT TO DAVIS BRYANT]

Chattanooga Tenn. Aug 16, 1863

Dear Davis—

... Aunt Julia has written me a long letter since her return; as you say, her influence is inspiring, and I always feel better satisfied with myself and the world in general, after reading one of her letters. She is full of the idea of our living together after the war ends, and seems to entertain the idea that I will go to Thomasville to live; the fancy pleases her, and is pleasing to me so far as our living together and her establishing a comfortable home for us is concerned, and I have no doubt but that the plan would work well as I have no marrying intention, and her influence would be invaluable to me, but as for burying myself in a country town, I can't make up my mind to that. I don't indulge in any bright plans for the future, and that time which all seem to think will bring everything desired—"when the war ends," but I do not think I shall live in Florida again; many of my oldest and dearest associations which have bound me to it have been broken, and I want a larger and more fertile and flourishing field for my tastes; I have always felt, and still think, that it was a mistake of Father's in establishing a home in Fla., and that I have committed the same mistake. If I *could* make up my mind to settle in Thomasville—which is in a thriving country—and away from more busy scenes of excitement, I have no doubt but that a pleasant and cheerful home might teach me to be satisfied, and I know I should live longer and happier.

You, now, I should think would be just suited. I want to hear more of the trips all the family have been talking about taking; I hope Mother may succeed in getting off, for a time at least, before the summer is over; *You* certainly will run up to Thomasville for a few days; if Mother can get off for 15 days, and spend 9 of them there, and am waiting to form my plans according to other's ...

Good bye for now—
Yrs Always Affectionately
Willie

[OCTAVIA STEPHENS TO WINSTON STEPHENS]

Rose Cottage Aug 18 1863

My dear husband

... Georgie has gone this morning to have my thread warped, I dread trying to put it in the Loom, but I have to try some time or another, so may as well now, I wish some one lived nearer that knew all about weaving and would lend me a helping hand, I am such a child any how I always dread doing anything alone, I think I never shall be a woman as I ought to be, I get perfectly disgusted with myself at times, I dont know what is to become of me, seems to me I am getting to be the crossest thing ever was seems the more I try to have patience and be good natured the worse I get, I am scolding at somebody all the time, I am afraid I am going to be a real scold. I think though if this war would end and you come home I might be better . . .

I am very busy getting ready for my trip, although I feel as though some thing will happen to prevent. I have not a great deal to fix but it takes me so long to contrive how to patch and piece, you would have thought so had you seen me yesterday working nearly the whole day trying to patch up and contrive a waist to a dress and by night I was not much better off than when I began, but this morning I nearly conquered before I began this, I dont know how it will look when finished, for I have just put the patches together. Rosa is lying across my lap and I scratching her back with one hand while writing this with the other, I think it is *all scratching* . . .

Burrel is still ginning on, very anxious to get done, I am going to write to Loulie to day and tell her again of my anticipated visit, I know she is dreading the next two weeks, her troubles will be over when I get there if I go, perhaps it would be best for me to have it so, but I wanted to be there to be company for her, I will feel very much disappointed if anything should happen to prevent my going for as you say, my heart is set upon it especially as I see my "doating" husband is so willing to have me go. I hope you will meet us at Baldwin that I may see as much of you as possible, but three weeks seems a long time to look forward to starting, I think we can start from here early Monday morning and get to Waldo Tuesday night and yet allow plenty time for the poking mules . . .

Mother sends love and accept a full share of love and kisses from Your

very affectionate
Wife

[REBECCA BRYANT TO WILLIE BRYANT]

Rose Cottage Aug 18, 1863

How are you to-day my dear Willie? Is the sun shinning over head and into your heart, making your duties appear light and Time move swiftly? Or is the atmosphere heavy, the clouds lowering, and the face of nature communicating a corresponding gloom to your mind? This is the 27th. anniversary of my marriage! As I look back through that long period of time a thousand mingled emotions fill my heart, and a thousand reminiscences of both a pleasing and melancholy character crowd upon me. What would I not give to know exactly how your father is situated to-day! How different everything is with both of us, from what we could have imagined on that bright and happy day when we stood at the altar in King's Chapel and then "plighted our troth" to each other, surrounded by so many nice friends, who are now in the spirit-land. Of those who composed the circle around us on that day, both my parents and three brothers are gone — the clergyman himself has departed . . . And how changed are those who remain! I wish I could transfer to your minds's eye as vividly as it *now* appears to mine, the image of your father as he stood by my side on that occasion — a rare specimen of manly beauty, such as I think you would allow you had seldom met; and his manner combining grace and ease. But I must leave these fond memories and pleasing fancies and come back to the realities of the present . . . Tivie, George and I are all promising ourselves a furlough of some weeks — "There is many a slip, between the cup and the lip" you know — But we propose the following programme — Tivie, Rosa and I to go in the buggy, Henry to drive the cart containing George, the trunks and one of the darkies (who will drive the cart back) to Waldo, Henry returns from there and we proceed thence to Baldwin where Winston will *try* to meet us, thence to Lake City, where we *hope* to be joined by Davis to proceed with me to Thomasville. Tivie and Rosa will leave us at Station 4 and go to Loulie's for a visit of a week.[53] George will go on with me to Thomasville and Tivie will come there for a few days after her visit to Loulie. She then intends to go down to the vicinity of Camp Cooper and stay at a house within a mile of Winston for a couple of weeks. Henry will probably go to Thomasville and return with me, after he gets through his engagement with Mr Stephens. He is very anxious to see his relatives there and may not have so good an opportunity for a long time. We are now making arrangements to leave here on Monday September 7th, bright and early so as to be at Baldwin on Wednesday the 9th. that being the day for the cars to come up from Camp Cooper — so that if nothing prevents our starting and no accidents befall us, we expect to reach Thomasville on the 10th of September.

If Davis goes with us, he will probably remain but a few days, and I wish you could manage to meet him there . . . What a delightful re-union it will be if we can all meet! Too much to *expect* I fear — but we will *hope* for it. Henry will stay at Mr Stephens' as he now does and come over every Sunday to see that all is right here, and give out the rations. We have not yet fully arranged as to the time of his coming for me, it will depend on circumstances — he will be very lonely when he is not on an Alligator hunt and I trust nothing will occur to disappoint him. Will you not write to him, so that the letter will reach him the week after we leave, say the 16th . . . ?

The talk in the news papers about intervention and recognition has raised my hopes again — But the recent riots in N. York have made me very uneasy with regard to your father — No one can be safe there in person or property when the

---

53. Station 4 was about three miles southeast of Monticello on the Pensacola & Georgia Railroad, a line that went to neither place but did connect Tallahassee to Lake City.

mob rise as they have done and may do again. There is no chance now of hearing directly from him . . .

Rosa has given me a sweet kiss to put in my letter. George sends "a pile of love." Tivie says "give him a great deal of love and tell him I would like very much to see him in Thomasville but do'nt expect he will happen there before I leave." Much love and God bless you, from

Mother

[WINSTON STEPHENS TO OCTAVIA STEPHENS]

Camp Cooper Aug 19, 1863

My Darling Wifey

. . . Drydale gives a horrid account of the treatment he received at the hands of the Yanks and he says it is impossible for him to describe their treatment to our men.[54] He tells me four of them were confined in a room six feet by six and locked up all night and then in the day they were thrown in to the yard and a small one at that. They had to stand in the hot sun all the day, diet bread, water and a small peace of salt pork, and constantly abused by white and black, but he says the blacks are better than the whites and they are sick of their trip to the yanks and nearly all of them wish they were back with their old Masters. He says the Yanks have a great many negroes in irons, some are shot and some hung for trifling offences and sometimes the negroes kill their officers and then in return they are butchered. He describes the prison in which he was confined as the most filthy place he ever saw, some 250 or 300 persons were confined, mostly Soldiers of the Yankee army, and some of them in irons, with dirt and filth and the lice were so thick that he said he could rake them up on the floor. Nothing that he tells gives them a place in the history of this war as civilized human beings but more on the *brutal savage* order. god help and deliver me from such a tryal as a six months confinement in one of their cells . . . Death is better than to submit to such a people. Drydale says their army is very much demoralized and he thinks they cant prep the draft in the north and the men whose time is now expiring will go home and they say they will not come back any more. When we get in the men up to 45 we will have a better and larger army than they have and I have every confidence in our ability to fight it out, but God knows I am heartily sick of it and wish we could have peace . . . You ask me what you shall do about letting travlers have feed for horses! I dont mind letting any one in the service have corn at a fair price, but the thieves of the Country I dont want to feed at any price and Clark has made more corn than he will use and I will have to buy and I rather

---

54. Jonathan Drysdale, previously mentioned, had been captured when Jacksonville was raided by the Federals in March 1863.

you would tell them to go to him, besides I dont care to have them troubling you when they can go where there is a man so near, and I cant afford to keep Hotel as its all I can do to feed my family, by no means I dont mean you shall not help a poor Soldier, but no others than those that cant well go some where else. In Henrys case he will have to join when he is sixteen but no one will have to go from home until the enemy invades the State and then they are called upon for active service as long as the enemy remain and then they return home as soon as the enemy leaves the State . . . Give love to all the family and Clarks family Howdie to darkies, and many kisses to Yourself and Rosa. tell Rosa I get no kisses but those sent. I am as ever your devoted Husband.

Winston Stephens

[OCTAVIA STEPHENS TO WINSTON STEPHENS]

Rose Cottage Aug 25, 1863

My dear husband

. . . I am very anxious to get off, but still feel as though something will prevent. I am afraid since the furloughs are stopped you can not meet us at Baldwin, four weeks seems a long time if I do not see you at Baldwin, but I guess the time will pass off quicker when I get amongst my kinsfolk, still I shall be anxious to see you and wish you were with us, we still hold to the same plan of trying to be at Baldwin on the ninth. I am so anxious to hear direct from you for I had [a] dreadful dream of you the other morning that at times worries me . . .

Pleasant news, if we get another beef we will have to pay 38 dollars for it, I guess your next letter will say as I have that I think we had better swear off, the darkies hint that it is hard, but do not as yet really grumble, Burrel killed one of his hogs last week. I hope in your next you will give me some directions about salt, Clark got out again and I could not refuse and let them have a little . . .

Mother sends love, Rosa sends a kiss and accept the whole devotion of

Your little Wife

[WINSTON STEPHENS TO OCTAVIA STEPHENS]

Camp Cooper Aug 26, 1863

My Dear Wife

I have just finished up my official communications sent up my report etc and am now ready to devote a short time to you. I am not feeling so well in my bowels this morning as I wish to, though not suffering much apprehension from them. My sick list is large! I have twenty one on it and have some new cases nearly every day. It is true some are constantly returning to duty keeping about 20 all the time sick . . . Lord how long must this bloody strife last! I do hope that something may turn up to bring us peace. I never was as sick of any thing in my life. Lincoln will soon test his strength as he has ordered the draft to proceed and many say it will bring about a conflict [in the] North. God grant it may with such a shock as to dethrone Lincoln the 1st. and produce permanent and lasting peace. I would sooner live in poverty with my family around me than with this uncertainty hanging over me, but it is now as Aunt Julia says we have no choice left but to fight on and fight forever rather than submit to the Tyrants yoke . . .

Love to all and Howdie to the darkies. Many kisses for Rosa and tell her Pa wants to see her very much. and all you wish take from your loving husband

Winston Stephens

[WILLIE BRYANT TO DAVIS BRYANT]

Catoosa Springs Ga. Aug 31, 1863

Dear Davis—

. . . Catoosa Springs Hospitals are near the R. Road, between Chattga. and Atlanta; nearest town Ringgold. I ran down here a day or two ago to seek relief for [what] turns out to be *camp itch*—d—n it!!—I have suffered with it for 7 weeks past, but owing to the bad state of my blood the Surgs. were misled as to its nature[55]—After so long service in the field I am finally doomed to contract the d——d disease at the Hd. Qrs of the army; when or how, I cant imagine; just think of it and you can imagine my feelings of disgust and anger, and will not wonder at my desperate curses—d—n the luck I say!

Today the eruption is better, from the effects of warm baths, but I am feverish and nervous; however, I must return to the office at Chattgn. this p.m. for a couple of days, to prepare our Field Return for Richmond, as it is highly important at this time and I am required for it; as soon as I can get that off I shall return here until the time for the next one (10 days) comes around and give my whole attention to this infernal disease, I will then write you a long letter . . .

When you write Mother you can mention my writing you from here, where I was for treatment of *an eruption,* I will write her that it is d——d itch.

If I had almost anything else the matter with me and wd. go at once to T-vlle until I get well, but not with this . . . Good bye for now—

Yrs Willie

55. Ringgold, Georgia, is about ten miles southeast of Chattanooga, Tennessee. Camp itch, also called scabies, was caused by mites and was similar to poison ivy or oak in that the victim could not refrain from scratching, which spread the infection. Camp itch was not a social disease, but in polite society it was associated with being unclean; like untreated lice, it was a social embarrassment.

[WINSTON STEPHENS TO OCTAVIA STEPHENS]

Camp Cooper Sept 2, 1863

My Darling Wifey

I have just finished my hard duties and now seat my self to have a chat with your dear self . . . You would perhaps like to know what I have been doing that I call hard duties. I have been obliged in the absence of my friend Greely to do all my Company work and the last of August was Muster day I had a great deal of writing to do—for instance 3 Muster and Pay rolls giving the names with Places of Muster date, age of men, where born, where mustered and what occupation, who last paid them and the names present with remarks etc and one Muster roll, Monthly report etc making three days hard writing. When Greely and I used to make them together it was not so heavy. I feel consoled that it is only to be done once in two months. I make monthly reports and ordinance reports every month etc which I do not mind. I have written until my fingers pain me and you cant expect this well written and hope you will be glad to see even this. I am glad to see yours no matter how short or how badly written, though yours is generally well done . . . When you get to Baldwin stay until the car returns from this camp as it will bring Your old man and I dont want you to be in Lake City and me in Baldwin. I think the cars will connect and we can both go to Lake City, they always connect unless something detains the cars from Camp. Arrange every thing with Henry and give him Money to get meat with while you are absent and I will replenish you when we meet. I want Burrel to geather the corn as soon as he can and if the hogs bother he must take the railes from the branch field and fix the fence and manage to keep them out until the Peas and potatoes and pinders are saved . . .

Tell Henry if any thing happens while you are gone to try and carry out the plan we adopted for the safety of negroes etc. I will trust him and Burrel to watch out for every thing, he must have beef if he has to kill it and I will stand the damage. If he cant buy one tell him to kill one and take the mark and brand and report to me and I will make it all O.K.

I have lost another Man. You know him I guess, his name is Isham Standley, he used to live with Granvill Priest. He died in Lake City at the Hospital on the 27th. August . . .

Give lots of love to all and accept for yourself and Rosa love and kisses from your aff

Winston

[WILLIE BRYANT TO DAVIS BRYANT]

Catoosa Springs Ga. Sept 3, 1863

Dear Bro. Davis—

I wrote you a few days ago from here and that I was to return again to Hd. Qrs. and then return here; well, you see I'm back; I was only gone from here a day and a half, and retd. Tuesday evng., as I was too unwell to attend to regular duties;—I commenced only yesterday a.m. to add medicine to my warm baths, and have already experienced great benefit, and think in a couple of days will be free from all annoyance, tho' my blood is in such a bad state that I shall remain until I am completely sound in every respect. When I see how much suffering I might have avoided if the surg's at Hd. Qrs. had had sense, and any interest in any but themselves, or if I had had sense and decision enough to give up my duties and come here earlier, I am provoked—I wonder if I ever will learn to sacrifice less of my own interests to the wishes and convenience of others! I begin to doubt it, I swear! I have taken a pencil for convenience, as my "sitting down place" is too sore for it to be comfortable to sit and write . . .

This trip I am obliged to make here knocks my expectations of being able to go to Thomasville in the head, as they can not well spare me from the office so long; on account of the facilities for bathing it is almost necessary that I should remain here; however, I will try to make the trip; the devil take this cursed ill luck! Mother was expecting to be able to reach Lake City on the 9th inst., in that event this will reach you about the time she gets there, and you will be able to tell her of the improbability of my being able to go to T— etc. I shall write her at T— in a day or two, however, and also enclose $150—to her . . . Good bye for now

Yrs always aff

Willie

[Rebecca] *Sept 6, 1863. A fine cool morng. but warm during the day. We leave home about 2½ p.m. and travel along well until within a hundred yards of the river, when one of the back wheels of the wagon breaks and we are compelled to remain in the woods sitting on a mattress and the floor of the wagon until Henry and Tom go to Mr Stephens and return with 2 wheels from the turpentine wagon. While they are gone George, Tivie and myself try to make ourselves contented, with a light wood fire, eat a lunch and sing a little as night comes on—Henry comes soon after dark—and after a cold supper we fix our beds for the night. Tivie, Rosa, Geo and I in the wagon—Henry and Tom on the ground with moss and branches of trees.*

[Rebecca] **Sept 7, 1863.** *Before daylight the boys are blowing the horn for the ferryman but we do not cross the river until after sunrise. We have a warm ride of 20 miles before we get accommodations for the night, being refused at the place where we expected to lodge. Tivie is very much fatigued but not made sick by the ride.*

[Rebecca] **Sept 8, 1863.** *A bright cool morng.—We start from Mr Cook's at 7 a.m.... All dine at Mr Guthries about 4 miles from Waldo— Arrive at W— at 4½ p.m. ....*[56]

[DAVIS BRYANT TO WINSTON STEPHENS]

Lake City Sept 8, 1863

Dear Winston

I have been full of remorse ever since last Wednesday for neglecting to write you ... I wished to particularly write you of a letter I rec'd from father some days before in which he mentioned some things that concern you. He, in fact, sent a message to you, advising you of the intended movements of the Yankees this fall and recommending your preparing against it. I am very sorry that I did not copy it word for word from the letter before sending it to Mother, but thought I could remember it, and could have given it correctly had I written as I ought to have done last week. The sum and substance of it was ... the Yanks and negroes were coming out in a short time to try to overrun Fla. and particularly the last and said he wished the folks were all at Thomasville or some where off the river. He did not think even Orange Springs a safe resort as their intention was to land *Cavalry* at Palatka and make raids into the interior. This letter was written June 19th. at Nassau N.P. and sent through the blockade via Wilmington. He was at Nassau on business and was to return to N. York in a few days. I don't know that this will change your plans now that it is so old but he evidently thought, and in fact *said* that this was to be undertaken *soon*. and the affairs at Charleston have delayed them, I have no doubt at all from what he writes and those who have been lately released from imprisonment by the yankees say that they are determined to give us trouble early this winter, and how I do wish you could get off long enough to make some changes. I should most certainly do so if possible even as late as October if impossible before, send most of the negroes off, all at any rate not needed about the house and yard, for they will come on very short notice the next time and run straight up to Palatka I think, or some where up there. However, I reckon you are worried enough by your own fears without my in-

---

56. A. W. Cook and his wife, Margaret, ran a hotel in Micanopy, about thirty-five miles west of Welaka. From Micanopy to Waldo is about twenty miles. Jasper and Amelia Guthrie had a farm about four miles south of Waldo. The family stayed at the Waldo Hotel, operated by J. G. and Anabell Stroble.

creasing them, but I merely wished to state the case according to the general belief, and what I know about it. I'll "dry up" now on that subject.[57] I hope you are able to meet Tivie and Mother at Baldwin and wish you could come up with them, I am impatiently expecting them tomorrow and shall be disappointed if they do not come I have engaged rooms at the "Hancock House"[58]—I could not get any as comfortable any where else—and will have the *ambulance* at the depot to *transport* them . . .

I would advise you to destroy this letter and all others that contain any information that could injure father in *certain events,* or anything of the sort might give him a great deal of serious trouble if known by the enemy. It is late and I must "dry up" *generally.* I will write more *sociably* soon.

Yours very truly

Davis

[Rebecca] *Sept 9, 1863. Weather clear and warm—we go on the cars few minutes before 8 a.m. . . . Arrive safely at Baldwin about 10 ½ o'clk . . . Wait for the cars from Camp Cooper until 4½ p.m. when Winston joins us and all proceed to Lake City. Arrive there just at dark, Davis meets us at the cars with an ambulance and goes with us to the Hancock House. After ten he passes an hour with us and all retire with the intention of rising at 3 o'clk to leave at 4 on the Cars.*

[Winston Stephens to Henry Bryant]

Lake City Sept 10, 1863

Dear Henry,

Your Mother, Tivie etc. all arrived in Baldwin and the Train from Camp Cooper made the connection and we all arrived about dark at this place . . . We will go in the morning. Davis goes with us. I am obliged to return to camps on next week and will have only a few days to attend to my business. I am going to get a place near Thomasville and move every thing that I cant dispose of. I wish you would fence the potatoes so that Burrel can turn the hogs on some of the peas. I want you to arrange to keep them on a good pasture all the time so as to get them as fat as possible . . . as I want to fatten enough to last me all next year, get a beef if you have not got one and allow the negroes to use the potatoes but tell Burrel not to allow theirs wasted, and tell him to save all the pinders he can when they

---

57. This information undoubtedly influenced Winston in his decision to move to Thomasville immediately.

58. Martin and Civility Hancock, with help from their three daughters and two slaves, owned and operated the Hancock House in Lake City.

get ripe as I shall want to take them with me. I want him also to get out all the cotton as it opens and keep the peas picked and any spare days he may have to *rake* around the fences a place at least ten feet wide so that it cant burn over ... I will try to come home with Tivie and we will at once commence moving. I think we will come some time about the 1st. of October. I will write you when to meet us ... Tell Burrel to have the mules fat and good collars and every thing in good order. Mother will write you from Thomasville as soon as I make my arrangements and tell you what to do ... Your attention to the above instructions will be greatfully received.

Howdie to darkies etc. yours truly
Winston Stephens

[Rebecca] **Sept 11, 1863.** *... The day very warm — We arrive at Monticello about 1 o'clk — dine at the Hotel ... About 3 o'clk we start in a hack for Thomasville and arrive at Aunt Julia's at 8 p.m. — We find Mother Bryant quite unwell, Julia the same as ever, all life and full of joy at seeing us all. After a bountiful supper all retire happy!*
Sept 14, 1863. *Mother, Aunt Caroline, Uncle Jared, Franky, Julie and Davis came to Aunt Mary's to spend the day.*[59] *I was taken sick just before dinner, After dinner the others had music etc, Towards eve. Aunt C— and Uncle J— went home and Mother, Winston, Davis and I returned to Aunt Julia's. Winston left us at 10 o'clk for Camp Cooper.*

[REBECCA BRYANT TO HENRY BRYANT]

Thomasville Sept 16, 1863

My dear Henry,

It seems a *very* long time since we left you at Waldo — yet the time has passed pleasantly. I am very impatient to hear from you, to know how you are getting along in our absence. I hope you have recd. a letter Winston wrote you from Lake City ... We arrived here about 8 o'clk last Friday night — Winston, Davis, Tivie, George, Rosa and myself all packed into a hack which we hired to bring us from Monticello, a distance of 22 miles. We did not know precisely where Grandmother and Aunt Julia lived but when I thought we were near it, Davis got out of the carriage to enquire at a pretty little cottage, which proved to be the house — and Aunt Julia stepped out when he rapped on the piazza. Your Grandmother

---

59. The Bryant relatives in Thomasville were Ann Andrews Bryant; Julia (Bryant) Fisher; Samuel and Mary (Bryant) Adams and their children, Lizzie, George, Willie, and Mary; and Jared and Caroline (Bryant) Everitt with the children from her first marriage, Paris Perham and Franky (Perham) Sharpe, wife of William H. Sharpe.

had been having chills and is more feeble than usual. She keeps [to] her room all the morning but usually passes the afternoon in the parlor. Aunt Julia teaches a school of 12 pupils and is all the time buying and packing for the soldiers, never still five minutes until she goes to her room at night . . . Winston left us Monday night at 10 o'clk to go to Lake City and is probably at Camp Cooper to-day. Davis will leave us next Monday night and if Tivie is strong enough she will go to Loulie's at that time and stay a week with her.

I suppose you will receive another letter from Winston, by the same mail perhaps that takes this to you, telling his plans and at what time he wishes you to be at Waldo to meet him and Tivie—I hope nothing will occur to prevent his carrying out his plans. When he left us he expected to get a furlough and to be at Waldo with Tivie on the eveg. of the 1st. Octr. He hopes to be able to get most of his furniture etc. moved by the middle of October. Tivie and Rosa are to stay with Aunt Caroline after they come back until 1st. Jany. when we are to have a house next to Aunt Julia's and all live together as at Welaka . . .

An ocean of love for yourself from
Mother

[WINSTON STEPHENS TO OCTAVIA STEPHENS]

Camp Cooper Sept 19, 1863

My Dear Wife

I wrote you to day that you may be sure to get this in time to prevent your starting with the intention of coming to this place . . . but I feel it is for your good not to come, in the first place we are having considerable rain and the creeks are very high and the road from the Depot to Mr Wingates is almost impassable and for you to ride over it in a cart would nearly jolt your life out of you, and resting the week longer at Lou's will better prepare you for the trip home and the packing after you reach home. I am willing to forgo the pleasure of having you here for the good I think you will derive from not coming. I have written . . . for Henry to meet us at Waldo on Wednesday the 7th. Oct . . . I slept last night under all the covering I had and was cold at that. I dont know what I am to do this winter unless I can get more blankets. I will try to draw some from the Q.M. and if I fail I guess I will have to hunt a bed companion. Shall it be male or female? I think there is more warmth in a female . . . ! I will write you again on Wednesday if any thing transpires in that time. Tell Loulie I would have been very glad to have seen her and her family around her. I suppose she looks like other married Women under similar circumstances but, I have her in my mind as I saw her last and cant associate babies with her.

Send Love to Thomasville friends when you write Love to Lou and the pair of darlings and accept much love from your old man and kisses to Rosa and the rest of the pritty girls Your ever aff

Husband

Winston Stephens

[WILLIE BRYANT TO DAVIS BRYANT]

Catoosa Station, Ga. Sept 21, 1863

Dear Bro. Davis—

... I am at last compelled to give up all hopes of my trip to Thomasville; I have been running up and down the R. Road, and trying with the greatest perseverance, for the past week to get an answer from Hd. Qrs., without success—Yesterday I tried to get there walked 3 miles and found I could only do so by walking 8 or more farther and not feeling equal to it turned back.[60] They have been fighting pretty hard the past two days about 11 miles from here; "the 3d." got into it yesterday a.m. . . . .[61]

Good bye for now—

Yrs Affctly Willie.

Sept 22, 1863. After dinner Uncle Jared drove me in the buggy to Aunt Julia's. I found Aunt Mary there. I repacked my trunk. Left Aunt Julia's in the hack for Monticello at 9 o'clk in the night, took breakfast at Monticello ... took the cars to No 4. arrived at Loulies a little while before dinner.[62]

Sept 24, 1863. Sewed all day in Lou's room. Mr Tydings went off to see a sick man to stay over night. Wrote to Mother.

---

60. Willie persevered and arrived in Thomasville on 25 September.

61. The Battle of Chickamauga, 19–20 September, was Bragg's greatest victory. His attack routed Rosecrans's army and might well have destroyed it but for the gallant stand of Major General George H. Thomas of the Union, the "Rock of Chickamauga." Casualties were staggering; Bragg listed 2,312 dead, 14,674 wounded, and 1,468 missing. Rosecrans reported that the Union had suffered 1,657 dead, 9,756 wounded, and 4,757 missing. Rosecrans, who was relieved of command on 19 October, found his army under siege at Chattanooga following the battle; but much to Confederate dismay, Bragg once again failed to follow up his success. Following his defeat by Grant at Missionary Ridge and Lookout Mountain, he resigned on 27 November and went to Richmond.

62. From Thomasville to Monticello was a twenty-two-mile trip and took all night. Station 4 was about three miles southeast of Monticello on the Pensacola & Georgia Railroad, and Panola was a few miles east-southeast of Station 4. Panola was a local name, the settlement consisting of only four families, and Monticello was the nearest town and post office.

[Rebecca] **Sept 25, 1863.** . . . *I have some fever through the day, but it abates towards night. Sister Mary nursing me all day—Caroline comes in the afternoon expecting to take me to her house. After 8 o'clk when all are preparing for bed and I am feeling exhausted from fever, Willie arrives! The surprise excites me a good deal and I pass a restless night.*

Sept 27, 1863. *Mr Tydings went in the morning to preach and be gone over night, Lou and I had a quiet day. Rosa had quite a fever.*

[Rebecca] **Sept 28, 1863.** . . . *I am feeling quite like myself again . . . Willie comes out to dinner and the afternoon passes merrily. I sit up until 10 o'clk, Willie leaves at 11 to take the hack for Lake City . . .*

[OCTAVIA STEPHENS TO WINSTON STEPHENS]

Panola Sept 28, 1863

My dear husband

. . . I had two gentlemen and a lady in the hack with me. I started under rather unfavorable circumstances as Rosa was taken with vomiting just before starting and I feared it might continue, and as she was feeling badly I had to hold her all the way which made me feel lame and badly fearing too I might get worse again, at the Depot at Monticello I came so near fainting I had to sit down on an old dirty salt sack. I arrived here safely but very much fatigued, but have improved much since the second day, I now feel better than I have since my weaving scrape and sincerely hope to keep so, but fear I never shall be as well again as I was last year, Rosa had fever last Friday and quite a high one yesterday, looks badly to day, I gave her a dose of oil this morning, but did not keep it down and will have to give another, I hope she will not have any more fevers, for there is no quinine here. I had to make my trip alone as Georgie was sick, we expect him here tomorrow, I hope he will get here safely, it is a troublesome little trip for one not accustomed to *going alone*.

I am so sorry you could not come here with me, this is a very pretty place, Mr Tydings and Lou both wished to see you . . . Loulie says she is a thousand times obliged to you for leaving me here another week, I dread starting off again and by myself, and I am so afraid something may prevent your meeting me at Baldwin, but the Lord seems to have favored us all through and I hope he will continue to favor us, I am anxious to get home again if it is true that we are to have an invasion, and am anxious to hear from home as I have not heard one word from there since I left, I hope the Yankees will not visit there before us . . .

Rosa sends a kiss and accept lots of love from

Yr loving

Wife

[Rebecca] **Oct 1, 1863.** *A fine rain last night has laid the dust—Our visitors leave soon after breakfast.*[63]

[REBECCA BRYANT TO HENRY BRYANT]

Thomasville Oct 2, 1863

My dear Henry,

... I feel very anxious about you, fearing that you are sick—I have not heard from you since we *parted at Waldo*—and I have been here 3 weeks to-night. When I last wrote you, I was just up from an attack of fever—a pretty bad one—But I am now quite well again—I am sorry to say that George had another slight chill and high fever *to-day*—He is up now however.

Willie stayed here with us three days and went to see Davis, he found him sick in bed with fever and staid with him until he was better—We expect Willie to-morrow night. You see we have all been taking our turn with the fever ...

I think you will like this place when you have been here a little while—George will not go to cousin Loulie's until he is stronger—

Company has come and the mail is about to close—so goodbye my dear boy. I hope to see [you] before long—Much love to Mrs Stephens and family—from

Your affectionate Mother

[WINSTON STEPHENS TO OCTAVIA STEPHENS]

Camp Cooper Oct 3, 1863

My Dear Wife

... I have a letter for you from Tina and I had one from Henry, he says he will meet us in the Buggy as it is now suspect but I learn through him that no hauling will be done before I get home, owing to the rains and waggon. no hogs were up when he wrote and not much of any thing else done on account of the heavy rain. He says he will hurry up and have all done he can by the time I get there. I fear I will be so much hurried that I will have to leave lots of things or only go on your return as far as Lake City. But we will see when we get home. I have written him to hire some waggons by the time I come and if he can all will yet be well ...

I will have from the 7th to the 28th. and in that time I hope we can get off the most valuable things, and the rest we will lock up and trust Providence ... love and a kiss to my two Rose buds.

Yours as ever
Winston Stephens

63. This is the last entry from Rebecca's diaries.

Oct 6, 1863. *Left Loulie's directly after breakfast. Mr Tydings took me in the buggy to the cars. Found a letter at the Depot from Winston. Arrived at Lake City about 4 p.m. Davis met me and spent the evening with me and gave me a letter from Winston, he also recd. one from Mother.*

Oct 7, 1863. *Met Winston at Baldwin and we then traveled together. Swep and Levi Branning were also on the cars.*[64] *We found Henry and Burrel at Waldo with the buggy and wagon. Winston and I took the buggy and went with Mr Greeley to his house to spend the night, arrived there at 10 p.m. had a terribly dark ride.*

Oct 8, 1863. *Left Mr Greeley's after breakfast and arrived home between 8 and 9 o'clk after another terrible dark and rough ride ... Henry and Burrel ahead of us.*

Oct 12, 1863. *Winston sent off two wagon loads to Waldo, he went a short way with them, Henry killed two turkeys.*

Oct 18, 1863. *Henry and the negroes left quite early for Waldo. Winston and I went to Clarks to stay until we leave. about 12 o'clk heard the ox team had broken down.*

Oct 19, 1863. *Winston, Clark and I left a little after daylight for Waldo, found the ox team at the Ferry nearly ready to start ...*

[REBECCA BRYANT TO HENRY BRYANT]

Thomasville Oct 19, 1863

My dear Henry,

I recd. a letter from Tina yesterday saying that . . . you want to continue Alligatoring with Mr Stephens sometime longer, and to attend to killing the hogs etc . . . I must say the thought is very painful to me and at first I thought I could not consent to it. But if Winston and Davis think the object to be gained is sufficient . . . I will yield my wishes to yours and try to be patient until the time arrives for you to come . . .

I suppose Winston is coming here with Tivie, from what he wrote to Aunt Julia. I had been counting on seeing you too, but am afraid to hope for it now. George will probably go down to Monticello in order to go to Cousin Loulie's on the team which is to go down on Friday next for Winston's baggage. I will be disappointed if he does not see you but I have prepared him for it and we must look forward hopefully to the 1st. of another year.

Dear Henry do not let *anything* make you forget what I have said about breaking the 4th. commandment and never omit your prayers at night if you are com-

---

64. David Levi Branning was a younger brother of Jessup Branning of Middleburg.

pelled to in the morning.⁶⁵ Those who would ridicule you for such a course are not worth your regard—I always remember you when I pray and hope you do the same—With a thousand kisses I remain most lovingly

Mother

Oct 20, 1863. We overtook the wagons and all stopped . . . and took our dinner and rested about two hours. When we got in sight of Waldo we found that Winston's haversack and my basket were missing, we then drove back two miles and he left me at a house and he went on horseback three or four miles back but did not find either. We arrived at Waldo at 8 o'clk in eve.

Oct 21, 1863. My 22nd. birthday. Left Waldo at 8 o'clk a.m. stopped several hours at Baldwin . . . arrived at Lake City at dark went to the Hancock House . . .

Oct 22, 1863. Tina's 32nd birthday. We staid over at Lake City. In the morn Winston was out attending to business so I made Rosa a pair of shoes. Henry and Burrel etc arrived about 4 o'clk p.m. with the wagon, Davis came after supper feeling badly . . .

Oct 23, 1863. Arrived at Thomasville at dark, found Aunt Julia sick . . . Met Georgie on his way to Lou's.

[WILLIE BRYANT TO DAVIS BRYANT]

near Chattanooga Oct 26, 1863

Dear Davis

It has been impossible for me to write you earlier, but from my letter to Mother, which she undoubtedly forwarded to you, you have learned that I am back again in the ranks. It goes devilish rough with me at first, particularly as the weather has been horrible ever since my return, rainy, cold, and windy, until to-day, and our Brigade is without tents—I have suffered greatly with rheumatism, and I am convinced will be unable to stand the service; I shall continue on long enough to establish the fact and a willingness to try it, and then on Surgeons certificate from Dr. Steele get a good situation and get out of it.⁶⁶ I feel sure I will be able to do so,

---

65. The fourth commandment is "Remember that thou keep holy the Sabbath day."
66. Willie transferred back to Company H, Third Florida Infantry at this time, but his motives remain unknown. He implies here that he has hopes of gaining a medical discharge from Captain Holmes Steele, who had transferred to the Medical Department as a surgeon in May 1862, but he had no intention of quitting the fight. He was looking for a better position than he had had at Bragg's headquarters but was not successful in his quest.

tho' I don't encourage the idea with Mother too strong for fear of disappointment; a little service now will do me good . . .

We have been out on picket twice since my return and are just off to-day; We go 1 ½ miles and in good weather will be a pleasant change.

Our videttes and the Yanks' are posted about 200 yds apart, but all comunication is now prohibited. I see no new plans. The Yanks have shelled 3 times lately, but can do little or no harm, our Regiment is just out of range I think — 2½ miles . . .

The 3r. is reduced to nothing, and no account for want of proper officers.[67]

The Yanks are thick as bees in and around Chattanooga. Our lines extend in a semi circle at the distance of 2 ½ miles from the river to Lookout Mountain on the river to the S.W.

We get just enough rations to make out on corn meal, poor beef, and 2 in 7 flour and bacon; I can make out on as little as any one, have a good appetite, and am not subject to diarrhoea, so can get along very well — I think of nothing of special interest to add and will close and go up to Hd. Qrs. . . . Good bye for now —

Yrs always Affctly
Willie

[REBECCA BRYANT TO WILLIE BRYANT]

At Aunt Julia's Oct 27, 1863

My dear Willie,

. . . I cannot but feel sad at the change in your situation, and think you are not *pleased*, altho' your consideration for me induces you to pretend you are. The Winter is fast approaching and you must necessarily suffer many privations — I know you will bear them patiently, even cheerfully, but still you have to bear them — I remember that your precious life is no more certain, no more exempt from casualties at Hd Qrs. than in the field — I will endeavor to imitate your philosophy and look with hopeful trust to the "Giver of all Good" . . .

Henry will stay at Dr Adams until we know whether Winston can get the place in the country — If we do, Winston wishes him to remain with us. He has gone to-day into the country to buy corn and fodder for Winston — He is afterward to attend to hauling his goods from Monticello. We expect to hear from the owner of the place in a week. I believe I have mentioned all that is of any importance or real interest. I neglected to say I was in no need of money — Davis sent

---

67. The Third Florida Infantry was drastically reduced by heavy casualties at Perryville and Chickamauga. After additional losses at Missionary Ridge, it was reorganized and combined with other units to form the western Florida Brigade.

me $50 and Winston sold things from the Office to the same amount—Henry has over $100 of his own earnings. God bless you

Mother

[WINSTON STEPHENS TO OCTAVIA STEPHENS]

Baldwin Oct 29, 1863

My Dear Wife

I write you again from this place as I find time having failed to make connection with the train going to Camp Cooper. We go down to day on a Special train. I will now give you an account of my trip. I found in the Hack a Lady and Gentleman and three small girls, the smallest about Rosa's age. We had rather a pleasant trip none of us being very disagreeable and we reached Monticello about 7 o'clock a.m. I started on at once for Depot to see and make arrangements about my baggage, I could not tell if all the baggage was right as it was piled in such a way that I could not see what was there. I made arrangements to have the goods and mules cared for until Henry called for them . . . I did not stop at Live Oak but made the luncheon do me to Lake City. I got a room at Hancock's house and spent a pleasant evening with Davis. I find he has not completed the arrangements for a transfer [to my company] but every thing is progressing finely. He has obtained the consent of the Officer of the other Company and will soon have his papers complete . . . If you want Joe before you learn if you can get the place I suppose Mr. Van will let you take him deducting his hire for the time you have him . . . Tell Franky the first time you see her that I hire Burrel and Jane for one year from the time she gets them as I may want to farm the year following and will want them in the Winter to make the necessary arrangements.[68] Mr Van takes the boys on the same terms and he understands it that way, and the parties furnish the negroes with clothing, shoes etc for this Winter and next Summer and I furnish for next Winter. You had better get the Dr or Mr Everette to tell you where you can get a pair of shoes for Rach and Sarah and the children can stay by the fire and will not require shoes and you had better get the two pair made as soon as possible. Make your arrangement to have a Loom at once so as to save money on clothing. You can advise with Your Mother about every thing and do what ever you determine is best and not wait to hear from me . . .

We are expecting the Cars so I must close. Love to all and many kisses and much love for yourself and Rosa from your devoted Husband

Winston Stephens

68. Winston leased Tom, Joe, Jess, and Mose to Elijah Vann for a year, but Tivie got Joe returned. Burrel, Big Jane, and Jane were leased to Frankie Sharpe while Sarah, Jane, Mary Polly, and Rachael stayed with or near Tivie. Vann was a small planter; in 1860 he and his wife, Rosey, had seven children and eight slaves and lived near Thomasville.

[OCTAVIA STEPHENS TO WINSTON STEPHENS]

Oct 30, 1863

My dear husband

I received your short but welcome letter yesterday . . . I guess I miss you more here than at home, I say home, I have no home . . . I went with Aunt Caroline to Mr Adams and went by that gloomy looking place we are trying to get, I was a little disappointed in the looks I was as usual prepared for *bad* but I believe it was worse than I expected, it is a framed house but such a one. I hope the inside is better looking than the outside, and such a mean road to go there, I suppose Aunt Julia would tell me to be thankful that there were thousands worse off, the house looks as though a good gust of wind would blow it down it is so old . . .

Burrel and Jane are still at Grand Mothers and of course will be there until Monday if not longer, no news from Frankie except that she had not heard a word from anyone since she went home, the day after you left Burrel and Jane were both quite sick with diarhoea, but were quite well to day and Burrel working for Grand Mother diggin up and transplanting strawberries and other things. Jane does all she can find to do, has waited on Mother in her sickness as little Mary was sick. Aunt Julia is very much pleased with them, but Jane says Grand Mother is always talking to her about her grim looks. Jane said to me "but Miss you know thats my common looks, I aint mad, I aint grim" she seemed very cheerful, only anxious to get to Frankie's. I hear that Rachel is doing well but have not heard whether or not Dr Adams is going to keep her, when Sarah came here she came without her meal or anything to eat, and when I came she was spinning and Jane in the pinder patch . . .

I hope when I write again to have better news to tell of our affairs. I hope I shall soon get some of your nice long affectionate letters to cheer up my lonely and homesick heart . . .

Well my dear I will bid you good night. God bless and protect you is the constant prayer of

Your loving
Wife

P.S. Day after tomorrow is the anniversary of our wedding day I wonder if you will think of it. I guess not.

Nov 1, 1863. The 4th anniversary of my wedding day. All went to Mr Adams expecting to go to church, but there was none, we spent the day there. Henry came with a wagon load of our things from Monticello just before ten.

[WINSTON STEPHENS TO OCTAVIA STEPHENS]

Camp Cooper Nov 4, 1863

My Dear Wife

... I hope I may get a good long letter from you tomorrow and hope every thing is progressing finely with you all up there. I would have been so much better satisfied if I could have remained a week longer and had every thing arranged. I fear we are calling on Mr Everett too much, he is getting old and requires his energy in his own matters, give them as little trouble as possible and call on Henry, he is young and willing to do and has an interest as he is more directly concerned, be guarded and never say any thing that will in any way wound the feelings of Your Aunt or Mr Everett and have Jane keep from interfering in their household business as she might take some things and cause hard feelings. You will understand what I mean to convey as I want all things to go on smoothley. I send a deed for you to sign and have it Witnessed by two persons, you will sign opposite the seal and they will sign where witness is written and send back to me by first mail[69] ... Give love to all friends etc and accept lots for yourself and Rosa from you ever aff

Husband

Winston Stephens

[OCTAVIA STEPHENS TO WINSTON STEPHENS]

Nov 6, 1863

My very dear husband

I received your letter, with shoes and limes, and two bars sweet soap ... I am much obliged for the things, the shoes are nicely fixed, the limes very acceptable as Mother and Rosa are both having fevers, and Mother drinking boneset. Mother had fever the day after you left, and broke it for a few days, but was taken down again out here, the day after she came, and Rosa with her, Mother is very much reduced, oh how many times a day I wish we never had left Welaka, I dread my turn every day, but have been very well excepting one day and night and that was only vomiting spells and headache, I think no fever ...

After supper, Well my dear I have just finished or not just finished for I have put Rosa to bed and she has gone to sleep with a little lime in her hand, how I do hope she will not have fever tomorrow, she went to bed in fine humor after worrying me much at supper, but I started to tell you of my supper, I thought of

---

69. This was the deed to the 60 acres called the "new ground" that Tivie owned; Winston sold their interest in the plantation, including the 60 acres, for $500 to Elijah W. Cannon on 12 December 1863.

you many times and wished you were here to help enjoy it and wondered if you had any like it, spare ribs, sausage meat, crackin and bread, things I know you love . . . I believe I wrote you that Sarah was spinning for Aunt Caroline, but the cotton gave out and as I could not get any beef I sent to Aunt Julia for bacon, and she let me have some of the soldiers. I sent to her for six or eight pounds but she sent me sixteen, and as she had cut a middling for me and would not like to cut it again I took it, for I thought it would keep even if I did get beef, and she let me have it at $1. a lb when it is selling at 1.50 and $2, and hard to get. Aunt Caroline was out of bacon, and to day she gave me two *heaping half* bushels of potatoes for [a] little over a lb of bacon so I have potatoes for Sarah too, but I am very economical with all, I give a little of each, instead of regular rations. Aunt C— gives her greens sometimes, and I am going to take Uncle Jared's advice and get a few peas to help out the meat, she has enough meat for this week of what you bought before you left, so I have not bought any more, I hope she will now be fixed . . .

Frankie came the very night that I wrote your letter and sent Burrel and Jane the next morning, and she came out here and staid until Tuesday, you dont know how glad they were to go, and you dont know how disagreeable Grand Mother made it to them and all by her fussing, but she got a good deal out of Burrel before he left, but the day I came out here, after you left, I left Mother with fever on, and Burrel and Jane quite sick with Diarhoea, but gave them a dose before I left and fifty cents to get some rice to boil soft and eat, and they soon recovered. Frankie took their baggage with her as Henry met the wagon and mules and brought a load the Sunday before, he has not been any more as he had to see about getting corn before hauling any more as he can not buy corn on the road, he got only fifteen and a half bushels and hauled it twelve miles and some fodder, two dollars a bushel, and borrowed Uncle Jared's wagon, ours has gone to have new fore wheels before hauling any more, and will cost about seventy dollars . . .

Well another pleasant thing last Sunday, Tom and the boys came to see Sarah, and to me complaining that Mr Van had whipped Mose for nothing, and that he said he had hired them cheap but they should work double to pay him, and he was going to take the bark off their back etc and so on, well that made me mad for I know Mose is a good boy, and I dont and wont like it, but the others dont believe it, and Mr Van told Aunt Mary of it and very differently said they were trying themselves, that they would stand and look over the fence, and that he spoke to Mose several times before he would mind, and that they talk to him as though they were white, asking him why he did this and that, but said they were smart boys, they say he *feeds well* but all the time they are eating hurries them, I tell you all that you may think as you wish, but I cant think it altogether the boys for I dont believe they are so mean, and could make up all those stories, I know he must talk that way to them, says he dont want Guinea niggers he wants Carolina niggers. Well I think I have given you a long enough string of my troubles for this time. I guess you are tired enough of it, so I'll try and say something else, but I tell you I get terribly downhearted sometimes . . .

I believe I wrote that Willie had returned to his regiment. Well my darling I must go to bed but hope my dreams of you to night may be pleasant, for I love to dream pleasantly of you when I can not have you with me, for I love my husband although I do not show it, and I think he must love me or he would not put up so well with my badness, I often think what a blessed thing it is I have such a good husband, and pray that we may never be any less happy. Good night.

Your loving
Wife

Nov 12, 1863. *Winston surprised us about 8 o'clk in the evening.*

[REBECCA BRYANT TO DAVIS BRYANT]

At Mr Everitt's Nov 15, 1863

My dear Davis

You may be sure we were surprised and delighted to see Winston on Thursday night . . .

I am very glad you are to be in Winston's Co. since you are obliged to return to the field. I hope the change in your duties may benefit your health. Nevertheless it is unpleasant to reflect that *all three* must be again exposed to the privations and dangers of this Winter's campaign. It is hardly to be expected that Florida will escape a visit from the enemy much longer, and I know that neither you or Winston are likely to keep out of danger . . . I believe too that we have as much to fear from the climate of Tennessee in Willie's case as from the shots of the enemy. I do hope he will, as you say, try to get some other position before long . . .

But I can only commend you both to the guardian care of Him who is all-wise as well as All-merciful, and pray that He will give us strength to do, and to bear, his whole will and pleasure. I have been writing to your father, that Winston may have a letter to send in case there shd. be a flag of truce. Not a word from him since 28th. of June! I think we must hear something soon. If he shd. come to Florida this winter do'nt encourage his coming up here—they say it will not do— Perhaps it could be arranged for me to go down and meet him.

I am glad on Tivie's account that Winston paid us this visit—She was troubled about getting corn and several other matters and was quite discouraged—We have two places in view in the country—I hope we shall succeed in getting one for living in town wd. be enourmously expensive . . . Tivie and Henry send much love, so does

Mother

[AUGUSTINA STEPHENS TO OCTAVIA STEPHENS]

Welaka Nov 15, 1863

My Dear Tivie

... You dont know how I miss you, as the Post says I feel like one who "left alone" without a friend or relation, on earth who cares one cent about my weal or woe, perhaps some brighter prospect may dawn upon us if the awful War ever comes to a close, my nature is not a desponding one or I should die of the hours. Clark arrived the second day after leaving you at Waldo, (on Thursday), on Saturday we went over to your place to bring the closet and peas, we found the Groundnuts *all* spoiled they are perfectly decayed, he immediately emptied them on the floor hoping there might be a few saved from the bunch, but they are all lost, those that look sound outwardly, when opened are soft and the skin slips as though they had been parched, their being put up damp in a closed room caused it ... Old Taylor is very happy and contented at his new home with us, I am glad to have him as he is to be depended upon. Clark tried to get him to follow him yesterday as a protector for the waggons but he "treed" something soon after leaving and then came home, for several days he would go back and forth, I suppose until he became convinced of the *final move* ...

I hope ere this you have all your things with you I think you will be better satisfied in the country, even if the place is a little objectionable you certainly can live cheaper and Henrys being with you will be a great help in hunting, gardening and lots of other ways, I only wish you more in reach of my fine "Turnip patch" you know I planted for you and I, but you got *proud* and concluded it was ungenteel to eat greens so you would go and get "flour goins and chicken fixins." Tell Henry I think of him nearly every day when a large dish of Turnip greens comes in and how he "berry lubs um" and tell him he is in honour bound to come back to get some oil to burn this winter, he and Clark were going right off and get me a plenty if I would not keep any out of the last they sold and my part has not come yet, we miss him *lots* and his partner grumbles and moans every day that is warm and pleasant, because he has to leave, tell your Mother she must let him come back next spring and stay part of the Summer anyhow ...

Clark has killed eight turkeys within the past fortnight, when will we enjoy Turkey together again? I fear not for a very very long time ... Ever Yours aff

Tina

Nov 16, 1863. In the morning Uncle Jared and Winston went to look at Mr McKinnon place.[70] *Winston went to town in the afternoon to take the hack tomorrow to return to camps . . .*[71]

[JULIA FISHER TO WILLIE BRYANT]

Thomasville Nov 16, 1863

Dearest Willie:

. . . Winston came up Thursday night and leaves tonight: they have a good deal of difficulty in finding a suitable place in the country, Tivy wont live in town and *she is right:* everything is scarce and high, *very* . . . one thing certain we are better off here than in most any section, and cannot expect to get along these times without care and anxiety: all share it: I only want to know you dear boys are comfortable: *if this could be:* it is only for your sakes we suffer; how can we forget a moment how you all are situated . . . God bless you! let us hope that in the future brighter days may obliterate the remembrances of these darker ones . . . but dearest boy let us remember that we cannot do this in our own strength — the best and bravest hearts that ever beat, trusted to a higher power than *self* to sustain them,

[REBECCA BRYANT TO WILLIE BRYANT, ADDED TO THE ABOVE LETTER]

My dear, dear Willie, it is a very long time since I wrote you a line but I wrote by proxy (Tivie) last week. I was then "under treatment" of Dr Adams — was up the next day and have been improving ever since. Yesterday afternoon Aunt C — and I rode in to see Aunt Julia — We found her in bed, looking miserably. She was sick on Monday when she began this letter, but would not give up until she was nearly crazy with the pain in her head — She is now much better, but the Dr has forbidden her writing at all until she is stronger and therefore she requested me to bring this with me and finish it — She says she wanted to write a *great deal* more but was obliged to take to her bed . . . The wagon is being repaired and next week Henry will begin hauling the household goods which were left at Monticello when they all came through. He has already brot. up one load of trunks etc but the wagon gave out. He will have four or five more and then he has about 200 bushels of corn to haul from the other side of Thosvlle. which will keep him busy . . .

I am most anxious to hear again from you Goodbye dear Willie. Take all the care of yourself possible for my sake.

Mother

---

70. Either J. N. McKinnon, Kenneth McKinnon, or S. R. McKinnon. The former was a merchant; the latter two were planters. The most likely owner is Kenneth, since he was listed nearest to the Adams and Fisher families in the 1860 census, and he was by far the wealthiest of the family.

71. This was the last time Winston and Tivie saw each other; he tried numerous times in the following months to obtain a furlough or short leave but was not successful.

[WILLIE BRYANT TO REBECCA BRYANT]

Camp 3d. Fla. Regt. Nov 21, 1863

My dear Mother—

Tivie's letter came to hand a few days since bearing the bad news of your being sick again; which I am most sorry too for I am afraid that the season is so far advanced now, and your fever not broken, that you will be liable to relapses all winter . . .

But now for the good news! The same mail that brought Tivie's letter brought one from Major George R. Fairbanks, Qt. Master at Atlanta offering me a situation with him if I could furnish a Certificate of disability for field service;[72] the certificate I have sent him, and he will probably apply for my detail immediately and I [will] know the results in a few days; I will write Col. Brent a note by way of advancing matters; the situation offered is one I would prefer to any I know, and unless they are unjust at Hd Qrs I will get it; however, there is many a slip etc; I am convinced I am not equal to a winter's campaign, and one thing is certain, if not I shall leave the field in spite of the a.a.g. office . . .

My object is accomplished, and as the weather is too uncomfortable excuse more this time.

Ever Affectionately
Willie

[OCTAVIA STEPHENS TO WINSTON STEPHENS]

Nov 27, 1863

My dear husband

. . . I feel glad to think that Davis is with you, but am sorry he is sick so much I hope your Dr will cure him now and that the exercise of Camp life will agree with him. I am so thankful that you keep so well, you and I are certainly blessed with health now when Rosa and so many of the others are sick . . .

Henry and Joe left this morning for Monticello, we thought the weather had cleared off but to day is cloudy again, the mules have appeared sick for some days, fell off and would not eat, but seemed better this morning. Jennie was much improved yesterday, Henry thought it was from eating sugar cane tops . . .

My dear you do not spell Uncle Jared's name right, it is Jared Everitt. I hardly know whether or not to expect a letter from you to day as you seemed to think the last so near the one before, but hope I may have the pleasure of getting one. I want you to describe to me how the inside of your house is fixed, I often think I

---

72. Major George R. Fairbanks served as the Atlanta quartermaster for most of the war. How Willie met him is not known since Fairbanks never lived in Florida, but it was probably through a relative, Jason Fairbanks, previously mentioned.

would like to look in and see how you are fixed, and how do you spend your Sundays, they are very dull here, do you read the bible as much as you did awhile back? or have you dropped it? I guess you'll think I am trying to make you good when I ought to be better myself, but I want you to keep good, I know I am not as good as I used to be . . .

Well my "Lord and Master" (do you think you are?) I must close for this time . . . I send you a Wife's devotion from Your

Unworthy

Wife

[REBECCA BRYANT TO WILLIE BRYANT]

At Mr Everitt's Nov 29, 1863

My dear, dear Willie,

. . . The Dr brought me a new medicine yesterday which he has tried with much success in elusive cases of fever—It contains a great deal of Arsenic—I have heard of it before, and shall take it according to directions, for I am uneasy of being so often burdensome to others, and of no assistance in any way. Besides, I am so tallow-faced my *beauty* is *spoilt*. I hope we may be able to send you a pair of gloves in Decr. But you will need your mittens before that time. Tivie sends much love and Rosa a kiss for you.

After waiting a fortnight for the wagon to be repaired, Henry started on Friday at 7 oclk a.m. with Joe, to bring up a load of Winston's goods from Monticello. The weather looked threatening but had been so a day or two and as all was ready it was thought best he shd. go. But it began to rain about 10 o'clk and in the afternoon it *poured*. He pushed on until nearly dark and finally put up at a house 3 miles this side of Monticello, where he got dry, had a *good supper* and good bed—but Saturday morng. proved as impropitious as Friday, so after breakfast he was obliged to leave the wagon and he and Joe took another pouring rain on mule-back all the way and reached here about 2 o'clk. To-day it is clearing off with a cold wind—and Tivie is having provisions cooked for them to start at daylight tomorrow and try it again. Henry will learn every hill on that road sure before he has done hauling the other four loads, then there will be two or three more to haul the last week in Decr . . . Henry does not seem to have any better opinion of this state than you have of Tennessee—there is no place like Florida for him—It would have saved a good deal of trouble if we could have left the furniture stored at Monticello, but the keeper of the warehouse threatened Winston with double storage, if he did not move them . . . Many kisses and prayers for my dear Willie from

Mother

[WINSTON STEPHENS TO OCTAVIA STEPHENS]

Camp Cooper Nov 30, 1863

My Dear Wife

... I write this earley as I expect to start out on a hog hunt and will not return in time to write on Wednesday. You may think strange of my going on a hog hunt from here and I will explain! Some hogs that was left in the neck are allowed to be killed by any one that feels like it, and I have concluded to catch a few and put them up and make some bacon to help you out up there and at the same time furnish something to eat down here ...

We had Inspection to day and the Maj's horse became restive and blistered his hands and I had to act in his place. The Maj throws nearly all of the duties of the Post on me. I have to act on all the dress parades and nearly all the Inspections. I am beginning to think him *lazy*. The Yanks are deserting quite rapidley from Fernandina, as 15 have come over in three installments, yesterday, four came over and they say there are about 800 in all in Fernandina and some 150 of them are black. They also state there are about 125 that will desert the first chance they get. We hear they are fighting in Chattanooga and I do hope God will give us the Victory. I have my doubts as Braggs force has been weakened by the Knoxville expedition. If we should lose that fight it will be a great calamity. We all have friends and relatives there and some must fall as sacrifice, but I hope their lives may be spared. I suppose you have rec'd my three letters ere this. I am sorry Henry has been so much disappointed about the waggon but hope he has got it and the hauling is progressing finely. I am in fine health and have a good apetite. Davis is rapidly improving and has received the appointment of Post Sergt Maj. This will give him quite an easy time and no exposure and enough time for exorcise to make him healthy. It is quite Cold and we have a nice fire burning and Davis and Lieut Shedd are reading while I write, we have quite a cozy time. Davis sleeps with me and make a tolerably good bed fellow, but I had rather have a Sister of his with me, and I often think how pleasant it would be to make the change. I hope Davis will be able to spend christmas with you and bring you something to eat ... Good night my dear and may angels guard you Love and kisses to you and Rosa

Winston

[OCTAVIA STEPHENS TO WINSTON STEPHENS]

Dec 4, 1863

My dear husband

... I am now obliged to tell you that that prospect [for the house] is all gone, and we are as bad off and worse than ever, when Uncle Jared went at the appointed time to finish up the bargain . . . found that someone else had secured it from some one else before our application. I declare it is too bad, we could have gone into the house so soon, for the McKinnons are going to move the last of next week. Well Uncle Jared and I went to look at a vacant house which he knew was not *nice,* but better than none, and intended going right on [to] the man to engage it but we found the house tumbling down so did not go any further . . . if we do not get that [one] Uncle Jared says our only chance is to build a one room house down by Sarah's house on his land, but I do not like that prospect at all, it will be so expensive to build and take so long, then we can only have a poor little garden and live so uncomfortably *in one room,* and the worst part give up Henry, Rachael, and Joe, the mules and wagon, and have no place for my Loom or stores, but I see no alternative, I suppose I must grin and bear it, and "look on the bright side" but where is any bright side—I have seen precious little appearance of any since I have been here. I wish you were here to help plan, I would do what you say more cheerfully but I feel as though you could fix to your notion better, but if we can not get an answer from you, I think if we have to build it will cost about as much in the end as it would have done to live in town . . .

Henry bought a pair of shoes for Joe from a black man on the road that are nice ones, the man charges six dollars for them, but as Henry had nothing but a ten dollar [bill], and the negroe no change, he gave him that rather than lose them, and said if they met again on the road they would square up, the man was hauling cotton. I was glad of them even at that price for it saved me twenty dollars on a pair for him . . . I received a long letter from Tina with your last, it is too bad the Pinders spoiled. I wish I had brought some and some peas, for I have not been able to get any yet, and fear will not, and if we get a place will need them. Henry feels as badly about the state of affairs as I do. Mose and Tom say they get along nicely now, but Rachael very much dissatisfied . . .

My health is better at present than I ever expected it to be again, my back has ached a good deal the past two or three days, but I must expect some of that for the next four months. I wish I knew whether I was to have pleasure or sorrow at the end of that time, at times I anticipate much pleasure but fear. Well my dear it is growing quite late so I will close. I hope to get your letter tomorrow.

We have the *biggest kind* of frosts and ice here. Give my love to Davis and for yourself accept the whole devotion of

Your aff. Wife

Sat. p.m. My dear I am happy to say I received your letter just before dinner I am very glad you are in such good health . . . I am glad you like Davis as a bedfellow, I hope you'll be satisfied with my *brother* and not get into *anybody else's sister's bed* . . .

lovingly your Wife.

[WINSTON STEPHENS TO OCTAVIA STEPHENS]

Camp Cooper Dec 4, 1863

My Dear Wife

... I was absent when [your letter] came but got in camp that night tired and sore from my hog hunt but yours was indeed refreshing. It is satisfactory to know that though the whole world should desert me I have one friend that will have faith and love me stil. The relation between man and wife is binding by Law but my feelings bind me more than all the Law in the world. When the natures of the Twain are at all congenial nothing save Death can seperate them ... I wish you would rent the field near the house containing about 50 acres if you can get it, I think Mr McKennan sayed it was one mile from the house. I presume the house question is fixed and settled by this time ... I hope that now the Waggon is in order that the team will go constantly until the corn fodder and the things at Monticello are hauled as it costs money every day ... get your Loom going as soon as you can as every thing is going *up! up!! up!!!*.

I had good luck on the hog hunt as I got 16 head to divide with three of us, and some of them very fine, my share will make me some 4 or 5 hundred pounds of pork when they are made fat ...

I hope Rosa is quite well again. Love to all and much love to yourself Rosa from your ever

Aff Husband
Winston Stephens

[WINSTON STEPHENS TO OCTAVIA STEPHENS]

Camp Cooper Dec 8, 1863

My Dear Wife

As Wednesdays are days of business I will attempt this p.m. to gratify your *Womans* curiosity, by giving you as near as I can the interior of our mansion etc and hope you may feel satisfied with the effort though it will be so incomplete. Imagine a common log house about 14 feet by 16 (about as high as our kitchen was at Rose Cottage) with the door in one end and the chimney in the other, built of logs like negroes generally build their chimneys and back and hobs made out of clay to protect the timber. The entrance of the fire place is about one third of the size of the end of the house. My door fronts to Fernandina being about an East course, on the right as you enter is my bed and at the foot of my bed is the one occupied by Lieut Shedd and Swep which reaches near the fire place, leaving just room for a chair. My bed is made by having a hole through the floor for a fork which makes one corner and the poles extend from that to the cracks and on those poles some plank make the foundation and on that rests my matrass and in front I have a pole fixed up to keep off intruders. Over the head of my bed hangs Davis' Carpet Bagg and on the back of the bed hangs my hat, at the foot of Lt Shedds bed on a pin is Sweps saddle b'gs and in the corner behind the chair is some 11 Rifles and 3 swords stacked in the corner, over the fire place Swep keeps his soap and over the door Davis keeps his and I keep my bottle of oil and a can of flee Powders for my pup. To the left as you enter is the glass, a Towell, neck tie, vest, my spurs and sword and in the corner is my shot gun, broom and 2 other swords, on the left side near the joist is a shelf on which I keep my saddle b'gs, hat, cap, candle stick and Lt S—keeps his sadle bags and some one has a bible. I dont know the owner as I never see them read it and under that shelf are 8 pegs, on the 1st. my haversack with contents 2d. pants of mine and Davis 3d. my clothes for wash, 4th. 2 rifles, 5 Davis cap and Lt S— a shirt, 5th a pr pants of Lt S— 6th. my Homespun Vest and Sweps Jacket, 7th. canteens etc. next is a small table with a writing desk upon which I write and on it is my Valise and some military books and my cap is off of my *head* and on the desk. In the desk are my papers and Books of Co etc. and in the corner next the fire place are 4 more rifles and 2 swords and some Haversacks and a pair of spurs of Davis. Under my bed I have a trunk, a box and some loose things and under the other bed Lt S—has 2 trunks and keeps a keg of powder etc and under the desk is a box of cartridges, on the floor near the wall the shoes, Boots etc are Strewn promiscuouly. We have 2 chairs, one bench upon which I sit while I am writing and a small box that one sits upon making four seats. One of us sweeps out once in the day generally in the morning after we feed our horses and ourselves. You cant conceive what a dirty house we live in but it cant be any better under the circumstances and the chimney is not high enough and when the wind blows as it has the past two days the Soot comes down and covers every thing. It would not do to have a scolding wife in such a house. You know the old saying? You may think from what I have said that I have no soap but I keep my soap in my Valise, under lock and key and I think Lieut Shedd does the same. I make a practise of bathing twice a week, so you see I keep my person clean if I dont my house and I sweep twice to any of the others once. I will give you our usual position at night. I sit on the left of the fire place, Lt Shedd on the right and Swep and Davis in the front between the bed and desk leaving no room for visitors. We generally read or I do and the others are engaged in a game of Chess. Sometimes one reads and the rest listen. We are pritty clever sort of fellows and behave as we should save now and then Lt S— swears and Swep and Lt S— make their pipes. I hope this will suffice, tomorrow I will write you. Love

Winston

[AUGUSTINA STEPHENS TO OCTAVIA STEPHENS]

Welaka Dec 9, 1863

My own Dear Tivie

... How pleasant my dear Tivie would it be if we could live near each other once more, where we might have some of our old cosy talks, I want to be near you and give you a whipping for being low spirited although I really feel very much for you for I know by experience what it is to feel as you do at times, no one knows how I used to feel before Charles was born and you know what a good time (if there is any good) I had, always try and look on the bright side and think how happy you will be with your little treasure, you cannot be sick at a better season of the year, you will have good medical attention and lots of kind friends around you, but I know there will not be one more anxious and interested in your welfare than I will be, you say you think I *like* you almost as well as you *love* me, you know I *really love* you, next best on earth to my Husband and children, I do not make any other exceptions, as to my own immediate relatives, I do not think they feel much if any interest in my welfare, so "as the Poet says" I care for nobody since nobody cares for me, they profess a good deal, now and then, but I believe in people showing a little affection more than once a year. After reading your letter last night I sat for hours thinking of you, and could so easily picture you in your lovely little room, I would find myself composing a letter to you and I could not half sleep for thinking of you and talking with you in my imagination, I have spent two days over at your place week before last and sad enough did I feel to be there. Every thing has such a deserted appearance and reminded me so forcibly of the many pleasant days we have spent there together, the Cat seemed rejoiced to have us there, she was well fed those two days, she is looking very well, in fact better than I ever saw her, we killed twelve of your hogs, the Mill bunch have strayed off ...

Sunday Morning. Tomorrow I intend hanging up all the meat and hope by the time Wins wishes it carried over to Waldo that it will all be safely cured. we have had some *very* warm weather upon it, but it is all very sweet, I would have commenced smoking it before but on account of the weather was afraid to risk it. Clark has just received a letter from Wins ... I would *not* build, for you know Winston will never make that his permanent home (so he writes us) and to spend so much money on a plan and then leave and perhaps get nothing for your trouble ...

Aint you worn out with reading this awful dry letter and worst writing, the pen is bad enough to make a Preacher swear, I have to mark and keep it *chock* full of Ink or it wont write at all ... Goodbye my dear Tivie may heaven bless you is the sincere wish [of] yours

Tina

[WINSTON STEPHENS TO OCTAVIA STEPHENS]

Camp Cooper Dec 9, 1863

My Dear Wife

I promised yesterday I would write you to day and I now seat myself for that purpose. I am as well as man could wish and I have plenty to eat and clothes to keep me warm and If it was not for this curse resting on us in the shape of War I would be about as happy as mans lot allow him to be, but God in his wisdom has seen fit to punish the wickedness of this generation in this particular way and it becomes us to submit to his will and wait his time to restore us to peace. I do think that the wickedness of the people increases dailey and for that reason we may be engaged in this strife until we are all consumed. I try as much as my weak nature will permit to discharge my duties both to God and man. I know I fall far short of what is required, but the sin of our flesh is great and the good book says none are free from sin, no not one! You state in yours that you want to keep me good, I wish I could be good and keep so, but I fall far short of that desire. We can all do better by constant watchfulness over our acts and by checking the evil spirit when it attempts to get the better of our feelings and judgment. If we give up to our passions we will go on increasing in sin until our concience becomes callous and we do not feel the compunctions that we do at first. It is by constantly resisting temptation that we are able to overcome sin and temptation and at last it is no effort to do right. I dont mean that we can become perfect, because that is impossible. I do hope your letter of to day will inform that Rosa has continued well. She has had so much fever I am fearful it will undermine her constitution and ruin her health for good, but you speak of getting medicine and of its breaking up her fever and I hope permanently. She is certainly a good girl to take her medicine so well and you must kiss her for me and tell her Pa sends it because she is so good. I think by giving medicine about the time the fever usually returns might prevent its return . . .

You ask how I spend my Sundays? I first get up feed three horses, my hogs, then wash and comb my head then eat Breakfast then water horses and hogs, then have inspection of the Company, then I read the bible some and sometimes I ride out, then I feed etc at dinner and night, and then read again in the evening, sometimes I get dull, but usually I manage to have enough to do to keep off the blues . . . Davis is improving fineley and I think camp life will suit him. We are having the most disagreeable weather imaginable. Cold and rain for the past week, I am sorry I get worse every day in my writing. Sometimes I get vexed and almost give up.

Love to Mother, Henry and George and to your Uncle and Aunt Everitt and accept oceans of love for yourself and Dear Rosa. Good bye and God bless you. Davis sends love to all Your old Man

Winston

[OCTAVIA STEPHENS TO WINSTON STEPHENS]

Dec 12, 1863

My dear husband

... Henry brought the piano up this week ... I hated to see him start those bitter cold mornings before day, he has been four times, and I suppose will have to go as many more, if we get all we expect. I think he is more cheerful than he was, and I believe I do not grumble quite so much, although things still go anything but straight. Mother says she intends paying one third of the storage and freight ...

I am afraid we will never be able to go to Dunlawton or any where else in Florida when the war does end, it is such a job to move. If *I* should live to see the end of this war I fear I will be a widow and will have to knock about the first place I can get. If I knew the end of this war would find us as when it began, a living happy couple, I believe I would say go anywhere. Do you really think your feelings bind you more to me than Law? I do not wish to live to see the time when it is any different ...

Henry has just returned with thirteen bushels of corn, and a receipt for the money. The lumber for the Loom had not been *sawed* last Sunday, and my reel is not made yet, Sarah is down sick for the first time since we've been here, and just as she had begun to spin *for me* but I hope she will be up next week, I forgot to say how or in what condition our things came, most of the legs broken to pieces off of both beaureaus, and my mattrasses all about ruined and the two chairs scratched. I have not yet looked into anything but the beaureaus, the roll of bedclothes which contained a white bed spread, musquitoe net and several sheets mildewed. A rain came up just as they were taking the piano out of the wagon but it did not get wet much, it was cloudy all that day and kept Henry and I in dread all day, it seemed Providential, he seemed so relieved when he got here.

Mother is better tonight and sitting up and Henry reading the paper to her. I am now writing after supper as I did not quite finish before night being housekeeper etc. Our little Rosa is sleeping sweetly, she has been well a little over two weeks now, and looks *very well,* how I hope she will continue so this is the first letter since I have been here that I have not had to speak of her sickness in, next Monday will be the anniversary of our "little Belles" birthday, I thought tonight how *pleasant* it would have been to see her a year old lying by Rosa but that pleasure has been taken from me, I can only look forward with hope to another, may the Lord spare us the next one, and my life to enjoy the pleasure. Good night my darling God bless you ever,

Affly
your little Wife

Mother sends love and says keep a "stiff upper lip" she thinks all will come right by the first of January . . .

[WINSTON STEPHENS TO OCTAVIA STEPHENS]

Dec 16, 1863

My Dear Wife

. . . I am now in as good health as a man can be in and I have been hardening myself in anticipation of building when I come up. I feel just like I can put up the house in short order. Davis does not grow strong so rapidly as I had expected and cannot bear much fatigue, as he has been helping a little and he grows weary quite soon, he thinks of not coming on the sixth if you fail to get a place as you will have no room for us both and it will be absolutely necessary for me to come to do the work. Davis would like to come and help what he can but under the circumstances thinks best to wait my return. This is if we have to build. I suppose if you get a house we will both come at the same time . . .

The Artilery has been ordered from this Post to Camp Finegan and I feel sure if the yankees should land at Jacksonville that my Company will have to go, as there was an alarm some two weeks ago and my Company was ordered over, but the order was countermanded before it reached us. Davis' pony has been crippled ever since he came down from Lake City and I fear he will be permanentley injured . . .

Give love to Mother, Henry and George and the family of your Uncle and accept much love for yourself and Rosa from your aff Husband.

Winston Stephens

[WINSTON STEPHENS TO OCTAVIA STEPHENS]

Camp Cooper Dec 19, 1863

My Dear Wife

I am sitting in the left corner writing by fire light and it is bad at that. Davis and Lieut Shedd are on my right between the desk and bed at a game of chess and Swep sits in the right corner lost in the misteries of a novel! I have just taken a bath and feel finely. Davis continues to improve and the rest of my family *here* are in pritty good health. It is now about 8 oclock at night, and my preperations are nearley complete for my trip to Camp Finegan, as I start to that place tomorrow with my Company. My orders are to be there on Tuesday the 22d. to take or form a part of a general review. The whole of the 2d. Fla Cav in the East will be there, and I suppose some of the elite of Lake City will be down to witness the affair . . . Davis will not go as his Pony is too lame to take the journey, he regrets not being able to go as I suppose he expects many of his friends from Lake City will be down. I think his Pony better than when I wrote you before, though he is quite lame yet, he has put a stifle shoe on and I think that does him good. Since writing you before an order has been rec'd from Dept Hd Quarters forbidding Genl Finegan giving furloughs to Officers for a longer period than 48 hours. I will see Genl Finegan at Camp Finegan and send an application for a furlough to take place on 6th. January and hope to come according to time appointed, but if I fail to get off I will send Davis along at that time, so you will be sure to get the things through at that time. It is a long way to go for a furlough and I fear they are to come few and far between in the future, but we must hope for the best . . . Good night and pleasant dreams to you, and May the King of Kings watch and protect you from harm. Yours as ever aff

Winston

[WINSTON STEPHENS TO OCTAVIA STEPHENS]

Camp Finegan Dec 22, 1863

My Dear Wife

We arrived at this Post yesterday about 3 oclock pm and to day at 8 oclock am we went out on the field and was kept on until about 2 p.m. We first had a Review before the Genl arrived so as to be sure to have any and every thing right. About 12 N the Genl arrived on the field and was saluted with 7 guns—then he took his position and the review was gone through in its usual stile and the men behaved very well and I think did themselves and Officers credit, for their Military appearance. I had command of the first or right squadron. Capt Dickison the 2d., and Capt Row the 3d., then came the Artilery and then the Batallion of Infantry commanded by Maj Bird[73] . . . I then took my squadron and escorted the Genl to the Cars—gave him 3 cheers for which he doffed his hat and expressed his thanks. Every thing passed off in good order and fine style. I feel pleased with every thing that transpired here, but it does seem foolish to order my Company so far and Capts Chambers and Dickison just to be present at a presentation of a flag. I think the time for such things has past. I am afraid My Dear you are to be disappointed on the 6th of Jany as an Order has been issued by Genl Beaureguard that no Officer will be allowed more than 48 hours unless granted by him. I will send the application up tomorrow but fear I will not get it. If I do not come Davis will . . .

I am sorry to hear so many of the things were damaged by hauling, or rather by getting wet and by the carelessness of handling. I do hope we will get all right

---

73. Pickens B. Bird, now a major in the Sixth Florida Infantry Battalion, would play a key role in the Battle of Olustee in February 1864.

once more and have a stop to this war then I will settle somewhere and hope we will be the same happy Couple we were before the War seperated us. I often look back on our past happiness with pleasure and wish we could renew the union, but God in his wisdom has seen fit for it to be otherwise and we must submit to his decree, let us wait and hope . . . I start to Camp Cooper soon in the Morning and will get there Thursday, and will not get your letter until that time. I do hope it will be a cheerful one giving me good news about the house and the health of all of you. I am so glad to hear that little Rosa is keeping so well and hope Mother is getting well and strong—I have secured the Syrup and Sugar . . . and it has been delivered and is now waiting on the road. Sugar 45 cts. and I suppose 4 dollars for the syrup. I have 6 good hogs in camp and 2 sows, one with pigs and one soon will have. I think I have written you all of any interest. Give love to Mother and boys and Your Uncle and aunt. Good night my dear lots of love to Rosa and yourself from your aff husband

Winston Stephens

[WINSTON STEPHENS TO OCTAVIA STEPHENS]

Camp Cooper Dec 24, 1863

My Dear Wife

. . . I hope the house question will have been settled before you write me again. You should in enumerating your objections to moving to Marion not bring up such things as you did as you must remember I have some pride and some feeling left, and my Wife should not bring up such unpleasant remembrances. I am faithful and have been and I was never such common property as your allusions would indicte. I know your motives in stating the case and think nothing of it, but I am obliged to destroy the letter, fearing it may some day fall into other hands, and this is the 1st. of yours I have ever given to the flames.[74] Some of it I would especially like to keep it for, but I cannot extract the bad from the good and I have to give the whole up. dont think I blame you My Dear as I know you think I have been a very bad boy, but do not, only it brings things up I had rather not have called up. I have sined and I have acknoweledged it to you and God and if you cant for give me how am I to expect forgiveness of Our heavenly father . . . I wish I could see Rosa and you but fate seems against it. Good by Love to those worthy of it. Your devoted old Man.

Winston

74. In her diary Octavia notes on 18 December that she wrote to Winston, but she did not mention the contents. She must have referred to Winston's love affairs specifically; otherwise, it is doubtful that he would have destroyed the letter.

[OCTAVIA STEPHENS TO WINSTON STEPHENS]

Christmas Day 1863

My dear husband

I want so much to know what you are doing to day to make the day seem like Christmas, but I suppose not much, if anything. I guess it seems as little like Christmas to you as it does to me, if I had not been knitting all the morning it would seem like Sunday, every thing is so quiet, all of the negroes nearly off of the place . . .

Poor Loulie is suffering the same grief that I have, she has lost her baby, he died the morning after Mr Tydings came to Conference, no one but Georgie was with her, and she had washed and dressed it before anyone got to her, something has always been imperfect about his heart, we heard of it last Sunday morning (he died Thursday) and Mr Tydings went right home, he is to remain at the same place another year. Mother left for Loulie's on Monday, will return with Georgie next Wednesday or Thursday, she had given up going but when Mr Tydings came she was persuaded to go back with him, as she was better . . . She looked very badly, I hope Florida air may restore her health and strength . . .

I am sorry I can not give you a long letter this time, I ought to especially as it is Christmas but I have nothing of importance to write. The darkies are to have a party tonight. I shall try and go in town tomorrow and get your letter so that I can answer it if there should be anything of importance to answer.

I must say good bye for this time with a heart full of love.
I am looking so anxiously for you to come.

Ever Affly
Tivie

[WINSTON STEPHENS TO OCTAVIA STEPHENS]

Camp Cooper Dec 29, 1863

My Dear Wife

I again commence a letter to you and fear this is our only means of communication for some time to come. Although my application has been sent on I feel like it would come back not approved, or sent back for some correction, or something is to happen that I will not be able to get off. If it should happen that I cant come dont give way to your disappointment but keep up like a brave Wife and hope for the best. Dont make any rash wishes, as it is perhaps best for the service that furloughs should cease for a time. I know we are selfish by nature and we would wish to come as often as possible, but think of the chances I have had compared to some others in other parts of the Confederacy, and you can but acknowledge that I have been one of the fortunate ones. Oh how much I want to come and how essential it is for me to come and how hard just now to have a *Boss,* but I must wait or perhaps do worse . . .

[On Christmas eve] Davis, Lt Shedd, Lt Gray and Myself took tea with Mrs Capps, and had a dance afterwards. I thought how much you would wonder if you could have droped down and seen us, and I was surprised at myself. I went to take supper and sit a few minutes, but I saw that any dignity on my part would destroy the amusement of all, so I took active part and tried to promote the good feelings of all and we had quite a lively time. I danced three or four times. Davis and myself left about 10 oclock. We had a good supper, a large roast, ham, chicken pie, pound cake, potatoe pies etc composed the fare. We have had no other Christmas. Davis took dinner at Mr Wingate. We lived on our usual diet and would not have known Christmas at hand only the boys were constantly wanting to go out to some frolic in the country. The best of the joke is that we got into a play the night we were at Capps and kissing was in it, Davis and myself did not know it until it was too late to withdraw, so I kissed one of the women and Davis was called on and tried to back out and they concentrated on him and they give him three kisses instead of one and Mrs Capps was one of them. you must not plague Davis too much about it but we had a good laugh at his expense. I never saw any one hate any thing so bad in my life. You can ask him how he spent Christmas eve etc and bring him out but if you see he dont want it named I would not pleague him. I must confess I was surprised to get such a good supper. It was not as well cooked as Felix could have prepared it but with that exception it was very good . . . Davis will not write this week and as he will come next week, your Mother may expect him and not a letter. I wish it was I . . . Kiss Rosa for Pa Pa and tell her she must send me a kiss. Good night my love.

Yours always

Winston

Dec 31, 1863. *Rainy. Uncle Jared and Aunt Caroline went to town to bring Franky and Mr Sharpe out. Uncle Jared rented the McKinnon house for me for $300. Heard that Mother and Georgie are to come to night from Lou Tydings. Henry carried a load of things to the house in the rain.*

chapter 6

Tragedy Strikes Again; and Again

The year 1863 had been an encouraging one for the Union with major victories at Vicksburg, Gettysburg, and Chattanooga, but there was little indication that the reduced Confederacy was on the verge of defeat. Indeed, for most of 1864 it appeared that Lincoln would not be reelected and that the Confederacy might very well achieve independence by simply wearing out the war spirit of the Union.

The war intensified in the spring of 1864, and the fighting became almost continuous. In the East, Grant moved against Lee in May and the bloodbath began; from then on the two armies were in constant contact, and the fighting never truly ended. In the West, Sherman maneuvered Joe Johnston's depleted force until he threatened to take Atlanta. Jefferson Davis relieved Johnston and replaced him with the aggressive John Bell Hood, who attacked Sherman's superior army until he had in large measure ruined his own, and Atlanta fell in early September.[1] The march through Georgia that Sherman then conducted convinced many Confederates that the war was lost; coupled with Lincoln's reelection and Grant's continuous pounding of Lee's army, even the most die-hard rebel had to concede that everything looked bleak indeed. The war went on, however, despite the horrible losses of 1864, a year that everyone who lived through it would remember with either satisfaction or sadness as the critical year of the war. The events of that year meant that the Union would survive, although many citizens would not.

It was the worst year of Tivie Stephens's life, a year that she would never completely recover from; but it started out on a rather joyous note, for she had at last secured a house and farm near Thomasville, Georgia.

---

1. Many historians cite various turning points of the war—Vicksburg and Gettysburg, for example—but few dispute the fall of Atlanta as essential to Union victory. Had Sherman failed, Lincoln would probably have been defeated, and there would have been a different end to the war.

[OCTAVIA STEPHENS TO WINSTON STEPHENS]

At Home, Jan 1, 1864

My dear husband

Good news for you at last, we have succeeded at last in getting a house, and the McKinnon house at that, after dancing around after about a half dozen others which I will have to tell you about some other time . . . we, or Uncle Jared got the house yesterday morning . . . for $300, and we sent a load in the afternoon in a rain to take possession . . . this morning we all came over, and we have the beds fixed so we can sleep tonight. Mother and Georgie came from Monticello last night and Aunt Julia brought them over here this morning . . . I am very much pleased with the house, it is lots more comfortable than I expected to be while the war lasted. All I want now for the present is to have you come with provisions . . .

All are delighted to get a "Home again," the clock is ticking away right easily, and Rosa and the boys gone to bed, and I am scribbling away to make haste and get there for my poor old back will hardly let me move . . .

Lovingly

Your Wife

[WINSTON STEPHENS TO OCTAVIA STEPHENS]

Camp Cooper Jan 4, 1864

Good morning my Wifey, happy new year to you, and I hope you are having better weather than we are. It is now raining and for the past two days it has been freezing. On Saturday morning we had ice about 2 inches thick and it remained in the sun all day as firm as it was in the morning, and yesterday it rained lightly and the icicles were hanging down from the roofs of the houses six inches long, taking it all together this is the coldest spell I have felt since the Spring of 1852. Then the snow was on the ground for several days without melting and nearly all the fruit trees were killed . . .[2]

Tuesday night after supper. My Dear Wife I am not feeling as well as I wish to as I am suffering with that pain in my right side. I have been busy all day taking stock, fixing up my lot, stables etc and yesterday I strained myself getting some wood and I suppose that has caused an increase of the pain . . . I fear unless things change very materially that I will not be able to feed you another year, that is, if I have every thing to purchase at present prices, but if you get a place and make something perhaps we can get along. I have just paid for the Syrup and

2. Winston was living in Marion County then, but 1852 was not regarded as a killer winter. The two worst winters of the nineteenth century were in 1835 and 1894–95.

Sugar and it cost 372 dollars and the freight will cost enough to make it nearly 400. The sugar is in a very large barrel and there is 480 pounds and it is not well driped, you must have it fixed so that you can loosen the hoops a little at one end and let it drip and catch the molasses that runs out as it costs enough to save all. The syrup I am afraid is so thin that it will spoil in summer . . . I want you to economize every thing you can when you commence keeping house and let us try to have something to go on as long as it lasts. I think you had better feed Jane from the table and perhaps others of the children and perhaps you can save in that way. You see you have no dog to eat the cold provisions as you must give it [to] the negroe children. I am glad you have no dog on that account and dont want Joe allowed to bring one on the place . . . I send you as a new years gift, 2 boxs soap, 1 bottle ink, some paper and envelopes and an orange, and for Rosa 2 pr shoes and small brush for hair, this with all the eateables I hope will be acceptable and when I am able I will do better . . . I regret to hear of Loulie's misfortune. She must have had an unfortunate time, both in loosing and then being compelled to wash and dress her child after death. Give my love to her when you write and tell her I can feel for her, knowing how great her los is. I hope we may have our next spared to us . . . I have lost several men lately by desertion and I expect they will continue to go as all furloughs are stoped and they have drawn no clothing and they are nearly naked and barefooted. A good many are deserting from Camp Finegan. Six Yankee deserters came to the Pickets Sunday night. It appears they are as tired of it as our men as they continue to desert. They are all fine looking fellows and say lots of them want to come over to us . . .

Give my love to Your Aunt and Uncle, Mother and boys and accept oceans of love for yourself and my darling Rosa. Oh that I could give each of you a kiss to night. Good night and God bless you.

Your aff Husband
Winston

[WILLIE BRYANT TO DAVIS BRYANT]

Atlanta Ga. Jan 6, 1864

Dear Davis—

. . . From my letters to Mother you will learn that I am "messing by myself"; I have now tried it nearly two weeks and manage finely, and rather enjoy it; I found it impossible to live on my pay, and was compelled to curtail my expenses by some means, besides, I shall try to save every dollar I can to assist Mother and the boys. I find that my eating expenses will reach $50 pr. month even at my present mode of living; this month I will not be able to save anything, as it cost me something to set up housekeeping and there have been many little contigent expenses I did not calculate upon . . . I found Tydings low in funds,[3] and such a clever fellow that I let him into my secret of my doing my own cooking, and invited him to share my bed and board, which he gladly accepted, and I have fed him better than he would have fared at an expensive hotel; I have given him beef steak, and onions, eggs, rice, potatoes, excellent bread, tea, genuine coffee (I managed to get a little from some for the Fla. hospital) besides some little "entrees"; excuse my mentioning these little details of my life as I thought it might interest you; you would be surprised to see what a *good* meal I can get up without soiling my fingers, scarcely; I know you would enjoy seeing my arrangements . . .

Just now I am very pleasantly situated, and have no cause for complaint, and I wish might be as much so all thro' the war; I am in comfortable quarters, have as little to do as I wish, and one good companion among the 5 clerks and employees; I get along well enough with all the rest but one, (you see I cant get along perfectly smooth anywhere) he is a mean, low-bred "cuss" who thinks himself as much of a gentleman as anyone, and wants to rule; just the style whom I can't get along with, and dont care to, and who hates me as the devil does holy water, fortunately I manage always to keep such fellows afraid to have a row with me or I would get licked sometimes; you cant get along with such fellows by having nothing to do with them . . .

Much love to you all.

Yrs Always affectly.
Willie

[OCTAVIA STEPHENS TO WINSTON STEPHENS]

At Home Jan 8, 1864

My dear husband

. . . I intend sending [the wagon] in town with corn and for a pig that Aunt Julia is going to let me have for $30, the same that Franky paid, Aunt Julia has been very kind, the day we moved here she hired a buggy and brought Mother and George out and a lunch for us all, and a bottle of syrup for our coffee, and the first time I sent to town she sent me a Kushaw and loaned me a half gallon of syrup without my asking, and again sent me some spare ribs and let me have a bushel of potatoes and to day knowing I had not sent to Monticello, sent me some meat to return if I had it to spare if not pay in money, she has the noblest heart of any of our relatives here . . .

---

3. Dr. Joseph Tydings was the brother of Richard Tydings. Willie had just secured a position in the Atlanta Quartermaster Department and moved into a house owned by his uncle, Lewis Bryant, who was absent during the early months of 1864.

I guess ere this your mind is relieved as regards the house question, and I know it is a great relief, perhaps you would like to know what we are all doing, Mother sewing, Jane the same, Georgie has been ripping out some old woolen socks to make Henry some mittens but is now in the yard with Rosa, Henry and Joe gone to Uncle Jareds for a load of corn, Sarah and Rachael spinning, and your humble servant is writing to her husband . . .

I am very sorry my husband could not spend his Christmas pleasantly without spending it in the company he did, and hope it is the last time you will honor Mrs Capps or any of those women with your company, I wish you *had* stood a little on your "dignity" and I think you *might* have done so when the games commenced, I would like to have had you have all the good eatables and more too, but the idea of your being in such company hurts my feelings, you have done enough now to have your name spread, you need not fear my plaguing Davis too much, it is too tender a subject to me, and I hope nothing will happen to bring up the conversation while he is here, I told Mother and the boys of your all taking supper and dancing at Mrs Capps' but that is all. I dreamed last night of being in some such company and it was a relief to me to wake, but enough, I hope you will not have any more invitations of that kind, if so that you will have dignity and respect enough for my feelings (if you should think them foolish) to refuse, I love my husband too well to want the least spot or suspicion to rest on his name, and his kisses are too precious to me to be thrown away. I expect you will be angry with me for writing this . . .

I know that all those who hired our negroes were trying hard sometime ago to clothe and shoe them so I feel sure they are taken care of as well as possible, I have not seen Tom and Mose since Christmas, they say they get on nicely . . .

I must say good night and close, Rosa threatens you greatly when you come, she is going to tickle you, she never forgets her Pa Pa's kiss at night, she is looking well now . . . Good night my dear may holy angels with our little one watch over you this night.

Ever your aff Wife

Jan 9, 1863. *Sent to town in the morning for Davis, but he was not there. In the afternoon he surprised us . . .*

[WINSTON STEPHENS TO OCTAVIA STEPHENS]

Camp Cooper Jan 11, 1864

My Dear Wife

It did my heart good to open your short letter of last Wednesday and see at the head of the page *At Home.* What a magic there is in those two little words! I am so glad to know that your home for this year is in so comfortable a house, I know the price is large, but that is nothing so long as we can be sure to meet the agreement. I want now to get the land Mr McKinnan spoke of as being one mile from the house, and the field contained 50 acres. I know that with the land at *home* is more than you can have cultivated but we can work about 50 acres with the mules and we can turn out some of the poorest spots. If I dont get to come home tell Henry to pick out about 2 acres of the best land at home for potatoes, then I want one planted in sugar millet and one in cotton and the rest in corn, the land for corn had better be plowed up as soon as he can . . . If you can get any turnip seed sow part of the ground saved for potatoes and the turnips will come off in time for the potatoes, the greens will help the meat and if you can get any seed you had better save a good spot for a garden. All the truck patches will help . . . I have so longed to be with you and hug you up these cold nights to keep me warm. I think of you and dream of you. I fear if they dont let me come I will be induced to come against orders, sometimes I feel like I would be willing to give up every thing on earth to be assured the priviedge of living with you as we used to. I think if this War lasts much longer I will go crazy and desert. We cant be more abject slaves than now and it appears to me it grows more and more so every day . . .

I suppose you have Davis sitting by your fire side swapping off yarns with you, *golly wish twas I* . . . I hope you will not take more work upon your hands than you can do as you must remember your delicate condition and how much you have at stake and do only what you can do not to injure you and by no means must you attempt to weave or put on any cloth or I dont want you to ride behind Mr Everitt's horse or any thing but Ginny or Flora as a fright in your situation might be fatal. Your short letter was very acceptable and I was glad you did not sit up to write any more. I love to read long letters from you, but I dont want you to injure yourself in writing them. I often wish I could make my letters more interesting but it appears that they get worse instead of better. I had rather talk to you . . . Give love to all. Good night my darling and may heaven soon allow us to live together in peace, pleasant dreams. Your affectionate old Man . . .

[OCTAVIA STEPHENS TO WINSTON STEPHENS]

At Home Jan 17, 1864

My dear dear husband

. . . I am writing in our parlor and I wish you could come and see how nice it looks. I looked for you until very late Thursday night and all the morning Friday hoping you might come but did not much expect you, I dont know what to say about your coming. I expect to be confined the last of March the first of April, I think the third of April the longest time that I can go, if that long any time, I am so "no count" I have to be amazingly particular in all my doings, I do not suffer so much with pain in my stomach as I have in former cases, but a great many little ways I cant describe, I dread being so far from every body, although I had such a comfortable time the last, it is over five miles to Dr Adams, but as I was going to say about your coming, I cant bear to wait until then to see you, fearing that then something might prevent for it is so far off, but still I dread the idea of being sick and not have you with me, you dont know how I feel sometimes when I feel badly and think perhaps I am going to be sick and you not here, sometimes I think perhaps you had better come now if you can, but I do want so much to see you, but fear if you do you cant come at the time I expect to be sick, I try to be very careful so to carry my time out, you must do as you think best, I fear that before long furloughs will be stopped until the end of the war, there is no telling what we will come to before this awful war ends, but my dear please dont go "*crazy and desert,*" do nothing rash, and I think you will not . . . I hope I did not hurt your feelings much by my last letter, I have been sorry since I wrote so strongly about your Christmas frolic, I must acknowledge that my jealousy is too easily aroused I am too selfish . . .

I will describe Mr Sharpe to you as well as I can, he does not look at all like you, I think the folks meant his manner was like you, I did not see a great deal of him, but enough to know or think that I would like him[4] . . . I will now tell you something to flatter your poor little no count wife and make you jealous, I hear he said I was the sweetest little woman he ever saw and wondered if you would exchange wives? do you think you would? Frankie's happiness seemed to make her think of us a great deal, she showed from many remarks that she wished and knew I wished that I had you with me, as happy as she was with her husband . . .

Rosa gave me a kiss for you. I hope my dreams to night will be of you and pleasant, I had all my grief over again in a dream last night of losing a baby, I suppose from receiving a letter from Lou. I must close as I have your little bundle to fix and Davis and the boys food to fix as they will probably leave at daylight in the morn . . . Good night my darling husband. God bless you is always the prayer of your

loving little
Wife

---

4. William Sharpe was the husband of Frances Ann (Franky) Perham, Tivie's cousin. He was serving in the Twenty-ninth Georgia Infantry Regiment when he was wounded and permitted to go home to recover.

[WINSTON STEPHENS TO OCTAVIA STEPHENS]

Camp Cooper Jan 18, 1864

My Dear Wife

Your letter, nice letter of *correction* was duly received and its contents duly considered. And I feel greatful that I have so *considerate and charitable* a wife. I have lived, moved and had existence for the last 34 years, with good councellers by me to prevent my going out of my path of duty, both to My God and Mankind. I have often erred and sometimes sinned and have as often repented not because of the correction of my friends so much, as the reproving of my concience, but in the last heinious sin I feel no compunctions of concience and no desire to change my views on the subject. I went to mrs Capps not knowing that any others were to be there but some of the Officers and men of my Company, when I had been there a short time three women came in. I did not know them! was I to feel that I was offended and get up and go from the house? No it was not my place to judge and condemn those women before I knowed them, so I remained for a time and joined in the amusements that good might be the result, as I hoped by example to make them behave. I will admit I had no notion of getting into the kissing arrangement, but I do not regret that as I did by them as I would like to be done by. I would not go with those women now because I have heard more of them, and dont feel disposed to bring my self in contact with such creatures. I feel thankful for the advise given, but I have *self respect and Pride* to keep me just where I belong . . . My men are deserting fast, four of them left Saturday night and I am expecting some more to go every night. Some one built a fire up against Lt Grays house the same night the men deserted, but fortunately it did not burn the house or the whole camp would have been consumed, as they are all built close together, it is believed it was fired by some of the men that left, but I think by some one in Camp and I fear we are some night to find ourselves in the midst of burning camps . . . I can see that discontent is growing rapidley in the ranks and I fear unless something is done soon in Congress that the men go off in squads until we will have no army.[5] The laws that have been passed generally protect the rich, and the poor begin to say it is the rich mans war and the poor mans fight, and they will not stand it. I used to have no trouble with my men but now I am in hot water all the time and some one is constantly under arrest and being Court Martialed. It does seem that some evil spirit is destroying the company, and yet they all appear to like me as well as ever and as enthusiastic as ever,

---

5. Desertions were up in all armies by this time, but quite often the men did not think they had really deserted; they sometimes came back to camp with the explanation that they had had to help their family out by getting in the crop or performing some other necessary task. Desertion in Florida was no worse than in other places, but it is true that more in-state troops went home for visits than did the Confederate regulars in the field.

but in some evil hour they go beyond the bounds of law or deceplin; ready to go off if my furlough came approved, but when the mail was delivered I saw my application and on the back of it in a large bold hand was written *Disapproved. Officers must remain with their Companies.* So my good old Lady you will not have your old man with you soon. I am bent on coming March or when you write me to come, if the Yanks dont land and occupy Fla before that time making it impossible for any one to come home. This is a hard sentence, but this is one of the prices of this Liberty we heard much talk about, among those that are at home out of range of all missels of death and not deprived of the society of those they love etc. I think it is dear bought liberty that keeps us slaves for years before we get our freedom, deprived of home, all that we love and no chance to see them or aid them! I hope next spring will bring with it peace in some shape, God knows I want all that a Southern man craves, but I am heartily sick of this state of affairs . . . Give Love to Mother and boys and all *friends,* and accept for yourself and Rosa a Husbands and Fathers devotion and many kisses.

Yours ever aff Winston

[WINSTON STEPHENS TO OCTAVIA STEPHENS]

Camp Cooper Jan 21, 1864

My Dear Wife

I received your nice letter by Davis on his return yesterday. It does me good to get such [a] letter full of love and affection and no counciling and scolding. I know I sometimes write you letters in which complaint is mixed, but I have tried to avoid all such expression of feeling, as I know from experience it harrows the good feelings of our nature and does no good, because we too frequently correct when no correction is required or necessary. I know it is our duty to each other to advise and counsil, but do it [in] an affectionate way that no offence may be felt. I am glad to see you are in such good heart about things generally . . . Davis tells me you have a few chickens and 2 pigs as you call them when in reality they are grown hogs and I suppose worth the $30 . . . I hope this with yesterdays letter will pay for yours. Love to all and many kisses and much love to you and Rosa from your Old Man.

[WINSTON STEPHENS TO OCTAVIA STEPHENS]

Camp Cooper Jan 26, 1864

My Dear Wifey

I have just finished parching and eating parched corn. You would have been amused to [have] looked in and seen the occupants of this cabin in that laudable occupation. One parching and the rest making music with the cracking of corn in their teeth. tonight we had some marsh beef and it has a very bad flavor and none of us made a hearty meal, and we have made up the deficiency by parching corn. You may judge if we did justice to it when I inform you we ate not less than eight or ten ears, and another advantage we may derive from eating parched corn is that we may yet come to that kind of fare in this revolution and then we will be used to it and will perhaps think less of it, than those unaccustomed to eating it. I spoke of having marsh beef for supper and left you to make up your mind as to what the objection might be to that kind of beef. I will tell you! when a beef uses on the marsh grass and is killed while using on it, the meat smells badley and tastes unpleasantly, and no one likes it. Such was the meat we had for supper, but now in this connection let me tell you what we had for dinner and what we had Sunday for dinner. We had on Sunday Oyster Stew in large quantities and with other good things and today we had Oyster pie and bird pie, nice rice, bake potatoes etc and so on I suppose that bill of fare will make your mouth water enough and I fear put you to longing for a dish of Oysters. I did think of you while eating and wished so much that I could place the dish before you or have [you] injoy them in some way. We do not as a general thing live half as well as we used to but now and then Felix gives us a good dish of something. A few days before we got the Oysters we had some of the nicest tripe and cooked the best you ever saw, Lieut Gray went after the Oysters and brought up a cart load so that we had them for several days . . .

The Maj does just about as much here as an automaton, he takes no part in drill and rarely ever comes out of his house unless it is to go hunting or fishing, he frequently issues orders and I suppose that is the reason we have so many orders, he does nothing but sit and think of an order and writes it and sends it out for others to have excuted. How easy it is for one to write an order but how difficult for others to execute. I think if all men that write and had orders issued would first think how they would like to execute the same if they had to change places with the privates that fewer orders would be issued and better feelings prevail every where.

I think from all I can see in the papers (if they can be taken as evidence of the feelings of the people) that the war will assume gigantic proportions next Spring and the result be known in a few months. If the North can throw the force in the field that they propose, it will either crush us or destroy them. I notice in their papers that they propose to throw one million of men in the service for ninety days and with that force they think they can crush out the rebellion. They offer large bounties and promise an early peace and no doubt they will get quite a large force, but I have no idea they can get the half they want, but if they should get one million of men and pay them seven hundred dollars bounty each it would take seven hundred million of dollars to pay the bounty then think of the amount of money necessary to equip that many men and the number of waggons necessary to take their baggage and the supplies and you will see that such an army will defeat itself as they could not feed them. If we offered no opposition they could not march with such an army through the south in less than one year and what time will take them when every mile will be disputed by Southern Sons and the damage they would sustain to their supply train would starve them. I hope they may either get the men or that the War feelings North is waining so fast that they cant recruit at all. I think their game is a desperate one, they have got to win soon or they know all is lost, and this last proposition looks like they feel as a gambler who becomes desperate by loosing, they stake all on a last effort to win and I hope that [we] may defeat them and wind up this unnattural and unholey war. I feel that we are to be hardley pressed and it will require all our fortitude to stand the coming campaign, but God has this far been mercifull to the south and I hope his strong arm will arrest this wicked enemy and send them howling back to their own soil and homes chastised in such a way as to make them glad to have peace... We have the credit of having some of the best Generals in the world and so far they have fully sustained that reputation and I think they will continue to prove to the world they are equal to the emergencies...

    I am sorry your back continues weak and you feel generally so good for nothing. I expect you underrate your usefulness. I know you have been very useful since I married you and I expect you are so yet. I know my not coming will be a disappointment to you but it cant be a greater one to you than it is to me. You cant imagine how much I want to see you and my dear Rosa. My thoughts are yours nearly all the time. I often think what would become of you and Rosa if I should get killed, for you would have nothing left you for a support as the Yankees would take your negroes from you leaving you nothing but a small peace of land in Marion and perhaps they would confiscate that. Then I think perhaps your Father might live through it and would perhaps take care of you, but then another thought pops in my brain and that is that you might be taken north and in a few years marry some Yankee that had been instrumental in destroying me! I want you to promise that no matter what befalls me that you will never marry a yankee, no matter what his calling or position. I dont ask you to promise me never to marry again, I want to know that I am not leaving such a good wife for a cursed Yankee and my child or perhaps children. I want them educated to hate a Yankee and glory in their Southern blood, and I want them never to go North and especially do I want them educated South and Southern principles instilled in their bosoms. Forgive me for speaking of this matter but I cant help thinking that such things might happen and I cant help but see how desperate your situation would be if I am lost and the cause lost also. But I hope God in his mercy will give us deliverance from such a people as the Northern people. I want you to keep me posted as to what is done and what you propose to do give me all your plans and if I can help by any suggestion I will give it...

I feel that my wife had quite a compliment paid her, but nothing more than I think she is entitled to, but I dont care to make the swap. I could I suppose have Frankie down here and make her *fat* and then she would be in as bad fix for traveling as you are, so I will hold on to my old Lady and [wait] for her to get in a traveling condition. You cant imagine how much I would give to be with you one week if no longer. I want to see how you are fixed about the place, but I would rather see you and Rosa than have forty such places . . . I want Henry to be sure to make the negroes work and not for him to do it all. I am going to try and get you some cooking utensils here and send them to you, and hope they may get through safe. I have sent word to Clark to try and get those through he started with and hope you will have enough after awhile. I hope all things will turn out well yet and that we may make enough to do us another year. Give love to Mother and boys and to inquiring friends my kind regards, and accept for yourself and Rosa my hearts devotion.

Your Aff Husband
Winston Stephens

[WINSTON STEPHENS TO OCTAVIA STEPHENS]

Camp Cooper Jan 28, 1864

My Dear Wife

. . . The Cars did not come yesterday . . . If you had seen the long faces as we returned to camp after waiting until nearley sun down you could then appreciate our anxieties on mail days, the only days in the week that we can hear from our dear families and then to have a disappointment is too bad . . . We are not only anxious to have our letters, but we have nothing to feed our horses upon and unless the cars come with corn soon we will be forced to go to the corn. Corpl Smith returned from the East side of the St Johns last night and gives a gloomy picture of affairs on that side, and an incident happened to him, that will illustrate the feelings on that side. He rode up to the house of one of my Deserters about daylight but the man was not at home, he then went on a few miles to another's home and there they saw both the men at work in the field, but the deserters saw them when they were about ¼ mile from them and ran for the swamp close by, Corpl Smith and party charged their horses as fast as they could, and the women (about a dozen) came out with hoes and axes and tryed to cut Smith off, but all the party were good horsemen but Smith and passed safely but his horse took fright and threw him in a bunch of palmettoes and the women shouted theres one of the d——d rascals off. Smith got up and the women blew the horn to let others know and told Smith if he would stay 15 minutes they would catch h—l, using all the time the most profane language they could think of. Some of the party would have got the deserters but they . . . got to the swamp before they could be overtaken, some of the party fired at them but missed. Smith says they have regular spies and that no party can go through the country without being found out by these persons on the watch. I think the Government should send over and have the whole party driven in the Augustine.

I must close. I hope I will get a letter today and that you may soon get this. Love to all.

Your aff husband
Winston Stephens

[OCTAVIA STEPHENS TO WINSTON STEPHENS]

Jan 29, 1864

My dear husband

I was pleasantly surprised Wednesday evening by the receipt of your letter of the 21st. which was as usual acceptable and very pleasant itself, much more so than the one before it which was *very* sarcastic and cutting, and I think I now deserve the name of a *"considerate and charitable"* wife not to write you what I first intended, any one would think from your first letter that I had written you a tremendous scolding and accused you of committing a "heinious crime" as you say, even in your last you speak as though I was in the habit of advising or scolding, in my letter "of correction" as *you call* it, I think I merely expressed a wish or hope that such a thing would not occur again.

We are getting on as well as usual, Sarah is sick though for the first time in a long time. Henry has brought the 1st things from Monticello safely, or the last that were there. I am now anxious to know when the other things are coming if at all . . . I am very sorry to hear that your men are deserting so, and that you have so much trouble with them, I hope it will not be thought to be your fault, I have said all along that I thought we or you more especially were buying our liberty very dear if we ever get it, which I fear will never be . . .

Good bye, Affly
Your Wife

[WINSTON STEPHENS TO OCTAVIA STEPHENS]

Camp Cooper Feb 2, 1864

My Dear Wife

I again seat myself to chat with you on paper. Oh! that I could have you by me to talk to instead of communicating by the art of letter writing. But what a pleasure it affords me to receive a letter from a friend who is far from us and that we cant see and converse with. I must admit the art of letter writing affords as much pleasure as any thing I know of that looks so simple in its performance. I wish I could accomplish letter writing in such a stile as to look and read like a well gotten up affair but I suppose there must be degrees in this as in other things and that all cant come to the same point of perfection. I am one of that class that write and give my meaning in common language and common form. My intention is as good as the best if not so elegantly expressed, and written in my blunt way. I say what I have to express and you have often expressed yourself satisfied with the effort and I therefore feel satisfied myself. I am aware that some of your correspondents write better letters than I do, but I am fully as sure that none of them love you half so well, and their fine letters are not worth as much in your estimation as my poor effort . . . We have but little excitement in Camps, every thing goes on in the same routine from day to day . . . We get no news here, still it does seem that something must be doing to make ready for a grand move. When the clouds that are gathering over and around us will burst with all its fury on our dear heads. I often think and wonder if our Government sees the awful truth and has or is preparing to meet and defeat the attempt to crush us. I fear for many causes, but I feel hopeful under all the circumstances. I pray God to avert the awful calamity and to shield us from the thratened danger and I believe he will do it. I know that this Nation has sined and that we are sinners yet and that this war has been visited upon us for the sins we have committed but remembering God is merciful, I feel by supplication he will hear our prayers and that we will yet be saved from total distruction. This War has not only punished the South, but the North at this moment feels the rod of afflication and they will be used as intruments in Gods hands to punish us and we to punish them.

Sometimes I know my Love, I write desponding letters and I feel just as I write my letters as a general thing is a true index of my feelings, sometimes I am *blue for true* and I cant see our way through this War, at other times I think God will see fit to have it stoped and at no distant day, then I feel cheerful and write good letters on that subject . . . I am getting better every day, My side does not trouble me but little and I take a great deal of active exorcise. I jump and do many things to strengthen my nerves and get rid of my surplus fat. I have got a breast like a lass of 15 years or older and some of the men remark that I have large tits. They are vulgar fellows, dont you think so. I would not care if I could feel some ones breasts tonight. I think I could appreciate the privildge.[6] I do want to see you so much to see how you look and see dear Rosa in her good health. I do feel that I could make any kind of a sacrifice to be with you for a short time. I cant bear the idea of being seperated from you much longer. I must come in march at all hazards . . .

6. Tivie worked diligently to cross out these four sentences, and it took a very long time to decipher them.

Keep Henry up to the point and tell him if the negroes dont mind him to fight, and keep fighting until they do their whole duty. If any thing turns up that you or Henry want advise about and you have no time to consult me, get the advise from some one of your neighbors that you can depend upon. You must be sure to raise your own sugar and syrup at home this year as I will not be able to purchase if it keeps up, plant the sugar millet certain, at least one acre and be sure to plant one acre in cotton to make our clothes . . . I hope you will not find this tiresome as I have written perhaps on subjects that dont interest you. Give my love to Mother and the boys tell George he must stop those chills and tell Henry I am sorry he is taxed so severely in his first effort at farming and I hope he may not take a disliking to it from what he now sees, as he has commenced with many disadvantages to contend against. I hope he may make a good crop on his account as well as for our common good. Give all my friends my kindest regards and accept for yourself and Rosa oceans of love and thousands of kisses. May God protect you through this unnatural War and once more unite us in that happy state when this War began, is the humble and sincere prayer of your devoted husband . . . Good night my darling Wife

Your as ever
Affectionately
Winston

[JAMES W. BRYANT TO REBECCA BRYANT]

Norfolk Va. Feb 7, 1864

My dear Wife

. . . I shall leave here tomorrow or next day for Washn. thence to N. Yk. I wrote you from N.Y. lately, and hope, and believe you received the letter, because I am told it passed the lines. This I presume will go through also, and hereafter I think I can have letters forwarded regularly. All are well in Boston—I am in good health—some cough yet—Hereafter Enclose letters addressed to me *69 Warren St. N.Y.* in an Envelope addressed to Maj. Genl. Butler Commdr. Dept. of No. Ca. and Virginia, *both unsealed* . . .[7]

The continued uncertainty as to our meeting is distracting, and I cannot make any calculations for the future with any confidence. I had supposed one year ago that we should be together long before this time. It is a cruel privation to me to be so long without seeing you and my dear children and other relatives. Was it not

---

7. Bryant was wrong in his assumption that the mail would be more regular in the future. Major General Benjamin Franklin Butler was known as "Beast" and "Spoons" Butler in the Confederacy because of his abolitionist views and because it was rumored that he had stolen the silverware from the residence he occupied in New Orleans while he was military governor of Louisiana in 1862.

that what I have heard from you, and about you has been so satisfactory as to your health and comfort I would be wretched, but I trust you may all continue well, and that this miserable and protracted war may cease soon.

I have been all the time engaged in private business, but only to a small extent thus far. Our Gas Comp'y is Progressing slowly, but think it will make dividends this year.

How cold and stiff appears a correspondence like ours, when our hearts are so full of affection and interest! But I know you feel Entire Confidence in my love, and sympathize fully with me in my sorrow and disappoinment. I am so glad that you are with our dear family, all together. We think here that the spring will End the war—My Prayer is for the speedy cessation of it, and I know yours is, and has been since its commencement. Give much love to Dear Mother and all the family

. . .

Oh, that I could see you all in health peace and prosperity, but the first wish is to see you. Good bye—God bless and continue to protect you in life until we can meet again.

Your affectionate husband JW Bryant

[WINSTON STEPHENS TO OCTAVIA STEPHENS]

Near Sanderson Feb 11, 1864[8]

My Dear Wife

I write you these few lines to allay the anxiety you may feel on my account. We have so far been able to elude the enemy, though we have at times been surrounded and from appearances we thought our prospect was fair for a northern prison. Our Command consists of 256 men in the Infantry and 52 Cavalry and we are trying to join Genl Finegan but so far the enemy's Cavalry have out traveled us. I dont know if we will be able to get out without being Captured. Davis left me at Camp Finegan and was on Pet and from all I can gather he has been captured or is lost. If he has gone through safe you will hear from him. We are having hard times and plenty of it. I think the Enemy are some ten thousand or more. I have lost some men Captured and some lost and not yet reported. I have but about 45 men with me. I must close as the Courier is waiting, love to all and

8. On 6 February 1864 some 7,000 troops under the command of Brigadier General Truman Seymore left Hilton Head, South Carolina, for another invasion of Florida. The first Federal contingent landed at Jacksonville on 7 February, and the stage was set for the only large battle to be fought on Florida soil, the Battle of Olustee on 20 February 1864. To oppose these forces, General Finegan had some 1,300 officers and men widely dispersed all over the state. He immediately asked for and began to receive reinforcements from Georgia, and the two armies were about equal in numbers when they met at Olustee. In the meantime, the Federals raided into the interior, capturing Camps Cooper and Finegan and sending the rebels back west of Baldwin to regroup.

may God bless you [and] protect you all. Do my dear Wife wait calmly and dont give your self unnecessarily trouble. We are about 8 miles from Sanderson. Ben Gaines is here with us.[9] Good bye, I hope to see you soon. your Devoted Husband

Winston

Feb 12, 1864. *Heard through a letter from Davis that Winston's Company was moved to Camp Finegan, and the Yankees at Jacksonville and Winston too busy to write.*

[OCTAVIA STEPHENS TO WINSTON STEPHENS]

Feb 12, 1864

My very dear husband

Your nice *very* nice long letter was received last Sunday and read and reread with delight, as you say it does "my heart good," to get such letters, your two or three last have been such nice affectionate ones . . . I want you to write all your letters just as you feel, desponding or not, I always want to know all your feelings and thoughts . . .

I dont know what to say of your getting so fat, perhaps though the Summer will take down some of it. I had rather have you fleshy than a sickly thinner one, you tell those "vulgar fellows" to stop making remarks on my husband . . .

Rachael has been spinning ever since we have had her home, when there is any fences to fix, wagon to unload, or corn to shell she helps, next week they will go to rolling logs etc. I try to make them work, I think sometimes you would think so if you should hear me scold, I guess you will say as you said once before that I was getting cross, I think so myself sometimes . . .

Yes, Joe has come and how his coming has changed my spirits. Oh my darling I dont know what to say, I am so anxious. Davis' letter was written nearly a week ago and there is no telling what may have happened since. God be merciful to us, and protect you from all harm, I wish I was so I could go nearer you that I might hear of you often. I do hope the Yankees will make a short stay . . . I will send in town tomorrow for your letter and hope to get it, still it will be but little later than Davis', do write *very often* if only two or three words to say you are well, I

9. Winston was ordered from Camp Cooper to Camp Finegan on 6 February and was forced to leave there in haste when the Federals captured it on the night of 9 February. He and Rowe's company fought a delaying action on 10 February at the St. Marys River and then retreated to Sanderson. The next day, they helped infantry units fire all supplies stored there and escaped just as the Federals arrived. Davis was not captured, but he had several narrow escapes. Ben Gaines, Winston's half-brother, is not listed in *Soldiers of Florida*, but he served in the Sixth Florida Infantry Battalion under the command of Major Pickens Bird. This unit turned the Union flank during the Olustee battle but took eighty-two casualties. Ben and James Gaines, Winston and Swepston Stephens, and Davis Bryant all fought at Olustee. Bird was killed at Cold Harbor, Virginia, on 3 June 1864.

can not say more now, I wish I could start off instead of this letter, oh I shall feel so anxious and fear for you but can only trust you to God and pray that he will protect you as before.

Your ever loving
Wife

[WINSTON STEPHENS TO OCTAVIA STEPHENS]

Lake City Feb 13, 1864

My Dear Wife

I write you a few lines to inform you of my whereabouts and what I am doing etc. You see I am in Lake City. I am also well. I am having the squadron formed to go to the front to join Genl Finegan. the enemy are falling back slowley. We have a good force, over 3 thousand in front and about 2 or 3 thousand coming from Georgia by way of Kings ferry, and they will fall in their rear and then we will have them all O.K.[10] God grant I may be spared to you. If not, grieve as little as you can for your lost husband and take consolation that I died a soldier defending a just cause. Davis is with me and is well and goes with me to the front. I have no time to write more, love to all. I will write at length when I can.

Good bye and love and kiss to Rosa

Your aff husband
Winston

Feb 14, 1864. No letter from Winston but one from Davis saying our forces were retreating to Starke, had narrowly escaped being taken . . .
Feb 16, 1864. Received a few lines from Winston at Lake City, he was preparing to join Gen Finegan in the front, he and Davis well . . .

[WINSTON STEPHENS TO OCTAVIA STEPHENS]

Camp Beaureguard Feb 18, 1864[11]

My Very Dear Wife

Your nice long and affectionate letter was received on my return to this place last night and you can imagine with what greediness I drank in it contents and it

---

10. Winston was mistaken here; all reinforcements from Georgia came to Live Oak, entrained for Lake City, and then marched east to fight the Federals. There was no way to get behind the Federals—that is, to the east of them—without command of the waterways, and this the Confederates never had.

11. Camp Beauregard was a temporary camp about six miles east of Lake City where the Confederates erected a barricade and intended to make a stand. As it turned out, the battle occurred several miles to the east of the camp.

did my heart good to know that you all are so well and doing as well as you represent . . . I wish I had time to write you a long letter in return for your nice one, but the fates of War decree otherwise as I have orders to be in the saddle by 10 oclock and it now H past 9 oclock giving me barely time to say a few words and again part with you. I have matter to write you a long and interesting letter but no time. On monday pm I left this camp and return at sun down yesterday and I rode some 150 miles and rested in the whole about six hours, riding night and day. We came very near making a good thing of it as a company of yankees (Cavalry) passed 6 hours ahead of [us] . . . As it happened we did nothing, only gave the Yanks a scare and made them fall back from Gainesville to Baldwin . . . Davis must keep you posted on the particulars, as I will be obliged to leave him all the time in Camp, as he lost his horse and I ride so much that I keep the mare and the big horse rode down, I lost the stud . . . Davis sent my trunk and valise to Lake City and saved them, but he sent my boots by a man and they are stolen. I am now so black and dirty that you would hardley know me and I see no hope for a change soon. I have worn one suit 2 weeks. we start on a scout towards the St Marys and I hope our force will soon be ready for an advance. I think we are nearley strong enough to drive them from their works. I have no hope of coming to see you now unless the Yanks are driven out by that time. I am quite well though very much jaded and if this thing goes on I feel sure I shall fail as we go night and day, no sleep and but little to eat, my horses are nearly broken down. I lost my hogs, chickens, cooking utensils and the Yanks have Felix, but he has sent word he will come out soon . . . I have some hope that he will save our things. I failed to get the letter of yours that should have reached me about the time the Yanks came, and I suppose they got it and read it. I wish I could have got it instead of them. I think we have from 7 to 10 thousand men here.[12] I am glad Henry is getting on so well, everything will be left to him. Good bye and may God bless you all. love to all yours as

ever aff husband

Winston

[WINSTON STEPHENS TO OCTAVIA STEPHENS]

Camp Beauregard Feb 21, 1864

My Dear Dear Wife.—I am now writing with a Yankee pen, Yankee ink and on Yankee paper captured on the battlefield. We had one of the hottest contested battles of the War on yesterday, commencing about 2 oclock pm and ending ½ past 5 pm and during the whole time there was not a moments cessation in the fire. Men never fought better than our men did and God seemed to shield them in

---

12. When the two armies met on 20 February, the Confederates had about 5,000 men, the Federals about 5,500.

a great measure from Destruction as the los on our side is comparatively light. We cant tell yet how much it is but, I think from all that I can learn that 300 will cover dead and wounded and the enemy think they have lost 1500 men killed and wounded.[13] I passed over the field this morning and the dead Yankees and negroes are strewn thick all over the field. we drove the Yankees inch by inch for about two miles and then they left in a hurry. I will give you some of the particulars, yesterday morning our Pickets reported that the enemy were coming towards us in heavy force. The 2d. Cav was at once put on the move with Col Clinch's Georgia cavalry and we met the enemy some six miles from our entrenchments and I was thrown to the front with my company to skirmish with them.[14] I engaged them and continued to fall back firing as I went until we got near our Infantry support which was one mile from the entrenchments, then I was drawn off and another company relieved me. When we got to the Infantry line I was thrown to the right flank some times Col McCormick Commanding and some times I was in Command and Col Clinch occupied the left flank. The enemy pressed us quite hard but our artilery and infantry opened and the boys yelled and went to work as men can only work who are in earnest, then the scene was grand and exciting. I felt like I could wade through my weight in wild cats. The 2d. Cav was dismounted to fight on foot and I think we did good work, we went on with a wild yell and the Yanks and negroes gave way, then we would remount and follow up and we continued that until the fight ended. Then we were thrown to the front and we got during the night some 200 yanks that were wounded and not able to keep up with the main body.[15] We were returned this morning after having been in the saddle one day and night without any rest or any thing for our horses to eat. We got the Yanks provisions and fared first rate. We followed the Yankees some ten miles from the battlefield and the Cav that relieved us are following them up now and I suppose they will stop at little St Marys as they have entrenched at that place. They say they only expected to find 1200 men here to fight and they had 11700 men and had provisions for four days and calculated to reach Tallahassee by that time. We had some four thousand

---

13. Federal casualties came to some 1,861, about 34 percent of those engaged, broken down as follows: 203 killed, 1,152 wounded, and 506 missing. The Confederates had 93 killed, 847 wounded, and 6 missing. Finegan ordered the Confederate cavalry to pursue, and the Federal retreat could have become a rout; but Colonel Carraway Smith, who was in command of the cavalry, found that his troops and horses had been largely used up and were not capable of rapid pursuit. There was much criticism of Finegan and Smith at the time, and the cavalry was decidedly slow in the follow-up.

14. Colonel Duncan L. Clinch and the Fourth Georgia Cavalry were a force of about 250 men. The Second Florida Cavalry, sometimes under the command of Lieutenant Colonel Abner McCormick and sometimes under Winston's command, numbered 202 men. As mentioned, Colonel Carraway Smith, in command of the Second Florida Cavalry Regiment, had overall command of the cavalry at Olustee.

15. All captured Federals, white and black, were sent to the new Georgia prison named Camp Sumter, soon known simply as Andersonville.

men in the fight against their immense numbers and we drove them as prettily as you ever saw any thing done. I had no men killed or wounded but had one horse shot and some very narrow escapes. Ben Gaines was in the fight and his company captured 3 peaces of artillery, some of the Company were shot but Ben got out without a scratch, how singularly our family are blessed, not one of us hurt yet. Davis was not quite well and was not in the fight but to day he got a wounded yankee horse and is going to try and cure him.[16] I [got] several things of Value, a blanket, tent, 2 oil cloths, Haversack of Provisions, and 2 flannel shirts, 1 pr Drawers, 1 pr Gauntletts, 3 canteens, and I have got a fine sword from one of my men that got it on the field. The old Georgia troops say they never have seen better fighting done any where but say our boys did better than any men they ever saw. They say they thought Fla boys would not fight here but now they say they will go even further than they will go, the fact is men cannot fight better than ours did. We lost some good and valuable officers belonging to the Ga troops, Col Charles Hopkins was slightly wounded in the thigh and arm though remained on the field and fought out the fight.[17] The Yanks are completely routed and unless they are strongly reinforced in a short time, they will not be likely to reach Tallahassee. our force is quite strong and I think we will advance soon. I got some very interesting letters directed to the 54th Mass Colored troops, you would be interested to read some of them.[18] The Genl is very much pleased with every one and I think he ought to be as he has no dout given the Yankees as complete a thrashing as any set ever carried. I am so tired and sleepy I can hardley keep my eyes open to write. Davis will write by this mail. I went over the battle ground this morning on my way to camp and never in all my life have I seen such a destressing sight, some men with their legs carried off, others with their brains out and mangled in every concievable way and then our men commenced stripping them of their clothing and left their bodies naked. I never want to see an other battle or go on the field after it is over. I could stand and count 20 or 30 dead yankees at one sight and I counted 12 fine horses killed in 20 steps of each other. We captured six peaces of artilery ... and a great many small arms and any quantity of baggage. I have only received one letter from you in nearly three weeks. I do wish you would write. I can get a letter any day here as the cars come through. when you feel like writing do so and dont wait for me. Tell the negroes if they could have seen how the negroes were treated I think it would cure them of all desire to go. one of the Yankee negroes offered to shake hands with one of the negroes in camp and the one in camp killed the other, telling him not to offer

16. Winston was mistaken; Davis found a horse and got into the fray about midway through the battle.

17. Colonel Charles F. Hopkins was in command of the First Florida Infantry Battalion.

18. These letters are missing. The Fifty-fourth Massachusetts Regiment was composed of free blacks, not recently freed slaves, and had been almost destroyed as a regiment during an assault against Battery Wagner on 18 July 1863. Battery Wagner was a heavily fortified earthwork that was part of the Confederate defense structure at Charleston. Since the Fifty-fourth had been so cut up six months earlier, it was assigned only a minor role in the Battle of Olustee.

to speak to him.¹⁹ I must close. Give my love to Mother and the boys and kiss dear Rosa and tell her Pa thought of her and Ma often while under fire and I feel thankful to god that he has been so merciful to me and Mine. Good bye my darling and may the giver of good continue to watch over us in mercy. I am as ever your devoted Husband.

[DAVIS BRYANT TO REBECCA BRYANT]

Camp Beauregard Feb 21st

My dear Mother

I write a few hasty lines to enclose with Winston, to send by train that has just arrived. I am glad Winston has been enabled to write so long a letter. I wished very much to write all day but felt obliged to go to the boys with provisions as early as possible; and after getting about two miles on the way learned they [were] coming in where as I was on the field concluded I had better avail myself of the chance to ride over it. And finding a fine wounded yankee horse undertook to bring him in which occupied a good deal of time; ever since I have been trying to revive him, as I am now virtually on foot, and fixing up some important papers for Col. McCormick. I have just finished the latter. I was with the cavalry only about two hours of the time during the fight, because I was sick and the mare in too poor a condition for use when they left, but when the firing became so terriffic as it was, I was too anxious to remain here idle. We had no idea of a general engagement when the Cav. left . . .

I have been running about too much lately to write to Willie do write him at once. Maj. Routh wants him much and look for him daily. Do not think for a moment that I am not heartily thankful for our preservation. The enemy is driven back about 18 miles.²⁰ But I must close with this and great deal of love to Tivie and *all*—Yr aff son—

Davis

[OCTAVIA STEPHENS TO WINSTON STEPHENS]

Feb 22, 1864

My dear dear husband

I will write a few lines and run the risk of your getting it, I have not known before where to direct, I received yours of the 18th. yesterday it was such a relief

---

19. There were certainly atrocities committed against blacks by Confederate soldiers during and after the battle, but we doubt the credibility of this story.

20. The Federals had retreated all the way to Jacksonville, some forty miles, and there they stayed behind fortified lines. This occupation lasted for the rest of the war, and Federal forces raided the area along the St. Johns River for its duration, but there were no more major attempts to invade the interior of the state. Willie was trying to transfer from Atlanta to Florida, and he finally succeeded in August 1864.

to me, for oh I have been so anxious, and am still, but your letter let me know that you were well three days before, and I am glad to hear that you have such a good force down there, affairs were so *hot* down there as I thought from reports, we thought the Yankees had Lake City as the cars did not come from there on Thursday and we had heard that the Yanks were advancing on it in two columns, I have never had such anxiety before as I have had since your removal to [Lake City], but thank the Lord you are yet spared to me, unless something has happened within the last three days, my thoughts are incessantly to the Lord in supplication for your protection, but my dear do be as careful of yourself as you can and do not run into any danger that you can avoid, do not forget how precious your life is to us, I hope the Yankees may soon leave but fear they have come for a long stay. I do want so much to see you, but I would willingly wait some time and go through my confinement without you if I could only know that you would return safely, I do not expect to see you before my confinement but hope we shall both live to see each other very soon after . . .

Mother sat up last night with the daughter of a neighbor who has been sick some time with Typhoid pneumonia, two sons were buried in the same grave two weeks ago from the same family . . .[21]

I am sorry the yankees have Felix but hope he may yet escape, as you have not mentioned our relatives in your company, I suppose they are all alive and with you . . . Do write when you can, I will write when I think there is any chance of your getting it. I can not say more now although my heart is full of love and anxiety for you, God grant that your life may be spared and we united soon in health here comes our little darling and sends you a kiss.

As ever your devoted
Wife

[REBECCA BRYANT TO WILLIE BRYANT]

Feb 22, 1864

My dearest Willie,

. . . We have been in great anxiety for the past week, as the various rumors from Lake City of the advance of the enemy seemed to be confirmed by the failure of the cars to reach Monticello on Friday last. But yesterday we recd. a letter from Winston of the 18th. which gave assurance of his safety up to that time and that Davis would be obliged to stay in camp as he has no pony and Winston keeps both his horses ridden down . . .

21. This is undoubtedly when Rebecca contracted the typhoid pneumonia with which she became ill. Before the war Octavia's diaries show that Rebecca often sat up with sick neighbors.

Davis and six others were completely surrounded by the enemy while on the road to Baldwin, but he and a sergt. of the company "made a break and escaped"—a narrow escape it was too, and how can we be sufficiently grateful that both he and Winston were unharmed! Winston is enduring great fatigue, riding night and day, often with but little food, but up to the above mentioned date he was well. I fear there will be very hard times in Florida yet. They estimate the enemy's force of 10,000—I *hope* you *may* be on your way from Atlanta before this reaches it, but thinking the confused state of affairs in Lake City might hinder the transmission of yr papers, I concluded to risk a post stamp rather than have you detained and without letters . . .

With an ocean of love from us all and hoping to see you here soon

Mother

Feb 25, 1864. *Rec letters from Winston and Davis written 21st the day after a tremendous fight with the Yankees in six miles from Lake City, our forces victorious, not a man in Winston's company killed or wounded . . .*

[WINSTON STEPHENS TO OCTAVIA STEPHENS]

On picket Near C. Finegan Feb 27, 1864

My Darling Wife

I know how anxious you are to hear from us and I write every spare time. You will see by this that we are gradually closing upon the Yanks and their brother negroe. We moved down from Baldwin yesterday . . . I learn we are having large reinforcements and siege guns sent on to us and I would not be surprised at any time to be thrown in the midst of battle with all grandure and at the same time with all dangers. Oh how much I wish I could never see such a sight as I witnessed after the battle near Olustee Station and then to think of the loved ones at home who have been left lonely in this life by the loss of husband, Son or Father or some young lady whose love had been centered upon some dear one whose life is so suddenly cut off. these reflections are not sweet and I'll not write of them. I think the Genl intends driving the Enemy to their gun boats and if he gets the force I learn is coming he will be able to do so. the sound drubbing we gave them before will prepare them to expect a second one when we meet. I dont suppose their has been a more dicisive battle fought since the War commenced . . . they did not stop running until they reached Camp Finegan. If we had only pressed them after the fight we could have captured the whole army. I hear that Genl

Colquitt wanted to follow them but Genl Finegan opposed.[22] Col Hopkins told me that Genl F— ordered Gen Colquitt to fall back during the fight but Colquitt sent him word it was no time to fall back and told him to send him more men which he did and we have one of best victories recorded. I want Genl Colquitt to have all the credit due him.

I like Genl Finegan more than I used to but I have not got the confidence I would like to have in my Commanding Officer. Our Genl seems to think that our men and horses can live on wind as [he] keeps us in the saddle all the time and we get but little to eat, the fact is if we had not got of the yankees waste we would have suffered very much. My horses are mere skeletons, they dont look like the same horses, it is nothing strange for them to go 24 and 36 hours without feed and then get a few ears of corn and go again. I was sent up to Middleburg on the 25th. with my Company and staid one night. Sister was well but Birtha looks badley and is almost constantly sick.[23] Sister has not heard from Ma in some time as the mail was cut off. I dont think from what I hear that the yanks have been above Palatka nor from Augustine farther than Dunns Creek. I think our old home has not been visited yet, and if we are successful they will not. lots of the people through here have taken the oath, I hear Greely has gone to Nassua with his family.[24] I dont know what point Davis is at . . . [he] has Pet with him I am well but as near worn out as any man you ever saw and so black that I am ashamed. I left Camp Cooper on the 6th. and had on a dirty shirt and I have changed but once since that time. I have clean clothes in Lake City but they had as well not be for the good they do as I am kept so constantly going I cant get them and we are not still long enough to wash once. I have had but one letter from you in the same time. I hope my letters have better luck and reach you regular. I hope God in his goodness will soon relieve us from this awful condition. give love to Mother and boys and kind remembrances to all friends . . . Give a kiss and love to dear Rosa and accept for yourself the love and devotion of a sincere and loving Husband . . .

Winston Stephens

22. General Alfred Holt Colquitt was in tactical command of the battle; Finegan stayed near the Olustee fortifications and sent in the troops as Colquitt requested them. As mentioned, Finegan did order Carraway Smith to pursue, but Smith was very slow in carrying out orders. Most probably his troops were too used up to effectively chase the enemy; horses and men alike had been without food, sleep, and rest for the better part of two weeks, and fewer than five hundred were present during the battle. Although many Confederates later insisted that the enemy could have been completely routed, Winston was mistaken in his belief that the whole army could have been captured. During the Civil War, when opposing forces were roughly equal, this never happened; the strength of the force on the defensive was simply too much to be overcome.

23. Mary (Gaines) Branning was Winston's half-sister; this was the last time they saw each other. Bertha was Mary's daughter.

24. As times became tougher and the Federal presence more ominous, residents of northeastern Florida were much readier to take the oath of allegiance to the Union and go home. This was true of civilians and military alike; the rate of desertion increased substantially after the Federal invasion, as the actions of J. C. Greely illustrate.

Feb 28, 1864. No letters. Mother taken quite sick, congestion of the brain, sent for Dr Adams. Aunt Julia came with him to stay over night . . .

[WILLIE BRYANT TO DAVIS BRYANT]

Atlanta, Ga. Feb 28, 1864

Dear Davis,

. . . Affairs in Fla. very suddenly assumed an exciting aspect and I suppose the end has not yet come, and perhaps not the worst, tho' I dont anticipate that the Yankees will try to carry out any plans they have laid for Fla. at a much greater Cost. The news we receive here from Fla. has been so long coming, and so "meager," that I have been greatly excited and irritated, and as I have been daily expecting for some time to be able to start for there I have felt it the more . . .

Atlanta possesses very few attractions to strangers and affords no ammusements . . . This evn'g I am to go to Church with Miss Steele, and for next week she has laid out a round of gaiety for me if she can draw me into it, and as I am "thawing out" somewhat . . . I think I shall indulge slightly.[25] A young lady friend of theirs whom I am not yet acquainted with, "fell desperately in love" with me upon my opening the gate for her in a very gallant style one afternoon . . . it is needless to say that the young lady in question is very susceptible, and highly flattered by attention from young gentlemen, and as that is my cue, unless I have forgotten my old taste and tricks I'll "amuse" her. I must tell you of an affair of love I have had on hand . . . I saw her at Church at first, she was pretty and plump and looked fast, I have been following her up for three weeks, and trying to learn her name, and she seemed flattered by it, for I plainly showed my intentions; I thought if I could become acquainted that there was a chance for some "fun" in that quarter . . . finally I learned her name, and with heart beating high with fond hopes, on yesterday morn'g wrote her a killing note seeking an acquaintance to commence with a walk home from church this morn'g, and engaging a nigger in the capacity of a "Mercury" and giving him his cue, sent the note by him . . . after some time the nigger retd. with a note in his hand, but alas for all my fond hopes it was the same I had sent, she had opened it and read it, turned scarlet, then pale and let out on me a tirade of abuse and finally burst into tears, telling the nigger who stood astounded at the serious turn of affairs had taken to tell the young gentleman that she would have nothing to do with him . . . O, ye gods and little fishes! what a pity! but the devil of it is that tho' I signed by name as *B. A. Williams* she knows me by sight . . . and [when we meet] I may expect daggers from her eyes . . .

Affairs have been very active in our front lately, some fighting has been going on and a general engagement was anticipated, but the intention was evidently

25. This is a niece of Captain Holmes Steele; her first name is unknown.

only a diversion on the part of the yanks and to prevent our sending troops to Mississippi — and they have now retired.[26]

If this good weather continues we may soon expect squally times in this section, and I must say I am not over sanquine as to the result; Genl. Johnston is too ready to fall back . . .

Much love to Winston and good luck to both of you — I wish I had a good pony and was with you.

Yrs. Always Affectionately

Willie

Feb 29, 1864. Mother still quite sick, Aunt Caroline came in the morning and Aunt Julia left just before dinner with the Dr . . . No letters.

Mar 2, 1864. Letter from Winston, he was near Camp Finegan again . . . Wrote to Winston and Willie. Mother better.

[OCTAVIA STEPHENS TO WILLIE BRYANT]

Mar 2, 1864

Dear brother Willie

Again I am seated to write you as Mother is sick but it will be but a few lines as I am expecting to send this off this afternoon and I have spent a long time in writing to Winston . . . [Mother] was taken Sunday morning with a kind of congestive chill which lasted three hours or more, which caused congestion of the brain and lungs and Sunday afternoon was quite delirious, she has been pretty sick since but not delirious but seems better to day, Dr Adams is of course attending her, Aunt Julia has been with her two nights, I hope she will now get well fast . . .

We all send love and still hope to see you very soon. You will hear from some of us soon if you do not come.

Very affly

Tivie

---

26. Bragg lost the Battle of Chattanooga during the months of October and November 1863. On 24 November, Federal forces threw the rebels from Lookout Mountain, and Bragg was forced to retreat to Dalton, Georgia. Bragg was relieved and General Joseph Johnston returned to command, but the Federals under Major General William Tecumseh Sherman now had a base from which to launch a spring offensive against Atlanta.

[Telegram, Davis Bryant to Willie Bryant]

March 8, 1864

Winston is killed. Mother and Tivie sick. Come if possible.

Davis

[Willie Bryant to Rebecca Bryant]

Atlanta Ga. Mar 8, 1864

My dear Mother—

I wrote you a hurried note on last Saturday p.m. when I first learned of Winston's death—As I could not get off the next morn'g I concluded to wait until I should learn something further of it and then be governed accordingly; The mail Saturday Evening brought me a letter from Davis but it was mailed the night before the sad event; Sunday brought me no intelligence, yesterday Major Fairbanks advised me as so long a time had now elapsed and the urgent need for my immediate presence was past, not to go at present unless I recd. intelligence requiring it; Capt. Doggett arrived here yesterday p.m. having left Madison last Thursday, and told me that he was told that Davis had passed on his way up to Thomasville with Winston's body, and was sure that it was so.[27] It was a great relief to me to know that Davis had been able to get off at such a time and be with you, and I felt comparatively easy, but this morning I am made more miserable by receiving a letter from Tivie written on the 2d., tho' not post marked until the 5th., containing the sad news that you have been very sick, and tho' better, that both you and Rosa are still sick;

The news of Winston's death at such a time must have been terrible upon you all and I fear for your health, and poor Tivie without your consolation and advice at such a trying time must be dreadfully stricken; my heart bleeds for you, and the thought that I am away from you and unable to do anything to relieve your situation, with the anxiety to know all, tortures me almost beyond endurance—

Thank Heaven! Davis was able to go to you if only for a short time, and with Aunt Julia and other loving ones around, you have all the consolation and atten-

---

27. Captain Aristides Doggett, who was in command of Company A, Third Florida Infantry, heard at Madison that Davis took Winston's body to Thomasville, but Davis took it to the Lake City cemetery for burial with the Olustee casualties. During the 1880s, with state financial aid, many Confederate remains were reinterred according to the families' request. This was true in the case of Winston. He was reinterred in the Westview Cemetery in Palatka at that time. His grave today is marked by a small headstone that reads, "W. Stephens C.S.A."

tion that can be of any avail; I hope that the Almighty who has sent this terrible visitation will in his mercy give strength to the afflicted ones, and by the grace of his holy spirit soothe their grief and help them to bear his chastenings with calm submission.

I can offer no consolation now acceptable to such a grief as Tivie's, at present she can only realise the fact that he is lost to her, and see nothing in his death and the circumstances to console her or call up other feelings to her support.

I am in no mood to write, sorrow, deep anxiety for you both, and hatred with the desire to avenge Winston's death, fill my mind with so many conflicting emotions that the words I write seem cold and hollow in comparison with what I feel and wish to express. The papers relative to my transfer to Fla. have been renewed . . . and by the last of the week at farthest expect to be with you.

I shall write Davis to-day—Much love to you all and may God be merciful to you in your distress. Ever Affectionately

Willie

[WILLIE BRYANT TO DAVIS BRYANT]

At Aunt Julias Mar 12, 1864

My dear brother

I came out here at 12.o.c. last night, when I learned our sad bereavment—my God, it is terrible![28]

I cant write of it now—Mine is not a grief that can relieve itself in words.

Aunt Julia, Georgie and I are now going out to Tivie's—Aunt Julia will add a line to and enclose a note Georgie brot over from Tivie last night . . .

Ever affectionately
Willie—

Near Thomasville, **Mar 15, 1864.** *With what a sad, sad heart I begin another journal. On Sunday Feb 28th, dear Mother was taken with a congestive chill. on Friday March 4th, Davis came with the news of the death of my dear dear husband, he was killed in battle near Jacksonville on the 1st. of March. Mother grew worse and on Sunday, Mar 6th, she too was taken from us, between 12 and 1 o'clk she passed quietly away from Typhoid Pneumonia. At 7 o'clk p.m. I gave birth to a dear little baby boy, which although three or four weeks before the time, the Lord still spares to me. Mother was buried on the 7th, and Rosa was taken with fever, but recovered after two days. Davis returned to Lake City on the 10th, and Willie arrived here on the 12th, and he and Henry left to day for Monticello,*

28. This is when Willie learned of the death of his mother six days earlier; Rebecca was buried on 7 March at Jones Cemetery, Thomasville.

Willie going to Lake City to see Davis, expects to return in a few days, our relatives and new made friends have been kind in visiting, Aunt Julia has devoted nearly her whole time to us since the first day of dear Mother's sickness. I have named my baby Winston, the sweet name of that dear lost one my husband, almost my life. God grant that his son whom he longed for but was not spared to see may be like him. I now begin as it were a new life and I pray that the Lord will give me strength to bear up under this great affliction, and with His help and the examples of those two dear ones now with him I may be enabled to do my duty in this life and be prepared when the Lord calls to meet them in that "better world" where there will be no more parting and no more sorrow.

[SWEPSTON STEPHENS TO OCTAVIA STEPHENS]

Ocala Oct 20, 1866[29]

My Dear Sister Tivie

... If it were possible I should never tire of talking with you of dear Winston, that I could be with you how happy I should be to sit and talk of the Dear Departed. You know not the anguish of my heart when he was shot. We were side by side and tho' I was not looking at him when the fatal ball pierced him I heard it and turned and asked him if he was hurt. He turned and looked the reply but could not speak and just at that time my spur was cut off and consequently he fell before I could reach him. I dismounted and took him up and sit him on my horse and got up behind him and took him out in that way leaning back against me. That look, the last look was full of love. His lips moved but no word escaped. I see that look now and ever will . . .[30]

Swepston

29. There is no accurate contemporary description of Winston's death; we include Swepston's account to remedy this deficiency.

30. The main Confederate force was at Camp Milton on the west side of McGirt's Creek, six to seven miles west of Cedar Creek. An advance force was on the east side of McGirt's Creek at Ten-Mile Station. On 1 March 1864 Winston made the notation "on picket" in a notebook he was carrying. Also on 1 March, Federal Colonel Guy V. Henry sent a patrol out of Jacksonville toward the Confederate position at Ten-Mile Station. After driving in the Confederate pickets, which included Winston, the patrol encountered a larger rebel force about three miles west of Cedar Creek, and a heavy skirmish ensued. About 11:00 A.M. the Federals began withdrawing and recrossed Cedar Creek, where they were reinforced. Winston rode up at the head of about eighty cavalry, most of whom were his own company. The cavalry, in column of fours, led a Confederate force in pursuit of the Federals, which consisted of cavalry, infantry, and artillery. The cavalry moved across Cedar Creek and the dry scrub pineland to the east of the creek, where it appears Winston was killed by a sniper with the first shot from Union forces waiting in ambush. The fighting became general, and the Federals were again forced to retreat, this time to prepared positions at Three-Mile Run. The Confederates withdrew about 3:00 P.M., and the fighting was over. The Federals reported one killed, four wounded (one of whom died), and five taken prisoner. The Confederate loss came to seven killed and twelve wounded.

Mar 16, 1864. Henry returned from Monticello about 9 o'clk a m brought the trunk containing dear Winstons clothes, and a barrel of irons and potware sent from Welaka. I sat up most of the day . . .

Mar 19, 1864. . . . Willie returned from Lake City about supper time, bringing Pet the horse with him.

[WILLIE BRYANT TO DAVIS BRYANT]

Thomas Co. Ga. Mar 21, 1864

Dear Bro. Davis,

I came thro' safely without any special adventure . . . I found Tivie about her room and the baby and all the rest well. Tivie now is able to come to the table and will soon be around and attending to all the household duties, and before I leave her will be able to take interest in matters around her and have something to occupy her thoughts and time . . .

I went to see the Judge of Probate or Ordinary, in Geo.—and found him a good and kind man who will give all information and attention he should. On the first Monday in May Tivie must appear before him with some one to give bond . . .

All send love.

Always Affectionately Willie—

[AUGUSTINA STEPHENS TO OCTAVIA STEPHENS]

Welaka Mar 21, 1864

My own dear Tivie

How shall I begin a letter to you, knowing how heart broken you are, but my dear dear Tivie you have not been absent from my thoughts ten minutes at a time since we heard the dreadful news of our dear dear Winstons death. I never had such a shock in my life and poor Clark, I dont hardly recognise as the same being never a word or smile unless spoken to, but as great as our grief must be at his loss I know it is nothing compared to what you must feel, I declare I think and think about you and cry until my brain seems to be on fire. If I could and had no hinderances I would go to see you for it seems as though I cant content myself from you, and my daily prayer is that the Almighty may strengthen and enable you to hold up under your dreadful afflictions. I cant realize the awful truth, we first heard the report two weeks ago last Sunday, but I could not or would not believe it, we hear so many things which are in a few days contradicted, but on the next Wednesday Wash Braning came and brought us the confirmation of the report.[31] Oh! my dear Tivie you certainly have your share of the worlds trials and none *can* feel or know what you suffer, but try my dear child and believe it is for some Wise purpose, I know words of consolation and sympathy at such a time wont lesson one moment of sorrow or trouble to you but still I want you to know and believe there is not one who feels for you more deeply than I do, although I cant find words adequate to convey my feelings . . . I want you *always* to remember my dear Tivie that our hearts and home are always ready to welcome you and yours not only for the sake of the dear one separated but for the love we have for you also, and for his sake and the little ones we treasure so dear to him.

Try and bear your afflictions with christian fortitude and poor Ma next to you her distress must be the greatest. I should not be surprised if it put an end to her sufferings on this earth, she is old and in such dreadful health and having already gone through with so much since this awful war commenced I fear to hear the result, if I ever hear . . . we are entirely cut off from the other side unless some one risks that chance of being taken by the Yankees which is not very often for the past two weeks they have been running up here and higher almost daily, you can well imagine what a state I am *all* the time in. Clark had determined to stay at home and if they did come to meet them . . . They have destroyed or taken off *everything* in Your Mothers office and Mrs Hopkins house, *nothing* has escaped his notice, all that remains at either place is scattered papers and broken furniture . . . All the wharves in town are open and cut away, and Mr Smiths store and warehouse broken open and everything cut to pieces and carried away. They know everything and everybody. They have the "Hattie" and "Sumpter" . . .[32]

When will this awful state of affairs end? as you said in your last "Liberty how dearly we are paying for it," if we ever gain it which I now very much doubt, our affairs really look gloomy but when I consider my situation compared with so many, with you my dear Tivie, I feel as though I ought to do nothing but return the thanks to our Heavenly Father that has still spared me my Husband, anything is easy to bear as long as he is still with me. Many wives have lost her Husband, but not such as yours, how short the time seems to look back when you were both so happy at "Rose Cottage" and then to see what a change to us all. My heart bleeds for you and it seems impossible for me to sit contented and not have the power to say one word of comfort or try to lighten your grief in any

---

31. Washington Branning was the mail carrier for the Middleburg region of Clay County.

32. Acting Master John C. Champion reported on 23 March that he had been told by Hampton Daniels, a pro-Union man who lived at Buffalo Bluff, about a supply of turpentine stored up the Ocklawaha River. He found and confiscated the supply and returned to Drayton Island in Lake George on 11 March. He was informed that the *Sumter* had been captured by the *Columbine*, and he took command of the *Sumter*, went upriver past Lake Monroe in Seminole County to Deep Creek, found the *Hattie Brock*, and captured her. On the way back to Jacksonville he reported that he stopped at Gardner's distillery below Welaka and took possession "of all the copper apparatus for distilling spirits of turpentine." ORN, ser. 1, vol. 15, 300–302.

way. Wash said Col McCormick announced the death of our dear Winston to the whole Regiment in the most feeling manner and said it had lost its best captain and his men their best Friend, he said there was not a dry eye in the whole command, he said he never saw men so affected or show it so openly, as they all did . . . Clark sends a great deal of love to you and kisses to dear little Rosa. Remember us kindly to your Mother and the boys and reserve oceans of love for yourself, my dear Tivie from your aff

Tina

[DAVIS BRYANT TO OCTAVIA STEPHENS]

Lake City Fla Mar 23, 1864

My very dear Sister

. . . It was such a satisfaction to see Willie and hear such good accounts of you, and I do hope and trust you have continued to improve. You cannot know how hard it was for me to leave you and dear little Rosa in such a state but I think it was best as it has proved, though I certainly could not have done so had I thought I could be of much assistance to you, but as it was I had every confidence that our dear and kind relatives would give you every attention in their power; and do much more than I could think of or suggest . . .

Kiss Rosa and little Winnie for me too. I hope you will feel well enough to write me soon, but don't attempt until you feel like it. I shall depend upon the boys writing me occasionally. I suppose Willie left for Atlanta today. I will want to know how every thing is going on with you all.

Your very affectionate brother
Davis

Mar 27, 1864. *Willie left just before night to take the cars in the morning to return to Atlanta . . . I walked to the Pond with Willie . . . and the children, the first time I've been out for three weeks . . .*

[WILLIE BRYANT TO OCTAVIA STEPHENS]

Atlanta Ga. Mar 31, 1864

My dear Sister Tivie—

I write a few lines to let you know of me up to date . . . It is hard, very hard upon us all, and it seems as if our loss is more sensibly brought before me now than while with you; then, thoughts for you and the desire to do all I could during my short stay engrossed my mind to a great extent and prevented my realising it so forcibly. I fear too that since I have left you there has been less to divert your thoughts, and that you have given way to them more. You have borne up nobly thus far, and your conduct through it all deserves the highest commendation, and has shown a character superior to most women many years older; but knowing your disposition so well, what I fear for you is that you may allow yourself to sink into a state of melancholy which will not only unfit you for the fulfillment of the duties which now the more strongly devolve upon you, but finally impair your health; let me warn you against this and implore you my dear sister to strive to bear up under your terrible visitation with calmness and resignation, and by endeavoring to become interested in matters around you keep your mind and body in a healthful state, that you may be enabled faithfully to perform your sacred duty toward your helpless children, in a manner that you know would best meet the approval of him whom you always wished most to please, and whose memory is dearest to you—

There is much yet left to you worth living for, and try to see and appreciate it. Grief does not sink so deeply into the hearts of men as women, besides their occupations are such as to help them overcome it, while woman is frequently such as to increase it, but if you will try to occupy your mind with active thoughts and duties, with your fortutude, I feel confident that after a time your life will not seem so gloomy and objectless to you . . .

Much love to you all and God bless and keep you.

Always your affectionate brother
Willie

[WILLIE BRYANT TO OCTAVIA STEPHENS]

Atlanta Apr 3, 1864

My dear Sister—

. . . For some time past I have written Mother Sunday Evn'g or some time during the day, and since she was taken sick and died on that day I will be the more impressed by the day when it comes around, and it seems *holier* to me now . . . On Sunday Evn'g too I shall feel that she and Winston are nearer, and more earnestly and with greater happiness, if it be possible, looking down upon us. Let Sunday Evn'g with us all, hereafter be a time when we will try to be all reunited in thought and spirit with those in Heaven, and feel that we can hold sweet Communion . . .

Our relations—I should say our whole family—are very demonstrative and expressive, and rather expect it in others, you are not so much so, and I hope in your intercourse with them at first you will endeavor by your manner to show them your appreciation of their kindness; these little things go a great way and give much pleasure . . . With a great deal of love to all. Always Affectionately,

Willie

[OCTAVIA STEPHENS TO DAVIS BRYANT]

Apr 4, 1864

My dear brother Davis

I did not intend so long a time should elapse before answering your letter, but Willie wrote just before he left, and I thought I would then wait awhile and now I know not how to write I am so bewildered . . . my grief now is almost more than I can bear and it is only at times that I can submit, all looks so gloomy now, I feel as though I had little to live for, I try to do my duty to my children and live for their sakes, but have not the heart to do anything, all the pleasure of my life was wrapt up in Winston, he was almost my life, it seems as though I could not do without him much longer, I can not realize the whole truth, it seems dark and mysterious.

The baby is fattening up fast, but has been sick a good deal, but I think only with colic, and has had a very bad cold, but has seemed better the past two days, I suppose he will be a great comfort after awhile but now I can not take half pleasure in him or anything.

I have not seen Aunt Julia for sometime, she has her hands full at home, Grand Mother has been sick, and she wrote me yesterday that Aunt Mary was *very* sick, Georgie was there a few days before and said she was so much better and looked better, Georgie still has chills, he will go to Loulie's next week, we have not set the day yet, I hate to have him go . . .

I hope when you write you will tell me all that is going on down there, I shall always take an interest in the company and shall want to know who are taken out of it to follow their Captain.[33] I must close this poor epistle . . .

Ever aff-ly
Yr Sister Tivie

[JULIA FISHER TO DAVIS BRYANT]

Thomasville Apr 4, 1864

My dear Davis:

. . . I wrote Tivy by Henry, a note on Saturday, and this morning received one from her: dear little thing: if others could read it they would see She has *heart-enough* for those she loves, but as it was *individual* in its application, I would not let others read it: If they cannot appreciate her disposition and win Tivy's confi-

---

33. Upon Winston's death, Henry A. Gray was promoted to Captain of Company B, which was subsequently attached to the command of Captain J. J. Dickison, commanding Company H of the Second Florida Cavalry. Gray served in Dickison's command for the duration.

dence and love, they will always misunderstand her: she is *peculiar* but not cold, and has a deal of character under that quiet exterior: . . . I love you all for your own sakes, but more especially and tenderly for the sake of *her* [Rebecca] that I loved almost *sacredly:* there was a nearer, dearer bond of love between us than any one knows: with how much satisfaction I recall it now! just a little while before she went in the country she said . . . "I could live *forever* with you dear, I think happily": not that I was amiable, but we had *confidence, and understood each other:* that is the key to social happiness and comfort: and she has so often told me that her love for me was only second to her love for William and you children, that I feel as if *that* love must ever unite us who are left: Willie left on Monday, (a week since:) in a much pleasanter state of mind than before he went to Lake City: his absence at the time of our sorrow, had just the effect I feared on him: he felt it *bitterly:* to you, who had the blessed privilege of comforting and blessing her last hours, grief had lost its bitterest sting: there was so much to *soothe and calm, and reconcile our hearts:* but to him, only the stern cold facts: and business details: nothing to soften or alleviate: poor boy how my heart ached for him: after seeing you he felt better, and your love is such a blessing to him! may God bless you boys . . .

With love from all,
Yours ever:
Aunt Julia:

[Willie Bryant to Davis Bryant]

Atlanta Apr 8, 1864

Dear Davis—

. . . I think it very probable that almost all the Infantry now in Fla. will soon be ordered to Va. to meet the expected advance of the Yankees, and only the Cavalry left in the State to prevent the incursions of those in Fla.; how glad I am that you belong to that arm of service, and in all probability will always be retained in the state . . .[34]

The evenings are now so sad to me that I almost dread them, and do so long to be where I might enjoy quiet and pleasant company—How I do wish I could occasionally spend one with you or Tivie . . . Ours is not a gloomy future, particularly, and we have much to look forward to, and there is much in our present afflication to comfort us, as all has been as well as it well could be under such

---

34. Most of the infantry remaining in Florida left for Virginia by June 1864. All units were thrown together with the remnants of the Second, Fifth, and Eighth Florida Infantry Regiments already in Virginia and called the Florida Brigade. Under the command of General Joseph Finegan, the Florida Brigade suffered heavy casualties in the forthcoming offensive launched by Grant. The only forces retained in the state were cavalry, cadets, convalescents, and a very few infantry units.

circumstances, but it does bear down so hard upon me, all that I have lived for has been taken from me, the mainspring of my life, my comfort and support in the present, and the object for which were my dearest hopes and wishes in the future—Heaven knows I loved my mother with all the fondness capable in my nature! for her I lived! and when I think how she was the centre of all thoughts and the motive of all that was best in me, I wonder that I can bear it so calmly— I mourn my own loss in her, tho' I could give her up resignedly under other circumstances, knowing it for her happiness, but I know that it would have been her wish to have remained with us longer, and when I reflect upon the life of trial that has been hers, buoyed up by hopes which I felt that she had a right to expect in the future, I cannot be reconciled to her having been taken away from earth without having realised one of those hopes—I know I should try to feel differently and sometimes I do, but there are times when in my heart I rebel against the Almighty and without caring. I am not unmanned for the work before me, nor is my spirit broken, tho' greatly bent, and I hope, and shall endeavor, to faithfully and cheerfully perform the duties assigned to me in life, and tho' I willingly accept a new care, it cannot at once take the place in my heart of the old one with it's fond hopes and plans . . .

Good bye again for a little while—As I wrote before, consult your own convenience and inclination as to writing me soon.

Ever affectionately
Willie—

[JULIA FISHER TO DAVIS BRYANT]

Thomasville May 3, 1864

Dear Davis:

. . . Yesterday Georgy came early with mules, and we took Mr. Vann's buggy and went to town. I went to a friend's with baby behaved so prettily and good: Tivy looked so sad in her deep black, so young and pretty, she touched all hearts: she bore it all well: the very exertion she had to make was a benefit:

Dr. Adams stood bondsman and Mr. Everitt having been clerk of the court etc (Judge of probate etc) can assist her with all necessary advice.

She has all the necessary papers and can now go on without any difficulty. She encloses in this the order for you to have to sell the horse and she leaves it to your judgement about selling him, price etc: she prefers he should be sold at private sale if possible: she will write herself . . . with love ever

Your, Aunt Julia.

[MARY BRANNING TO OCTAVIA STEPHENS]

Hill Side Cottage Middleburg May 4, 1864

My dear dear Tivie

I have for some time past thought of writing to you, but could not summons courage though to do so untill now and how can I write? You have passed through firery trials dear Tivie since last I saw you and I longed to fly to you and comfort you in your time of sore trouble but it was impossible for me to do so and I know that such affliction as yours there is nothing that can comfort you but the hope of a reunion here after. God alone knows how deeply I sympathise with you and earnestly I pray that his blessings may rest upon you and your little ones. O! that he may comfort you in your desolation and heal your broken heart; dear Tivie I saw my darling brother only 5 days before his death. he with his company passed through this place on a scout. I never saw him in better health and spirits and as I pressed my lips upon his in parting how little I thought it would be the last time on earth, I watched them as far as I could see them . . . when I heard of his death the next week it almost broke my heart but I know my grief is nothing in comparison to you and my poor old broken hearted Mother . . .

Now dear Tivie I must close as I have to write to Jessup and it will soon be mail hour. Give my best love to Your Grand Mother and Aunt Julia. kiss both the children for me and accept much for your self from your

Loving and Affectionate Sister
Mary

[WILLIE BRYANT TO OCTAVIA STEPHENS]

Atlanta May 16, 1864

My dear Sister—

. . . There has been no general engagement but considerable hard fighting. From my disposition you will know that I have been much excited ever since active operations commenced on our front,[35] and it has been with the greatest difficulty that I have restrained myself from going up to take a part; most of the time I have been perfectly miserable, as I have seen comparatively so little service with my Regt. and more than ever am desirous to join them in a fight; but I knew that just at this time it would be particularly hard upon you should anything

---

35. Sherman began his campaign to capture Atlanta on 1 May. His army of about 98,000 men headed south from Chattanooga against Johnston's 53,000-man Army of Tennessee. It was a little over a hundred miles to Atlanta, and the campaign took more than four months; but the city fell on 2 September, one of the most decisive victories of the war.

happen to me, and as I felt that there was no especial call upon me to go, and as it was Maj. Fairbanks advice, I concluded to remain here—I am now able to go through a fight, and Heaven knows that I regret the circumstances which deter me from it and that I wish to do my whole duty . . .

I must close now with an ocean of love to you all. I imagine that little Mr. Winnie is becoming "interesting" and long to see the little gent; I want him to make haste and get big enough to know some one besides his ma and be able to talk some.

Good by Tivie dear!

Ever affectionately

Willie

May 22, 1864. The Anniversary of Mother's birthday I hope she is passing it in a better world . . .

May 25, 1864. As Winnie was wakeful I spent part of the morning tending him and reading in some of my journals of the many happy hours spent with my dear husband. Oh that they could return . . .

[WILLIE BRYANT TO OCTAVIA STEPHENS]

Atlanta May 26, 1864

Dear sister Tivie—

. . . I am so glad you went over to Aunt Julia's again and with such inclination; you dont know how happy I am on account of the good feeling and congeniality between you; you will always find her what you wish in her and it will be such a comfort and help to you, and the pleasure will be mutual, for you know what gives her most happiness is to do for others and have them repay her with love and confidence; she can fill many wants of your woman's heart which with all my desire and efforts would be impossible with me . . .

There has been more fighting near us, within 35 miles, and the cannonading could be distinctly heard here to-day . . .

Ever affectionately

Willie

[WILLIE BRYANT TO OCTAVIA STEPHENS]

Atlanta May 31, 1864

Dear Tivie—

... To-day I am much engrossed by business, and the arrival of many wounded Floridians who claim my attention, but will write you tho' it be a short and hurried letter ...

A Florida Relief association has been organised here and I am one of the members. The Fla. Brigade with the Ky. Brige. have just been terribly slaughtered, the Floridians losing 219 and the Kentuckians 207.[36] Several of my warmest friends in the army have been killed and severely wounded. What makes the affair more sad is that quite a general charge had been ordered, but the other Brigades had recd. an order countermanding it, and it was too late in reaching these two and they were led into the slaughter unsupported; it is very sad. Excuse more now, I have two lists of the casualties in the Fla. Brige. to make out and then am to go with Maj. Fairbanks to see some of the wounded. An ocean of love to you all.

Good bye for a little while—

Always affectionately
Willie

[DAVIS BRYANT TO OCTAVIA STEPHENS]

Lake City June 1, 1864

My dear Sister Tivie

It has been a long time since I have written you much longer than I intended should elapse ... I suppose you have heard of the exploits—recently—of Capt. Dickison on the St. Johns—his having captured 56 yankees at Welaka ... and ... a gunboat or rather a transport carrying two guns, with 65 prisoners killing

---

36. The Florida Brigade in the west (not to be confused with the Florida Brigade fighting in Virginia), under the command of Brigadier General Jesse Johnson Finley, was created during the interim between the Battles of Chickamauga and Chattanooga and consisted of the remnants of the First Cavalry and First, Third, Fourth, Sixth, and Seventh Infantry Regiments. The brigade was constantly engaged until the fall of Atlanta and suffered heavy casualties throughout the campaign. Willie's figures seem to be accurate; the brigade was crushed and very nearly routed by a greatly superior force outside of Dallas on 28 May. Finley was wounded at Resaca on 15 May, and Colonel Robert Bullock, Seventh Florida Infantry, took command. After this battle the brigade was about used up and did not fight well in any of the later engagements. The First Kentucky Infantry, the famed "Orphan Brigade," so-called because their state never seceded, was also terribly cut up at this time. Of the more than 4,000 in the unit when it left Kentucky in 1862, barely 600 men returned when the war ended. *OR*, ser. 1, vol. 38, pt. 3, 645.

and wounding some.[37] He was obliged to burn the boat, this was done below Palatka. The yankees have had a small force at Welaka some time and still have quite a cavalry force on the Haw Creek to guard the crossing to St. Augustine and get up cattle . . .

There is news from the front this morning that the yankees are making an advance. They know that we are weak here now and wish to draw forces from other parts probably. I am afraid, however, that we will have to depend upon what we have and that they will reach Baldwin before we can check them, as we have but a small force and cavalry only . . .

Yr. very aff brother

Davis

[CATHERINE PARKER TO OCTAVIA STEPHENS][38]

Dedham [Massachusetts] June 6, 1864

My dear darling Tivie,

I have written you one letter since we received the distressing news of our sad bereavement, and your two fold affliction. Words can not express what I and your other Aunts felt for you and how keenly we suffered at the loss of our dearly loved sister — your sainted Mother. If ever Mother and sister deserved affection and our veneration she did and it is very hard for us poor Kind mortals to be reconciled to the decree which took her from us. But we must remember that to her — to die was gain — and that she is now beyond suffering — joined to them who have gone before — Her pure spirit has found kindred spirits in Heaven. The daily beauty of her life on earth — her unwearying self sacrifice — strict fulfilness of every Christian duty — have found their reward. And he whom you so loved — the kind devoted husband! My heart bleeds for you, dear — when I think of your trial in parting with him so suddenly and at *that time*. May God sustain and comfort you — as He alone can! I hope he will spare your boy and the darling Rosalie whom you and your dear mother have so often described. I hope they will be a solace to you — and that you may yet bring them to see us. I wish if it is possible, you would convey some intelligence to us — of your health and situa-

---

37. Dickison's command, including a detachment from Company B, surprised the Federal post at Welaka on 20 May 1864 and captured the entire 41-man garrison. On 23 May, his command, including one battery of the Milton Light Artillery and a detachment from Company B, forced the *Columbine* to surrender after a fierce fight in which 20 Federals were killed and 65 were taken prisoner. The Confederates ambushed the ship near Horse Landing and sunk her to prevent her loss to Federal gunboats that were on the way. *OR*, ser. 1, vol. 35, pt. 1, 393–96; *ORN*, ser. 1, vol. 14, 440–54.

38. Catherine (Hall) Parker (Rebecca's sister) and her husband, Richard Parker, previously mentioned, were the aunt and uncle with whom Tivie lived in Boston in 1856 and 1857.

tion . . . God bless and give you that comfort "the world cannot give." Your affectionate

"Aunt Kate"

[OCTAVIA STEPHENS TO DAVIS BRYANT]

June 11, 1864

Dear brother Davis

I scarcely know how to begin my letter to you, but I know you will not be much surprised at the sad news I have to tell. Death has again visited us and taken another one from our midst, I hope to a better world, Aunt Mary died last Wednesday afternoon, her death was *very* similar to dear Mother's, they tell me they have laid her beside Mother and I hope they are together in peace in another world . . . Oh what a strange world this is, it seems like a new world and a new life to me and so hard to toil on in, though I know the hardships have hardly yet begun, it has seemed a hardship to do my *small* work about the house without the love and advice of that dear one who was almost my very life, but Henrys approaching birthday reminds me that I must make up that there is much ahead to be done, every thing has been left entirely to him regarding the farming, and you and Willie have been and are still kindly bearing the burden of my other matters for they have not burdened my mind in the least, but when I think of it I know it rests upon your minds, will I ever be able to take care of my children? Oh how often Winston has told me that I ought not to be so dependent upon him, but learn how to manage in case he was taken from me, but I always prayed that I might die first, that I might never have to mourn for him, I think I never shall become reconciled to his death . . .

It did me some good to hear of Capt Dickison's exploits, and to know that a part of the Old company, Capt Grey's took a part in the affair . . .

Rosa is asleep but Henry joins me in much love to you.

Ever affly yr
Sister Tivie

[AUGUSTINA STEPHENS TO OCTAVIA STEPHENS]

At Sweps June 19, 1864

My own dear Tivie

You will no doubt be surprised to see from where this is dated and doubly so to hear that we are homeless, how full of meaning that little word is and so much of ones happiness wrecked by it, two weeks ago to day we arrived here worn out in soul and body.³⁹ I had to ride on horse back from "Horse Landing" 70 miles here, you may judge of my condition. I know you take an interest in our welfare so to begin at the beginning, Soon after I wrote my last to you Welaka was occupied by a portion of the 17th. Connecticut troops, they were all very gentlemanly as much so as I ever saw, and we hoped and believed we would remain unharmed during the war but about a week after their arrival the Lieutenant in command saw Willie and Louis in town and asked them,⁴⁰ what had they been to horse landing for, that two small bare foot tracks had been tracked from our gate to within speaking distance of the "Rebel Pickets," the boys denied having been there (and they had not for nearly three months) and we supposed satisfactorily the tracks were made by two of William Priests negro women who were left on that side when their mistress was sent off and they came to our house enquiring the way to the Landing and it was their tracks Old Daniels saw and reported to the Lieut.⁴¹ Clark did not see him after that to explain matters to him but spoke to some of the men about them and supposed that every thing was right, about two weeks afterward Dickison captured them all except this Lieut and Daniels who had left about a half hour before for Augustine, as soon as they returned to "Haw Creeks" where the principal Yankee forces were stationed they informed Col Harms of it (their company being captured confirmed the suspicion) and he ordered Tom Peterson with fifteen men to go to Mr Barbers and kill him and burn all he owned and then to come to our house and shoot Clark on sight show him no quarters and destroy all we had. Mr Sikes had been taken by them and sent on an express somewhere and happened to return in time to hear the order given and see the men start, this was on Tuesday morning, he reached home on Wednesday about noon and went to Mr Bassfords to beg him to come and let us know, Mrs Marlow came down about dusk and that night her Father came down at midnight and went to the Ferry with Clark to see him safely over and he crossed on a *log*, as Barber lived above Enterprise some distance.⁴²

He knew they would be several days going there and returning so he told me to pack all I could in my trunks and have things ready to move at any moment in the night, Mr Bassford saw him over safely and let me know that morning (Thursday) and you may imagine my feelings all alone no one to exchange a thought with and in hourly expectation of those Devils riding up and burning the house over my head, but they did not and on Sunday night just after I had lain down Clark called me in a whisper to the door, he had got a portion of Dickisons and Grays men, Swep in command with a couple of Boats to take what they could. I

39. Swepston lived near Ocala in Marion County.
40. Tina's sons were William Winston and Lewis Isadore.
41. This was probably Hampton Daniels of Buffalo Bluff, previously mentioned.
42. Captain H. Harms was in command of Company A, German Artillery, First Regiment Artillery, South Carolina Militia. Thomas H. Peterson, a Welaka farmer, had evidently "gone over to the Yankees" if he assisted in burning out Cornelius Barber, a sixty-three-year-old farmer who lived several miles south of Welaka. John B. Sikes was a sixty-six-year-old Putnam county farmer. James Bassford, about sixty-four, lived in Welaka with his wife, Polly. We have not been able to identify either Mrs. Marlow or her father.

had the oxen up and had borrowed Mr Bassfords horse cart, expecting the Emergency, so in a short time one Boat was full of our things and the other filled with men, I could only bring my trunks packed closely. My Bedding, (I had to empty all the mattrasses), Bureau, the chest packed with crockery, the Centre Table, old chest of Drawers a few chairs, my Pot ware and a few of Sophia's things, some of the men offered to risk carrying the oxen cart and Horse around by land and they did so safely and swam them over, our splendid crop, hogs Poultry and the many little comforts and my great little home all left and now what is to be our fate, turned out of doors upon the Charity (I may almost say) of a cold selfish speculating world . . . Minnie and I rode on old Charley (we could not get a cart for love or money, every one seemed panic stricken and were moving away with the companies) Willey, Louis and Sophia walked nearly every step of the way, and Minja with Charlie and Mary, rode on the cart, we reached here Sunday afternoon about sun set, and received a hearty welcome from Vicky she has been very kind to us and insists on our remaining with her until we can do better.[43] You are also a sufferer by their occupying Welaka, as the old place and all of your things were burned to the ground. The Yankees denied doing it but I do not believe them it was either them or old Daniels, they first set the fence and palings on fire supposing the house would catch but it did not and then they set the house on fire all the buildings that are left are the two negro houses and the Cotton house . . .[44]

Poor Ma your heart would ache to see her, she looks *awful* for she is not long for this world her whole conversation is of you and dear Winston and she is almost all the time in tears now her anxiety about James and Ben makes her destress double. James was wounded in a skirmish but is now better and Ben is before Richmond, he went through the last fight unhurt. It was our intention when we first came up here to go to Ma's to stay but we found out how destitute her situation is so we did not go only for a few days, she will not remain down there any longer than this year . . . Ma sends a great deal of love and kisses to the children, she never speaks of either of you but in tears, she said this morning to think she would never live to see you all once more, seemed too hard, but I trust and pray that there is a little day in store for us all, Clark unites with me in kind love to you and the children, how I long to see that dear little Baby . . . good bye and May the Almighty bless protect you and yours, love to Henry,

aff your sister

Tina

43. Minnie was Tina's daughter, Mary Jane, born in 1855. Willey, Louis, and Charlie were her sons, previously mentioned. Sophie, Minja, and Mary were slaves. Vicky was Swepston's wife, Victoria Mills, whom he married at Fellowship, Florida, on 7 October 1860.

44. Rose Cottage and most of the other buildings were burned at this time, but it is not clear why since Winston was dead and none of the property belonged to Tivie. Neither White Cottage, the Bryants' house in Welaka, nor Clark and Tina's house was destroyed, although both sustained considerable damage. It may be that the Federal denial was accurate and that a mob led by Hampton Daniels fired the place, perhaps out of personal animosity toward the new owner. At any rate, no remains of the buildings have been located.

July 3, 1864. ... *a letter from Tina written at Swep's at Ocala, she writes of shameful doings of the Yankees and deserters at Welaka* ...

July 12, 1864. In the morning found Willie *had come in the night and gone into Henrys bed, and in the afternoon who should surprise us but* Davis, *he also came last night* ...

July 17, 1864. Willie and Davis went to ... *visit Mother's grave returned to late dinner* ...

[AUGUSTINA STEPHENS TO OCTAVIA STEPHENS]

At Sweps July 17, 1864

My own Dear Tivie

... My heart is sometimes fit to sink ... at my troubles and state of dependence I am obliged to live in, I think what you have had to endure and now have to breast the storms of this selfish world alone without your dear dear Husband and then think mine is still spared to me, I quell every rising morning and fear the Almighty would send some awful curse upon me for being so unthankful, but it is so hard to realize that every *mouthful* I eat, is given by others. My house was a humble one, but still I always had a plenty of the necessaries of life and a great many of the comforts, sometimes I get so worked up that I almost determine to go back and run all risks, yet I know in my calmer moments that I could not endure to live there alone and Clark on this side for I know he would slip over *sometimes* and I would always be in dread ...

I received a very kind letter from Lewis poor fellow he has his hands full, he gave me the particulars of our dear Seton death.[45] I cannot realize that it is so, he had passed through so many battles unharmed that I really believe he was to be one of the spared ones his poor Mother is almost crazy ... I have several of his letters and feel certain from the spirit breathed in them that he was prepared for a change, but it seems so hard to be cut down in the prime of manhood, he was 26 last Feb ...

I suppose I ought to be thankful for any favor but there are times when my situation is very forcibly brought to mind, it is dangerous to write too plain always, Swep is just as kind as can be when he was home and I believe him to be a christian at heart he seems to feel deeply for us and always charges Vick to do all she can for our comfort and she is *generally* very kind but there are times (I suppose she feels troubled and worried and all allowances ought to be made) when she seems distant and reserved and my being over sensetive on the subject makes me imagine *all sorts of things* ... I am so glad to hear that you have heard

---

45. Colonel Lewis Fleming was Tina's brother, and Captain Charles Seton Fleming was her half-brother. Seton was killed on 3 June 1864 at the Battle of Cold Harbor in command of Company G, Second Florida Infantry.

from your Father, I hope he did and will ever feel your Mothers death, but I fear not enough to allow for the neglect he was guilty of, whenever he thinks of that sainted and pure wife he so long neglected he ought to be consicience stricken...

God bless you my dear Tivie and may we be permitted at some future time to meet, I am

Ever Your aff Sister,
Tina

[Davis Bryant to Octavia Stephens]

Lake City July 24, 1864

Dear Tivie

I wrote Henry on my arrival here (last Wednesday) enclosing a furlough of ten day from Capt. Abell and Transportation tickets for his fare from Thomasville to Columbus Fla. which I hope reached him promptly[46] ... I enclose $10.00 for him which is all I can spare just now. I hope it will not be long before he will receive his Bounty ($50.00) and if the company is not paid off before the last of August he will get regular pay—at the rate of $12.50 per month ...

When I returned I found that the horse seemed worse than ever, and what has been told me by many before that he would soon become worthless unless he could have pasturage good grooming etc. etc. was so apparent I decided to sell him ... and accordingly, sold him yesterday for $1000.00 cash ...

Yr. very affecte. brother
Davis

July 27, 1864. . . . Henry left us in the p.m. and went to Aunt Julia's and is to leave on the hack for Columbus Bridge to join an Artillery Company.

[Octavia Stephens to Davis Bryant][47]

Aug 1, 1864

Dear brother Davis

... I am sorry to hear the Yankees are again creating a commotion down there, I fear they may yet take possession of Lake City, and when they do it will be so sudden that Winston's body could not be removed, and I would dislike very much to have it there if they have possession, but if there is no danger I would not

---

46. Henry enrolled in Company B, Milton Light Artillery, under the command of Captain Henry Abell and served for the duration of the war. Columbus, on the east bank of the Suwannee River, is present-day Ellaville. The destruction of the Columbus bridge had been one of the key objectives of the Federal invasion in February 1864.

47. This is the last letter in the collection written by Tivie in the period covered by this work.

have it disturbed, and I know you could not have it done easily. Oh I cannot realize the truth of what I am writing it seems so strange to speak of him in that way, I wanted so much to talk more of him when you were here, it seemed as though we had not talked together at all, writing is not satisfactory, I had been longing for you to come and talk with me, and when you were here I kept thinking until the last that I would have a chance, and now it seems so long before I will see you again. I feel very grateful to you for the attention to the grave of my lost one, I had felt that he was so far off and that no loving one ever visited the place, none but almost strangers, it is five months to-day since he left this world of trouble.

I am glad on your account that the horse is sold, for I know it was a great care to you and I am very much obliged to you for your trouble . . .

I shall be very anxious to hear from Florida again, my papers come *very* irregular. I generally get two or three at a time, I think they are taken out and read. I must close this miserable affair for this time. With much love

Aff-ly your
Sister Tivie

[WILLIE BRYANT TO OCTAVIA STEPHENS]

Macon Aug 7, 1864

Dear Tivie—

. . . Atlanta is in a deserted and dilapidated condition which is sad to behold— All the families of any note have left the city, tho' a few living out on the South side still remain . . . While I was in the old office packing up some things a shell entered the building joining and within a few feet of me, thro' the wall, took off a man's leg; several times the fragments of bursting shells and pieces of stone knocked off flew within 15 feet of me. My stay was quite exciting you may be assured, as my business kept me the whole time in the most exposed part of the city. Night and day it is kept up; not a continual heavy fire, but a few pieces playing upon the city at regular intervals, say each piece firing once in from 5 to 10 minutes. It is astonishing how people become accustomed to even these terrible missiles; even women and children may be seen about the streets, merely dodging behind some place to avoid the fragments when they hear a shell coming. And it is surprising how little damage is done by the hundreds of shot and shells thrown into the city during every 24 hours . . .

Good bye! Much love to you all, and may God bless and keep you.

Affectionately
Willie

[WILLIE BRYANT TO OCTAVIA STEPHENS]

R. Road [Macon] Aug 22, 1864

Dear Tivie—

Here I go, en route to Fla. at last![48] and will reach Lake City to-morrow p.m. at 4. As I have left you but so recently I thought you would not expect me to come thro' Thosville and therefore keep right on. Let me have a few lines from you very soon unless you have written Davis quite recently and there is nothing new with you—I shall write directly after I arrive at Lake City—I will "open Communication" with Henry at once . . .

Much love to you all—

Always lovingly

Willie

[HENRY BRYANT TO OCTAVIA STEPHENS]

Camp Jackson E. Fla. Aug 23, 1864[49]

My dear Sister

. . . I started from Columbus a week ago last Thursday, I came down with the drivers on horse back. We started Thursday afternoon and went to Houston that night . . . we started from there early next morning, that day we stopped at a house to buy some watermelons and peaches, and the lady gave us one melon, and told us we could get as many peaches as we wanted, if we would not shake the trees, I tell you what, we had a good *feed* . . . After we arrived at Lake City and fed our horses, I went down to Maj Routh's office . . . and staid with Davis until five o'clock and then I went to feed my horse, we drew some hard bread that had weavels enough in it to give it a *splendid* taste, and bacon that you would only have to smell to get enough [of] it. I took supper with Davis at his tent . . .

As we were coming down we stopped at Olustee . . . I rode over the battle field with some of the men that were in the fight and they showed me where our troops were, and where the Yanks had their batteries. We arrived here late that afternoon . . .

While I [was] putting on dinner Monday, orders were given . . . and . . . I had to leave dinner, and fall into ranks to see what was to be done, after all came out,

48. Willie's transfer was finally approved, and he reported to Quartermaster H. R. Routh in Lake City.

49. Camp Jackson, named for Brigadier General John King Jackson, who received the District of Florida command in July 1864, was located on the south fork of the St. Marys River at the railroad trestle, about four miles west of Baldwin. It was renamed Camp Turney in September and was only a temporary encampment.

the cannoneers were ordered to help the drivers harness up the horses, as we were to go on a scout with some of the cavalry, as the Yankies were advancing from Baldwin, we expected to come back that night so did not carry any blankets or raw rations, (for we didn't have time to cook any.) After we had started we heard that the Yankies had changed their course and were going toward Stark so *we* started for Stark too, *that* afternoon just after dark we came to a creek where the Yanks had cooked that afternoon and cut trees down across it so as to keep any of our troops from crossing, we halted there and made our fires, and as most of us had had no dinner we were pretty hungry so we went into a corn field close by and got some corn to roast for supper . . .

We found out that the Yankies were too strong for us at Stark, so we started for Waldo to join Capt Dickison, we arrived there about eight o'clock at night, we fed our horses and laid down to sleep and just as I was dosing off, Capt Dickison came riding up and told us to hurry and harness up our horses that the enemy were right upon us . . . we started on the road to Palatka and went a few miles on that road, when our piece took a right hand road and went across to the Gainesville road, Capt Dickison went right on . . . toward Gainesville, and came out a head of us on account of our having infantry for a support and could not travel fast on account of them, and our horses had not fared any better than we had and were nearly worn out and we had no horses to change . . . About daylight we stopped awhile for the infantry to catch up, and I laid down in the corner of a fence and went to sleep, and as I had not slept but very little since Sunday night, I slept so sound that I didn't hear the gun when it started, and nobody saw me, so I was left behind, when I woke up the sun was a good ways up, and I had to run about three miles before I got in sight of the cannon, just before I caught up two negroes came along with four mules and I got on one and we soon caught up with the cannon, Capt Dickison had sent back word, that he had nearly caught up with the Yankies, and we must hurry on as fast as possible, we took out our horses, and put the four mules in, with two of the best horses and left the infantry behind, we hurried on as fast as we could to try and get there in time for the fight, but did not get there until it was over, most of the prisoners were brought in after we got there, I didn't get any thing but a new calico shirt that had never been worn and a haversack . . . The Yanks had no idea that Capt Dickison was any where near Gainesville so they did not put out any pickets and were taken completely by surprise[50] . . . Give lots of love to *all* my relatives, and How-die to the

---

50. On 15 August Baldwin was burned by Federal cavalry. A column moved from there by night to Starke, where they burned warehouses and railroad cars, and then moved on to Gainesville early on 17 August. The place was almost deserted. As they began firing the buildings, they were surprised by Dickison and about 175 Confederate cavalrymen. A savage fight resulted in a reported 28 Federals killed, 5 wounded, and some 200 captured, with about 125 escaping back toward the coast. Confederate losses were reported to be 1 killed and 5 wounded. William Watson Davis, *Civil War and Reconstruction*, 304–5; OR, ser. 1, vol. 35, 22–23, 427–40.

Darkies. I would have written more but we will have to leave in about an hour and a half. From your

aff brother

Henry

Sept 8, 1864. Heard of Cousin Edward's death, he was killed in battle near Jonesboro.[51] *Uncle Jared and Aunt C— return home in haste and Frankie and Julia with them . . .*

Oct 21, 1864. My 23rd. birthday, a sad one, so many changes since the last. My dear Husband and Mother both gone, beside many other changes . . .

[DAVIS BRYANT TO OCTAVIA STEPHENS]

Head-Quarters, Military District of Florida,
Tallahassee Oct 27, 1864

Dear Tivie

You see I am at Tallahassee at last, though, I guess you are not much surprised, unless, it may be, because I have written so frequently that the Hd. Qr's were soon to be removed, and they failed to do so . . .

I am very much pleased with the appearance of Tallahassee, but from accounts and some evidences fear will not like the inhabitants so well as they (those of the class I would visit) are said to be very formal and full of high notions. However, I have not yet found any of that kind, and I have met several. I have passed most of my time, or, rather have taken most of my meals at Mrs. Longs. Her son (Dick) is a courier in the office and as we have not been able to get board as cheap or easily as we expected we have accepted their pressing invitation to remain with them until we can make an arrangement.[52] Last evening I called, with young Long, on a young lady, by way of commencement, and was very favorably impressed with the specimen . . .

We have a very pleasant office in the capitol, and have been sleeping there, but will probably soon have to give it up, so I am in a very unsettled state. I was very

---

51. Edward Everitt, son of Jared Everitt by his first wife, was twenty-five when he died. As a result of the Battle of Jonesboro, Georgia, 31 August–1 September, Sherman's army cut the railroad into Atlanta, which made it mandatory that the Confederates evacuate the city. The Atlanta campaign was finally over when the city fell on 2 September. On that date Sherman sent his famous telegram to Washington stating, "Atlanta is ours, and fairly won."

52. Richard C. Long, of Company C, Fifth Florida Battalion, was the nineteen-year-old son of Ellen (Call) Long of Tallahassee. Ellen was the daughter of Territorial Governor Richard Keith Call, and she married Medicus A. Long in 1844. In 1860 the Longs declared their real estate value as $14,000 and their slaves worth $30,000. After the war, Ellen wrote a book about her recollections entitled *Florida Breezes or Florida New and Old*. Although highly romanticized, it is a valuable work about how the antebellum upper classes lived.

comfortably settled at Lake City and was sorry to change. However, it is far preferable as far as the comfort and many other considerations concerned, but when among *respectable* people it is natural to want to be like them . . .

Yr. very aff'cte brother
Davis

Nov 1, 1864. The 5th. Anniversary of my wedding day, but my dear Husband is not with me to celebrate it, he is in a better world and how many years may pass before I meet him there I know not. Georgie the children and I spent the day at Aunt Carolines . . . About 8 o'clk p.m. Davis arrived on horseback from Tallahassee.

[WILLIE BRYANT TO OCTAVIA STEPHENS]

Lake City Nov 23, 1864

Dear Tivie—

. . . I have a late letter from Davis—he is flourishing at Tallahassee—I knew he would take there. A charming girl has just gone there from Madison and I am anxious to learn his opinion. She is my "charmer," tho' I am having a most interesting flirtation with a "vidder" here and [am] succeeding as well as I could wish. Dont be afraid of my getting into a *matrimonial trap,* I am too shrewd and experienced for that, but I cant get along without a little courtship on hand, where can get loving smiles and words and an occasional kiss; it's good for me too. I have lost none of my old tricks and tastes by being out of practice so long, and since Davis left have quite come out of my shell, and am again a "favored gallant," tho' I find but little time for such pleasures . . .

I am frequently asked concerning you, and there are many who manifest much interest in your welfare, of Winston's friends as well as our own. I occasionally see men from his old company whom I do not know and who on learning my name speak in praise of Winston and inquire about you . . . A bushel of love to all you dear ones and *two* kisses to sweet faced little Rosa.

Always affecty,
Willie

[WILLIE BRYANT TO OCTAVIA STEPHENS]

Lake City Nov 27, 1864

Dear Tivie—

. . . You will be greatly surprised, and I know pained, to hear that Abell's Battery has been ordered out of the state to report at Savannah, tho' the order stated *temporarily*. The Battery left on short notice passing here Thursday p.m. I knew it the night before and wrote Henry a short note and sent by Capt. Abell, telling him that I would be on the lookout for him. There were two cos., the first train got here about 2 hours before the second and I got permission for Henry to remain and go on the second . . . Henry is in fine health and spirits and went off with the bearing and excitement of an old soldier. As sorry as I was to have him leave the state I knew the trip would be beneficial to him in many respects, and my regrets were much relieved by his cheerfulness and willingness . . .

The *likenesses* have been a great satisfaction to me, and you were very thoughtful to send so many. What a train of reflection is brought to my mind as I look at the picture of the little girl standing by the side of her mother! my own darling little sister Tivie, and my dearly loved and loving mother . . . !

What I would not give to be with you this Sunday afternoon and evening, quietly and happily! how much better I could bear the little trials and crosses of every day life if I could at least spend my Sundays with you, life would present a new charm, an incitement, now, I live on from day to day without attaining anything or much to satisfy me but passing pleasures. To the world I seem perfectly happy, as I am a careless gay fellow, but there is still a longing it cannot see and cannot minister to . . .

God bless you

Always affly,
Willie

[HENRY BRYANT TO OCTAVIA STEPHENS]

Savannah Nov 29, 1864

My dear Sister

. . . We left Baldwin Friday morning and arrived at Madison about nine oclock at night. I stopped about an hour at Lake City and ate dinner . . . and much to my surprise saw Ben, he looks very thin, but is improving quite fast, I only had time to speak a few words to him, he said all were well when he left.[53] Willie had not seen him, but I hope he will find out which Hospital he stays at, and see him, when you write to Mrs Stephens or Mrs Gaines tell them I send lots of love to *all* and think about them a great deal.

We marched across from Madison to Quitman Saturday, and left there Sunday morning on the train, for Savannah where we arrived about 12 oclock night before last, we are camped nearly four miles from town.[54]

---

53. Benjamin Gaines was up from Marion County, where he had been on sick leave; his health had been ruined in Virginia during the summer and fall of 1864.

54. There was no rail connection between Florida and Georgia at this time. It was approximately a twenty-five-mile march from Madison to Quitman.

I saw lots of pretty girls as we passed through town yesterday, they were dressed a *heap to* fine for these war times, they don't think much of soldiers. I hope our Battery will be able to do some good in helping to whip Sherman. I dont think he will be able to get down this far if all accounts are true.[55] The Battery is well equiped now, and all the boys in fine spirits. I am in fine health now and wheigh more than I ever did . . .

Tell the Darkies How-die, kill or give away my dog if he troubles about sucking eggs for they are too good for dogs. When you write direct to Savannah. Yours always lovingly

Henry

[DAVIS BRYANT TO OCTAVIA STEPHENS]

Tallahassee Dec 2, 1864

My Dear Sister Tivie

. . . Tallahassee is very gay now but I have not participated in it [to] much extent and do not intend to do so. There has been an entertainment here every night this week. I attended quite a stylish wedding at the Episcopal Church Tuesday evn'g, that of a Lt. Grant and Miss Annie Ward of this place.[56] They made quite a display. This Tallahassee is famous for that you know. After the ceremony an elegant entertainment was given and on the next evening they had a grand reception . . . I have made up my mind not to think seriously of matrimony until I have some means of supporting some one besides myself. I don't often see any one any how who would suit my fancy . . .

Give . . . the little ones much love and, also, all relatives. Aunt Julia particularly after taking lots for yourself from

Yr. affch bro.

Davis

---

55. Sherman began his march to the sea, which culminated with the capture of Savannah, then the largest city in Georgia, on 15 November 1864. His army of some 62,000 forced the 10,000 Confederates out of Savannah on 20 December and entered it the next day.

56. First Lieutenant J. B. Grant was an aide-de-camp to General William M. Gardner, who was in command of the District of Middle Florida. Anne H. Ward was the daughter of the late George T. Ward, one of the wealthiest planters in Florida. In 1860 he declared assets of real estate valued at $70,000 and a slave force valued at $130,650. He was a staff officer of the Second Florida Infantry and was killed at Williamsburg, Virginia, in May 1862.

[WILLIE BRYANT TO OCTAVIA STEPHENS]

Lake City Dec 11, 1864

My dear Sister Tivie—

... My visit to Tallahassee was not as pleasant in all respects as I anticipated; the weather was rainy the whole 5 days I was gone and I was so unwell, rheumatic, and disappointed that the trip hardly paid me my share. I saw a great deal of Davis however, and was much gratified at that, and to see him so pleasantly situated and generally appreciated. It is of much value to Davis being there, and his manners qualifications, and *good looks* will undoubtedly secure him some valuable friends. Tallahassee has been shamefully gay and I know of no place that so justly deserves a visitation by the Enemy. I attended a large party there Thursday night, which was a grand but very pleasant affair, and enjoyed myself considerably, tho' I dont enter into such things with the spirit I once did—A *flirtation,* however, is still agreable to me; *I cant help it,* and am sorry you condemn it in me so strongly; I always choose my subjects from those who are inclined to it themselves and havn't much feeling, or if I find they have always shown some consideration for them; in seeking my own pleasure I never will sacrifice the happiness of another ...

I am not well, that is hearty, and so thin I am ashamed of myself ... Love to the little darlings Geo. and yourself in abundance from yrs. ever fondly

Willie

***Dec 25, 1864.** While at breakfast Burrel came, after breakfast Georgie and the negroes with the wagon returned to town with him for big Jane and their things*[57] ... *A Christmas day but a sad instead of a merry one.*

57. Burrel and his family returned to Tivie at this time and remained with her as freedmen after the war ended.

chapter 7

End of an Era; Farewell Dixieland

The fall of Atlanta, Sherman's march through the heartland of the Confederacy, Lincoln's reelection, the failure of peace overtures, and Grant's merciless siege of Lee's army took the heart out of most Confederates by 1865. They fought on in ever dwindling numbers, and some died, but more became despondent and deserted and went home. By the spring there were very few rebels who were still as steadfast in their beliefs as Willie, who fought once again at the Battle of Natural Bridge south of Tallahassee in March.[1] After Lee's surrender on 9 April 1865, Willie wanted to continue participating in the war by departing for the Confederate forces west of the Mississippi River but was unable to do so.

Davis was much more realistic in his assessment of the situation. He harbored no illusions about the Confederacy in the West and was more than ready to quit when the surrender came, but he absolutely hated it when his comrades cheered the end even though it meant their defeat.

Henry remained confident of victory and served until the surrender of Johnston's forces in North Carolina on 26 April.[2] That May he made his way back to Georgia, where he was reunited with Tivie and his brothers. Of them all, he was the only one who knew exactly what he wanted to do; Henry could not wait to return to Welaka.

Tivie was relieved when the war ended and happy when her father and brothers joined her, but for the rest of her life she looked back to what had been rather than ahead to the future. Like other widows of that war, including Mary Lincoln, she never really came to terms with her loss. The end of Rose Cottage was a minor matter; the end of her life there with Winston was almost unbearable.

1. Floridians were fond of bragging that their capital, Tallahassee, was the only one east of the Mississippi River that was not conquered.
2. Hood virtually destroyed the Army of Tennessee by attacking at Franklin (30 November 1864) and Nashville (16 December 1864); when he turned over command to Joseph Johnston in mid-January 1865, there were fewer than 20,000 troops left to confront Sherman's 85,000.

[WILLIE BRYANT TO OCTAVIA STEPHENS]

Lake City Jan 2, 1865

My dear sister Tivie—

... The past year has been the saddiest of our lives to all our little family; we have been truly tried in the measure of sorrow, and thank God it has been productive of some good—I know that I have not received it as I should, but I have lately learned to look upon it with more resignation ...

I hope you have heard from Henry since the troops left Savannah and that he is well—I have learned that the battery was engaged but without loss.

I am glad that he has seen some fighting, since he came thro' safely, for I know he wished it. The fall of Savannah is a heavy blow to our cause and I fear will lead to others; I hope on, in the faith that the Almighty will bring us thro' safely in his own good time, tho' I see but little encouraging.

Surely he will not allow such a people as the Yankees have shown themselves to be, to crush us under foot.

Much love to George and a kiss to the little ones; with an ocean of love for yourself.

Yrs. always affectionately
Willie

[AUGUSTINA STEPHENS TO OCTAVIA STEPHENS]

"Bruton Place" Jan 8, 1865[3]

My own dear Tivie

Your long looked for letter I received last night ... Oh! Tivie no one knows the mortification one has to endure to get barely enough to keep soul and body together. I went yesterday and tried to get a little cotton for spinning from Col Martin (enormously wealthy) and as a great favour and only to accommodate me let me have a few pounds for two dollars and a half a pound.[4] 'Aint that patriotism just such we meet with every day ...

---

3. F. B. Bruton was a planter who lived near Ocala in Marion County.
4. Colonel John Marshall Martin was very well known all over northeastern antebellum Florida. Born in South Carolina in 1832, he came to Marion County in 1856; four years later he listed assets of $55,000, including fifty-five slaves. He raised and was the captain of the Marion Light Artillery until he was severely wounded in the head at Richmond, Kentucky, in August 1862. He resigned his commission in March 1863 to serve in the Confederate House of Representatives but declined to run for another term and returned to the field that September. He commanded the newly organized Sixth Florida Infantry Battalion at Olustee and in Virginia after the unit joined Lee's army. In December 1864 Lee granted Martin leave, and he never returned. He lived until 10 August 1921. He was a prosperous Ocala citrus grower and the last survivor of the Confederate Congress.

Sometimes I feel out of humor with the whole world nearly and then I think how wrong it is as long as I have my dear good husband spared to me, it is presumption to murmur at any thing, for as long as he is near every thing seems to be lighter, and I feel when he has to go from home as though the only friend I had, had left . . . I see no Earthly hope for our success now, we hear that [Jefferson] Davis has gone to Europe deserted in time to save his neck and that his Coffin was taken out and buried in Richmond to express his fate and the public sentiment, but I do not credit any such a report, it is only raised by some enemy or friends to the Yankees, but I really believe we are whipped . . .

How I wish I could see your darling Boy, dont call him Winnie it is a womans name and an ugly one, call him as you did the dear one after whom he is named, of course you cant right away but when time has done its healing work you will then be able to, I sometimes get to thinking of you my dear Tivie and knowing so well how you loved and almost worshipped Winston, that I am only surprised at your ever living through your afflication, God grant that I may never experience such grief as yours or know what it is to lose a good Husband . . . Clark and all unite with me in much love to you and kisses to the dear children I am as ever your sincere Sister

Tina

[HENRY BRYANT TO WILLIE BRYANT]

Near Salkehatchee S.C. Jan 26, 1865[5]

Dear brother Willie

I have not written to you or Davis since I left Florida, but I will now try to write you about everything that has happened since I left there . . .

Well I will commence at Madison. The train I was on arrived . . . pretty late, but I had to go on guard, and just as I was relieved the rations came and I helped issue them and didn't go to bed until twelve o'clock, but I slept mighty well when I did crawl in.

The next morning we started across to Quitman and arrived there pretty late in the night, we slept in the piazza of the *Hotel*. The next morning (Sunday) we put all our Battery on the train except one gun, Caisson and wagon, and started off for Savannah. The most of the cars were flat cars that had been used for hauling sand, the wind was pretty high and we were going quite fast which made the sand fly in our eyes and *all over everything,* so our trip was not a very pleasant one. Capt Abell was presented with a flag, by a lady, between Quitman, and Sav.

We didnt get to Savannah until very late in the night, the next morning, we

---

5. Salkehatchie is about thirty miles north of Savannah and forty-five miles west of Charleston.

went out about three miles from town, where they were building breastworks, we staid there three days and were then ordered to carry two guns, to a redoubt fourteen miles from town, on the Augusta road, the other gun was carried to a redoubt, just to the left of us on another road, and when the one that was left at Quitman came it went still farther to the left. It was three miles from the first redoubt, to the third, there were no troops between them, only a support at each redoubt, we staid there over a week before the Yanks came, they attacked all the redoubts at once, we held them in check at the first redoubt until night, when we had to "git up and git," for fear they would cut us off from town, at the second redoubt after fighting some time they had [to] leave under fire, and were cut off at one time, but turned back and took another road, so they came out all right, the yanks flanked them out of the third redoubt, so that there was no fight there at all. We got the whole Battery together, and then fell back to the breastworks near Sav, then two of our guns were ordered to Rose Dew on the Ogeechee, and the other two to the breastwork at the Canal.[6] We had to work hard throwing up works at both places, but the boys at Rose Dew got a gill of whiskey a day for working, and we didnt get any at the Canal, I worked harder filling and carrying sand bags and throwing dirt than I ever did before. There are [a] great many thousand yards of cloth wasted on the works around Sav. When we left Sav. we joined Wheeler, and staid with him until Christmas morning when we started for Grahamville, when we got there we were ordered to Pocotaligo while I [was] there I saw George Adams, the day after we got there his Regt was ordered to Coosawhatchee and I didnt see him again until the other day, I dont know where he is now.[7] A week ago last Saturday, the Yank advanced on us at Pocotaligo, and we opened on them with all of our guns and made them fall back, the Infantry didn't fire much, but the Yanks made the balls whistle around us, a little more than was pleasant. I dont admire the sound of the balls, when they are come towards me, *at all,* and when they come *so* close *I cant help dodging.*

We staid at Pocoligo until two o'clock so that the troop could come up from Crosawhatchie, and then we fell back to this place. We had to wade through mud and water coming down here and the night was powerful cold, I have seen more muddy roads since I left Florida than I ever saw before. There is nothing hardly but mud and water from Savannah here, Florida is the State for *me.*

The other day we heard that the Yankies were about to make an attack, and there was a scoutting party sent out from where we were up the river and a Col sent another party from up the river down, and they met each other, and each

---

6. Rose Dew, on the Ogeechee River, was part of the defensive fortifications around Savannah.

7. Major General Joseph Wheeler's cavalry was about the only Confederate unit available to skirmish with Sherman. Grahamville, Pocotaligo, and Coosawhatchie were all on the Savannah-to-Charleston railroad between Savannah to the south and Salkehatchie to the north. George Henry Adams, son of Samuel and Mary (Bryant) Adams, was born 9 January 1847 and was now eligible for military service. He and his sixteen-year-old brother, John William Adams, were prison guards atr Macon, Georgia.

party thought the other was Yank and pitched into each other, and didn't find out their mistake until they charged, there was one Lieut and three privates killed, it was raining and the guns snapped a good deal without firing or more would have been killed. The rain has made the river rise so, that we had to come out here (about a quarter of a mile from the works) to find ground high enough to camp on, we had to wade nearly the whole quarter, in some places up to our waists, the water was nearly as cold as ice.

I thought we would get bacon after we left Florida, but we still get beef, there was ever so much bacon on the wharf at Sav. but they kept a guard over it . . . and then had to throw it all over board after all, we have pretty short rations, I am willing to hold out as long as any body. I am in good health and pretty fat. In Fla I could buy *something* once in a while, but there is nothing here at all not even rice although it is a great rice country . . .

Give my best respects to all of our friends. I believe I have written all I know about . . . With much love. Always affecly

Henry

[WILLIE BRYANT TO OCTAVIA STEPHENS]

Lake City Feb 20, 1865

Dear sister Tivie,

. . . Henry's letter was a great pleasure, so full in its details and written in such a cheerful, manly spirit—The boy holds out well, and I am most proud of him—May Heaven sheild him from all harm—Since Sherman has cut off our communication with that army there is no telling when we can hear from him again, and I shall be most anxious until we do . . .

The report you had at Thomasville that the Yanks were on their way to Geo., via Lake City, extended all down that road—

They only came out on an extensive raid; nearly all the Military in the state started out to meet them when they put back, but didn't get back without some punishment, for Dickison with part of 3 cos. overtook them and gave them fight, altho' against great odds, and succeeded in killing about 50, which were left on the field, but only got 3 wounded, losing but 5 men wounded of his own . . .[8]

Yrs. always with affection

Willie

---

8. A Federal force of approximately 400 men moved north from Cedar Key on 8 February 1865 and was met by Dickison's command of about 145 men, including a detachment from Company B of which Swepston Stephens was a member, on 13 February near Station Number 4 (four miles inland from present-day Cedar Key). The Federals had 5 killed, 18 wounded, and 40 captured; Confederate losses were 2 killed and 5 wounded. William Watson Davis, *Civil War and Reconstruction*, 313.

Feb 21, 1865. Flora died with colic.⁹

Feb 22, 1865. Georgie went to Uncle Jared to borrow a mule to help haul corn...

Mar 1, 1865. The first Anniversary of my dear Husband's death. As Aunt Caroline sent the buggy for us we all went and spent the day. Franky there for a week. Davis received a letter from Willie.

Mar 6, 1865. . . . This is the 1st. Anniversary of dear Mother's death and my little Winnie's birth.

[WILLIE BRYANT TO JULIA FISHER]

R.R. below Tallahassee Mar 9, 1865

Dear Auntie—

While we are awaiting the train to go to Tallahassee I will scribble a few lines to say I am O.K., and send to you, and after, you can send to Tivie by first chance, as I presume you have all learned of the fracas down here and that I was a participant and naturally feel a little uneasy like.

Just after dinner Sunday p.m. at Lake City I was notified that I was wanted at once to get our local company together to come down here, and as I am orderly Sergt., and really the head and manager, I had no oppt'y to write a line before leaving that Evn'g...

We came down to this point on the R.R., 4 miles from Newport, and that morn'g about ½ p. 11. were led into the fight at the "Natural Bridge," after a quick and hot march of 8 miles in a round about way. The Enemy had 2 Regts. of negroes, and part of 4 co's of Deserters at the Bridge, with 3 pieces of artillery— We had a Regt. of Reserves, a Battallion of 260 men, a good co. of cavalry and 5 pieces of artill'y.¹⁰ We at first fought across a small stream, (East River,)¹¹ our Batty. doing all the fighting after we got there, the Reserves having been there some hours and tired; It was a regular Indian swamp fight, being at close range and our men being behind trees mostly, and the Enemy behind entrenchments and logs—At about 3 o'clk p.m. the Enemy abandoned their first line near the stream, as Our fire was too hot for them, and the firing ceased almost entirely for

---

9. The loss of Flora the mule was severe, for she was the only one broken to both saddle and plow. She was a gentle animal; neither Tivie nor Rebecca had hesitated to ride her.

10. The Battle of Natural Bridge took place some sixteen miles south of Tallahassee. Federal forces, about 900 strong, consisted of the Second and Ninety-ninth United States Colored Infantry, and the Second Union Florida Cavalry was under the command of Brigadier General John Newton. These troops were opposed by Confederate Brigadier General William Miller's force of some 1,500 boys and men. With G. W. Scott's Fifth Battalion Cavalry, three companies of the Second Florida Cavalry (dismounted), Dunham's artillery battery, the cadet corps of the West Florida Seminary, and a few convalescents and old men, Miller won a decisive victory.

11. Willie was probably mistaken in identifying this as the East River; it was most likely the St. Marks River.

more than ½ an hour, when skimishers were ordered to cross the Natural Bridge and find the Enemy—It was a ticklish piece of business for a few men to advance into a thick swamp to find a hidden foe, and the men did not step forward with alacrity and details were obliged to be made; I didn't like to make a detail from our co. and stepping forwd. called for men to follow me, tho' I was so lame and exhausted I could scarcely get up a good walk; but 3 volunteered with me—as soon as the skirmishers crossed, the Enemy opened a terrible fire upon us, as far as noise was concerned, and then fell back—random shooting and an irregular fight was kept up until we were brought up standing by another smaller stream, the bridge torn and burning and another line of entrenchments just where the pine woods joined the swamp confronting us—It was impossible to get the men to charge in a body, I tried in vain with those around me, then dashed onto the road and on the Bridge myself, to try example, a volley opened at once and no man came to me, I fired my gun, then stepped behind a tree and loaded again, and my blood being up to fighting heat by that time I took my hat in my hand and cheering made another start, just then the word was given that we were being reinforced, when a few followed me, I being the first to cross the Burning Bridge and in the face of the Enemy, almost the whole Battallion being witnesses. Before I got to the entrenchments the Enemy seeing us reinforced abandoned that line also and scampered across the open woods like black sheep, only a part of them going to their main works still further back—There was fun, as the black devils, with only white men, as officers among them, were scampering for dear life, while the 5 or 6 of us in advance who reached the open woods first had nothing to do but shoot and yell at them—That tune was soon changed however, for as soon as our main body appeared in view such a volley of small arms, grape and canister, was opened upon us that we very quickly sought shelter behind trees and the entranchments we had just taken. Not satisfied with what I had done, calling to the same men who came thro' with me I crawled some 200 yds into the open woods where we commenced sharp-shooting, but were soon spied out when we were peppered so warmly that we dared expose ourselves only occasionally to shoot—Presently we observed our main line giving way, and the first thing we knew 4 of us were left out there to take care of ourselves—Two jumped up and ran at once, but from the fire they drew, the other chap and myself thought prudence decidedly the better part of valor and concluded to *crawl* off; which we did with credit to ourselves, for you never saw men flatten out so thin and hug the ground closer; he would crawl a piece while I watched to tell him when, and when not to move, and then he for me, until we got at the edge of the swamp, when we rose and fired and giving back a yell broke like good fellows into the swamp to overtake our retreating companions, who were truly replused tho' some gave as an excuse that they were out of ammunition—Let the papers and blowers say what they please, it was *disgraceful,* and the men (that is, all) could not be made to hold their ground until ammuntn. should be brought, and if the Enemy had had the pluck of old troops and charged us then, we would have been slaughtered; but too glad of the chance they at once took advantage of it to beat a retreat, and later when another force was sent over to reconnoitre no enemy was in sight, and about an hour and half after they started we commenced a pursuit[12] — We marched 8 miles to Newport by 9 o'clk, or later, when so many of the men were broken down that only the few cavalry continued the pursuit — From that time Monday night until this a.m. we have been at Newport waiting until the last Yankee vessel should leave . . .

We only *know* of 35 killed, as they carried off all white men but one, and tho' there are many negroes still scattered thro' the woods from all I can learn up to the present time 75 will cover all prisoners, add 150 for wounded and you have an outside number of casualties — of our loss I know; 3 killed, 17 wounded, and one captured with a piece of artillery at Newport.[13] At any rate it was quite a brilliant little affair, but it should have been *much* more so. Two Deserters were found hid at Newport and executed before all the troops. At Newport the Yanks burned a dwelling on the other side of the river — The men there came across, firing the mill and destroying the Bridge to prevent the Yanks crossing, and Mr. Ladd and 3 *others* kept them from rebuilding it until assistance reached them from our troops.[14] Many shot and shell were thrown by the Enemy into the town and they killed a mule and five negroes belonging to Mr. Ladd. I breakfasted with Mrs. Ladd Tuesday a.m. when I first got there (not being able to reach them the night before.) and again this a.m.[15] They were kind, and pressed me to stay there altogether but I prefered remaining with the co., — or rather thought I ought to do so — Mrs. L. tried to write you but has been kept too busy by the troops and confusion — I will write you more at length of my stay there; of course my first letter must be expected to be full of what *I* did, what *I* saw and know, and "bragg" generally — But honor bright! I have long wanted a chance to show I am not in the B.P. Dept. thro' aversion to lead, and said when I went down there I should distinguish myself if it cost me my life.[16] I did it, and if I did not get killed numbers will vouch for it's not being "my fault," and I have been repeatedly pointed out as the man who led the way across the burning bridge in the "great charge," and as one who is fearless, while all who know me have given me praise

---

12. The Federals retreated to St. Marks, where they gained the protection of the naval guns of their fleet.

13. Willie's estimate was fairly accurate; Federal casualties came to 148, with 21 killed, 89 wounded, and 38 captured. Confederate losses were slight — 3 killed and 22 wounded — and none of the young cadets were hurt. William Watson Davis, *Civil War and Reconstruction*, 315.

14. Daniel Ladd was a prominent merchant and town builder before the war. See Shofner, *Daniel Ladd*, for an excellent biographical account that details antebellum commercial life in Florida.

15. In 1860 Ladd owned real estate worth $20,000 and other property, including twenty-six slaves, worth $100,000. He and his wife, Elizabeth Ann, had two sons, George and Joseph.

16. Willie is referring to the "bomb proof department," meaning that staff officers were usually safe from bombardment of any kind.

and say that they heard of my conduct throughout—no one vies with me in the lead tho' many claim to have been next to "Sergt. Bryant."

I did act thro' motive and dont think I should again, but no one can resist being flattered when they think they deserve the praise. This trip has completely used me up for a few days and yesterday was fearful of pneumonia in addition to my rheumatiz. One good effect it has had has been to cure me again of all desire to go to my command at once—I *cant march,* and wading thro' mud and water and the bad weather the past few days has used me up so that I can only hobble along—

Will write as soon as I can to Tivie—suppose I will see Davis to-morrow. There was to have been a grand review at Tallahassee to-morrow but I think it has been given up and that we will go right on—Much love to Everybody.

Always affectionately
Willie

Mar 17, 1865. Went to Aunt C—s, Georgie went on to town and got $162, for my rag carpetting . . .

[DAVIS BRYANT TO OCTAVIA STEPHENS]

Waldo Mar 28, 1865

Dear Tivie,

. . . I find camp life pretty rough, of course, and disagreeable—as it always has been at best to me—after my long respit from camp duty—but was prepared for it, and reckon, from the manner in which it commences I will soon become initiated, as I have been on the go almost ever since the day after I returned, the duty being very hard in consequence of the small number to perform it, and the extent of country it is necessary to protect, (just reverse these last two clauses and you'll get my meaning).[17] I returned last night from a long scout of two days, which, though very fatiguing, as I am not yet broken in well—I enjoyed considerably, I have up to this time been doing regular duty, but as I am needed occasionally to do the writing of the company, will probably have rest once in a while . . .

Love to George and *all others* and kiss to the little ones as usual from

Your very affe. bro.
Davis

Apr 8, 1865. Georgie the children and I started early for Aunt Julia's, in the p.m. Aunt Julia and I went to . . . Mother's grave and planted some flowers . . .

---

17. Davis was back with Winston's old unit, Company B, Second Florida Cavalry.

[WILLIE BRYANT TO OCTAVIA STEPHENS]

Lake City Apr 10, 1865

Dear sister Tivie—

I was greatly relieved to know you had heard from Henry tho' the letter was of so old date, but since that terrible fight with Sherman I shall feel anxious until we hear from him again.[18]

If reports are at all true we must have got a good whipping lately. The fall of Richmond is very severe upon us, and will depress our people greatly I am afraid, while it will encourage the Enemy.[19]

The fact of my being in the fight at the Natural Bridge and having behaved well even reached my friends in Jacksonville. Good bye for now!

Much love to you all, and God bless you.

Yrs. Always affectionately
Willie

Apr 25, 1865. Aunt Julia and Dr came in the p.m. with the news that the Yankee President Lincoln was killed and Seward badly stabbed and that there was an Armistice of 90 days . . .[20]

[WILLIE BRYANT TO OCTAVIA STEPHENS]

Lake City Apr 27, 1865

Dear Sister Tivie—

. . . We will soon know better what calculations to make for the future, and almost everyone is so sanguine that peace will result from this armistice, and that there will be no more fighting, that I hope there is reason for it, but I still fear the worst has not come yet. In ordinary times all of us boys could certainly make you comfortable, and tho' I prefer a lifetime of such a life as the present, or worse, to the South compromising on terms which will not be for the general good, yet I long for the time when we may all establish a comfortable home together as is our object, or at least be near each other with the same spot to call home . . .

---

18. The Battle of Bentonville, North Carolina, 21 March 1865, happened when Johnston attacked one wing of Sherman's army under the command of Major General Henry W. Slocum. Sherman brought up more troops, and the Confederates were forced to retreat. In this fight, the last major confrontation, Federal losses were put at 1,645, and Confederate casualties were 2,606.

19. Unknown to Willie, Lee had surrendered to Grant the previous day, 9 April 1865.

20. Johnston surrendered to Sherman on 26 April; for all intents and purposes the long war was over.

Lincoln was assassinated in the theatre at Washington and Seward and son mortally wounded.[21] Andy Johnston, vice President, called for an armistice; of course he thinks he can make best terms with us now, but the troubles at the North and with foreign powers it is thought will compel him to accept terms favorable to us. I feel sure with others that France will not allow our subjugation or a restoration of the union, and hope for some good to arise out of this armistice . . .

I shall pass Davis to-morrow and expect to spend saturday and sunday with him, which we will both enjoy so much and therefore the trip promises me great pleasure. I must say good night now. With an ocean of love to you all.

Always affectionately
Willie

[WILLIE BRYANT TO JULIA FISHER]

Baldwin Friday Apr 28, 1865

Dear Aunt Julia—

I am en route down Fla. R.R. on business and will see Davis two days. Having just seen a most important communication I beg a piece of paper to drop you the substance of it—Sherman telegraphs from Raleigh, and Genl. Vogdes, comd'g at Jv'lle, sends copy thro' to Genl. Jones at Tallahassee, that stipulations of treaty have been forwarded to Washington for approval.[22] *The Confederate armies to be disbanded and a permanent and lasting peace to be established;* the terms of treaty of course not stated in a tel. dispatch, the intention being only a notification with an order for no more destroyal of property.

Of course we can but wait in anxious suspense for particulars, and I must say I do so in dread, from our present condition . . .

I shall write soon after I return to Lake City and gain new items. In haste but none the less lovingly to all.

Willie

---

21. Secretary of State William H. Seward and his son Fred were severely wounded when Lincoln was murdered, but both survived the attempted assassination.

22. Federal Brigadier General Israel Vogdes was a brigade and district commander in Florida during the last month of the war. He notified Confederate Major General Samuel Jones, who had been given command of the Military District of Florida on 11 January 1865, of the terms of the treaty, and Jones formally surrendered Tallahassee on 20 May 1865. The Federal occupation began that day, and the war in Florida was finally over.

[DAVIS BRYANT TO WILLIE BRYANT]

Camp Baker May 4, 1865

Dear Willie

Your several favors received yesterday. The painful intelligence that Johnston had been compelled to surrender all the troops in his Dept. (So. Ca. Ga. and Fla.) was announced to us in General Orders from Dist. H'd Qr's yesterday . . . The majority of this Comd.—and nearly all in our Comp'y seems rejoiced and do not hesitate to express themselves to that effect. After the orders were read yesterday, when the ranks were broken a majority of our co. set up a hearty yell, much to my annoyance and their disgrace and it was remarked upon by some of the other Comps. It is too bad I declare and I think a judgment should be sent upon such men. I have felt wretchedly and am at a loss to know how to act. That the war is at an end so far as we are concerned I suppose there is not a doubt, as we can never be exchanged even if it is continued in Texas and west of the Miss—which I am inclined to think will be the case. Therefore, the only course left us is to try to get into business. I must to begin with, first sell my horse, and the most certain way of accomplishing that is to take him to Jacksonville, which I presume would be allowed, but I hate like thunder the thought of going there so soon, and would not think of it for a moment if there was any probability of my being enabled to get current money any where else . . .

Yr very aff bro.
Davis

[WILLIE BRYANT TO OCTAVIA STEPHENS]

Lake City May 7, 1865.

My darling sister—

. . . All the troops in Johnston's Depmt. have been surrendered, which includes those of us down here, and the war on this side of the Miss. River is virtually ended. The Yankee Commander at Jacksonville has received no instructions yet, but I presume will soon, and within a week all in the state will be paroled and disbanded. It was my intention to go to you to-morrow, but the train running west will neither take Confed. money or Govmt. Transportation any longer and of course I have nothing else . . . Of course none of us can form any definite plans for the future, but as far as you are personally concerned I think you can feel sure of being none the less comfortable; you have more than enough current money to meet your wants until matters become settled and business somewhat established; Henry will be with you in a day or two if he is not already, and Davis before long, each of them have a taste for and some knowledge of farming, and could no doubt earn a good living for you all in that way even if your negroes should leave you, or be taken away, which I do not think probable for some time; even after they find they are freed I feel sure Burrel will prefer to remain with you on some terms to the good of you both. If Father is alive he will no doubt soon come on and be able to render you some assistance. You no doubt have observed that I have made all these calculations without including myself and perhaps wonder at it; it is not for the reason that I have any plans separate from you but merely to show you that you are independent of me entirely . . . I will tell you frankly that I have tried to arrange to go over the Mississippi, and still cling to our president and our cause as long as it remained; had confed. money held good a little longer I could have done so, but those of us who would go havn't the means, and it would be worse than folly to start on foot from way down here in Fla. without them. As far as I can now see *clearly* I will be obliged to take a parole in the event I get transportation to go to wherever I call my home.

If I remain I shall try as soon as possible to get into some business with some old friend, and in the meantime can manage to scratch along somehow. There will be much more that is humiliating and hard for us to bear, but of the ability of us boys to take good care of you I havn't a doubt. I must say I have but few feelings of anxiety, mortification, hate, and rage fill my breast . . .

An ocean of love always from

Yr. aff. brother
Willie

[WILLIE BRYANT TO DAVIS BRYANT]

Lake City May 7, 1865

Dear Davis—

. . . Everything looks quiet and gloomy here but there are some who show in their faces that they would like to be jubilant if they dared. By order Genl. Jones 60 days rations have been promiscuously issued to soldiers and families, but on Thursday night (I was away) a party clubbed together to sack the . . . store houses, to go over to Maj's T. and R. houses to demand stores stored there and to help themselves to public property generally[23] . . . Genl. Jones was here and tried to pacify them, and then Smith (now Lt.) was ordd. out with a guard with instructions to fire into the crowd wherever he found them unless they dispersed.[24]

---

23. The Commissary Department served rations while the Quartermasters Office was concerned with equipment, clothing, and logistics. Willie's "Majors T. & R." were Teasdale and Routh, previously mentioned.

24. M. Smith, the former Welaka merchant and mailman, was promoted to third lieutenant late in the war.

They were finally dispersed tho' there was some excitement—The next night it was feared again but the thing blew over . . .

Some of our paroled prisoners in passing thro' Jv'lle are cursed and insulted by yankees and the nigger troops and dare not reply—a nice state of affairs and an idea of what we may expect! I am at boiling heat the whole time and can scarcely be quiet any time . . .

If I had not heard to-day of the state of affairs in Jv'lle, and the impracticability of our people going back to live as they desire, I would have hoped to be able to get into business there soon and felt somewhat reconciled to remain about here, as it is if I can leave the country I wish to do so for the present . . .

Our private affairs give me comparatively little anxiety, but I am so filled with sorrow, hate, mortification and anger over our public affairs that at times I am half distracted I believe. We are doing nothing but lying around the office . . .

Yrs. always

Willie—

May 10, 1865. Joe went to town for meal and brought the news that the Yanks were in town.

May 11, 1865. Aunt Julia and Willie took us by surprise in the morning . . . Willie perhaps to join Pres Jeff Davis on the trans Mississippi . . .

May 14, 1865. . . . just as dinner was ready who should surprise us but Henry, has been away ten months . . .[25]

May 31, 1865. Willie and Davis arrived from Monticello in the afternoon.

June 17, 1865. . . . The Confederacy entirely subjugated, *terrible! terrible!! and negroes all emancipated.*

[JAMES W. BRYANT TO OCTAVIA STEPHENS]

New York, July 5, 1865

My dear daughter Tivie,

. . . The loss of Winston I very deeply deplore and I am only consoled by knowing that your health is good and that you have your dear little ones to

---

25. In later reminiscences Tivie wrote, "Willie, Davis, & Henry came home from the service with nothing. Henry until nearly home with his pants off up to his knees, & a lady gave him a pair. He had 60 cts. & he said the 50 should be a Souvenir of the war—the ten cents he hung around my Baby's neck. Davis brought his pony 'Panic' home, & I will never forget the day he laid 50 silver dollars on the table & his expression when he said—'Theres the proceeds of my pony (A fine pony).'"

engage and interest you. The high estimation in which Winston was held by every one who knew him at all must be gratifying to you, as his memory will be cherished for a long, long time with respect and affection by a great many . . .

I am of course very anxious to be with my loved and loving children again, and shall hasten the time. Alas, that your dear mother cannot be with you to receive me! Great as our loss has been, yet I can but remember how much we have left. We must not repine over past grief and calamity, but meet the present and prepare for the future with a full sense of the duties we are called upon in life to perform, and act cheerfully.

My affection for all of you and for my home has not decreased by my long absence, on the contrary I feel it *strengthened* and my whole heart is with you.

Farewell dear Tivie—it will not be long before I will see you I am sure. Ever Your Affectionate father

J. W. Bryant

chapter 8

The Sad Times Continue

We have not been able to account for the later activities of some members of the cast, particularly the Stephens-Gaines clan. When the war ended, Winston's mother, Mary Ann Jane Gaines, and her three youngest daughters were staying with her son Richard Stephens in Marion County. Mary Ann later moved to live with her daughter Mary Branning in Middleburg, where she died on 7 March 1875. Swepston moved to nearby Levy County and died in Hillsborough County early in the twentieth century. Benjamin Gaines moved to Hernando County and became a commercial fisherman. His brother James Gaines became a citrus grower in Volusia County. Clark and Tina Stephens returned to Welaka in December 1866. Once home again, they never left it. Tina died on 20 August 1900, and Clark on 19 December 1904; both are buried in Oakwood Cemetery in Welaka.[1]

Burrel Stephens and his family apparently returned to Welaka in January 1868. Burrel resumed his ministry and preached and farmed in Welaka until his death in September 1884. His wife Jane died sometime in the 1870s, and Burrel had remarried by 1880. All of their children were also living in Welaka in 1870, as was Sarah Stephens, the former cook.[2]

The correspondence reveals the fate of the rest of the cast in some detail, and we feel that it is only just to begin with Tivie.

1. Mary Branning to Octavia Stephens, 7 March 1875; Tenth Census of the United States, 1880, Hernando County; Tenth Census, 1880, and Twelfth Census, 1900, Volusia County; Augustina Stephens to Octavia Stephens, 22 January 1867.

2. Ninth Census, 1870, Schedule I, Putnam County, lists all the family except Sarah's daughter Mary Polly, who may have died young. In the 1880 census, Burrel, his wife Linda, and four children surnamed Lucas comprise the household; Sarah was listed with her son-in-law Richard Reddick. We have not been able to determine what happened to Rachael, Tom, and Sarah's daughter Jane or to discover either the obituaries or the grave sites of any of the former slaves.

Octavia Louisa (Bryant) Stephens

After the war ended, Tivie remained in Thomasville, while Willie formed a partnership with his old friend John Bouse in a mercantile venture in Savannah. She joined them in 1866, but the firm folded and the family split up.[3] Willie moved to Baltimore, Maryland, and Davis joined his father in New York City. Henry came back to live in Welaka with Clark and Tina, who had returned there late in 1866.[4] Early in 1868 Tivie and the children followed Henry to Welaka, and Tivie wrote on 1 April:

> After an absence of four years and a half I begin another journal in my old home (before I was married) and what changes! I return here with my two children, without husband, Father and Mother, brothers scattered except Henry, who is at present living with Clark.[5] I find the old place in shocking condition, in fact all Welaka going to ruin and my little home on the plantation burned down. Clark and Henry and the negroes, Burrel, Sarah, etc. met us at the Wharf.

Life in Welaka was hard following the war, but Tivie's activities were very similar to those she experienced during happier times: frequent visits back and forth with Tina and family, teaching school, tending the sick and dying, huckleberrying, cutting bee trees, planting the garden. During the early 1870s Tivie made occasional trips to Palatka and Jacksonville to visit the Reeds and other friends. She also entertained company at White Cottage.

Tragedy continued to stalk the family. On 7 January 1876 Tivie wrote:

> Words cannot express the sorrow I have endured the past two weeks. My brother Georgie, dear, dear, brother was taken sick Dec. 30 and died Jan. 3rd. Oh, what a darkness is again thrown over my life. It seems almost impossible to struggle on ... oh, how much, how much has transpired. The neighbors were very kind. My precious brother was laid by the side of my little Belle, on the 4th of Jan.[6]

Five years later Tivie lost another family member when the irrepressible Willie died, but it appeared that her daughter, Rosa, might have a bright

---

3. They planned to operate a general commission store, and although both of them were experienced in this business, they did not succeed. Willie Bryant to Davis Bryant, 29 September 1865.

4. Clark and Tina returned to Welaka on 14 December 1866; Augustina Stephens to Octavia Stephens, 22 January 1867.

5. Her father, J. W. Bryant, died on 26 July 1867.

6. The tombstones of all the family buried at Oakwood Cemetery in Welaka are extant except for a marker for the infant daughter, Isabella Gertrude, 1862–63, who is believed to have been buried to the right of Tivie. The marker was made of wood and disappeared in recent years.

future. On 14 June 1882 Rosa married Albert Postell in the Welaka Episcopal Church. She soon told her mother that she was with child, and Tivie's old fears from her own pregnancies resurfaced. On 27 January 1883 she recorded that having to give up

> my only girl to enter the matrimonial state was a *real grief to me* . . . the very thing I dreaded came to pass very soon and she was soon in a delicate way and although very well for her most of the time, had to be very careful . . . I have felt that we must be with her all we could for I feel that *every day is precious* . . . her time of sickness should be about the middle of April, but I fear she will not hold out as long.[7]

Once again Tivie's fears were more than justified, as shown by her diary entry of 24 February 1883:

> In the afternoon I went to see Rosa and found her in bed. Some fever but not seeming much sick. At 4 o'clock I was fixing her hair when she got up for a little she had a convulsion . . . She had a dozen or more in a few hours . . . at 1 o'clock my poor darling died."[8]

Tivie's grief was partially assuaged by the presence of her son, who continued to be called Winnie despite Tina's objections. He attended one year of school at South Georgia College to become a teacher and began teaching in Welaka, where Amy Gaston, whom he had known for a few years, was also teaching. They married on 11 October 1886.[9] The young couple built a house behind White Cottage. There, on 20 December 1888, Amy gave birth to a baby boy, who was named Winston Bryant Stephens. Winnie left Amy in Welaka while he went to Baltimore to study dentistry. He graduated in March 1894 from the Baltimore College of Dental Surgery and decided to open his practice as a dental surgeon in New Bedford, Massachusetts.[10]

Although Tivie continued to live in Welaka, she spent long vacations with Winnie and Amy. She arrived for her last visit in June 1908. She died three months later, on 6 September, no doubt happy that she had finally joined her parents, husband, children, and other loved ones in that "far happier place" she had written about so often.

---

7. Octavia Stephens to Mary Hall, 27 January 1883.
8. Tivie also lost her first grandchild, who was about two months from term. Rosa is buried at Oakwood, but there is no mention of this infant.
9. Amy Gaston was the daughter of Horace Munson and Elizabeth (McFarland) Gaston, from Massachusetts and New York respectively.
10. Winston Stephens, dentist, is first listed in the New Bedford city directory in 1895; from 1897 to 1921 he lived and practiced at 12 South Sixth Street.

WILLIAM AUGUSTUS BRYANT

Willie's first hope was to continue playing a role in the war by joining Confederate forces west of the Mississippi River, but he was thwarted in the attempt. Jefferson Davis was captured by Federal forces on 10 May 1865, and Willie soon accepted that the cause was lost and joined Tivie in Thomasville for a short stay.

Willie and John Bouse opened their Savannah business in December 1865. Henry joined his brother in January 1866; Tivie, with her children and George, followed in November 1866. Tivie kept house for them all while Henry and George returned to school. The family grew by another member the next month when Willie brought home a wife, the former Marianna (Mamie) Gilbert, whom he had met during the war. They were married in Rochester, New York, on 26 December 1866.[11]

Willie settled in Baltimore early in 1868. Over the next few years he tried several business ventures, mostly involving new inventions. He was the most ambitious of the family to succeed financially; he was forever hoping, as he would have put it, to hit it big. He was no more successful in this endeavor than his father had been, but he continued searching for new inventions to patent and market.

Willie's personal life was troubled as well. A baby girl, who was not named, lived only six weeks; a second child, William Augustus Bryant Jr., died at the age of four months.[12] Despite these heartbreaks and Mamie's declining health, the couple determined to try again and were rewarded on 29 May 1872 with the birth of another daughter. They named her Julia May after Willie's aunt and the child's birth month but called her May or Maysie. She soon assumed a very special place in the hearts of her parents, or at least in Willie's; Mamie never completely recovered her health and apparently lost the will to live. She moved back to Bridgeport in 1874 and died on 15 May 1876.[13]

Willie's business was severely hurt by the Panic of 1873, and he also had a serious health problem. The condition was diagnosed as a cancerous tumor, caused no doubt by a lifetime of cigar smoking, and Willie underwent an operation in June 1880. His health did not return, and he was forced to move

---

11. Willie Bryant to Octavia Stephens, 22 April 1866; *Bridgeport Daily Standard*, 26 December 1866.
12. Willie Bryant to Octavia Stephens, 13 March 1871; Marianna Bryant to Octavia Stephens, 4 April 1871.
13. Mamie died in Jacksonville after visiting Tivie and her family at Welaka. Willie took the body back to Bridgeport, Connecticut, for burial.

in with Davis and his family in New York City. He died on 24 April 1881 at forty-three; May continued to live with Davis and his family.

DAVIS HALL BRYANT

In January 1866 Davis visited his father in New York City. He found that his father was in bad physical health and not in a financial position to help further his plan to open a business in Savannah. Davis helped his father carry on the business of editing the *Mining and Petroleum Standard and American Gas-Light Journal,* and by June 1867 he had found a place for the two of them to live in Bloomfield, New Jersey.[14] He wrote Tivie that "as soon as we have clear mild weather he [father] will begin to gain." This was not to be the case; James William Bryant died that summer.

Davis remained in New York after his father's death and married Lucy (Loulie) Spiers on 7 July 1870. A daughter, Blanche Rosalie, was born on 30 May 1871. Davis specialized in the imported lace business. Of all the family, he was the most successful in business and in his private life as well.

Although he lived in the North, Davis remained a Southern man at heart. He became involved with the United Confederate Veterans organization and, as he put it, kept himself "pretty well informed of important events connected with the 'lost Cause.'" He most probably would have approved of his obituary that appeared in the January 1915 issue of *Confederate Veteran:*

> While of Northern parentage and justly proud of his ancestry, he was by birth, by choice, and by nature a true Southerner. His love of the South and her people, her customs and traditions was one of the strongest elements that contributed toward a personality of unusual charm and sterling worth ... He became remarkably familiar with all that pertained to Florida—its history, its beauty, and its possibilities—and cherished for the State a deep affection.
>
> When the war broke out, he at once enlisted, first as a member of the Jacksonville Light Artillery [sic] and later in the 2d Florida Cavalry, and for the entire four years he was in the service of the Confederacy, having during this time many thrilling experiences as scout, special messenger, and in the ranks, where he fought under Gen. Joseph Finegan and Gen. Patten [sic] Anderson and saw particularly hard service in the battle of Olustee ...
>
> Comrade Bryant engaged in business in New York City until his retirement, seven years ago, when he returned to the State he loved, making his home in Orlando, Fla. ... As a soldier he was plucky and steadfast, with the

---

14. Stationery used by Davis also has the letterhead *American Gas-Light Journal and Mining Reporter.*

highest sense of honor, duty, and fidelity. As a man he clung always to the finest ideals—a true gentleman of the old school, whose courtesy and courtly manner, whose fine temperament and rare magnetism, drew to him all, of high or low estate, with whom he came in contact.[15]

HENRY HERBERT BRYANT

The end of the war found Henry anxious to return to Welaka, but he was pressured by Tivie and his older brothers to go to Savannah and attend school with his younger brother, George. This was an intolerable state of affairs. Henry was nineteen years old and a war veteran, and he left for Welaka in January 1868 and lived with Clark and Tina Stephens for the next several years. Of all the family, Henry was soon again in his element. He farmed with Clark and his sons and once again killed alligators for their oil. His relationship with Clark and Tina became closer in 1875, for on 22 June he married Mary Jane, their eldest daughter.

Henry and Mary Jane remained in Welaka for the rest of their lives and raised a family of five children, many of whose descendants still live in Florida.[16] He had several orange groves and was the local agent for the Clyde Steamship Company.[17] Henry served as a tax assessor and collector and as a school trustee. He also served as a model for young people. A simple, hardworking, generous man, he was much like his father-in-law, Clark Stephens. And like Clark and Tina, as well as Tivie, Henry no doubt had many memories when he drove north from Welaka on the new road to Palatka, for the vacant rolling countryside through which he was passing had once been a plantation highlighted on his right by a small log home called Rose Cottage. All that was left were the memories and these chronicles.

---

15. Davis and his family moved to San Jose, California, in 1900 and to Orlando, Florida, in 1907. He died there on 24 May 1914. *Confederate Veteran* 22 (January 1915): 38.

16. Henry and Mary Jane both died in 1930 and are buried in Oakwood Cemetery.

17. Information supplied by granddaughter Cordelia (Bryant) McIlwain, April 1993.

Bibliography

PRIMARY SOURCES

United States Documents

U.S. War Department. *Official Records of the Union and Confederate Navies in the War of the Rebellion*. 26 vols. Washington, D.C., 1901.
———. *War of the Rebellion: A Compilation of the Official Records of the Union and Confederate Armies*. 128 vols. Washington, D.C., 1880–1901.

Unless otherwise stipulated, the following census documents are on microfilm at the University of Florida Library, Gainesville.

U.S. Bureau of the Census. Fourth Census of the United States, 1820, Population and Slave Schedules, Oglethorpe County, Georgia.
———. Fifth Census of the United States, 1830, Population and Slave Schedules, Choctaw, Dallas, and Washington Counties, Alabama; Duval and Madison Counties, Florida.
———. Sixth Census of the United States, 1840, Population and Slave Schedules, Choctaw, Dallas, Shelby, and Washington Counties, Alabama; Duval County, Florida.
———. Seventh Census of the United States, 1850, Population and Slave Schedules, Marion and Putnam Counties, Florida.
———. Eighth Census of the United States, 1860, Population and Slave Schedules, Thomas County, Georgia; Population, Slave, and Agricultural Production Schedules, Clay, Putnam, and Nassau Counties, Florida.

State and Local Documents

Boston, Massachusetts, City Directory, 1816, 1818. Massachusetts State Archives, Boston.
Cahaba County, Alabama, Register of Certificates, Cahaba Land Office, Books 304, 318, 547. Alabama Department of Archives and History, Montgomery.
Dallas County, Alabama, Probate Judge Records, Orphans Court Minutes, LG 2627, microfilm reel 10; Mscl. Probate Records, vols. E, F, and L; Mscl. Probate Records—Accounts, Administrators, Guardians, etc., Vol. D, LG 2625, microfilm 3. Alabama Department of Archives and History, Montgomery.
———. Register of Certificates, Dallas County Office, Books D and E.

Florida Department of Military Affairs, Special Archives, Publication no. 76, Florida Military Master Rolls, vol. 10.
Marion County, Florida, Records, Deed Books C, D, E, F. Courthouse, Ocala, Florida.
———. Marriage Records Book B. Courthouse, Ocala, Florida.
Putnam County, Florida, Records, Deed Books A, B, C, D, E, F, G. Courthouse, Palatka, Florida.
Washington County, Alabama, Probate Judge Records, Book D, and Mscl. Probate Records, Book H.

Unpublished Manuscripts

Greely, Mellen Clark. "Musings of Mellen Clark Greely, Written in His Anec-Dotage" (Jacksonville, 1963). P. K. Yonge Library of Florida History, Gainesville.
Reed, A. M. "Diary of A. M. Reed, 1848–1899." P. K. Yonge Library of Florida History, Gainesville.
Stephens, Winston. "The Little Boston Rebel." P. K. Yonge Library of Florida History, Gainesville.

SECONDARY SOURCES

Articles and Compilations

Dodd, Dorothy. "Florida in 1845." *Florida Historical Quarterly* 24 (July 1945).
Lainhart, Ann S. "The Descendants of Abraham Bryant of Reading [Massachusetts]." *New England Historic Genealogical Register* 137 (1983).
Shofner, Jerrell, and William Warren Rogers. "Confederate Railroad Construction: The Live Oak to Lawton Connector." *Florida Historical Quarterly* 43 (January 1965).
———. "Sea Island Cotton in Ante-Bellum Florida." *Florida Historical Quarterly* 40 (July 1961–April 1962).
Smith, Mrs. Herschel W., comp. *Marriage Records of Greene County, Georgia (1787–1875) and Oglethorpe County, Georgia (1795–1852)*. Winder, Ga., 1962.

Books

Anderson, Bern. *By Sea and by River: The Naval History of the Civil War*. New York: Alfred A. Knopf, 1962.
Biddle, Margaret Seton. *Hibernia: The Unreturning Tide*. New York: Vantage, 1974.
Blakey, Arch Fredric. *Parade of Memories: A History of Clay County, Florida*. Green Cove Springs, Fla.: Clay County Bicentennial Steering Committee, 1976.
Buker, George E. *Sun, Sand and Water: A History of the Jacksonville District United States Army Corps of Engineers 1821–1975*. Washington, D.C.: U.S. Army Corps of Engineers, 1976.
Covington, James W. *The Billy Bowlegs War, 1855–1858: The Final Stand of the Seminoles against the Whites*. Chuluota, Fla.: Mickler House, 1982.

Davis, T. Frederick. *History of Jacksonville, Florida, and Vicinity, 1513 to 1924.* Edited by Richard A. Martin. Gainesville: University of Florida Press, 1964.

Davis, William Watson. *Civil War and Reconstruction in Florida,* ed. Fletcher M. Green. Gainesville: University of Florida Press, 1964.

Dodd, Dorothy. *Florida Becomes a State.* Tallahassee: Florida Centennial Commission, 1945.

Faust, Patricia L., ed. *Historical Times Illustrated Encyclopedia of the Civil War.* New York: Harper and Row, 1986.

Florida Board of State Institutions. *Soldiers of Florida in the Seminole Indian, Civil and Spanish-American Wars.* Tallahassee, 1903.

Gold, Pleasant D. *A History of Duval County, Florida.* St. Augustine, 1929.

Hayes, John D., ed. *Samuel Francis Du Pont: A Selection from His Civil War Letters.* 3 vols. Ithaca: Cornell University Press, 1969.

Higginson, Thomas Wentworth. *Army Life in a Black Regiment.* Boston: Fields, Osgood, 1870.

Long, Ellen Call. *Florida Breezes or Florida New and Old.* Facsimile. Gainesville: University of Florida Press, 1962.

Martin, Richard A., with Daniel Schafer. *Jacksonville's Ordeal by Fire: A Civil War History.* Jacksonville: Florida Publishing Co., 1984.

Martin, Sidney Walter. *Florida during the Territorial Days.* Athens: University of Georgia Press, 1944.

Michaels, Brian. *The River Flows North: A History of Putnam County, Florida.* Palatka: Putnam County Archives and Historical Commission, 1976.

Mueller, Edward A. *Ocklawaha River Steamboats.* Jacksonville: Edward A. Mueller, 1983.

———. *St. Johns River Steamboats.* Jacksonville: Edward A. Mueller, 1986.

Nulty, William H. *Confederate Florida: The Road to Olustee.* Tuscaloosa: University of Alabama Press, 1990.

Partridge, Eric. *A Dictionary of Slang and Unconventional English.* New York: Macmillan, 1970.

Pettengill, George W. *The Story of the Florida Railroads, 1834–1903.* Boston: Railway and Locomotive Historical Society, 1952.

Rinhart, Floyd, and Marion Rinhart. *Victorian Florida, America's Last Frontier.* Atlanta: Peachtree Press, 1986.

Rosengarten, Theodore. *Tombee: Portrait of a Cotton Planter.* New York: William Morrow, 1986.

Shofner, Jerrell. *A History of Jefferson County.* Tallahassee: Sentry Press, 1976.

———. *Daniel Ladd: Merchant Prince of Frontier Florida.* Gainesville: University Press of Florida, 1978.

Tebeau, Charlton W. *A History of Florida.* Coral Gables: University of Miami Press, 1971.

Williams, Edwin L., Jr. "Florida in the Union, 1845–1861." Ph.D. diss., University of North Carolina, Chapel Hill, 1951.

Index

For place names, Florida is assumed unless another state is specified

Abell, Henry, 345, 351, 356
Acosta: Domingo, 14; Jany, 14
Acosta Creek, 14, 52
Acosta Creek Marina, 52
Acosta Grant, 14, 22–23, 31
Adams: George, 271, 357; John William, 357; Mary, 271; Lizzie, 271; Mary Frances (Bryant), 8, 14, 159, 271, 341, 357; Samuel Seth, 14, 143, 159, 250, 271, 278, 325–26, 336, 357; Willie, 271
Alabama, 15
Alachua County, 4, 22, 160
Albany, N.Y., 250
Alberti, E. R., 199
Alberti's Mill, 199
Allisonia, Tenn., 170, 177
Allen, Dan, 60–61, 66, 157
Alligator, Fla., 11
Alligator hunting, 137, 219, 221, 225, 234, 243, 263, 276
Amelia Island, 75, 82, 93, 102
America, 109
American Gas-Light Journal and Mining Reporter, 11, 373
American Party, 53
Ammen, Daniel, 113
Anderson, James Patton, 149, 164
Andersonville. *See* Camp Sumter
Antietam, Md., battle of, 142, 150, 187
Apalachicola, 133
Apalachicola River, 1, 76
Appomattox, 129
Archey. *See* Slaves
Armed Occupation Act, 15
Army of Northern Virginia, Confederate, 120, 226
Army of Tennessee, Confederate, 187, 197, 226, 337, 354
Army of the Cumberland, Federal, 142, 226
Army of the Potomac, Federal, 120, 130, 226
Army of the West, Confederate, 148
Army of Virginia, Federal, 130

Atlanta, Ga., 15, 266, 286, 300, 302, 321, 325–27, 332–33, 335, 337–39; evacuated, 346; fall of, 149, 349, 354; campaign, 337–39
Augusta, Ga., 167, 357

Baker, Archibald, 93
Baldwin, Abel S., 9
Baldwin, 11, 80, 86, 102, 103, 117, 212, 259, 262–63, 265, 267, 270, 274, 276–77, 279, 315, 318, 323, 340, 347, 351, 364; burned, 348
Baltimore, Md., 370, 372
Baltimore College of Dental Surgery, 371
Banger. *See* Slaves
Barber, Cornelius, 342
Bardstown, Ky., 159
Barnes: Caroline H. (*see* Stephens, Caroline H. [Barnes]); David, 21; E. Sylvester, 99, 156; Henrietta, 21
Bassford: James, 342–43; Polly, 342
Battery Wagner, S.C., 320
Beauregard, Pierre Gustave Toutant, 117, 235, 237–39, 296
Bell, John, 56
Bentonville, N.C., battle of, 363
Big Jane. *See* Slaves
Bill. *See* Slaves
Bird, Pickens B., 176, 296, 316
Bisbee, Cyrus, 213
Bisbee and Canova, 213
Black Creek, 4, 116, 122
Black troops, 207
Blakey, Arch Fredric, x, 6
Bob. *See* Slaves
Blockade runners, 71, 74, 86, 100, 269
Bloodgood and Bouse, 67, 73
Bloomfield, N.J., 11, 373
Boston, Mass., vii, 6, 8, 31, 314, 340; Octavia sent to, 30
Bostwick, W. M., 235–36
Bouse, John, 34, 370, 372

Bowling Green, Ky., 148
Braddock: James, 63, 158, 162, 228; John, 63; Joseph, 63; William, 63; Winny, 63
Bradley, Nicholas, 23, 52
Bragg, Braxton, 74, 76, 98, 142, 149, 159, 173, 177, 182–83, 185, 187–88, 197, 226, 241, 244, 247–48, 256, 273, 277, 288, 326
Branch, Thomas H., 61
Brannan, John Milton, 156
Branning: Bertha, 324; David Levi, 276; John, 57; Mary, 57; Thomas Jessup, 57, 141, 215, 276; Washington, 330–32
— Mary (Gaines), 18, 31, 33, 141, 143, 324, 369; letters from, 337; as bridesmaid, 49; marriage of, 57
Breckinridge, John C., 56
Brent, George W., 177, 183–84, 188, 229, 241, 252, 286
Brevard, Theodore W., 146, 151–52, 162, 216
Brice. *See* Slaves
Bridgeport, Ala., 248
Bridgeport, Conn., 372
Bright, George W., 119, 137, 242
Brock, Jacob, 35, 78, 102
Brown: John, 53; William, 22, 157
Brunswick, Ga., 68, 78
Bruton, F. B., 355
Bryan: Henry, 160; Stephen, 160
Bryant genealogical chart, 7
Bryant: Ann (Andrews), 6, 8, 70, 101, 118, 271, 280, 282, 334; Abraham, x; Blanche Rosalie, 373; George Lawton, 8, 12, 14, 22, 31, 52; Julia A., 33–34, 38, 44; Julia Maria (*see* Fisher, Julia Maria [Bryant]); Julia May, 372; Lewis Henry, 8, 11, 33, 303; Louisa (*see* Tydings, Louisa [Bryant]); Louisa H. (Burritt), 33; Lucy (Spiers), 373; Marianna (Gilbert), 372; Mary Frances (*see* Adams, Mary Frances [Bryant]); Mary Jane (Gaines), 21, 36, 157, 219, 343, 374; William Augustus, Jr., 372
— Davis, viii, ix; letters from, 109, 182, 189, 202, 213, 237, 269, 321, 332, 339, 345, 349, 352, 362, 365; letters to, 64, 67, 69, 72, 77–79, 84, 90, 93, 95, 111, 114, 121, 124, 131, 137–38, 142, 148–49, 157, 169, 183, 208, 217, 219–21, 228–29, 240, 244, 246–47, 252, 257, 261, 266, 268, 273, 277, 283, 302, 325, 328, 330, 334–35, 336, 341, 345, 366; birth of, 8; sees father in Jacksonville, 111; becomes 4th corporal, 182; ; becomes clerk, 182; and burning of Holmes Mill, 190; skirmishes with Federals, 203; detached duty of, 230, 238; duties of, as clerk, 238; becomes sergeant major, 288; visits Thomasville, 304–5, 344, 367; with Winston's company, 316–17, 323, 350, 362; at battle of Olustee, 321; narrow escape of, 323; sends telegram to Willie, 327; returns to Company B, 362; returns to Thomasville, 367; in business with father, 373; marriage of, 373; in business in New York City, 373; death of, 374; obituary of, 373–74
— George Perham, viii, 50, 246; letters from, 137, 212, 246; birth of, 12; death of, 370
— Henry Herbert, viii, ix; letters from, 149, 347, 351, 356; letters to, 270–71, 275–76; birth of, 12; and deer and turkey hunting, 50, 149, 212, 214; and alligator hunting, 137, 219, 221, 225, 234, 246, 263, 276, 374; enlists at sixteen, 256, 265; moves from Welaka, 275–76, 278, 287, 294, 312; Confederate service of, 345; at Gainesville, 348; in battle of Savannah, 357; returns to Thomasville, 367; returns to Welaka, 374; marriage of, 374; death of, 374
— James William, vii, viii, 29, 34, 73, 118, 147; letters from, 48, 54, 111, 113, 179, 314, 367; letters to, 47, 209; birth of, 6; father of, 6; editor, 11; merchant, 11; state representative, 11; and founding of Welaka, 12; and smallpox epidemic, 12; in Cuba, 37; reaction of, to Octavia's marriage, 48; in New York, 91; attempts to see family, 86, 111–13, 114; military governor of Florida, 86, 121, 124; renounced by sister, 120–21, 124; on gunboat, 111–12; sees Davis in Jacksonville, 111; in Massachusetts, 138; in Palatka, 178; whereabouts during war, 181, 269; death of, 370, 373
— Rebecca (Hall), vii, viii; diary entries by, 87, 89, 102, 104, 110–13, 115–17, 119–20, 122–23, 136, 138, 141, 156–57, 161, 164, 167, 169, 174, 178, 180, 184–85, 189, 191–92, 194, 207, 212, 214, 218–19, 221, 230, 245, 257, 268–71, 274–75; letters from, 64, 67, 72–73, 77, 79, 84, 90, 93, 95, 114, 124, 131, 142, 147, 157, 169, 173, 175, 180, 184, 187, 196, 202, 208, 219, 221, 228, 234, 245, 249, 256, 262, 271, 275–76, 278, 283, 285, 287, 322; letters to, 55, 60, 101, 107, 115, 117, 126, 133, 139, 144, 158, 167, 170, 177, 179, 187, 196, 223, 232, 249, 286, 314, 321, 327; marriage of, 8; comes to stay with Octavia, 64; reaction of, to Julia's renunciation, 122, 124–25; teaches the boys, 143; sees husband in Palatka, 178, 180–81; catches typhoid fever, 322, 325–26; death of, ix, 328

William Augustus, ix; letters from, 60, 78, 84, 115, 121, 126, 138–39, 144, 148, 158, 167, 170, 177, 183, 187, 196, 208, 219, 221, 229, 232, 240, 244, 247, 252, 261, 266, 268, 273, 277, 286, 302, 325, 327–28, 330, 332–33, 335, 337–39, 346, 347, 350, 353, 355, 358–59, 363, 364–66; letters to, 73, 90, 93, 147, 173, 175, 180, 182, 184, 187, 189, 196, 202, 208, 212–13, 218, 234, 237, 245, 249, 256, 262, 278, 285, 287, 322, 326, 356, 365; birth of, 8; groomsman, 49; enlists, 58–59; on furlough, 79; leaves Florida with regiment, 115; reaction of, to reports of father, 126; and Tennessee-Kentucky campaign, 139, 148, 160, 167, 177; at battle of Perryville, 159–60, 167; clerk in adjutant general's office, 177, 229, 232, 241; visits hospital, 188; on getting ahead in the world, 208; on furlough, 217–218; with Paris in Savannah, 222; on Bragg's retreat, 247–48; on future, 261; in hospital, 266, 268; visits Thomasville, 273–74, 344; returns to 3rd Florida Infantry, 277; tries to transfer to Florida, 321, 325; social life of, in Atlanta, 325; transferred to Florida, 328, 347; on mother's death, 336; in Atlanta during shelling, 346; social life of, in Tallahassee, 353; on "bomb-proof department," 361; on going west of the Mississippi, 365–66, 372; returns to Thomasville, 367; marriage of, 372; settles in Baltimore, 372; death of, 370, 373
Bryantsville, Ky., 158
Buckner, Simon Bolivar, 149
Buell, Don Carlos, 142, 144, 147–48, 159
Buffalo Bluff, 52, 110, 114, 135, 157, 331, 342
Buffington House, 12
Bull Run, Va., battle of, 83, 129–30, 142, 150
Bullock, Robert, 339
Burrel. See Slaves
Burritt: Louisa A., 8; Louisa H. (see Bryant, Louisa H. [Burritt]); Samuel, 11; Samuel L., 8, 212
Butler: Benjamin Franklin, 314; John G., 213

Calhoun, John C., 3
Call, Richard Keith, 2, 349
Camp Baker, 365
Camp Beauregard, 317–18, 321
Camp Cooper, 128, 182, 190–91, 202–3, 213, 249–50, 252, 254, 257–59, 263–65, 267, 270–72, 279, 281, 288, 290, 293, 295, 297–98, 301, 304, 307–8, 311–12, 315–16, 324; description of, 90, 253, 315

Camp Dunlawton, 96–97
Camp Finegan, 107, 126, 161, 164–65, 168, 171, 176, 189, 191, 195, 198–99, 207, 212, 216, 218, 220, 223, 225–26, 228, 230, 235, 237–39, 243, 249–50, 295–96, 302, 315–16, 323, 326
Camp Hateley, 124, 126, 129
Camp Hopkins, 76
Camp Jackson, 347
Camp Milton, 329
Camp Porter, 67
Camp Stephens, 124, 130, 132, 134–35, 141
Camp Sumter, Ga., prison camp, 319
Camp Turney, 347
Cannon, Elijah W., 281
Canova: Anthony, 213; Paul, 110, 156–57
Cape Hatteras, 8
Capps: Elizabeth, 258, 299, 304, 307; Michael, 258
Carolina (blockade runner), 100
Catoosa Springs, Ga., 273; hospital, 266, 268
Cecil (blockade runner), 100
Cedar Creek, 126, 329
Cedar Key, 11, 358
Chambers, William E., 124, 146, 152, 156, 162, 176, 183, 213, 215, 237, 243, 296
Chambersburg, Pa., 243
Champion, John C., 331
Champion's Hill, Miss., 231
Chancellorsville, Va., battle of, 226
Charleston, S.C., 6, 8–9, 68, 88, 167–68, 249, 252, 269, 320
Charley. See Slaves
Chattahoochee, 115
Chattanooga, Tenn., 138–39, 167, 173, 247–48, 252, 261, 266, 273, 277–78, 288, 300, 337; battle of, 326, 339
Cheatham, Benjamin Franklin, 148–49
Chestnut, Mary, vii
Chickahominy River, 120
Chickamauga, Ga., battle of, 273, 278, 339
Choctaw County, Ala., 17
Cimarron (Federal gunboat), 179
Clark: F. J., 190–91, 203–4, 230, 249; John, 34
Clay County, 4, 21, 52–53, 160, 331
Clifton, Jack, 204
Clinch, Duncan L., 319
Clyde Steamship Company, 374
Cold Harbor, Va., battle of, 316, 344
Colquitt, Alfred Holt, 164, 324
Columbine (Federal gunboat), 331, 340
Columbus, Fla., 345, 347
Columbus, Ga., 115, 117
Columbus Bridge, 345

Conant, Larkins, 83
Confederate Veteran, 373
Connecticut, 8, 372
Connell, James R., 74
Conscription Act: Confederate, 111, 264; Federal, 111, 250, 264, 266
Constitutional Union Party, 53, 56
Cook: A. W., 269; Margaret, 269
Cooper, James G., 128
Coosawhatchie, S.C., 357
Corinth, Miss., 98, 115, 117, 120
Cortez, Augustina, 18
Crandall, 203
Crane: E. P., 74; L. G., 146
Crescent Lake, 109, 158
Crespo House, 129, 131, 136, 176
Crosby, Michael, 6
Crosby Grant, 6
Crows Bluff, 157
Cuba, 11, 37, 55, 58–59, 73, 91, 111
Cuban Messenger, 11, 120
Cumberland Gap, 142
Cumberland Ridge, Tenn., 144
Currel, Dr., 156, 165, 191–94

D. H. Mount, 8
Dallas, Ga., 339
Dallas County, Ala., 15, 17–18
Dalton, Ga., 326
Daniels, Hampton, 331, 342–43
Darien, Ga., 101
Darlington, 35, 57, 68–69, 77–78, 95, 113, 157–58
Davis, Jefferson, 97, 118, 197, 248, 300, 356, 366–67; capture of, 372
Decherd, Tenn., 247
DeCottes, Edward Augustus, 12
Dedham, Mass., 340
Deep Creek, 331
Delk, William, 20
Democratic Party, 2, 53, 56
Department of East Tennessee, 138
Department of the South, 199
Department of the West, 197
Deserters: Confederate, 302, 307, 311, 354, 359, 361; Federal, 288, 302
Dicey. *See* Slaves
Dickison, John J., 181, 194, 215–16, 243, 255, 296, 334, 339–42, 348, 358
Dilworth: C., 131; W. S., 131
District of Middle Florida, 352
Doggett, Aristides, 327
Domingo. *See* Slaves
Donaldson: George W., 96; John F., 96
Douglas: Hannah, 9; Stephen A., 56; William, 9

Drayton Island, 331
Drysdale, Jonathan, 213, 264
Du Pont, Samuel, 68
Dukes, Theodore, 162
Dunham, Joseph L., 132–33, 135, 141, 146, 151, 162
Dunlap, Tenn., 144
Dunlawton, 71, 96–97, 99, 294
Dunn, Mary Ann. *See* Stephens, Mary Ann (Dunn)
Dunns Creek, 109, 324
Dunns Lake, 109
Duval County, 21, 53, 189, 213, 216; demographics of, 4

E. B. Hale (Federal gunboat), 179
East Florida, 1, 2, 15, 76, 104, 114; demographics of, 4; map of, 5; Unionists in, 54
East River, 359
Elephant: seeing the, 176
Ellaville, 345
Ellen. *See* Slaves
Emancipation Proclamation, 85, 150, 156, 186, 207
Enterprise, 4, 9, 35, 56, 78, 98, 100, 110, 342
Erwin, Robert, 57
Erwin and Hardee, 57
Eveline. *See* Slaves
Everitt: Caroline Ann (Bryant) (Perham), 70, 101, 271, 281; Edward, 349; Jared, 70, 101, 271, 279, 281, 286, 336, 349

Fair Oaks, Va., battle of, 120
Fairbanks: George R., 286, 327, 338–39; Jason, 177, 182, 184, 188, 286; Juliet, 177; Samuel, 111, 177
Fatio: Francis Phillipe, 18; Sophia, 18
Fawn, 34
Federal blockade, 58, 61, 62, 68, 85–86, 109, 114, 186, 254
Federal conscription, 264
Federal gunboats, 80, 83, 86, 114, 128, 132, 134–35, 146, 150, 156, 161, 171, 180, 189–90, 201, 213, 233, 243; threatening Welaka, 102–3, 105–6, 108, 113, 157, 217, 257–58; at Palatka, 112; on St. Johns River, 151–53, 155; at Welaka, 158, 163; *Cimarron*, 179; *Columbine*, 331, 340; *E. B. Hale*, 179; *Isaac Smith*, 179; *John Adams*, 204; *Ottawa*, 111; *Patroon*, 179; *Paul Jones*, 179; *Seneca*, 111–12; *Uncas*, 181; *Water Witch*, 179
Federal troops: captured in Welaka, 339–40; in Thomasville, 367; in Welaka, 331

Felix. *See* Slaves
Fellowship, 343
Fernandina, 60–62, 68, 70, 74, 75–76, 79, 80, 82–84, 87–88, 90, 92–93, 102–6 111–14, 116–17, 129, 142, 179, 190, 199, 203–4, 288, 290
Finegan, Joseph, 126, 128–30, 134–35, 146, 152, 155–56, 161–62, 164–65, 169, 195, 200, 213, 215, 217, 224, 227, 233, 237–39, 243, 245, 253, 255, 296, 315, 317, 319–20, 323–24, 335
Finley: Jesse Johnson, 339; Virginia, 339
Fisher: Ellis, 12, 14
—Julia Maria (Bryant), viii, 6, 8, 12, 14, 86, 124, 131, 147, 163, 174, 196, 208, 245, 261, 266, 271–72, 325–26; letters from, 69, 107, 117, 133, 209, 223, 249, 285, 334, 336; letters to, 359, 364; works for soldiers, 118, 223; and Ladies Aid Society, 118; renounces brother, 120; receives Rebecca's forgiveness, 133; article by, in Savannah paper, 249
Flagler County, 158
Fleming: Augustina (Cortez), 18; Augustina Alexandria (*see* Stephens, Augustina Alexandria [Fleming]); Charles Seton, 344; George, 18; Lewis Isadore, 22, 344; Lewis Michael, 18; Margaret (Seton), 18, 344; Sophia (Fatio), 18
Flemings Island, 18
Florida: banks in, 2; cotton production in, 23; demographics of, 1, 3, 4; and panic of 1837, 1; great freeze of 1835, 1; and constitutional convention, 2; map of East and Middle, 5; planters of, 29; railroads in, 11; secession of, 57, 59, viii; slave owners of (chart), 29; slavery in, 2–3; and statehood, 3
Florida Atlantic and Gulf Central Railroad, 11, 86, 102
Florida Railroad, 86, 102, 129
Florida Relief Association, 339
Florida State Museum, 36, 142
Flynn: Catelina, 216; George, 216
Foreign intervention, 131, 150, 163, 186, 250–51, 254–55
Fort, B. I., 17
Fort Beauregard, S.C., 68
Fort Donelson, Tenn., 98, 149
Fort Gates, 158, 162
Fort King, 15
Fort Pickens, 62, 74
Fort Pulaski, Ga., 68
Fort Steele, 59–60, 64, 90, 104
Fort Sumter, S.C., 58
Fort Walker, S.C., 68
Frank. *See* Slaves

Frankfort, Ky., 159
Franklin, Tenn., 354
Fredericksburg, Va., 226
Futch: James, 257; Joshua, 257; Lavina, 257
Gaines: Alabama, 38; Benjamin, 58, 65, 316, 320, 343, 351, 369; Ida, 369; James, 316, 343, 369; Lewis Clark, 17–18, 20, 29, 57–58, 141, 143; Mary (*see* Branning, Mary [Gaines]); Mary Ann Jane (Taylor) (Stephens), viii, 14–15, 22–23, 76, 143, 369; Mary Jane (*see* Bryant, Mary Jane [Gaines]); Phillip Pendleton, 17; Rubannah, 369
Gainesville, 36, 142, 147, 318, 348
Gamble, Robert H., 146
Gardner: Bryan, 60–61, 66, 69, 80, 112, 331; William M., 352
Gardner and Branch, 60
Gaston: Amy (*see* Stephens, Amy [Gaston]); Elizabeth (McFarland), 371; Horace Munson, 371
General Sumter, 56, 78, 331
George. *See* Slaves
Gettysburg, Penn., battle of, 186, 243, 250, 251, 300
Gilbert, Marianna. *See* Bryant, Marianna (Gilbert)
Glisson, D. W., 112
Goosepond Creek, Ga., 15
Governor Milton, 104, 110–11, 156–58
Grahamville, S.C., 357
Grant: J. B., 352; Ulysses S., 98, 149, 186, 192, 197, 231, 254, 273, 300, 335, 354, 363
Gray, Henry A., 63, 73, 76, 78, 107, 112, 129, 157, 214–15, 227, 299, 307, 309, 334, 341–42
Greeley, Mrs., 224
Greely, Jonathan Clark, 142, 176, 267, 276, 324
Groverville, Ga., 101
Gulf of Mexico, 143
Guthrie: Amelia, 269; Jasper, 269

Hall: Abigail Mary, 63; Catherine (Davis), 8; Catherine (*see* Parker, Catherine [Hall]); James, 8; Rebecca (*see* Bryant, Rebecca [Hall])
Halleck, Henry W., 130
Halliday: Mary J. (Fleming), 22; Soloman F., 22
Hancock: Civility, 270; Martin, 270
Hancock House, 270, 277, 279
Hardee: Charles H., 57; William Joseph, 138, 222
Harms, H., 342
Harpers Ferry, Va., 53

Harriet. *See* Slaves
Harrison, Robert, 116, 131, 183, 191, 203, 253, 255, 288, 309
Harrodsburg, Ky., 159
Harts Road, 128, 189
Hastings, Joseph, 14, 22–23
Hatcher's Run, Va., 176
Hateley, John C., 124
Hattie Brock, 35, 104, 111, 154, 331
Havana, Cuba, 11, 54
Haw Creek, 109, 157–58, 162, 340, 342
Hawes, G. E., 56
Hawes Creek, 109
Hawkinsville, 157
Helen Getty, 68
Hemming: Charles, 159; Charles C., 159
Henry. *See* Slaves
Henry, Guy V., 329
Hernando County, 369
Hibernia Plantation, viii, 18, 22
Hickman, Enos, 79
Higginson, Thomas Wentworth, 199, 203, 213, 216
Hillsborough County, 369
Hilton Head, S.C., 157, 199, 315
Hoeg, H. H., 104
Holmes, Henry E., 189
Holmes Mill, 189
Hood, John Bell, 187, 300, 354
Hooker, Joseph, 226, 243
Hope, 111
Hopkins: Benjamin, 26, 44, 57, 63, 65, 68–69, 74, 76–77, 80, 82, 88, 93, 97–99; Charles F., 56, 82, 156, 161–62, 164, 176, 320; Edward, 82; Henry T., 44, 76, 97; Isabella, 44, 97, 218, 228
Joseph, 44, 76, 96–97; Susan, 76, 96–98, 113, 135, 218, 228, 331
Hopkins Plantation, 110
Horse Landing, 112, 116, 120, 340, 342
Houston, 347
Hundred Pines, battle of, 203–4
Hunter, David, 199

Indian artifacts, 35–36, following p. 84
Iowa, 3
Isaac Smith, Federal gunboat, 113, 116, 121, 179
Jackson: Andrew, 2; John King, 347; Thomas J., 226
Jackson, Miss., 231
Jacksonville, 4, 8, 33–35, 37, 49, 56–58, 61–62, 67, 78, 80, 84, 86, 90, 110–11, 113–14, 121, 124–26, 128–29, 140, 146, 158–60, 162, 164, 177, 179–80, 183, 189, 212, 222, 235, 258, 295, 328–29, 331, 363–65, 367, 370, 372; description of, 9–12;

antebellum map of, 10; Unionists in, 59; first occupation of, 102, 104, 107–8; second battle of, 156; third occupation of, 213–19, 220; Federals evacuated from, 218; fourth occupation of, 315–16, 321
Jacob. *See* Slaves
Jane. *See* Slaves
Jefferson County, 131
Jenny. *See* Slaves
Jess. *See* Slaves
John Adams, Federal gunboat, 204
Joe. *See* Slaves
John. *See* Slaves
John Bull. *See* Slaves
Johnson, Andrew, 364
Johnston: Albert Sidney, 85, 98; Joseph E., 120, 197, 222, 231, 300, 326, 337, 354, 363, 365
Jones: Jesse N., 203; John Beauchamp, vii; John D., 190, 204; Samuel, 138, 364, 366
Jones Cemetery, 328
Jonesboro, Ga., battle of, 349
Judah, blockade runner, 74
Judson House, 104

Kansas-Nebraska Act, 53
Kentucky campaign, 149, 167, 173, 248
Kernerly, E., 26
Kiel, Morris, 9
King's Chapel (Boston, Mass.), 263
Kings Ferry, 199, 201, 317
Know-Nothing Party, 53
Knoxville, Tenn., 167, 170, 288

Ladd: Daniel, 361; Elizabeth Ann, 361; George, 361; Joseph, 361
Lainhart, Ann S., ix
Lake Broward, 149
Lake City, 11, 97, 194, 199–200, 205, 220, 230, 235, 237, 240, 245, 257, 259–60, 263, 267–68, 270, 272, 274–77, 279, 295–96, 317–18, 322–24, 327–28, 330, 332, 335, 339, 345, 347, 350–51, 353, 355, 358–59, 363, 365–66
Lake County, 23
Lake George, 110, 331
Lake Monroe, 9, 331
Lancaster: Eliza, 9; William, 9
Latham: Amanda W., 30–31, 39, 41; Carrie, 30–31, 41; Emma, 31; Horatio, 31
Lee, Robert E., 74–75, 82, 93, 120, 124, 130, 142, 150, 186, 226, 243, 252, 254, 300, 354, 355
Levy, David. *See* Yulee, David Levy
Levy County, 369
Lexington, Ky., 158

Lincoln: Abraham, 56, 57, 74, 80, 84, 85, 105, 143, 150, 199, 201, 230, 250, 254, 266, 300, 354, 363–64; Mary, 354
Live Oak, 279, 317
Livingston, J. L., 69
Logrolling, 89
Long: Ellen (Call), 349; Medicus A., 349; Richard C., 349
Lookout Mountain, Tenn., 138, 186, 273, 326
Louisville, Ky., 142, 144, 148, 159, 188
Lynch: Adeline, 178; Charles G., 178; Harriett, 178; Mary, 178, 181

Mackall, William W., 241
Macon, Ga., 346, 347
Madison, 8, 86, 102, 238, 327, 350–51, 356
Madison, John H., 20
Magara, 74
Magnolia, 56, 68, 124
Magnolia Spring, 36
Malvern Hill, Va., 124
Manassas, battle of, 83
Mandarin, 112
Marietta, 126
Marion County, 4, 15, 18, 20, 23, 58, 76, 96, 108, 297, 301, 342, 369
Marlow, Mr. and Mrs., 342
Martin, John Marshall, 355
Mary. *See* Slaves
Mary Polly. *See* Slaves
Mayport, 4, 59–60, 72, 104, 146, 156
McBlair, Charles, 75
McClellan, George B., 120, 124, 130, 142, 150
McCormick: A. H., 183, 192, 218, 220, 321, 332; Abner, 319
McEaddy, W. J., 181
McGirt's Creek, 329
McIlwain, Cordelia (Bryant), ix, 8, 374
McKinnon: J. N., 285, 305; Kenneth, 285, 305; S. R., 285, 305
McLeod: D. C., 215; R. H., 68, 83, 155, 215, 227
McMilland, John C., 49
McMinnville, Tenn., 144, 148
McNelty, William, 68
McRae, G. W. A., 26
Meade, George Gordon, 243
Melia. *See* Slaves
Memphis, 109
Mercer, Hugh Weedon, 223
Meredith: David, 111; James S., 96, 111, 119, 141, 215
Mexico, 3, 251
Micanopy, 269

Middle Florida, 1, 76; demographics of, 2; map of, 5; district of, 352
Middleburg, 21–22, 31, 39, 45, 57–58, 160, 324, 337
Midway, 115
Milanich, Jerald T., 36
Military District of Florida, 364
Military units: 2nd U.S. Colored Infantry, Federal, 359; 99th U.S. Colored Infantry, Federal, 359
—Connecticut, 17th, 342
—Georgia: 4th Cavalry, 319; 29th Infantry, 306
—Florida
  1st Cavalry, 339
  2nd Cavalry, 152, 156, 195, 213, 237, 295, 315, 319; Company B (*see also* St. Johns Rangers), 44, 63, 70, 182, 240, 334, 340, 358, 362; Company C, 124, 162, 183; Company F, 124; Company G, 204; Company H, 116, 121, 181, 334; Company K, 116, 182–83, 190–91, 203
  5th Battalion Cavalry, 359
  5th Battalion Infantry, 159; Company C, 349
  1st Infantry, 82, 135, 159, 176, 320, 339; Company A, 135
  2nd Infantry, 129, 176, 335, 352; Company G, 344
  3rd Infantry, 60, 79, 98, 110–11, 115–16, 118, 131, 170, 173, 175, 189, 232–33, 278, 286, 337, 339; Company A, 59, 138, 159, 327; Company B, 160; Company H, 138, 159, 277
  4th Infantry, 82, 138, 339
  5th Infantry, 124, 129, 159, 335
  6th Infantry, 296, 316, 339, 355
  7th Infantry, 142, 339
  8th Infantry, 129, 335
  10th Infantry, 82, 135, 176
  11th Infantry, 152
  2nd Union Florida Cavalry, Federal, 359
  Brevard's Partisan Rangers, 146, 151–52, 216
  Florida Brigade, Virginia, 335
  Florida Brigade, West, 278, 339
  Gamble's Light Artillery, 146, 217
  Independent Florida Volunteers, 111
  Jacksonville Light Infantry, 59, 138
  Marion Light Artillery, 355
  Milton Light Artillery, 134, 135, 340; Abell's Battery, 350, 351, 352, 355, 357; Battery A, 146; Company A, 133; Company B, 345; Dunham's Artillery, 237, 359

St. Augustine Marion Artillery, 82
St. Johns Rangers (*see also* 2nd Florida Cavalry, Company B), 26, 44, 63, 65, 74, 75, 77, 79, 87, 93, 98, 114, 116, 121–22, 130, 152, 156, 182, 195
—Kentucky
  1st Infantry, 339
  Orphan Brigade, 339
—Massachusetts
  54th Regiment, Federal, 320
—Mississippi
  41st Infantry, 159
  24th Regiment, 82
—South Carolina
  1st Volunteers (Colored), Federal, 199, 203, 213
  2nd Volunteers (Colored), Federal, 199, 213
  Militia: 1st Regiment Artillery, German Artillery, Company A, 342
Miller, William, 359
Mills: Archibald, 21; Caroline T., 21; Victoria (*see* Stephens, Victoria [Mills])
Millstone Creek, Ga., 15
Milton, John, 56, 76
Mining and Petroleum Standard and American Gas-Light Journal, 373
Minja. *See* Slaves
Minorcans, 131, 136, 205
Missionary Ridge, Tenn., battle of, 197, 273, 278
Mississippi, 57, 85, 326
Mississippi River, 354
Missouri Compromise, 53
Mizell, John, 96
Mobile, Ala., 121–22, 126, 128, 140, 167, 182
Montgomery, Ala., 85, 115, 117, 120
Montgomery, James, 199, 213
Monticello, 83, 170, 201, 263, 273–74, 276, 278–79, 285–87, 290, 301, 303, 312, 322, 328, 330, 367
Mooney: Ella, 214, 216; George, 214–16
Moragne, N.H., 193–94
Mose. *See* Slaves
Moseley, William, 80
Mosquito Inlet, 71, 86
Mt. Tucker, 6
Murfreesboro, Tenn., 167, 177–78, 183, 187, 196, 222, 226; battle of, 187–88

Napoleon III, 250, 251, 254
Nashville, Tenn., 98, 139, 144, 147–49, 247, 354
Nashville and Chattanooga Railroad, 177, 226
Nassau, 64, 80, 100, 269, 324

Nassau County, 128
Nassau River, 80, 189
Natural Bridge, battle of, 354, 359–61, 363
Nelson, William, 142
New Bedford, Mass., 371
New Berlin, 152
New Ground, 22, 51, 281
New Orleans, La., 314
New Smyrna, 71
New Smyrna Beach, 71
New York, 8–9, 73, 179, 181, 243, 269, 314, 367, 370, 373; draft riot in, 250, 263
Newport, Fla., 359, 361
Newport, R.I., 109
Newton, John, 359
Newton, Mass., 9
Nicholson, J. W. A., 113, 116
Nick King, 68
Norfolk, Va., 314
Norton, Nathan, 68

Oakwood Cemetery, 369, 370, 374
Ocala, 15, 18, 21, 58, 102–4, 108, 329, 342, 344, 355
Ocklawaha River, 34, 66, 86, 102–3, 111, 137, 202, 331
Ogeechee River, Ga., 357
Oglethorpe County, Ga., 15
Olustee, battle of, 164, 296, 315–16, 318, 319–21, 323, 347, 355
Orange County, 90
Orange Park, 160
Orange Springs, 86, 102, 111, 147, 216, 221, 246, 269
Orlando, 374
Ottawa, Federal gunboat, 111

P. K. Yonge Library of Florida History, ix, 6
Palatka, 9, 35, 49, 55–56, 63–65, 68, 70, 73–74, 77–80, 86, 97, 108, 110, 112, 117, 142, 147, 153–54, 178, 180–85, 193, 208, 216–17, 257, 269, 324, 327, 340, 370; demographics of, 4, 6
Panola, 201, 273, 274
Parker: Catherine (Hall), 30, 44, 62, 340; Richard Green, 30, 44, 340; Rosalie (Geer), ix; William B., Sr., ix
Parson, John, 69
Parson and Livingston, 69
Parsons, William, 204
Patroon, Federal gunboat, 113, 116, 231
Paul Jones, Federal gunboat, 179
Peacock, Hugh A., 23
Pemberton, John C., 192, 231
Pennypacker, Galusha, 128
Pensacola, 62, 74, 85, 88, 102

Pensacola and Georgia Railroad, 11, 263, 273
Perham: Benjamin, 70; Caroline Ann (Bryant) (see Everitt, Caroline Ann [Bryant] [Perham]); Franky (see Sharpe, Franky [Perham]); Paris, 70, 101, 222–23, 271
Perryville, Ky., battle of, 142, 149, 159–60, 173, 183, 278
Peterman, Peter, 63, 88, 97
Peterson, Thomas H., 342
Picolata, 4
Pine Grove Plantation, 14, 22, 35, 38, 45
Pocotaligo, S.C., 357
Ponce de Leon Inlet, 71
Pope, John, 130, 142, 150
Port Royal, S.C., 68, 75–76
Porter, J.W., 65
Porterville, 65
Postell, Albert, 371
Price: Mr., 224; Sterling, 148
Priest: Gabriel, 252; Granville, 95, 168, 172, 267; James, 113; Martha, 113; William, 113, 342
Putnam County, 6, 20, 158, 257; demographics of, 4; planters in, 26; slave owners chart, 27; cotton growers chart, 28

Quincy, 115
Quitman, Ga., 86, 102, 351, 356–57

Rachael. See Slaves
Raleigh, N.C., 364
Rappahannock River, Va., 226
Reading, Mass., x
Reddick, Richard, 369
Reed: Arthur M., 9; Harriet, 9; Louisa, 9
Republican Party, 53, 230
Resaca, Ga., 339
Richard: Eugenia (See Stephens, Eugenia [Richard]); John C., 135, 146
Richmond, Ky., 142, 355
Richmond, Va., 120, 124, 130, 147, 197, 226, 229, 266, 273, 343, 356, 363
Ringgold, Ga., 266
Rochester, N.Y., 372
Rose Cottage, viii, ix, 14, 22–23, 25, 31, 40, 49, 50, 86, 110, 186; description of, 51, 52; location of, 52; burned, 343
Rose Dew, Ga., 357
Rosecrans, William S, 159, 187, 226, 244, 247–48, 273
Rou, Samuel F. See Rowe
Routh, H. S., 230, 238, 321, 347, 366
Roux: George, 105; Louis F, 105, 190
Rowe, Samuel F., 124, 237, 296, 316

Salkehatchie, S.C., 356–57

Salt Springs, 246
Sammy. See Slaves
Sandy. See Slaves
San Jose, Calif., 374
Sanderson, 315, 316
Santa Rosa Island, 74
Sarah. See Slaves
Satilla, Ga., 12
Savannah, Ga., 8–9, 11, 57, 68, 75, 77, 100–101, 120, 167–68, 222–23, 350, 351, 356, 370, 372; battle of, 352, 355, 357
Savannah Republican, 120–21, 124
Scott: Edmund G., 121; G. W., 359; James E., 121; William Washington, 176, 181
Selma, Ala., 15
Seminole, 68
Seminole County, 331
Seminole Wars, 1, 3, 8, 21, 27–28, 31, 50, 82, 95
Seneca, Federal gunboat, 111–12
Sequatchie Valley, Tenn., 144
Seton, Margaret. See Fleming, Margaret (Seton)
Seven Days Campaign (Va.), 120, 124
Seven Mile Camp, 107, 110, 213
Seven Pines, Va., battle of, 120
Seward: Fred, 364; William H., 363, 364
Seymore, Truman, 315
Sharpe: Franky (Perham), 271, 279, 306; William H., 271, 306
Shedd, William W., 63, 288, 290–91, 295, 299
Shelbyville, Tenn., 226, 240, 244, 245, 247
Sherman, William Tecumseh, 68, 300, 326, 337, 349, 352, 354, 357–58, 363
Shiloh, Tenn., battle of, 98, 149, 187
Sikes, John B., 342
Silver Spring, 35, 78
Silver Springs, 78
Simkins, E. C., 56
Slaves: afraid of Yankees, 163; leased out in Thomasville, 279–80, 282; and possum hunting, 71; rations of, 25, 71; sick, 71, 75, 117, 153, 198, 258; slave patrols, 58, 80; task system, 24
—Archey, 26
—Banger (Old Bangs), 18, 20
—Big Jane, wife of Burrel, 17, 20, 23, 58, 62, 71, 80, 94, 99, 166, 193, 198, 225, 236, 251, 279–80, 282, 353, 369
—Bill, 18
—Bob, 18
—Brice, 18, 22
—Burrel, 17, 20, 23, 64–65, 69, 71–72, 75–77, 82, 98, 100, 102–6, 123, 130, 153–54, 156, 168, 181, 198, 226, 234, 242, 245–47, 252–55, 260, 265, 271, 276–77, 279–80, 282, 353, 366; preacher, 24, 39, 41,

46, 49, 52; lifestyle of, 50; children of, 52; Christmas visit of, 58; works on Winston's farm, 66, 87, 89, 94, 99, 134, 136, 144, 161, 166, 172–73, 200–202, 205, 211, 232, 236, 239–40, 251, 262, 267, 270; and killing hogs, 81; and logrolling, 92; returns to Welaka, 369–70
—Charley, 18, 22
—Dicey, 18, 20
—Domingo, 22
—Ellen, 40
—Eveline, 20
—Fanny, 26
—Felix (mess cook), 74, 78, 97, 135, 212, 299, 309, 318, 322
—Frank, 97
—George, 26
—Harriet, 97
—Henry, 26
—Jacob, 53, 157–58
—Jane (Burrel's wife). *See* Big Jane
—Jane (Burrel's daughter), 23, 52–53, 64, 117, 128, 132, 279–80
—Jane (Sarah's daughter), 20, 23, 52, 57, 61, 64, 71, 75, 100, 232, 279, 302, 369
—Jane (owned by Swepston Stephens), 26
—Jenny, 26
—Jess, 23, 61, 64, 81, 128, 132, 225, 232, 279
—Joe (owned by Winston Stephens), 20, 23, 57, 70–71, 75, 119, 130, 212, 279, 282, 286–87, 289, 302, 304, 316, 367
—Joe (owned by Swepston Stephens), 26
—John Bull, 97
—Mary, 18, 22, 343
—Mary Polly, 52–53, 123, 134, 224–25, 232, 241, 279, 369
—Melia, 26
—Minja, 343
—Mose, 20, 23, 117, 134, 258, 279, 282, 289, 304
—Rachael, 20, 23, 39, 52, 64, 71, 100, 198, 279–80, 289, 304, 316, 369
—Sammy, 26
—Sandy, 26
—Sarah, 20, 23, 52–53, 57, 64, 66, 71, 75, 95, 117, 119, 123, 134, 150–51, 153, 161, 166, 198, 232–33, 236, 251, 279–80, 282, 294, 304, 312, 369–70
—Solomon, 26
—Sophie (owned by Tina Stephens), 22, 343
—Sophie (owned by Hopkins family; wife of Felix), 97, 212
—Tom, 20, 23, 61, 71, 75, 81, 89, 110, 112, 136–37, 154, 161, 172, 198, 202, 246–47, 258, 268, 279, 282, 289, 304, 369
Slocum, Henry W., 363
Smith: Carraway, 183, 319, 324; Edmund Kirby, 142, 149; Joseph F., 154; M., 70, 117, 119, 150, 157–58, 185, 195, 224, 311–12, 331, 366; Miss, 49; Mr., 69
Smyrna, 71, 72, 86, 88, 96–99, 100–102
Solomon. *See* Slaves
Sopchoppy, 143
Sophie. *See* Slaves
South Carolina: secession of, 56–57
South Georgia College, 371
Soutton, M., 182–83
Spain, 1
Sparta, Tenn., 144
Spiers, Lucy. *See* Bryant, Lucy (Spiers)
St. Augustine, 4, 56, 67, 70, 82, 132, 158, 213, 324, 340; occupied, 102, 108; exiles from, 199, 204
St. Johns, 68
St. Johns Bluff, 146, 151–52, 155–56, 161–62
St. Johns County, 4
St. Johns Hotel, 178
St. Johns River, 4, 6, 9, 14–15, 23, 34, 60, 68, 72, 86, 98, 101–2, 107, 109, 121, 142, 151, 157, 171, 179, 238, 311, 321, 339
St. Johns sandbar, 68, 72, 104, 153, 179
St. Marks, 361
St. Marks River, 359
St. Marys, 68, 102, 109
St. Marys, Ga., 189
St. Marys River, 199, 203–4, 213, 316, 318–19, 347
St. Simons Island, Ga., 68
Stanley, Isham, 95, 267
Starke, 317, 348
Station Number 4, Cedar Key, 358
Station Number 4, Monticello, 263, 273
Steele: Holmes, 60, 277, 325; Miss, 325; Rebecca, 60
Stephens genealogical chart, 16
Stephens: Adolphus, 21; Amy (Gaston), 371; Caroline H. (Barnes), 21; Charles Seton, 94, 292, 343, 374; Eugenia (Richard), 21; Isabella Gertrude, 180, 182, 185, 189, 191–93, 194, 370; Joshua, 15, 17; Lewis Isadore, 71, 157–58, 219, 342–43; Linda, 369; Mary Ann (Dunn), 17, 21; Minor Richard Goolsby, 3, 15, 20, 21, 26, 33, 49, 57, 76, 369; Rosalie, viii, 56, 227, 232–33, 239, 371; Thomas Peter Goolsby, 15, 18, 19; Tina (*see* Augustina Alexandria [Fleming]); Victoria (Mills), 21, 343–44; William H., 21; William Winston, 18, 342; Winston (Winnie), 328, 371; Winston B., Jr., ix, 36, 61, 142
—Augustina Alexandria (Fleming); letters from, 284, 292, 330, 341, 344, 355; marriage of, 18; approves of engagement, 37; pregnant, 94; forced to leave Welaka,

—Augustina Alexandria (Fleming), *continued*, 341–43; at Swepston's, 344; returns to Welaka, 370
—Octavia Louisa (Bryant), vii, 8; diary entries of, 33–39, 41, 43–49, 55–57, 64, 72, 79, 95–96, 103, 110–13, 116, 119, 122, 140, 156–57, 178, 189, 191, 193, 216–18, 271, 273–74, 276–77, 280, 283, 285, 299, 304, 316–17, 323, 325–26, 328, 330, 332, 338, 344–45, 349–50, 353, 359, 362–63, 367; letters from, 31, 34, 37–41, 46–47, 62, 65, 70, 75, 81, 83, 89, 91, 94, 95, 97, 99, 103, 105, 108, 117, 119, 123, 128, 130, 134–35, 137, 143, 145, 150, 153–54, 156, 163, 166, 168, 172, 174, 192–93, 197–98, 201, 206, 211, 217, 224–25, 227, 231, 233, 236, 239, 241–42, 245, 251, 253, 258, 260–61, 265, 274, 280, 281, 286, 288, 294, 298, 301, 303, 305, 312, 316, 321, 326, 334, 341, 345; letters to, 42–46, 48, 54–55, 57, 61, 63, 65, 67, 73, 76–77, 79, 82, 87–88, 90, 92, 96–98, 100, 102, 104, 106–7, 112–13, 116, 120, 124, 129–30, 132, 134–35, 141, 146, 151, 155, 160–61, 164–65, 168, 171, 176, 191, 195, 198–200, 205, 207, 214, 223, 225–26, 228, 230, 235, 237, 239, 243, 250, 252, 254–55, 259, 264–67, 272, 275, 279, 281, 284, 288, 290, 292–93, 295–98, 301, 304, 307–8, 311–12, 315, 317–18, 323, 329–30, 332–33, 337–341, 344,-347, 349–53, 355, 358, 362–63, 365, 367; birth of, 9; courtship of, 30; physical description of, 32, 50, 51; begins diaries, 32; breaks engagement, 34, 41; renews engagement, 37, 44; tells father of planned marriage, 47; marriage of, viii, 49; gives birth to Rosa, 56; and disciplining of slaves, 100, 128; buries silver, 103; comments on uniform, 151; writes of Isabella's death, 197; visits Isabella's grave, 206; visits Winston, 212, 216, 259–60, 262; on spinning and weaving, 208, 227–28, 233, 236, 242, 261, 294; on taking "morphine," 227, 234; mentions Winston's affair before marriage, 243; pregnant with Winnie, 260; visits Lou Tydings, 273–74; moves from Welaka, 276; and new home in Thomasville, 280, 289, 301; reaction of, to Christmas party, 304; at probate court, 336; concern of, for Winston's grave in Lake City, 345; returns to Welaka, 370; death of, 371
—Swepston Benjamin Whitehead, 20, 76, 141, 216, 276, 290–91, 295, 316, 341–44, 358, 369; letters from, 329; in 3rd Seminole War, 3, 33; birth of, 15; marriage of, 21; slaves of, 26; 2nd corporal, 129

—William Clark Taylor, viii, 374; birth of, 15; marriage of, 18; slaves of, 18, 20, 22; medical discharge of, 111; and alligator hunting, 137, 219, 221, 225, 234, 246, 263, 276; forced to leave Welaka, 341, 342, 343; returns to Welaka, 370
—Winston John Thomas, vii; letters from, 42–46, 55, 57, 61, 63, 65, 67, 73, 76–77, 79, 82, 87–88, 90, 92, 96–98, 100, 102, 104, 106–7, 112, 116, 120, 124, 129–30, 132, 134–35, 141, 146, 151, 155, 160–61, 164–65, 168, 171, 176, 191, 195, 198–200, 205, 207, 214, 218, 220, 223, 225–26, 228, 230, 235, 237, 239, 243, 250, 252, 254–55, 257, 259, 264–67, 270, 272, 275, 279, 281, 288, 290, 293, 295–98, 301, 304, 307–8, 311–12, 315, 317–18, 323; letters to, 31, 34, 37–41, 46, 62, 65, 70, 75, 81, 83–84, 89, 91, 94–95, 97, 99, 103, 105, 108–9, 117, 119, 123, 128, 130, 134–35, 137, 143, 145, 150, 153–54, 156, 163, 166, 168, 172, 174, 192–93, 197–98, 201, 206, 211, 224–25, 227, 231, 233, 236, 239, 241–42, 245, 251, 253, 258, 260–61, 265, 269, 274, 280–81, 286, 288, 294, 298, 301, 303, 305, 312, 316, 321; birth of, 15, 371; in 3rd Seminole War, 3, 31, 33; slaves of, 18, 20, 22–24, 52; on slave rations, 25, 71; crops of, 22, 24–25, 27; social standing of, 29–30; courtship of, 30; reaction of, to broken engagement, 42; engagement of, renewed, 44; marriage of, viii, 49; physical description of, 50, 51; and hunting, 50; politics of, 53; political candidate, 54–56; and cotton growing, 61; shoots slave, 61; mustered in, 63, 64; moves contraband, 102; skirmishes with gunboat, 116, 146; uniform of, 142; politics of, in company, 152; troubles of, with Gen. Finegan, 155, 164–65; describes surrender of St. Johns Bluff, 161–62; feelings of, about Tina, 200; on depending on Burrel, 215; on taking "morphine," 228, 235, 253; at military review, 235, 237; and love of family, 240; comments on speculators, 254; moves from Welaka, 276; and disposition of slaves in Thomasville, 279–80, 282; describes quarters at Camp Cooper, 290–91; premarital affairs of, 297; on Christmas party, 299, 307; thoughts of, about getting killed, 310; and battle of Olustee, 317–21; death and burial of, ix, 327, 328–29
Stevens: Naaman, 116; Susan, 116; William B., 116
Stones River, Tenn., battle of, 149, 159, 186–89, 226
Stroble: Anabell, 269; J.G., 269

Stuart, J. E. B., 226
Sturtevant, William C., 36
Sumter County, Ala., 17
Suwannee River, 1, 345

Taft Mercantile, 6
Tallahassee, 2, 8, 11, 23, 57, 76, 82, 86, 110, 113, 115, 130, 143, 263, 320, 349–50, 352–54, 359, 362, 364
Tampa, 31, 111
Taylor, Mary Ann Jane. *See* Gaines, Mary Ann Jane (Taylor) (Stephens)
Teasdale, H. R., 90, 152, 366
Ten-Mile Station, 329
Tennessee River, 139, 226, 244, 248
Texas, 3
Thomas: George H., 273; Jane, 224; Judana, 224; Mary E., 223–24, 227
Thomasville, Ga., viii, 14, 69, 83, 107, 117, 121, 125, 159, 163, 209, 222–23, 246, 249, 261, 266, 273, 275, 300, 327, 370; move to, 256–57, 263, 265, 267–71, 277
Thorn, 35
Three-Mile Run, 329
Tom. *See* Slaves
Tortugas Island, 230
Township Landing, 203
Trans Mississippi, 354, 365–67
Trapier, James Heyward, 76, 104, 129
Tredinick, Don, 52
Tullahoma, Tenn., 196–97, 208, 221, 226, 229, 232; campaign, 244, 247–48, 252
Tupelo, Miss., 138, 147
Turner, William J., 111
Tybee Island, Ga., 68
Tydings: Joseph, 303; Louisa (Bryant), 33, 38, 83, 107, 143, 163, 201, 235, 246, 253, 262–63, 272–74, 276, 298, 299, 302; Richard, 83, 107, 110, 143, 163, 201, 273–74, 276, 298, 303
Tyler, John, 3

Uncas, Federal gunboat, 181; James W. Bryant on board, 179
United Confederate Veteran, 373
University of Pennsylvania, 15

Vallandingham, Clement Laird, 230, 231
Vann: Elijah, 279, 282, 336; Rosey, 279
Vicksburg, Miss., 186, 192, 231, 244, 249, 251–52, 300

Villipique, F. L., 146, 162
Virginia, 17
Vogdes, Israel, 364
Volusia, 98, 100–102, 104, 106–7
Volusia County, 369

Walden's Ridge, Tenn., 139
Waldo, 86, 212, 216, 221, 262–63, 269, 271–72, 275–77, 284, 292, 348, 362
Waldo Hotel, 269
Wall, Elijah, 26
Ward: Anne H., 352; George T., 352
Washington County, Ala., 17
Washington, D.C., 91, 179, 181, 314, 364
Wassaw Island, Ga., 68
Water Witch, Federal gunboat, 179
Webb, William A., 75
Webster, Daniel, 57
Webster, 57
Welaka, 68
Welaka, vii, viii, 4, 15; founding, 6, 12; antebellum map, 13; demographics of, 14; threatened by gunboats, 105–6, 108, 217, 259; Federal troops land at, 157; Federal troops occupy, 331, 340, 342–44; Federal troops captured at, 339
Welaka Springs, 112
West Florida, 1
West Florida Seminary, 359
Westview Cemetery, 97, 327
Wethington, John Wesley, 159
Wheeler, Joseph, 226, 357
Whig Party, 2, 53
White Cottage, 12, 14, 21, 60, 343; description, 51–52
Whitesville, 57
Whitney, Eli, 23
Williamsburg, Va., 352
Wills Branch, 126
Wilmington, N.C., 269
Winchester, Tenn., 187, 196
Wingate, Margaret, 257; William, 257, 259, 272, 299
Wisconsin, 3
Woodall, M., 179
Woodward, C. Vann, vii
Woonsocket, R.I., 31

Yellow Bluff, 146, 152, 155–56, 162
Yulee, David Levy, 2–3, 129
Yulee, Fla., 189

Material from the Bryant-Stephens letters and diaries is reprinted in this book courtesy of the P. K. Yonge Library of Florida History and the following descendants: Henry Herbert Bryant III, Henrietta Bryant Cox, Stephen Russell Davis II, Lucile W. Ellis, Amy E. Goulart, Ellie Kartrude, Ann Smith Lainhart, Catherine Bryant Lainhart, Ann Ball Stephens Leemon, Sarah Lillian Bryant Lomax, Elizabeth Stephens Marsh, Cordelia Bryant McIlwain, Amy S. McNeill, Henry Yeates Reeder, William Franklin Reeder, William S. Reeder, Louis C. Stephens, Wesley Pecora Stephens, Winston Bryant Stephens Jr., William Ernest Tydings, Linda S. Vidal, Mary Louise Tydings Whatley, Edward S. Wilkinson, Ernest C. Wilkinson, Henry Bryant Wilkinson, John Wilkinson, and Julia May Bryant Williams.

The photographs following page 84 are reproduced courtesy of the following: the P. K. Yonge Library of Florida History (photos 1, 2, and 3); Winston Bryant Stephens Jr. (4, 7, 8, 9, 10, and 11); Cordelia Bryant McIlwain (5 and 6); the Florida State Museum (12 and 14); and Henry Reeder and the Putnam County Archives (13).

www.ingramcontent.com/pod-product-compliance
Lightning Source LLC
Chambersburg PA
CBHW052230230426
43666CB00035B/2598